DISPARITIES IN ECONOMIC DEVELOPMENT SINCE THE INDUSTRIAL REVOLUTION

Also by Paul Bairoch

REVOLUTION INDUSTRIELLE ET SOUS-DEVELOPPEMENT
THE WORKING POPULATION AND ITS STRUCTURE *(editor)*
LE TIERS-MONDE DANS L'IMPASSE
URBAN UNEMPLOYMENT IN DEVELOPING COUNTRIES
THE ECONOMIC DEVELOPMENT OF THE THIRD WORLD SINCE 1900
COMMERCE EXTERIEUR ET DEVELOPPEMENT ECONOMIQUE DE L'EUROPE AU XIXE SIECLE
TAILLE DES VILLES, CONDITIONS DE VIE ET DEVELOPPEMENT ECONOMIQUE

Also by Maurice Lévy-Leboyer

LES BANQUES EUROPEENNES ET L'INDUSTRIALISATION INTERNATIONALE DANS LA 1ERE MOITIE DU XIXE SIECLE
L'AVENEMENT DE L'1ERE INDUSTRIELLE EN FRANCE, 1789–ANNEES 1880
LA POSITION INTERNATIONALE DE LA FRANCE: ASPECTS ECONOMIQUES ET FINANCIERS/XIXE-XXE SIECLE *(editor)*

Disparities in Economic Development since the Industrial Revolution

Edited by
Paul Bairoch and Maurice Lévy-Leboyer

M
MACMILLAN

First edition 1981
Reprinted 1985

Published by
THE MACMILLAN PRESS LTD
Houndmills, Basingstoke, Hampshire RG21 2XS
and London
Companies and representatives
throughout the world

Printed in Great Britain by
Antony Rowe Ltd
Chippenham

ISBN 0–333–26801–6

Contents

Preface ix
Notes on the Contributors xi

PART 1 ECONOMIC DISPARITIES AMONG NATIONS

A *INTERNATIONAL DISPARITIES*

1 The Main Trends in National Economic Disparities since the Industrial Revolution *Paul Bairoch* 3
2 Inequality among Nations: 1950 and 1975 *Robert Summers, Irving B. Kravis and Alan Heston* 18

B *THE THIRD WORLD*

3 Industry and Empire: The Beginnings of French Industrial Politics in the Colonies under the Vichy Regime *Catherine Coquery-Vidrovitch* 29
4 Constraints to Economic Development in Africa: Some Determinants of Economic Disparities *Richard O. Ekundare* 34
5 Notes on the Patterns of Economic Growth in the British North American Colonies in the Seventeenth, Eighteenth and Nineteenth Centuries *Stanley L. Engerman* 46
6 Decolonisation and the Multinational Company: Unilever in India, 1917-65 *D.K. Fieldhouse* 58
7 Egypt, Iran and Turkey, 1800-1970: Patterns of Growth and Development *Charles Issawi* 65
8 Technology Transfer, Population Growth and the Development Gap since the Industrial Revolution *Priyatosh Maitra* 78
9 The Economic Underdevelopment of the United States South in the Post-Bellum Era *Jay R. Mandle* 86
10 Export Growth and Capitalist Development in Colombia in the Nineteenth Century *José-Antonio Ocampo* 98
11 Terms of Trade between France and Latin America, 1826-1856: Causes of Increasing Economic Disparities? *Jürgen Schneider* 110
12 The Unevenness of the Socio-economic Development and Prospects for the Economic Self-sufficiency of the Countries of the East *N.A. Simoniya* 120

C *THE DEVELOPED WORLD*

13 Methodological Aspects in Describing the Bourgeois and Industrial Revolutions *Walter Becker* 131
14 Economic Integration and Regional Development in Austria-Hungary, 1867-1913 *David F. Good* 137
15 The Process of Industrialisation in General and the Process of Industrialisation in Italy: Some Suggestions, Problems and Questions *Giorgio Mori* 151
16 On the Economic Development of the Habsburg Monarchy *György Ránki* 165
17 Structural Change and Industrialisation in Inter-war Central-East Europe *Alice Teichova* 175

PART 2 REGIONAL ECONOMIC DISPARITIES

A *NORTHERN, WESTERN AND CENTRAL EUROPE*

18 Regional Economic Inequality in the Netherlands since 1600 *Jan de Vries* 189
19 Regional Differences, Differential Development and Generative Regional Growth *Herman Freudenberger and Gerhard Mensch* 199
20 The Development of a Growth Pole in the Nineteenth Century illustrated by the example of Nuremberg *R. Gömmel* 210
21 Market Integration during the Period of Industrialisation in Norway *Fritz Hodne and Ole Gjølberg* 216
22 Regional Wages in Sweden during the Nineteenth Century *Lennart Jörberg and Tommy Bengtsson* 226
23 Regional Differences in the Position of Peasants in the European Part of Russia in the Nineteenth Century *J. Kahk and I. Kovalchenko* 244
24 Regional Disparities in Wages: the Cotton Industry in Nineteenth-century Germany – Some Methodological Considerations *Hubert Kiesewetter* 248
25 Regional Disparities in Brabantine Urbanisation before and after the Industrial Revolution (1374-1970): Some Aspects of Measurement and Explanation *Paul M.M. Klep* 259

B *FRANCE*

26 Regional Inequalities and Economic Development: French Agriculture in the Nineteenth and Twentieth Centuries *Marc Auffret, Michel Hau and Maurice Lévy-Leboyer* 273

27 The Spread of Agricultural Growth over the Departments of France from the Mid-nineteenth to the Mid-twentieth Century *Nicole Soubeyroux* 290
28 The Uneven Growth of Regional Incomes in France from 1840 to 1970 *Jean-Claude Toutain* 302

C *SOUTHERN EUROPE*

29 Regional Inequalities in Italy *A. Graziani* 319
30 Regional Development in Portugal (1929-1977): an Assessment *Jean Mayer* 331

D *THE THIRD WORLD*

31 Regional Inequalities in Brazil during the Second Half of the Nineteenth Century *Mircea Buescu* 349

PART 3 RELATION BETWEEN REGIONAL AND NATIONAL DISPARITIES

32 Regional and International Economic Disparities since the Industrial Revolution: the Indian Evidence *Dharma Kumar and J. Krishnamurty* 361
33 Inequality and Regional Development: the View from America *Jeffrey G. Williamson* 373

PART 4 METHODOLOGY FOR MEASUREMENT OF ECONOMIC DISPARITIES

34 Comparison of Development Levels: Inequalities in the Physical Structures of National Economies *Eva Ehrlich* 395
35 National Product Series in Historical Analysis: a Case Study of Sweden, 1861-1975 *Olle Krantz and Carl-Axel Nilsson* 411

Index 420

Preface

This book assembles all the contributions to one of the four major themes of the 7th International Economic History Congress which took place in Edinburgh on 13-19 August 1978. The papers have been revised since the Congress.

When a few years ago the two co-editors of this book were asked to prepare the theme of disparities in economic development, one of the most important tasks involved was to ensure that the contributors would be chosen from among the best international specialists in this field. Taking into account the nature of the subject, this led the editors to avoid selecting only economic historians, and economists specialising in development problems were also invited to participate. For the same reason, the contributors were chosen not only from the developed world, but also from the Third World. As the conference was organised by the International Economic History Association, it meant that in some rare cases a delicate geographical balance had to be preserved. The overall result has exceeded the already high expectations of the two editors. Thus the thirty-three papers (not counting the editors' own two) represent probably one of the best and certainly one of the most complete collections of essays devoted to this very important problem: the inequality of economic growth. It is a problem which is of the utmost interest not only to the academic world, but also to the student and the layman.

We have abandoned the traditional procedure of presenting a short summary of each paper. In view of the extreme complexity and concentration of most of the papers, this could only introduce unnecessary distortion of the authors' arguments.

Part 1, which includes seventeen papers, is devoted to national disparities, and Part 2 (fourteen papers) to regional disparities. The difficult problem of the relation between regional and national disparities is the subject of both papers in Part 3. Two papers form Part 4, dealing with the methodological aspects of the measurement of economic disparities. Within each part and sub-part, the papers follow the alphabetical order of the authors' names.

The word 'billion' is used in the US sense, i.e. a thousand million, throughout the book.

April 1979

Paul Bairoch
Maurice Lévy-Leboyer

Notes on the Contributors

MARC AUFFRET was born in 1944. He holds a doctorate '3e cycle' and is currently *maître-assistant* in contemporary history at the Faculty of Arts of the University of Maine, Le Mans. His publications include: *L'industrie linière en Normandie au XIXe siècle; La France de l'entre-deux-guerres, 1919-1939; La France actuelle, 1958-1970;* in collaboration with P. Bois, *L'Histoire du Mans et du pays manceau.*

PAUL BAIROCH was born in 1930. Since 1956 he has specialised in the field of development of industrialised and Third World economies. He has taught at the University of Brussels; Sir George Williams University (Montreal); Ecole Pratique des Hautes Etudes (Sorbonne, Paris). He has been a professor at the University of Geneva since 1972. His books include: *Révolution industrielle et sous-développement; Le Tiers-Monde dans l'Impasse; Urban Unemployment in Developing Countries; The Economic Development of the Third World since 1900; Commerce extérieur et développement économique de l'Europe au XIXe siècle; Taille des villes, conditions de vie et développement économique.*

WALTER BECKER was born in 1921. Since 1970 he has been Professor of Economic History at the Hochschule für Okonomie 'Bruno Leuschner' of Berlin, Department of Marxism-Leninism. He specialises in the economic history of Germany since the industrial Revolution. He was awarded a doctorate in economics (1960) for a thesis on 'The history of the German mechanical engineering industry from 1860 to 1870', published in *Studien zur Geschichte der industriellen revolution;* and a doctorate in economic science (1967) for a thesis on the economic history of the Weimar Republic, contained in the chapters 'Inflation' and 'Relative Stabilization of Capitalism' of the textbook *Wirtschaftsgeschichte Deutschlands*, vol. 3 (in collaboration with Mottek and Schröter).

TOMMY BENGTSSON, is a member of the research programme on 'Mortality, fertility and economic development – studies in the demographic transition in Sweden' at the Department of Economic History, University of Lund. His PhD thesis deals with the modern Swedish textile industry. He has written articles in Swedish journals.

MIRCEA BUESCU is a graduate of the Law Schools of Bucharest and Paris. He is Professor of Economic History at the Pontificial Catholic University and at the Bennett Colleges in Rio de Janeiro. He is editor of APEC's economic publications and a member of the Brazilian Historical and Geographical Institute. His books include: *Historia Economica do Brasil; Pesquisa e Analises; 300 Anos de Inflaçao; Guerra e Desenvolvimento; Evoluçao Economica do Brasil; Disparidades de Renda no Passado.*

CATHERINE COQUERY-VIDROVITCH was born in 1935 and graduated from the Ecole Normale Supérieure. She holds a doctorat d'Etat and is a professor at the University of Paris VII and director of the laboratory 'Connaissance du Tiers-Monde'. She is a specialist in the socio-economic history of Africa in the twentieth century. Her books include: *La découverte de l'Afrique; Le Congo (A.E.F.) au temps des grandes compagnies concessionnaires, 1898-1930; L'Afrique noire de 1800 à nos jours* (with H. Moniot); *Connaissance du Tiers-Monde, Approche pluridisciplinaire* (editor).

JAN de VRIES was born in 1943. He is a professor of the University of California at Berkeley. His books include: *The Dutch Rural Economy in the Golden Age, 1500-1700; Barges and Capitalism: Passenger transportation in the Dutch economy, 1632-1839.*

EVA EHRLICH is a senior research worker in the Hungarian National Planning Office's Institute and teaches at the Karl Marx University of Economics. She has worked as a short-term consultant to the EEC in Geneva and has been working for twenty years on Hungarian long-term economic planning. Her books include: *Infrastruktura. Korok ës orszagok,* in collaboration with Dr A. Csernok and Dr. Gy. Szilagyi; *An International Comparison of Infra-structural Development; International Economics – comparisons and interdependences; Japan: the Anatomy of Closing Up* (forthcoming).

RICHARD O. EKUNDARE was born in 1932. He graduated in economics (with honours) in 1957 at the University of Durham, England, and was awarded postgraduate degrees in economics and law. He is a barrister of Lincoln's Inn. He began his academic career as a lecturer in economics in 1958 and in 1976 was appointed the first Nigerian Professor of Economic History at the University of Ife, Ile-Ife. His books include *An Economic History of Nigeria*, 1860-1960.

STANLEY L. ENGERMAN was born in 1936. He is Professor of Economics and History at the University of Rochester. His books include: *Time on the Cross* (in collaboration with R. W. Fogel); *The Reinterpretation of American Economic History* (co-editor with R. W. Fogel); *Race and Slavery in the Western Hemisphere: Quantitative Studies* (co-editor with E. D. Genovese).

DAVID FIELDHOUSE was born in 1925 and served as a pilot in the Fleet Air Arm during the war. He graduated in history at Oxford in 1949. He was a lecturer in history at the University of Canterbury, New Zealand from 1953 to 1957. Since then he has been Beit Lecturer in Commonwealth History at Oxford and a Fellow of Nuffield College. He has been a visiting professor at Yale and Stanford. His books include: *The Colonial Empires; Economics and Empire; Unilever Overseas.*

HERMAN FREUDENBERGER was born in 1922 and is Professor of Economics at Tulane University. His books include: *The Industrialization of a Central European City; The Waldstein Woolen Mill; Von der Provinzstadt zur Industrieregion (Brünn-Studie)* (in collaboration with G. Mensch).

OLE GJØLBERG was born in 1949 and holds a degree in economic history and economics from the Norwegian School of Economics. At present he is a research fellow at the Institute of Economic History there. His publications include articles on wages and the standard of living. He is now finishing a book on Norwegian shipping, 1865-1914.

R. GÖMMEL was born in 1944. He studied political economy at the University of Erlangen-Nuremberg, from where he graduated in 1977. Since 1977 he has been assistant at the Institut fur Finanzwissenschaft, Statistik und Wirtschaftsgeschichte, University of Regensburg. His books include: *Growth and Business Cycles of the Economy of Nuremberg 1815-1914;* 'The Importance of Entrepreneurs in Franconia (Northern Bavaria) during Industrialisation and the Causes of their Rising', in *Festschrift for Hermann Kellenbenz* vol. 3.

DAVID F. GOOD was born in 1943. He received his PhD from the University of Pennsylvania in 1972 and is now Associate Professor of Economics at Temple University in Philadelphia. His publications include several articles on the late nineteenth-century Austro-Hungarian economy. He is currently writing a book on the Habsburg Monarchy as a case study in modern economic growth.

A. GRAZIANI was born in 1933. He was a postgraduate student at the LSE and at Harvard University from 1957-9, and in 1962 became Professor of Economics at the University of Catania (Sicily). Since 1965 he has been Professor of Economic Policy at the University of Naples. He is the author of a number of works on Italian economic development.

MICHEL HAU was born in 1943. He graduated from the Ecole Normale Supérieure de Saint Cloud and from the Institut d'Etudes Politiques, and holds a doctorate in history. He has been *maître-assistant* of contemporary history at the University of Human Sciences of Strasbourg since 1974. His books include: *La Croissance économique de la Champagne, de 1810 à 1969;* 'L'étude de la croissance régionale de 1810 à nos jours, données et lacunes', in *Pour une Histoire de la Statistique;* 'Coûts de transport du charbon et industrialisation des régions françaises de 1847 à 1911', in *Transports et Voies de Communication.*

ALAN HESTON was born in 1934. He gained his MA in Washington in 1957 and as a Ford Foundation fellow was awarded his PhD at Yale in 1962. He was visiting lecturer at Bombay from 1960-61, assistant professor at Yale from 1960-62, assistant professor in South Asian Economy at the University of Pennsylvania in 1962 and was a member of the American Institute of Indian Studies from 1965-66. He specialises in the economic history of Asia, monetary economics and economic development, and the economic history of Western India, 1850-1947.

FRITZ HODNE was born in 1932. He gained an MA degree in American history from Claremont University Center, California in 1960, and a degree in history from the University of Bergen in 1961. He is a senior lecturer at the Norwegian School of Economics and Business Administration, Bergen.

His books include: *An Economic History of Norway 1815-1970* and numerous articles. He is Corresponding Editor of *Economy and History*, Lund, Sweden.

CHARLES ISSAWI was born in 1916. He has taught at Columbia, The American University of Beirut and other universities and has served in the United Nations Secretariat and the Egyptian Ministry of Finance and Central Bank. His books include: *Egypt in Revolution; Issawi's Laws of Social Motion; The Economic History of the Middle East; The Economic History of Iran; The Economics of Middle Eastern Oil* (co-author).

LENNART JÖRBERG is Professor of Economic History at the University of Lund, Sweden. He was visiting professor at the Institut fur Weltwirtschaft, Kiel, in 1964 and at the University of California at Berkeley from 1965-66. His books include: *Growth and Fluctuations of Swedish Industry 1869-1912; Studies in the Process of Industrialisation; The Industrial Revolution in the Nordic Countries.*

J. KAHK was born in 1928. He graduated from the Faculty of History, Tartu State University, in 1951 and completed his postgraduate studies in the Department of History of the University of Leningrad. Since 1968 he has been Director of the Institute of History of the Academy of Sciences of the Estonian SSR. In 1973, he was appointed Secretary Academician of the Department of Humanities of the Academy of Sciences of the ESSR. He has been a member of the Academy of Sciences of the Estonian SSR since 1978. His main publications are in the field of Estonian agrarian history.

HUBERT KIESEWETTER was born in 1939. After nine years working as an engine-fitter and engine-driver, he studied history, philosophy, economy and psychology at Frankfurt, Kiel, the London School of Economics and Heidelberg. He obtained his PhD in 1973 at Heidelberg. Since 1975 he has been an assistant at the Free University of Berlin. His books include *From Hegel to Hitler: An Analysis of Hegel's Ideology of a Power-State, and the History of the Political Effects of Right-Hegelianism, 1820-1945.*

PAUL M. M. KLEP was born in 1948. He studied at the University of Nijmegen, the Agricultural University of Wageningen, and the University of Leuven, where he obtained his doctorate in 1978. He is Senior Lecturer in Economic and Social History at Nijmegen. His publications include *The Historiography of Cliometrics, The Methodology of Historical Statistics,* and *The Process of Growth, Stagnation and Transformation in 18th and 19th Century Brabant.*

I. KOVALCHENKO was born in 1923 and served in the Second World War. He graduated in 1952 from the Faculty of History of the Moscow State University and in 1955 became a lecturer there. In 1966 he was appointed Professor of Historiography. Since 1969 he has been chief editor of the journal *History of the USSR* and in 1973 he was elected a corresponding member of the Academy of Sciences of the USSR. He has been chairman of the Commission for Applying Mathematical Methods and Computers in Historical Sciences since 1966. His main publications deal with the agrarian history of Russia.

OLLE KRANTZ is a Research Fellow at the Faculty of Social Sciences of the University of Lund. His publications include: *Swedish National Product 1861-1970: New Aspects on Methods and Measurement* (with C. Nilsson); *Structural Changes in the Swedish Economy 1950-75* (forthcoming).

IRVING B. KRAVIS was born in 1916 and obtained his PhD at the University of Pennsylvania in 1947. He served in the US Department of Labor from 1946-48 and as a consultant from 1949-52. He has been a professor at the Department of Economics of the University of Pennsylvania since 1949, and was chairman of the department from 1955-58 and from 1962-67. He was Assistant Dean, Wharton School from 1958-60; a Ford Foundation faculty research fellow from 1960-71; Guggenheim fellow from 1967-68; staff member of the National Bureau of Economics in 1962. His publications include: *Domestic interests and international obligations; Structure of income; National products and the purchasing power of currencies* (co-author).

J. KRISHNAMURTY is currently Reader in Economics at the Delhi School of Economics and Associate Editor of the *Indian Economic and Social History Review*. His publications include: *The Industrial Distribution of the Working Force in India, 1901-61: a Study of Selected Aspects*. He has published a number of papers on the structure of the Indian work force since 1881 and on problems of employment planning.

DHARMA KUMAR is currently Professor of Economic History at the Delhi School of Economics, and managing editor of the *Indian Economic Review* and of the *Indian Economic and Social History Review*. She is acting as one of the general editors of the forthcoming Cambridge Economic History of India. Her publications include: *Land and Caste in South-India; India and the European Economic Community;* 'Changes in Income Distribution and Poverty in India: A Review of the Literature', in *World Development*, vol. 2, no. 1, 1974.

MAURICE LÉVY-LEBOYER was born in 1920. He is Professor of Economic History at the University of Paris X, Nanterre. His books include: *Les banques européennes et l'industrialisation internationale dans la 1 ère moitié du XIXe siècle; L'avènement de l'ère industrielle en France, 1789 – années 1880; La position internationale de la France: aspects économiques et financiers XIXe – XXe siècle* (editor).

PRIYATOSH MAITRA has been with the Indian Statistical Institute, Calcutta, and the East African Institute of Social Research, Makerere, Kampala. He is a Visiting Fellow of the University of Tokyo and is currently a member of the Economics Department of the University of Otago, New Zealand. His books include: *Import Substitution Potential in East Africa; Underdevelopment Revisited; Economic Development with or without an Industrial Revolution* (forthcoming); *Economics of Underdevelopment in Bengali.*

JAY R. MANDLE was born in 1941. He has been a Fulbright-Hays Lecturer in Economics at the University of Guyana. He is Professor of

Economics at Temple University, Philadelphia, and an associate editor of *Marxist Perspectives*. His books include: *The Plantation Economy: Population and Economic Change in Guyana, 1838-1960* and *The Roots of Black Poverty: The Southern Plantation Economy after the Civil War.*

JEAN MAYER was born in 1931. He holds a doctorate in law and a diploma in regional planning development. Since he joined the International Labour Office in Geneva in 1963 he has undertaken numerous technical co-operation missions to Africa, Asia and Latin America. In 1977 he assembled a team to assist the Portuguese planning authorities, and himself prepared the regional chapter of the plan. His publications include a socio-economic essay on Chile, and several papers and articles on regional planning development.

GERHARD MENSCH was born in 1937. He is Professor of Management Science at the International Institute of Management of Berlin. His books include: *Ablaufplanung; Stalemate in Technology; Gemischtwirtschaftliche Innovations-praxis; Von der Provinzstadt zur Industrieregion* (with H. Freudenberger).

GIORGIO MORI is Professor of Contemporary Economic History at the University of Florence. He has specialised in the history of European industrialisation. His books include: *La Rivoluzione industriale. Economia e società in Gran Bretagna nella seconda metà del secolo XVIII; Il Capitalismo industriale in Italia; L'industrializzazione in Italia (1861-1900); L'industria del ferro in Toscana dalla restaurazione alla fine del Granducato (1815-59).*

CARL-AXEL NILSSON is a senior lecturer at the University of Copenhagen. His publications include: *Swedish National Product 1861-1970: New Aspects on Methods and Measurement* (with O. Krantz); *Structural Changes in the Swedish Economy 1950-75* (forthcoming).

JOSÉ-ANTONIO OCAMPO was born in 1952. He graduated in A.B. (Economics and Sociology) in 1972 at the University of Notre Dame and obtained his PhD in economics at Yale University in 1976. He is Professor of the History of Economic Thought and the Economic History of Colombia, Department of Economics, Universidad de los Andes, Bogotà, Colombia. His books include: *Capital Accumulation and International Relations;* 'Las importaciones colombianas en el siglo XIX', in M. Urrutia (ed.), *Ensayos sobre historia economica colombiana* (forthcoming).

GYÖRGY RÁNKI was born in 1930 and holds a PhD in history and economics. From 1972-73 he was Visiting Fellow at All Souls College, Oxford, and in 1976 he was Visiting Professor at the Ecole des Hautes Etudes en Sciences Sociales, Sorbonne, Paris. He is Deputy Director at the Institute of History, Budapest. His books include: *The Development of Manufacturing Industry in Hungary, 1900-44; Economic Development in East-Central Europe in the 19th and 20th Centuries; Hungary: A Century of Economic Development; East Central Europe in the 19th and 20th Centuries.*

JÜRGEN SCHNEIDER was born in 1937. He obtained his doctorate in 1972 at the University of Erlangen, Nürnberg. From 1969-77 he was assistant to Hermann Kellenbenz in Cologne and Nürnberg. Since 1977 he has been a professor at the Zentralinstitut für Fränkische Landeskunde und Allgemeine Regionalforschung der Universität Erlangen-Nürnberg. His books include: *Handel und Unternehmer im französischen Brasiliengeschäft 1815-1848; Wirtschaftliches Wachstum im Spiegel der Wirtschaftsgeschichte* (co-editor with H. Kellenbenz and R. Gömmel); *Festschrift for Hermann Kellenbenz* (editor); *Beiträge zur Wirtschaftsgeschichte* (co-editor with H. Kellenbenz).

N. A. SIMONIYA is currently professor at the Institute of Oriental Studies, Academy of Sciences of the USSR.

NICOLE SOUBEYROUX holds a doctorate in economic sciences. She graduated from the Political Studies Institute in Paris and has been at the National Scientific Research Centre since 1955, where she is currently a research assistant. She specialises in French regional economy and is at present working on the relationships between growth and agricultural space over a long period of time.

ROBERT SUMMERS was born in 1922. He obtained his PhD in economics at the University of Stanford in 1956. He taught at Stanford from 1950-51 and at Yale from 1952-56, and was an assistant professor in the Department of Economics of the University of Pennsylvania from 1956-59. He has been Professor of Economics there since 1960, and has also been a member of the Ford Foundation and a faculty fellow. His books include: *Studies in the Micro-economy of Development* (co-author); *The Wharton Index of Capacity Utilization.*

ALICE TEICHOVA obtained a BA (hons) in economics at Leeds University in 1945, a PhD at Charles University, Prague, in 1952, a CSc in historical sciences at Charles University in 1960, and in habilitation in 1964. She has been a reader at Charles University and a Fellow of Girton College, Cambridge from 1969-71. She is a professor at the School of Social Studies, University of East Anglia, Norwich. Her books include: *An Economic Background to Munich: International Business; and Czechoslovakia 1918-38.*

JEAN-CLAUDE TOUTAIN was born in 1931 and holds a doctorate in economics. He is *Maître de Recherches* at the Centre National de la Recherche Scientifique, and Director of the Laboratory 'Histoire et Analyse de la Croissance Economique' at the University of Paris I. His books include: *La Produit de l'agriculture francaise de 1700 à 1958; La population de la France de 1700 à 1959; Gérer l'environnement* (with B. Desaigues).

JEFFREY G. WILLIAMSON was born in 1935. He has been Professor of Economics at the University of Wisconsin since 1963. He has served as co-editor, associate editor or editorial board member of *Explorations in Economic History*, the *Review of Economics and Statistics,* and *Economic Development and Cultural Change.* He was Chairman of Program Arrangements for the Madison Cliometrics Conference from 1970 to 1976, and has published widely in cliometric history. His books include: *American Growth and the Balance of Payments, 1820-1913; Dualistic Economic Development: Theory and History; Lessons from Japanese Development: An Analytical*

Economic History; Late Nineteenth Century American Development: A General Equilibrium History; A Macroeconomic History of American Inequality (forthcoming).

Part 1

Economic Disparities Among Nations

Part 1a International Disparities

1 The Main Trends in National Economic Disparities since the Industrial Revolution

Paul Bairoch

1. THE STARTING-POINT

If we exclude a certain number of small countries, which for specific reasons could benefit from exceptional resources, it appears that the differences in the international levels of income were very limited before the strong upheaval introduced by the industrial revolution. The gap between the least developed or poorest country and the richest was probably in the range of only 1.0 to 1.6. If we refer to broader economic entities, such as Western Europe or China, the gap was even more limited, of the order of 1.0 to 1.3 or less. In the framework of traditional economies, a favourable natural resource endowment brought in general a more rapid increase in population, which in turn led to a new equilibrium at a lower level of resources per capita.

It appears very likely that differences in income levels were more important at micro-regional levels than at international levels (defining micro-region as a country or region of less than two million inhabitants). Indeed, high per capita income levels could only derive from exceptional factors, and the probability that such factors are present everywhere in a large region is close to zero. Among those factors, we have on one hand natural elements such as a very fertile land or a rich subsoil or a favourable geographical situation; and on the other hand factors resulting from human activity such as industrial specialisation or, even more important for that period, commercial activity. Such commercial activity led in general to a situation where a small country performed the commercial activities of a much broader region.

Still referring to micro-regions, it should be taken into account that inside a specific region the value added per worker in industry certainly did not exceed that of agriculture by more than 100 per cent. The inter-regional disparities in agricultural productivity, even resulting from the combined effect of natural factors and of technology (but pre-agricultural revolution technology), were more important, but probably did not exceed the ratio 1.0 to 3.0. This implies that if we exclude the cases of small micro-regions specialising in international trade (e.g. the Italian republics before the sixteenth century) the greatest difference in average regional income could not exceed the ratio 1.0 to 3.0.

The concept utilised here to measure income will be the real per capita gross national product (GNP) at market prices. A very brief summary of the methodology will be presented later (see section 2). The fact that GNP per capita is used as a measure of income does not imply that it is a perfect yardstick; it is not only an inadequate measure of economic levels, it is an even more inadequate indicator of living conditions. External costs of growth are imperfectly, if at all, taken into consideration in national accounting. The same is true for such important elements in living conditions as the climate and the urban and rural environment. But at the present stage of research for alternative indicators, and especially as far as historical data are concerned, real GNP per capita remains the least questionable single indicator of level of income – no more, but no less, than that.

In a recent study, I tried to estimate the greatest spread of national income per capita before the industrial revolution.[1] This was done by six different approaches which all provided very converging results.

Table 1.1 provides GNP per capita figures for 13 countries at a stage of

TABLE 1.1 Real GNP per capita for selected countries at a stage of development close to that of traditional societies (in 1960 US dollars and prices)

	Coefficient used to correct 1960 data [(a)]	*GNP per capita*	
		Periods	*Data*
COUNTRIES NOW DEVELOPED			
Great Britain	1.30	1700	160 – 200
United States	1.00	1710	200 – 260
France	1.15	1781 – 1790	170 – 200
Russia	1.14 [(b)]	1860	160 – 200
Sweden	1.20	1860	190 – 230
Japan	1.75	1885	160 – 200
COUNTRIES NOW LESS DEVELOPED			
Egypt	2.10	1887	170 – 210
Ghana	1.70	1891	90 – 150
India	2.80	1900	130 – 160
Iran	1.75	1900	140 – 220
Jamaica	1.30	1832	240 – 280
Mexico	1.60	1900	150 – 190
Philippines	1.70	1902	170 – 210

(a) To correct the 1960 GNP data expressed in local prices (converted at the prevailing rate of exchange) into 1960 US dollars and prices.
(b) Correction not only for price differences, but also for the translation of net material product into GNP.
Note: Not necessarily comparable with data provided in the other tables since the methodology is not strictly comparable (see text).
SOURCES: P. BAIROCH: 'Ecarts internationaux des niveaux de vie avant la Révolution industrielle', *Annales, Economies, Sociétés, Civilisations,* 34ᵉ année, No. 1, January-February 1979 (pp. 145-71).

development preceding or close to traditional societies. Those figures derive from the application to the corrected 1960 levels of GNP per capita of the various available historical series of growth of the volume of per capita GNP. If we exclude the USA and Jamaica, then two micro-regions of some 300,000 inhabitants, the spread of income lies between some 130 and 200 dollars, a gap of 1.0 to 1.5. After taking into consideration various elements tending either to increase or reduce this spread, the probable maximum spread was in the order of 1.0 to 1.4 – 1.6.

Among the other methods used, the most significant is that of the determination of the minimal cost of living in current prices for countries which, in the first half of the nineteenth century, had already reached a level of development leading to an average standard of living higher than those of the richest countries (but not micro-regions) in the framework of traditional societies. Comparing the minimal cost of living to the average level of consumption per capita provides an excellent indicator of the extreme spread of income before the industrial revolution. The data were assembled, and the computation was made for four countries; the result was a probable spread of 1.0 to 1.5 – 1.7.

The other four methods and the results they provided in terms of the probable extreme range of income are as follows:

situation of European countries at the beginning of the nineteenth century in terms of real GNP per capita: 1.0 to 1.4 – 1.6;

long-term (for more than two or three centuries) evolution of real wages in traditional societies: 1.0 to 1.4 – 1.6;

per capita income of European cities in the sixteenth and seventeenth centurie (the GNP was provided by an indicator method[2]): 1.0 to 1.5 – 1.7;

last but not least, the contemporary views of national inequalities as assessed by seventeenth and eighteenth-century pioneers of national accounting: 1.0 to 1.3 – 1.5.

Thus, it is possible to conclude that before the industrial revolution, the income gap between the poorest and the richest country was certainly smaller than the ratio 1.0 to 2.0, and probably of the order of only 1.0 to 1.5. In terms of 1960 US dollars and prices, the lowest level for traditional countries lay around $130 – 150, the highest around $190 – 240. This does not take into account primitive societies, the poorest of which had probably an 'income level' some 30 per cent below the poorest traditional country at a stage beyond that of the neolithic revolution. Obviously, there existed (and may still exist) primitive societies that were richer than very poor traditional societies.

2. NATIONAL ECONOMIC DISPARITIES SINCE THE INDUSTRIAL REVOLUTION: METHODOLOGICAL SUMMARY

The data and analysis that follow are based on personal research published or in process of being published as three articles.[3] Our ambition has been to provide better figures than those presently available, but 'better' does not mean perfect and does not necessarily mean that the margin of error has become very small. The fact that those figures are reproduced without rounding does not imply that the margin of error is correspondingly low. For developed regions, per capita GNP figures have a probable margin of some 8 - 10 per cent for pre-1913 data, and some 5 per cent for post-1913 data. For Third World regions, this goes up to some 15 per cent. On individual country levels those margins are higher, ranging from a minimum of 7 per cent to a maximum of 30 per cent. Although recent data as a rule obviously have a lower margin of error, it should be taken into account that the narrow spread of per capita income until the 1850s contributes to lessening the amount of error. Lastly, it should be considered that, in general, the margin of error for the trends is smaller than that for levels.

It is impossible to provide in the present framework all the methodological aspects involved in the various stages of calculations and estimations that led to the data used in this text. The methodological appendixes of the three articles where this data is presented in full cover more than 60 printed pages. This implies that the few short paragraphs that follow can only provide a very crude summary of the major aspects.

All the series concern the gross national product at market prices, for which we use the abbreviation GNP. The concept of gross national product at market prices is based on what is now called the former SNA (System of National Accounts) adopted by the Statistical Commission of the United Nations. We have not used the new SNA for the simple reason that some 99 per cent of the pre-1970 data and practically 100 per cent of the pre-1950 data are available in the former SNA. The new SNA, which was adopted in 1968, is only beginning to be progressively implemented. Furthermore, for the present purpose, the differences between the two concepts are negligible.

For the developed countries, the starting-point for the calculations was to correct each country's GNP per capita in 1960 for the differences in real purchasing power of the currencies. For this, the available results of international price comparison studies, as well as those of the various physical indicators approach or other short-cut methods of real income, were used. Thus, all individual country GNP per capita is expressed in 1960 US dollars and prices. The available historical series of growth of the volume of the GNP was applied backward and forward to these corrected levels. For countries and periods for which no historical series of GNP were available, I calculated them on the basis of the major aggregates. The figures for real GNP per capita resulting from the above calculations were compared with a series of physical indicators, and adjusted accordingly. This was done for four periods: 1970, 1928/29, 1899/1901, and around 1860. The intermediary figures were adjusted to those corrected benchmarks.

Calculations for the Third World were restricted to five regions: Africa, America, Asia (except China), China, and Oceania. For each region, an index of the volume of the GNP was calculated for the 1900-77 period. This index resulted from the aggregation (using adequate weighting) of the six series of production: food, export crops, mining, industrial production, construction, and services. For the 1900-50 period, these production series were obtained through calculation. On the basis of the various available data for individual countries' real GNP per capita levels, the average for each region was calculated for 1960. This was tested for both 1900 and 1960 by the use of physical indicators. As far as the pre-1900 figures are concerned, they were based on a systematic survey of the existing literature on historical GNP series or other indicators of standard of living (real salaries, production series, etc.). Pre-1900 data should be regarded as very conjectural.

3. DISPARITIES BETWEEN THE DEVELOPED WORLD AND THE THIRD WORLD

It is very likely that, in the middle of the eighteenth century, the average standard of living in Europe was a little bit lower than that of the rest of the world. This was due to the high level achieved by the Chinese civilisation, and the relative importance of that country in the rest of the world (some 36 per cent). Till the years 1815-20, the impact of the industrial revolution was negligible for what would later become the developed world. There was still a parity of average income levels between the two regions, since at its outset the industrial revolution concerned only a small fringe of the future developed countries, and since growth was very slow in the beginning.

TABLE 1.2 Real GNP per capita trends of major economic regions and of the world (in 1960 US dollars and prices)

	Total GNP (billions)			*GNP per capita (dollars)*		
	Developed countries	*Third World*	*World*	*Developed countries*	*Third World*	*World*
1750	35	112	148	182	188	187
1800	47	137	183	198	188	191
1830	67	150	218	237	183	197
1860	118	159	277	324	174	220
1880	180	164	344	406	176	250
1900	297	184	480	540	175	301
1913	430	217	646	662	192	364
1928	568	252	819	781	194	405
1938	678	293	971	856	202	433
1950	889	335	1224	1054	203	490
1960	1394	514	1909	1453	250	633
1970	2386	800	3185	2229	308	868
1977(a)	3108	1082	4190	2739	355	1001

(a) Provisional figures.
Notes: The degree of rounding off of the figures does not imply a correspondingly low margin of error.
Regional appellations apply to actual status.

But already in the 1830s, owing to the combined effects of the spread of the industrial revolution and to the regression in standards of living in some countries outside the developed world, the gap became significant (see Table 1.2). The regression of income in those countries was due not only to the negative effects of increased economic relations between the two regions, but also to a negative phase of classical long-term cycles. The income gap increased substantially between 1830 and 1872-76, when the total GNP of developed countries probably exceeded that of the Third World. Around 1872-76, the developed countries, with some 31 per cent of the world population, concentrated 50 per cent of the world's income. This implies that the gap in average incomes was then already in the range of 1.0 to 2.2. This reached 3.4 by about 1913; 5.2 in 1950; 7.2 in 1970 and 7.7 in 1977. If the trend prevailing during the period 1950-77 persists, the gap in real income will be of the order of 1.0 to 10.8 in the year 2000.

From the beginning of the nineteenth century until the 1950s (and to a small degree later) this evolution of relative average income reveals only imperfectly the divergent evolutions of standards of living of the local population, since it is not possible to take into account the high level of income of the European settlers and the transfer of income resulting from the export surpluses of colonial trade.

TABLE 1.3 Gaps in terms of real GNP per capita

	GNP per capita in 1960 US dollars and prices				*Gaps between developed countries and Third World*		
	Developed countries		*Third World*				
	Total A	*Most developed B*	*Total C*	*Less developed D*	*A/C*	*B/C*	*B/D*
1750	182	230	188	130	1.0	1.2	1.8
1800	198	240	188	130	1.1	1.3	1.8
1830	237	360	183	130	1.3	2.0	2.8
1860	324	580	174	130	1.9	3.3	4.5
1913	662	1350	192	130	3.4	7.0	10.4
1950	1054	2420	203	135	5.2	11.9	17.9
1960	1453	2800	250	140	5.8	11.2	20.0
1970	2229	3600	308	140	7.2	11.7	25.7
1977(a)	2737	4220	355	145	7.7	11.9	29.1

(a) Provisional figures.
Notes: The degree of rounding off of the figures does not imply a correspondingly low margin of error.
Regional appellations apply to present status.

But even more significant is the gap between the more developed countries of the industrialised world and the Third World, since it is from the former that the domination effects originated. In this case, the gap was already of

1.0 to 2.0 in the 1830s and of 1.0 to 7.0 in 1913. And the consequences of this gap on the Third World were aggravated by the fact that the more developed regions (e.g. the United Kingdom) achieved such a level through a combination of industrialisation and foreign trade. From 1.0 to 2.0 the gap increased to 1.0 to 7.0 in 1913 and to 1.0 to 11.9 in 1950 (see Table 1.3). Since 1950, owing to the slower growth of the United States, the gap remains stable.

A similarity to the loss of relative speed of the United States can be found in the nineteenth century: it concerned the United Kingdom, beginning with the years 1860-70. And those two evolutions had similar consequences on the domination effects: a multiplication of centres of gravity. From 1780-90 to 1860-70 the spread of colonial possessions essentially concerned the United Kingdom, while after that period practically all European countries participated in the colonial scramble. From 1946 to 1960-65, the United States had a predominant position in the areas of trade, international investment and international aid. Since the 1960s, the intervention of the other powers has become more important.

Finally, it should be noted that, if the comparison of real incomes made above provides relatively valid indicators of the average levels of income inside the countries of the Third World, these real incomes underestimate what could be called 'purchasing power on international markets'. This is due to the fact that, in order to provide figures in relatively comparable international prices, Third World GNP data had to be increased substantially. For the Third World market economies, this implied a multiplication by 1.95. Therefore the gap expressed in monetary terms is much more pronounced. For 1977, the average income of developed countries expressed in 'purchasing power on international markets' is some 15 times that of Third World countries.

4. DISPARITIES INSIDE INDUSTRIALISED REGIONS

The scope of the two world wars, the severity of the depression of the 1930s and the emergence of new economic regions led to deep breaks in the process of economic growth of the developed countries. It is therefore necessary to divide into three the period that separates us from the beginning of the nineteenth century.

The nineteenth century is the period *par excellence* of the formation of disparities among developed countries, disparities which resulted essentially from the differences in the periods when those countries started their process of development and to a lesser extent from differences in natural resources (mainly between Europe and North America). Whether this process of development was concentrated in industry or in agriculture seems to imply no important difference as far as the increases in standards of living were concerned. Indeed, and this is a major conclusion that derives from a single observation of GNP levels before the First World War, among the eight richest countries in the world there were four non-industrialised countries (Canada, Australia, New Zealand and Denmark).

Around 1800, the gap between the three poorest and the three richest of the developed countries was only in the range of 1.0 to 1.5; as early as 1860 this had reached 2.9, and in 1913, 4.0. At this period the most developed country (the USA) had a GNP per capita of some $1350. This means an income that is more than sixteen times higher than the physiological minimum, estimated to be around $80.

If in terms of GNP per capita the United States overtook the United Kingdom around 1875-80, in terms of total GNP this was already the case ten years earlier. But the United States had to wait till around 1892-99 before becoming the country with the largest total GNP, since till that period, due to her large population, China held this position.

TABLE 1.4 Real GNP per capita for constant geographical boundaries (in 1960 US dollars and prices: actual boundaries)

	1830	*1860*	*1913*	*1929*	*1950*	*1960*	*1970*
Australia	–	580	1095	990	1640	1970	2650
Austria	–	390	700	715	765	1300	1960
Belgium	240	400	815	1020	1245	1520	2385
Bulgaria	–	215	285	340	420	725	1380
Canada	280	405	1110	1220	1785	2205	3005
Czechoslovakia	–	–	500	560	810	1340	1980
Denmark	225	320	885	955	1320	1710	2555
Finland	190	245	525	600	1005	1430	3285
France	275	380	670	890	1055	1500	2535
Germany, West	240	345	775	900	995	1790	2705
Germany, East	–	–	–	–	690	1380	2100
Greece	–	235	335	405	410	635	1255
Hungary	–	–	375	430	515	875	1530
Ireland	–	–	655	710	805	990	1520
Italy	240	280	455	525	600	985	1670
Japan	180	175	310	425	405	855	2130
Netherlands	270	410	740	980	1115	1490	2385
New Zealand	–	420	800	1060	1895	1860	2390
Norway	225	325	615	845	1225	1640	2405
Poland	–	–	–	420	545	845	1400
Portugal	250	290	335	380	440	550	985
Romania	–	215	370	365	360	575	1060
South Africa	–	–	350	410	620	710	905
Spain	–	325	400	520	430	640	1400
Soviet Union	180	200	345	350	600	925	1640
Sweden	235	300	705	875	1640	2155	2965
Switzerland	240	415	895	1150	1590	2135	2785
United Kingdom	370	600	1070	1160	1400	1780	2225
United States	240	550	1350	1775	2415	2800	3605
Yugoslavia	–	225	300	370	360	610	1035

Note: The degree of rounding off of the figures does not imply a correspondingly low margin of error.

If for all the developed countries the inequality of income increased rapidly in the nineteenth century (see Table 1.5), it should be noted that if we restrict the analysis to the ten countries that began their development before 1860[4] the picture is a different one. For those countries, there was a process of equalisation, especially after 1860. For those ten countries the coefficient of variation of GNP per capita passes from 23.0 to 23.2 between 1860 and 1913. If the USA is excluded, it is from 21.8 to 17.5.

For the developed countries as a whole, the First World War brought an increase in the spread of incomes, since among the countries that did not suffer from the war there was a majority of rich countries. In terms of global economic potential, the upheaval was even deeper, leading to a shift of gravity from Europe to North America. In 1913 Europe's total GNP was in the range of $265 billion, compared to 140 for North America; in 1920, the comparable figures were 213 and 160, and in 1925, 275 and 195.

If the First World War led to stronger inequalities in incomes, this was mainly restricted to the more developed countries, since the others (except the USSR) reached a higher level in 1929 than in 1913. This leads to a quasi-stability of the coefficient of variation of GNP per capita. Where between 1830 and 1913 this coefficient (for 25 developed countries) increased from 18.2 per cent to 46.8 per cent (see Table 1.5), from 1913 to 1929 it gained only 0.7 of a point, and from 1929 to 1938 it regressed to 41.0 per cent. But this amelioration in the equality of income distribution in the developed world is to be linked to the differences in the impact of the depression, which affected the less industrialised countries more mildly; and to the differences in armament policies.

TABLE 1.5 Coefficient of variation of per capita Gross National Product of developed countries (%)

	Twenty-five countries (a)	*Thirty countries* (b)
1830	18.2	–
1860	34.7	–
1913	46.8	–
1929	47.5	–
1938	41.0	–
1950	56.0	56.1
1960	45.7	44.5
1970	34.9	32.3
1977	31.2	29.8

(a) Countries in the boundaries of 1970 and for which fairly valid series exist on this definition even before 1913.
(b) All developed countries of more than three million inhabitants in 1977 (see list in Table 1.4).

But besides those rather cyclical developments, mention should be made of more fundamental changes, the most important of which was the loss of ground of the United Kingdom. In 1913, this country still exceeded by some 20 per cent the GNP per capita levels of the other three richest countries in Europe (30 per cent around 1860). In 1938 six European countries had a level of only 10 per cent below that of the United Kingdom, and around 1977 eleven European countries (and six outside Europe) had a higher GNP per capita.

In this context, one should stress the time-lag which generally exists between a change in the relative economic position of a country and its intervention (or desire to intervene) in the international arena. It would seem that a time-span of at least one generation is needed for political leaders to become aware of their country's relative advance or falling behind.

The Second World War had more or less the same impact as the first. But the 30 years of rapid growth that followed were characterised by an even more rapid development of the poorest of the developed countries. This brought about a very sharp reduction in the disparities of income. In 1950, the gap between the three poorest and the three richest countries in the developed world was still 1.0 to 5.4; in 1977 it was reduced to 1.0 to 3.0. The coefficient of variation regressed from 56.1 per cent to 29.8 per cent, falling back to the level reached in the years 1840-50. Another expression of this reduction of inequality can be provided by the Gini coefficient of income distribution (on national bases) inside the developed world; from 0.3384 in 1950, this coefficient is reduced to 0.1620 in 1977.[5]

TABLE 1.6 Real GNP per capita of developed regions (in 1960 US dollars and prices)

	Western Europe	*Eastern Europe*	*North America*	*Japan*	*All developed countries*
1750	190	165	230	180	182
1800	215	177	239	180	198
1830	270	196	322	180	237
1860	379	231	536	175	324
1880	455	279	724	199	406
1900	588	328	1052	290	540
1913	693	412	1333	310	662
1928	784	426	1657	430	781
1938	868	566	1527	660	856
1950	928	588	2364	405	1054
1960	1354	932	2748	855	1453
1970	2098	1606	3547	2130	2229
1977 (a)	2491	2149	4168	2830	2739

(a) Provisional figures.
Notes: The degree of rounding-off of the figures does not imply a correspondingly low margin of error.
Regional appellations apply to present status.

For what could be called the big economic blocks, the recent reduction in economic inequality was also very rapid (see Table 1.6). Western Europe was catching up with North America. In 1950, its GNP per capita represented 39 per cent of that of North America; in 1977, 60 per cent. The USSR was coming close to the level of Western Europe, and Japan overtook Western Europe probably as early as 1967-70.

This process of equalisation in development levels, which was also noted during the period 1860-1913 for countries already affected by the industrial revolution, is a very important fact. It allows us to postulate the possibility of a historical constant. To each phase of development there could be a corresponding logistic growth curve.

However, it should be stressed that the rapid catching-up in levels of GNP per capita gives only an imperfect picture of the catching-up in the standard of living. GNP is essentially a measure of flows and not of stocks. Furthermore, even if we exclude external costs of growth, the two following elements should be taken into account. The first is simply the fact that rapid economic growth implies a high rate of investment, thus leaving a smaller share of GNP for consumption. The second element, the more often neglected stock component, is the fact that the standard of living of a given period is also dependent on the standard of living prevailing during the preceding years which allowed the accumulation of what could be called a 'welfare capital'. This can have many aspects, ranging from the stock of private goods to the quality of public infrastructure, and from the level of education to that of health. In fact, the standard of living of a given year should be expressed as a weighted average (decreasing with time) of the level of consumption for a period of ten to thirty years. Such correction could lead in some cases to a difference of some 30 per cent between the 'real standard of living' and GNP per capita.[6]

5. DISPARITIES INSIDE THE THIRD WORLD

We shall restrict ourselves here to disparities at the continental level. A valid analysis on a country level could only be performed beginning with the 1960s, and is therefore excluded from our framework. But it is worth mentioning that, at the present time, the disparities in national levels of income are greater inside the Third World than the developed one. Even excluding the oil producers, the gap between the poorest and the richest less developed country is in the range of 1.0 to 12.0.

For the nineteenth century, the data are very approximative, but it is very likely that the trends depicted in Table 1.7 are close to reality, at least for Asia and Latin America. While the GNP per capita in Asia probably declined, that of Latin America progressed by some 45 per cent, leading to an increasing gap. Most of the progress made in Latin America was due to a fairly rapid growth in the temperate countries (Argentina, Uruguay, Chile). The latter three countries could in fact hardly be included then in the Third World. To a large extent, the same pattern persisted till the 1950s.

TABLE 1.7 Real GNP per capita of Third World regions (in 1960 US dollars and prices)

	Market Economy Countries					
	Africa	*America*	*Asia*	*Total*	*China*	*Total Third World*
1800	130	245	180	171	210	188
1860	130	260	164	164	195	177
1913	142	357	182	195	188	192
1938	158	400	187	211	187	202
1950	183	467	178	222	166	203
1960	220	520	210	261	230	250
1970	268	610	246	309	306	308
1977 (a)	283	723	288	359	346	355

(a) Provisional figures.
Notes: The degree of rounding-off of the figures does not imply a correspondingly low margin of error.
Regional appellations apply to present status.

The economic growth of the last thirty years has been rather uniform in the different regions forming the so-called developing market economies. But the salient fact for these years is the more rapid growth of China, whose GNP per capita overtook that of the rest of Asia around 1955-60, and which, in 1977, had some 15-25 per cent higher income. However, and this is often neglected, part of this rapid growth is a recovery process from the very low levels of 1948-50. Furthermore, it is certain that China's figures have a larger margin of error, but it is very likely that the data presented in Table 1.7 reflect the fundamental trends quite adequately.

However, it should be underlined that the more rapid growth of China's GNP per capita was mainly the result of a more moderate population increase compared to that of the rest of Asia. China's population data also have a wider margin of error. Around 1950, China's population can be estimated as in the neighbourhood of 545 millions. For 1977, the likely figure is 910 millions, but the probable range goes from a minimum of some 840 to a maximum of 980. Thus between 1950 and 1977 the annual increase of population was of the order of 1.9 per cent, with a range from 1.6 per cent to 2.2 per cent. For the rest of Asia, it was 2.3 per cent (probably a little underestimated). If we apply the population increase of the rest of Asia to China's total GNP growth for the period 1950-77, we get for 1977 a GNP per capita of some $310, i.e. only 5 per cent above that of the rest of Asia (instead of the probable 20 per cent).

6. NON-EXHAUSTIVE INVENTORY OF THE PROBABLE FACTORS OF LONG-TERM INEQUALITIES IN ECONOMIC GROWTH

The day we can claim that the problem of understanding the causes of inequality in economic growth has been solved, a large part of the difficulties, as well as the joys, of economic history will disappear. But unfortunately, or perhaps fortunately, the time is still far away. Probably the answer to the problem will come (if ever it comes) in the form of a large group of factors specific to each medium-term time-period for each individual country. So the purpose of this final part is limited to listing the specific factors for which a practically unlimited number of combinations (weighted) include the probable answers.

But, before going over this inventory, I would like to exclude from it what can be called tautological factors. Among those, for example, are explanations of rapid economic growth through high levels of investment or by strong increase in productivity. Both of those are modalities of growth rather than causes. At the same time, to explain rapid growth by the urbanisation process, or by the changes in the structure of active population, leads also to confusion between causes and consequences.

The list of the main causes will be divided (only partly arbitrarily) into four groups: Human factors; localisation effects; social environment; and historical accidents. 'Causes' and 'factors' will be used as synonyms.

(a) Human factors

It is obvious that human factors cannot be treated as constants derived from geographical or ethnic determinants; rather, they are mainly the results of an acquisition process. This is true, but it leaves open the problem of the form and causes of this process. The major human factors are essentially the result of the dominant attitude of the population about amount and quality of work; level of savings (and consumption); utilisation of savings (and the problem of risk and security in general); and geographical and sectoral mobility. In this context, the presence of minorities with attitudes differing from the general society may lead them to play an important role. But this is only possible when social tolerance is at a sufficiently well developed level.

Other aspects of the problem concern levels of education and health. But these can be more easily modified in the short run.

(b) Localisation effects

Here, one is faced with one of the major causes of inequality of income before the industrial revolution. The main factors involved in this case are the quality and the quantity (per capita) of land, the extent of natural resources, the geographical location (in relation to other important economic regions), the natural communications network, the climate and the size of the country.

If for the short and medium term these factors can be considered as constant, the problem is quite different for the long term. In this case almost no localisation benefit or handicap can be considered as stable. Such is obviously the case of mineral resources, which are always limited and nonrenewable. The value of those resources depends on effective demand, which can totally disappear. The positive aspect of geographical location is a function both of the nature and direction of exchange flows; those in turn can be radically modified through changes in demand and in the technology of transportation. Such things as changes in political boundaries can drastically modify the situation. Local handicaps and benefits can both appear and disappear. Both can be present at the same time: for example, trade routes are very often also paths of war, which can bring about the destruction of the accumulated capital which they had contributed to create. Agricultural assets can be drastically modified by climatic changes as well as by technological innovations and by shifts in demand.

(c) Social environment

The list of factors that can be included under this heading is large as well as very disparate. Furthermore, some of those are very closely linked to the human factors. Broadly speaking, in this group one should include all aspects of social institutions whether religious, political, legal or strictly social. By their mere form most of those factors can be considered as unstable in the long run, even if in some cases they lasted for centuries (and some still last).

(d) Historical accidents

All positive or negative results from international relations belong to this group of factors. Among those the two most important are the extent (and frequency) of military conflicts (including civil wars) and the colonisation process. This last aspect leads to two series of inequalities: between colonised or non-colonised countries (depending on the form of colonisation); and between countries having more or less economically gainful colonies. The consequences of those situations are not always uniform. Thus if being colonised implied in general a negative effect on growth, in some cases the opposite was true. If the absence of military conflict is generally a positive factor, in other cases the destruction of industrial capacity can be a positive element.

Among the accidents of history one should also include the general tendencies of international economic policies (especially in the field of trade) and the adoption (forced or not) of specific economic regimes. A further and very important element to include here is the choice of a specific national economic policy. A good minister of economics capable of implementing a good policy is certainly a rare historical accident. This leads us to another rare historical accident: the industrial revolution. It has been a very strong and unique factor in growth and well-being as well as a unique contributor to economic inequalities at international and regional levels.

NOTES

[1]Bairoch, P., 'Ecarts internationaux des niveaux de vie avant la révolution industrielle', *Annales, ESC,* 34e annẽe, No. 1, January-February 1979, pp. 145-171.

[2]Bairoch, P., 'Estimations du revenu national dans les sociétés occidentales pré-industrielles et au XIXe siècle', *Revue Economique,* vol. XXVIII, no. 2, Mar 1977, pp. 177-208.

[3]Bairoch, P., 'Europe's Gross National Product, 1800-1975', *Journal of European Economic History,* vol. 5, no. 2, Fall 1976, pp. 273-340; 'Le volume des productions et du Produit National dans le Tiers-Monde, 1900-1977'; 'World Gross National Product, 1750-1977: Computations, Estimates and Guesses' (both forthcoming).

[4]Belgium, Canada, Denmark, France, Germany, Norway, Sweden, Switzerland, United Kingdom and United States.

[5]Bairoch, P., 'Historical Evolution of Inequality of Levels of Income among Developed and Underdeveloped Countries, 1800-1977', paper presented to the Social Science History Association, Second Annual Meeting, Ann Arbor, October 1977. A revised paper will appear.

[6]This estimate used the cases of the United States and Japan as examples of divergent rate of growth and levels of capital formation. For the estimation of the possible effect of the divergent growth rate, it was postulated that the 'real income' of a given year is the result of the weighted average of that final year plus the nineteen years preceding it. The weight attached to the final year was presumed to be 100 and for the nineteen preceding years the weight was arbitrarily presumed to decline at a constant rate (– 14.6 per cent) from 20 to 1 (thus for final year minus 1 = 20, final year minus 2 = 17.1, final year minus 3 = 14.6, etc.). This implies a difference of 16 per cent in real income. (If the weight for the nineteen preceding years were taken to decline from 10 to 1, the difference would be 13 per cent; from 30 to 1, 18 per cent.) The effect of the difference in the share of investment leads to a 12 per cent difference in 'real income'. Thus by summing up the two effects, the total difference is of the order of 30 per cent.

2 Inequality among Nations: 1950 and 1975

Robert Summers, Irving B. Kravis and Alan Heston

Differential growth rates of both national product and population among countries lead over time to changing patterns of relative affluence and poverty. In this chapter the consequences of these differential growth rates are investigated by examining their implications for the world distribution of income over the period from 1950 to 1975. The results reported here are preliminary to a more comprehensive effort in progress which takes account of intra-country as well as inter-country income inequality.

The term 'world' exaggerates the geographic coverage of this chapter. Out of the 150-odd political jurisdictions listed in the United Nations *Yearbook of National Accounts Statistics,* 106 industrialised and developing countries are included which contain about 62 per cent of the world's population in 1950 and 64 per cent in 1975.[1] More complete coverage of the world is under way.

1. DATA AND METHODS

The starting-point for the derivation of the data used is a set of international comparisons of real gross domestic product for 1970 reported in Kravis, Heston and Summers (1978b). These comparisons avoid the usual procedure of converting GDPs in domestic currencies to dollars via exchange rates, because, as is widely recognised, a country's exchange rate is often a misleading indicator of the purchasing power parity (PPP) of its currency. The pattern of the discrepancy between the exchange rate and PPP for 15 countries uncovered in the research of the International Comparison Project of the United Nations,[2] plus other structural relations subsequently unearthed, was exploited[3] to estimate 1970 real product per capita comparisons for a large number of countries. The 1970 estimates were extrapolated backwards in time to 1950 and forwards to 1975, using a procedure which drew principally on the growth rates in real product for each of the 106 countries as reported by the World Bank.[4]

The World Bank real product series for the various countries refer to gross domestic product (GDP), a concept which assumes constant terms of trade over the years. Because the assumption of fixed terms of trade was inappropriate for a study of world inequality, the GDP estimates were adjusted to allow for terms of trade changes.[5] The resulting estimates of gross domestic income (GDY) used in what follows incorporated each country's gains or losses from changes in the terms of trade and are expressed relative to the base year (1970).[6]

For the purposes of this chapter, since only inter-country income differences are considered, it is assumed that each resident of a country receives his or her per capita share of the country's GDY.[7] The exercise to be carried out is to look at the size distributions of income of individuals all over the world for both 1950 and 1975. The object is to see how global inequality arising from inter-country differences in growth has changed in the last quarter-century.

The problems with such a simple exercise are manifest. Inequality measures for size distributions in each of the years ignore the additional inequality inherent in intra-country inequality and they take no account of differences in need arising out of differences among countries in demographic composition, geography and climate. In addition, the GDP per capita and GDY per capita estimates are subject to well-known theoretical and statistical deficiencies, the theoretical issues arising out of the inadequacy of conventionally measured GDP itself as a proper measure of material welfare, and the intertemporal and interspatial statistical problems including those resulting from the crudeness of deflation procedures, especially for sectors such as construction, durable goods, and services in the health, education and government areas. Furthermore, for some purposes it might be regarded as more useful to examine the global distribution of private consumption rather than that of GDP.

In what follows, inequality of each income distribution is measured by a single summary number, the so-called Gini coefficient, also known as the concentration ratio. The simplest intuitive interpretation of this index is that, apart from a scale factor relating to the total income that is distributed, the index measures the average absolute income difference of all pairs of income recipients. The Gini coefficient is intimately associated with the Lorenz curve, which is a geometric representation of the relationship between each cumulative percentile of the income distribution and the proportion of total income that is received by all recipients up to but not above that percentile. The Gini coefficient is simply twice the area between the Lorenz curve and the straight line joining the points (0.0) and (1.1). One income distribution may be judged more unequal than another unambiguously under a broad set of social views if its Lorenz curve lies wholly below that of the other. If the Lorenz curves of two distributions do not intersect, then the differences between Gini coefficients can be used to determine which distribution is more unequal. But if the Lorenz curves intersect, equality of Gini coefficients cannot be taken as clear evidence that the inequality displayed by the two distributions is the same. That this is of some practical significance will be apparent in what follows below.[8]

2. CHANGES IN INEQUALITY

The quarter of a century 1950-75 was a period of unprecedented growth in the world economy. For the part of the world under scrutiny here, gross product tripled while population increased by two-thirds.[9] Early in the period, the emphasis was on growth, but it was not very long before voices came to be heard claiming with increasing force that growth was very uneven, and uneven in a particularly unfortunate way. The rich countries were growing rapidly while the poorest countries were being left further and further behind. The per annum growth in per capita GDY for 18 industrial countries[10] was 3.05 per cent for the 25-year period. For the remaining 88 developing countries the corresponding rate was 2.96 per cent, but for the 27 poorest of these countries the rate was much lower. (Six of the 27 with about 2½ per cent of the population of all 106 actually suffered declines in per capita GDY.)

One might expect on the basis of these developments that world inequality – or at least the between-country component of it, which is what is being measured here – would rise. In fact, the Gini coefficient for the 106 countries showed virtually no change, moving from 0.546 in 1950 to only 0.555 in 1975.[11] It is surprising that a period of such rapid and uneven growth should be characterised by stability in the distribution of income.

The obvious explanation is that there must have been offsetting changes, some pushing in the direction of more equality and others towards less equality.[12] The way in which the composition of these changes can be described, it will be seen, is sensitive to the principle which is followed for grouping the countries in order to summarise the shifts. Reliance is placed here on a classification widely used both in international political discourse and in the work of the World Bank. Countries are divided into low-income, middle-income and industrialised groups, with the oil exporters (mainly middle-income) sometimes separated out.[13]

Gini coefficients and related basic data for these groups of countries are set out in Table 2.1. It can be seen that the overall constancy of the Gini coefficient masks both changes in intra-group inequality and differential growth rates of the groups. There were small increases in the coefficient within each of the two groups of developing countries (0.096 to 0.113 and 0.273 to 0.311) and a sharp drop in the coefficient in the industrialised countries (0.302 to 0.131).[14] In connection with the latter point, a part of the underlying phenomena was the relatively rapid growth of Japan, Germany, France and others that enabled them to attain incomes closer to the US. However, this was by no means a complete explanation; the Gini coefficients for the 17 industrialised countries excluding the US declined from 0.242 in 1950 to 0.094 in 1975. On either basis, the per capita incomes of the industrialised countries are now relatively similar compared to the income diversity found among these countries in the past or among the middle-income countries in the past or at present. Less happily, there is also a high degree of income similarity among the low-income countries. Comprising

TABLE 2.1 Population and Level and Distribution of Real Per Capita Gross Domestic Income, 1950 and 1975

	Low Income	*Middle Income*		*Indus-trialised*	*World*
		All	*Exc. Oil Exp.*		
No. of countries	27	61	51	18	106
Percentage distribution of population					
1950	40.8	26.9	20.4	32.3	100.0
1975	43.5	31.0	22.5	25.5	100.0
GDY					
1950	10.1	16.1	12.9	73.8	100.0
1975	8.2	24.4	17.0	67.4	100.0
Growth in per capita real GDY per annum					
1950-75	1.33	3.59	3.18	3.05	2.45
Per capita GDY (US 1970=100)					
1950	4.2	10.2	10.8	38.9	17.0
1975	5.9	24.5	23.5	82.5	31.2
Gini coefficient					
1950	0.096	0.273	0.264	0.302	0.546
1975	0.113	0.311	0.294	0.131	0.555

over 40 per cent of the population of the 106 countries included, the 27 low-income countries earn only about 10 per cent of the total income, leaving them in 1975 with an average per capita real GDY of only 5.6 per cent of the level of the US's per capita GDY for the same year.[15]

Table 2.1 also shows the offsetting effects on world equality in the average growth rates of the three groups of countries: 1.33 per cent for the low-income LDCs, 3.59 per cent for the higher-income LDCs, and 3.05 per cent for the industrialised nations. The slow growth of the low-income countries relative to the other two groups tended to push the world Gini coefficient up, while the more rapid growth of the middle-income countries relative to the industrialised ones tended to push it down. The essential point remains the same whether the oil-exporting countries are included or excluded from the middle group.

With such similar Gini coefficients for 1950 and 1975 and such pronounced cross-currents in the movements of individual country incomes it is not surprising to find that the Lorenz curves for the two years cross (see Figure 2.1). As would be expected from the growth lag of the low-income countries, the 1975 curve falls below that of 1950 for the lower portion of the population distribution. Then, as the effects of the relative gains of the middle-income countries are felt, the 1975 curve crosses the 1950 curve and runs above it. It is no coincidence that the crossing-point is in the neighbourhood of the percentile of the world distribution dividing the industrialised nations from the developing ones. It was observed above that the industrialised countries together experienced an annual per capita growth rate of 3.05 per cent while the rate for the others in the aggregate was very close, 2.96 per cent. If the two rates were exactly the same and the population composition remained unchanged, the ordinates of the Lorenz curves would be exactly the same at the percentile dividing the two groups. That percentile was at 0.68 in 1950 and 0.75 in 1975, and, as can be seen in Figure 2.1, the curves cross just above 0.70.

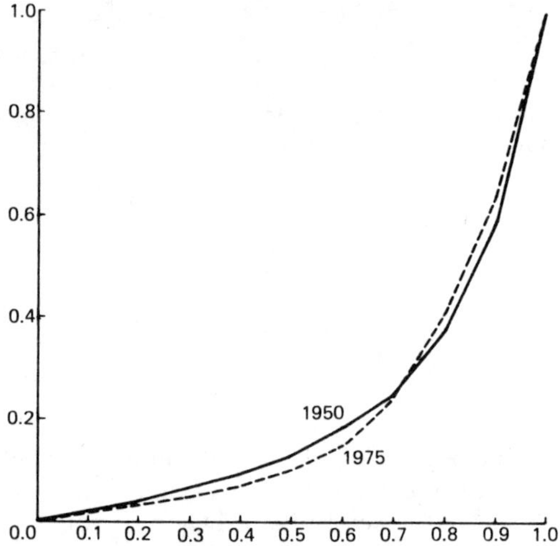

Fig. 2.1 Lorenz curves for the world, 1950 and 1975

It was mentioned earlier that the classification of countries can affect the way in which the overall stability of the Gini coefficients may be explained. The World Bank's classification which has been employed thus far has the sanction of widespread current use. Furthermore, the list of industrialised countries has been pretty standard for almost the whole of the period. Japan, the most recent addition to the list, was added, at least in official presentations of trade statistics, in 1954.[16]

Nevertheless, it is of interest to look at the same phenomena when countries are classified on the basis of 1950 per capita GDYs. The numbers of countries in each of three income groups – low, middle, and high – are standardised at 27, 61 and 18 to match the numbers in the groups in the previous classification. The chief differences are that Japan, Austria and Italy are in the middle-income group rather than in the top group, while Chile, Uruguay and Argentina are classified with the top group. Growth-rates and Gini coefficients for the three groups of countries classified by 1950 per capita GDY are as follows:

	No. of countries	Growth in per capita real GDY per annum 1950-75	Gini coefficient	
			1950	1975
Low	27	1.76	0.064	0.156
Middle	61	4.28	0.202	0.366
High	18	2.48	0.203	0.125

The results are similar but the increases in inequality are much sharper in the two lower groups, the impetus to greater inequality in the latter group being attributable largely to the addition of fast-growing Japan. Also, the decline in inequality in the high-income group is smaller; indeed, the decline disappears if the US is excluded. (Without the US, the Gini coefficients become 0.116 for 1950 and 0.111 for 1975.)

In either classification, the between-group differences in income obviously play a major role in pushing the world Gini coefficients to a level, 0.55, well above that found within the three groups. The 0.55 level is also high relative to the degree of inequality generally found within countries; most nationwide Gini coefficients, casual observation suggests, tend to be under 0.40.[17]

CONCLUSION

While world income has increased significantly over the past 25 years, and has been shared by almost all countries (all but six countries accounting for 2½ per cent of the population), the sharing of the increase has not been the same for all countries. This preliminary assessment of the shifts in world inequality over the past 25 years suggests offsetting changes. Equality increased sharply among the industrialised countries and decreased slightly among the developing countries. The effects of these within-group changes taken in conjunction with large between-group differences in income produced a relatively high world Gini coefficient for 1975, which remains virtually at the 1950 level.

In the future, work is planned to examine changes within the 25-year period, to extend coverage to socialist countries, and to expand the measures to take rough account of the possible contribution of within-country inequality to world inequality.

NOTES

1 All non-socialist countries were included for which adequate data for both 1950 and 1975 could be obtained. The population of the excluded socialist countries constituted about 32 per cent of the world population in 1975.

2 See Kravis, Kenessey, Heston and Summers (1975) and Kravis, Heston and Summers (1978b).

3 See Kravis, Heston and Summers (1978a).

4 The calculations were carried out using the World Bank's current (July 1978) computer tape rather than its earlier published estimates in World Bank (1976).

[5]Described in Kravis, Heston and Summers (1978a). Note that the World Bank also offers a series corrected for changes in the terms of trade for each country, though by a different method from that used here.

[6]For a few countries inadequate information on exports and imports made it necessary to estimate 1950 GDY on the assumption that the country's 1950 terms of trade were the same as those of a later year in the 1950s for which export and import data were first available.

[7]This is essentially the procedure of Andic and Peacock (1961).

[8]In the work in progress, alternative measures of inequality are being applied.

[9]The total population for the 106 countries grew from 155 billion in 1950 to 244 billion in 1975 while gross product per capita increased from 17 in 1950 to 31 in 1975 (US 1970=100).

[10]The classification of countries was taken from that used in World Bank (1978), p. ix.

[11]The Gini coefficients for GDP were virtually the same as for GDY: 0.544 in 1950 and 0.556 in 1975. In 1970 the exchange-rate-converted GDPs per capita relative to the US were all understated compared with the corresponding figures based upon estimates of purchasing-power-parities. Therefore the degree of world inequality is exaggerated by the use of exchange-rate-converted GDPs, with the result that Gini coefficients derived from them were much higher: the coefficient for 1950 based upon exchange-rate-converted GDPs was 0.653 and for 1975 it was 0.662.

[12]The decomposition of the world income distribution that follows is an informal but informative procedure. The substantial literature on this subject (e.g. Paglin (1975), Pyatt (1976) is taken into account more explicitly in the work in progress.

[13]The low-income countries were taken as having real per capita GDYs of $250 or less in 1975.

[14]It might appear inconsistent to judge the change in intra-group inequality using the Gini coefficient in view of the evidence that the similarity of the world Gini coefficients for 1950 and 1975 does not reveal the important differences between the two distributions. However, the judgements made about intra-group inequality are substantiated by comparisons of corresponding Lorenz curves.

[15]The 1975 figure of 5.9 per cent for the low-income group shown in Table 2.1 is based on the US 1970 real per capita GDY as 100.

[16]See GATT (1955) p. 148.

[17]The median for 67 nationwide distributions reported in Jain (1975) was 0.36; it must be said, however, that the distributions differ widely with respect to definitions of income, recipient units, etc.

REFERENCES

S. Andic and A.T. Peacock (1961), 'The International Distribution of Income', *Journal of the Royal Statistical Society,* vol. 124, series A.

General Agreement on Tariffs and Trade (1953), *International Trade* (July 1955).

S. Jain (1975), *Size Distribution of Income* (Washington, D.C.: International Bank for Reconstruction and Development).

I.B. Kravis, Z. Kenessey, A. Heston and R. Summers (1975), *United Nations International Comparison Project: Phase I; A System of International Comparisons of Gross Product and Purchasing Power* (Baltimore, Md.: Johns Hopkins University Press).

I.B. Kravis, A. Heston and R. Summers (1978a), 'Real GDP per Capita for More than One Hundred Countries', *Economic Journal,* vol. 88 (June).

I.B. Kravis, A. Heston and R. Summers (1978b), *United Nations International Comparison Project: Phase II; International Comparisons of Real Product and Purchasing Power* (Baltimore, Md.: Johns Hopkins University Press).

M. Paglin (1975), 'The Measurement and Trend of Inequality: A Basic Revision', *American Economic Review*, vol. LXV (September).
G. Pyatt (1976), 'On the Interpretation and Disaggregation of Gini Coefficients', *Economic Journal*, vol. 86 (June).
United Nations *Yearbook of National Accounts Statistics* (1976), vol. 1 (New York, N.Y.).
World Bank (1978), *World Development Report* (August 1978: Washington, DC).

Part 1b The Third World

3 Industry and Empire: The Beginnings of French Industrial Politics in the Colonies under the Vichy Regime

Catherine Coquery-Vidrovitch

1. THE LOW LEVEL OF INDUSTRIALISATION BEFORE THE SECOND WORLD WAR

(a) The industrial condition of the Empire

After the First World War, the equipping of the colonies was the order of the day. It was a question of remedying the exploitation, typical of the first colonial phase, of an almost exclusively commercial nature by planning infrastructural investments: the Sarraut plan (Sarraut was Minister for the Colonies in 1921) was partially assimilated into the Maginot programme (Maginot had succeeded Sarraut in the same post in 1929); and it finally approached realisation through the great laws of loans to the colonies (1931).

TABLE 3.1 Projects realised on long funds till the Second World War (situation at 1 Jan 1942: millions of francs)

	Endowment	*Of which unstarted works*	*Industrial amount*	*Equipment[1] %*
Indochina	1872	239.5	–	–
French West Africa	3370	797	65	1.9
French East Africa	1513	–	–	–
Madagascar	835	5	15	1.8
Togo	118	–	–	–
Cameroons	57	–	–	–
Reunion	63	–	–	–
Somaliland	44	5	–	–
Martinique	150	35.7	88[2]	58.7[2]
Guadeloupe	240	18	66[2]	27.5[2]
Oceania	15	15	–	–
New Caledonia	130	9	–	–
TOTAL	8455	1153	264	2.8

SOURCES: Derived from *Plans d'équipment colonial*, tableaux récapitulatifs, S.O.M., Aff. Eco., 58.
[1]Industry and Mine and Electricity.
[2]Electrification only.

Therefore, up until the Second World War, industrialisation at the government level appeared only in sectors, that is, in a limited way (see Table 3.1). If the truth be told, the industrial sector *stricto sensu* received nothing. Only by extrapolation in the fields of mining and energy – particularly electrical energy – does one discern the aid provided.

The primary reason: industrialisation remained the province of the *private sector,* which was more than unforthcoming about its overseas establishment. Local business circles, the majority of which were commercial, were unenthusiastic about an industrial policy that risked disturbing the traditional 'trading' system; metropolitan business circles, as well, did much to retard the maximum industrial development of the dominated territories, whose competition, above all things, had to be avoided. Thus, on the eve of the Second World War, industry in the colonies was still faltering. Nowhere did an ironworks exist; these continued to be considered 'problematical', at best.

In AOF*, for example, the only working-class concentration of any importance was the group of railway-workers in the local railway workshops. These concentrations were the first – and only – hotbeds of social demands as exemplified by the strike at Thiès, on the Dakar-Niger, in 1939). Likewise, the principal enterprises for invested capital were dedicated to construction or to the furnishing of the cities.

In brief, aside from public works the only sector of any importance was limited to localised and partial transformation of agricultural products for export: in AOF the shelling of peanuts – these constituting in value more than half the exports of the entire AOF – remained the most outstanding industry. With the possible exception of Morocco, it hardly seems that the condition of modern industry in Maghreb was perceptibly better – including Algeria and perhaps especially there, in spite of a colonisation process going back over half a century – if we make an exception of the important phosphates industry.

(b) The attitude towards industrialisation in the colonies by the period between the two World Wars

The Great Depression brought no immediate notable innovation. However, the crisis had the effect of crystallising a major contradiction: the necessity for structural reforms likely to meet the new demands of imperialism, through the access of the colonial domain to a superior development of production, collided with the defensive reflex of 'the Empire's closing ranks' felt by a metropolis anxious to maintain exclusive rights to the colonies and private property, while simultaneously eliminating all productive overseas activity likely to compete with the French economy.

The economic conferences of metropolitan and overseas France, held in the thick of the crisis (1934), raised the problem, for the first time, to an official level. But it was with the Popular Front that technicians of colonial economy would face the problem.

* AOF = Afrique Occidentale Francaise: French West Africa.

The colonial programme of the Popular Front, limited as it was, lacked no less than one essential element: time, to leave behind it much more than tracks. Thus, the colonial domain entered the war in approximately the same state as it had been since its creation: in large part, the industrial idea was yet but an idea. The total of the actual balance-sheet proved quite lean; the delay, willed by the companies even more than caused by the action – non-existent – of politicians, considerable.

TABLE 3.2 Ten-year plan: breakdown of overseas investments (1942-52)

			Millions of francs	%
I	*Public investments: colonial possessions: North Africa and Middle East*			
1.	Agriculture equipment		2,976	5.5
2.	Irrigation		4,243	7.9
3.	Town-planning		2,000	3.7
4.	Public building		961	1.8
5.	Teaching sport and scientific research		1,127	2
6.	Railways		15,108	28
7.	Post-office and telecommunication		1,943	3.6
8.	Roads and bridges		7,568	14
9.	Harbours and rivers		5,460	10.1
10.	Aviation and meteorology		831	1.5
11.	Mines		2,730	5
12.	Electricity including hydraulic power		4,260	7.9
13.	Industrial equipment		2,807	5.2
14.	Public health, population		1,939	3.6
		Sub-total	53,953	100
II	*Private investments*			
1.	Colonial possessions		18,800	
2.	North Africa			
	(a) electrification		4,000	
	(b) real private investments		6,000	
3.	Middle East		1,400	
		Sub-total	84,153	

SOURCE: derived from: *Notes documentaires et Etudes,* no. 267, 22 Mar 1946.

2. VICHY POLITICS: THE PLAN FOR INDUSTRIALISATION IN THE COLONIES

It is in this context that the Vichy 'technocrats' were to intervene.

(a) Global evaluations (see Table 3.2)

Overall, the ten-year plan anticipated (1942-52) – which, incidentally, was not in the end ratified by its own government – left a mediocre part to the colonial domain: in spite of the imperialist pretensions of its authors, only 84 million francs out of an estimated total of 723 million in public and private investments (in 1942 francs), or 11.6 per cent of the total (metropolitan and Empire).

(b) Stages and limits of industrialisation

Three stages can be distinguished: industry of 'rescue' and of penury, imperial defence and the economic future. Innovations were made especially in the field of energy. The accent was put on the systematic electrification of Algeria. Finally, there was no hesitation about launching projects characterised as 'grandiose'. For example, the upkeep and development of the Ogooué network and, most of all, of the Congo River in Equatorial Africa, were launched, because all the technocrats envisaged – which was novel – large units, established by great works, thereby implying a productive capacity far superior to the foreseeable average consumption of the zones concerned: whence the idea, equally 'revolutionary' at that time, of long-distance transportation of resources and materials (including the furnishing of high voltage to the European continent!).

Also proposed was the idea of a powerful colonial chemical industry, which would provide materials for arms factories in North Africa. It is – paradoxically as compared with the preceding period – in the sector of industries-in-transformation that the Vichy technocrats, under pressure from metropolitan businessmen, committed themselves with the most circumspection.

CONCLUSION

All of this shows, of course, both the novelty and the limits of the plans proposed by Vichy. To industrialise? – politicians and especially the technocrats in power became quite conscious of this necessity. But French industrial policy in Africa appears only mediocre and retarded. Need we remind the reader that, at that time, the plans of Vichy remained a 'dead-letter' programme, all the more because they were not ratified? However, one fact was becoming certain: the Empire was about to enter its 'productive' era; the traditional opposition between 'agricultural' and 'industrial' countries was violently attacked by the colonial expansionists themselves, and modern political economy would henceforth continue to come up against the delays overseas and against the ditch dug by more than half a century of inertia and uneven industrial development.

TABLE 3.3 Ten-year plan: public equipment (millions of francs)

	Total	*Industrial equipment (a)*	*Mining equipment (b)*	*Electrical equipment (c)*	*Total (a) + (b) (d)*	*Total (a + b + c) (e)*	*% (d) Total*	*% (e) Total*
Indochina	13,243	525	205	2766	730	3511	7.3	26.5
Madagascar	2,300	103.5	749	10	825.5	862.5	37	37.5
French West Africa	13,661	1135	158	50	1293	1343	9.4	9.8
Togo	347	–	–	–	–	–	–	–
French East Africa	2,200	150	180	50	330	380	15	17.2
Cameroons	3,250	80	55	50	135	185	4.1	5.6
Somaliland	241	–	–	15	–	15	–	6.2
Reunion	392	–	–	–	–	–	–	–
Martinique	268	–	–	15	–	15	–	5.6
Guadeloupe	339	–	–	30	–	30	–	8.8
Guyana	328	2	20	13.5	22	35.5	6.7	10.8
Oceania	210	6	–	9	6	15	2.8	7.1
New Caledonia	405	5	55	15	60	75	14.5	18.8
New Hebrides	100	3	–	10	3	13	3	13
St Pierre et Miquelon	111	–	1	12	1	13	0.9	11.7
Total colonies	37,766	2009.5	1423	3045.5	3432.5	6478	9	17.2
Maghreb	11,187	797.5	1307	1214.5	2104.5	3319	13	20.5
Grand Total	53,953	2807	2730	4260	5537	9797	10.3	18.1

Derived from: Tableaux récapitulatifs, S.O.M., Aff. Eco., 58 et *'Les plans francais d'équipement'*.

4 Constraints to Economic Development in Africa: Some Determinants of Economic Disparities

Richard O. Ekundare

1. INTRODUCTION

It appears that the world has now reached the stage when one can attempt to take stock of the impact of technological progress which has spread in varying degrees to most countries, if not to all, and which has produced some expected and some unanticipated results, thus complicating the concept of economic development. The differences in political systems, cultures, social and economic values have added, in no small measure, to the problem of measuring economic progress since the Industrial Revolution.

Africa, being a very large continent, has its inherent disparities in the endowment of natural resources. Apart from geographical location, which dictates the nature of primary production, there are differences in the size and quality of population, known natural resources, and some basic social and cultural values. Most of the African countries have also passed through three main political changes – the pre-colonial period, the colonial period and the post-independence era. The implications of these will be explained presently. It is important to add that the modern industrial revolution did not originate in Africa. In other words, Africa has to grapple with the 'unique' problems of imported technology. Apart from its own inherent political social and economic differences, Africa has, therefore, been exposed to foreign politics, laws, religion, technology, economic order and culture over, at least, the past century. The contemporary economic history of Africa reflects, amongst other things, the best and the worst of economic, political, and technological ingenuities of the developed countries. It is therefore very difficult to explain economic inequalities in Africa merely with the aid of conventional economic tools. An attempt will be made to explain some of the unconventional constraints to economic development in Africa.

I would like to think that in a broad sense economic development concerns primarily the study of production, exchange and consumption and their interrelationship as they affect the national economy and the welfare of the people within the context of a particular socio-political system. Most economists who first dealt with the problems of economic development emphasised the need to increase the growth rate of each country, particularly that of the so-called underdeveloped nations. It was fashionable to compare the per capita incomes of various countries, particularly those of industrialised Europe and America, with those of some African, Asian and Latin American countries. Per capita income became the magic word which was synonymous with level of development and along with it was the concept of the growth rate which was used to dazzle and embarrass a number of countries which could not attain an arbitrarily fixed level. It became a 'stigma' for a nation to be called underdeveloped, backward or developing. In recent years, however, some modifications have been introduced into some conceptual issues on development. These modifications have arisen because a number of assumptions on which the concept of underdevelopment was based were either no longer valid or needed to be modified. For example, the concept of per capita income on which the whole measurement of underdevelopment was based has been proved to be of limited value in the assessment of the general economic progress of a nation. One could not agree more with the view that:

> The arbitrary nature of the current distinction between developed and underdeveloped countries on the basis of the per capita incomes is compounded by the fact that per capita income is in itself a seriously inadequate index of development.[1]

It is clear that the more industrialised, monetised and educated (in the modern sense) a country is, the easier it is for that country to compute a fairly accurate estimate of its national income and hence of the per capita income. Indeed, most African countries are still unable to obtain reliable population counts. For example, Nigeria has been unable to conduct any successful population census for over two decades. In underdeveloped countries many 'economic' activities are still not exchanged for money and hence could not be added to the estimates of the national income. Such services include personal services, intra-family services, subsistence or near-subsistence production. The notion of per capita income, which is a monetary indicator, is far from being either fully accurate or sufficiently comprehensive.[2] The per capita income concept is an aggregative approach to measuring economic growth and does not indicate the structure of the growth. In other words, it does not concern itself with equitable rates of the increases in the incomes of individuals and/or sectors of the economy. It is therefore absurd to argue that closing the relative per capita income gap between the less developed countries and the developed countries should be the prime objective of development planning.[3]

Also, I believe that the use of the growth rate concept as a mathematical indicator of progress is an unsatisfactory method of assessing the general economic progress and welfare of the people. Indeed, the growth rate concept by its very nature can only indicate the material growth of the economy. It follows, therefore, that only quantifiable variables will form the basis for estimating any growth rate. You can prove a lot with statistics, but not everything.[4]

Lastly, the applications of concepts developed in one country cannot be readily applied to another country. Stolper has pointed out that 'the application to country B of lessons learned in country A may be as much a source of error as of wisdom. There is no substitute for a direct study of the peculiarities of country B'.[5] The inability of economists to study adequately the peculiar social, political and economic conditions of the underdeveloped countries has added to the great confusion in the minds of many economic planners as to what type of development, and how much, should be pursued at any given period for a particular country.

2. SOME CONSTRAINTS TO DEVELOPMENT

One could start to identify some constraints by first examining some aspects of the very concept of 'development'. There seems to be the basic assumption that 'development' means the same thing in the minds of the people in a community. It is my contention that, on the contrary, development-consciousness is neither spontaneous nor of uniform degree among the various groups of people or within the age-groups of any community or among nations. The mental attitude to development, or in other words development-consciousness, can be explained in the context of the 'utility' of social values which an individual or a group of people attaches to material wealth. Different age-groups and indeed different societies place different valuations upon goods and services relatively to their valuation of such non-material satisfactions as leisure, security, equality, the extended family system and religious salvation.[6] The various scales of the 'utility' of social values naturally create some conflicts in the minds of people as to what constitutes economic development in material terms, and to what extent it should be pursued individually or collectively.

Remembering these points, what constitutes economic development in the mind of one individual may not be so considered by another person. It is the aggregate assessment of the various levels of social values, at least in a free-enterprise economy, which goes into the vague concept of national development. It can be concluded, therefore, that various individuals and generations of a society have their peculiar social values attached to particular levels or rates of economic development and as such there are bound to be some problems – purely human and invariably unconsciously – in the acceptance and pursuit of activities and policies which constitute or lead to economic development.

Secondly, the economic development of a society is a function of its political system. It is assumed that a centrally administered country lends itself more readily to clear-cut economic policies than a federal system of government where there are heterogeneous groups of people. By the very nature of federalism, the preoccupation of any policy, be it social, political or economic, is to ensure a kind of equilibrium which may not in itself be conducive to economic development. Again, since the attainment of political independence most African countries have faced internal political unrest, basically arising from ethnic differences and sectional interests, but sometimes masterminded or aided by foreign interests. Although political stability or instability cannot be predetermined, yet both remain important variables in planning, executing and achieving economic progress.

Thirdly, the economic system which is operative in any community must necessarily affect the mechanism for achieving economic development. It is very clear that the economic goals of a free-enterprise economy at the macro level are not the same as those of a socialist economy. The former system believes in the spontaneous economic interests of individuals which if allowed to operate within a reasonably free and unrestricted atmosphere will produce the greatest contribution to economic development, while the latter believes that without central control of all economic activities optimum economic growth cannot be achieved. An element of uncertainty is introduced into the whole argument if a country cannot be strictly categorised as either capitalist or socialist. Although the behaviour of a typical capitalist in Africa needs to be investigated further, yet from all known indications he does not behave strictly as an American or European capitalist. Similarly, some of the traits of social behaviour in Nigeria which are often linked with the extended family system cannot be compared with the strict socialist principles of Russia or China. The 'African' economic man does not exactly answer Adam Smith's description, because his everyday economic pursuits are often influenced and determined largely by his social and cultural background, which is essentially different from that of a typical capitalist or socialist country.

Fourthly, and following from the last paragraph, the extended family system exists in most African countries. The system has often been described as semi-socialist or at least anti-capitalist and as impeding economic growth.[7] Of course, these assertions arose from a lopsided assessment of the system. The fact is that the extended family system is a peculiar socio-economic phenomenon which has been influential in the African brand of a free-enterprise economy.[8] The economic aspect of the extended family system involves essentially an exchange of goods and services which can be termed 'family-care'. The major variables of the system include the number of people within what can be accepted as the extended family, the variation in the levels of incomes of both the giver or donor and the recipient of family-care, and lastly the standard of family-care as determined from time to time by the generally accepted standard of life expected of a recipient of family-care. What is often overemphasised is the dependence of a large number of people within the extended family on the income of say one well-to-do member – an income which by Western standards is below the subsistence level even if it remains the disposable income of the earner. It is needless to say that what constitutes income in an African context differs from that of a modern monetised and technologically advanced country.

The extended family system has an in-built positive multiplier effect. The positive multiplier in this context is taken to mean a general economic development multiplier. Not only has an individual got to depend on his own hard work, he must be well disposed at all times to put any less fortunate member of the family firmly on his feet economically, e.g. by training him or setting him up in a trade or business. The system, apart from providing social security, is a development promotion technique socialised by philosophy.[9]

Next, the decision to engage in ostentatious expenditure is another important non-quantifiable constraint. This kind of expenditure involves lavishing money on such things as naming, funeral and house-warming ceremonies. Ostentatious spending is partly a psychological issue and partly an economic phenomenon in Africa. Generally, such expenditure is regarded as wasteful and unproductive. I believe that this general condemnation should be re-examined in the light of the African's cultural background which affects his social values. First, it must be realized that in a free-enterprise economy any expenditure at all creates utility to the spender, whether the expenditure is productive, wasteful or ostentatious. Secondly, expenditures which are now often regarded as wasteful arose from the old custom of maintaining social equilibrium. It must be admitted, however, that in recent years some by-products of maintaining the so-called social equilibrium are bribery, corruption and nepotism, which are making it increasingly difficult for any African government to operate a viable economy. Lastly, ostentatious spending has now been modified into a means of maintaining and possibly improving one's social position and even more so of promoting one's business by retaining the goodwill of people. It is a kind of 'advertisement'.

Also most African countries have to contend with the problems of 'dualism'. Dualism may be defined as the continuing coexistence of a 'modern' sector and a 'traditional' sector within the national economic framework of the country.[10] A region in a country may be advanced in terms of general economic development, while another may be backward. There are usually a number of reasons for this kind of situation. It might be that a region had an earlier contact with modern civilisation, or that one region responds more quickly to changes than the other, and so on. Dualism is therefore the result of the varying degrees of economic civilisation of the various groups or sectors of the economy. The backward or forward linkages of dualism tend to obstruct the smooth path to economic progress. It is not only the problem of the psychological battle of reconciling different approache to development, but also that of running virtually two different economic systems with different orientations within the same economy.

Lastly, one should mention briefly the problems of imported technology. Since modern technology originates outside Africa, African countries have no choice but to purchase the kind of technology they can easily afford and whicl the advanced countries are prepared to offer. Industrialisation is seen in most African countries as the only answer to solving 'economic' poverty.

In an attempt to achieve some degree of industrialisation, European and American technologies are imported indiscriminately. Inevitably the economic climate of the advanced countries tends to dictate the pace of economic progress in these countries. With the limited resources at the disposal of most African countries, it has been impossible to purchase the best of the most modern technologies. Indeed, the rapid changes in the technologies of the advanced countries make it impossible for the African countries to keep pace. In simple language, obsolete machines, by American, European and Russian standards, are the best 'modern' technologies in Africa. The money cost of obtaining these machines keeps fluctuating according to the internal economic conditions of the advanced countries, thus creating some economic uncertainties in the importing countries. Indeed, it is common knowledge that increases in the prices of imported technologies have contributed in no small measure to the peculiar inflationary pressure in some African countries. Perhaps most important of all is the fact that the 'fruits' of modern technology are maximised with inherently trained technological manpower. Whereas modern technology has become an aspect of life in developed countries, it is by no means fully understood in most African countries, where technical education is very backward. Africans are hurriedly trained to handle and manipulate machines, the origin, function, limitations and dangers of which they know very little or nothing about – a sword in the hands of a virtually blind warrior. A handful of educated elite in each African country have now engaged in the 'rat-race' of modern industrialisation without adequate planning and regard for the majority of their ill-prepared people, who will be exposed inevitably to some degree of suffering.

3. THE NIGERIAN EXPERIENCE

Nigeria has been having development plans since 1945[11] and it seems that one single non-quantifiable factor which has affected each development plan is 'political change'. In other words, 'up till now, all the development plans in Nigeria have run into social problems – mainly of political origin'.[12] In 1947 a constitutional change brought into being a central legislature for the whole country and three Regional Houses of Assembly, one for each group of administrative provinces. The next constitutional change occurred in 1952 with increased regional autonomy, but by 1954 a federal system of government was introduced. This brought the first plan to an 'official' end, as it was clear that regional government had deviated substantially from the original plan. Consequent upon the new political changes, five separate development plans emerged in 1955 – the three Regional Development Plans, the Plan for the Federal Government, and one for the Southern Cameroons, which ceased to be part of the Federation of Nigeria in 1959. The 1955-60 Economic Development Plans, as they were called, were modified in 1958 and extended to 1962. During the seven years of these plans, inter-regional rivalry prevented the normal flow of resources, the national allocation and location of development projects, and the necessary maximisation of the relatively scarce economic resources. These shortcomings resulted inevitably in the duplication of projects, and in unhealthy competition among the Regions with consequent economic waste. The political events of the plan period completely overshadowed the economic significance of the plan itself. In fact, the rivalries among the political parties and their leaders had widened the social gap which already existed among the peoples by reason of the different ethnic groups which made up the Federation.[13]

It was under this socio-political pressure that the First National Development Plan 1962-68 was formulated. Within a month of launching the plan, Nigeria was plunged into a prolonged period of serious political and social disturbances. The public disorder which followed, particularly in the south, finally led to the military takeover in January 1966. For a period of about eighteen months, social and political uncertainties increased the agitation for the creation of more states in Nigeria. In May 1967 the Federation of Nigeria was divided into twelve states.

Within a couple of months of the creation of new states, the 'Biafran' civil war began and lasted until January 1970. Again, the political crises of the plan period led to the modification of the plan and extended it to 1970. Once again, in 1975, Nigeria went through yet another political change with far-reaching consequences. The Gowon regime was overthrown and the late General Muhammad took over with a different style of administration which has so far been hailed as dynamic and progressive. In 1976, the Federation of Nigeria was broken into nineteen states. There could have been yet another drastic political change in February 1976 when Dimka with some collaborators attempted his abortive coup. Although the coup was unsuccessful the then Head of State, General Muhammed, was killed and a new administration was established under Lt.-Gen. Obasanjo. Nigeria is still going through the wind of change in the political sphere. The local government elections have taken place, the draft of the new Nigerian Constitution has been produced and the country is looking forward to a return to civilian rule in 1979.

The political changes I have enumerated above are enough to throw any meaningful development plan out of gear. It appears to me that a total period of over thirty years of political uncertainty is a sufficient constraint to rapid and sustained economic growth. It is a constraint over which the economist is powerless. It cannot be quantified and by its very nature cannot be predicted. It appears, therefore, that continued growth rests on the collective goodwill of the majority of the people to give the system of government the chance to operate.

In an attempt to maintain a socio-political equilibrium in Nigeria a number of non-quantifiable factors have been either deliberately or inadvertently introduced into the development plans, which in the end have affected the plan implementation and fulfilment. If one starts with the Second National Development Plan, 1970-74, a set of objectives were deliberately enumerated as follows:[14]

(i) a united, strong and self-reliant nation;
(ii) a great and dynamic economy;
(iii) a just and egalitarian society;
(iv) a land of bright and full opportunities for all citizens; and
(v) a free and democratic society.

The Third National Development Plan, 1975-80, went further to elaborate on the basic objectives of the Second National Development Plan. It was stated that 'the specific short-term objectives aimed at facilitating the ultimate realisation of the five national objectives and the Third Plan are as follows:[15]

(*a*) Increase in per capita income.
(*b*) More even distribution of income.
(*c*) Reduction in the level of unemployment.
(*d*) Increase in the supply of high-level manpower.
(*e*) Diversification of the economy.
(*f*) Balanced development.
(*g*) Indigenisation of economic activity.'

Without examining the details of the expenditure on various specific projects one could ask: how realistic are these basic objectives? The Second National Plan rightly argued that

> For planning purposes, a set of national objectives must deal simultaneously with the community's standard as well as quality of life. . . The first is a quantitative phenomenon and easier to measure. The second is a qualitative notion which is not susceptible to quantitative analysis but which is crucial to the pace of economic development and social change. It is relatively easy to quantify targets such as outputs, growth rates or changes in per capita income. Yet it is becoming increasingly appreciated that the development process is a function of the innate forces of a society.[16]

In concrete terms most of the national objectives as contained in the Second National Plan, and their 'corollaries' enumerated in the Third National Development Plan, are themselves non-quantifiable and those that can be to some extent quantified are also invariably affected by non-quantifiable constraints. I have already mentioned a number of non-quantifiable constraints in the last section and these can be applied appropriately to these objectives. However, I intend to deal with one or two such problems briefly.

In trying to diversify the economy, reduce the level of unemployment, and achieve balanced development, two major sectors of the economy must necessarily be exposed to changes – the agricultural sector and the industrial sector. As for the agricultural sector, it has long been recognised that the much-needed agrarian revolution is overdue. It has also been accepted that the agrarian revolution cannot be achieved without a modification to the land tenure systems.[17] Yet, because of the delicate social non-quantifiable nature of the attitude of the people to the land tenure system, the plan remained very vague as to what changes are necessary. It suggested that in the southern

States the local communities should consolidate the fragmented holdings and redistribute them into economic units suitable for tree crops and mixed food crops. Any spontaneous move among the people for the consolidation of land is however very unlikely and whatever initiative there is will have to come from the government. The Third National Development Plan has not tackled the issue. After admitting that 'the under-utilization of agricultural land itself is a function of some institutional constraints, in particular, the land tenure system and the seasonal labour shortages',[18] it went on to say that 'the problems of land-use and tenurial reform are somewhat explosive issues requiring long-term and careful solutions'.[19] This obviously represents a classical example of a non-quantifiable constraint to economic development in Nigeria. It cannot be strongly disputed that the neglect of the constraint has increased the rural-urban migration problems with the resultant pressure on food production, employment and the provision of social amenities.

Turning to the industrial sector, the Second Plan listed eight objectives of the new industrial policy. The first objective, which is 'to promote even development and fair distribution of industries in all parts of the country'[20] is most relevant to the issue of maintaining social equilibrium[21] – a non-quantifiable factor. This objective suggested that economic considerations – quantifiable – are secondary when deciding where to locate new industries. The government gave itself the opportunity to use its discretion as to what is in the public interest as far as industrial location is concerned. It means in effect that even if the siting of an industrial project in a given area is uneconomic but can help to promote political and social unity, the government may disregard those economic considerations which favour its establishment elsewhere. It may be possible for the government to adhere to this policy in respect of any industrial project which is to be financed from public funds. It will be difficult, however, to expect private enterprise under our present economic system to cooperate with the government in establishing industry in any area where optimum production and profit cannot be achieved.

Undoubtedly, the main obstacle to any definite policy of full employment is that of mobility of factors of production, particularly the mobility of capital and labour. The greatest obstacle to such mobility in recent years has been the mistrust and lack of understanding among the various ethnic groups. Although the Federal Military Government is struggling to eradicate this non-quantifiable constraint, it is regrettable that many of the State Governments have so far insisted on recruiting labour and encouraging capital investment largely from within their own boundaries, irrespective of the size and quality of such investment and labour. The issue of the free mobility of factors of production contributes to the main social barrier – a non-quantifiable constraint to economic and social stability in Nigeria.

Lastly, indigenisation of economic activity is a basically good thing in itself, in so far as one expects that such a policy will not lead to greater exploitation of the lower or fixed income groups by a few rich citizens. The exploitative nature which the operation of our free-enterprise economy has exhibited in recent years and which has resulted in a series of measures to protect the 'ordinary' consumer calls for a critical examination. As has already been pointed out, recent events cannot be divorced from the fact that those Nigerian businessmen who now set themselves up as what I might call 'economic monsters' are not detached from religious, political and socio-cultural relationships. For example, much of the behaviour of a business proprietor can be explained by his membership of a traditional cult, his family ties and his ethnic loyalty. His ostentatious spending is partly a condition of maintaining his exploitative tendencies.

CONCLUSIONS

From the brief analysis above, there is no doubt that one needs a more realistic, rather than a theoretical approach; or, if you like, call it a more practical and human approach to the problems of economic development in Africa. It has been said that: 'The new approaches to economic history are definitely positivistic, in that for positivism nothing matters unless it can be counted, measured, or weighed.'[22] It must be realized, however, that quantifiable variables or constraints are products of history and, as such, are not entirely relevant to the rapidly changing world, because history hardly ever repeats itself without some substantial modifications. 'An attempt to understand the conditions of economic progress in the developing countries will require the full and sensitive application of the insights and methods that have been devised by the economic historians of the past, together with imaginative use of the newer contributions of sociology and anthropology. . .'[23]

African economists, particularly those involved in planning, in conjunction with other relevant areas of study must formulate clear research programmes in order to examine many of the variables and constraints which are so far non-quantifiable and which inevitably affect economic phenomena in Africa. 'Economic growth or industrialization are surely not the only acceptable meanings of change for economic history!'[24]

It cannot be over-emphasised that Africans and their socio-economic lives are quite different from those of other countries. The readiness to look for quick solutions and seek refuge under capitalism and/or socialism is an unrealistic approach to solving the African problems. This is not to say that experiences in those countries where these systems operate are not useful, but they cannot be looked upon as ready answers to all the questions which modern economic development pose to Africa.

In quantitative terms one could examine briefly some changes in the structure of the Nigerian economy as an example. One significant feature of the economic changes was the declining percentage contribution of agriculture to GDP as shown in Table 4.1. The contribution of agriculture fell from 53.8 per cent in 1966/7 to 48.8 per cent in 1970/1 and to 37.0 per cent in 1973/4. It is projected that by 1979/80 it would have fallen further to 18.9

TABLE 4.1 Sectoral contribution to GDP of Nigeria at factor cost (selected sectors)

Sectors	*Percentage contribution*			
	1966/7	*1970/1*	*1973/4*	*1979/80**
Agriculture, livestock, etc.	53.8	48.8	37.0	18.9
Mining and quarrying	7.2	10.1	23.5	37.5
Manufacturing and crafts	7.0	7.2	77.0	6.9
Others†	32.0	33.9	32.5	36.7

*Projected percentage contribution.
†Others include electricity and water; building and construction; distribution; transport and communications.
SOURCES: *Second National Development Plan,* 1970, p. 4; *First Progress Report; Economic Indicators,* Vol. 11, Sept. 1975; and *Third National Development Plan,* 1975. p. 80.

per cent. In contrast, the contribution of mining and quarrying increased from 7.2 per cent in 1966/7 to 10.1 per cent in 1970/1 and to 23.5 per cent in 1973/4. The projected percentage contribution in 1979/80 is put at 37.5. Undoubtedly, the increased production of petroleum oil contributed to the substantial shifts in the percentage contributions of agriculture on the one hand and mining on the other. The percentage contribution of the manufacturing and crafts sector has remained fairly static. Unless a greater proportion of the earnings from the mining sector is continually invested in agriculture and in manufacture, the disparities in the earnings of the various sectors will continue to widen. Industrialisation has not benefited all the sectors in the Nigerian economy. Agriculture remains very backward and the little industrialisation that can be claimed to exist is concentrated heavily in the mining sector, with little left for light industries. The incomes of the peasant farmers continue to drop in relation to incomes in the other sectors, e.g. mining, construction and distribution.

There is need for careful and meaningful research into the ordinary way of life in Africa. We need to know more about the various standards of life which the size of the continent and the heterogeneity of the people make possible. We need to know more about what motivates production, exchange and consumption. It seems to me that the consumption pattern of each group of workers, and even the various levels within each group should be carefully examined so as to ascertain, or at least obtain meaningful indications about, savings and investment habits. The sociologist could also help in examining some of the social values which are more important to Africans than material wealth; and how such social values affect attitudes towards economic development at the micro and macro levels.

Lastly, every country in Africa needs at least twenty-five years of uninterrupted political stability. It must be realised that frequent constitutional or political changes, however socially desirable, tend to slow down the wheel of economic progress and sometimes stop it altogether. Even if the mechanism for economic progress could be restarted to work at full capacity after such changes, the loss of momentum and time constitutes a serious impediment to smooth and greater development. Africa can ill afford political instability now or in the future. This calls for greater self-re-examination on the part of Africans as to what politico-economic goals should be pursued at any given time.

Most important of all, African countries should be more vigilant in checking or better still, in eliminating those forces within and from without which are capable of dislocating the socio-political structure, which in turn disrupts the normal process of development.

NOTES

[1] P.T. Bauer, *Dissent on Development* (Weidenfeld & Nicolson, London, 1967) p. 53.
[2] Paul Alpert, *Economic Development* (Collier-Macmillan, London, 1964) p. 1.
[3] V.P. Diejomaoh, 'Towards a more realistic view of Development', *Nigerian Journal of Economic and Social Studies,* July 1973, p. 197.
[4] Arthur Hazlewood (ed.), *Industry and Underdevelopment* (Addison-Wesley Publishing Company, 1971) p. 1.
[5] Wolfgang F. Stolper, *Planning Without Facts* (Harvard University Press, Cambridge, Massachusetts, 1966) p. 3.
[6] W. Arthur Lewis, *Theory of Economic Growth* (Allen & Unwin, 1972) p. 11.
[7] Bauer and Yamay, *The Economics of Underdeveloped Countries* (Nisbet, Cambridge, University Press, 1957) p. 64.
[8] R.O. Ekundare, Capitalism: An Aspect of Yoruba Economic Philosophy, *Proceedings of Seminar on Sociology and History,* March 1975.
[9] Ekundare, op. cit.
[10] H. Myint, *Economic Theory and the Undeveloped Countries* (Oxford University Press, 1971) p. 315.
[11] *A Ten-Year Plan of Development and Welfare in Nigeria,* Sessional Paper No. 24 of 1945.
[12] R.O. Ekundare, 'Nigeria's Second National Development Plan as a Weapon of Social Change', *African Affairs,* London, vol. 70, No. 279, April 1971, p. 147.
[13] R.O. Ekundare, op. cit. (see Note 12) p. 148.
[14] *Second National Development Plan, 1970-74* (Federal Ministry of Information, Lagos) p. 32.
[15] *Third National Development Plan, 1975-80* (Federal Ministry of Economic Development, Lagos) p. 29.
[16] *Second National Development Plan,* p. 31.
[17] Ibid., p. 110.
[18] *Third National Development Plan,* p. 63.
[19] Ibid., p. 66.
[20] *Second National Development Plan,* p. 143.
[21] Ekundare, op. cit., (see Note 12) p. 154.
[22] Fritz Redlich, ' "New" and Traditional Approaches to Economic History and their Interdependence', *Journal of Economic History,* Vol. xxv, No. 4, Dec. 1965, p. 481.
[23] Cater Goodrish, 'Economic History: One Field or Two?', *Journal of Economic History,* Vol. xx, No. 4, March 1960, p. 538.
[24] Barry E. Supple, 'Economic History and Economic Growth', *Journal of Economic History,* Vol. xx, No. 4, March 1960, p. 553.

5 Notes on the Patterns of Economic Growth in the British North American Colonies in the Seventeenth, Eighteenth and Nineteenth Centuries

Stanley L. Engerman

The growth and development of Great Britain in the Industrial Revolution and afterwards was heavily influenced by the economic characteristics of its settlements in the Western Hemisphere. While these colonial areas may not have been indispensable conditions for British industrialisation, their production characteristics and the high levels of income achieved did provide a major market for British exports, as well as an important source of imports to be consumed in Britain or to be re-exported to the continent. In addition, the economic performance of these areas figured in several of the major debates about British economic and social policy in the seventeenth, eighteenth and nineteenth centuries. The discussions of mercantilism, of the economics of slavery and its abolition, and of the effects of production methods upon long-term colonial growth, all drew heavily upon the interpretation of the economic performance of the British New World colonies. In this note I should like to draw together some of the available data to discuss the economic conditions of these British colonies (with the exception of Canada) from settlement until the twentieth century. The statistical series presented are drawn from widely-known secondary sources, and their limitations are well-known. Nevertheless it is felt that they can provide useful information on the nature of colonial economic growth, as well as cast light on the impact of slavery and its abolition.

1. SETTLEMENT TO c. 1770

The data in Table 5.1 show both the growth in total populations of the three main regions of British settlement (the West Indies, the area on the mainland that came to be the northern United States, and the area which became the southern United States) and the racial breakdown of settlement – important because, with few exceptions, the black population was enslaved and used to produce a different set of crops from those produced by free labour. Clearly the mainland colonies were larger in terms of population than were

TABLE 5.1 Total population and percentage black, British West Indies and Mainland North America

	British West Indies		*Northern United States*		*Southern United States*	
	Total ('000)	*% Black*	*Total* ('000)	*% Black*	*Total* ('000)	*% Black*
1650	59	25.4	27	3.3	23	3.1
1680	118	64.4	82	2.3	69	7.3
1710	178	83.1	181	4.6	151	24.3
1740	285	87.7	490	4.9	415	30.4
1770	479	90.6	1101	4.4	1047	39.3
1780	537	91.1	1390	3.9	1390	37.5
1830	811[a]	90.8	7153	2.3	5708	37.9

[a]This estimate is for the 1830s, and includes British Guiana.
SOURCES: J.J. McCusker, 'The Rum Trade and the Balance of Payments of the Thirteen Continental Colonies', (unpublished PhD thesis, University of Pittsburgh, 1970) p. 712; R.M. Martin, *History of the Colonies of the British Empire* (London, 1843); US Bureau of the Census, *Historical Statistics of the United States* (Washington, 1975) pp. 1168, 22.

the West Indies after the mid-seventeenth century, and the population in each of the component regions of the mainland exceeded the population of the Caribbean islands by the early eighteenth century. The racial composition and characteristics of the labour force of these areas differed dramatically. Even before 1700, the West Indies was more than one-half black, and the share of blacks, almost all of whom were slaves, rose from about 80 per cent to 90 per cent of the population during the eighteenth century. In the northern United States blacks were only a small part of the total population, while the ratio for the southern states rose sharply in this period; but at no time were the shares of slaves in the population equal to that reached by the West Indies in the seventeenth century. Particularly rapid expansion of the slave population occurred in the South between 1680 and 1710, a period which also saw a rapid increase in the number of slaves imported into the West Indies. As Curtin has reminded us, the total black populations of these areas are a most imperfect guide to the total number of Africans imported, because of the marked differences in the fertility and mortality patterns in the two areas. The total slave imports into the British West Indies between 1680 and 1808 were at least 1.7 million, more than twice the number of blacks there at the end of the slave trade. On the other hand, the United States areas received many fewer Africans, approximately 0.6 million, less than one-half of the black population there when the slave trade ended.[1] The number of slaves imported into both areas rose throughout the eighteenth century, as did their prices, reflecting the increased New World demand for involuntary labour.

The pattern of labour demand reflected the different crops produced in the various parts of the British Empire. For reasons apparently related to climate, scale of technology, and the unwillingness of whites, even indentured servants, to work on larger units in tropical areas, each of the three major regions had crop specialisations which implied a different importance for forced black labour. The West Indies early specialised in sugar, grown in large units based almost exclusively upon slave labour. In the southern United States, the export staples were mainly tobacco and rice, the former being grown on relatively small slave units, and the economy had a more diversified agriculture than did the West Indies. In the North, with specialisation in grain and livestock, there were few of the large-scale units which seemingly required slave labour for production.

The net outcome of these crop patterns, combined with English needs for consumer and producer goods, is indicated in Table 5.2. It can be seen why the West Indies was considered so important a part of the mercantile empire, exporting considerably more to the home country than did the larger mainland colonies, with a sharply increasing quantity of per capita exports over the eighteenth and early nineteenth centuries. The southern mainland colonies were more important than the northern in providing exports to the British. Yet, because of the nature of trade balances, the mainland was the more important source of total demand for British exports (though lower in per capita terms). Given the nature of West Indian and southern demands for northern output, Deane and Cole argue, as had Arthur Young, that 'directly

TABLE 5.2 Official values of exports to England and Scotland, total and per capita, from Mainland North America and the British West Indies (annual averages)[a]

	British West Indies		*Northern United States*		*Southern United States*	
	Total ('000)	*per capita*	*Total* ('000)	*per capita*	*Total* ('000)	*per capita*
1697-1704			48	0.3	243	2.3
1705-14	725[b]	4.1	49	0.3	239	1.6
1715-24	1022	4.8	87	0.3	353	1.8
1725-34	1351	5.2	96	0.3	482	1.8
1735-44	1324	4.6	91	0.2	643	1.5
1745-54	1398	4.2	106	0.2	834	1.5
1755-64	1976	5.2	122	0.1	967	1.3
1765-74	2999	6.3	274	0.2	1390	1.3
1775-84	2883	5.4	117	0.1	307	0.2
1785-94	4051		217[d]	0.1	796[d]	0.4
1795-1804	6211					
1805-14	8077					
1815-22	8001	9.9[c]				

[a]England and Wales to 1754 and Great Britain thereafter for the West Indies; England to 1744 and England and Scotland thereafter for the mainland colonies.
[b]1710-14.
[c]1830 population used for illustrative purposes.
[d]1785-91.
SOURCES: B. Mitchell (with the collaboration of P. Deane), *Abstract of British Historical Statistics* (Cambridge, 1962) pp. 309-11; US Bureau of the Census, op. cit., pp. 1176-8 (corrected). For population data, see Table 5.1.

TABLE 5.3 Estimates of sugar output and 'real revenue' from sugar production, British West Indies, 1700-1850 (annual averages)

	(1) *BWI sugar output ('000 tons)*[a]	(2) *'Real revenue' from sugar output (1765-74=100)*	(3) *British total sugar imports (official values; £'000)*	(4) *'Real revenue' value of British Sugar imports (1865-74=100)*	(5) *UK sugar imports from BWI ('000 cwts)*	(6) *'Real revenue' value of UK sugar imports from BWI (1830-34=100)*
1700-4	19.4	30	£ 525	31		
1705-14	20.5[b]	30[j]	584[l]	32[n]		
1715-24	31.7	34[k]	885	36		
1725-34	39.3[c]	38[c]	1181	39		
1735-44	40.1	40	1134	42		
1745-54	42.9	59	1230	64		
1755-64	62.7[d]	87[d]	1770	93		
1765-74	80.8	100	2154	100		
1775-84	77.0[e]	115[e]	2025	106		
1785-94	95.6[f]	179[f]	2624	134		
1795-9	–	–	3429	197		
1800-4	120.9[g]	107[g]	4882	178	3603	122
1805-9	142.7[h]	103[h]	5019	153	3479	101
1810-14	147.5[i]	163[i]	5608[m]	190	3690	116
1815-19	178.6	184	5351	208	3713	135
1820-4	179.5	147	5496	168	3764	113
1825-9	195.3	154	5716(6366)	168	3964	117
1830-4	204.0	144	(6890)	167	3856	100
1835-9	174.0	164	(6535)	211	3363	115
1840-4	126.5	129	(6670)	234	2363	88
1845-9	145.1	106	(9872)	248	2767	75

[a]Includes British Guiana after 1745. [b]1705 omitted. [c]1727 omitted. [d]1755 and 1759 omitted. [e]1775-80 only. [f]1792 only. [g]1800 only. [h]1807 and 1809 only. [i]1810 and 1814 only. [j]1705 and 1711 omitted. [k]1717 and 1720 omitted. [l]1712 omitted. [m]1813 omitted. [n]1705, 1711, and 1712 omitted.

SOURCES:

Col. (1) N. Deerr, op. cit., pp. 193-203.

(2) Col. (1) times the sugar price divided by an overall index of British prices. Sugar prices are from (prior to 1728) McCusker, op. cit., p. 1143, and Deerr, op. cit., pp. 530-1 (using midpoints where Deerr provides the range). The Schumpeter-Gilboy consumer price index is used prior to 1819, and linked to the Gayer-Rostow-Schwartz index of domestic prices. See Mitchell, op.cit., pp. 468-70.

(3) Mitchell, op. cit., pp. 285-91. The figures in parentheses refer to the United Kingdom. Coverage is England and Wales to 1791, then Great Britain to 1829, and United Kingdom after 1826.

(4) Computed by method described for Col. (2) with Col. (3) substituted for Col. (1), with the post-1829 period linked to the earlier estimates to adjust for change in geographic coverage.

(5) Parliamentary Papers, 1852/53, Vol. XCIX (567), p. 568.

(6) Col. (4) times the price of sugar divided by the Gayer-Rostow-Schwartz index of British domestic prices.

and indirectly, the fortunes of the most rapidly growing section of Britain's export trade were closely bound up with the fortunes of the southern planters.'[2]

They also emphasise the role of a rising British demand for imports after 1745 in explaining the sharp rise in West Indian exp rts, thus denying an exogenous role to the empire as the source of the demand spurring British economic growth. Table 5.3 shows that sugar output grew rapidly after the middle of the eigh.eenth century, while the relative price of sugar was falling slightly, so that clearly more consideration needs to be given to the sources of increased supply in the West Indies. Table 5.3 provides several measures which indicate the rapid growth of sugar output and revenues in the eighteenth century, output rising to about five times its early level, a rate of increase sharply in excess of the rate of growth of population.

2. *RELATIVE LEVELS OF PER CAPITA WEALTH c. 1770*

Debates on colonial settlement often distinguished between two types of settlement – one based on the production of export commodities by forced labour and the other based upon settlement by whites in small, family-type farms. The contrast was drawn by Adam Smith and was probably most specifically examined by Merivale in the 1830s.[3] It was argued that the slave-based settlements might, because of the availability of fertile land, initially show high levels of income and growth, but that, in some undefined long run, the production structure and income distribution patterns of the other colonies would mean they would benefit from higher growth rates and income levels. While it is often unclear as to how long the long run would be, and thus some confusion exists between describing the expected tendencies in contrast to the achieved levels, clearly the nineteenth and twentieth-century patterns indicate that, for whatever reason, these predictions were accurate. More attention, however, can be paid to the earlier patterns based upon some of the wealth data prepared by Alice Jones for the mainland and Richard Sheridan for Jamaica.[4]

Table 5.4 provides estimates of the relative wealth per capita of three regions of the mainland and of Jamaica around 1770. The first three were

TABLE 5.4 Wealth per capita, English colonies, c. 1770

Mainland	*Wealth per capita*[a] *(pounds sterling)*
New England	36.4
Middle colonies[b]	40.2
South	36.4
Jamaica	43.0

[a]Wealth excludes value of slaves. The population totals include both free and slave.
[b]Vermont and Delaware are considered as Middle colonies.
SOURCES: Jones, *Wealth of a Nation to Be*, Chap. 4; Sheridan, op. cit., pp. 229-32, with population estimates from McCusker, op. cit., p. 692.

prepared by the same person and are therefore comparable, while the Jamaica estimate is provided for suggestive purposes. Clearly the United States South was a wealthy colony, with a value of physical assets nearly equal to that of the rest of the nation. If we measured the value of wealth per free person the differences would appear dramatically in favour of the South. Comparing Jones' estimates with that of Sheridan, the per capita wealth in Jamaica was above the wealth of the mainland areas. Thus in the years before the American Revolution it does appear that those regions producing commodities for export to England were among the wealthiest of the English areas of settlement. It should be noted that, for the South, cotton was not exported until after the Revolution, so this high level of wealth was achieved while there was primary specialisation in tobacco and in rice.[5]

3. THE UNITED STATES, 1770-1880

Table 5.5 points to a sometimes neglected aspect of the effect of the American Revolution upon United States regional economic development. Clearly one net effect of the Revolution and the freedom from the regulations governing trade with the British empire was a significant impairment of the economic conditions in the southern states. Southern shares of both wealth and exports fell dramatically, with there being a marked increase in the relative position of the Middle Atlantic states which specialised in mixed agriculture. The economic decline was pronounced throughout the South, affecting

TABLE 5.5 Effect of the American Revolution on regional shares of wealth, exports and population

	Wealth (net of slaves)		*Exports*		*Population*	
	1774	*1799*	*1768-72*	*1791-92*	*1770*	*1800*
New England	25.1%	29.6%	17.0%	22.4%	27.0%	23.4%
Middle Atlantic	29.3	38.5	19.3	29.2	24.2	26.7
South	45.6	31.9	63.6	48.4	48.7	49.9

SOURCES:
Col. (1) Jones, *Wealth of a Nation to Be,* Chap. 4. Vermont and Delaware are considered in the Middle Atlantic only in this column; in all others Vermont is in New England and Delaware is in the South.
Col. (2) T. Pitkin, *A Statistical View of the Commerce of the United States of America* (New Haven, 1835) p. 313. Wealth is defined as the 'value of houses and lands'.
Cols. (3), (4) J. F. Shepherd and G. M. Walton, 'Economic Change after the American Revolution; Pre- and Post-War Comparisons of Maritime Shipping and Trade', *Explorations in Economic History,* Vol. 13, No. 4, Oct 1976, pp. 397-422. These estimates exclude invisibles. If they were included the shares of the northern regions in both years would increase, but the basic changes over time would not be altered.
Cols. (5), (6) US Bureau of the Census, op. cit., pp. 1168, 24-37.

areas of both rice and tobacco production. If any other year were chosen the decline would seem even sharper, since tobacco production returned to the pre-war heights only in a few years prior to 1840, and was at its highest in the years 1890-92.[6] Clearly leaving the British empire imposed costs on the South, and was beneficial to the Middle Atlantic areas. This was reflected in the falling price of slaves during the war, but it should be noted that slave imports rose sharply to 1808 and that, with the recovery to pre-war levels in the 1780s and the sustained rise after 1800, the price of slaves did not fall below subsistence costs. This indicates that despite the setbacks an economic ending of the slave economy was not anticipated.

After the Revolutionary period, the rate of growth of southern per capita income and wealth was at or slightly above that of the rest of the nation until the onset of the Civil War.[7] This occurred in a period of particularly rapid growth for the nation, with major industrialisation in the northern states. In the South there was little change in industrial structure, the slave-based economy being specialised in the production of export crops, particularly cotton. On the eve of the Civil War, per capita incomes in the South were at a level equal to nearly three-quarters that in the rest of the nation. Looked at as a separate nation, the South was the world's fourth or fifth richest nation, with only Great Britain and the North, among the major 'countries', having higher incomes.[8] In the North, the industrialising north-eastern states were those with highest incomes, the per capita incomes in the states of the 'Old Northwest' being below those of the South. Further, for the free population, the inequalities of income and wealth distributions did not differ dramatically among the sections, the sharp inequalities due to urbanisation and industrialisation in the North offsetting the impact of large, slave-based farms in the South.[9]

The marked decline in relative southern incomes which characterised the late nineteenth and early twentieth centuries did not occur during the slave era, but came, rather, with the emancipation of slaves after the Civil War. There was a decline in labour force participation, and a movement to production on units smaller than the efficient antebellum plantations.[10] Some of the benefits of emancipation were taken in the forms of increased leisure and more favourable working and living conditions, an adjustment which characterised all slave-based economies upon emancipation. It took about one-quarter of a century after the war for the south to reach the level of measured per capita income it had reached in 1860, and almost a century to reach its antebellum level relative to the rest of the nation. Incomes in the South declined sharply with emancipation, but, perhaps because of the technology of cotton, the South was unique among ex-slave areas in an increase in the share of exports in regional income after emancipation, albeit produced less efficiently than before. Thus whatever its long-run effects, the relative decline of the South came after slavery ended, not before. Care must be taken to examine separately the declines in per capita income and per worker output. The latter did fall in the immediate aftermath of the

Civil War, but, because of the measured changes in labour force participation, not as rapidly as the former. And, after the initial decline as a result of the impact of the Civil War, southern per capita incomes generally rose or remained constant relative to the increasing level of national per capita income. While marked convergence did not occur until after the 1930s, the absence of widening relative per capita incomes between North and South thus characterised the post-Civil War years as it had the antebellum decades. Within the northern states a convergence of per capita income relatives has marked the past century, with perhaps the most prominent features being the relative declines in the older north-eastern states as well as in the western states which had high relatives in their frontier period. Thus the one marked case of regional divergence, the South during the Civil War era, represents a profound structural shift directly attributable more to political, military, and social factors than to the operation of purely economic forces.[11]

4. THE WEST INDIES, 1770-1930

Despite wartime fluctuations, territorial changes, and the generally unsettled state of the European political and economic situation in the late eighteenth and early nineteenth centuries, the British West Indies continued expanding its sugar output and revenues derived from sugar production. Column (1) of Table 5.3 indicates that the output of sugar in the British West Indies expanded at an average annual rate of 1.8 per cent from 1700 to 1834, a rate in excess of that of population growth. While there were fluctuations in the price of sugar, both in absolute terms and relative to other prices, the 'real return' to sugar production rose throughout the eighteenth century. There were sharp fluctuations in the early nineteenth century, mainly reflecting changes in the prices of British goods in the Napoleonic War period, and, while atypically high 'revenues' were achieved in 1795-1804 and 1815-19 because of these British price changes, the returns from sugar production remained above eighteenth-century levels and sugar output was increasing prior to slave emancipation.

There are several changes which must be considered when examining Table 5.3. First, in the nineteenth century some shifts were occurring in the West Indies, and other crops, such as coffee, were becoming more important as exports. Thus expansion was more rapid than projections based on sugar alone would suggest. Second, as indicated by the different patterns of change in columns (3) and (5) the share of West Indian sugar in total British sugar imports was declining. Through 1830 the West Indies accounted for about 90 per cent of British sugar imports, the share falling to about three-quarters in the 1830s, and then to one-half by 1850.[12] The very sharp decline in the West Indian share of British sugar came after, not before, slavery ended. Third, within the British West Indies, there were dramatic shifts in the sources of sugar production. From 1770 to 1810 the older areas of the British West Indies accounted for over three-quarters of sugar output, their share fell to 60 per cent by the early 1820s, and then to about one-half afterwards. Jamaica suffered a particularly sharp loss in relative terms, from accounting for over one-half of British West Indian sugar production in 1810 to about one-third when slavery ended, and to about one-fifth by 1850.[13] This decline was mirrored in the increased share of the output coming from the ceded colonies, particularly the areas of British Guiana.[14] Fourth, and perhaps most crucial for examining the long-term consequences of settlement, is that the major decline in sugar output and revenues came with the end of slavery and the transformation of the regional agricultural economies. The emancipation of slaves led to sharp drops in sugar output as well as in the output of other plantation crops. While this reduction in output of plantation crops reflected an increased leisure and more desired working conditions for the ex-slaves, clearly the decline was not a phenomenon of the slave period but rather the result of its abolition.

There were important differences in the adjustments to emancipation of the older and the newer areas of the West Indies.[15] The newer areas, such as British Guiana and Trinidad, soon began to import indentured labour from Asia, and these labourers provided the basis for reinstalling the plantation

TABLE 5.6 Population, per capita income, sugar production, and output structure, Jamaica and British Guiana, post-1832

Jamaica	*Population ('000)*	*Per capita income*	*Sugar production ('000 tons)*	*Share of exports in total output*
		(1910 prices)		*(Current prices)*
1832	370.0[a]	£15.6	72	43.5%
1850	400.5[a]	12.2	29	24.3
1870	506.1	11.9	25	20.2
1890	639.5	12.4	17	19.1
1910	831.4	13.7	20	22.6
1930	1017.2[a]	15.7	65	19.8
British Guiana		*(1913 prices)*		*(1913 prices)*
1832	98.0	£23.9	55	43.3%
1852	127.7	19.9	49	22.8
1871	193.5	–	92	–
1891	270.9	–	114	–
1911	289.1	–	86	–

[a]Computed by using Eisner's estimates of total product and per capita product.
SOURCES: The population estimates are for census years different from the year of output estimates in several cases, but these differ by only one or two years.
Col. (1) Eisner, op. cit., pp. 134, 289; Mandle, op. cit., p. 19.
(2) Eisner, p. 289; Moohr, op. cit., p. 589; Mandle, p. 19.
(3) Deerr, op. cit., pp. 198-9, 203.
(4) Eisner, p. 237; Moohr, p. 589.

production of sugar. As shown in Table 5.6, the initial income declines in British Guiana and Jamaica were similar, as were the changes in the importance of exports in total production. Yet, British Guiana began large-scale imports of indentured labour, and within 40 years of the end of slavery produced more sugar than prior to emancipation. Jamaica, on the other hand, was quite different, the levels of per capita income not returning to the pre-emancipation level for one century, and output per worker did not return to earlier levels until the early twentieth century.[16] The sugar economy collapsed, and the levels of sugar output of the 1820s were not achieved until one century later. Indeed Jamaica did not exceed its 1805 quantity of sugar output until 1936.[17] In part this decline reflected the dramatic rise in exports of bananas, logwood, and other crops after 1870, sugar falling from 60 per cent of Jamaica's exports as late as 1850 to less than 10 per cent in 1910. Despite these shifts, however, it was not until after 1890 that the total value of domestic exports returned to the 1832 level.[18] Thus in the West Indies, as in the US South, the end of slavery meant falls in measured income and shifts in the production structure, although in some areas the possible uses of a new form of forced labour limited the decline and permitted a recovery of the plantation production. The US was unique in its maintenance of export production, indicative of different conditions of demand in the world market for cotton and for sugar as well as the technological scale requirements of cotton as contrasted with sugar.[19]

5. SUMMARY AND CONCLUSIONS

This paper has presented some data to describe the relative fortunes of the different parts of the British New World settlements in the period from the seventeenth to the nineteenth centuries. It indicates that in the eighteenth century the areas based on the use of the forced labour of African slaves to produce export commodities were quite wealthy, but due to changing economic and political forces their relative positions declined in the nineteenth century. Particularly marked were the impact of the Revolutionary War on the American South, and the ending of slavery in both the South and the West Indies. In general, however, the absolute levels of per capita incomes were growing in all regions until the end of slavery, and it was emancipation which lowered measured per capita incomes and, in the West Indies, led to significant shifts in the composition of output. In the US South emancipation caused significant changes in the scale of production and in efficiency, bringing the white population more heavily into the production of export commodities although there was little change in the output mix. The different effects upon crop-mix in the South and in the West Indies were influenced by the different world market demand conditions for cotton from the South, which remained the world's major supply source to the First World War and for West Indian sugar, which quickly lost its dominant position both within the British Empire, and, with the changing sugar duties, as a source of supply to the British consumer. Yet there may also have been some impact of technology, which permitted cotton production to occur on smaller units, with some loss in productivity, but precluded sugar production without the introduction of forced labour.

In the late nineteenth century the regions which had been dominated by slave labour were clearly those with lower incomes than those to the north. The extent to which this was due to the direct or indirect impact of slavery, and the extent to which climate and resources would have restricted the possibilities for large-scale development along alternative paths, remain to be examined. One point seems clear, however: during the period of slavery economic growth was more rapid and measured output was higher than they were after emancipation. With emancipation, and the ability of the labour force to work on smaller units in peasant-type agriculture, measured output fell. It may, of course, be argued that slavery led to a form of specialisation which precluded the development of an appropriate structure for sustained long-term economic development after slavery ended. Alternatively, perhaps the combination of climate, resources, technology, and worker preferences would not have permitted such development in the absence of slavery. The resource base of the northern United States was richer and more appropriate for industrialisation than it was in areas to the south, and the ability of northern entrepreneurs to instil a specific type of work-discipline and to attract workers into industry by some mix of voluntary and other methods remains a perhaps unique New World achievement in this period. In any event, with our increasing knowledge and improved statistical data on actual patterns of economic change we shall be in a better position to evaluate the causes and consequences of the income disparities which arose in the period of the Industrial Revolution.

NOTES

1Curtin, P. D., *The Atlantic Slave Trade* (Madison, 1969) pp. 119, 216; and the adjustments of Carey's data for the United States in Fogel, R. W. and Engerman, S. L., *Time on the Cross* (Boston, 1974) II, p. 29. On the demographic patterns, see the summary presentation in Klein, H. S., and Engerman, S. L., 'The Demographic Study of the American Slave Population' (unpublished, 1976).

2Deane, P. and Cole, W. A., *British Economic Growth, 1688-1959* (Cambridge, 1962) p. 86; Young, A., *Political Essays* (London, 1772).

3Smith, A., *The Wealth of Nations* (New York, 1937); Merivale, H., *Lectures on Colonization and Colonies* (London, 1861).

4See Jones, A. H., *Wealth of a Nation to Be: Wealth of the Colonies on the Eve of the American Revolution* (New York, 1979) as well as her *American Colonial Wealth: Documents and Methods* (New York, 1977); Sheridan, R.B., *Sugar and Slavery* (Baltimore, 1973) pp. 229-32. Cf. M. Craton, in *Sinews of Empire* (New York, 1974) pp. 132-56.

5Although tobacco was the more important commodity, rice was increasing in importance in the eighteenth century, rising from an amount equal to about 1 per cent of tobacco exports at the start of the century to about 40 per cent of the value of tobacco exports just prior to the Revolutionary War. Shepherd, J. F., and Walton, G. M., *Shipping, Maritime Trade, and the Economic Development of Colonial North America* (Cambridge, 1972) pp. 38, 98.

[6] Gray, L. C., *History of Agriculture in the Southern United States to 1860* (Washington, 1933) pp. 214, 602-6, 1035. See also Bjork, G. 'The Weaning of the American Economy, Independence, Market Changes, and Economic Development', *Journal of Economic History,* Vol. XXIV, No. 4, December 1964, pp. 541-60, and Fishlow's discussion.

[7] Engerman, S.L., 'A Reconsideration of Southern Economic Growth, 1770-1860', *Agricultural History,* Vol. XLIX, No. 2, April 1975, pp. 343-61.

[8] Fogel, R. W. and Engerman, S. L., op. cit., I, p. 250.

[9] Soltow, L., *Men and Wealth in the United States, 1850-1870* (New Haven, 1975).

[10] Ransom, R. and Sutch, R., *One Kind of Freedom* (Cambridge, 1977).

[11] Engerman, S. L., 'Some Economic Factors in Southern Backwardness in the Nineteenth Century', in Kain and Meyer (eds), *Essays in Regional Economics* (Cambridge, 1971) pp. 279-306. Cf. Easterlin, R. A., 'Regional Income Trends, 1840-1950', in Harris (ed.), *American Economic History* (New York, 1961) pp. 525-47.

[12] Parliamentary Papers, 1852-53, Vol. XCIX (567), Sugar etc.

[13] Deerr, N., *The History of Sugar* (London, 1949-50) pp. 193-203.

[14] Green, W. A., *British Slave Emancipation* (Oxford, 1976) p. 36. Cf. Drescher, S., *Econocide* (Pittsburgh, 1977).

[15] Green, W. A., op. cit.; Adamson, A. H., *Sugar Without Slaves* (New Haven, 1972); Mandle, J., *The Plantation Economy* (Philadelphia, 1973); Moohr, M., 'The Economic Impact of Slave Emancipation in British Guiana, 1832-1852', *Economic History Review,* Vol. XXV, No. 4, November 1972, pp. 588-607; Nath, D., *A History of Indians in British Guiana* (London, 1950); Hall, D., *Free Jamaica, 1838-1865* (New Haven, 1959); Hall, D., *Five of the Leewards, 1834-1870* (St Lawrence, Barbados, 1971); Laurence, K. O., *Immigration into the West Indies in the 19th Century* (St Lawrence, Barbados, 1971).

[16] Eisner, G., *Jamaica, 1830-1930* (Manchester, 1961) p. 290.

[17] Deerr, N., op. cit., pp. 198-9.

[18] Eisner, G., op. cit., pp. 237, 238.

[19] Engerman, S. L., 'Quantitative and Economic Analysis of West Indian Slave Societies: Research Problems', in Rubin and Tuden (eds), *Comparative Perspectives on Slavery in New World Plantation Societies)* (New York, 1977) pp. 597-609.

6 Decolonisation and the Multinational Company: Unilever in India, 1917-65

D. K. Fieldhouse

No references are given for the sources on which this paper is based because they are all in the archives of Unilever, which are neither catalogued nor available for general study. The substance of the essay forms part of chapter 4 of my Unilever Overseas: the Anatomy of a Multinational *(Croom Helm, London, 1978).*

In the controversy over the role of multinational companies emphasis is normally placed on the effects of their activities on host countries. In this paper the standpoint is reversed. An attempt is made to answer, from evidence relating to Unilever's subsidiary in India, one question: what difference political independence made to the character of the company's operations in that country.

No two multinationals are the same and no two colonial dependencies reacted identically to colonialism or independence. It is therefore necessary to put the Unilever enterprise in India in a broader perspective. Multinationals broadly do one of three things: they extract or grow commodities; they manufacture for a world market; or they manufacture for a local market. Unilever is almost entirely concerned with the first and third of these; and in India, as in most less-developed countries, its main function is to manufacture consumer goods – detergents, edible oil and other food products – for local consumption. Thus, if this evidence has any general significance, it must relate to those multinational companies which manufacture consumer goods for local consumption in parts of the less-developed world which most closely approximate to India.

With the subject area defined it is possible to break down the general question into four topics which follow chronologically. (1) Why, during the colonial period, Unilever decided to undertake local manufacture in India rather than serve that market with exports from Europe. (2) What advantages or limitations flowed from colonialism. (3) What attitude Unilever adopted to Indian independence. (4) In what ways independence affected the business in India.

Local Manufacture. In assessing the relevance of colonialism to Unilever's overseas activities the main point is that as late as 1947 there were only five manufacturing subsidiaries in the colonial world – India, Ceylon, Indonesia,

Nigeria and the Belgian Congo. This may seem surprising. If colonial status provided economic advantages for the imperial power, one would have expected many more colonial factories. One obvious and continuing deterrent was the limited size of most colonial markets, but the Indian case suggests that, where this was not a major factor, the lack of local competition with imports, possibly due to low tariffs, was the main cause. Until the early 1920s India provided a very satisfactory import market for Lever soap products. There was then a dramatic decline in the volume of sales and profit margins in 1921-22 which may have been affected by the post-war slump and a decline in the value of the rupee, but which William Lever, the first Viscount Leverhulme, attributed to the *swadeshi* movement led by Gandhi, which called for a boycott on imports from Britain. Such a boycott would have stimulated native Indian producers, and Tatas were already involved in oil-milling. Lever's instinctive reaction to such a situation in other countries had always been to establish local manufacture, preferably by buying out an established producer. In 1922 he therefore acquired a controlling interest in the Premier Soap and North West Soap Companies, two parts of a company flotation undertaken by members of a British family banking concern, Boulton Bros, whose assets included a small soap factory in Garden Reach, Calcutta. Significantly this was done by an exchange of shares because Levers were then in serious financial difficulties: there was no question of using 'surplus capital'.

In retrospect this can be seen as the foundation of one of Unilever's largest overseas subsidiaries. But for a decade after 1922 this seemed unlikely. Almost immediately the case for local manufacture disappeared. The *swadeshi* movement died, soap was not among those products given tariff protection during the 1920s and soap imports recovered to reach an all-time peak of 20,238 tons in 1928. Production in the Calcutta factory remained very small and was limited to local, not Unilever, brands. Thus the reason for reviving the project for local manufacture as a substitute for imports was that between 1929 and 1932 sales of imported Unilever soap fell from 18,830 to 11,305 tons and net profits from £196,900 to £33,000. The slump was an obvious cause; but, since Indian-made soaps were not affected to the same extent, it seemed likely that the decline resulted from one or both of two other factors – the revived boycott on imports and the protective tariff introduced in 1931 which imposed duties of about 25 per cent *ad valorem* on imported soaps. No one in Unilever House was certain which was primarily to blame, but together these indicated that local manufacture was essential to save the established market for Unilever brands. Early in 1933 it was decided to build a substantial factory in Bombay alongside another factory making *ghee* substitute (*vanaspati*) which had been undertaken a year earlier on identical grounds.

Local manufacture in India was thus a defensive step taken to protect established import markets. The critical moment came when this dependency was allowed to break free from the principle that a colony could not protect its domestic market against imperial products and was thus no longer to be constrained by colonialism.

Colonial Status and the Multinational. But if empire itself was not an incentive to establish local manufacture in India, its significance for Unilever's operations there was considerable. Colonial rule provided favourable conditions for foreign companies once established. First in importance was political stability and predictability. The Indian government might not do what a British firm wanted, but it was not arbitrary, faction-ridden or corrupt. Above all it was consistent and law-abiding. Second, colonial India had an 'open' economy in which the government imposed virtually no constraints on the operation of market forces. As a result Unilever did not have to ask permission to manufacture and no official controlled its output, prices or inputs. There was no possibility that Unilever's Indian business would be taken over or that it would be forbidden to transfer its profits or capital. The Indian company was registered locally, but it was not obliged to have any indigenous shareholders, managers or directors. Finally corporate and income taxes were low – under 30 per cent before 1939. All these things encouraged business confidence. Moreover, at least in India, colonialism had few if any adverse features, once an adequate protective tariff had been established. Unilever might well fear the prospect of Indian independence.

Decolonisation. Nevertheless Unilever appears to have faced the prospect of the transfer of power, which was clearly imminent after the Cripps mission of 1942, with extraordinary equanimity. This may have been due in part to a misconception about the consequences of independence: thus a visiting director commented in 1944 that 'It must require many years in which to build up the machinery for an efficient national government, and in the process the assistance of Britain is essential. It is therefore hard to picture a state of complete independence for India before the lapse of 15-20 years.' On this assumption Unilever discounted the threat of nationalisation made by many Congress members in the mid-1940s: the only steps taken in 1947 were to hedge against a rapid devaluation of the rupee by declaring interim and final dividends for 1946 earlier than usual, capitalising reserves as a bonus share issue (of course a recurrent measure) and remitting surplus cash to Europe. In the event the rupee stood firm and no further steps were necessary. The most pressing problem resulted from the partition of India, which made it necessary to establish a separate enterprise in West Pakistan.

The Effects of Independence. The experience of the following two decades none the less showed that independence did substantially affect Unilever's position in this and other ex-colonial territories. Expropriation was not the main threat: only in Egypt and Burma were Unilever enterprises permanently nationalised before 1978. Yet the new world was substantially different. The most important fact was that the 'open' economy of colonial times was replaced in India and most other ex-colonies by 'managed' economies. India declared itself to be a 'socialist' state, adopting as its stated objective central control of all aspects of economic life and, in varying degrees, public control of the means of production and exchange. In practice this meant close bureaucratic control of the private sector, whether foreign or Indian-owned. Productive capacity was regulated by licence. Imports of all capital goods, intermediates and raw materials required a licence and, where suitable local substitutes were available, this would not normally be given. Some prices were subject to formal control, others were informally regulated. Tax rates rose far above rates common in Europe and America: by the 1960s the 'statistical' tax rate, which assumed that all profits were distributed, rose above 70 per cent. Thus the business could not expand, diversify, use imported inputs or even reduce its labour force without formal or informal official consent. It had, in effect, been allocated a specific role in the economy and its future depended largely on how favourably it was regarded by the government and its agencies.

Two other aspects of state policy significantly affected Unilever: on Indian ownership of part of the capital of foreign companies and on the Indianisation of management. As a general rule Unilever has preferred not to sell equity in overseas companies because to do so gives part of the profit to third parties, limits a company's freedom in using its profits and might ultimately make effective control impossible. It is thus not surprising that when the Indian government, long committed to partial disinvestment by foreign companies, first put informal pressure, unsupported by law, on Unilever to sell shares in the Indian business in 1954 Unilever House refused flatly. The significant fact is that the company quickly saw that to sustain this attitude would result in such hostility in official circles that their operations might be seriously endangered. In the event Unilever not only sold 10 per cent of the equity in its Indian business (consolidating its several companies into a single Hindustan Lever in the process) but had to do so on unfavourable terms laid down by the authorities. Although the proportion of the total equity held by Indians was small and was still under 15 per cent in 1965, the events of 1954-56 had great symbolic importance as the moment when a great multinational found it necessary to accept dictation from a host government conveyed informally by a senior minister.

It could, however, be argued that localisation of management was more important as a way in which a multinational can come to terms with a host society, and that this has generally been understressed in the literature. In this process decolonisation played an important part. Unilever had never excluded non-Europeans from management and during the Second World War a policy of rapid Indianisation was adopted to meet a shortage of expatriates. But merely to replace British by Indian managers would have little effect on the character of the enterprise. Full localisation involved two further steps: first, a majority of the local board must be drawn from the indigenous managers; second, the board must be given effective control of long-term planning as well as day-to-day administration. Such freedom of action could never be total so long as the Indian company remained part of a multinational. But, provided the centre used its reserved powers sensitively, the end-result might be a genuine 'socialisation' of the subsidiary into the host economy. The importance of Hindustan Lever in this context is that it was the first Unilever subsidiary in any country without a predominantly European population to fulfil these conditions for full autonomy. It was also the first British subsidiary in India, and may well have been the first subsidiary of any multinational company in the Afro-Asian world to reach this point. The first Indian director was appointed in 1949. In 1952 progressive Indianisation of the board was projected, but without a date for its realisation. The decisive point came in 1955 when a director of Unilever recommended that 'final responsibility and essential initiative should be transferred as soon as possible' to an Indian management. Six years later, in 1961, this point was reached with the appointment of the first Indian Chairman and a board of six, of whom only two were expatriates. There is no doubt that this achievement was substantially the result of Indian independence, which created an environment in which refusal to localise management would have cast a slur on the ability of Indians to run a company of this kind successfully.

It remains to assess the impact of decolonisation on the performance of the Unilever companies in India. The two central questions are what effect the physical and fiscal controls imposed by post-independence governments had on the pattern of production and growth of the business; second, how independence affected profitability.

It is not easy to give a confident answer to the first question. If one considers first the established Unilever products – soap, *vanaspati* and toilet preparations – one would expect to find that the system of controls, notably licensing of productive capacity, would affect the scale and pattern of production. In practice, however, these seem to have had less effect than market forces. Sales of Lever soaps expanded roughly in proportion to the growth of the market for quality products and were even helped by import licensing which largely excluded international rivals. The main effect of controls was to restrict the rate of investment in non-soapy detergents, the main growth point of the industry in Europe and America, but pre-tax profits on soap remained very satisfactory. *Vanaspati* did much less well and became relatively unprofitable by the 1960s. This was partly due to legislation in the interests of the dairy industry which imposed a common specification on all manufacturers and so excluded the possibility that Hindustan Lever might pioneer a premium product more closely resembling natural *ghee*, on the analogy of Stork or Blue Band margarine in Europe. But overproduction and a saturated market were also important causes of low profitability and static sales, and these were due to overinvestment in the industry by Indian firms. Finally, Unilever had little success in toilet preparations, but again the main constraint was a limited market and failure to compete successfully with Indian and foreign competitors.

It was therefore as regards diversification that official controls had the greatest effect. Negatively, New Delhi limited the range of options because it would not permit foreign firms to start new enterprises in fields where Indians were already operating. Positively it was official policy to encourage foreign firms to invest in new products, particularly those which by the 1970s were described as part of the 'core' segment of the economy: that is, those concerned with the transformation of raw materials into industrial or consumer products, preferably with backward linkages into the agricultural base or forward linkages into other manufactures. In the later 1950s Hindustan Lever attempted to meet these requirements by an investment of over £3 million in processing milk, peas and cotton-seed and making cattle and poultry feeds. By the 1970s it was clear that these enterprises were technically successful but financially unsatisfactory: Hindustan Lever still depended mainly on soap for its profits and was considering new enterprises in fields still further removed from its original industrial base. How far this setback was the result of governmental constraints is uncertain. The new 'managed' economy had undoubtedly blocked many potential lines of development; yet the problem of finding new consumer products suited to Indian conditions was bound to be difficult, given the limitations of the market. It is at least arguable that the business might have looked much the same if the Union flag had still been flying in New Delhi.

Finally there is the question of profits. There are gaps in the surviving records, but Table 6.1 shows average net profits as a percentage of average capital employed for four quinquennial periods, the first two during the first decade of local manufacture, the others during the decade before 1965.

TABLE 6.1 Unilever's Indian companies: Average net profit as a percentage of average gross capital employed

1935-9	17.8
1940-4	17.6
1956-60	10.6
1961-5	8.1

At first sight these figures seem conclusive: decolonisation very substantially reduced the net profitability to Unilever of its business in India. From the standpoint of London this was undeniable. But if one asks whether this was due to the effect of governmental management of the economy it becomes clear that it was not. Table 6.2 shows that pre-tax profits were on average less before 1939 than they were in 1962-5. Indeed, the Indian government in the modern period so managed the economy that less efficient indigenous manufacturers could obtain an acceptable return and this ensured that a more efficient firm such as Unilever could get relatively high pre-tax profits. The cause of reduced net profitability, and therefore of funds for reinvestment or transfer to Europe as dividends, was the high rate of taxation characteristic of most post-independence developing countries.

A short general conclusion to the argument might thus be that neither colonialism nor decolonisation had a decisive influence on the character of Unilever's operations in India. The initial motive for local manufacture was

TABLE 6.2 Comparative profits made by Unilever in India, 1935-8 and 1962-5 (Rs.'000)

Year	A *Capital employed*	B *Trading profit before tax*	*B/A per cent*	C *Net profit after tax*	*C/A per cent*
1935	10,883	892	8.2	736	6.8
1936	10,968	1,377	12.5	1,060	9.7
1937	11,408	2,988	26.2	2,345	20.6
1938	11,526	3,698	32.1	2,903	25.2
Average	11,196	2,238	20.0	1,761	15.7
1962	152,200	42,810	28.1	14,983	9.8
1963	163,000	43,660	26.8	11,788	7.2
1964	167,900	32,062	19.1	11,767	7.0
1965	179,800	35,972	20.0	12,015	6.7
Average	165,725	38,626	23.3	12,638	7.6

NOTE: The data for 1962-5 exclude Pakistan.

to defend an established export market that was threatened by local competition within a tariff barrier. This was certainly not a situation characteristic of colonialism in most parts of the world. Decolonisation forced Unilever to adapt in many ways to the fact of Indian sovereignty, and the new 'managed' economy had a significant effect on the business. Yet thirty years after the transfer of power Hindustan Lever was still a thriving enterprise; and this suggests that, provided a multinational accepts the fundamental changes implicit in decolonisation, it may have a continuing and profitable role in any new state which continues to allow foreign capital to operate there.

7 Egypt, Iran and Turkey, 1800–1970: Patterns of Growth and Development

Charles Issawi

An assessment of the relative economic performance of Egypt, Iran and Turkey[1] from 1800 to 1970 is more meaningful than most such comparisons. Throughout the period, the three countries have had populations of much the same size and degree of development, and around 1800 their per capita incomes must have been roughly equal and their economic structures basically similar. Until the Oil Revolution of 1970-73, which drastically changed their relative positions, there was no significant difference in their resource endowments. All three share a common historical and cultural legacy: each had originated one of the major ancient civilisations, each had greatly contributed to the formation of Islamic society and culture, and all three had experienced the stagnation and decline that characterised the Middle East in the modern period. Lastly, all three were integrated in the world economy at much the same time and subjected to the same major forces: the thrust of European imperialism, the expansion of world trade, the spread of mechanical transport and electric communications, the flow of vast amounts of foreign capital, the unsettling Western ideas of nationalism, secularism and political liberty, and the influx of hundreds and thousands of Europeans with the technical, business or administrative skills required for the modernisation of society which the Middle Eastern governments were, with various degrees of commitment and success, attempting to carry out.

This paper falls into two parts. In the first, an appraisal is made of the economic development of the three countries at certain significant dates: 1800, 1860, 1913, 1950 and 1972. The second consists of an analysis in terms of some factors that may account for the differences observed.

I

1800

The end of the eighteenth century marks a low point in the economic history of the Middle East. Population had declined considerably from its late medieval and early modern levels, standing at some 3.5 million in Egypt, 6 million in Turkey (1831) and perhaps 5 million in Iran. The cultivated area had shrunk, and many villages and their surrounding fields had been abandoned. The crafts were still active, but their technology had stagnated and in many quality had fallen off; moreover some branches were already suffering from the competition of cheaper or better European goods. As for trade with Europe – which is the only one about which we have any information at present – it was definitely diminishing in Egypt, where both British and French merchants were leaving the country, and in Iran where the East India Company's business had declined so much that it was planning to close down its establishments in the Gulf. The Ottoman Empire's trade with Europe grew appreciably between 1715 and 1790, but this was largely attributable to the development of the Balkan provinces; the trade of Izmir showed a comparable increase, due partly to the diversion of the Persian silk trade from Aleppo, but otherwise no trend can be discerned in the trade of Istanbul or Anatolia. At the outbreak of the French Revolution Egypt's trade (exports plus imports) with Europe may have totalled £0.6 million and Turkey's £1.5 million, while Iran's *total* trade in 1800 was put at £2.5 million. The Revolutionary and Napoleonic Wars greatly reduced the trade of Egypt and Turkey and the War of Greek Independence led to further diminution in Turkey's trade. This economic decline was accompanied by reduced intellectual activity. One has only to compare the curriculum of the leading Muslim university, Al Azhar in Cairo, with the sciences taught in the heyday of Islam, or to recall the fact that when Muhammad Ali started his reforms he could not find a single native Egyptian who knew any European language, to realise how low Egypt had fallen. Iran was no better off but in Turkey there had been some hopeful developments in the eighteenth century, including the introduction of a Turkish printing press, some translations from European works and the opening of Western-type military academies.

Many causes led to this decline, of which only one will be mentioned here: the breakdown of government. In Iran this occurred early in the eighteenth century, with the collapse of the Safavi dynasty and the Afghan and other invasions. In Egypt anarchy grew steadily throughout the same century. And in the Ottoman Empire the central government gradually lost its control until, by the beginning of the nineteenth century, it was confined to a small area in Europe and Asia Minor centred on Istanbul.

1860

On the eve of the American Civil War, which by creating a shortage of cotton was to stimulate Egyptian growth so greatly, the Middle East presented a very different picture. Steam navigation had linked Egypt, Turkey and the Levant with Europe for nearly three decades, though Iran was still unprovided for. Steamers were also sailing on the Nile and Tigris-Euphrates, as well as the Aegean and Black Sea waters. Telegraphs had been laid down in Egypt and Turkey and would soon be in Iran. Some 500 kilometres of railway had been built in Egypt and work was under way on the Izmir-Aydin Line. The Ottoman Empire had been opened up by the Anglo-Turkish Commercial Convention of 1838 (applied to Egypt in 1841) and Iran by the

Russo-Persian Treaties of 1813 and 1828 and the Anglo-Persian Treaty of 1841; these replaced the former monopolistic, prohibitive and arbitrary practices with non-discriminatory, permissive provisions and very low import duties. European merchants increasingly supplied the expertise, market connections and short-term finance required by the import-export trade. At the same time various reformers – Muhammad Ali in Egypt, Mahmud II and the 'Men of the Tanzimat' in Turkey and Amir-i-Kabir in Iran – were attempting to modernise their countries.

Thanks to all these developments, the various parts of the Middle East began to be integrated, in different degrees, in the international trade network. Foreign trade expanded, in Egypt from about £2 million in 1823 to over £5 million in 1860, in Iran from about £2.5 million in 1800 to some £5 million and in Turkey from £5 million in the 1840s to £25 million in the 1870s. On the export side, the growth was due to greater output and sales of cash crops like cotton in Egypt and silk and opium in Iran and Turkey. By far the greatest increase in imports was that of cotton and other textiles, which drove many handicraftsmen out of business. There was also a rise in imports of colonial goods such as sugar, coffee and tea. Except under Muhammad Ali in Egypt, almost no capital goods were imported.

During this period all three countries were engaged in numerous wars, which drained a large part of their resources, but Iran enjoyed a longer period of peace than the other two. Nevertheless, its development was much slower. Its population grew little if at all. Its transport system saw no improvement except for the appearance of a few Russian steamships on the Caspian and an occasional British one in the Gulf and the revivial of the ancient Tabriz-Trabzon caravan route that shortened communications with Europe. Only a very small part of its agriculture was commercialised and there was no discernible change in either techniques or land tenure. Its efforts at industrialisation, in the 1850s, were very feeble. Its currency depreciated by over half in relation to sterling and its government revenues increased very little. Very few foreigners settled in the country and fewer Iranians went to Europe, with a consequent lack of intellectual stimulus.

Egypt, by contrast, experienced considerable change. Its population rose to some 5.5 million, or at about 0.8 per cent a year. The cultivated area was considerably extended; more important, large-scale irrigation works (diversion dams, dykes and canals) made it possible to grow more than one crop per annum, including the valuable 'summer' crops such as cotton and sugar, and agricultural output greatly expanded, with a corresponding increase in exports and imports. Agriculture had become market-oriented, and tenure had been radically transformed and almost all farmland was privately owned by landlords or peasant proprietors. Navigable canals and roads were built and in 1853 the first section of the Alexandria-Cairo-Suez railway was opened. An adequate port was built at Alexandria. Many foreign technicians and businessmen came to Egypt and hundreds of Egyptians were sent to Europe for study or training; technical and secondary schools were set up and a large-scale programme of translation and publishing initiated, thus starting a far-reaching intellectual awakening.

These developments did not proceed smoothly. Muhammad Ali (1805-49) attempted to set up a state-owned and managed industry and transport, financed by compulsory deliveries of cotton and other crops and a foreign trade monopoly. His success was considerable but after 1841 the system broke down under its own weight and because of foreign pressure. The monopolies were abolished and the factories dismantled but the improvements in agriculture and transport served as a foundation for future development.

Turkey was engaged in major wars throughout the period, against foreign powers or rebellious subjects. It was not until the 1840s that serious attempts at industrial development – only partly successful – began, not till then did foreign trade expand significantly, and Turkey was less integrated in the international network than Egypt. The commercialisation of agriculture and the transformation of land tenure was less advanced than in Egypt and, in all probability, population growth was slower. But Turkey's educational efforts matched those of Egypt and its intellectual progress was at least as great.

1913

In the next fifty years the processes described above accelerated. In real terms Egypt's foreign trade multiplied twelve-fold, Iran's four-fold and Turkey's almost three-fold; the League of Nations' estimates for 1913 were: Egypt $291 million, or $24 per capita, Iran $93 million or $9, and Turkey $273 million or $15. Thanks to improved hygiene and, probably, to greater food supplies, population about doubled in all three countries, with the towns growing a little faster. The rise in the labour force, and the availability of arable land, made it possible to expand cultivation. Output of cash crops like cotton, tobacco, silk, opium and dried fruits rose very fast and capitalist relations increasingly prevailed in agriculture, Egypt being again in the lead. This was aided by the adoption, in Egypt and Turkey, of Western-style agricultural and commercial codes and law courts that made it possible to sell or mortgage land and facilitate the collection of debts. Numerous foreign banks opened branches in Egypt and quite a few in Turkey but only two (British and Russian) in Iran; they concentrated heavily on the moving of the crops for export and the financing of imports. Transport expanded greatly: in 1913 Egypt had 4300 kilometres of railway and Turkey 3200 but Iran was still without any; similarly, modern ports had been built at Alexandria, Port Said, Suez, Istanbul, Izmir and Beirut, but in Iran the only noteworthy improvement was at Enzeli. Currencies were a little more stable and the governments were handling their finances somewhat better, on both the revenue and the expenditure side.

The Middle East received more than its share of the outflow of European capital in the last third of the nineteenth century. By 1913, Egypt's foreign debt, public and private, stood at about $1000 million, and that of the

Ottoman Empire at an equal amount, some 60 per cent of the private capital being in Turkey; Iran's was a little over $100 million. Much of the public debt had been spent on wars or wasted by monarchs but some had been used for railways and other public works. In all three countries the servicing of the debt absorbed a large proportion of government revenues and remittances of interest and profits were a heavy burden on the balance of payments. In Egypt and Turkey a small, but growing, industrial nucleus had come into being, but in Iran there were only a few factories struggling hard to survive. Another hopeful sign was the increasing proportion of capital goods in imports and the rising proportion of GNP devoted to investment – over 10 per cent in Egypt, a little less in Iran and Turkey.[2] Still another was the rapid growth in education and the emergence of an intelligentsia.

A review at this point brings out significant differences between the three countries. By any criterion, economic or social, Iran stood far behind the others. Both Egypt and Turkey had a per capita income of about $50 – a figure that was not too low by contemporary standards – but in other respects there were marked contrasts. The level of living of the masses in Turkey seems to have been higher and the distribution of income and wealth – notably land – more equal. Turkey also had a more experienced political and administrative elite. But in purely economic terms Egypt was distinctly more developed. On a per capita basis its foreign trade was considerably greater, its industrial output somewhat larger, its transport system far more serviceable and its financial structure much more elaborate and widespread. Its economy was distinctly more monetised and a much larger proportion of its agricultural output reached the market. Few countries could match its superb irrigation system, which made it possible to intensify agriculture and greatly raise output per acre – but only slightly per man. Its cities enjoyed amenities unrivalled in the Middle East until well after the Second World War. Its debt burden was also heavier and a larger proportion of its national product was absorbed by foreigners, including the 250,000 foreign residents in Egypt – a figure much larger than that of Turkey and many times as great as Iran's.

1950

During the First World War and its aftermath, Turkey suffered more than most belligerents and large parts of Iran were overrun and devastated. Egypt, on the other hand, was unscathed militarily and accumulated large sterling balances; hence its lead over the other two countries lengthened, as is shown in Table 7.1.

In the inter-war period the same general forces were at work in the three countries. Like other underdeveloped regions, the Middle East suffered from deteriorating terms of trade, shrinking exports and balance of payments strains in the late 1920s and 1930s. This reinforced the desire to industrialise, which had already been strengthened by the shortages felt during the war,

TABLE 7.1 Iran, Egypt and Turkey, 1925

	Iran	*Egypt*	*Turkey*
Population (millions)	(12.5)	14	13.1
Imports (millions of dollars)[a]	88	250	246
Railways (kilometres)	250	4,555	4,700
Automobiles[b]	4,450	17,740	7,500
Cement output (metric tons)	–	90,000[c]	59,000[c]
Refined sugar output (metric tons)	–	109,000[c]	5,000[c]
Students in schools	74,000	635,000	413,000

[a]In this and subsequent tables, only import figures are shown; exports are omitted, since both the inclusion and the exclusion of petroleum would be misleading.
[b]1926.
[c]1928.

and the recovery of tariff autonomy around 1930 enabled all three governments to protect and foster manufacturing. And in all three an attempt was made – most far-reaching in Turkey – to transfer economic control from foreigners or members of minorities to ethnic Egyptians, Iranians or Turks. But there was also a marked contrast. Egypt essentially maintained its 'open', private-enterprise economy and kept its link with sterling, while in Iran and Turkey the government was largely responsible for industrialisation, set up various state banks and agencies and conducted most foreign trade under bilateral agreements and blocked accounts. As is shown by Table 7.2 Iran, starting from a very low level, made the greatest relative progress and somewhat reduced the gap between it and the others, but Turkey also advanced quite rapidly, overtaking Egypt in several respects and, although no reliable figures are available, probably slightly surpassing it in per capita GNP.

TABLE 7.2 Iran, Egypt and Turkey, 1938

	Iran	*Egypt*	*Turkey*
Population (millions)	15	16.4	17.1
Imports (millions of dollars)	55	184	119
Railways (kilometres)	1,700	5,606	7,324
Automobiles	(15,000)	33,700	11,300
Cement output (metric tons)	65,000	375,000	287,000
Refined sugar output (metric tons)	22,000	238,000	247,000
Cereals output (million metric tons)[a]	3.09	3.63	6.46
Cotton output (metric tons)[b]	34,000	400,000	52,000
Energy consumption[c]	1.55	2.05	2.18
Students in schools[d]	234,000	1,309,000	810,000

[a]Wheat, barley, maize, rice – annual average, 1934-38.
[b]Annual average, 1934-38.
[c]Million metric tons of coal equivalent.
[d]1936/37.

During the Second World War the three countries just escaped becoming a battlefield, but once again the impact was uneven. Iran suffered most, being occupied by British and Soviet troops and experiencing severe disruptions. Turkey remained neutral, trading with both sides, but was forced to keep 500,000 men under arms, with serious effects on its agricultural output. Egypt was a base for British troops and cut off from Europe; this caused shortages and hardships but greatly stimulated industrial growth and once more enabled it to accumulate large sterling balances, which were gradually drawn down after the war. On the whole, however, as Table 7.3 indicates, there were no significant changes in the relative position of the three countries. But after 1950 their growth paths began markedly to diverge. Egypt went through two great upheavals. First, the 1952 Revolution which, following the beneficial land reform of that year, led to the wholesale nationalisation of industry, transport, finance and foreign trade of 1957 and 1961; on balance, the latter had an adverse effect on economic development. Secondly, Egypt was involved in successive wars with Israel, suffering increasing damage to its economy; a further drain was the war in Yemen, and more generally, the huge burden of defence expenditures, which in recent years rose above 20 per cent of GNP and, of course, were made possible only by massive outside aid. As a result, growth was rather slow – an average of 4 per cent per annum in 1960-73, or little above the population increase of 2.5 per cent.

TABLE 7.3 Iran, Egypt and Turkey, 1950

	Iran	*Egypt*	*Turkey*
Population (millions)	19.3	20.4	20.9
Imports (millions of dollars)	191	564	286
Railways (kilometres)	3,180	6,092	7,634
Automobiles	38,300	77,900	32,600
Cement output (metric tons)	54,000	1,022,000	396,000
Refined sugar output (metric tons)	69,000	218,000	186,000
Cereals output (million metric tons)[a]	3.09	3.72	6.74
Cotton output (metric tons)[b]	26,000	364,000	99,000
Electricity output (million kWh)[c]	200	642	676
Energy consumption[d]	4.51	4.42	5.40
Students in schools	743,000	1,597[e]	1,798

[a]Wheat, barley, maize, rice – annual average, 1947-51.
[b]Annual average, 1947-51.
[c]1948.
[d]Million metric tons of coal equivalent.
[e]1949.

Turkey got off to a very good start, with Marshall Plan aid, after 1948, but soon developed severe imbalances that slowed down its advance. After 1963, a fresh spurt was made, and progress continued on a broad front, with a rapid increase in industry, trade, finance and infrastructure and a rather slow one in agriculture. The government made a notable contribution but growth was most marked in the private sector, which saw the emergence of a large entrepreneurial class, the expansion of the managerial and technical salaried middle class, and the rapid growth of a skilled labour force; of particular significance was the migration of nearly one million workers to Germany and other parts of Western Europe: not only did their remittances reach a peak of $1.4 billion in 1972, but they brought back skills and attitudes which are bound to have far-reaching effects. In 1960-72 Turkey's rate of growth was 6.4 per cent, compared to a population increase of 2.5 per cent. In social terms it is certainly the most advanced of the three countries, its literacy rate in 1970 being 55 per cent, compared to 40 per cent in Egypt and 35 per cent in Iran, and its crude death rate 1.3 per cent compared to 1.4 and 1.6.

After the dislocations caused by the Soviet occupation of Azerbayjan and the oil nationalisation crisis of 1951 and its aftermath, Iran entered a long period of political stability and very rapid economic growth. In 1960-72 GNP increased at 9.6 per cent a year, one of the highest rates recorded, and population at 3.2 per cent. Here too there was a happy mix of public and private endeavour and, like Turkey, Iran has seen the very rapid growth of both an entrepreneurial and a salaried middle class. Here too development was widespread, agriculture being the lagging sector. Over the whole period, Iran received much less foreign aid than either Egypt or Turkey, but by the

TABLE 7.4 Iran, Egypt and Turkey, 1972

	Iran	*Egypt*	*Turkey*
Population (millions)	31.2	34.8	37.0
Per capita GNP (dollars)	490	240	370
Per capita energy consumption[a]	954	324	564
Per capita steel consumption (kilograms)	59	30	55
Per capita textile consumption (kilograms)[b]	5.1	4.6	6.7
Per capita sugar consumption (kilograms)	28	16	20
Imports (million dollars)	2,410	899	1,508
Railways (kilometres)	4,944	5,500	8,133
Railway freight (million ton kilometres)	3,693	2,976	6,641
Automobiles (thousands)	481	206	372
Cement output (thousand metric tons)	3,372	3,822	8,424
Refined sugar output (thousand metric tons)	598	550	811
Electricity output (million kWh)	9,100	8,030	11,242
Cereals output (million metric tons)[c]	7.7	6.7	17.1
Cotton output (thousand metric tons)[d]	209	495	536
Students in schools (thousands)[e]	4,820	5,708	6,720

[a]Coal equivalent, kilograms.
[b]1971-72.
[c]Wheat, barley, maize, and rice, annual average 1972-74.
[d]Lint, annual average 1972-74.
[e]1971.

late 1960s oil was making a large contribution to economic growth and after 1971 the increase in oil revenues was explosive. Table 7.4 shows how, by 1972, Iran had overtaken the other countries by most economic, but not social, criteria. Since then its advance has been extremely, and indeed unsustainably, fast.

II

Analysis of the factors determining the course of events surveyed above may be carried out under the following headings: location and topography, resources, social structure, political structure, and the interplay of international political forces.

Location and Topography

Location largely explains Egypt's early and Iran's belated start. Egypt was only a few days' journey by steamship from Europe, which made it easy for thousands of foreigners to settle in the country and many more to visit it. At their peak, just before the First World War, Europeans constituted 16 per cent of the population of Cairo, 25 per cent of Alexandria and 28 per cent of Port Said, forging strong economic, social and cultural links between Egypt and Europe. Iran, on the other hand, was inaccessible to European-based steamers until the opening of the Suez Canal in 1869, and remained remote until the air age, being thus deprived of a powerful stimulus. Turkey's location was almost as favourable as that of Egypt; it was further from Western Europe, a handicap that was not offset by proximity to Central Europe until the completion of the Vienna-Istanbul railway in 1888. Turkey received many fewer foreigners than Egypt, and Iran far fewer still.

Location also explains Egypt's head-start in transport. Both the Alexandria-Cairo-Suez railway and the Suez Canal were designed to serve European-Asian trade rather than Egyptian economic needs, but the railway in particular was also very beneficial to Egypt. Iran, by contrast, lay well of the main international trade routes and, except for some chimerical British and Russian railway schemes, was never envisaged as a transit route. The same was true of Turkey. The only alternative to the Suez Canal that was seriously considered was the Syrian-Mesopotamian route. The Istanbul-Baghdad railway was designed mainly to serve Ottoman, not German, political and economic objectives.

Egypt's topography is also much more favourable than that of Iran and Turkey. The flatness of the land and the omnipresence of the Nile and its branches means that the whole country is accessible to water transport, which greatly facilitated the spread of a cash-crop agriculture geared to foreign markets. Neither Turkey nor Iran have any significant stretches of navigable rivers. In Turkey this is partly compensated by the length of the coastline and the concentration of the population on the rims of the peninsula, but it still left large stretches of the country without water or mechanical transport and therefore virtually outside the world market. Iran was far worse off: its coastline on the Gulf is short and inhospitable and the bulk of its population and agriculture lies in the north, cut off from the oceans by formidable mountain ranges and deserts. It was only when regular steam navigation was established on the Caspian and the Russian railways reached Baku in 1884 that Iran was linked to a large and expanding market.

Resources

Egypt had only one major resource, fertile land, but until the First World War this was fully adequate to sustain rapid growth. With the introduction of long-staple cotton in 1821, Egypt had an export staple that was not produced by any industrial country except the United States, that constituted the raw material of the main item in international trade, cotton textiles, and that therefore enjoyed a rising demand. With increasingly elaborate and expensive irrigation works, Egypt could steadily expand its cultivated area and output and between 1848-52 and 1908-12 the volume of cotton exports rose more than twenty-fold. By then, however, the limits of cultivation had been reached, output and exports stagnated and, in addition, the terms of trade deteriorated. Accelerated population growth resulted in a falling land/man ratio and per capita income began to decline. When supplementary resources were sought in industrialisation it was too late for speedy relief.

Turkey lacked the counterpart of Egyptian cotton, but it had a much broader and more diversified agricultural and mineral base. For the reasons given above and below, this was developed much more slowly, but when it was, it generated greater momentum. Partly for the same reasons, industry followed the same course and by the 1950s Turkey forged ahead.

Iran's great and at present decisive resource, oil, was not discovered till the eve of the First World War. After that output expanded rapidly but the impact on the economy was slight, partly because the industry had remained relatively small and partly because only a small fraction of these revenues was devoted to development. It was only in the 1960s that oil tipped the balance of resources in Iran's favour; since then the enormous increase of revenues has pushed it far ahead, and the government is trying to use this windfall capital to create other resources, in agriculture, industry and mining, that can sustain future growth when oil gives out.

Social Structure

The Middle East entered the period of this study with a very unfavourable social structure, which is only now being slowly improved. First, it had experienced neither Renaissance nor Enlightenment, its cultural level was extremely low, its technical and scientific skills almost non-existent and its masses illiterate. But the trouble went even deeper: in contrast to the European, the Middle Eastern entrepreneurial bourgeoisie was too weak to influence policy and make its interests respected; no measures to protect handicrafts, manufactures, agriculture and shipping, like those of Elizabeth, Cromwell, Colbert and other European statesmen, are recorded until the nineteenth century. Power lay in the hands of soldiers and bureaucrats whose concern, apart from enriching themselves and increasing state revenues, was to ensure the provisioning of the cities to keep the populace quiet – which explains the strange phenomenon of higher duties being levied on exports than on imports and illustrates the fact that policy was based on 'fiscalism', not mercantilism. Hence when economic development came its main agents had to be foreign. In all three countries the large-scale enterprises were established by European capital – British and French, then German and in Iran Russian – and Europeans supplied the requisite entrepreneurial, managerial and technical skills. For the rest, Egypt imported its bourgeoisie *en bloc,* from Europe or neighbouring lands: Lebanese Christians, Armenians and Greeks and Jews. In the inter-war period, and to a greater extent during and after the Second World War, these were gradually squeezed out by a Muslim bourgeoisie, whose development may well have been inhibited by their overwhelming presence. The latter had hardly got into its stride when it was felled in the 1960s. Iran's much feebler development required a correspondingly smaller bourgeoisie; here too, Armenians, and to a much lesser extent Jews, played an important part but there was also a small Muslim trading class which formed the nucleus of the present powerful Iranian bourgeoisie. In Turkey the situation was more complex. From the eighteenth century, or even earlier, an active bourgeoisie had emerged among the Greeks, Armenians, Jews and other non-Muslims, and in the course of the nineteenth century it controlled the greater part of foreign trade, finance and shipping and a considerable part of cash farming. When industry began its promoters, in so far as they were not foreigners, were Greeks or Armenians. Clearly these groups greatly stimulated Turkey's economy but, in view of the rising tensions between them and the Turks, one wonders how long development on that basis could have been sustained. In a series of explosions between 1895 and 1923 Turkey eliminated its minorities and then settled down to the task of creating its own bourgeoisie.

Political Structures

Only two questions will be examined under this heading: the governments' ability to promote development and their desire to do so. For a long time Egypt was in far the best position: Muhammad Ali (1805-49) controlled his country much more effectively than any other Middle Eastern monarch and, as noted above, initiated a massive, though only partly successful, development programme. Another spurt occurred under Ismail (1863-79) whose extravagance contributed to Egypt's loss of independence but who also greatly developed its infrastructure. Under British rule (1882-1922) Egypt was efficiently administered and much investment took place in irrigation and transport, but with a neglect of such important sectors as industry and education. After that, however, Egypt enjoyed less freedom of action than Iran or Turkey and its government showed less interest in economic development.

The Ottoman government, preoccupied with wars and uprisings, did not seriously attempt to promote economic development until the reign of Abdul Hamid (1876-1908), which witnessed a fairly rapid and broad-based advance in agriculture, mining, transport and foreign trade. The Young Turks paid more attention to economic affairs and industrialisation and railway-building accelerated, but the country was soon engulfed in the Italian, Balkan and First World Wars. Mustafa Kemal (1919-39), renouncing imperial ambitions, carried out a far-reaching social and political revolution and laid the groundwork for subsequent development.

The Iranian government was by far the weakest, and with increasing British and Russian intervention, its authority actually declined in the decade preceding the First World War. It was left to Reza Shas (1925-41) both to re-establish central government control and to initiate economic and social development. After the setbacks caused by the Second World War and its aftermath, his task was taken up, with greater success, by the present shah.

International Forces

The Ottoman Empire was by far the strongest of the three states and, consequently, suffered least from the presence of external forces. The Turks soon mastered the art of playing off the Powers against each other, thereby not only preserving their independence but sometimes securing valuable concessions. Thus when Turkey declared bankruptcy, in 1881, its foreign debt was cut by half, in contrast to Egypt which had to accept responsibility for all its outstanding debts. Similarly, there is little doubt that German interest in Turkey, and its massive and beneficial investments in railways and other enterprises, were at least partly due to the desire to draw the Empire to its side. But this multiplicity of outside forces also had disadvantages, best seen in the attempts of the various Powers to block each other's railway projects and in the British refusal to allow the Turks to modify their tariffs, for fear this would benefit the Germans.

Egypt suffered twice from foreign interventions, in 1841 when the Powers forced Muhammad Ali to dismantle his economic system and in 1882 when the British occupied the country. Thereafter, until the Entente Cordiale of 1905, the French and Russians could be relied upon to use their position in the Caisse de la Dette and elsewhere to thwart any British schemes for the development of Egypt.

But in a way the main victim of international rivalry was Iran. After fruitless attempts by Britain and Russia to sway it to their side, both countries tacitly agreed that their interests were best served by keeping Iran undeveloped. The British were haunted by the nightmare of Cossacks charging on India while the Russians were equally scared of British economic and political penetration of their vulnerable Caucasian flank.[3] Hence, until the Anglo-Russian agreement of 1907, which in effect partitioned Iran into spheres of influence, both Powers opposed railway and other projects, a fact that ranks high among the causes of Iranian lack of development.

One final point may be mentioned – the disadvantage of an early start. For the reasons given above, Egypt's natural resources began to be exploited very early but its human resources were not correspondingly developed, immigration supplying the necessary skills. By contrast Iran – like Iraq, the Sudan and the Arabian peninsula – was almost untouched until the twentieth century. As a result, it did not experience the early and rapid population growth, and the ensuing population pressure, of Egypt. Nor was its development distorted by the presence of large foreign settlements and economic institutions. When it did start building, in the 1920s, it could do so on relatively unencumbered ground.[4]

In 1800 Turkey was somewhat ahead of the other two countries in economic and social development, and Iran may possibly have been a little better off than Egypt. In 1913 the order was: Egypt, Turkey, Iran. Today it is Iran, Turkey, Egypt. The preceding analysis attempts to explain these changes.

NOTES

[1]The term 'Turkey' designates the area within the borders of the Republic. 'Ottoman Empire' refers to the area directly ruled by the Sultans at the given date.

This paper draws heavily on my three books: *The Economic History of the Middle East* (Chicago, 1966), *The Economic History of Iran* (Chicago, 1971) and *The Economic History of Turkey* (in press), and the sources cited therein.

[2]Samir Radwan, *Capital Formation in Egyptian Industry and Agriculture* (London, 1974) p. 236; Julian Bharier, *The Economic Development of Iran* (Oxford, 1971) p. 55; Vedat Eldem, *Osmanli Imparatorlugunun iktisadi sartlari hakkinda bir tetkik* (Istanbul, 1970) p. 309.

[3]Both sides had ample justification for their fears; for the Russian see the correspondence, in 1878 and 1885, from the 'Comité patriotique', representing 'all nationalities in the Caucasus' and headed by various Georgian and Armenian notables, promising an insurrection in case of an Anglo-Russian war – PRO, F078/3902, Trebizond, 1886; British fears of Russian expansionism have been often described and explained.

[4]See Charles Issawi, 'Asymmetrical Development and Transport in Egypt, 1800-1914', in William R. Polk and Richard L. Chambers (ed.), *Beginnings of Modernization in the Middle East* (Chicago, 1968); idem, 'Middle East Economic Development, 1815-1914; the General and the Specific' in M.A. Cook (ed.), *Studies in the Economic Development of the Middle East* (London, 1920).

8 Technology Transfer, Population Growth and the Development Gap since the Industrial Revolution

Priyatosh Maitra

INTRODUCTION

Disparities in per capita output and in the structure of economies between rich and poor nations apparently have been increasing over time[1] but at a greater rate in recent years than in the past despite the fact that the per capita output in poor countries has been increasing at a faster rate over the last decades than ever before.

This rise in income has been achieved through a massive transfer of technology, capital and skill from the developed to underdeveloped countries; low productivity and the high population growth rate in poor nations are widely regarded as causes of this gap.

Another important explanation of the widening gap between rich and poor nations is based on a Marxian concept, i.e. the rule of monopoly capitalism and imperialism in the advanced countries and economic and social backwardness in the underdeveloped countries are immediately related.[2] But this analysis does not tell us anything about the effects of technology and capital transfers from a labour-short socialist economy to another, but labour-surplus, socialist economy (e.g. Soviet capital and technology assistance to China in the early 1950s) or to a labour-surplus underdeveloped free-enterprise economy (e.g. Soviet aid to India).

In this paper I have attempted to re-examine the interrelationship between population growth, technology transfer and the gap, which will also explain the above question.

THE POPULATION QUESTION AND THE GAP

Population 'take-off' or population 'revolution' in the late eighteenth and early nineteenth centuries played a vital role in the industrial revolution in England. An important study made by E. Boserup[3] points out that population pressure spurred agricultural innovation that led to the industrial revolution. Habakkuk[4] and others have suggested that population took off because economic development necessitated a sharp increase in the size of the labour force, and this 'stimulus to fertility' brought about by increasing employment opportunities may have been a significant determinant of 'population take-off' in England.

Most studies of the period, however, indicate a general rise in the level of economic and social activities – a contribution of agricultural and industrial revolution of the period, which created tremendous demand for labour, stimulating fertility, particularly at a time when organisation, management and methods of doing things were simple and labour-absorbing. Improvement in living conditions, food supply and medical treatment reducing the mortality rate also contributed to population growth.

However, with the pace of development, technology has become more and more sophisticated, thus creating the need for relatively skilled labour. This need for quality replacement acted as a disincentive towards high fertility, causing it to drop particularly since the early twentieth century. But increase in the demand for labour as a stimulus to the fertility rate as an explanation of population explosion in other parts of Europe has been questioned by many authors.[5] In contemporary France the primary mechanism at work seems to be declining rather than rising fertility as was the case in England. That 'population take-off' in Continental Europe has been influenced by the decreasing mortality rates due to improvements in medical treatment rather than by increasing fertility rates can be explained by examining the fundamental differences in the pattern of industrial development of the UK and Continental Europe in the nineteenth century.

One of the most vital factors that explains this divergence in the pattern of population growth between England, France and other Western European nations is traceable to the difference in the process of their industrialisation, as mentioned earlier.

In England, economic growth was characterised by the rapid and simultaneous development of all three main branches of the economy – agriculture, industry and commerce – as a result of the process of the industrial revolution.[6] Obviously, this process had a greater impact in terms of demand for labour. The modest but quite definite upturn in the pace of economic activity in England after 1750 was largely due to the simultaneous increase in rates of population growth;[7] whereas France or Germany, for example, followed the process of imported industrialisation from England. Paul Bairoch[8] has pointed out this difference in terms of the growth of the iron and steel industry in England to meet the growing need of the agricultural economy, whereas in France and Germany the iron and steel industries owed their origin to the needs of railways, shipbuilding and the consumer goods industries. W.O. Henderson[9] and others have shown how imported capital and skills from England played the initial role in the development of these industries on the Continent. Consequently, in contrast with England, on the Continent simultaneous development of three sectors of the economy did not take place.[10]

For our present analysis, the implication of England supplying capital and skills to the Continent is that the employment effects of industrialisation acting as a stimulus to fertility in Western European countries were much less compared to England. Because the technology was simple at the initial stage of the industrial revolution, imported industrialisation at that time was labour-intensive which was sufficient to absorb this moderately growing population.[11] These economies, however, had to face a dualistic structure composed of a modern industrial sector on the one hand and a labour-surplus rural sector on the other.[12]

The effect of economic development on long-term variations in the level of human fertility appears to vary according to the particular stage of economic development concerned. Thus in the late eighteenth and early nineteenth centuries, the initial growth of the industrial economy acted as a positive stimulus to earlier marriage and higher rates of marital fertility; it did so because of the enormous opportunities it offered for child labour.[13] This is Stage I; and this happened only in England.

Certain key influences led to a shift in the supply of labour. These included the laws relating to child labour, reduction in child and infant mortality, the introduction of old age security, widening opportunities for female employment, new and optimistic attitudes towards material standards of living, and the skill requirements of new and sophisticated technologies. All these factors and the impact of the 'keeping up with the Joneses' attitude, produced and nurtured in developed capitalist economies, have played a forceful role in keeping fertility rates down.[14]

High rates of population growth from the mid-eighteenth to the early twentieth centuries were associated with, and particularly responsible for, industrial 'take-off' and sustained and rapid economic advance. Underdeveloped countries have been deprived of the beneficial effects of such industrialisation, i.e. the demand-for-labour effects. Rapid population growth in underdeveloped countries has been mainly due to a steady fall in the mortality rate. It may be termed 'population inflation' (to use Bairoch's term) which is unlike the 'population take-off' of the nineteenth century as the population growth in underdeveloped countries has not been accompanied by the growth of productivity.

In the Third World of today, the death rate has shown a down-turn due to the availability of modern medical technology and food aid, while birth rate is more or less constant. Obviously, a fall in mortality rates has very little to do with the national income and economic activities of these countries. Industrialisation of these countries, being essentially based on imported capital and technology and other resources, has created, on the one hand, little demand for labour and on the other, opportunities, although very limited, for sophisticated living, both acting as a disincentive to high marital fertility and nuptiality in very limited urban areas. Secondly, a large subsistence sector of surplus labour is dependent on labour-intensive techniques and organisation, which produces an attitude of indifference, if not acting as an incentive towards a larger family entirely for economic and social security reasons.

The industrialising sector of these countries, transplanted from overseas, has led these economies to skip over the first demographic effects of industrialisation, i.e. of creating demand for labour. In the case of France and Germany, the initial process of imported industrialisation did not create a stimulus to fertility but created opportunities of employment for the growing population resulting from declining mortality rates. The reason, as stated before, was that the technology and capital that France and Germany imported was simple and labour-absorbing. Population history shows that population control has never been associated with the process of economic development at its take-off stage. What were the effects of transfers of manufactured goods, capital and technology from developed countries to underdeveloped countries since the industrial revolution? It led to deindustrialisation but with a fundamental difference from that in Europe.

Thorner[15] wrote about the alleged phenomenon of the deindustrialisation of India in the nineteenth century that there can be no dispute with a flat statement that India's national handicrafts have declined slowly from their pristine glory. This falling-off, however, was not a phenomenon peculiar to India but a world-wide development affecting different countries at different times. The skill, sooner or later, of the old-style craftsman was as integral a part of the industrial revolution as the coming of the factory system. His conclusion is a result of a serious omission to take into account the vital point of difference in the process of industrialisation in the UK, other European countries, and the colonies.

In Britain it was her own industrial revolution which led to the destruction of handicrafts, so that employment was being created in one branch of secondary industry while it was shrinking in another; after a point, the rate of creation of employment in the new branch of secondary industry was far higher than the rate of loss in the other branch. The same process worked in other parts of the Continent although with some difference, as discussed before. The impact of industrialisation in the West on employment and income in the secondary industry of today's underdeveloped countries was almost entirely destructive. John Hicks wrote: '. . . what of the Indian weavers who were displaced by the same improvement? . . . The most likely is that it will suffer long-lasting damage now and then, from a backlash of improvements that have occurred elsewhere'.[16]

According to a recent study of the deindustrialisation of India, the proportion of industrial to total population in Bihar fell from 18.6 per cent around 1809-13 to 8.5 per cent in 1901.[17]

According to another estimate of the Bengal area, taking cotton weavers, cotton growers, spinners, dressers, embroidery, etc., together, one million people of Bengal (including Bihar and Orissa) were thrown out of employment by 1828.[18]

In his well-known work, *Conditions of Economic Progress,* Colin Clark has shown that in India from 1881 to 1911 the proportion of the workforce engaged in 'manufacturing, and construction', fell by half from 35 per cent to 17 per cent.[19] There are numerous studies testifying to the above contention.

The imported industrialisation process in the Third World today is more negative in its demand-for-labour effects for obvious reasons.

TECHNOLOGY TRANSFER AND THE GAP

It is a well-known fact of history that there has been a great deal of technology transfer from the East to West in the past. During the pre-industrial days this transfer did not create any gap in the West; while using this technology the West produced modern science and technology. Singer[20] in his elaborate study of the history of technology observes that up to the sixteenth century the Near East was superior to the West in skill and inventiveness and the Far East was perhaps superior to both; whereas, technologically, at that time the West had little to offer to the East. It has also been pointed out by scholars that yield rates per man and yield rates per unit of land were higher in India than in the more progressive of the West European countries in the seventeenth century. Comparisons of seed yield ratio for individual crops were also more favourable for India.[21] India hadlarger and richer urban areas than Europe before the Industrial Revolution.[22]

In the pre-industrial epoch, production technique and technology embodied a gradual accumulation of empirical knowledge, handed down from generation to generation through apprenticeship in the skilled trades. In this process some changes in the techniques took place to suit the need of the time and place. But the technique was simple and labour-intensive for obvious reasons. Productive activity gave rise to further productive activity, just as one generation gives birth to the next. In the East, because of the congenial weather and resources provided by nature, this simple process of technological change was considered sufficient to provide the people with a simple living.[23] Pressure of population was not high, a high death rate cancelling out a high birth rate. In the cases of some parts of Africa and Latin America, slavery, and Portuguese and Spanish colonisation respectively, led to depopulation which had a serious implication in terms of the impact on prevailing technology; whereas in the West a very harsh and uncongenial climate forced the people to improve upon the productive techniques required by the growing volume of population, leading to the development of modern technology.

Marx wrote:

> It is not true that the most fruitful soil is the most fitted for the growth of the capitalist mode of production. This mode is based on the dominion of man over nature. Where nature is too lavish, she keeps him in hand, like a child in leading strings. She does not impose upon him any necessity to develop himself. It is not the tropics with their luxuriant vegetation, but the temperate zone that is the Mother Country of Capital. It is not the mere fertility of the soil, but the differentiation of the soil, the

> variety of its natural products, the changes of the seasons, which form the physical basis for the social division of labour, and which, by changes in the natural surroundings, spur man on to the multiplication of his wants, his capabilities, his means and modes of labour. It is the necessity of bringing a natural force under the control of society, of economising, of appropriating or subduing it on a large scale by the work of man's hand, that first plays the decisive part in the history of industry.[24]

We have noted earlier how in the seventeenth and eighteenth centuries in England the increased pressure of population forced the change in agrarian technology and economic organisation.

However, in the nineteenth century, in England and other European countries, rapid population growth was accompanied by a more rapid growth in income resulting from the expansion of modern industrialisation which was largely helped by the practice of international division of labour. Since the late nineteenth century, rapid growth of technology based on modern science to meet the fast-growing need of international trade enabled these economies to substitute labour, the supply of which was not keeping pace with the economic growth rate. The result was the rapid growth of income and a high level of living in the industrialised countries of the West. Why has this rapid growth of industrialised countries failed to transmit its growth effects to the present-day poor nations? This question tempts us to assume with the mercantilists that the enrichment of one community inevitably meant the impoverishment of the other, and the mercantile character of trade has not changed.[25] The prime force behind industrialisation in latecomer countries of today has been foreign trade helping imported industrialisation.

Since the nineteenth century there has been a considerable transfer of technology and in particular since the 1950s, but this time from the West to the East, paradoxically, accompanied by an increasing gap between the two. This, however, did not happen when the technology was transferred from the East to the West in pre-industrial days, the reason being that the technology of that period was simple and labour-absorbing which led to more productive utilisation of domestic resources.

In the modern period, however, with the growing importance of an equipment industry based on advanced technology, technology transmission took the form of a straightforward commercial transaction and it became possible to transfer an entire productive sector at an unprecedented speed. England set the process in motion by developing a transport equipment industry, which transformed the means of transport throughout the world. Further, by providing adequate financing for this industry it created a mechanism for exporting capital which was to be a decisive factor in shaping the world economic and social system.[26]

The result was the growth and integration of the world economy in the nineteenth century and an intensification of international specialisation based on the international division of labour. It resulted in the emergence of a few industrialised countries with rapidly rising income, on the one hand, and, on the other, a large number of primary producing countries with a stagnating economy and income. World trade expanded rapidly; but the external trade of underdeveloped countries was confined to those primary products which were needed by the economies of the industrial centres and investments in these productions in underdeveloped countries were financed by them.

Obviously, industrialisation having been confined to Western countries has determined the type and requirement of natural resources. Most suppliers of these natural resources have had nothing to do with them in terms of the needs of their economies at the time, when the cultivation, mining, plantation or extraction of these resources was undertaken.

There has been a tremendous increase in the output of the extractive industries in the countries of the Third World since the nineteenth century, but 'it was in no way due to the demand of local industry, indeed local industries absorbed only a fraction of production'.[27]

CONCLUSION

This analysis shows that the development patterns in LDCs in recent times have not stimulated demand for labour, the development process being essentially based on imported technology and capital which are products of a different historical and consequently of a different factor-endowment situation. Consequently, problems of so-called overpopulation and income inequality have been and are being aggravated and therefore, the gaps between rich and poor – intra-national and international – are widening as the days go by.

NOTES

[1] Ranis, G. (ed.) 1972, *The Gap Between Rich and Poor Nations,* (Macmillan): articles by Kuznet, S., Boulding, R.E. and Pfaff, Tolly, R., Jaquier, N.

[2] (*a*) Baran, Paul, 1957, *The Political Economy of Growth.*
(*b*) Frank, A.G., 1971, *Capitalism and Underdevelopment in Latin America.*

[3] Boserup, E., 1965, *The Conditions of Agricultural Growth* (Chicago) p. 12.

[4] Habakkuk, H.J., 1971, *Population Growth and Economic Development since 1750.*

[5] (*a*) Tranter, N., 1973, *Population Since the Industrial Revolution.*
(*b*) Drake, M., 1969, *Population and Society in Norway, 1735-1875.*

[6] Habakkuk, H.J., op. cit.

[7] Ibid.

[8] Bairoch, P., 1969, 'Agriculture and the Industrial Revolution', in Cipolla (ed.), *The Industrial Revolution,* pp. 488-92.

[9] Henderson, W.O., 1954, *Britain and the Industrialisation in Europe, 1750-1870,* pp. 139-67.

[10] (*a*) Hohenburg, 'Changes in Rural France, 1830-1940', *Journal of Economic History,* Vol. 32, March 1972, pp. 223-40.
(*b*) Landes, D., 'Industrialisation and Economic Development in Nineteenth-century Germany', *1st International Conference on Economic History,* 1960, pp. 85-6.

[11] Tranter, op. cit., pp. 146-53.
[12] Landes, D., op. cit.; Hohenburg, op. cit.; Maitra, – *Economic Development with or without an Industrial Revolution* (Croom Helm, 1978).
[13] Tranter, op. cit., pp.150-1.
[14] Maitra, P., 'Population, Poverty and Pollution', *Mainstream,* Vol. 17, 1974, pp. 11-14.
[15] Thorner, D., 1960, 'De-Industrialisation of India', in *1st International Conference on Economic History.*
[16] Hicks, J.R., *A Theory of Economic History* (1969) p. 165.
[17] Bagchi, A.K., 'De-Industrialisation in India', *Journal of Development Studies,* Vol. 12, No. 2, Jan. 1976, pp. 132-50.
[18] Sinha, N.K., *The Economic History of Bengal, 1793-1948* (Firma KLM, 1970), Vol. 2.
[19] Clark, C., *The Conditions of Economic Progress* (1957) pp. 499, 515.
[20] (*a*) Singer, C., 'East and West in Retrospect', in *A History of Technology,* Vol. II (C. Singer *et al,* 1956).
(*b*) Benedict, R., *Race, Science and Politics,* 1959.
[21] Slicher Van Baih, B.H., *The Agrarian History of Western Europe A.D. 500-1850,* pp. 239-41.
[22] Habib, I., *The Agrarian System of Moghul India, 1556-1707* (1963) p. 35.
[23] Moreland, W.H., *India at the Time of Akbar* (H. Ram, Delhi, 1962)– *From Akbar to Aurangzeb* (Macmillan, 1923). Geye, P., *Jehangir's India* (Cambridge, 1925) pp. 60-1.
[24] Marx, K., *Capital,* Vol. I, pp. 563-4 (1906).
[25] Furtado, C., *Economic Development of Latin America* (CUP, 1970) pp. 27-34.
[26] Ibid., p. 30.
[27] Bairoch, P., op. cit., pp. 44-51.

9 The Economic Underdevelopment of the United States South in the Post-Bellum Era

Jay R. Mandle

In 1900, per capita income in the Southern United States stood at 51 per cent of the national average. This was roughly the same relative position it had experienced in 1880. However, it was significantly below the levels achieved in 1840 and 1860 when it stood at 76 and 72 per cent, respectively, of the national average.[1] In the recent literature, these data have been interpreted to mean that the causes of Southern economic backwardness can be isolated in time to the 1860 to 1880 period. On the one hand, Stanley Engerman has argued that the decline from 76 to 72 per cent between 1840 and 1860 is within the usual margin of statistical error, and there is 'no clear evidence for any marked change in the southern income position relative to that of the North' for this period.[2] On the other hand, the fact that the relative income of the South remained constant between 1880 and 1900 indicates that the region's economy grew as rapidly as that of the rest of the country during these years. It was only between 1860 and 1880 that a marked deterioration in the region's relative income occurred. It is to that period, therefore, that attention has been directed.

Following this line of reasoning, two hypotheses have emerged in the recent literature to explain Southern underdevelopment. The hypotheses associated with the names of Roger Ransom and Richard Sutch speak to the problem by emphasising the supply side and constraints to output. They, however, explicitly rule out wartime destruction as the major obstacle to production. Asserting that 'historians and economists have exaggerated the impact of destruction, they attribute the relative decline in the South's position to the labour supply consequences of emancipation. With the ending of slavery, Ransom and Sutch argue, there was a substantial reduction in the availability of labour in Southern agriculture, a reduction they estimate at between 28 and 37 per cent.[3] The leftward shift in the supply function of labour occurred, they argue, because 'rather than work like slaves, the freedmen chose to offer an amount of labor comparable to the standard for free laborers of the time.'[4] This reduction in labour, they believe, accounts for virtually all of the decrease in output which occurred between 1860 and 1880 and thus is responsible for the region's relative decline in per capita income.

Gavin Wright, by contrast, points to demand considerations as accounting for this decline. Noting that 'southern incomes were still very largely tied to the course of world demand for cotton', Wright estimates that, in the aftermath of the war, the world demand for cotton grew at a decreasing rate.[5] Wright's thesis is that the relatively weak demand for the South's staple was responsible for the South's lag in income growth. He writes that it was the sluggish demand curve which 'was the proximate cause of the slowness of the return to pre-war income levels'.[6]

Strictly speaking, the views of Ransom and Sutch and Wright are not mutually exclusive. A withdrawal of labour services certainly can occur at the same time that sluggish demand in the product market is encountered. Each might well have occurred and have separately contributed to the region's economic difficulties. Indeed, Peter Temin has concluded that both of these conditions did prevail and their respective impacts were about equally strong on the post-bellum Southern economy. Agreeing that wartime destruction was of relatively little importance, Temin's work is supportive to both the labour withdrawal and weak market demand theses.[7]

There is an unstated, but none the less crucial, hypothetical alternative which underlies these two theses. Implicit in each position is the view that if these shocks had not occurred, the Southern economy would have been able to keep pace with the economy of the rest of the country. By assigning responsibility for the decline in the South's relative income level to the withdrawal of labour and to weak market demand, these authors are implicitly assuming that if these conditions had not prevailed the decline would not have occurred. That is, they are assuming that in the absence of a shift to the left of the supply function of labour and a stable demand function for cotton, the South's economy had the capacity to grow at a rate equal to that of rest of the country. The two hypotheses under investigation here, then, share one very important common element. That element is the view that the relative decline which occurred was not due to a flaw in the Southern economy, a weakness which prevented it from experiencing economic expansion. Rather, the failure of the region to keep pace with the rest of the country according to both positions was due to exogenous factors not central to the functioning of the region's economy.

Constructed in this way, these hypotheses appear to fit the time pattern of the Southern experience. Especially in the case of the Ransom and Sutch thesis, the timing of the withdrawal of labour appears to correspond to the period in which the region suffered a marked deterioration in relative income. This lends support to the view that by explaining the 1860 to 1880 decline, the authors have solved the analytic problem of Southern backwardness. This is presumably the case, since thereafter the growth rate of the South approximated that of the rest of the country.

This argument is, however, not theoretically sound. For economic theory predicts that, over time, income levels in two regions within a free trade area will tend to approximate each other. By attracting mobile factors of production to the poorer region where rates of return are assumed to be relatively high, the anticipation is that the income level of the poor region will grow relative to the richer region. Assuming that there are no underlying constraints to economic development, the region which is less advanced is expected to grow at a higher rate than the more developed one. Specifically, this means in the current context that if the capacity to achieve economic development in the South had been equal to that of the North, its relative income level should not have remained constant at 51 per cent of national income between 1880 and 1900, but should have increased. That this did not occur, contrary to the prediction of economic theory, raises a problem which requires explanation. The fact that the South did not grow more rapidly than the rest of the country is suggestive of an underlying flaw in the region's economy which interfered with the operation of the market equilibrating mechanism. As we shall argue, that underlying flaw appears to centre on the South's capacity to achieve technological advance.

None of the authors discussed in these pages takes up the issue of technological change systematically. We know, however, that it, broadly defined, is the proximate source of long-term economic development. A society which has not mastered the capacity to sustain advances in productivity cannot be expected to sustain long-term economic expansion.[8] Thus data indicating that the South (compared to the North) found it more difficult to achieve productivity advances would tend to cast doubt on the implicit alternative which underlies the views of Ransom and Sutch and Wright.

In point of fact, both Ransom and Sutch and Wright do mention the issue of productivity advance. However, they do so only to show how unimportant it was in cotton cultivation. This they then take as justification for ignoring it in their analysis. Thus, Gavin Wright remarks that 'throughout the period before World War I cotton expansion was largely a matter of increasing the total improved acreage in cultivation.'[9] Similarly, Ransom and Sutch note the labour-intensive technology which prevailed in the industry and point out that 'the slow growth of agricultural output following 1870 reflects the fact that further expansion had to wait for population growth to increase the available supply of labor'.[10] Neither considers the possibility that

TABLE 9.1 Percentage decrease in man-hours required per 100 bushels of wheat and corn and 500 pound bales of cotton, 1840-1920

Years	*Wheat*	*Corn*	*Cotton*
1840-80	34.8	34.8	30.8
1880-1900	28.9	18.3	6.9
1900-20	19.4	23.1	0.7
1840-1920	62.7	59.1	36.0

SOURCE: Calculated from Martin R. Cooper, Glen T. Barton and Alber P. Brodell, *Progress of Farm Mechanization,* United States Department of Agriculture, Miscellaneous Publications No. 630, Table 1.

productivity advance could have achieved increases in output in the absence of a growth in inputs employed. In making the assumption of little or no productivity advance, these authors acknowledge the experience in the industry. But, in failing to deal with the significance of this fact, both Ransom and Sutch and Wright are led to make overly optimistic assumptions about the growth potential of the South in the absence of the exogenous shocks which concern them.

There is direct evidence that the South lagged in technological advance. The US Department of Agriculture has prepared estimates of the man-hours required to produce wheat, corn and cotton over time. The first two, of course, were Northern and mid-Western crops and the latter, the Southern staple. Decreases in man-hours per unit of output reflect improved productivity. Table 9.1 reports the results of calculating the percentage decrease in man-hour requirements over the period 1840-1920. It is clear from this table that the rate of technological change in cotton over the entire period was only about one-half that of the other crops. Furthermore, the relative performance of cotton was even worse between 1880 and 1920 than it was between 1840 and 1880.

At least partial confirmation of the impression that cotton lagged behind the other crops in mechanisation throughout the nineteenth century is provided in Jacob Schmookler's data on patent grants. Schmookler collected data on the number of patents granted by commodity and process, letting these time series stand as a proxy for levels of inventive activity and technological change. In this case, his data are confined to the harvesting of cotton, corn and grain. They demonstrate a similar trend by crop as is reported in the Department of Agriculture's estimates of mechanisation. As is seen in Table 9.2, over the entire period annual patent activity in cotton was lower than for the other two crops; but by the twentieth century, this shortfall had to be narrowed when cotton was compared to grain.

These data, then, make it clear that the rate of technological change in the South's principal agricultural product was below that of comparable crops

TABLE 9.2 Average annual number of patents granted for grain and corn harvesting, threshing and cutting and cotton harvesting, picking and chopping ploughs, 1837/1859 – 1900/1919

Years	*Grain*	*Corn*	*Cotton*
1837-59	10.3	12.4	1.2
1860-79	35.4	34.2	11.1
1880-99	57.2	48.7	25.9
1900-19	47.1	63.0	45.1
1837-1919	35.9	37.8	20.5

SOURCE: Jacob Schmookler, *Patents, Inventions and Economic Change, Data and Selected Essays*, edited by Zvi Griliches and Leonard Hurwicz (Cambridge: Harvard University Press, 1972) pp. 100-3.

produced elsewhere in the United States. The importance of this finding is that with it the hypothetical alternative which gives rise to the conclusions of Ransom and Sutch and Wright is rendered dubious. To argue that either labour supply or market demand factors were the causal variables impeding Southern economic growth, it must be assumed that other potential sources of expansion were equally present in the two regions. In particular, given the importance of technological change and productivity advance in economic development, the assumption which has to be made is that this variable experienced a similar pattern in the regions under consideration. Precisely such a comparable pattern, however, is what appears not to have been present, with the South's performance in this regard substantially below that of the rest of the country. Thus, the logic which gives rise to the causal statements in the theses advanced by Ransom and Sutch and Wright appears to be deeply flawed.

Given these data on productivity, it is possible, in fact, to turn the argument completely around and hypothesise that it was the slow advance in productivity in cotton which underlay the region's lag in economic development, and not the exogenous shocks cited by Ransom and Sutch and Wright. If labour withdrawal produced a constraint to output, it could be argued that productivity advances could have helped to overcome that problem. Similarly, if sluggish demand confronted the region's cotton producers, technological change in cotton could have freed resources and permitted the emergence of new sectors of economic activity. Seen in this way, productivity advances represent a potential offset to the kinds of events cited by Ransom and Sutch and Wright. It is the fact that productivity advance was relatively slow and that as a result the offset effect was relatively weak, which produces the impression that the impact of these events was decisive.

To get to the root of the South's limited economic expansion, then, it is necessary to analyse why technological change in the region was as slow as it was. Recent work in explaining differential rates of technological advance has used a framework which sees such achievements as a form of economic behaviour whose level is explainable through the use of economic reasoning. In particular, this means that the hypotheses which are developed to account for differences by product or region in the rate of technological change centre on the cost of engaging in inventive activity or introducing new methods of production compared to the benefits which are received from such activity. Differences among the suggested explanations show up with regard to the factors held dominant in raising or lowering the cost of the process of innovation. In general, a line can be drawn between those hypotheses which emphasise the degree of difficulty and feasibility which exists in achieving productivity advances and those which emphasise the degree of incentive which exists to engage in technological advance. Those in the first category can be considered supply hypotheses, and those in the second can be viewed as demand hypotheses. A region which experiences slow rates of productivity advance, then, would be a region in which either there is a relatively limited incentive to engage in technological change or there is little capacity to do so even if there were a strong motivation in that direction. It is, of course, also possible that both supply and demand factors were operating in a negative direction independently.

One demand hypothesis which does not fit the Southern experience postulates a connection between the product market and the incentive decision-makers would have to introduce new methods of production. The argument would be that where there is a weak product market, there would be relatively little incentive to introduce new capital equipment, and as a result the rate of technological advance as embodied in new machines and tools would be relatively low. The reason that this hypothesis does not fit the Southern experience is that even though its rate of productivity was the slowest among these products, its market was not the weakest. In fact, the product market for cotton was stronger than it was for wheat or corn. Table 9.3 reports the price and output experience of cotton, wheat and corn during this period. Panel A shows that during these years the production of cotton grew more rapidly than was the case for corn or wheat. But Panel B indicates that while this was occurring, the price of cotton rose, an increase comparable to that of corn and superior to that of wheat. Increases in price in the face of increasing output suggest that the demand for the product grew even more than did supply. These data thus indicate that the market for cotton was stronger than for the other crops. That cotton output increased much more than corn and yet their price trends were similar suggests a more favourable shift in demand for cotton than corn. Similarly, the superior experience of cotton in both production and price suggests a stronger market

TABLE 9.3 Comparison of production and price trends, corn, wheat, cotton, 1881/85 – 1906/10

	PANEL A *Production* Percentage Change		
	Corn	*Wheat*	*Cotton*
1881/85 – 1906/10	+58.0	+40.1	+95.1
	PANEL B *Price* Percentage Change		
	Corn	*Wheat*	*Cotton*
1881/85 – 1906/10	+21.6	+ 0.6	+17.1

SOURCE: *Historical Statistics of the United States,* Colonial Times to 1957, Series K265-73 and K298-306 (Washington: Government Printing Office, 1960).

for cotton than corn. In combination, these results strongly rule out an explanation of cotton's poor performance in productivity as due to relatively unfavourable market circumstances.

One hypothesis which could account for cotton's slow advance in technology and which has received some support in the literature concerns technical difficulties in the cotton harvest.[11] There is some evidence that technical problems, particularly in harvesting, were more difficult in cotton than in other crops. As we shall see, however, it does not seem likely that these were the principal sources of the slow pace of technological change in the industry.

James H. Street lists two complicating factors which made difficult the mechanising of the cotton harvest. First was the fact that soil types varied, with the result that machinery suited to some circumstances was unworkable in others. Differences in the genetic characteristics of the cotton plant and variations in cultivation practices similarly made the adoption of a mass-produced harvester difficult. These, however, appear to be unlikely sources of a long-term or a considerable lag in technology. This is so since, as Street points out, such problems might have affected a mass-marketed harvester but still would have permitted the development of a set of machines each suited to local conditions.[12]

A potentially more serious problem was the fact that cotton bolls on the cotton plant do not ripen at a uniform rate. This means that a method of harvesting is required which strips the plant of the ripened boll, but skips over and does not injure the unripened bolls. With handpicking, this problem meant that pickers went over the same crop three or four times. The same repetition was required of a mechanised picker, with the added complication that the machines had to be selective and not damage unripened bolls.

Notwithstanding this problem, Street, the principal historian of cotton technology, argues that these technical difficulties were not the principal reasons that technology lagged in cotton.[13] In this connection, Schmookler's patent data seem to support Street's scepticism. For what the patent data indicate are efforts to find solutions, not the viability of the solutions themselves. Seen from this perspective, what is significant about cotton is that so few efforts were made to solve the technical problems, not that the technical problems remained unsolved at a relatively later date.

The difficulties encountered in the harvesting of cotton were mechanical. They did not require the application of new scientific principles; only the solving of the physical problem of not injuring the cotton plant while stripping it of the fibre. The fact that there were relatively few patents granted in cotton suggests that efforts made in this area were few, and it was this limited effort which was the key to the delay in achieving a mechanical breakthrough. Furthermore, in principle, the problems of leaving undamaged, unripened cotton bolls were not different from that faced in corn, where there was a need to separate the ear from the stalk while preserving the stalk for forage. It thus appears unlikely that technological supply considerations –

emphasising the level of theoretical science and technology – adequately account for the lagging technological advance experienced in cotton.

The hypothesis which seems most plausible in accounting for the slow pace of technological change in the South is one which emphasises the social context in which cotton cultivation was carried out. Even after the Civil War, cotton cultivation took place within a plantation economy – an economy which continued many of the aspects of the old slave regime. As such it continued a social structure and way of life which, as we shall argue, militated against the introduction of new technology. This, parenthetically, is not to say that the planters in such a society did not attempt to maximise profit or function effectively in markets. Rather, the argument is that the incentive system which they confronted in a plantation setting made it precisely 'rational' to be technologically stagnant.

William O. Jones argues that plantations are 'different from other kinds of farms in the way in which factors of production, primarily management and labor, are combined'.[14] Specifically, plantations are characterised by the use of a plentiful supply of low-productivity/low-wage labour which is mobilised under the close supervision of management to achieve substantial private returns.

Plantations were instruments of colonisation. The settling of the tropical and semi-tropical New World was, in considerable measure, accomplished by the ceding or sale of large tracts of potentially cultivatable agricultural land to individual landholders. Given the prevailing level of technology for the commodities which could be produced in these settings, profitable large-scale production could only be carried on by using masses of labourers. How to mobilise such numbers of workers became the key to successful production, in a region which extended from the north-east of Brazil and the Guianas through the Caribbean and the Caribbean coast and into the United States.

That such a number of disciplined workers was not indigenously available in this region, nor would be forthcoming voluntarily from elsewhere, quickly became apparent. As a result, non-market methods of allocation and control became essential in order to carry out profitable production. Force was required to supply the manpower the plantations required, and continued coercion was needed after the workers arrived on the plantations to ensure that the goals of the plantations were achieved. These goals, to be sure, were the cultivation and sale of agricultural commodities. But the circumstances in which these ends were essayed were such that the planters, or their agents, were compelled to assume extra-economic authority. A plantation economy then is one in which profit-maximising agricultural landowners depend upon some mobilising mechanism, not simply the operation of a free labour market, to satisfy the need of their farms for disciplined unskilled workers in large numbers.

It is this situation that leads Thompson to argue that plantations are best defined not in terms of territory or even in terms of agricultural production, but in terms of the authority of the planter; where the authority of the planter ended so too did the plantation as a viable institution. Not only did the planters have to bind workers to the estates for the duration of the crop year, they also were required to induce this essential involuntary labour force to cooperate in production. To accomplish this, wide-ranging authority governing estate behaviour was required by plantation management.

Power was vested in the planter and employed to achieve the latter's economic advance. Thompson writes that in such a setting when a worker 'steals, fights, assembles unlawfully, plots, marries secretly, indulges in fornication, has illegitimate children, spends his time in gambling, cock-fighting or courting, the planter suffers some loss or threat of loss'.[15] As a result, laws and regulations governing these and many other aspects of plantation life were established, resulting in the plantations' developing a high degree of autonomy and sovereignty.

Plantation economies survived emancipation in many parts of the New World. Thus, in some parts of the West Indies emancipation meant practically nothing to the social organisation because of the absence of unutilised land. With legal freedom, the ex-slaves had no alternative employment opportunities available to them and thus *de facto* were compelled to continue to work on the estates as before. In other parts of the West Indies, where land was available and where the ex-slaves did vacate the plantations, indentured immigration became the mechanism by which the plantation-dominated societies remained intact. In Trinidad, Guyana and to some extent in Jamaica, a state-supported programme of immigration resulted in an annual supply of new labour above and beyond the supply which came from the resident population. In this way, the plantations were provided with a sufficiently large and cheap supply of labour, independent of the operation of a labour market. These immigrants were legally required to work for a specified number of years on sugar plantations and it was this process, combined with official discouragement of the creation of alternative industries, which allowed the plantation to continue to earn profits on the old labour-intensive and low-labour-productivity basis for more than a century after emancipation.

In each of these cases, the essential social relations of production of plantation agriculture were retained; monopolisation of the productive assets by a small planter class, a continued close managerial and supervisory role by this class which extended to 'non-economic' aspects of plantation life, production of a staple for external markets, absence of a vital domestic labour market, use of low-productivity, low-wage labour, and a highly uneven distribution of income.

The plantation economy survived emancipation in the United States South as well.[16] This persistence was the consequence of the functioning of mechanisms of control which inhibited the mobility of the ex-slave population and effectively confined it to southern cotton plantations even after the Civil War. Within the South, blacks had little access to land because of discrimination. This was the case especially in those parts of the South dominated by plantations and where soil and climate conditions would have meant potentially lucrative opportunities as commercial farmers. Additionally, alternative employment opportunities within the South were further limited by the slow pace of industrialisation which was experienced in the region as well as by the discriminatory hiring practices which existed within the manufacturing sector. Confinement was also reinforced by anti-enticement and anti-recruitment legislation passed by governments within the region, which inhibited employers from seeking out potential black workers. In the North, employer discrimination, favouring immigrants from Europe rather than Southern blacks, tended to shut this market off as a potential escape from plantation labour. Finally, sharecropping itself, by delaying payment until the end of the crop year, had the effect of limiting mobility seasonally, thus allowing planters to be confident with regard to the reliability of their labour force when it was needed. In concert, these mechanisms confined the ex-slaves to plantation work in ways similar but not identical to those which existed under slavery. In turn, this meant that in basic ways a high degree of continuity existed in the South between the ante- and post-bellum periods.

It is in this context that we are able to account for the slow pace of technological change in cotton. In a plantation setting, the extent to which planters were motivated to seek out new methods of production was limited in at least two ways. First, assuming that the mechanisms of control which surrounded black labour rendered that labour relatively inexpensive, economically rational planters would tend to use relatively more labour, compared to other resources, than they otherwise would have. The typical plantation production function was labour-intensive.[17] Such a pattern of production, however, militates against technological advance since new technology is often embodied in new capital equipment and tools. The effect, therefore, of confining black labour to cotton was to reduce the amount of capital used in production. In doing so, the carrier of new technology too was minimised, tending to depress the rate of productivity advance. The issue here is not the profit-making intentions of the planter. Indeed, it was because the planter was oriented to profits that he minimised the use of capital in production. But it was in doing so that the plantation society suffered compared to market economies where labour may have been relatively more expensive.

In addition to the fact that the factor proportions employed by planters tended to reduce the extent of technological change, there is a second reason to believe that the search for new techniques was limited in plantation economies. In reviewing historical episodes, the outcomes of which were advances in production techniques, Nathan Rosenberg identified three 'focusing devices' – experiences which tended to intensify the search for new methods of production.[18] The three focusing devices cited by Rosenberg were technical imbalances in the production process, the threat of labour shortages and disruptions in the supply of essential materials. Both the first and third of these mechanisms are more appropriate to manufacturing than agriculture. It is, therefore, not remarkable that they were not present in plantation economies. For, in agriculture, the sequencing of the stages of production occurs over a longer time-span than in manufacturing. Problems of coordination are less acute than in manufacturing. Similarly, the availability of raw materials is a less serious problem in agriculture than in manufacturing because of the greater self-reliance in agriculture's production process. The problem of the labour supply, on the other hand, is not one which agriculture escapes. It is in this regard that the functioning of the plantation economy tended to reduce the incentive to adopt technology.

Rosenberg cites England during the industrial revolution as an illustration of a case where the reluctance of labour to accept factory discipline provided an incentive to adopt labour-saving technology. According to him, the threat of withdrawal of labour and the development of labour scarcities focused the attention of decision-makers on this potential threat to profits. As a result, this threat acted as a focusing device and spurred businessmen to change methods of production.

The plantation economy was an unlikely place to find this kind of mechanism. For the very foundation of the plantation economy – the denial of freedom to the labour force – was structured exactly to avoid production disruptions from this direction. To the extent that these institutions were successfully functioning and allowing for the viability of plantation agriculture at all they were also acting to minimise the appearance of such a focusing device.

What all of this meant was that cotton planters had less incentive to search for and implement new methods of production than did farmers elsewhere in the United States. The data on cotton's slow decrease in man-hour requirements cited above are consistent with such an incentive system. Planters were faced neither with profit-threatening disruptions nor with an incentive to substitute capital for labour. They were thus more content with existing production methods than they would have been if either a focusing device had been present or if they had been given price signals through the capital market to increase the relative extent to which they employed machinery in production.

Technological advance, then, did not find fertile soil in the plantation economy. The nature of the class relations between planter and plantation worker were such as to constrain the search for productivity advance. It is, therefore, the thesis of this paper that it was this structurally-induced retardation of technological advance which underlay southern economic backwardness. Specifically, the argument here is that so long as the bias to slow technological change persisted, a tendency for the region to lag behind other more technologically progressive regions of the United States existed in the South.

NOTES

1 Easterlin, Richard A., 'Regional Income Trends 1840-1950', in Robert William Fogel and Stanley L. Engerman, *The Reinterpretation of American Economic History* (New York: Harper & Row, 1971) p. 40.

2 Engerman, Stanley L., 'Some Economic Factors in Southern Backwardness in the Nineteenth Century', in John F. Kain and John R. Meyer (eds), *Essays in Regional Economics,* p. 286.

3 Ransom, Roger, and Sutch, Richard, 'The Impact of the Civil War and of Emancipation on Southern Agriculture', *Explorations in Economic History,* Vol. 12, No. 1 (1975) p. 6.

4 Ransom and Sutch, 'The Impact of the Civil War and of Emancipation on Southern Agriculture', pp. 13, 14.

5 Wright, Gavin, 'Cotton Competition and the Post-Bellum Recovery of the American South', *Journal of Economic History,* Vol. XXXIV, No. 3 (September 1974) p. 634.

6 Wright, Gavin, 'Cotton Competition and the Post-Bellum Recovery of the American South', p. 633-4.

7 Temin, Peter, 'The Post-Bellum Recovery of the South and the Cost of the Civil War', *Journal of Economic History,* Vol. XXXVI, No. 4, December 1976, p. 907.

8 For a full development of this theme and its implications see Simon Kuznets, 'Modern Economic Growth: Findings and Reflections', in Simon Kuznets *Population, Capital and Growth* (New York: W. W. Norton, 1973).

9 Wright, Gavin, 'Cotton Competition and the Post-Bellum Recovery of the American South', p. 634.

10 Ransom, Roger, and Sutch, Richard, 'The Impact of the Civil War and of Emancipation on Southern Agriculture', p. 21.

11 Parker, William N., 'Agriculture', in Lance E. Davis, *et al. American Economic Growth: An Economist's History of the United States* (New York: Harper & Row, 1972) p. 385.

12 Street, James H., *The New Revolution in the Cotton Economy* (Chapel Hill: The University of North Carolina Press, 1957) pp. 100-3.

13 Street, James, H., *The New Revolution in the Cotton Economy,* p. 118.

14 Jones, William O., 'Plantation', in David Sills (ed.), *The International Encyclopedia of the Social Sciences* (1968), Vol. 12, pp. 154-5.

15 Thompson, Edgar T., 'The Plantation: The Physical Basis of Traditional Race Relations', in Edgar T. Thompson (ed.), *Race Relations and the Race Problem* (New York: Greenwood Press, 1968) pp. 192-4.

16 This paragraph is based on my *The Roots of Black Poverty: The Southern Plantation Economy After the Civil War* (Durham: Duke University Press, forthcoming)

17 Evidence that lower levels of capital investment occurred in cotton than in corn or wheat is contained in data on capital per acre by product compiled in the 1900 census. In that year, capital per acre in corn stood at $7.93, in wheat $7.91, and in cotton at $4.78.

18 Rosenberg, Nathan, 'The Direction of Technological Change: Inducement Mechanisms and Focusing Devices', *Economic Development and Cultural Change,* Vol. 18, No. 1, Part 1 (October 1969) pp. 6-22.

10 Export Growth and Capitalist Development in Colombia in the Nineteenth Century

José-Antonio Ocampo

Basic support for this research has been provided by a Tinker Foundation Fellowship.

Two basic methodological conceptions derived from the Latin American Dependency School are taken as the starting-point of our work. First of all, it is conceived that the question of the historical origins of international economic inequalities should be primarily posed as the question of the historical origin of different socio-economic *structures,* and not as a question of the divergent quantitative growth of the same underlying economic variables. It is only by understanding how these different structures arose that we can hope to understand the specific laws of motion that tend to produce what are commonly conceived as 'international economic inequalities'. Secondly, it is conceived that the historical origins of the socio-economic formations which are usually called 'underdeveloped', 'dependent' or 'peripheral' capitalist formations are not independent of the historical process by which the advanced capitalist nations have reached maturity. Rather, one must conceptualise advanced and dependent capitalism as arising out of the same historical process. From the point of view of the study of dependent capitalist formations, this implies that one must search for a basic dependence of their laws of motion on their articulation within the world capitalist economy.

Using these two basic conceptions as a starting-point, our specific task here is to reconstruct the *logic* of capitalist development in Colombia in the nineteenth century, and the crucial role played by the relations of Colombia with the evolving world capitalist economy in that process. We attempt to briefly outline the dynamics of nineteenth-century economic development in Colombia as characterised by a basic contradiction: on the one hand, export-led growth presented itself, and was conceived by the Colombia bourgeoisie as the only feasible form of expansion given a specific historical heritage and world economic conditions; on the other, the particular articulation of Colombia within the world economy (its status as what can be called a secondary region within the periphery) severely limited the possibilities of successful export expansion, and helped to reinforce internal conditions, which also hindered export growth.

1. THE HISTORICAL NECESSITY OF EXPORT EXPANSION

Our historical starting-point is what nineteenth-century liberals used to call the 'colonial economy' – i.e., the economy that was inherited after political independence from Spain. The term 'colonial economy' must be used, however, with great care. It almost carries within it a tendency to place Colombia under one and the same category which includes other colonial economies of the late eighteenth and early nineteenth centuries, or even later times, and this might lead us to try to analyse Colombian evolution by standards which may be adequate to other colonial economies, but not to the specific historical conditions of Colombia. As will become clear below, this would constitute a fundamental mistake. It must then be emphasised that the term 'colonial economy' refers here to the specific historical conditions we are analysing, and it is not used in its generic sense.

From the point of view of the historical process of capitalist development, the colonial economy can be defined by three basic features. First of all, it was an economy only very loosely integrated into the world market. Secondly, it was characterised by a very underdeveloped internal mercantile system. Finally, regardless of the underdevelopment of both the internal and the external mercantile networks, the colonial economy contained within itself the basic elements of capitalist development, the internal dynamics, the search for expansion, typical of processes of capital accumulation, albeit only in very underdeveloped and primitive forms relative to capitalist development at the time (particularly, it was still very far from calling into existence a modern proletariat and the factory system). Let us analyse this general characterisation of the colonial economy in detail.

The degree of articulation with the world economy of the time was so low that one is tempted to characterise the colonial economy by the absence of any significant integration into the world market. Existing links were obviously important for certain regions and economic groups. But, for the economy as a whole, they served only the purpose of procuring a few luxury consumer goods, and allowing a very small degree of fiscal exploitation by Spain. In all these senses, Colombia constituted a socio-economic formation which only remotely resembled the colonial export economies that existed at the time, for example in the West Indies, the Southern United States, or the more expansive Spanish colonies of the late eighteenth century (Cuba, Argentina). A late colonial writer was struck by the fact that the level of per capita exports of Colombia was only Col. $1.75, which compared very unfavourably with Venezuela ($6.25), the United States ($8.5), Cuba ($17.5), Jamaica ($40) and Haiti before the revolution ($133.3).[1] Under the conditions of weak articulation into the world economy, internal forces tended to dominate the evolution of the economic system, rather than externally generated pressures. The colonial economy thus evolved under conditions of a 'relative autonomy' with respect to the world economy. It is precisely this relative autonomy that explains basic characteristics of the evolution of productive relations in the eighteenth century: the limited development and early crisis of slavery;[2] a general tendency towards a superabundant labour force, which rendered unnecessary the old forms of forced Indian labour, and created a pressure upon the land in Indian reserves which (instead of a labour scarcity created by an expansive economy) finally led to their dissolution.[3] All these conditions manifest the presence of features quite unlike those of an export economy either in a period of expansion or crisis. They rather point to the complete absence of any sector with the expansive dynamics typical of an export economy.

In a very important sense, however, it can be argued that this weak articulation within the world economy depended on the conditions of the world economy at the time. In fact, the world economy was then only in its first phases of development, and was thus incapable of true world-wide integration. In its relations with peripheral regions, not only did it leave vast territories entirely untouched (in Asia and Africa), but even among those regions under its domination in one form or another, only a few could claim the status of economically integrated regions. It was a world economy that, due to its own underdevelopment, necessarily left most of the world outside its control, and even in regions which it somehow controlled vast locations were only partially touched, remaining a sort of 'secondary periphery'. This was precisely the status of the Colombian economy.

The second major characteristic of the colonial economy was the narrow extent of the internal market. This was determined by the nature of the dominant forms of production – the absence of any important division of labour, and the low level of productivity. It had reproductive mechanisms of its own: the means of transportation to serve such a narrow market remained very backward, a factor which tended to aggravate the tendency of Colombian geography to segment the existing market. Moreover, the extent of the market significantly conditioned the role of the state. In an economy in which most production was not mercantile, direct taxation was rendered impossible or strictly limited in its scope. This made the state dependent on indirect taxation or government monopolies (tobacco, liquor), whose revenues were also conditioned by the extent of the market. The scant revenues were only sufficient during the late colonial period to extract a very small fiscal surplus to Spain, and this only after the Bourbon reforms had been successful in expanding the revenues from a new government monopoly (tobacco).[4] In republican times, the necessary increase in government expenditures that resulted from the development of the State (and thus a more encompassing bureaucracy and military machine) and periodical civil strife, together with the weight of an internationally small, but domestically huge foreign debt acquired during the years of the independence wars, precipitated a continuous fiscal crisis which left the state little room for manoeuvre.[5] Under those conditions, the state could hardly have played a significant role as a promoter of economic development. Rather, because its revenues were being determined by the extent of the market, it helped to reproduce the conditions upon which it grew.

The colonial economy was thus, from the point of view of capitalist expansion, a very underdeveloped mercantile economy, both internally and in its relations to the world economy. It was, none the less, a dynamic economy, since it contained within itself the most primitive but still expansionary forms of capital, the urge to grow which is typical of all forms of capitalist development.[6] In the late colonial period, this urge to expand may appear as the product of the process of semi-autonomous development. It must not be forgotten, however, that the 'colonial economy' was itself a historical product, the result of a process of evolution which had originated in the European expansion of the sixteenth century. Such expansion had been based, at least partly, on the dynamics of merchant capital. It was this same dynamics which, regardless of the many obstacles it encountered for its development in the seventeenth century, was able to assert itself with greater strength in the late colonial period.

We thus meet an economy that was in a very significant sense expansive, but also greatly limited in its expansionary urge by its own internal and external market conditions. It is in this sense that economic expansion became in late colonial times the fundamental economic *problem.* It is also in this connection that the historical *necessity* of export growth was first posed by late colonial writers. In the nineteenth century, however, a further element was added: the development of capitalist production in England, and later in the rest of Europe. The tendency of capitalist production to constantly increase productivity and the size of the firm rendered the production of commodities competing with European-produced goods completely illusory in Colombia – for, with existing techniques and the primitive extent of capital accumulation, domestic producers could not hope to compete, even within their own market, with commodities produced in industrial capitalist countries. A process of independent industrialisation was in this way made more illusory than it would have seemed in the late eighteenth century or, at the very best (provided that tariff policy could be made as protective as necessary, a fact which depended primarily on the ability of the State to control contraband trade), a process seriously limited by the very narrow market that it hoped to serve. Moreover, in the nineteenth century, the development of the internal market was made dependent on export expansion in a new sense. The development of a modern transportation system to unify the existing market required the importation of the means of communication typical of a modern economy, and this in turn the expansion of exports to pay for them. In the nineteenth century, thus, to the necessity for export expansion based on the need to meet the existing urge to expand, two new elements were added: on the one hand, independent industrialisation was made more unattainable than ever; on the other, export expansion became the only conceivable road to develop (in a very contradictory way, of course) the internal market itself.

We can thus see that the primacy of export growth in the capitalist development of Colombia in the nineteenth century was not the result of an act of choice on behalf of the Colombian bourgeoisie, an 'economic policy' that was chosen among an array of possible alternatives, as some historical interpretations seem to imply. It resulted from very specific material conditions, both internal and external. The ideology of 'free trade', which manifested precisely this primacy of export development, was thus the result of very specific historical conditions – a historically *necessary* and thus not, in any meaningful sense, a 'misguided economic policy'. In the Colombian experience, the historical necessity of this export-orientation of capitalist development, and of the ideology of free trade that corresponded to it becomes evident. The ideology of free trade was asserted very clearly since the late colonial years, by both royal officials and private individuals.[7] In republican times, however, the free trade ideology appeared not only as a colonial legacy, but also as the product of a failed industrialisation and protectionist attempt in the 1830s.[8] After this attempt failed to produce significant development, it became clear both to conservatives and liberals that export growth was the only feasible road of development. The issue of free trade and protectionism became a minor political issue afterwards, except in so far as the artisan class was involved in the debate.

2. *THE EXPORT RECORD OF THE NINETEENTH CENTURY*

Against the background of an economy with a very low base for its expansion, and a more or less clear consensus among the upper class that exports were the crucial facet of economic development, the historical record of export expansion in the nineteenth century appears extremely dismal. The record of export growth since the 1830s can be seen in Table 10.1.

Given a population growth of 1.5 per cent,[9] only the export expansion in the 1850s and 1870s was capable of significantly increasing the value of per capita exports. For the whole period 1850-82, the yearly rate of growth in the value of exports was 4.4 per cent, 2.9 per cent in per capita terms.[10] On the other hand, between the peak of this expansion and the end of the century, per capita exports remained more or less constant. During the Colombian Civil War of 1899-1902, exports decreased, and had not yet recovered the pre-war level by the late 1900s. Since in the first decade of the nineteenth century exports were probably no less than $3 million,[11] the value of per capita exports in the early twentieth century was very similar to that of the late colonial period.

The expansion, from 1850 to 1880, can be characterised by the following features:[12] first of all, it was very diversified in its composition; secondly, most export commodities had a very short cycle of expansion, stagnation and decline (e.g. cinchona bark, cotton, indigo, straw hats), most especially if the export cycles are looked at from a regional standpoint. Tobacco was charac-

TABLE 10.1

	Value of exports (million gold pesos)	*Yearly rate of growth to:*					
		1854/58	*1867/71*	*1878/82*	*1890/93*	*1895/98*	*1906/09*
1834/39	3.4						2.1%
1844/48	3.4	6.4%		4.4%			
1854/58	6.3		1.9%				
1867/71	8.0			6.1%			
1873/82	13.6				0.8%	1.4%	
1893/87	10.6						
1890/93	15.0					3.1%	
1895/98	17.5						–1.4%
1906/09	15.0						

SOURCES: Reports of Ministers of Finance and Statistical Yearbooks. Although there existed minor differences in the definition of the gold peso from 1834 to 1909, it can be considered equivalent to 5 French francs. The data from 1834/39 to 1878/82 refer to averages of fiscal years (September/August);for 1883/87 they refer to the period September 1883 to December 1887, and from 1890/93 to calendar years.

terised by somewhat longer periods of expansion, but it was not immune to this tendency towards short export cycles (the great expansion of Ambalema, for example, lasted only about seven years, and decline clearly started six years later). In fact, only coffee, among nineteenth-century commodities, presents a clear tendency towards long-run expansion throughout the century.

After 1882, this picture was completely altered. While many of the booming exports of the previous decades became insignificant, exports of coffee and precious metals tended increasingly to dominate the picture. Whereas in the late 1870s exports of coffee and precious metals amounted to about 50 per cent of total exports, their share had increased to over 75 per cent in 1888-91, and to over 85 per cent by 1895-98; by the end of the century, coffee alone made up two-thirds of total exports.[13] This change was due not only to the decline of other export products, but also to the expansion of coffee production in central Colombia and to a precious metals boom in Antioquia, the latter largely dependent on foreign capital.

A significant export expansion is thus, in the case of Colombia, a twentieth-century phenomenon. It was characterised, however, by certain features which significantly differentiated it from the nineteenth-century experience. First of all, it was based almost uniquely on coffee. Secondly, it was based on independent peasant production, a significant break with respect to nineteenth-century coffee production in Colombia. Finally, it occurred under conditions in which Brazil had come to dominate the world market, and started to use restrictive policies to regulate the international price of coffee. On the basis of these specific conditions, the value of exports increased at a yearly rate of 10. 8 per cent from 1905/9 to 1925/29.[14] It is not the purpose of this paper, however, to analyse the specific conditions that allowed for successful expansion in the twentieth century and thus broke with all those limitations that we will consider below.

3. LIMITS TO EXPORT EXPANSION IN THE NINETEENTH CENTURY

We have seen that export growth was the only feasible form of development open to the Colombian economy in the nineteenth century, and that the Colombian bourgeoisie clearly understood this to be so. At the same time, however, the record of exports in the nineteenth century appears as a very dismal one and, when looked at in terms of commodities, as very unstable. The present section hopes to explain what the conditions were that account for the latter result.

When we analyse the external and internal conditions for export growth, three basic limits to export expansion can be differentiated.

First of all, the particular articulation of Colombia within the world economy (its status as a secondary region within the periphery) made Colombian producers weak competitors in the international market. The status of secondary peripheral region was closely associated with backward financial, mercantile and communication systems in relation to both important independent countries within the periphery (e.g. Argentina, Brazil), and major European colonies (e.g. Java). Whereas in these 'preferred' regions within the periphery, European capital invested considerable amounts of money into the development of modern financial, mercantile and communication networks, Colombian capitalists were largely left to their own efforts – which, of course, never could hope to match the advantages of the former. Among all these disadvantages, financial weakness was probably the most important. It implied that a modern plantation system, with the significant fixed capital investments associated with it, remained beyond the possibilities of the Colombian bourgeoisie. Closely associated with all these sources of international uncompetitiveness lay the fiscal weakness of the State itself. The fiscal weakness of the state affected the ability of the private sector to compete in the international market in several ways. First of all, it made the Colombian state a poor promoter of modernisation of the transportation system. Secondly, it made it a poor promoter of new export products. This contrasts heavily, for example, with the efforts of the Dutch government in Java to experiment with new primary products and techniques, including expensive experiments such as the cultivation of cinchona.[15] Finally, it made the Colombian state a very poor agent in the promotion of economic recovery at the time of crisis.

A second basic limit to export growth lay in the dominant forms of production in Colombia itself, forms of production which were being increasingly pushed aside by the rise of free labour. The form of tenant farming typical of tobacco production in Ambalema (in which the tenant had to sell all produce to the landowner at a fixed price) was considered by many as a factor conducive to poor-quality production.[16] Analyses of the coffee sector in the twentieth century, on the other hand, have claimed that the system of tenant farming typical of coffee production in the nineteenth century (in which rent was sometimes paid in labour) was less productive than the system of peasant farming which tended to become predominant in the twentieth.[17] Similar comments on productivity could be made about the techniques which were typical of gold production until mechanisation was gradually introduced in the second half of the nineteenth century. Finally, aside from the question of productivity, the forms of exploitation typical of extractive industries (cinchona bark, rubber, etc.) were characterised by their inability to sustain a high level of production.

A final limitation to the expansion of exports in the nineteenth century was the tendency of the Colombian capitalists to behave as what can be called producer-speculators. The conception of producer-speculator is intended to emphasise the fact that capitalists did not have a serious commitment to productive investment, with all the tying-up of capital intrinsically associated with it. They felt more comfortable in commercial, usury and speculative ventures, or in the investment in those traditional assets (e.g. land, cattle) that, due to the special role they play in the economy as 'safe assets' acquire some of the liquidity characteristics typical of a monetary unit. This type of capitalist invested in production only when prices were extremely high, and then only to enjoy what can be called the 'speculative gain' associated with great scarcity. Consequently, they had no interest in the reinvestment of profits for building productive capacity. Their interest lay only in making easy profits under conditions in which almost any type of production would do. They were thus only 'half-committed' to production, and consequently never ready when a crisis came either to sustain production at a lower price, or to innovate on the basis of their productive experience to profit under lower price conditions. When a crisis came, they simply abandoned any attempts to keep producing the specific commodity, and looked for other outlets for their investment. The mobility of their capital was facilitated by the fact that the capital tied up in production was actually minimal, so that the losses from a crisis were also minimised.

The interplay of these three limits to export development explains some basic characteristics of export expansion in the nineteenth century. First of all, taking all of them together, they explain why export industries tended to remain backward by world and general capitalist standards – i.e., in terms of their ability to supply a uniform-quality product in increasing quantities. Expansion could only take place during periods of world scarcity, when almost any supplies would be welcome. Under these conditions, the expansion was always very unstable, and thus contraction rapidly ensued once stable, trustworthy suppliers appeared in the world market. In other words, Colombian capitalists in the nineteenth century were in general unable to overcome their status as temporary suppliers in the international market in times of great scarcity. This explains the tendency for export products in the nineteenth century to undergo very short cycles of expansion and contraction. Capital would be rapidly mobilised to a promising sector, but any sector would also be rapidly abandoned once it did not promise easy profits. It also accounts for the great diversification of exports. Since the objective was never to build a strong productive base, the scale economies associated with both individual and social large-scale production (in terms of input availability, adequate processing, common use of certain facilities, association of producers for technical development and other common purposes, etc.) were irrelevant. There were thus no incentives to concentrate efforts in any one industry on a large scale. Moreover, since exportation always remained a sort of a gamble, each capitalist had the incentive to diversify his activities. Only coffee remained outside this limited circle of production-speculation, for it necessarily involved fixed capital investments. Its development remained, however, geographically limited until the late nineteenth century. Its geographical spread in the nineteenth century seems also to be closely associated with the failure of other export products and, more generally, with an international conjuncture which significantly narrowed down the possibilities for production-speculation.[18]

These three limits to export development are intrinsically related. First of all, the backwardness of the mode of production was dependent on the tendency for the centre of the world economy to remain a passive element in the expansionary process. Significant amounts of capital and labour power were not mobilised towards a secondary peripheral region such as Colombia to facilitate the expansionary process. In a sense, the international economy always remained indifferent to the expansion of Colombia, in complete contrast to the serious commitment of advanced capitalist nations to the development of important peripheral regions such as Brazil, Argentina and Java. The lack of mobilisation of capital towards a secondary peripheral region restricted the possible growth of total exports in expansionary times, and this made overall growth compatible with the preservation of old forms of exploitation of labour. On the other hand, the scant opportunities for productive investment which resulted from the status as a secondary peripheral region tended to discourage capitalists from seriously engaging in productive ventures, and thus gave a special rationality to their producing-speculating behaviour. Finally, the little manoeuvre for expansion provided by the internal modes of production, and the low commitment to productive investment helped to reinforce the status of Colombia as a secondary peripheral region. There existed, in other words, mechanisms in operation quite similar to those that determine the process of concentration of capital in a few firms, and the growth of poles of development within a capitalist nation. Those mechanisms were manifested in the tendency for internal and external factors to interact in reproducing the status of certain regions of the world economy as either primary or secondary regions within the periphery. Such mechanisms were simply the manifestation of a specific law of uneven development operating at the level of the periphery of the world economy.

In this interaction of the three limits to export development, however, the status of the region within the world economy played a predominant role. The reason for this dominance of external over internal limits to export growth can be most clearly understood in the context of the history of primary peripheral regions. In this case, no internal factors seem to have hindered expansion in the nineteenth century, since any internal limitation broke down under the dynamic pressure of an expansionary process which was called forth from the centre of the world economy. The modes of production in the primary peripheral region were significantly and rapidly transformed by the dynamic pressure of an expansionary capitalist economy which required that all labour power be available for capitalist exploitation. In so far as they were not transformed rapidly enough to serve the purpose of capitalist exploitation, then labour power was imported, and new 'modern' sectors developed alongside the old modes of production. Finally, the opportunities to profit from production and credit facilities available were apt to remove any prejudice against productive investment by local capitalists. In so far as this did not happen, or local entrepreneurship did not suffice for the expansion to take place, then entrepreneurship flowed into the region to facilitate export expansion. The process had, of course, its own contradictions. In the long run, however, the dynamics of an expansionary process called forth by the centre of the world economy was capable of destroying any internal barriers it encountered in the way of capitalist development.

In the Colombian case, on the other hand, internal limitations to export expansion appear so important precisely because of the peculiar status of Colombia within the world economy. In the context of regions for which the centre of the world economy played a purely passive role in the expansionary process, internal conditions tended to acquire a life of their own in the determination of export development. The dependence of internal on international conditions was most clearly manifested, however, at the time of a crisis. In this case, internal factors were completely overshadowed by the laws of uneven development of the world economy. The international uncompetitiveness of Colombia in the late nineteenth century had indeed very little to do with internal conditions. It was basically a by-product of the rapid development of the great raw material producers of the world economy, and of the significant mobilisation of capital and labour power from Europe which allowed this rapid development to take place. It was thus no coincidence that the era of export growth of Colombia in the nineteenth century started with the increase in the demand for tropical products as the result of the general capitalist development of Europe and the United States in the second half of the nineteenth century, and that it ended with the rise of the great peripheral regions capable of supplying those tropical products on an ever-increasing scale. Whereas the first of these developments tended to call for the expansion of any peripheral region (and to produce it, provided that the minimal internal conditions for expansion were present), the second made export growth without the adequate bases completely illusory, and thus tended to discard as a sort of hindrance to capitalist development all those regions which did not enjoy the best of all conditions for expansion-conditions which, left to their own efforts, they could have hardly hoped to create.

NOTES

[1] Sergio Elias Ortiz (ed.), *Escritos de dos economistas coloniales* (Bogotá, 1965) pp. 125-7, 130. See also David Bushnell, *El Régimen de Santander en la Gran Colombia* (Bogotá, 1966) pp. 19-20.

[2] Gabriel Giraldo Jaramillo (ed.), *Relaciones de Mando de los Virreyes de la Nueva Granada: Memorias Económicas* (Bogotá, 1954) p. 165; Jaime Jaramillo Uribe, *Ensayos sobre Historia Social Colombian* (Bogotá, 1968) pp. 71-5; Germán Colmenares, *Cali: terratenientes, mineros y comerciantes, siglo XVIII* (Cali, 1975) pp. 76-7, chs 3 and 4.

[3] Juan A. Villamarin, 'Haciendas en la Sabana de Bogotá, Colombia, en la época colonial', in *Haciendas, Latifundios y Plantaciones en América Latina* (Mexico, 1975) p. 373; Margarita Gonzalez, *El Resguardo en el Nuevo Reino de Granada* (Bogotá, 1970) pp. 72-3; Orlando Fals Borda, *El Hombre y la Tierra en Boyacá* (Bogotá, 1973) pp. 82-3; Juan Friede, *El Indio en la lucha por la tierra* (Bogotá, 1972) pp. 91-7.

[4] Giraldo Jaramillo (ed.), op. cit., pp. 198, 230.

[5] Bushnell, op. cit., pp. 113-17; José Manuel Restrepo, *Historia de la Neuva Granada,* Tomo I (Bogotá, 1952) pp. 137-8, 141, 145, 164, 179.

[6] For a development of the idea of the 'Spirit of Capitalism' in Bogotá, see Frank R. Safford, *Commerce and Enterprise in Central Colombia, 1821-1870* (Ph D thesis, Columbia University, 1965) ch. 2. For a characterisation of the capitalists of the time, see the analysis of the concept of 'producer-speculator' in section 3 below.

[7] Giraldo Jaramillo (ed.), op. cit., pp. 64-5, 75-6, 122, 177; Anthony McFarlane, 'El Comercio exterior del virreinato de la Nueva Granada', *Anuario Colombiano de Historia Social y de la Cultura,* 1971-2, pp. 94-106. For forceful expressions of free trade thought, see the writings of Antonio de Narvaez and José Ignacio de Pombo in Ortiz (ed.), op. cit., especially pp. 41-60, 123-34, 137-44, and Pedro Fermin de Vargas, *Pensamientos Políticos* (Bogotá, 1968) pp. 19-20, 94-102.

[8] Frank R. Safford, *Aspectos del siglo XIX en Colombia* (Medellín, 1977) pp. 237-9, and *Commerce* . . . , ch. 4; Luis Ospina Vásquez, *Industria y Protección en Colombia, 1810-1930* (Bogotá, 1955) ch. III.

[9] Calculated from the 1835 (Fernando Gomez, 'Los Censos colombianos antes de 1905', in Miguel Urrutia and Mario Arrubla, *Compendio de estadisticas históricas de Colombia* (Bogotá, 1970) Table 3 and 1912 (Official Publication)) population censuses. In intermediate periods, calculations are in the 1.3–1.8 per cent range. According to Fernando Gomez (*Análisis de los censos de población en el siglo XIX* (thesis, U. de los Andes, 1969) ch. 3) a consistency analysis of the 1835, 1843, 1851 and 1870 censuses gives a population growth of 1.7 per cent.

[10] The rate of growth in the value of imports from the late 1840s to 1878/83 was 3.7 per cent, and from 1878/83 to the late nineteenth century, 1.9 per cent (José Antonio Ocampo, 'Las importaciones colombianas en el Siglo XIX', in Miguel Urrutia, ed., *Ensayos sobre historia económica colombiana* (forthcoming) Table 3). Comparable rates of growth in Table 1 are 4.4 per cent and 1.4 per cent. Since we are considering long periods of time in which capital mobility was not very important, the rates of growth in the value of exports and imports should be approximately equal. The rates of growth of Table 1 could thus be overestimated for the period 1844/48–1878/82, and underestimated for the latter part of the century.

[11] In 1801-10, legal gold production was $ 2.3 million a year (José Manuel Restrepo, 'Memoria sobre amonedación de oro y plata en la Nueva Granada', in *Historia de la Nueva Granada,* (Bogotá, 1963) Vol. II pp. 455, 459). On the other hand, in its

highest point (1802-4), merchandise exports through Cartagena were $ 784.500 a year (*Semanario del Nuevo Reino de Granada* (Bogotá, 1942) Vol. 1, p. 230). However, this was a period between two international wars and the value of exports can thus be considered exceptional (Ortiz, (ed.), op. cit., pp. 72-4, 95-9). Excluding illegal gold production, but including merchandise exports through all Colombian ports, however, total exports were probably no less than $ 3 million.

[12] Safford, *Commerce . . .*, chs. 5 and 6; Luis Eduardo Nieto Arteta, *Economía y cultura en la historia de Colombia* (Bogotá, 1973) chs 17, 18, 20.

[13] Calculations of the author based on the 1882, 1891 and 1905 (Henrique Arboleda) Statistical Yearbooks.

[14] Calculation based on Jorge E. Rodríguez and William P. McGreevey, 'Colombia: Comercio Exterior, 1835-1962' in Urrutia and Arrubla (eds.), op. cit., Table I-B.

[15] Alle M. Sievers, *The Mystical World of Indonesia: Culture and Economic Development in Conflict* (Baltimore, 1974) pp. 104-5, 142.

[16] John Parker Harrison, *The Colombian Tobacco Industry, from Government Monopoly to Free Trade, 1778-1876* (PhD thesis, University of California, 1951) pp. 290-1, 296-7; Safford, *Commerce . . .*, pp. 241-5.

[17] Salomón Kalmanovitz, *Desarrollo de la Agricultura en Colombia* (Bogotá, 1978) p. 18; Absalón Machado, *El Café: de la aparcería al capitalismo* (Bogotá, 1977) ch. 4, p. 338. Nevertheless, Mariano Arango (*Café e Industria, 1850-1930* (Bogotá, 1977) p. 125) claims that *labour* productivity was very similar in both forms of production.

[18] Mariano Arango, 'Comentarios al Trabajo de Absalón Machado', in *El Agro en el desarrollo histórico colombiano* (Bogotá, 1977) pp. 233-40; Safford, *Aspectos . . .*, pp. 274-5.

11 Terms of Trade Between France and Latin America, 1826–1856: Causes of Increasing Economic Disparities?

Jürgen Schneider

Speaking about theories of economic development, M. Bohnet distinguishes between (*a*) theories of dualism, (*b*) theories of strategy, and (*c*) theories of foreign trade. The latter ones may be divided into Perroux's theory of the dominant economy, the theory of a secular deterioration (as enunciated by Singer and Prebisch), and Bhagwati's theory of immiserising growth.[1] The commodity terms of trade can be measured fairly exactly; statistically the figure results as the quotient of export price index and import price index.[2] The problem lies, of course, in the contents of the 'baskets' standing for 'export goods' and 'import goods' and forming the basis for those indices. The commodity terms of trade will be negative if cheap export goods are given in exchange for expensive importations; in the opposite case, a positive exchange relation results.[3] According to Singer and Prebisch export prices for raw materials from the developing countries will fall in the long run, whereas prices for manufactured import goods will rise; the consequence will be a deterioration of (real) terms of trade.

> For the industrially developed countries technical progress will lead to rising incomes as well as to decreasing import prices for raw materials from the developing countries. Accordingly, being at the same time the producers of manufactured goods exported into the developing countries and buyers of agricultural raw materials therefrom, the former countries will gain in two ways from this intercourse with the latter ones. The result will be an increasingly unjust distribution of welfare between those two parties.[4]

Prebisch's investigations were presented to a United Nations Conference on World Trade held at Geneva in 1964; from that time onwards, his ideas have also been discussed by economic historians.[5]

A. G. Frank concludes that the 'metropolis', for the sake of its own development, deprives its satellites of their economic surplus.[6] According to this author it is not to be expected that the industrially less advanced countries will be able to perform the steps of economic progress executed by the highly developed ones.[7] Against this opinion, however, one may hold Karl Marx's dictum – expressed in the introduction to the first edition of his *Das Kapital* – that the industrially developed country demonstrates the future path of development to the less advanced nation.[8] Frank believes that, in the case of the Latin American countries, the five decades following independence must be considered the crucial period of development.[9]

The latest state of information on this subject may be gathered from Carlos Manuel Peláez's 'The theory and reality of imperialism in the coffee economy of nineteenth-century Brazil (1857-1906)'.[10]

The present author will try to examine the Latin American countries'[11] position in their trade with France during the decade 1847-56, as compared with the year 1826. Beside the 'official values' fixed in 1826, the Direction generale des douanes et des contributions indirectes used, from 1847 onward, 'real values', established by a special commission in concurrence with the chambers of commerce.[12] Thanks to this actualisation of the statistical tables we have available a practical instrument for investigating price developments in export and import goods. For either branch of foreign trade there was a strict differentiation between the 'commerce général' and the 'commerce spécial'; 'A l'importation, le commerce général embrasse tout ce qui est arrivé par terre ou par mer, sans égard à la destination ultérieure des marchandises soit pour la consommation, soit pour l'entrepôt, soit pour la réexportation ou le transit. Le commerce spécial ne comprénd que ce qui est entré dans la consommation intérieure.' And: 'A l'exportation, le commerce général se compose de toutes les marchandises qui passent à l'étranger, sans distinction de leur origine, francaise ou étrangère. Le commerce spécial comprend seulement les marchandises nationales et celles qui, ayant été nationalisées par le payement des droits d'entrée, sont ensuite exportées.'[13] For the sake of as broad a basis of statistical comparison as possible we shall use here the figures of the 'commerce général' only.

The general impression is that the 'official' prices exceeded the 'actual' ones from 1847 to 1852, whereas during the following years, due to an increase in real prices, the reverse situation appears. Looking more closely into the matter, however, we find quite different circumstances for exports and imports, respectively. As to exportations, 'actual' prices for silk cloths, floss-silk, wine and spirits, metal and wood manufactures, hardwares, ready-made skins, clothes and clothing, were higher during the decade 1847-56 than the 'official' ones. On the other hand, the 'official' prices for cotton and woollen manufactures, linen manufactures, earthenware, glassware, painters' colours, and perfumery, exceeded the 'actual' prices, which meant that these goods in part were considerably cheaper in 1847/56 than they had been in 1826 (see Table 11.1). As to importations from Latin America, there were these two tendencies as well: prices for wool, sugar, raw skins, coffee, copper, cocoa and guano were higher in 1847/56 as compared with the year 1826, whereas prices for cotton, tobacco, indigo, cochineal and Peruvian bark had decreased during the same period (see Table 11.2). The question of whether

TABLE 11.1 'Actual' and 'official' prices of goods exported to Latin America, 1826 and 1847-1856 (in francs per kilogram)[a]

Goods exported	*Official price 1826*	*'Actual' prices*									
		1847	*1848*	*1849*	*1850*	*1851*	*1852*	*1853*	*1854*	*1855*	*1856*
Silk goods											
uni-coloured printed foulards	120	110	60	63	70	70	72	72	72	72	78
tulle	88	100	110	115	1265	126	130	135	128	128	140
Cotton goods											
shawls, handkerchiefs	26	8	8.5	9.6	10.5	9.6	10	10	9.2	8.8	8.8
tulle	200	125	140	88	88	88	88	130	120	120	88
Woollen goods											
merino cloth	47	25	20	27	26	25	25	25	238	26	26.5
miscell. goods	27	24	20	22	22	22	23.4	24.3	24.5	25.6	26.8
Linens											
white or half-white	20	16	10	10	10.5	9.8	9.8	9.2	8.7	8.2	8.2
Table wines											
Not from Gironde (hectolitres)	20	20	15	15	19	21	24	36	90	90	100
in barrels from Gironde, (hectolitres)	48	38	29	31	31	34	43	79	145	130	150
Salted butter	1.35	1.40	1.40	1.40	1.40	1.40	1.40	1.50	1.50	2.40	2.40

[a]Tableau decennal 1847-1856, S.XXII.

TABLE 11.2 'Actual' and 'official' prices of goods imported from Latin America, 1826 and 1847-1856 (in francs per kilogram)[a]

Goods imported	*Official price 1826*	*'Actual' prices*									
		1847	*1848*	*1849*	*1850*	*1851*	*1852*	*1853*	*1854*	*1855*	*1856*
Indigo (from countries outside Europe excl. India)	16	9	9	9	9	10.5	10.5	12	11	16.5	15.75
Cochineal	30	15	12	12	10	9	9.5	12	10	10	10.5
Cocoa	0.90	1.20	1.20	1.30	0.9	0.9	0.9	1.2	0.9	1.5	1.7
Foreign sugar	0.45	0.60	0.52	0.57	0.53	0.55	0.49	0.52	0.59	0.62	0.89
Raw skins	1	0.60	0.65	0.65	0.65	0.70	0.70	0.90	1.05	1.15	1.80
Dried skins	1.80	1.50	1.25	1.15	1.15	1.60	1.50	1.85	1.95	2.30	2.80
Coffee (not from French colonies)	0.85	0.90	0.78	1.05	1.20	1.10	1.10	1.24	1.28	1.26	1.38
Peruvian bark	8	8	8	9.5	10	8	4	4	4	4	4
Guano	0.08	0.08	0.15	0.20	0.20	0.20	0.25	0.25	0.30	0.35	0.35
Copper (once smelted)	2.0	2.20	2.20	2.15	2.15	2.15	2.30	2.90	3.20	3.20	3.25
Dyewood	0.2	0.2	0.15	0.16	0.16	0.16	0.25	0.23	0.23	0.2	0.2
Mother of pearl	2.2	0.53	0.53	0.62	0.72	1.14	1.07	1.28	0.98	1.18	0.92
Vanilla	250	115	45	65	60	60	60	120	120	200	200

[a]Tableau decennal 1847-1856, p. XXII; prices for dyewood, mother of pearl, and vanilla are based on the values indicated in the Tableau, pp. 194, 32, and 158.

TABLE 11.3 France's trade with several Latin American countries 1847-56[a] (annual averages for general trade, in francs)

	Exports		*Imports*	
Countries	*Official values*	*Actual values*	*Official values*	*Actual values*
Brazil	45,531,520	39,637,888	22,579,074	26,165,714
diff.		−3,893,632	+3,586,640	
Chile	21,264,876	20,366,466	3,358,555	3,948,364
diff.		−898,410	+589,809	
Peru	17,820,392	17,863,386	3,847,094	6,857,957
diff.	+42,994		+3,010,863	
Venezuela	5,102,669	4,599,457	3,694,409	4,201,858
diff.		−503,212	+507,449	
Uruguay	7,117,470	7,565,351	6,512,955	6,132,209
diff.	+447,881			−380,746
Argentine	13,676,412	14,657,123	9,988,522	9,674,203
diff.	980,711			−314,319
Colombia	4,423,161	4,329,606	1,654,718	1,125,986
diff.		−93,555		−528,732
Ecuador	321,881	334,038	458,165	570,057
diff.	+12,157		+111,892	
Guatemala	857,332	825,944	564,835	630,141
diff.		−31,388	+65,306	
Mexico	22,511,288	20,355,147	6,109,852	3,667,808
diff.		−2,156,141		−2,442,044
Total	1,483,743	−7,576,338	7,871,959	−3,665,841
Total diff.	−6,092,595		+4,206,118	

[a]Compiled and calculated from Tableau decennal 1847-56, pp. 38-53.

there was an improvement in 1847/56 (as compared with 1826) can be decided only if we take into consideration the assortment of goods exported to, or imported from, the several Latin American countries (see Tables 11.3 and 11.4).

In these terms, two groups of trading partners emerge. In the first group appear those countries with favourable terms of trade in their relations with France, viz. Brazil, Chile, Peru, Venezuela, Ecuador and Guatemala. *Brazil,* in exchange for her exportations of sugar, coffee, raw skins and cocoa, received higher prices in 1847/56 than had been the case in 1826, whereas

TABLE 11.4 Progress/declined state of several Latin American countries' general trade with France during the decade 1847-1856, as compared with the year 1826 (annual averages in francs)[a]

	1st group: progress		*2nd group: decline*
Brazil	7,480,272	Argentine	1,295,030
Chile	1,488,219	Uruguay	828,627
Venezuela	1,010,661	Colombia	435,177
Peru	2,967,769	Mexico	285,903
Ecuador	99,735		
Guatemala	96,694		
Total	13,143,450	Total	2,844,737
Latin America's average annual progress:	10,298,713		
Latin America's net progress 1847-56	102,987,130		

[a] Calculated and compiled from: Tableau decennal 1847-56, pp. 38-53.

prices for her importations from France had decreased appreciably; the consequent improvement of her situation amounted to 74.8 million francs.[14] *Chile's* net proceeds for her exportations had increased by nearly 600,000 francs, whereas she had to pay about 900,000 francs less for her importations. Her exportations to France consisted of more than 50 per cent of raw copper, the price of which had risen considerably. The improvement of Chile's situation in her trading relations with France amounted to nearly 15 million francs. *Peru's* shipments to France consisted of saltpetre, guano, raw copper, Peruvian bark, and cotton; the prices for these goods had risen by 80 per cent during the period under consideration. On the other hand, prices for importations had remained unchanged so that the improvement of Peru's situation in her relations with France may be calculated as 29.68 million francs. For *Venezuela* the improvement totalled 10.1 million francs; her exportations to France consisted of coffee (50 per cent), indigo, cocoa, cotton, dyewood, and skins, whereas importations therefrom were mainly composed of cotton goods (42 per cent), prices for which had decreased considerably. The 'actual' prices for cocoa exceeded, in 1847/56, the 'official' ones of 1826 uninterruptedly; since this product accounted for 80 per cent of *Ecuador's* exportations to France, that country's improvement amounted to about 100,000 francs. During the years 1837-46, 36.5 per cent of *Guatemala's* exportations to France had consisted of indigo; during the following decade, however, the first rank in the list of exportations was occupied by coffee, the 'actual' price for which again exceeded the 'official' one of 1826 so that for Guatemala an improvement of about 100,000 francs emerged.

For a second group of countries, namely Argentina, Uruguay, Colombia and Mexico, the structure of exports and imports caused a deterioration in their terms of trade with France. Three-quarters of *Argentina's* exports to France consisted of skins, the prices for which were considerably lower in 1847 than they had been in 1826; that year's level was reached again during the years 1853/54, rising further during the following years. Importations from France were at higher prices than in 1826, whereas Argentina received less for her exports to France. It was mainly wines and brandy (14-17 per cent of Argentina's importations from France) and silk goods (about 20 per cent) that had risen considerably in prices. A very similar situation may be stated with regard to *Uruguay*. The deterioration for Argentina amounted to about 13 million francs, for Uruguay to about 8.28 million. *Colombia* exported dyewoods (30 per cent), Peruvian bark (10 per cent), and skins, all of which saw price reductions. On the import side, 18 per cent were made up of silk goods. The deterioration for this country amounted to 4.35 million francs. *Mexico's* main exports consisted of cochineal, dyewoods, and vanilla – not to mention silver. After Mexico had declared her independence, the cultivation of cochineal was, from 1820 onwards, successfully tried in southern Spain. Since prices for all three products receded appreciably, Mexico's receipts for her exportations during the decade 1847/56 had decreased by about 40 per cent as compared with the year 1826. Although importations from France were produced as well, the situation on balance deteriorated by 2.85 million francs.

SUMMARY

During the decade 1847/56 France's proceeds for her exportations of French and foreign produce to Latin America had diminished by 60.926 million francs compared with 1826, whereas her expenses for importations from Latin American countries had risen by 42.06 million. Consequently, the total improvement witnessed by those countries amounted to nearly 103 million francs. The industrialised countries competed against each other for the sale of their products on the Latin American markets as well as for the purchase of raw materials coming from there. Thus, the terms of trade improved considerably in favour of those countries which could make profits out of the industrial nations' rising productivity, their economic growth, and their rising purchasing power. Owing to decreasing costs of production, prices for industrial products abated in relation to quotations for raw materials; from this development, during the period under consideration, the Latin American countries derived high profits. Consequently, all the advantages of technical progress were shared by those countries as well. Their relative position was determined by the structure of their imports: low shares of agricultural products of European origin (such as wines and spirits) and high proportions of European textile products (in particular cotton textiles) were, simultaneously, indicative of favourable terms of trade.

These results correspond with similar studies by Imlah[15] Maurice Lévy-Leboyer,[16] Paul Bairoch[17] and Carlos Manuel Peláez,[18] whereas they refute A. G. Frank who, relying on Celso Furtado's studies on Brazil, applied his opinions to Latin America in general.[19] Regarding the first half-century following upon the declarations of independence – which period was, according to A. G. Frank, of essential importance for any further development – the terms of trade cannot be considered to have been the cause of growing economic disparities. Empirical investigations on the terms of trade between Great Britain and Latin America will probably have the same result; the Latin American countries' exportations to Great Britain were of much the same structure as those to France, and Great Britain's exportations to Latin America largely consisted of cotton manufactures, prices of which had considerably decreased.[20] There is good reason to presume that there was an improvement in the terms of trade in favour of Latin America from the beginning of independence up to the First World War. Prebisch does not start his investigations until the year 1870.

When the Latin American countries grew independent at the beginning of the nineteenth century, there were only few manufacturing districts there. When in Western Europe the 'take-off' set in, the countries concerned were advanced ones already, and this advantage increased continually. For the Latin American countries there was, at that time, no alternative between industrialisation and an increase in the cultivation of produce which might be purchased by other countries; the latter was indeed the only means of economic development, all the more so after the destruction following independence. The situation was aggravated by those countries' financial weakness, 80 per cent of their expenditure being financed by import duties.

Moreover, the present author is convinced that, with regard to economic growth, capital had not the importance imputed by Marxist historians. A preparatory accumulation of capital may have had relevance in certain respects, but for the whole of capitalistic growth that theorem does not appear to be a sufficient explanation. According to Alfred Müller-Armack,[21] the speed of capitalism is maintained by a form of growth in which the capital necessary for expansion is accumulated in the course of the process of expansion itself. This opinion has been verified by investigations undertaken by Knut Borchardt,[22] Francois Crouzet,[23] Harald Winkel,[24] and Hermann Kellenbenz, Gerhard Kaiser and Jürgen Schneider.[25]

Historical evidence suggests that peripheral countries did not have a decisive importance for Western Europe's early industrialisation but that this process developed largely independently of that periphery.[26] The 'theory of dependence' not proving sufficiently apt for the explanation of growing economic disparities, the economic historian must look for novel approaches to the problem. Joseph Needham's studies on China might exercise a stimulating effect in this direction.[27]

NOTES

[1]Bohnet, Michael, 'Die Entwicklungstheorien. Ein Uberblick', *Das Nord-Süd-Problem. Konflikte zwischen Industrie- und Entwicklungsländern,* Michael Bohnet (2nd ed. München: Piper, 1971) pp. 50-5.

[2]Haberler, Gottfried, article on Aussenhandel (Theorie), *Handwörterbuch der Sozialwissenschaften,* vol. I (Stuttgart, etc., 1956) p. 465.

[3]Hebga, Joseph, 'Uber die Terms of Trade der Entwicklungsländer', *Wirtschaftspolitische Chronik. Beiträge zur Ordnung von Wirtschaft und Gesellschaft. Festgabe für Alfred Muller-Armack,* ed. by Institut für Wirtschaftspolitik der Universitat zu Köln (Köln, 1966) p. 273.

[4]Bohnet, M., loc. cit., p. 54.

[5]R. Prebisch, 'Towards a New Trade Policy for Development', UN/E/Conf.46/3, dated 12 February 1964 in *Mitteilungen,* ed. by Vereinigte Wirtschaftsdienste in cooperation with Bundesstelle für Aussenhandelsinformationen (Frankfurt) vol. 40, No. 80, 1964). For a critical discussion on Prebisch's opinions cf. Sieber, Hans, 'Die realen Austauschverhaltnisse zwischen Entwicklungslandern und Industriestaaten. Eine Verifizierung der These Prebischs, in *Schriftenreihe für Wirtschaftsprobleme der Entwicklungsländer,* ed. by Schweizerisches Institut für Aussenwirtschafts- und Marktforschung an der Hochschule St. Gallen für Wirtschafts- und Sozialwissenschaften, vol. 4 (Tübingen and Zürich, 1968) p. 168. Sieber concludes that the correlation between terms of trade and real factor-incomes in the developing countries' export sectors, as argued by Prebisch, appears to be questionable as well from a theoretical point of view as with regard to our – rather scanty – statistical material.

[6]Frank, Andre Gunder, *Kapitalismus und Unterentwicklung in Lateinamerika* (Dritte Welt, Frankfurt, 1969) p. 27.

[7]Idem, loc. cit. p. 12.

[8]Marx, Karl, *Das Kapital* (ed. Institut fur Marxismus-Leninismus beim ZK der SED) Vol. 1 (Berlin, 1966) p. 12. According to Marx development into capitalism was inevitable.

[9]A. G. Frank, loc. cit. p. 16.

[10]Peláez, Carlos Manuel, 'The Theory and Reality of Imperialism in the Coffee-Economy of Nineteenth Century Brazil (1857-1906)', in *Economic History Review,* 2nd ser., vol. XXIX, No. 2, May 1976, pp. 276-90.

[11]Under the term 'Latin America' we embrace here Brazil and the former Spanish colonies. The British, French, Danish, and Dutch possessions are consequently excluded from our views.

[12]Tableau decennal 1847-1856, I, p. xxii.

[13]Tableau decennal 1837-1846, p. xiii. For the problems connected with 'official' and 'real' values in the British foreign trade statistics cf. Imlah, Albert H., 'Real values in British foreign trade, 1798-1853', in *Journal of Economic History*, vol. VIII, 1948, No. 2, pp. 133-52.

[14]Schneider, Jürgen, 'Handel und Unternehmer im französischen Brasiliengeschäft 1815-1848. Versuch einer quantitativen Strukturanalyse', *Forschungen zur internationalen Sozial- und Wirtschaftsgeschichte,* ed. by Hermann Kellenbenz, vol. 9. (Köln and Wien, 1975) pp. 155-62.

[15]Imlah, Albert H., 'The terms of trade of the United Kingdom, 1798-1913', in *Journal of Economic History,* vol. X, 1950, pp. 170-94.

[16]Lévy-Leboyer, Maurice, *Les banques européennes et l'industrialisation internationale dans la première moitié du XIXe siècle,* Publications de la Faculte des Lettres et Sciences humaines de Paris, Série 'Recherches', vol. XVI (Paris, 1964) pp. 208 seq.

[17]Bairoch, Paul, *The Economic Development of the Third World since 1900* (London, 1975) pp. 111.

[18]Peláez, Manuel Carlos, loc. cit., see particularly his conclusions on pp. 286-97.

[19]Frank, A.G., loc. cit. p. 170.

[20]Regarding Great Britain in general, Albert H. Imlah states (op. cit., p. 176): 'Among the more striking trends indicated by these indexes none stands out more clearly than the deterioration in the net barter terms of trade in the early years of the series. It was caused by more rapid fall in export than in net import prices, and much the greater part of decline in the net barter terms occurred by the year 1839.' See also Platt, D. M. C., *Latin America and British Trade, 1806-1914* (The Merchant Adventurers: general editor Ralph Davis, London, 1972) and in particular Humphreys, R. A. (ed.), *British Consular Reports on the Trade and Politics of Latin America* (London, 1940).

[21]Muller-Armack, Alfred, 'Konjunkturforschung und Konjunkturpolitik', in *Handworterbuch der Staatswissenschaften,* Ergänzungsband (4th ed., Jena, 1929) p. 652.

[22]Borchardt, Knut, 'Zur Frage des Kapitalmangels in der ersten Hälfte des neunzehnten Jahrhunderts', in *Jahrbücher für Nationalökonomie und Statistik,* vol. 173 (1961) pp. 401-21.

[23]Crouzet, Francois, 'Die Kapitalbildung in Grossbritannien während der Industriellen Revolution', in *Industrielle Revolution. Wirtschaftliche Aspekte,* ed. Rudolf Braun *et al.* (Köln, 1972).

[24]Winkel, Harald, 'Die Ablösungskapitalien aus der Bauernbefreiung in West- und Süddeutschland', *Quellen und Forschungen zur Agrargeschichte,* vol. XIX, 1968.

[25]Kellenbenz, Hermann, Kaiser, Gerhard and Schneider, Jürgen, 'Kapitalbildung und Finanzierung von Aktiengesellschaften Oberfrankens in der sweiten Hälfte des neunzehnten Jahrhunderts, 1854-1914', in *Jahrbuch für Fränkische Landesforschung,* vol. 38 (Erlangen, 1978) pp. 191-218.

[26]Fischer, Wolfram, 'Die Rohstoffversorgung der europäischen Wirtschaft in historischer Perspektive', in *Wirtschaftskräfte und Wirtschaftswege,* IV: *Ubersee und allgemeine Wirtschaftsgeschichte. Festschrift für Hermann Kellenbenz,* ed. Jürgen Schneider, in *Verbindung mit dem Vorstand der Gesellschaft für Sozial- und Wirtschaftsgeschichte,* Karl Erich Born, Alfred Hoffmann, Hans Mauersberg, Hans Pohl und Wolfgang Zorn (Stuttgart, 1978) pp. 675-93.

[27]Needham, Joseph, *Wissenschaftlicher Universalismus. Uber Bedeutung und Besonderheit der chinesischen Wissenschaft,* ed., introduced and translated by Tilman Spengler (Frankfurt, 1977).

12 The Unevenness of the Socio-economic Development and Prospects for the Economic Self-sufficiency of the Countries of the East

N. A. Simoniya

When analysing and evaluating the prospects for the attainment of economic self-sufficiency by the countries of the East, it is very important to take into account considerable differences in the levels of socio-economic development between separate countries or groups of countries. Due to the unevenness of economic development caused by differences in social, historical, political, geographical, ethnic and other conditions, the gap between developing and highly developed capitalist countries will be eliminated in different ways and in considerably different periods of time. Since the overwhelming majority of developing countries function to a large extent within the framework of capitalist world economic ties, the unevenness of their development will get more accentuated and deeper. Some countries and some industries and enterprises in these countries may forge ahead, while others will be standing still or even lag behind. In this connection I would like to touch on the questions of methods of summary evaluation and of the methodology of forecasting on that basis the prospects of social and economic development of the countries of the East.

1. Inaccurate estimates of the prospects of the economic development of these countries and related socio-political forecasts are often the result of using methods of general regional 'overall Third World' and the like calculations, of using 'gross' indicators for all developing countries. This means leaving out not only differences in the present levels of socio-economic development of these countries, but also differences in the available and potential possibilities of their further growth and modernisation. When we stated, for example, that during the 1960s the real national product of the developing countries grew annually by 5.5 per cent on the average (that is, exceeded the 5 per cent target set for the first UN Development Decade); or that the average growth rates of the national product in 1970-74 were about 6 per cent, and the rates of growth in industry (8 per cent) and the

share of accumulations (20 per cent) considerably exceeded UN forecasts, this did not produce even an approximate estimate of the concrete economic situation in the developing countries. For in one numerically small group of countries these indicators have been considerably exceeded, in another group they have not been reached by a large margin and in a third group they fluctuate around this level. And the difference between any two countries of these groups may be as considerable as between a developed capitalist country and one of the liberated countries. (India or Singapore are economically rather far removed from Britain or Sweden, but countries like Nepal or Northern Yemen are likewise considerably behind India or Singapore.)

2. One of the most often recurring shortcomings of a methodological nature in analysing the prospects of the socio-economic development of the Eastern countries lies, in our view, in the absence of a dialectical approach to the relationship of quantitative and qualitative factors. Comparisons are usually made of purely quantitative indicators of the economic growth of developing and highly developed capitalist countries and then a mathematically quite correct conclusion is drawn about the extent of the lag of the developing countries. But what we have is a comparison not of abstract or homogeneous (uni-type) economies, but economies of such social organisms which are at different levels of social and historical development.

The main distinctive feature of the given stage of the economic development of the multi-structural countries of the East is the decisive importance of a definite qualitative, rather than quantitative, factor. Far be it from us to belittle the significance of quantitative economic growth, but it does not determine the essence of the present development process in the East. The aim of the present stage is not a simple accretion of the economic potential, nor the increase of the national income on this basis (gross and per capita income) and the elimination in this way of the gap in development levels. There is not yet an appropriate basis for attaining this aim. The aim is precisely to create this qualitatively new basis, and this requires the concentration of main efforts and relies not on an accelerated quantitative growth of the national income but on reshaping the existing economic structure and creating fundamentally new productive forces. Given this approach, comparatively low rates and scale of economic growth at the start are objectively inevitable and reflect, paradoxically, a specific manifestation of the process of eliminating backwardness. (This refers, of course, not to all countries of the East indiscriminately, but *only* to those of them which have really launched the building of the new basis.)

In other words, the newly free countries of the East are developing according to the model: the evolutionary process of accumulating elements of a new quality (economic basis) – a leap to a new quality (completion of the modernisation of the nucleus of the economy in basic outlines) – accelerated quantitative growth (national income) – modernisation on this basis of other backward structures (patterns) of the economy. In those countries whose governments (at times following recommendations from outside) hoped to achieve the final result through mere economic growth, the actual outcome was lagging. This course has no prospects from the standpoint of closing the gap. And in this case indicators of economic growth may indeed serve as a criterion of the 'remoteness of the prospect'. But similar yardsticks cannot be applied to countries actually involved in the modernisation process.

3. When the prospects of the developing countries' economic progress are evaluated, there are cases when the significance and role of the political factor are underestimated in a two-fold way. On the one hand, almost entirely overlooked is the negative aspect of the operation of the political factor, which played a particularly big role at the initial stages of the independent development of the Eastern countries. On the other hand, there is an underestimation of the great positive impact of an active, well thought-out and coordinated economic policy characteristic of the latest stage in the development of Asian countries.

Viewed from this angle, the post-war period of social and economic development of the countries of the *East* may be conditionally divided into three stages: (*a*) The first decade (the second half of the 1940s and the first half of the 1950s) – a stage of rearguard battles of colonialism in Asia and political self-affirmation of the young Asian states. At this stage there can be no question of any 'normal' economic development, for there were neither objective nor subjective conditions. (*b*) The second decade (the second half of the 1950s and early 1960s) – a stage of offensive on colonialism on the economic front. But in some countries this stage was characterised by 'leftism', by belief in the omnipotence of political actions, which substantially disrupted the usual process of economic growth and in some cases even caused a crisis of the economy. In other countries this stage was characterised by attempts to solve problems of economic development through cooperation with foreign monopoly capital, which likewise failed to produce any tangible results. (*c*) The third stage, which took shape in the second half of the 1960s and reached its peak in the middle of the 1970s, is characterised by a transition to a more realistic and effective anti-imperialist struggle on the economic front which is fought increasingly not in isolation but on a regional and even global inter-continental scale.

The already mentioned shortcoming in evaluating the prospects of the economic development of the countries of the East (and, with a certain adjustment, also the developing countries in general) lies precisely in the fact that no consideration is given to differences between these stages and summary data are taken for the entire post-war period, that is the calculations include also negative indicators of the first two stages when in the majority of countries there was no actual development in the proper meaning of the term. This not only reduces the general evaluation of the existing potentials of economic development, but also obscures the real scope of the first serious successes achieved by a number of countries at the present stage of development. There is a tendency to view these successes most often as something isolated and accidental rather than as the first manifestations of a qualitatively new tendency in the economic development of the Eastern countries.

4. Overall indicators also blur the unevenness of development of the internal economic structure of the developing countries and, in particular, the unevenness of the development of town and country. To be sure, summary indicators too may give a general idea that in agriculture the situation is worse than in industry. Rather revealing, for example, is the fact that the annual growth of agricultural production in the developing countries during the first four years of the second Development Decade hardly reached a *half* of the 4 per cent target, as a result of which there was even a reduction of per capita production in this branch. But again the situation was different from country to country and the pressure of the 'burden' of agricultural lagging on general economic development differs so much that attempts to build a concrete policy on such generalisations are rather non-effective.

Glancing back on the historical experience of the formation of capitalism in Europe, we can easily see that nowhere and at no time did it develop evenly in all sectors of the national economy. Forced industrialisation invariably required appropriate accumulations either at the expense of the countryside or at the expense of outside sources. Besides, capitalism never, especially at the early stages of its development, set the task of radically solving the agrarian, food or other problems. In the East the majority of countries are developing their industry at the expense of the village and some of them use mainly substantial export receipts (from oil, rubber, tin, copra, tea, etc.) in foreign exchange. And it appears that today too the governments of many Asian countries with a capitalist orientation, which have embarked on the road of industrialisation and are carrying it out mainly with the help of internal accumulation, adhere to the following policy in the food sphere: (1) achieving the supply of a minimum necessary level of food consumption in new centres of industrial development; and (2) maintaining rural consumption at the lowest possible level (from the standpoint of a threat of social explosion). And this necessarily means that these countries temporarily turn from being exporters to being importers of food. Leaving out countries with extreme socio-political and economic circumstances (Bangladesh, etc.), we will see that large imports were

TABLE 12.1

	1960 (or 1961)	*1970-72 (on average)*	*1973*
India	5,145	2,703	4,563
Pakistan	1,510	424	1,373
Sri Lanka	763	905	1,001
Egypt	1,371	1,843	1,872
South Korea	347	2,965	3,284
Philippines	341	992	1,004

characteristic of countries or territories which carried out a more or less large-scale industrialisation, as indicated by the data shown in Table 12.1 (in thousand metric tonnes).[1]

It is obviously necessary to realise quite clearly that an important reason (though not the only one) for the lag in agricultural modernisation and food shortage in the majority of Eastern countries lies not only in rural conservatism and traditionalism, not only in the resistance of landowners and the inconsistency of the bourgeoisie (all these factors undoubtedly contribute their great 'share'), but also in the deliberate orientation of the governments of a number of such countries at the initial stage to forced industrialisation at the expense of the agrarian sector.

Here we have a manifestation of the traditional law-governed regularity of evolving capitalism, of its unevenness and one-sided emphasis at the early stages of development on industrialisation encouraged by the neo-colonialist strategy of multinational corporations.

But already today there are clear indications of a tendency to show heightened attention for some problems of agriculture in the capitalist-oriented countries. After the first steps in industrialisation it became evident that further progress in this field in the majority of countries is held up by unsolved agrarian problems, growing foreign exchange expenditure on food imports, and instability of the agrarian source of industrial accumulation due to its strong dependence on natural and business fluctuations. Besides, growing unemployment and social instability in the agrarian sector of the majority of densely populated countries jeopardised in general the prospects of the capitalist orientation. The process of industrialisation carried out mainly at the expense of rural areas has revealed its failure to absorb surplus labour generated in the agrarian sector on a more or less large scale.

In the past also industrialisation at the early stages revealed its inadequate ability to involve large masses of people dislodged from traditional social structures in the modernisation process, thereby creating considerable *lumpen* and pauper strata in European societies. In many developing countries this problem is today even more pressing. As pointed out in the 1975 review of the Development Assistance Committee, in the developing countries 'the growth rate of the labour force, overall, is at least double the rate typical in Europe during the industrial revolution. Technology has changed considerably since that time: its emphasis is on the intensive use of capital which means fewer jobs per unit of investment than was the case 20 or 30 years ago.'[2]

It is not surprising therefore that the need for shifting the centre of attention to the solution of urgent agrarian problems is more and more often mentioned in the developing countries of the East and elsewhere.

5. The unevenness of the development of the Eastern countries is accentuated by the fact that processes of gradual economic evolution alternate with *leap-like* acceleration of development of separate groups and individual countries, giving rise to fundamentally new relationships of economic and political forces between the developing countries themselves. Thus, we

witness today the beginning of a new and rather significant leap-like acceleration of economic development of a whole group of oil-exporting countries. And contradictory consequences of this are bound to affect a broader range of countries rather substantially.

One of the consequences of the 'oil confrontation' of 1973-74 was the emergence of a new centre or source of financial resources which may be used both to boost the internal economic development of the oil-exporting states and to render aid to other developing countries.

Before the energy crisis the economic assistance given by the OPEC countries to other developing countries was in the area of 400-500 million dollars annually in 1970-73. The total allocations made at the end of 1973 amounted to three billion dollars. But already in 1974 total aid commitments by OPEC countries in relation to a far greater number of developing countries reached eight billion dollars.

The sudden multiplication of foreign exchange resources already has as its consequence a tendency towards the *financial-economic integration* of a number of petroleum-exporting countries with imperialist state-monopoly capitalism.

This tendency is manifested not so much in growing portfolio investments by petroleum-exporting countries in the West as in large-scale deals for the construction of the most up-to-date industrial enterprises and for the modernisation of the entire social and economic structure.

We cannot help mentioning also this qualitatively new phenomenon: integration, no longer just bilateral, is becoming multilateral. There have begun to appear so-called 'triangle agreements', the substance of which is the combination of petroleum dollars with Western technical aid and equipment to build industrial projects in third world developing countries.

6. What are, most generally, the prospects for the attainment of economic self-sufficiency?

The European countries first accomplished the industrial revolution, completed capitalist industrialisation, successively passed through the stages of monopoly and state-monopoly capitalism and only at the present stage of the latter have arrived at the modern scientific and technological revolution. But does this mean that the developing Asian and African countries too are to go successively through all these stages of social development? In our view, in the present historical conditions this is not only undesirable but practically ruled out. The modern world is so much interconnected and the balance of world forces is steadily tilting in favour of social progress in such a way that the skipping of separate stages of the traditional pattern of social development in some Asian countries is becoming today a universal law.

It stands to reason that this process of skipping cannot develop in an absolutely pure form, smoothly and harmoniously, and that social, economic and political 'overhead expenses' will inevitably be incurred. Thus, the rapid borrowing from the more developed countries of modern productive forces and scientific and technical achievements and the skipping on this basis of certain stages of socio-economic development often produce 'gap' situations when the social and psychological reorganisation of the main section of society does not keep pace with socio-economic shifts. In short, such societies enter a more or less prolonged period of discrepancy between the incipient rapid economic modernisation and largely persisting traditional survivals in the socio-political and psychological spheres. The way this 'gap' situation is resolved and its consequences largely depend on the relation of class and political forces within a given country and outside it and on its place and role on the world scene.

The fact that many Afro-Asian countries are only in the initial stage of their industrial development while the scientific and technological revolution is unfolding in the rest of the world has, paradoxically enough, negative as well as positive aspects. These countries get the 'advantage of the lagging', i.e., they may begin modernising their economic structure taking into account the latest world achievements of science and technology and overleap certain intermediate stages of technical progress, sharply reducing the time of transition to the machine stage of production and then to its highest forms – comprehensive mechanisation and automation of production. Incidentally, the conversion from coal to oil constituted a whole epoch in the history of the European countries' industrial development. The subsequent tempestuous development of petrochemistry was another important landmark. In the developing countries hundreds of petrochemical plants have already appeared or are under construction. Some of them have made first steps in the use of electronics in production, etc. It goes without saying, of course, that so far all this is done on a small scale compared with the world standards. But the new always begins with small things. And though the above facts do not yet signify a radical reshaping of economic structures of the countries concerned, they nevertheless indicate the trend of this reshaping.

7. In the last few years the economic struggle of separate 'raw material' groups and all developing countries in general has received a new strong impulse with the result that we witness a whole series of special international forums. It is characteristic that in the van of this new movement have always been the states with a progressive orientation which have relied on the support of world socialism. Thus, the Sixth Special Session of the UN General Assembly on problems of raw materials and development was held in April 1974 on the initiative of Algeria. It adopted a Declaration on the Establishment of a New World Economic Order and a Programme of Action.

If anyone were to advance as a *practical task of the day* the global alteration of the international economic order ten or, at most, fifteen years ago, he would be dismissed as a utopian. Today this problem is on the agenda at all more or less significant international forums. Of course, definite changes have taken place in the world economic order in earlier periods (say, the 1940s), but they were connected with regrouping within the circle of developed capitalist states, with a changing balance of forces between leading imperialist monopolies and, lastly, with technological changes within the world capitalist economy. Today, in conditions of a global change in the balance of forces between the two world systems, the developing countries raise the question not of just purely technical changes in the world economic order, but of its overhaul on a new and fair basis ruling out injustice and relations of exploitation.

NOTES

[1] *Development Co-operation. Efforts and Policies of the Members of the Development Assistance Committee. 1975 Review* (Paris, 1975) pp. 74-5.

[2] Op. cit., p. 78.

Part 1c The Developed World

13 Methodological Aspects in Describing the Bourgeois and Industrial Revolutions

Walter Becker

The industrial revolution in Europe had been preceded by urban changes. Since the eleventh century not only had thousands of towns been founded, particularly, in northern Italy, southern and western Germany, north-eastern France, southern England and some other areas, but this process had also been accompanied by the emergence of the bourgeoisie, by the spreading of simple commodity production and by the development of capitalist production relations in the form of firms putting out work and of manufactures.[1] Due to the autonomous position of the bourgeoisie *vis-a-vis* the feudal lords it had in many towns become possible for the first time in economic history to politically safeguard the results of commodity production. The consequence was that the profit mechanism—the appropriation of surplus labour of journeymen and even wage-labourers by master craftsmen, by firms putting out work and by manufacturers—became effective as a new motive force for the rapid development of the productive forces and, thus, for economic growth. In the feudal states of Europe the sector of non-agricultural production expanded, although to a different degree. It contributed to weakening the feudal basis, to stimulating – to a certain extent – the expansion by European feudal lords of mercantile and trade capital and, eventually, also of the colonialism of the absolutist states. All this leads to the formation of the world market during the sixteenth century and conditions the further development of capitalist production relations.

As a function of the intensity of urban changes and their historical results, the basis developed for the weakening of many European feudal systems. Since the early sixteenth century favourable conditions had matured in feudal countries with a strong bourgeoisie for new convulsions such as the Great German Peasants' War in 1525, which had been characterised by certain traits of an early bourgeois revolution, and the revolutionary mass uprisings (1566-83) in the Netherlands, which eventually ended in the foundation of the first bourgeois republic in world history in connection with the struggle against the Spanish oppression. According to Marx, the bourgeois Netherlands were the chief capitalist nation of the seventeenth century.[2] The European feudal system had in one place been broken by the bourgeois Netherlands, a republic which from now on guaranteed the political rulership of the bourgeoisie on a national level too, thus creating the most favourable conditions for the further development of capitalist production relations.

Antwerp and later on Amsterdam were considered to be centres of the world market. But it had become obvious by that time that even the first chief capitalist nation needed the resources of Europe and also the world market, the extra profits as well as colonialism, in order to '. . . safeguard the political rulership of the conservatively and cosmopolitically oriented mercantile oligarchy'.[3]

These historically progressive trends were hampered by the reduction of non-agricultural production during the first half of the seventeenth century, by the weakening of capitalist production relations in connection with the Thirty Years War in central Europe and, in addition, by the consolidation of the feudal forces in eastern and south-eastern Europe, who intensified their feudal rulership as an economic basis of their power, which they could utilise to deliver even grain and also, at a later stage, crude iron to western Europe. But in western Europe too there were reactions in the feudal states aiming at the stabilisation of the system by means of reforms of enlightened absolutism, e.g. a mercantilistic economic policy. However, under these historical conditions feudal exploitation as it had existed in south and south-east Europe could be intensified only to a limited extent.

In a country which is situated at the periphery of the European continent – England – favourable conditions had evolved in the form of primitive accumulation and the related methods of a protectionist policy, in the form of taxes, gross national debts of colonialism and the massive emergence of wage-labourers as well as the precipitate expansion of the home and foreign markets for the further development of capitalist production relations. Here the historical conditions for another bourgeois revolution matured in the first half of the seventeenth century – a revolution which had its basis in a stronger position of the manufacturers and firms putting out work in relation to trading capital. At the same time changes occurred in agriculture which led to a 'bourgeoisification'. The years between 1644 and 1688 saw the victory of the bourgeois revolution, the smashing of the feudal superstructure and the creation of the prerequisites necessary for an efficient capitalist mode of production. As compared with the revolution in the Netherlands, a more radical transformation of the social base had without doubt taken place in England in connection with primitive accumulation, i.e. simple rural commodity production had largely been restrained and capitalist production relations were introduced in agriculture, a fact which had huge consequences also for the subsequent industrial revolution. In the century following the bourgeois revolution, England as the chief capitalist nation of the eighteenth century broke the hegemony of the Netherlands, thus subjugating trade capital to industrial capital.[4] Once capitalist commodity production, the growth of the bourgeoisie and the class struggle of the masses of rural craftsmen had created the prerequisites for the bourgeois revolution, the historical results of this revolutionary development released new motive forces. The smashing of the feudal basis and of its superstructure had eliminated all obstacles that hampered capitalist development. The social division of labour increased at an enormous rate, the home and foreign markets developed to a hitherto unknown extent. On this basis a contradiction developed between the precipitously increasing profits and the level of production technology which, at the stage of manufacturers, had still been characterised by craftsmen's production. It was this contradiction which, finally, ushered in the industrial revolution, i.e. that technological, economic and socio-economic change which resulted in the massive investment of constant tied-up capital, the triumph of factory production over other forms of commodity production, in production for the factories' own requirements and in the development of the two main classes of capitalism – bourgeoisie and proletariat. The industrial revolution brought about a precipitous increase in labour productivity by introducing machine tools and other machines as well as a rapid increase in industrial production. Industrial production increased to such an extent that the former main branch of production (agriculture) was outmatched; for some time England had become 'the workshop of the world', accounting for about 90 per cent of the overall industrial production. The transition to a massive investment of constant tied-up capital occurred in the most important branch of non-agricultural production, in the textile industry. The demand for spinning machines and looms, transmission belts and driving machines represented that demand for means of production that permitted capital investments in the fields of heavy industry, mechanical engineering and transport. The growing purchasable demand had repercussions on the historical starting-point of the industrial revolution, i.e. the textile industry, and accelerated its development.

During the eighteenth century a contradiction had developed in countries with a powerful non-agricultural sector, as the markets were growing faster than the productive facilities, so that the number of persons employed in the textile industry could not be further increased at will. In many European countries, but in particular in England, there was a shortage of spun yarn, a fact which fundamentally stimulated the invention of the spinning machine and other machines and machine tools. The solutions which had been found empirically for the first generation of machine tools ushered in the, so to say, 'British phase' of mechanical engineering. Up to the early seventies of the nineteenth century British spinning machines, looms, metal-working machines and steam engines largely determined technological progress. In the subsequent phase of the development of European mechanical engineering, the influence of science, of technical knowledge became obvious, above all in Germany, and ushered in the phase of the so-called universal mechanical engineering. Until 1844, mechanical engineering on the European mainland had been facilitated to a certain extent by the British machine monopoly. Machine tools for meeting the requirements of the European countries had in the first stage to be produced by those countries themselves. After 1844 British exports to France and Germany played a minor role from the quantitative, but a big role from the qualitative point of view. The shortage of qualified labour, a huge national market, almost inexhaustible resources and, last but not least, the utilisation of European experience contributed to the development in the USA of another generation of machine tools which were manufactured in large series for industrial mass production.

Machine tools and other machines made it possible actually to rid production of the physical barrier in so far as the operational energy of man could be restrained. But human control energy was more and more coming to the fore in production. 'The bourgeoisie has created more massive and more colossal productive forces than have all preceding generations together. Subjugation of Nature's forces to man, machinery, application of chemistry to industry and agriculture, steam-navigation, railways . . .'[5] The bourgeois revolutions of the sixteenth, seventeenth and eighteenth centuries as well as the industrial revolution in England, which entered into its golden period in the eighties of the eighteenth century, may be considered another stage in the formation of the capitalist system, which also formed the first elements of a world system. This system was founded on the bourgeois countries England, France and Holland, and on the capitalist development which took place in many feudal states, in particular in Germany, Russia, Sweden, Austria and, last but not least, the USA.[6] After 1780, England became the centre of this system with the material and technological basis of the capitalism of free competition, which culminated in the first beginnings of industrial capitalism and initiated an irreversible development. In many countries this historical lead of England combined with the bourgeois revolution in France aggravated the antagonistic contradictions between feudalism and capitalism. On the other hand, the attempt made by the British bourgeoisie to preserve their monopoly in the field of factory production hampered the further development of capitalist production relations on the European mainland – a process which, by the way, had its basis also in the cheap British industrial consumer goods, in particular textiles.[7] The result of all these influences was that in France, Germany and some other countries the role of the textile industry as the element which had ushered in the industrial revolution had been weaker during its main period than in England;[8] impulses such as the manufacturing of means of transport or railways were needed in order to unleash waves of investments of constant and tied-up capital. Due to the industrial revolution and specific historical conditions, heavy industry developed more rapidly on the European mainland than in England during its classical revolution. This statement applies, in particular, to those countries which underwent their industrial revolution much later (50 to 100 years). The competition between different countries with a developed capitalist industry rendered the industrial revolution in east and south-east Europe more complicated. The weakness of the bourgeoisie in eastern Europe should also be taken into account. In great parts of Prussia, for instance, it made it necessary to follow the 'Prussian path of the bourgeois revolution', i.e. the path of reforms from 'above' as a consequence of the pressure brought to bear by the masses from below, and of the pressure from outside. In the course of this development former feudal lords changed into capitalists of agriculture.[9] In this connection it was also important that the working class had emerged already in the bourgeois and bourgeois-democratic revolutions of the nineteenth century. The result was that the bourgeoisie was inconsistent in its struggle against the feudal class enemy and that it was prepared to enter into an alliance with the feudal lords, which took on the form of 'Prussian reforms'.

The more the industrial revolution advanced in the main capitalist countries, the more difficult became its realisation in other countries and the more contradictory became capitalist industrialisation. This applies to countries which had achieved the manufacturing stage of capitalism, although to a different degree. Outside Europe and with the exception of the USA and Japan the industrial revolution had negative impacts on the non-agricultural sectors of colonial countries. As a result, capitalism as a world system had fully developed by the early seventies of the nineteenth century; it comprised countries where the industrial revolution had taken place (England, France, Germany, Switzerland, Belgium, the USA), countries which had made the first steps on the path towards the industrial revolution (Russia, Austria, Italy, Japan) and many more or less dependent countries and states, which, in the majority of cases, may be considered colonies of capitalist industrialised countries. An 'international division of labour, a division suited to the requirements of the chief centres of modern industry, springs up and converts one part of the globe into a chiefly agricultural field of production for the supply of the other part, which remains a chiefly industrial field.'[10]

The development of industrial capitalism was marked by a profound inequality which finds its expression not only in the lead of one group of capitalist European countries but also in the fact that its level differs between west, central, east, north and south Europe, and in the colonial system. From time to time considerable differences as regards their growth existed also among the countries of the first-mentioned group. These differences aroused political contradictions which developed into open conflicts during the imperialist phase. The application of British experience, the leading role of the state in the industrial revolution, the Prussian path of capitalism temporarily proved to be more efficient than the classical path England was treading. A regional site analysis of the course of the industrial revolution also shows that the centres of urban changes, apart from a few exceptions, had later on also become the centres of industry. Only the coalmines brought about new centres of mechanical engineering and of heavy industry as a whole. To the same extent as, internationally, a group of capitalist industrialised countries developed and as other countries were increasingly being transformed into agricultural countries, there developed a difference in level also within the capitalist industrialised countries themselves, a difference in level between the industrialised urban agglomerations and agricultural areas that were left behind. This shows that capitalist industrialisation neither contributes to overcoming the backwardness of weakly developed countries nor to approximating the economic development within the capitalist countries themselves.

An analysis of some indices which are characteristic of the economic growth reveals that England's lead over the other European countries reached its peak probably between 1820 and 1830. Temporarily, England was 50 to 60 years ahead of other countries. This lead diminished from the fifties of the nineteenth century to the early seventies without, however, disappearing. The most rapid development took place in Germany, which by the early seventies had already overtaken France. In Germany industrial production doubled every five years as a result of the cyclic upswing in the fifties. When comparing some of the machine constructions with their British counterparts, German mechanical engineering production, which increased by five times between 1850 and 1870, showed a certain advance. Round about 1870 England's lead continued in shipbuilding, in some branches of machine tool engineering, in coalmining, cotton processing and power economy.

In the early seventies the approximation of the four most important countries of Europe reached its peak, at any rate since the beginning of the industrial revolution in England. During the last third of the nineteenth century, during the transition to monopoly capitalism, the USA became the leading capitalist industrialised country and Germany was set on the path towards becoming the strongest economic power in Europe.

NOTES

[1] Cf. Mottek, H., *Wirtschaftsgeschichte Deutschlands. Ein Grundriß* (Economic history of Germany. An outline) Vol. 1 (Berlin, 1964) pp. 144 ff.

[2] Marx, K., *Capital,* Vol. I (Foreign Languages Publishing House, Moscow) p. 752.

[3] Marx, K., op. cit., unauthorised translation.

[4] Marx, K., op. cit., unauthorised translation.

[5] Marx/Engels, *Selected Works,* Vol. I, *Manifesto of the Communist Party* (Progress Publishers, Moscow, 1969) p. 113.

[6] Tchistosvonov, A., 'The stadial and regional research into the bourgeois revolutions of the 16th to 18th centuries', *Social Sciences,* published by the USSR Academy of Sciences, No. 1, 1975, p. 123.

[7] Blumberg, H., 'Die deutsche Textilindustrie in der industriellen Revolution' (The German textile industry in the industrial revolution) *Publications by the Institute of Economic History of the 'Bruno Leuschner' College of Economics, Berlin,* Vol. 3 (Berlin, 1964) p. 23.

[8] Ibid.

[9] Cf. Mottek, H., *Wirtschaftsgeschichte Deutschlands. Ein Grundriß,* Vol. 2 (Berlin, 1964) p. 20.

[10] Marx, K., *Capital,* Vol. I (Foreign Languages Publishing House, Moscow) p. 451.

14 Economic Integration and Regional Development in Austria-Hungary, 1867–1913

David F. Good

This is an abridged version of a larger paper, 'Growth and Integration in the Austro-Hungarian Economy, 1867-1914', Working Paper No. 31, Temple University, revised 1978, which contains a more detailed description of the methodology, data and data sources. My thanks to Temple University for generous financial support for this project and to Robert Billinger, Scott Eddie, Rainer Fremdling, Edward Hewett, Thomas Huertas, Franklin Mendels, Zora Pryor, Hugh Rockoff, Gene Smiley, William Stull and Martin Wolfe for very helpful comments on earlier drafts.

INTRODUCTION

The persistence of regional disparities in levels of economic development continues to threaten political stability throughout the world. The most dramatic example is, of course, the growing conflict between rich nations and poor nations. But even within nations of the developed world, there is a growing impatience over the failure of regional differences to narrow.[1]

The forces behind this situation are not fully understood by social scientists and policy makers. It seems clear, however, that the current disparities between rich and poor regions both within and among the nations of the world are deeply rooted in a dynamic process extending far back in the past. For this reason, economic historians can play a vital role in the analysis of present-day regional economic problems.

The Habsburg Monarchy offers a particularly instructive historical case for studying the dynamics of regional economic development.[2] In the latter part of the nineteenth century, regional economic issues became important in the political arena of the multinational state. Although the various nationalities of the Monarchy were not perfectly segregated in a spatial sense, they did tend to cluster in well-defined geographical areas. With time the economic differences among regions were translated into political terms by aggrieved national groups. As a result, the process of modern economic growth unfolded in Austria-Hungary within a political system whose viability was increasingly problematical. The ultimate collapse of the Monarchy after the First World

War suggests the value of the Habsburg experience in understanding the complex link between regional economic development and the political institutions within which this development proceeds. Was the political disintegration of the Monarchy mirrored in the behaviour of the economy? This question has largely been ignored by historians, who have chosen instead to concentrate on the political manifestations of the disintegration process.[3] My paper fills this gap by measuring quantitatively both the process of economic integration within the Monarchy and the path of economic disparities among her regions.

THE PROCESS OF ECONOMIC INTEGRATION AND ITS EFFECTS

The economic linkages among regions in any given territorial unit can be viewed either at the institutional level or at the level of market transactions.[4] If regions are governed by a common set of economic institutions and policies, they will tend to be part of a single, integrated economy. If regional authorities, however, are permitted autonomy in fiscal and monetary policy, economic integration will be hindered and economic separation the likely result. Market, as opposed to institutional integration, is related to the actual flow of goods and resources across boundaries. If goods and resources are spatially mobile, economic integration is likely to be high. A diminishing interregional exchange of goods and resources implies a lack of integration.

Whether institutional and market integration lead to a narrowing of regional differences in economic well-being is a major concern. Unfortunately economic theory offers no clear-cut answer on this issue. At one extreme are the neo-classical models which stem from the early work of Heckshер and Ohlin in trade theory.[5] Assume there are two regions with identical production functions but differing resource endowment. Each region will tend to specialise in the production of goods utilising its abundant factor while trading for goods whose production requires heavy use of its scarce factor. Thus, the labour-scarce, high-wage region will specialise in capital-intensive goods and trade for labour-intensive goods, with the labour-abundant, low-wage region specialising in labour-intensive goods and trading for capital-intensive goods. With resource mobility, labour will flow from the low-wage to the high-wage regions, while capital will flow in the opposite direction. As a result, factor returns will tend to equalise and income per capita converge between the two regions.

As noted in the introduction, the rather optimistic predictions of neo-classical models have not always been verified by experience. As an alternative framework, many economists have settled on some variant of Gunnar Myrdal's cumulative causation model.[6] According to this model, the development process begins in regions which by historical circumstance are blessed with conditions favourable for sustained economic growth. Market forces lead to a series of 'backwash effects' which tend to widen rather than reduce regional inequalities. For example, the agglomeration of increasing return activities in the favoured growth regions encourages capital and skilled labour to migrate from the lagging regions. The lagging regions thus are drained of the very elements needed for sustained growth. In contrast to neo-classical models, interregional flows in the cumulative causation model become 'the media through which the cumulative process evolves – upwards in the lucky regions and downwards in the unlucky ones'.[7] The positive value of any 'spread effects' – the benefits which the growth centres might provide the lagging regions in the form of new technology and new markets – are dwarfed by the 'backwash effects'. Only some exogenous event, e.g. a compensatory government policy, is capable of reversing this process of uneven growth.

Many regard these positions as unnecessarily dichotomous. For example, Jeffrey Williamson agrees that regional differences may increase sharply in the early phase of economic development for the reasons cited by Myrdal.[8] However, he argues that as market imperfections are overcome, the transfer of growth impulses to the lagging regions begins to dominate the 'backwash' effects and regional disparities diminish.

THE DEBATE ON ECONOMIC UNITY IN THE HABSBURG MONARCHY

Traces of these formal models have long been implicit in most discussions of regional development in the Monarchy. For example, the cumulative causation framework is reflected in the early work of Oscar Jaszi, who argued that in 1913 the Monarchy was already a 'defeated Empire from the economic point of view'. The customs union was a 'pseudo free-trade organization [whose] tendency of economic evolution was toward the emancipation of [Austria and Hungary with] a similar tendency also operative among the various territories of Austria.'[9] Using less emotive language, Nachum Gross has echoed this position. 'We know from theoretical analysis . . . that the mere joining together of [the industrial west and the agricultural east] into a common customs area was likely to perpetuate and reinforce the structural differences, rather than levelling them out.' In fact, 'Habsburg tariff policy . . . aimed . . . at consolidating and conserving the economic and cultural supremacy of the western, "hereditary" Austro-Bohemian provinces.'[10]

On the other hand, the neo-classical view is reflected in the well-known work of Friedrich Hertz, who pointed to the Monarchy's 'great economic achievement [resulting from] the natural division of labor between the Austro-Hungarian territories [and] the absence of trade barriers'. He argued that 'all nationalities and all parts of the Empire derived almost equal profits from the general development.'[11] More recently William Ashworth has come to a similar conclusion in viewing the Austro-Hungarian Customs Union as a device through which the impulses for economic growth were transmitted from west to east. 'Recent . . . study has suggested that [the Customs Union] gave opportunities of economic advance to most, though not all, of the non-German population.'[12]

A priori it seems that the Austro-Hungarian experience could conform to the cumulative causation model. Within the Monarchy, a well-defined east-west continuum of development prevailed. Because of their close proximity to western Europe, Austria's western provinces were more capitalistic and industrial than were her eastern provinces and the provinces of Hungary, which resembled the Monarchy's agrarian, feudal neighbours to the east.[13] Although firm statistical evidence is lacking, it is likely that the regions of Austria-Hungary were characterised by wide disparities in levels of development in the early nineteenth century. Such wide divergences may well have provided fertile soil for the cumulative causation mechanism. Furthermore, the available evidence suggests that the process of modern economic growth was initiated in the western territories in the middle decades of the nineteenth century and spread to the eastern lands after some delay.[14] One might expect, therefore, that these disparities, already substantial by the mid-nineteenth century, would widen over most of the period up to the First World War.

Most discussions of economic unity in the Habsburg lands do not treat this hypothesis directly but instead concentrate on the institutional aspects of economic integration. Superficially, the Monarchy appears to have satisfied the conditions for institutional integration. In 1850 the internal barrier (*Zwischenzollinie*) between Austria and Hungary was removed and the Monarchy became a full-fledged customs union.[15] Monetary union was established even before this with the founding of the Austrian National Bank (1816), which as the only institution permitted to issue paper money, provided the Monarchy with a common currency. As noted earlier, Hertz has pointed to these institutions and to the 'natural' division of labour between the agricultural east and the industrial west as strong reasons for his belief in the viability of the Habsburg lands as an economic union. On the negative side, many have cited the geographical obstacles which blunted the potential gains from economic union.[16] For example, Galicia and Bucovina, provinces of Austria in the eastern part of the realm, and the Dalmatian Littoral on the Adriatic were cut off from the economic heartland of the Monarchy by mountains. The chief waterway of industrial rich Bohemia did not flow south to the Danube and Vienna, but north to the North Sea. In addition, some have argued that the supranational institutions, despite their continuous existence until the final collapse, failed to nurture economic union. In fact, participants in the customs union 'paid more attention to wrecking each other's trade than to actively promoting "free trade"'.[17] The debate on unity at this level remains quite inconclusive.

In contrast to discussions of institutional integration in Austria-Hungary, analyses of the degree of market integration are scarce. Fortunately such studies have the potential for being more conclusive. Market integration involves increased interdependence among regions in the exchange of goods and factors. This interdependence becomes manifest when goods and factors flow on an interregional basis. Thus, market integration is more amenable to empirical investigation since, for example, the relative importance of interregional as opposed to intraregional flows can be measured.

In the only quantitative research of this type, Scott Eddie has measured the relative importance of Austria and Hungary as trading partners for one another. His results show a high degree of interdependence between the co-partners of the Monarchy from 1882 to 1913.[18] Austria remained Hungary's major trading partner with her share of Hungarian exports at roughly 73 per cent, while her share of Hungarian imports declined somewhat from 83 to 74 per cent. In addition, the dominant feature of the trade relationship remained the exchange of Hungarian foodstuffs (mainly grain) for Austrian manufactures (mainly textiles). The Austrian share in Hungarian imports of manufactures was stable at 86 per cent, while the Austrian share of Hungarian agricultural exports declined only slightly from roughly 65 to 61 per cent. Data on interregional trade flows between other sub-regions of the Monarchy are not available and their estimation would be a herculean task. Fortunately, alternative indicators of market integration can be constructed.

THE MEASUREMENT OF ECONOMIC INTEGRATION IN AUSTRIA-HUNGARY

Economists and economic historians have used several measures of regional price and income dispersion to examine various issues of regional economic development.[19] For my analysis, regional data on agricultural prices and interest rates were collected and several proxy indicators for income per capita were generated for the regions of Austria-Hungary. Dispersion measures were computed for these data to provide evidence on regional disparities in prices and incomes within the multinational state. The process of integration is examined by observing the time trends of these dispersion measures.

To measure the extent of integration in the product market three commodities were chosen: wheat, beef and wine. The coefficient of variation is an appropriate measure to chart the process of market integration. This statistic is computed from a sample of regional prices as the standard deviation divided by the mean. If the standard deviation falls relative to the mean price, i.e. if the coefficient of variation falls, regional price differences are narrowing. For each commodity a sample of cities was chosen and an unweighted coefficient of variation was computed for any year in which data were available for the entire sample. The coefficients were estimated for the combined sample of Austrian and Hungarian cities and for Austria and Hungary separately. Essentially the computed coefficients of variation form a time-series for each commodity. Each of these series was regressed on time with the resulting trend coefficients appearing in Table 14.1, lines 1-3. A negative sign indicates that regional prices converged, a positive sign indicates that the dispersion of regional prices increased over time. With the exception of beef prices in Hungary the trend coefficients for Austria and Hungary as a single unit and for each separately are negative and statistically significant. This trend toward regional price convergence is consistent with the hypothesis of increased market integration. The findings are also consistent with those of G. Szabad in the only other statistical analysis of regional price differences in the Monarchy.[20] Using five-year averages from 1831 to 1861 Szabad computed index numbers for wheat prices in various regions in the Monarchy. I have computed coefficients of variation using the means and standard deviations of these index numbers. The data for the Austrian provinces suggest a movement toward price convergence some time in the early 1840s. The coefficient of variation for regional prices was 0.27 in the 1830s, dropped to 0.169 in the early 1840s and to 0.125 in the late 1840s. It stabilised at roughly 0.15 in the 1850s, which is roughly comparable to coefficients computed from my data for the early 1860s.

TABLE 14.1 Indicators of economic integration: trend coefficients for measures of regional dispersion

Indicator	*Period*[a]	*Constant*	*Trend coefficient*	r^2
1. *Wheat prices*				
Austria (13 cities)	1862-1910	0.157	–0.0017 (0.0003)	.42*
Hungary (8 cities)	1872-1910	0.085	–0.0013 (0.0003)	.38*
Monarchy	1872-1910	0.154	–0.0017 (0.0005)	.30**
2. *Beef prices*				
Austria (11 cities)	1862-1909	0.221	–0.0029 (0.0003)	.63*
Hungary (8 cities)	1872-1909	0.119	+0.0014 (0.0005)	.18***
Monarchy	1872-1909	0.168	–0.0013 (0.0003)	.40*
3. *Wine prices*				
Austria (11 cities)	1862-1909	0.441	–0.0018 (0.0007)	.13**
Hungary (11 cities)	1872-1909	0.389	–0.0079 (0.0013)	.58*
Monarchy	1872-1909	0.623	–0.0084 (0.0013)	.61*
4. *Interest rates*[b]				
Austria (15 cities)	1872-1913	0.168	–0.0013 (0.0003)	.40*
Hungary (16 cities)	1875, 80-89	1.322	–0.0337 (0.0077)	.68**
Monarchy	1875, 80-89	1.609	–0.0447 (0.0113)	.64**

5. *Deposits*[c]				
Austria (15 regions)	1869-1913	0.921	−0.0061 (0.0005)	.75*
Hungary (8 regions)	1890-1909	0.694	−0.0096 (0.0011)	.82*
Monarchy	1890-1909	0.865	−0.0023 (0.0004)	.66*
6. *Physicians*[d]				
Austria (15 regions)	1864-1906	0.568	−0.0012 (0.0003)	.33*
Hungary (8 regions)	1892-1913	0.475	+0.0046 (0.0015)	.44**
Monarchy	1892-1906	0.579	−0.0023 (0.0009)	.35***

[a]Generally a complete time-series was not available for these indicators. For missing years see my working paper 'Growth and Integration'.
[b]Interest rate on bills of exchange discounted by savings banks.
[c]Deposits in savings banks.
[d]Physicians per 10,000 population

NOTES AND SOURCES
See text for details. The equations were generated from a regression of each dispersion measure on time. The asterisks indicate the level of statistical significance: * = 0.001, ** = 0.01, and *** = 0.05. Austrian data from *Statistisches Jahrbuch der österreichischen Monarchie, Osterreichische Statistik and Osterreichisches Statistische Mitteilungen, Statistisches Jahrbuch für Ungarn* and *Magyar statisztikai évkönyv*. For more details on the data and their sources see my working paper 'Growth and Integration'.

An analysis of the capital market produces similar conclusions. Elsewhere I have shown that in the late nineteenth-century Austrian provinces the process of financial integration was under way as indicated by the narrowing of interregional interest rate differences.[21] In testing for regional interest rate convergence the appropriate measure is not the coefficient of variation but the standard deviation of regional rates, a measure of absolute dispersion. Time-series were generated for the standard deviations of regional interest rates with the resulting trend coefficients reported in Table 14.1, line 4. For the Austrian data the sign of the trend variable is negative and statistically significant at the 1 per cent level, indicating a movement toward financial integration. The results are the same for Hungary and for the entire Monarchy at least for the short period 1875-89.

Conclusions on the extent of integration in the labour market must be highly impressionistic since no systematic analysis of the Austro-Hungarian labour market has been carried out. Some inferences are possible from data on interregional migration within Austria. Although a high percentage of the population emigrated abroad, interregional flows were substantial. The direction of these flows is consistent with neo-classical predictions. Provincial data for Austria in the immediate pre-World War period show a strong, positive correlation between rates of net migration and levels of income per capita. Provinces having the lowest levels of income per capita tended to have the highest rates of out-migration.[22]

Was the process of economic integration accompanied by a narrowing or widening of the substantial differences among regions in income per capita? Statistical data on regional growth at a disaggregated level are scarce. Except for the immediate pre-First World War years regional estimates of income per capita do not exist. Fortunately other types of socio-economic data are available. In particular three statistical indicators – savings bank deposits per capita, physicians per 10,000 population, and the rate of literacy – can be derived for the Monarchy on a regional basis. These indicators appear to be reasonable proxies for income per capita based on 1910/13 data.[23]

To test whether economic integration was accompanied by a reduction in regional differences in levels of economic development I have used the same methodology as in the previous section. The deposit data and the data on physicians are available annually for regional units in Austria and Hungary. Coefficients of variation were calculated to measure the degree of regional dispersion in each of these variables over time. The trend coefficients from the resulting time-series were computed and appear in Table 14.1, lines 5, 6. For the deposit indicator the equations show a statistically significant (at the 0.01 level) narrowing of regional differences. In the case of the physicians indicator the convergence trend is more uncertain. Regions converge significantly for Austria, diverge somewhat in Hungary and converge slightly for the Monarchy as a whole. Literacy rates are available only at census years, so a time-series showing regional dispersion has less meaning. But for the available years Table 14.2 shows a declining coefficient of variation giving further evidence that economic development was more rapid in less developed than in more developed regions.

Was this overall tendency toward integration and reduced regional disparities due to trends in only a few regions or did all regions participate in this process? This is an important question because much of nineteenth-century Habsburg history is written in terms of the relationships among large

TABLE 14.2 Coefficient of variation of literacy rates* in regions of Austria-Hungary

	Austria[a]	*Hungary*[b]	*Austria-Hungary*
1880	.502	N.A.	N.A.
1890	.423	.279	.421
1900	.325	.228	.326
1910	.252	.187	.258

*Measured as percentage of population over 6 years old, able to read and write.
[a]15 Provincial units.
[b]8 Regional units.

SOURCES
Osterreichische Statistik and *Statistisches Jahrbuch fur Ungarn.* See 'Growth and Integration' for details.

sub-units of the Monarchy. Such a focus is especially used for the period after the Compromise of 1867 which gave the most important sub-units, Austria and Hungary, some limited political autonomy.

To deal with this issue the disaggregated regions are combined into eight larger units, four each for Austria and Hungary. These regions are of approximately the same size in terms of population and are composed of sub-regions having contiguous boundaries. Since political forces within the multinational state increasingly coalesced along nationality lines, the regions have been constructed so that where possible each has one or two nationality groups with a population majority.[24] The regions of Austria are Alpine Austria with a substantial German majority (85.6 per cent), the Bohemian Crownlands with a Czech majority (62.5 per cent) and a German minority (34.9 per cent), the South Slav regions with no majority but substantial Serbo-Croat and Slovenian minorities (39.4 per cent and 33.2 per cent), and the eastern provinces of Galicia and Bucowina with a slight Polish majority (53.7 per cent) and a strong Ukrainian (Ruthenian) minority (40.0 per cent). The regions of Hungary are the lands bordering on Austria around Budapest with a Hungarian majority (76.4 per cent) and a small German minority (13.3 per cent), the northern regions with strong Slovak and Hungarian minorities (43.6 and 42.0 per cent), the eastern lands with sizeable Rumanian and Hungarian minorities (39.9 and 40.7 per cent) and Croatia-Slavonia with a Croat majority (62.5 per cent) and a large Serbian minority (24.6 per cent).

Using the same time-series data as above, mean values for each variable were derived for each of the eight regions. These values were then converted to index numbers where for each year the mean for all regions was 100.0. For any indicator the convergence of regional values toward 100.0 over time implies increased economic integration and/or reduced regional disparities. Overall the data indicate that the process of economic integration and regional convergence was a general phenomenon and not the result of trends in just a few regions.[25] For most of the indicators initially high-price regions and regions with high levels of economic development experienced a relative decline up to the First World War. Conversely low-price regions and regions with low levels of economic development experienced a rise in their relative position among the eight regions. In some cases this pattern is violated. However, there seems to be no evidence that specific regions were systematically excluded from the convergence process.

Direct estimates of growth rates in output per person give somewhat ambiguous results about the relative performance of large sub-units within the Habsburg economy. Estimates of growth in aggregate output per capita for the period 1865/70 to 1908/13 show virtually identical rates for Austria (1.8 per cent per annum) and Hungary (1.7 per cent per annum).[26] These estimates suggest that in relative terms Austria held her lead over her partner in the Dual Monarchy. On the other hand, estimates of growth in industrial output per capita indicate that Hungary was substantially cutting into Austria's industrial lead on the eve of the Monarchy's collapse. In the four decades after 1865/70 the rate of industrial growth per capita was 3.5 per cent per annum in Hungary and 2.6 per cent per annum in Austria.[27]

There have been few attempts to estimate growth rates for output in sub-regions of either Austria or Hungary. One exception is Anton Kausel, who has estimated the growth of Gross Domestic Product per person in the portion of the Monarchy later becoming the Republic of Austria.[28] His estimate of 2.2 per cent per annum from 1870 to 1913 should be compared to my estimate of 1.8 per cent for all of Austria. It suggests that the disparity between income per person in the more developed regions and the less developed regions may have increased rather than decreased over time.

A persistent, if not strong, tendency toward economic integration and regional income convergence is apparent in Austria-Hungary. Yet significant regional disparities still existed in the last pre-World War decade. How do they compare to those existing in other countries at this point in time?

The only directly comparable data on the dispersion of regional prices is for India. In the period 1906/10 the coefficient of variation of regional wheat prices in India averaged 0.177 while my data show a figure of 0.079 for Austria-Hungary.[29] Comparable studies of interregional interest rate differences exist for the United States and Japan. The coefficient of variation of regional interest rates in Austria averaged 0.119 over the period 1906/10, which compares favourably with the figures for Japan (0.145) and for the United States (0.140).[30] The regional dispersion of income per capita can be computed for the provinces of Austria and then compared to similar measures which are available for other countries. Using 1910/13 data the coefficient of variation of regional income per capita in Austria was 0.309, which is lower than that for Italy (0.313 as late as 1928) and Sweden (0.440 in 1920) but higher than that for Germany (0.226 in 1913).[31] The Austrian figure was roughly the same as that of the United States (0.299 using 1900 state data and 0.330 using 1900 regional data). Regional dispersion of income per capita in Austria also falls in between two separate measures of dispersion in 1913 using all of Europe as the geographic unit and a sample of countries as the individual regional units. The 0.309 figure for Austria is higher than a computed coefficient of 0.230 based on Maddison's estimates of output per head in 12 European countries but is lower than Bairoch's computed coefficient of variation, 0.433, for a sample of 19 European countries.[32]

The greater degree of regional dispersion in Austria than in Germany is more dramatic if regional data on physicians per capita are utilised. The coefficient of variation computed for this indicator is only 0.273 for the regions of Prussia in 1903 but 0.503 for Austria and 0.561 for the Monarchy as a whole in 1906.[33] A comparison using other indicators, however, makes this difference less pronounced. For Prussia the coefficient of variation of income tax collected per person is 0.546 for the regions of Prussia in 1910.[34] In contrast, a relatively low level of regional dispersion in Austria-Hungary is shown for the coefficient of variation of literacy rates (0.258 in 1910). These data for Prussia and the Habsburg Monarchy suggest the difficulties in making international comparisons of regional disparities. Much depends on the indicators chosen and on the precise nature of the data used to measure these indicators. Yet on balance the results seem to suggest that by 1913 the degree of economic unity and regional convergence displayed by Austria-Hungary was comparable to that attained by several of her contemporaries.

SUMMARY

The time-series data on regional differences within Austria-Hungary show trends toward increased economic integration and reduced regional income inequalities. The evidence for this conclusion is not overwhelming but strong enough to argue against the opposite conclusion. There is no systematic tendency toward economic separation or increased inequality among the regions of the Habsburg Monarchy.

This finding is significant in two respects. First, from a theoretical point of view one might have expected the regions of the Monarchy to have experienced a widening and not a narrowing of differences. The Monarchy appears to have begun the process of modern economic growth under conditions of a rather sharp regional dualism which could have fostered the operation of Myrdal's model of cumulative causation. Either the initial differences between west and east were not sharp enough to produce Myrdal's backwash effects or these effects were over by mid-century. In any case from the 1860s and 1870s the data show no tendency toward regional divergence. The Monarchy entered the most critical phase of its long history with an increasingly integrated economy and declining regional inequalities.

Second, the Habsburg experience is instructive from the standpoint of economic policy. Most observers view a reduction of income inequalities as a prerequisite for political harmony among regions and nations. The case of Austria-Hungary casts doubt on this assumption since the Monarchy collapsed after the First World War. The dramatic collapse of the Monarchy was the end-result of a long, dynamic process. The significance of my findings is that this process of political disintegration occurred within the context of a growing, increasingly unified economic structure. The economic integration of the regions of Austria-Hungary was apparently insufficient to produce political harmony within the multinational state.

Was the Habsburg Monarchy unique in her failure to forge a political system consistent with the dynamic forces of modern economic growth? Or is this task inherently difficult for all multinational political structures? If the political tensions arising from persistent regional inequalities are to be reduced, these questions deserve serious study.

NOTES

[1]For example, theoretical and empirical issues of regional economic development are discussed within the context of present day Europe and the United States in A. J. Brown and E. M. Burrows, *Regional Economic Problems: Comparative Experiences in Some Market Economies* (London, 1977). See also the articles in 'Problems of Regional Economic Development', *The American Economic Review,* 68 (1978) pp. 99-117, and 'Strangers at the Feast: A Survey of the Development Regions of the EEC', *The Economist,* 25 January, 1975.

[2]The terms Habsburg Monarchy, Austria-Hungary and Austro-Hungarian Empire are used interchangeably to refer to the entire territory which fell under Habsburg rule until the First World War.

[3]For a useful compendium of the conflicting opinion on the viability of the Habsburg Monarchy see Harold J. Gordon and Nancy M. Gordon (eds.), *The Austrian Empire: Abortive Federation?* (Lexington, MA, 1974).

[4]This distinction is made by Richard Cooper in his 'Worldwide versus Regional Integration: Is There an Optimum Size of an Integrated Area?' in Fritz Machlup, ed., *Economic Integration: Worldwide, Regional, Sectoral* (London, 1976) pp. 42-3, and by Fritz Machlup in his *A History of Thought on Economic Integration* (New York, 1977) pp. 16-24.

[5]These models are summarised in Harry Richardson, *Regional Economic Growth Theory* (New York, 1973) pp. 22-9.

[6]These models are also summarised in Richardson, op. cit., pp. 29-34.

[7]Gunnar Myrdal, *Economic Theory and Underdeveloped Regions* (London, 1957) p. 27.

[8]Jeffrey Williamson, 'Regional Inequality and the Process of National Development: A Description of the Patterns'. *Economic Development and Cultural Change,* XIII (1965) 3-10.

[9]Oscar Jaszi, *The Dissolution of the Habsburg Monarchy* (Chicago: University of Chicago Press, 1961) pp. 210 and 212.

[10]Nachum Gross, 'The Industrial Revolution in the Habsburg Monarchy, 1870-1914', in Carlo Cipolla, ed., *The Fontana Economic History of Europe,* IV, 1 (London, 1973) pp. 241-2. The negative aspects of economic forces in Habsburg unity is stressed by other scholars. See, for example, Krisztina Fink, 'Die österreichisch-ungarische Monarchie als Wirtschaftsgemeinschaft' in *Südosteuropa-Schriften,* IX (1968) p. 2; Jurij Krizek, 'Beitrag zur Geschichte der Entstehung und des Einflusses des Finanzkapitals in der Habsburgermonarchie in der Jahren 1900-1914', in *Die Frage der Finanzkapitals in der österreichisch-ungarischen Monarchie 1900-1918* (Bucharest, 1965), pp. 5-52; and Hans Rosenberg, *Grosse Depression und Bismarckzeit* (Berlin, 1967) pp. 227-52.

[11]Friedrich Hertz, *Economic Problem of the Danubian States* (London, 1947) pp. 41, 49-51.

[12]William Ashworth, 'Typologies and Evidence: Has Nineteenth-Century Europe a Guide to Economic Growth?', *Economic History Review,* 2nd ser., XXX (1977) 79. The positive role of economic forces is also emphasised by Heinrich Benedikt, *Die wirtschaftliche Entwicklung in der Franz-Joseph-Zeit* (Vienna, 1958); William A. Jenks, 'Economics, Constitutionalism, Administrative Class Structure', *Austrian History Yearbook,* III, 1 (1967) 46; and Andrew Whiteside, 'The Germans as an Integrative Force in Imperial Austria: The Dilemma of Dominance', *Austrian History Yearbook,* III, 1 (1967) 168. Others have taken a more intermediate position. See Eduard März, 'Einige Besonderheiten in der Entwicklung der österreichischen Volkswirtschaft in 19. Jahrhundert', *Sozialwissenschaftliche Annalen,* I (1977) 87-107; Péter Hanák, 'Hungary in the Austro-Hungarian Monarchy', *Austrian History Yearbook,* III, 1 (1967) 281-4, 299-302, and György Ranki, 'Comments', *Austrian History Yearbook,* III (1967) 68.

[13]On early industrialisation in the Alpine provinces see Ferdinand Tremel, *Wirtschafts-*

und Sozialgeschichte Osterreichs (Vienna, 1969) pp. 230-80. For the Czech Crownlands see Herman Freudenberger, 'Industrialisation in Bohemia and Moravia in the Eighteenth Century', *Journal of Central European Affairs,* XIX (1960) 347-56, and Arnost Klima, 'Industrial Development in Bohemia, 1648-1781', *Past and Present,* XI (1957) 87-99.

[14] A discussion of this point and the relevant sources are in my working paper 'Growth and Integration', pp. 2-3.

[15] For a discussion of the key events leading up to the Customs Union see Fink, *Wirtschaftsgemeinschaft.* Thomas Huertas has measured the actual gains from the removal of the customs barrier between Austria and Hungary and found them to be minimal. See his *Economic Policy and Economic Growth in a Multinational Setting* (New York, 1977) pp. 18-25.

[16] These obstacles are described in Gross, *The Industrial Revolution,* pp. 237-8.

[17] George Macesich, 'Theory of Economic Integration and Experience of the Balkan and Danubian Countries Before 1914', *Florida State University Slavic Papers,* I (1967) p. 13.

[18] Scott Eddie, 'The Terms and Patterns of Hungarian Foreign Trade', *Journal of Economic History,* XXXVII (1977) 334-6 and 350-1.

[19] Several of these studies are discussed below.

[20] György Szabad, 'Das Anwachsen der Ausgleichstendenenz der Produktenpreise in Habsburgerreich um die Mitte des 19. Jahrhunderts', in V. Sandor and P. Hanák (eds), *Studien zur Geschichte der österreichischungarischen Monarchie* (Budapest, 1961) pp. 213-37.

[21] See my 'Financial Integration in Late Nineteenth-Century Austria', *Journal of Economic History,* XXXVII (1977) 890-910.

[22] On this point see my 'Growth and Integration', footnote 36.

[23] Using provincial data regressions of each of these variables on income per capita show a positive relationship and the following r^2 all significant at the 0.01 level or lower: literacy, $r^2 = 0.77$; savings deposits per capita, $r^2 = 0.51$; and physicians per 10,000 population, $r^2 = 0.66$.

[24] Compiled from 1910 data in *Osterreichisches Statistisches Handbuch,* 31, Table B.4, and *Statistisches Jahrbuch für Ungarn,* pp. 11-12, 22-5.

[25] The results appear in detail in my 'Growth and Integration', Table 4.

[26] Austrian estimate from my 'Stagnation and Take-Off in Austria, 1873-1913', *Economic History Review,* 2nd ser., XXVII (1974) 81, and my 'The Great Depression and Austrian Growth After 1873', *Economic History Review,* 2nd ser., XXXI (1978) p. 293. Hungarian estimate from Lászlo Katus, 'Economic Growth in Hungary During the Age of Dualism (1867-1913)', in E. Pamlényi (ed.), *Social-Economic Researches on the History of East-Central Europe* (Budapest, 1970), Table 49.

[27] For Austria the estimate is based on Richard Rudolph, *Banking and Industrialization in Austria-Hungary* (New York, 1976) p. 11, and his 'The Pattern of Austrian Industrial Growth from the Eighteenth to the Early Twentieth Century', *Austrian History Yearbook,* XI (1975), Table 1. For Hungary the estimates are from Katus, 'Economic Growth', pp. 5-57 (see Note 26, above).

[28] My thanks to Dr Kausel for transmitting this estimate in private correspondence. Toussaint Hocevar cites estimates of NNP per head in Slovenia for 1880 and 1913 made by Ivo Vinski in a 1959 study. See Hocevar's *The Structure of the Slovenian Economy (1848-1963)* (New York, 1965). The 1880 estimate was derived simply by assuming that the Slovenian economy grew from 1880 to 1913 at the same rate as Germany (1.4 per cent) so the figure cannot be taken seriously.

[29] The data for India are from John Hurd, 'Railways and the Expansion of Markets in India, 1861-1921', *Exploration in Economic History,* XII (1975) 263-88, Appendix 7.

[30] For Japan see Kenneth Lewis and Kozo Yamamura, 'Industrialization and Inter-

regional Interest Rate Structure, The Japanese Case: 1889-1925', *Explorations in Economic History*, VIII (1971), Appendix A; and for the United States see Gene Smiley, 'Interest Rate Movement in the United States, 1888-1913', *Journal of Economic History*, XXXV (1975), Tables A-5 and A-7.

[31] Austrian provincial income per capita estimates from David F. Good, 'Financial Institutions and Economic Growth: The Evidence from Pre-1914 Austria' (PhD dissertation, University of Pennsylvania, 1972), Table D-2. Other data from Williamson, 'Regional Inequality', Table 4, pp. 25-6.

[32] The data appear in Angus Maddison, 'Phases of Capitalist Development', *Banca Nazionale del Lavoro*, 121 (1977) p. 126, and in Paul Bairoch, 'Europe's Gross National Product: 1800-1975', *Journal of European Economic History*, 5 (1976) p. 287.

[33] Prussian data from Helmut Hesse, 'Die Entwicklung der regionalen Einkommens-differnzen in Wachstumsprosess der deutschen Wirtschaft', in Wolfram Fisher (ed.), *Beiträge zu Wirtschaftswachstum und Wirtschaftsstruktur im 16. und 19. Jahrhundert* (Berlin, 1971).

[34] Prussian data from Hesse, 'Einkommensdiffernzen', Table 2, p. 276.

15 The Process of Industrialisation in General and the Process of Industrialisation in Italy: Some Suggestions, Problems and Questions

Giorgio Mori

1. In 1861 Italy was united under the House of Savoy as a result of the war which had been fought against Austria in 1859 in alliance with Napoleon III and of the expedition of Garibaldi and his Thousand volunteers to the South. This was the event which realised the hopes of the small groupings of the urban and intellectual petty bourgeoisie, who had at the end been drawn into the dispassionate but highly effective political and military operation energetically carried through by the firm and victorious alliance created and led by Cavour, in which the land-owning classes had assumed a hegemonic position. Their interests were expressed, however, in a great variety of ways, and they were in particular increasingly drawn towards commercial and financial activities.

The new state covered an area of 250,000 km^2 with some 22 million inhabitants (ranking tenth in Europe in the first respect, and fifth in the second). There were more than 15 cities with over 50,000 inhabitants (totalling 1,900,000); six were larger than 100,000 (Turin, Milan, Bologna, Genoa, Palermo and Naples – the biggest of all with 439,000). The communications network on the peninsula was not the most backward on the continent, with 2000 km of railways, 85,000 km of roads (although the majority were in a terrible state), 1032 post offices, 10,000 km of telegraph wires, a merchant navy of some 644,000 tons (only five per cent of which was steam-powered, however). Foreign trade was valued at 65 lire per head of the population (against 116 lire in France, 325 lire in Great Britain, and only 25 lire in Russia), although exports (35 per cent of which were made up of raw and worked silk) accounted for only two-thirds of the value of imports. The shortfall of income over expenditure in the State's annual budget was very nearly the same percentage.[1]

Agriculture was still far and away the most productive sector of the economy, but even here it was only in certain northern areas that it was organised in such a way as to resemble the advanced zones of Central and Northern Europe (e.g. the small peasant farmers of Piedmont and the large capitalist leasehold farms of the Po Valley). Throughout the rest of the peninsula, technological stagnation and very low levels of production and essentially pre-capitalist modes of production (e.g. sharecropping tenures such as *mezzadria,* short leases encouraging soil exhaustion and preventing improvements etc.) survived unchanged.

In the secondary sector, which consisted overwhelmingly of artisan activities and domestic service, and in which there was as yet very little differentiation from agriculture, the new form of industrial production which had been born of the Industrial Revolution, and which united in the factory both the new productive machinery and the wage-earning labour force, had made its appearance.[2] The principal field in which these precocious industrial nuclei were to be found was, as in the case of the take-off stages in the industrial development of other countries, the production of consumer goods, especially textiles. But the realities of the industrial preparedness of the new state are illustrated quite unambiguously by the following comparative figures:

	Cotton spindles	*Pig iron output*	*Steam engines*
England	N.30,387,000	3,772,000 tons	700,000 h.p.
France	5,500,000	967,000	178,000
Italy	450,000 (in 1867)	27,000	54,000 (in 1866)[3]

The table shows clearly that while Italy was experiencing the phase of *proto-industrialisation*[4] and was not therefore part of that material backwardness and social and economic immobility which still gripped entire continents, nor was she as yet part of that large area of Europe within which the Industrial Revolution had opened out and become established.

Only sixty years later, by the time of the close of the 1914-18 War, Italy had become part of that advanced area, and with full recognition. Article 393 of the Versailles Treaty included Italy as one of the eight most industrialised nations of the world, and this was no more than the recognition of fact. Is it possible to consider in any other way a state which held sixth position in the world for the production of steel, fifth for that of cement, sulphuric acid, automobiles and hydro-electric power, fourth for superphosphates and artificial textile fibres, not to mention fifth and seventh places respectively for the numbers of mechanical spindles and looms in her cotton industry, together with impressive plants in other sectors? In addition, both the size and capital value of business enterprises had reached impressive degrees of concentration, and compared favourably with those of the most advanced nations. For some time there had also been a general movement towards an osmotic relationship between banks and industry of major importance, and at the same time both the factory owners and the workers had been forming highly politicised, aggressive and powerful class unions.[5]

This would certainly not have caused any surprise to those in the late nineteenth century like Alfred Marshall, and even in a certain sense Karl

Marx, who had taken it for granted that this would be, albeit at varying paces and by different paths, the common fate of mankind, like it or not. But now we are better aware that history in fact followed a number of quite separate paths. In particular, it is clear that there came into being at a certain moment an invisible, but no less insurmountable, barrier in the path of aspirant 'newcomers', and that there were very few countries, other than the eight indicated in the Treaty of Versailles, which proved capable of fulfilling the expectations of the nineteenth-century observers.

The Italian case therefore provides the unusual example of a race to catch up which was successful, the example of a country which escaped from the no-man's land between the countries in which industrial growth was self-sustaining and 'complete', on one hand, and the vast strata of backwardness on the other, to which the impetuous industrial developments of the early nineteenth century had relegated the peninsula.

2. Sidney Pollard took up and revived an issue first identified by Schumpeter when he claimed some time ago that the industrial 'plants' which were nourished in the different European states all had the same roots, and that therefore the industrialisation of the continent should be understood and studied as a single and unified phenomenon.[6] We are entirely in agreement with such a line of interpretation, and as far as Italy is concerned one can go even further. Some forty years after unification, one of Italy's most eminent thinkers, Antonio Labriola, in reflecting on the weak state of the country stated: '. . . Above all else it is in direct proportion to the differences which exist between conditions in Italy and those in other countries; it is this which measures effectively what Italy is and might become in face of the great movements of "active" history and it is this which provides an evaluation of the nation's place within what is now the world of the ruling peoples. . . .' This is a view which perfectly fits the process of industrialisation at that time occurring on the peninsula, and it was this that we had in mind when claiming that it was possible to go beyond Sidney Pollard's statement. The methodological coherence and value of the same concept has in other contexts been noted independently first by Braudel in *La Mediterranee* and then by Perroux and by a group of English and American economists.[7] In fact, it would be difficult to deny that the industrial development of the area which shortly after became the Kingdom of Italy had encountered grave difficulties and obstacles in its slow and tormented phase of take-off, which can be fixed in the period of French occupation at the start of the century,[8] due to the shifts in the 'world market' which arose from, and were increased by, the application of Ricardo's theorem of comparative costs by the industrial powers. As a result of these shifts, the Italian regional states, and after them the national state, saw themselves forced into a bond of dependent reciprocity with the industrial states.[9] More controversial, although in our view not unduly so, is the argument that thanks once again to another shift of the 'world market' in what Lenin called the 'latest stage' of capitalism, the imperialist phase, Italy's industrial development received

a major stimulus, in the 'completion of the process'.[10] This was the founding of the new mixed banks, undertaken by and large by leading financial interests in the German Reich. The new banks, the *Banca Commerciale* and the *Credito Italiano*, saw the creation of a coke-based steel industry, of the massive hydro-electric power industry, and later gave essential aid to the major concerns in other decisive industrial sectors (among them Fiat and Montecatini). To take up not entirely by chance a phrase used by Gerschenkron in his masterly paper at the Aix-en-Provence Congress, can one ask whether it is appropriate to see Italian industrialisation as a process of 'derived industrialisation', let loose by the mighty 'invisible hand of the world market, the nerve centres of which were Labriola's 'ruling peoples', Braudel's states of major size and power, and Perroux's 'independent nations'?[11] *In looking at Italy are we not in fact confronted with the case of a pursuit which was undertaken, and which succeeded, due to the exogenous propulsion which first pushed in the wrong direction, but which subsequently made it possible for the Italian economy to enter into the right orbit? In certain respects, and in very general terms only, the answer is yes.*

We must also pay careful attention, however, to another phenomenon which is to our mind beyond doubt, and that is the visible parallelism between the formation of a market which stretched beyond Europe to embrace the world, riding the crest of the most advanced processes of industrialisation, and the birth and the gradual strengthening of the nation states and their governmental apparatus. The latter, of course, had the consequence of introducing, or at the very least of aggravating, important degrees of separateness and, more often than not, conflict amongst the industrialised nations, between those which were not and still are not industrialised, between the two groups and within the two groups, now on an individual basis, now on a collective basis. For the same reasons, the same problems appeared within the national groups of the ruling classes both within and outside Europe. Only deep and heartfelt devotion to his own benign understanding of the world, therefore, could have led a man like Karl Polanyi to refer to the century between 1815 and 1914 as 'the Hundred Years Peace'.[12] Even if it means falling back on a problematic generalisation, it is important to draw attention to the dynamic contradiction which existed between the tendency toward *economic internationalisation,* on the one hand, and the *political fragmentation* of the planet on the other. Certainly this is an issue which is far from clearly or precisely expressed, but, if we accept that it contains a degree of truth, it merits a more serious discussion of the problem of the relationship between politics and economics. In particular, given that the state represents the highest and most concentrated form of political activity, we must examine the political options adopted at a strategic level in each country confronted by the onset of industrialisation. This in turn must involve the decisions, tendencies, and values of the local ruling classes, and the nature of the divisions and conflicts among them; and equally important, if not more so, the phenomenon of class struggle, once it has attained a mass character, must also be taken into account. If we agree with Gerschenkron that '. . . simple availability of wealth will be helpful for industrialisation only if it is assembled in the hands of the peoples who are . . . willing to invest it in industrial ventures themselves . . .' and that '. . . apprehensions on the part of the landowning classes lest industrial development should deprive them of their position of pre-eminence within the community . . .' might constitute an insuperable barrier to this, what we have said above takes on an even greater heuristic significance in so far as Italy is concerned.[13] Let us look again at what Labriola had to say: '. . . I use the terms *active* and *passive* as examples of the theoretical extremes of comparative value, which are established through . . . a multitude of transactions. No one I think could deny that Italy was in a certain historical sense *active* even in the period in which national unification was being prepared.'[14] There can be little doubt that the forces, interests and programmes which arose from and were bound together by the complementary economic conditions of the peninsula, on one hand, and by the economic weaknesses and by the social groups which dominated the pre-unitary states on the other – and which then became the same interests, forces and programmes of the socio-political alliance which achieved national unification – *operated* with exceptional energy, intelligence and realism. The effect of this was that within the value system and culture that came into being as a result, and also in practice, a single general notion prevailed which proved binding in the long term and which was in total harmony with a dependent and subordinate development of the national economy. What might from outside appear to have been essentially *passive* characteristics, resulting from unavoidable necessities, were in fact *also* the product of *active* tendencies and desires.

In our view this general line had three principal features: a foreign trade policy which was dominated by the extreme free-trade ideas of the commercial and financial groups, and in particular by the land-owners who were directly involved in the highly profitable export of raw and worked silk (which until the end of the century continued to account for 30-35 per cent of all exports), and which found their fullest expression in the commercial treaty of 1863 with France; a willingness to allow massive and continuous exports of the country's natural resources – iron ores, mercury, lead, zinc, sulphur (over which Italy enjoyed a natural world monopoly up to 1890)[15] to take place; an unyielding defence of the relations of production in the countryside which we have mentioned, which prevented any strengthening of the internal market, itself the indispensable basis for consolidating a developing industrial structure.

The ways in which the unified state – which Rosario Romeo has rightly described as 'the most important event in our history in the nineteenth century',[16] and this is equally true from the point of view of economic development – came into being did not prevent certain social groups within the country remaining *actives*, and amongst them the industrialists in particular, who could not fully identify their interests with the general objectives which were becoming established. The larger market now in theory available, the defeat of the traditional ruling forces (the former sovereigns, the nobility, the Church), together with the incomparably greater material opportunities of the new state and the obvious uncertainties of the political leadership, all served to keep the industrialists in touch with events and encouraged them to work patiently and constructively. This is shown by the tone of certain parliamentary debates, by the national industrial survey conducted in 1872, by the struggle for a more rigid tariff policy which culminated in the new tariffs of 1878 and 1887, and by the growing public interest in and sympathy for the industrialists' difficulties. It is revealed even more fully by the continuous, albeit slow and lurching, growth in the country's industrial plant. Although this experienced periods of great difficulty and even crisis, it must also be remembered that it was the result of a political and social struggle the outcome of which remained unpredictable for a considerable time. In any case, this was the period which saw the founding of a whole series of new vast industrial concerns, the Terni steel works, the Pattison iron foundry, the Orlando shipyards, Moncenisio, Riva, the Armstrong shipyards, the Voltri steelworks, the Franco Tosi engineering works, the Cirio and Peroni food and drink industries, the Montecatini mineral industries, the Pirelli rubber industry, the Balzaretti and Modigliani glassworks and the De Angeli Frua and the National Hemp and Linen Manufacturers in textiles (which after 1866 included the Rossi and Marzotto woollen industries too), and Italcementi. The number of spindles in the cotton industry exceeded 1.5 million, the total factory power availability reached 400,000 h.p., the capital assets of public companies rose from 200 million lire in 1872 to over 500 millions in 1891, and even the banks were drawn in some measure into the financing of industrial ventures.[17] For the reasons described above a less sullen attitude on the part of the state began to emerge – although neither the extent nor the effects of this should be exaggerated – but also, and above all, an opportunity for the industrialists, which they defended to the very last, to press down on the cost of labour to the loss of a dispersed working class which was still weak and disorganised despite the few although endemic strikes and disruptions: Stefano Merli's recent important study provides valuable evidence of this entire process.[18]

The profound crisis which struck the country in the early 1890s seemed to throw open to doubt even these achievements when stability and the liberal regime returned. It should be noted that the country's industry would not have come out of that crisis into the phase of massive growth which was to change radically both its appearance and structure, had it not been for the drastic reorientation which was brought about by the influx of capital, techniques and entrepreneurial leadership from Germany. The process was then politically rationalised in the years generally referred to as 'the Giolittian age' (the years between the beginning of the twentieth century and the First World War).

Was this then the consequence of a parallelogram of endogenous and exogenous forces which, at a certain juncture, made it possible for the

barriers to be broken down and for Italy to move into the industrialised zone? In many respects, and as a second-degree generalisation, the answer is yes.

3. As we have already pointed out, industrialisation in Italy can be said to have been achieved about 1920. But that is also the period which coincides with the collapse of the liberal regime and the Fascist seizure of power. The debate on the relationship between industrialisation and the victory of Fascism is still one that is very open, and little general agreement has so far been reached. The problem is that the debates have not yet been accompanied by adequate critical research and analysis. The result is that opposing interpretations, many of which are extremely lucid in their own terms, and the general ideological assumptions from which they derive, tend to clash head on to little useful purpose. This means that even today the debate tends to be polarised round two extreme positions established quite some time ago, even though the originals may have been altered and refined in one way or another. The first position takes Fascism to be 'the means by which the agrarian elite attempted to hold back the speed with which industrialisation was advancing, and to control the ways in which it developed', while the second is based on the contrary conviction that Fascism was the functional result of 'the needs of productive capital, and especially those of heavy industry'.[19]

Let us try to identify some of the features of the problem on which there is a certain degree of agreement: (*a*) as in the case of national unification, Fascism provides a further example of a *political* event which was to have an enormous influence on the country's industrial development and which accentuated the originality of the turn which it was to take; (*b*) the coincidence between the moment in which the full completion of the process of industrialisation was achieved and the Fascist victory is, if we are not mistaken, unique in the process of national industrialisation. Starting from these assumptions, we should again draw attention to the fact that, in our view, the completion of the process of industrialisation took place in Italy within a very short time-span, roughly between the turn of the century and 1920. It is well known that it was during this period that the following industries came into being: coke-based steel production, hydro-electric power production (and the geothermal energy industry, which was unique in the world), the motor car industry (Fiat and others), the aeronautical industry (Caproni), the Solvay soda, the chlorine, synthetic ammonia, dyes and intermediate colour industries. Similarly there was expansion in the consumer goods industries, and the development of the artificial textile fibre industry was accompanied by an increase in the number of cotton spindles from 2 to 4½ million, and from 200,000 to 500,000 in the case of wool. The number of sugar factories rose from 28 to 55; breweries from a mere handful to some 89, and the dairy industry was rapidly modernised. Table 15.1 gives an impression of the enormous leap in production which accompanied this structural step forward.

TABLE 15.1

Year	Electricity mill. kWh	Steel tons	Chloric acid tons	Sulphuric acid tons	Cotton yarn tons	Cement tons	Sugar tons	Beer hl.
1898	100	108,501	7,251	139,271	118,000	100,000	5,973	132,696
1920	4,690	773,761	17,425	563,200	148,220	1,200,000	124,392	1,157,024[20]

Clearly the effects of a leap of this sort could not be confined within the boundaries of the factories alone nor even within their boardrooms.[21] To trace the full direct and indirect consequences of this change would however involve recounting the entire history of the country in these twenty years. For our present purposes it is enough to bear in mind that from the background of an unmistakable political and cultural movement which tended to exalt nationalist sentiments, and which drew substance from the development of a political alliance which was both hostile to Giolitti and favourable towards the Entente powers, emerged a demand for what one of the nationalist leaders described as 'economic independence' – in other words, independence from the German economy (and from the banks which were held to be its tools). This tendency is best known for the inflammatory and scandalous journalistic features which it assumed, rather than for the realities which lay behind it. But there can be little doubt that while it grew in certain branches of heavy industry which were not connected with the 'mixed banks' – Ansaldo provides a good example of this – there is also evidence that such views were also held by men who were connected with the 'mixed banks'.[2] On one hand, such views were not uninfluential in bringing about the declaration of war on the central Empires, but they also served to sanction a split within the industrial and banking ruling group over the strategy and management of the country's economic development. In the long run this also serves to aggravate even further the political and social divisions within the country resulting from the declaration of war, which were made all the deeper by the existence of the mass socialist and Catholic opposition.

It was not possible to bring about any reconstitution of the ruling group either during the four years of war or after the victory. For complex reasons rooted in the need to convert and reconvert twice within a short space of time the country's productive capacity, in the heated open controversy over who should bear the material costs of the war, which had been increased by the heavy burden of war debts, and in the unprecedented militancy of the working classes whose forces, albeit divided and uncertain, were growing from moment to moment, the clash of interests, the class struggle, and the political battle group became embittered as never before. It is for this reason that we are more inclined to see the rise of Fascism as a means of 'reconstituting from above' the unity of the dominant classes, rather than as a 'preventive counter-revolution'.

As we have already said, what we are concerned with at present is the way in which the changes in the political regime were related to the development of the country's industrialisation. Let us pause to consider the quantitative aspects of (*a*) structural evolution, and (*b*) productive development, in Table 15.2.

TABLE 15.2

(a)	*1*	*2*	*3*	*4*	*5*	*6*	*7*	*8*
1927	3,391,310	26.5%	20.6%	3,257,466	43.39%	33.40%	12,500 (1922)	24.96%
1937	4,360,054	31.4%	24.72%	6,154,639	51.54%	44.22%	37,720	68.31%

1. Total numbers employed in industry; 2. Percentage of industrial employees in concerns with over 250 employees; 3. Percentage of employees in iron and steel, chemicals and engineering alone; 4. Total industrial horsepower; 5. Percentage of the total energy supply in concerns employing more than 250; 6. Percentage of energy supply (hp) in metallurgical, chemical and engineering industry; 7. Total capital of manufacturing joint-stock companies (in thousand million lire); 8. Companies with over 50 millions of lire in share capital as a percentage of column 7.

(b)	*1*	*2*	*3*	*4*	*5*	*6*	*7*	*8*	*9*	*10*	*11*	*12*
1923	5,610,000	1,142	26.5	993	37	164	2,300	319	1,465	4.8	229	0.9
1939	18,417,000	2,283	65.8	2,055	69	192	5,024	441	830	53.6	531	518

The figures are in thousands of tons except where otherwise indicated:
1. electrical energy (1000 kW); 2. steel; 3. chloric acid; 4. sulphuric acid; 5. motor cars (N.); 6. cotton yarn; 7. cement; 8. sugar; 9. beer (1000 hl); 10. artificial textile fibres; 11. paper and cardboard; 12. petrol.

The value of annual industrial production was calculated at the time of the industrial census for 1937-40 to be about 150 thousand million lire (about one-third of the English figure for 1935), and shortly after it was shown that in the principal industrial sectors decisive shares were held by only a very limited number of companies.[23]

Figures of this sort indicate that it is very difficult to distinguish Italy's industrial development from that of other countries. However, the most recent studies on the Italian economy in the Fascist period have in the first place tended to reject conclusions of this nature;[24] and, secondly, instead of treating 'the Fascist economy system' as an 'alternative' – a 'third way' – to capitalism and socialism, they have been more concerned to reopen the whole issue. Let us first consider the government's economic policies. Although the reasons for the continuing subordination to foreign economies remained unchanged (in fact the burden of war debts together with the strengthening of the nation's industrial capacity, which had the result of increasing the need for raw materials and supplies of energy, may well have served to make this dependence even greater), and although the identities had changed (in that the USA had become Italy's principal creditor and partner in place of Germany), the impression given by recent studies is that immediately after the seizure of power the Fascist government embarked on a series of measures which were designed to reduce that dependence. Examples of this are the cancellation of the Sinclair franchise for prospecting and exploiting combustible fuels in the Italian subsoil, and the later rejection of the Ford proposal to establish a motor car factory in Italy, and then the deflationary tendency which culminated in the '*quota 90*' and the 'battle for grain', together with the centralisation of the banking system.

A careful examination of the development of the Italian industrial system in the first ten years of Fascist rule gives the same impression. The available sources, however, mean that it is virtually impossible to attempt anything more than a theoretical assessment of the distribution of investments and their movements over time, and the difficulties are even greater when it comes to differentiating between specific industrial sectors. But if we take as a crude indicator the capital of the joint stock companies – which according to estimates in the 1930s held about 40 per cent of the country's industrial patrimony – we can devise Table 15.3 showing the percentage distribution of this capital, following the current statistical groups, in the period between 1916 and 1931.[25]

TABLE 15.3

Industry	*1916*	*1920*	*1923*	*1926*	*1929*	*1931*
Manufacturing	72.33	73.79	68.56	63.61	59.35	54.60
Mining	5.69	6.39	7.85	7.43	6.93	6.80
Building	3.17	3.06	4.24	4.05	4.65	5.03
Electricity	18.81	16.76	19.35	24.91	29.07	33.57
	100	100	100	100	100	100

There is hardly any need to comment, and a comparison of the development of the manufacturing and electrical sectors shows the solid and massive growth of the latter during the period in question. Between 1923 and 1931, the electrical industry absorbed about 50 per cent of the 18 thousand million lire increase in the country's joint-stock capital. Was it the case that the demand for 'economic independence' which had grown popular before the war was then taken up subsequently – and at once, rather than in the 1930s – in the shape of a strategy of creating independent energy resources? (Between 1923 and 1939 electrical power rose from 32.6 per cent to 48.6 per cent of the total energy consumption.)[26] More research is needed, but there is already sufficient evidence to justify the question, and indeed another. Was there any significant connection between the change in pattern and the trend towards investment in electrical energy, which the table shows to have taken place between *1920* and *1923,* and the advent of a regime which was by nature likely to be sympathetic to such a strategy?

Despite the support of American finance – and it should be noted that, as the Sinclair and Ford affairs demonstrated, the attitude towards finance was different from that towards industry – the effort was immense. It was made all the more difficult by the struggle which took place again on this issue (although it is doubtful whether it had ever really died down) between the overwhelmingly powerful industrial and banking groups who were involved up to the hilt in the development of the electrical power industry – the *Banca Commerciale Italiana* and the *Credito Italiano-Edison* group (whose policy was quite different from that of the *Confindustria*).

It is probably to this effort and to the struggles which surrounded it, as well as to the consequences of the world slump and the series of gambles taken by bankers and entrepreneurs, that we should look to discover the origins of the massive operation which in 1933 led to the creation of *IRI*, and the resulting transfer into state ownership of a large number of concerns previously tied to the mixed banks, and later of the banks themselves. Thereafter in no other capitalist country did the state own as large a proportion of the national industry as in Italy.[27] Clearly the whole nature, implications, and wider significance of such an event, which in many ways seemed to anticipate similar experiments elsewhere, need to be looked at much more closely than is possible here. But we should at least point out that it constituted a second possible 'distinguishing factor' in Italy's industrial development between the wars in comparison with other industrial countries. A third can be found – and despite the fact that Meier argues that this was not important and Sarti has claimed that it can be discounted I have absolutely no doubts on this score[28] – in the destruction of political freedom and therefore of the freedom of the unions which resulted from the establishment of Fascism. As a result, the industrialists gained enormously increased profit margins and a much greater degree of control over the running and organisation of industry and the labour market than had even been the case before. The decline in real wages of some 15 per cent between 1923 and 1939 was only one facet of the conditions which made Italian industrialists amongst the most 'privileged' and envied internationally.[29]

With her attack on France in June 1940 Italy entered the Second World War as Germany's ally, but only on paper were they on an equal footing. The reality was that despite the major advances which had been made in the electrical industry and in the hunt for locally produced raw materials and their substitutes, despite the vaunted launching of the campaign for autarchy and the conquest of an empire, it was soon all too obvious that the dreams of 'economic independence' were still no more than dreams. In an international situation such as that which developed after 1929, where autarchy was not simply talked about but put into practice as warlike military and political formations took up their positions, a country such as Italy whose industries required ever-increasing supplies of raw materials,[30] at a time when she could no longer count on the remittances of her emigrants to right her balance of payments as in earlier years, when she had to renounce the dollars of her financial tutors across the Atlantic, quickly found herself confronted by the necessity of making a choice. The government and the Fascist party, and with them the group who controlled Italian industry, albeit with some misgivings and doubts, ended up by allying themselves to their aggressive northern neighbour. From that moment onwards it became increasingly difficult to withdraw from what Mussolini called the 'test of the war', and equally, once again, from a situation of growing subordination.[31]

Military defeat and the profound changes in international relations after the war brought about radical changes in Italy's industrial structure and its development, as is well known. But the parallelogram of endogenous forces which had brought about the completion of Italy's industrialisation process continues to influence, perhaps more than ever and perhaps more than in any other industrial country, the structure of Italy's economic development, even though the nature of the pressures change and are changed. Unless we are dealing with a 'historiographical illusion', studies on Italian industrialisation are still very far from being able to provide a coherent and detailed picture of the workings of this dual mechanism. And this, to conclude, will be evident from the general problems, sketches and questions, together with the silences, international and otherwise, which run through and dominate this paper.

NOTES

[1]Corbino, E., *Annali dell'economia italiana,* vol. I (Citta di Castello, 1931); *Cento anni di vita nazionale attraverso le statistiche delle regioni* (Rome, 1961); *Almanacco statistico europeo per il 1865* (Milan, 1865); Mitchell, B. R., *European Historical Statistics* (London, 1975).

[2]For a recent reference to the importance of this distinction see Crouzet, F., 'Quelques problemes de l'histoire de l'industrialization au XIXe siecle'. *Revue d'histoire economique et sociale,* vol. 53 (1975) pp. 529-30. Among the factories already in activity in Italy in 1861 were Ansaldo, Pignone, Guppy Macry & Henry (later I Granili), Breda (at that time called Elvetica), Pietrarsa, Crespi, Poma, Mazzonis, Sella, Manifatture Cotoniere Meridionali (under various commercial names), Ginori, Cini and Richard (see: Fossati, A., *Lavoro e produzione in Italia dalla metà del secolo XVIII alla seconda guerra mondiale,* (Turin, 1951).

[3]Mitchell, B.R., op. cit., passim, Rioux, J.P., *La Révolution Industrielle* (Paris, 1971) p. 87; Corbino, E., op. cit., vol. II, p. 93.

[4]This is to use the term in a different sense from that adopted by Mendels, F.F., 'Proto-industrialization: The First Phase of the Industrialization Process'. *Journal of Economic History,* vol. XXXII (1972) pp. 241-61, and is meant to characterise the period during which there is, once industrialisation has actually begun, a clear predominance of consumer goods, following the well-known typology of Hoffmann, W., *Stadien und Typen der Industrialisierung* (Kiel, 1931), which is in turn derived from Marx. The problem is discussed in Mori, G., 'Il Tempo della Protoindustrializzazione', *L'Industrializzazione in Italia (1861-1900)* (Bologna, 1977).

[5]For levels of production see the still very valuable Svennilson, I., *Growth and Stagnation in the European Economy* (Geneva, 1954). On economic and technical concentration see Caracciolo, A., 'La crescita e la trasformazione della grande industria durante la prima guerra mondiale', *Lo Sviluppo Economico in Italia,* vol. III (Milan, 1969) pp. 187-240.

[6]Pollard, S., 'Industrialization and the European economy', *Economic History Review,* vol. XXVI (1973) pp. 636-48. A similar interpretation can be found in Hobsbawm, E., 'The XVIIth century in the Development of Capitalism', *Science and Society,* vol. XXIV (1960) pp. 97-112.

[7]Braudel, F., *La Méditerranee et le Monde méditerraneen a l'epoque de Philippe II,* vol. II, ch. VI (Paris 1949); Perroux, F., *Indépendance de la nation* (Paris, 1969); Robinson, E.A.G. (ed.), *Economic Consequences of the Size of Nations* (London, 1960).

[8]As is indicated by a number of recent studies which have served to weaken the older thesis put forward by Tarle, E.V., *Le Blocus Continental et le Royaume d'Italie* (Paris, 1928).

[9]A fine example of this in Richard Cobden's statement to D'Azeglio in 1847: '. . . the Italians' steam is their sunshine' (cf. Fossati, A., op. cit., pp. 344-5). Somewhat earlier he had expressed his disappointment that 'the finest raw cotton which ought to be sold to us' was being worked domestically in Egypt as a result of the initiative of Mohamed Ali (see Morley, J., *The Life of Richard Cobden,* vol. I, ch. 3 (London, 1893).

[10]For an examination of this concept with reference to the appearance and subsequent predominance of the sector devoted to the production of the means of production, see: Mori, G., 'Processo d'Industrializzazione e Storia d'Italia', *Belfagor,* a. XXIX (1974) pp. 609-32 (now in Mori, G., *Il Capitalismo Industriale in Italia* (Rome, 1977). For the definition of imperialism as the 'latest' stage of capitalism, rather than the 'highest' or 'final', in the first edition of Lenin's essay, and its implications, see Kula, W., *Problemi e metodi di storia economica* (Milan, 1972) pp. 138-9.

[11]For an incisive methodological discussion of this see De Rosa, L., 'La Rivoluzione Industriale in Italia', *Rassagne Economica,* a. XXXV (1971), reprinted in De Rosa, L., *La Rivoluzione Industriale in Italia e il Mezzogiorno* (Bari, 1973).

[12]Polanyi, K., *The Great Transformation,* ch. 1 (New York, 1944).

[13]In this context the pioneering remarks made by Habbakuk, H.J., during the round-table debate held in 1952 by the International Economic Association at St Margherita Ligure on the types of imitative and non-imitative reactions to Britain's industrial primacy in the different European states are still worth remembering. The issue of imitation naturally relates to objectives. The quotations of Gerschenkron are from G., A. 'Reflections on the concept of "pre-requisites" of modern industrialization', *L'Industria,* a. XLII (1957) p. 363, reprinted in *Economic Backwardness in Historical Perspective* (N.Y., 1962). For an example of the case of a bank with extensive capital available which was not attracted to industrial investment, see Luzzatto, G., *L'Economia Italiana dal 1861 al 1914* (Milan, 1963) pp. 151-2.

[14]This and the earlier quotation from Labriola come from Labriola, A., 'Da un secolo all'altro' in Labriola, A., *La Concezione materialistica della Storie,* ed. Garin, E. (Bari, 1965) pp. 347-8.

[15]On the treaty with France see Fohlen, C., 'Il trattato di commercio franco-italiano del 17 gennaio 1863', *Archivio Economico per l'Unificazione Italiana,* s. I, vol. XII (Rome, 1963). The figures on silk and natural products are from *Sommario di Statistiche storiche 1861-1955* (Rome, 1958). On the termination of Italy's sulphur monopoly see Colonna, M., *L'industria zolfifera siciliana* (Catania, 1971) pp. 188-92; also Haynes, W., *Brimstone, the stone that burns* (Princeton-New York, 1959); the slenderness of the internal demand for industrial products has not been discussed by anyone.

[16]Romeo, R., *Risorgimento e Capitalismo* (Bari, 1963) p. 110.

[17]Fossati, A., op. cit., passim.

[18]Merli, S., *Proletariato di fabbrica e capitalismo industriale* (Florence, 1972).

[19]For the two extremes see Organski, A.F.K., *The Stages of Political Development* (New York, 1965) p. 157; FOA, V., *Introduction* to Grifone, P., *Il Capitale Finanziario in Italia* (Turin, 1971) p. xxiv.

[20]*Sommario* (*see* Note 15, above) passim. Overall horsepower must have more than doubled between 1900 and 1920. In the same period industrial joint-stock companies increased their share capital four-fold (in constant *lire* prices). See Coppola d'Anna, F., 'Le societa per azioni in Italia', Ministero per la Costituente. *Rapporto della Commissione economica,* II. *Industria,* III. *Appendice alle relazioni* (Rome, 1946) pp. 259 and 263.

[21] As has rightly been pointed out: '. . . it is too frequently not taken into account that a rushed, violent and chaotic renewal of some sector of the economy may in the short term lead to . . . a rapid increase in production and to intense growth, but that it may also bring about a profound fracture between what is modern and what is not in the economic system. As a result a whole series of tensions and conflicts come into being which tend to upset the social, political, spiritual and cultural life of a nation, even their very moral and religious foundations' (Rosenberg, H., *Grosse Depression und Bismarckzeit* (Berlin, 1967) pp. 57-60).

[22] On this last point see Galli della Loggia, E., 'Problemi di sviluppo industriale e nuovi equilibri politici alla vigilia della prima guerra mondiale', *Rivista Storica Italiana,* a. LXXXII (1970) p. 862, which is also useful on the attitudes of Ansaldo, and also Mori, G., 'Le guerre parallele', *Studi Storici,* a. XIV (1973), now reprinted in Mori, G., *Il Capitalismo . . .,* pp. 170-3. Maraviglia, M., 'Per l'indipendenza economica d'Italia', *L'Idea Nazionale,* 3 March 1915, was among the first, if not the first, to use the phrase.

[23] On this, see the report in Ministero per la Constituente, *Rapporto . . .,* II, I, vol. 2, pp. 216-17. The production values are taken from the industrial census for 1937-40. Table (a) is reconstructed from data to be found in that census, together with that of 1927, and for columns 7 and 8 we have drawn on the *Notizie statistiche sulle societa italiane per azioni* (Rome, 1928, 1938). Table (b) is based on the *Sommario . . .*

[24] Although Gualerni, G., *Industrie e fascismo* (Milan, 1976) seems to do so, albeit departing from a new line of argument.

[25] We have drawn on the *Notizie statistiche . . .,* (various years).

[26] Ministero per la Costituente, *Rapporto . . .,* II, I, vol. 2, pp. 74-5.

[27] As was stated shortly after: 'IRI is involved in a complex of share-holding companies whose capital amounts to 44.15% of the capital of all share-holding companies in Italy; it holds majority shares equivalent to 17,80% of that total and minority shares equivalent to 2.37% (Lefebvre d'Ovidio, O., 'L'azione dell'I.R.I. per la riorganizzazione dell'industria', *Rassegna Economica,* vol. VIII (1937) p. 192). The best reconstruction of the events leading to the founding of IRI is in Toniolo, G., *Crisi economica e smobilizzo pubblico delle banche miste: 1930-1934* (a discussion paper delivered to the Convegno of Ca' Foscari, Venice, 15-16 April 1977).

[28] See Sarti, R., *Fascism and industrial leadership in Italy* (Berkeley, 1971) and Maier, C.S., *Recasting Bourgeois Europe* (Princeton, 1975).

[29] On wages see Zamagni, V., 'La dinamica dei salari nel settore industriale', *L'economia italiana nel periodo fascista,* ed. Ciocca, P. and Toniolo, G. (Bologna, 1977). For a local study see Sapelli, G., *Fascismo, grande industria e sindacato. Il caso di Torino* (Milan, 1975). On an aspect of employer-worker relations which is of great interest see Preti, O., 'La regolamentazione delle controversie "individuali" di lavoro in regime fascista', *Studi Storici,* a. XVIII (1977) pp. 125-69.

[30] A striking picture of the situation can be found in Ministero dell'Industria, Commercio e Lavoro, *Relazione del servizio minerario nell'anno 1939* (Rome, 1945) pp. 5-6.

[31] It even came to the point that the German Minister of Economics, Walther Funk, argued openly that Italy should be asked to strengthen its agriculture, while all industrial growth was reserved for Germany. This is evident from the memoirs of the former Italian Minister Guarneri, F., *Battaglie economiche tra le due grandi guerre,* vol. II (Milan, 1953) pp. 312-13.

16 On the Economic Development of the Habsburg Monarchy

György Ránki

A modern economic history that would summarise and evaluate a given period – in this case, the years when capitalism was taking shape – of a country's economic development must necessarily address itself to three main issues. (1) It needs to ascertain the particular country's role in the world economy at the beginning and at the end of the period; (2) it needs to give an idea of the nature and pace of the economic development that took place – to show the extent of the economic growth and of the structural changes that transpired; and (3) it needs to analyse the socio-political context that determined the direction and rate of this economic growth.

It is no easy task to get a clear picture of the level of any country's economic development at the beginning of the nineteenth century. Nevertheless, the sophistication of the means of production, the nature of the relations of production, trade, industry, urbanisation, the wealth of the royal court, and other non-quantitative indicators clearly show the Habsburg Monarchy – one of the arbiters of contemporary European – and thus, world – politics to have been one of the countries where the potential for development was the greatest. If we compare Austria-Hungary to the rest of Europe, we find the western provinces of the Empire to have been hardly less developed economically than the area of Western Europe where industrialisation began and whence economic growth originated.

If we compare the Austrian and Czech parts of the Empire to pre-Revolutionary France, to say nothing of the German states, we can hardly find the Empire to have been behind in respect either of its (mercantilist) economic policy, of its regulation of feudal services and dues, or of its educational system. Industrialisation, too, took root relatively soon after its English flowering. The handicrafts provided a pool of skilled labour, and though capital accumulation was considerably weaker than in England or Western Europe, we can hardly speak of a shortage of capital.

Recent works on the economic backwardness of the Habsburg Empire distinguish two major phases.

The first time the Empire is claimed to have fallen behind is in the first half of the nineteenth century, and estimates are given of the extent of its backwardness by mid-century in quantitative terms. The gross domestic product of the Western half of the Empire around 1840 is estimated to have been around 7 million forints. In terms of per capita income, this was but

25 per cent of England's, and but 75 per cent of the German states' per capita GNP.[1] M. Mulhall, that pioneer of statistical analysis, estimated the Habsburg Empire's industrial production around 1850 to have been about 60 per cent of the German figure; his estimate for other economic indicators – for instance, trade figures – showed the Empire to have been even further behind.[2]

Both economic and social factors contributed to this difference. For one thing, the countries of Western Europe started with a number of potential economic advantages: they were more advanced to start with; they were in the immediate proximity of the most developed economic areas of the world; and, consequently, shipping costs were of minor consideration in their contacts with these areas. Moreover, we must not forget that the new technology of the industrial revolution rested on a raw material base which differed considerably from that of the past; with this shift, the economic value of a particular region also changed, often radically. In this respect, Austria (by which we shall mean the entire western half of the Empire, unless we explicitly specify the developed Austrian and Czech areas, in this case without Galicia, Bukovina and Dalmatia, three extremely underdeveloped areas of the Hereditary Lands) was definitely worse off than, for instance, Germany.

But significant as the economic and technological causes of backwardness were, they can by no means obscure the socio-political context that made it almost inevitable. The mercantilism of the enlightened absolutism of the eighteenth century was more or less adequate to the economic needs of the age; the artificially restored semi-feudalism and reinvigorated absolutism that characterised the years after the French Revolution and especially the age of Metternich, however, was by its very nature the chief impediment to economic development. It is no coincidence, then, that the reforms initiated in the eighteenth century were taken up again only more than half a century after 1789, that the abolition of serfdom had to wait until 1848, and the abolition of the guild system until as late as 1859. Modern capitalist relations of production, thus, could begin to take shape but much later than in the West, a circumstance that fundamentally impeded modernisation and growth as much in agriculture as in industry.

The tariff wall set up against Hungary was part of this feudal, absolutistic economic policy, and quite unlike the protective tariff Kossuth had urged Hungary to set up in the 1840s. The tariffs that were put into operation were part of Metternich's and Kubeck's plans for making the eastern half of the Empire primarily a supplier of foodstuffs and raw materials; it was an economic policy that preferred Hungary's economic exploitation and low living standards as being of definite advantage to Vienna.[3]

Recent economic histories regard the 1848 revolution as a major turning-point for the Empire's economic development. The abolition of serfdom means that one of the most vital preconditions of industrialisation and modern economic growth was now met.[4] Many other social reforms that were the *sine qua non* of a bourgeois society were, paradoxically, to be espoused by the centralised neo-absolutism that defeated the Hungarian Revolution and War of Independence, which found itself checked by a number of feudal and traditional forces. It was, thus, the central government which was obliged to carry through – albeit half-heartedly and incompletely – a number of social and administrative measures permitting and promoting the development of capitalist relations of production. The second, incomparably more successful, phase of Austria-Hungary's economic development can be said to have started with the 1848 revolutions, or rather, with the institutionalisation of the societal prerequisites of capitalist development which culminated in the 1867 Compromise.

What part did the western half of the Monarchy play in the economy of the rest of Europe before the First World War? If we look at the employment distribution of the population, we will be struck first of all by the preponderance of the agricultural population.

TABLE 16.1 Employment Distribution, in %

Year	*Austria*		*Germany*	
	Agricultural population	*Industrial population*	*Agricultural population*	*Industrial population*
1869	67.2	19.7	50.9	27.6
1900	58.2	22.2	38.0	36.8
1910	53.1	24.0	35.1	37.9[5]

We find that the initial figures not only reflect greatly discrepant levels of development, but that all of them show that Austria's industrial population grew at a much slower rate and much less than Germany's. (The drop in the agricultural population figures is about 15 points in both cases, but in Austria's case this means an actual decline of 20 per cent, while in Germany's, a real drop of 30 per cent.)

There might have been purely demographic reasons for this difference had the Monarchy's population growth been faster than Germany's. This, however, was not the case. Even the above data, then, indicate that, its relatively favourable growth rate notwithstanding, the Austrian economy was not as dynamic as the German. Other indicators, too, support this conclusion. The difference in per capita GNP also grew, so that by the 1910s Austria's was but 60 per cent of Germany's per capita GNP.

In the 1910s, Austrian industry was contributing 4.5 per cent of Europe's industrial production; her population of 30 million, on the other hand, was 9 per cent of Europe's population (Russia not included). This, too, indicates a relatively low industrial productivity; the leading industrial nations – England, Germany and France – contributed a substantially higher percentage of Europe's industrial production than the percentage they constituted of its population. The picture would be even bleaker if we tried to compare Mullhall's pre-1900 estimate (which put the Monarchy's industrial production at 9 per cent of that of Europe – Austria's alone, then, would have been around 7 or 7.5 per cent) with the more precise calculations available for the 1910s.[6] Other evidence – for instance, a look at the most important industry of the age, the textile industry – is no more encouraging. To England's 54 million spinning jennies, Germany's 10 million, and France's 7 million, the Monarchy had only 4.7 million spinning jennies in operation – 4.2 million of them in Austria. Thus, even Austria's relatively developed textile industry was nowhere near that of the West in productivity.

Steel production in England was 6.5 million tons per annum, in France 3.8 million tons, in Germany 14.5 million tons; while in the Habsburg Monarchy it was but 2.4 million tons, 1.6 million of it coming from Transleithania. Raw material consumption was in similar ratios, as was the production of coke.

The table that follows presents a picture that is unambiguous enough. The Austro-Hungarian Monarchy was one of the great powers of Europe, but, as in the case of Russia, its economic strength was by no means commensurate with its great power status and its political influence. While the three Western countries we have been referring to owed their great power status in no small degree to their economic strength, Austria-Hungary's economic development was hardly adequate to sustain its position as a great power. What is more, the foreign policy decisions made to preserve this great power status were often a direct impediment to economic development – for instance, during the years of neo-absolutism.

TABLE 16.2 Production and consumption indicators for the leading European countries, in %

Country	*Population*	*Coal production*	*Steel production*	*Machine industry*	*Chemical industry*	*Cotton consumption*	*Industrial production*
England	13	52	20	27	19	43	27
Germany	21	34	46	48	41	19	32
France	12	7	12	5	14	11	13
Austria	9	8	5.5			7.5	4.5[7]

Europe, without Russia = 100%

All this brings us to the issue of the dynamics of Austrian development. How did the rate of growth compare to that of the rest of contemporary Europe; and how did this economic growth tie in with whatever structural changes there were? It had long been maintained that the Monarchy's relative backwardness *vis à vis* both the most developed and other smaller western European countries indicated an extraordinarily slow rate of growth. Recent quantitative examinations, however, have totally discredited this view. Besides a number of studies concentrating mostly on structural problems, two works using the quantitative approach to the issue of economic growth have also come out in the past few years. The first, a doctoral dissertation by Nachum T. Gross,[8] uses time-series to show the rate of industrial development. These time-series indicate the growth of per capita industrial production in the Hereditary Lands to have been an annual 3.46 per cent in the period from around the Compromise to about the First World War. Gross's computations, however, show the growth rate in the first two decades (1865-85) to have been 4.09 per cent; but in the last three decades (1880-1911) only 3.42 per cent.

Gross made calculations also for the 1841-65 period, and found there a very slow growth rate of but 2.25 per cent. On the basis of the above, he puts the annual per capita industrial growth rate between 1841 and 1911 at 3.09 per cent.[9]

Gross's calculations are for discrete years, and are based on adjusted national income and GNP figures.

Another American economic historian, Richard L. Rudolph,[10] looked at the trends of the major industrial products to construct an industrial production index. The index is based on five statistical series – mining, metallurgy, the machine industry, the food industry, and the textile industry. These five branches provided 70 per cent of Austria's pre-war industrial production;[11] statistically, they are thus certainly representative.

Rudolph's findings are given in Table 16.3.

TABLE 16.3

Year	*Industrial production index*	*Mining*	*Metallurgy*	*Machine industry*	*Food industry*	*Textile industry*
				1900 = 100%		
1880	44	46	20	10	48	50
1890	72	76	51	41	72	88
1900	100	100	100	100	100	100
1910	130	122	160	171	113	136
1912	150	135	195	208	120	164
1913	144	140	189	196	116	153

In about three decades, then, Austria's industrial production had grown more than three-and-a-half-fold. Growth was slowest in the traditional industries – mining, the textile industry, and the food industry; and fast in the modern industrial branches – metallurgy, and the machine industry. Growth in the former was ten-fold; in the latter, more than twenty-fold.

The overall rate of industrial growth between 1880 and 1913 was 3.6 per cent per annum. The slowest rate of growth we find in the food industry, with an annual 2.7 per cent; the textile industry was next, with 3.7 per cent; mining followed with 3.4 per cent. Metallurgy grew at an annual rate of 7 per cent; the machine industry, at 9.5 per cent.[12]

Rudolph's figures are somewhat lower than Gross's estimates; the latter had put the per capita industrial growth at 3.42 per cent per annum. Given the annual population growth rate of .9 per cent, Rudolph's index would give us a per capita growth rate of less than 3 per cent. One might rightly point out, however, that Rudolph's index ignores a number of new, dynamic branches of industry – the electrical and chemical industries, for instance – which would presumably raise his figures too.[13]

We will, thus, be quite safe to assume an annual production growth of 3-3.5 per cent for the western half of the Monarchy. It is a rate that can hardly be said to reflect explosive or really dynamic growth. It is, however, but a little short of the estimated German growth rate of 3.7 per cent per annum; in terms of per capita industrial production growth, the Austrian is quite equal to the German growth rate.

We find the industrial growth rate in Hungary to have been even somewhat faster. There are three sets of computations that we can make use of here. The first of these is a study of ours that appeared in 1966, 'National Income and Capital Accumulation in Hungary 1867-1914'.[14] We started with well-grounded estimates for Hungary's national income and industrial product before the Compromise. Using Frigyes Fellner's pioneering calculations of the national income for 1900 and 1913, as well as the figures available for gross production, we calculated the industrial growth rate to have been about 6 per cent per annum.[15]

Péter Hanák, in a study written not long thereafter,[16] calculated the rate of industrial growth on the basis of net output, and found an annual growth rate of 5.2 per cent.

Undoubtedly the most systematic and best grounded are László Katus's calculations.[17] To start with, he used quantitative indices to adjust the estimates for 1867, concluding that Hungary's national income at that point was probably 20-25 per cent higher than what we had figured. (Katus used the 1913 prices; we had worked on the basis of the prices in 1900.) With the base value thus adjusted, Katus found an annual industrial growth rate of 4.2 per cent; without the adjustment, the growth rate was found to be 5.1 per cent. The per capita industrial growth rate on Berend and Ránki's calculations is 4.9 per cent on Katus's adjusted calculations, 3.5 per cent; on his unadjusted calculations, 4.2 per cent.

Even if it is the lowest of all the above figures that we accept as accurate, we cannot help but conclude that the economy of the Monarchy as a whole was showing, if not an explosive, at least a stable growth. Recent research thus supports our contention that it would be simplistic to seek the roots of the Monarchy's problems primarily in the underlying economic factors. More precisely, we can hardly hope to find a mechanistic correspondence between the contradictions inherent in the Monarchy's political, social, constitutional and multinational structure, and the problems of its economic development. We will be closer to the truth if we see the feudal elements in the social and political life of the Monarchy, the unequal balance of power among its various nationalities, and the economic development the Monarchy was capable of as mutually determinative one of the other. For though the social and political milieu did not, as we have seen, obstruct economic development as such, it certainly set a number of impediments to it. Economic problems, developmental disproportions, regional disparities were, in turn, extraordinarily magnified in this unusual, multinational political context, so that they acquired a significance that was much more than purely economic – acquired, in fact, the dimensions of national and power struggle. In other words, problems peculiar to this stage of capitalist development in quite a few countries – the fact, for instance, that market factors, raw material supplies and so on predetermined some regions for prosperity, others for decline – took on quite a different aspect within the framework of the Monarchy, so that the problems of development and underdevelopment served but to aggravate national conflicts. The fact that economic development tended to characterise the areas inhabited by the ruling nationalities, and backwardness or much slower development in the politically oppressed areas lent a political hue to the most minute of economic problems. The disparity could be attributed to the use – or rather, abuse – of political power even when it was due merely to the free operation of capitalist market forces which, undoubtedly, favoured the strong.

The industrial revolution initiated fundamental and dynamic changes in the territorial distribution of the economy: the location of industry came to be determined by considerations of maximal rationality and the demands of modern technology. The railway brought radical changes in economic concentration. Capitalist railway building, however, was determined by considerations of profitability; railways were, thus, likely to be built in areas where maximal returns on the investment seemed guaranteed by their high level of economic development, or extremely great potential for development.[18]

Besides railways, technology, too, played a great part in economic development. New raw materials and a new technology had undoubtedly a great deal to do with the fact that, of the two developed western areas of the Monarchy in Austria and Moravia, the balance tilted in favour of the latter in the second half of the nineteenth century. There can be no doubt, however, that economic policy decisions, too, greatly influenced the regional development of industry. But though duties, taxes, and other measures influenced the pattern and pace of development, they were not decisive in how and how energetically capitalist development penetrated the various regions of the Monarchy.

An analysis of the industrial population on the basis of both the 1869 and 1910 censuses shows both a great increase in the traditional industrial regions, and the growing importance of the – likewise traditional – Czech-Moravian industrial zone. In the more backward regions (Galicia, Bukovina and Dalmatia) there was no area where the industrial population came to as much as 15 per cent of the population as a whole, in either 1869 or 1910. In the Czech and Moravian areas there were 368 and 595 factories, respectively, per 1 million inhabitants, and 11.3 and 7 factories, respectively, per 100 sq. km; and the respective figures for Lower Austria were 904 and 16.1; for Upper Austria 542 and 13; and for Steirmark 693 and 9.4. But in Dalmatia, Bukovina and Galicia for an average 1 million inhabitants there were 12.7 factories, with more than one factory per 100 sq. km. only in Galicia. True, there were less industrialised regions in the German-speaking areas, too, for example Tyrol, but this gave rise to no comparable social tensions.

By contrast, the Czech areas and the Vienna Basin were, effectively, on a Western level of development. Recent Austrian economic research on the area presently constituting the country has rightly shown that these regions – and, we might add, the Czech regions, too – had a technology on a par if not with German, at least with most Western technology. Industrial growth after the turn of the century computed on the basis of the per capita GNP figures is 3.1 per cent.

These calculations (which can be taken as roughly valid for the Czech areas, too), taking Austria's 1913 per capita GNP as 100, put Japan's at 30, Russia's at 32, and Italy's at 66 per cent. Austria's national product was nearly equal to that of Holland and Sweden, fell 25 per cent short of that of Germany and Switzerland, and was 40-50 per cent behind that of England and the United States. The Austrian (and Czech) per capita GNP, however, was 50 per cent higher than the Cisleithan average, and 70 per cent higher than the per capita GNP of the Monarchy as a whole.[19] These calculations coincide with those of Péter Hanák, who, taking the per capita GNP of the Austro-Hungarian Monarchy as a whole to be 100, arrived at a figure of 197 for the area that is today's Austria, of 192 for the Czech areas, but at only 97 for Galicia, Bukovina, and the South Slav (among them the Slovene) areas.[20]

If we compare Hungary and Austria (including here all the Transleithan areas of the Monarchy), we find that after the industrial revolution got off the ground in Hungary, too, the differences between the two areas grew considerably smaller. All calculations give Hungary's rate of growth as being somewhat the faster of the two; and while the ratio of Austria's industrial production to Hungary's had been 84:16 at around the time of the Compromise, by just before the First World War this had changed to 76:24. The contribution of the two halves to the national income had changed from 70:30 to 63:37. Per capita national income in the middle of the nineteenth century was 107 crowns in Austria, and 62 crowns in Hungary; on the eve of the War, the figures were 426 crowns and 319 crowns, respectively. While earlier, Hungary's national income had been three-fifths of Austria's, it was now three-quarters.

Before the Compromise, the horsepower used by Hungary's manufacturing industry was a quarter that used by Austria's; before the First World War, it was a third. During the same time, the industrial population–population ratio in Hungary had grown by 8.3 per cent; in Austria, by 4.6 per cent.

Any examination of the growing parity or growing inequality in the economic development of the various regions of Austro-Hungary must account for the discrepancies that existed among these regions by the time the industrial revolution reached Austria in the mid-nineteenth century in terms of the graduality of capitalism's progress from west to east. That development was gradual was a function of the actual historical unfolding of the capitalist world economy, though naturally, the form it took was influenced also by the natural and economic conditions of the region or country in question. Research has shown that the economy of a particular area 'took off' when the first wave of the industrial revolution reached it, leaving behind the areas lying to the east of it. The differences between the two were, then, bound to grow, in no small part because the capital accumulation of the more developed area went on at the expense of the more backward. As soon as the wave of capitalist development reached Hungary, the rate of economic growth accelerated here too, and there were even signs of her catching up to some extent with the more western areas.

We can, however, hardly generalise our findings for Austria and Hungary. The developmental trend just described is peculiar to the given period of historical and economic development, and to these two countries.

In conclusion, we can list the following as the economic, social and political factors of development: Hungary's derivative economic development was boosted in no small measure by the foodstuff and raw material demands of an industrialising Austria. Capital accumulation owed much to the favourable terms of trade enjoyed by Hungary's agricultural exports, which also provided the foreign capital needed to build up the country's infrastructure. In this respect, the free trade area that was the Austro-Hungarian Monarchy proved of definite advantage in facilitating the free movement of the factors of production, and in compensating for the insufficiency of the domestic capital accumulation. This free movement of the factors of production meant not only the availability of capital, but also experts, technology, and a market, and even promoted a kind of comparatively advantageous specialisation.

There are two other aspects that we must take into consideration. It was an essential feature of Hungary's potential for development that Austria's economic dominance within the Monarchy was perceptible, though not overwhelming. As a political unit, the Monarchy was founded, if not on equality, at least on a certain parity. Hungary's political weight within the Monarchy was greater than her economic weight. This not only generally prevented Austria from using political pressure to ram her economic interests down Hungary's throat, but even permitted Hungary to ward off economic pressure through political means.

There can be no doubt that Hungary's economic growth would have been less rapid whatever advantages the Monarchy's being a free trade area might have brought her had she not had an independent government to speak for her with economic and political arguments of its own.

NOTES

[1]Nachum T. Gross, 'An Estimate of Industrial Production in Austria in 1841', *Journal of Economic History,* 1968.

[2]Michael G. Mullhall, *Industries and Wealth of Nations* (London, 1896) p. 32.

[3]Nachum T. Gross, in 'Die Sellung der Habsburger Monarchie in der Weltwirtschaft', *Die Habsburger-Monarchie 1848-1918,* Band I, (Wien, 1973) point out that this policy was mistaken from the point of view of modern economic theory, too, in that it misunderstood the market concept. His critique, we feel, lacks historical perspective, for both the absolutist economic policy, and free trade capitalism's attempt to maximise profit rested on postulates quite different from those of contemporary capitalist consumer society and the welfare state.

[4]This is a claim not only of Marxist historians, but also of, among others, Herbert Matis, in his 'Konjunkturelle Dynamik und gesellschaftlicher Wandel im Zeitalter Franz Joseph I', in *Osterreichs Wirtschaft 1848-1913* (Berlin, 1972) p. 32.

[5]György Ránki, 'A Monarchia gazdasági fejlodésének problémái' [Some problems of the Monarchy's economic development], *Valóság,* 1968/5.

[6]Mullhall's calculations are given by Nachum T. Gross in his 'Die Stellung der Habsburger Monarchie'.

[7]Iván T. Berend and György Ránki. 'Das Niveau der Industrie Ungarns zu Beginn des 20. Jahrhunderts im Vergleich zu dem Europeas', in P. Hanák and V. Sándor (eds), *Studien zur Geschichte der Osterrichisch-Ungarischen Monarchie* (Budapest, 1961).

[8]Nachum T. Gross, *Industrialization in Austria in the Nineteenth Century* (Berkley, 1966), manuscript, sections of which were later published. The author sent us a copy of his manuscript in 1967, giving us the opportunity to make reference to it in an earlier publication.

[9]See 'Austrian Industrial Statistics, 1880-85, and 1911-13', *Zeitschrift für die gesamte Staatswissenschaft,* 1969.

[10]Richard L. Rudolph, 'The Role of Financial Institutions in the Industrialisation of the Czech Crownlands 1880-1913' (Wisconsin, 1968), manuscript dissertation, sections of which have been published. Published from *Industrial development in the Austro-Hungarian Monarchy* (Cambridge, 1976).

[11]Richard L. Rudolph, 'Quantitative Aspekte der Industrialisierung in Oisleithanion', *Die Habsburger Monarchie 1848-1918.*

[12]For some data on this, see Richard L. Rudolph, 'Austria's Banking and Economic Development' in Rondo Cameron, (ed.) *Banking and Economic Development. Some Lessons of History* (Oxford, 1972).

[13]For the data, see Herbert Matis, op. cit.

[14]Ivan T. Berend and György Ránki, 'Nemzeti jövedelem és tokefelhalmozás Magyarországon 1867-1914', *Történelmi Szemle* [Historical Review], 1966/2.

[15]The published article contains a misprint of the industrial growth rate; this mistake was corrected in the German-language version.

[16]Péter Hanák, 'Tulsuly vagy foggoség' [Preponderance or dependence], *Századok* [Centuries] 1971/5.

[17]László Katus, 'Economic Growth in Hungary', *Social Economic Researches on the History of East Central Europe, Studia Historica* (Budapest, 1970).

[18]H. Matis, op. cit., gives a fine illustration of this, pointing out that at the time the Kaiser Ferdinand railway was built, there were 384 factories situated along its route; by 1888, there were 983.

[19]A. Kaisel, 'Osterreiche grosser Sprung nach vorn', *Europäische Rundschau,* July 1973.

[20]Péter Hanák, op. cit.

17 Structural Change and Industrialisation in Inter-war Central-East Europe

Alice Teichova

This paper is based on work within a research project supported by the SSRC, and their financial aid is gratefully acknowledged.

This study attempts an assessment of changes in the relative rank order of branches of industry within the economic structure of six Central-East European countries and puts forward some tentative explanations for the specific industrialisation process which took place since the Industrial Revolution in Western Europe. It analyses economic structures; examines the significant growth of certain industries, especially the textile industry in twentieth-century conditions; then looks into the reasons for this phenomenon when, at the same time, industrial advance in the West proceeded on quite different lines; and finally, discusses the question whether this specific development can without reservations be regarded as a sign of economic backwardness.

Geographically, the countries East of the Elbe and along the Danube are taken into consideration (Poland, Czechoslovakia, Hungary, Romania, Yugoslavia and Bulgaria) whose different levels of industrialisation show a marked West to East-South-east gradient. The only exception is presented by Czechoslovakia, whose pattern of industrial development did not conform to that of the other Central-East European countries but progressed similarly to that of Western European economies. The Western regions of Czechoslovakia – Bohemia and Moravia – had already under the Habsburg Monarchy undergone an industrial revolution essentially of the nineteenth-century type, starting with the textile industry, then penetrating to the agricultural industries (sugar, brewing, distilling) and to heavy industry and engineering (iron, coal, agricultural and textile machinery). In all its phases Czech industrialisation was supported by a continuous inflow of labour and by a fairly substantial domestic capital accumulation derived mainly from a relatively advanced agriculture which had developed simultaneously. Such a gradual rise of industrial development permeating the whole economy was largely bypassed in the other East European countries as they were faced with the need to industrialise in twentieth-century conditions alongside and in unequal competition with high-powered industrial economies.

The main obstacle to modern economic development remained the overwhelming weight of agriculture in the economies of that region, and any assessment of economic growth or stagnation can only be made by taking into account the basic relationship between agriculture and industry. Under the prevailing political and socio-economic conditions between the wars it was impossible to overcome effectively the enormous differences between the advanced agriculture of Western Europe and its backward state in Eastern Europe. Agricultural reforms had become a political necessity but were neither incisively carried through nor economically sound; modernisation and capitalisation of agriculture, particularly in the Balkan area, were frustrated both by fragmentation of land and by relative rural overpopulation. The only viable solution to economic backwardness lay in industrialisation. However, its pace and extent were impaired by the stagnant conditions in agriculture which tended to emphasise rather than redress the imbalance in the economies of Central-East Europe. Notwithstanding, industry was the crucial and most dynamic sector which contributed most to any economic growth registered in this area.

The newly-established states entered the inter-war phase of industrialisation with the disadvantages of latecomers and with the heritage of war, revolution and counter-revolution. They had to adapt themselves to new conditions; their economic life had been orientated towards Vienna and Budapest, and in the case of Poland her component parts had even been tied to three centres: St Petersburg, Berlin and Vienna. Thus, initially, they did not form individual economic units and recovery was a long-drawn-out and painful process. Only Czechoslovakia escaped the worst economic upheavals by an incisive and early currency reform (1919) and a complete separation from the Austrian monetary and banking system. She was first to succeed in stabilising her economy.

The different points in time of stabilisation in the social, political and monetary spheres diminished the generally weak opportunities for domestic capital formation and delayed the badly needed inflow of foreign long-term investment into the capital-starved industries of Eastern Europe until late in the 1920s. The constant lack of capital and the dependence on foreign loans and investments were in a varied measure common to all.

Closely related to this phenomenon was another feature common to all investigated countries, which consisted of a chronically insufficient demand on the domestic market. When the Czechoslovak state was established it acquired, like all Successor states, part of the Habsburg Monarchy's uneven distribution of resources and levels of industrialisation. On the whole, Czechoslovakia comprised 21 per cent of the territory, 26 per cent of the population but no less than about 70 per cent of the industrial capacity[1] and also 44 per cent of the entire labour force of the Dual Monarchy.[2] The widespread areas of the Habsburg Empire had provided a convenient outlet for the industries of the Czech Lands and until 1918 had been their home market; after 1918 the relatively highly developed Czechoslovak industry was faced with an immensely diminished home market which was unable to absorb its products. This so-called Austro-Hungarian structure of Czechoslovak industry emphasised the problem of foreign trade, for the country had to export at least 30 per cent of its total output in order to survive. From the point of view of a drastically shrunken domestic market and, as a result of this, a relative over-capacity of industrial production post-war Hungary had to grapple with similar problems, but in most other aspects her situation was very different from that of Czechoslovakia. Within her new boundaries Hungary retained only 32.7 per cent of her pre-war area and 41.6 per cent of her former population; 47 per cent of her industrial enterprises had remained on her territory, producing about 55 per cent of the former value of production. As well as being separated like the territory of Czechoslovakia from the Monarchy's nearly self-sufficient trade network her industries were largely cut off from essential raw material sources which now lay beyond her frontiers and became increasingly surrounded by tariff walls. Thus imports of raw materials became essential to keep the wheels of the relatively expanded ironworks, engineering factories, spinning and weaving mills turning. Even the strongest branch of industry, flour milling, was unable to utilise its capacity, for domestic supplies of grain on the diminished territory could not reach more than between a third and a half of available capacity at the best of harvests. As a result of the territorial changes of 1919-20 Hungary was transformed into a more industrial country, but the domestic market was unable to absorb the produce of Hungarian industry and agriculture in sufficient quantities; therefore, securing export markets became of critical importance.[3] Fundamentally, the persistently low level of incomes, descending from West to East-South-east, could not generate any buoyant demand on domestic markets throughout the entire region over the whole inter-war period (cf. Table 17.1). This problem was most pressing in the predominantly agricultural countries, i.e. in Yugoslavia, Bulgaria and Romania, where more than 70 per cent, and in Poland and Hungary, where more than 50 per cent of the population were dependent on agriculture.

The comparative economic structure of the six Central-East European

TABLE 17.1 Per capita manufacturing and per capita national income in six European countries

Country	*Gross value of manufacturing in US$ in 1930-38 at 1926-29 prices per capita*	*Per capita national income in US$, in 1938 prices*	
		in $	*CSR=100*
Czechoslovakia	100	176	100
Hungary	60	112	64
Poland	30	104	59
Yugoslavia	–	–	–
Bulgaria	28[x]	68	39
Romania	20		

SOURCE: W.E. Moore, *Economic Demography of Eastern and Southern Europe* (Geneva, 1945) p. 125. [x] refers to 1937. The figures for Bulgaria were supplied by L. Berov based on his book *Ikonomitsheskoto razvitie na Bulgarija prez vekovete* (Economic Development of Bulgaria throughout the Centuries) (Sofia, 1974).

TABLE 17.2 Percentage distribution of the gainfully occupied population in six European countries

Country	Year	Agric. and fishing	Mining	Manufact. and handicraft	Commerce and transport	Administration, dom.service. etc.
1. Among typically industrialised:						
Czechoslovakia	1930	28	2	40	14	16
2. Among less industrialised						
Hungary	1930	54	1	23	10	12
Poland	1931	65	1	16	8	10
3. Countries lagging in industrial development:						
Romania	1930	78	–	7	5	10
Yugoslavia	1931	79	–	11	4	6
Bulgaria	1934	80	–	8	4	8

SOURCE: *Industrialisation and Foreign Trade* (League of Nations, 1945) pp 26-7.

countries shown in Table 17.2 clearly divides them into three categories. Czechoslovakia alone belongs to the typically industrialised countries of the inter-war years, Hungary and Poland fall int the category of less industrialised countries and Romania, Yugoslavia and Bulgaria range themselves with countries lagging behind in industrial development.

The countries which form the centre of interest in this study took up about one third of the area of Europe and represented just under a quarter of Europe's population but, even at the end of the inter-war period, their combined contribution to Europe's industrial production amounted to no more than 7 or 8 per cent whilst the three leading industrial powers alone (Britain, France and Germany) produced 67 per cent of the total industrial output of Europe.[4] The great disparities existing in the inter-war period fundamentally influenced the course of industrialisation in the Central-East European countries. They were particularly powerfully affected by the expansive financial and business operations of the world's most advanced economies of Britain, France and the USA, with whom they suddenly found themselves in imminent contact after having attained formal political independence.

In the immediate post-war years the new states sought the support of the Western Powers in their efforts to stabilise their political and economic systems, and later they leant heavily financially on the West in their endeavour to arm and to industrialise. In this way they became increasingly dependent on the capital mainly of France, Britain and the USA, although the degree of dependency varied in the different countries according to the strength or weakness of industrial development in their economies.

Throughout the inter-war period, notwithstanding cyclical fluctuations and the shock of the world economic crisis, industrial production registered faster growth rates than other sectors of the Central-East European economies. Average annual growth rates in South-eastern Europe were significantly higher than the European average. Bulgaria's annual growth rate between 1904 and 1941 was calculated at 6.3 per cent as against the European average of 1.4 to 1.6 per cent between 1913 and 1936/38, whilst Romania's was 4.5 per cent over the same period.[5] Still, this could not outweigh the dragging influence of agriculture on economic growth generally, as it was neither able to contribute significantly to domestic capital formation nor to induce an expansion of purchasing power for industrial goods on the home market in this area. Thus agriculture could not play the same role as it had played in the nineteenth-century industrialisation of Western Europe when part of the fast-growing population on the land was transferred into industry. In Eastern Europe the rapidly growing rural population could not be adequately absorbed into industry precisely because industrial growth, hindered by backward conditions in agriculture, was not rapid enough to do so.

In spite of the largely unfavourable conditions of the inter-war period, the bulk of these countries' economic growth did take place, above all, in industry. This was reflected in occupational distribution by a continuous movement away from the land, resulting in a decline of the agricultural proportion of the labour force accompanied by a rising proportion of people engaged in industry, commerce, transport and services. In Hungary there was an absolute drift away from agriculture into other occupations; in Poland figures are somewhat misleading for her total agricultural population increased from 17.4 to 19.5 million between 1921 and 1931 at the same time as the share of gainfully occupied persons in agriculture diminished absolutely; in Yugoslavia the volume of agricultural occupations still grew but the flow into other sectors was proportionately greater; whilst in Bulgaria by far the bigger part of the increase was absorbed by agriculture although industrial and other occupations grew as well.[6] Hungarian industries were able to absorb the net increase in the potentially active population between 1935 and 1937, yet industry and mining in Bulgaria, Yugoslavia and Romania were able to siphon off only approximately a quarter of the annual increase in their potentially active population.[7]

Structural changes in occupational distribution have progressed gradually but they reflected a tendency towards greater industrial employment. Thus the countries most lagging behind (Bulgaria, Romania, Yugoslavia) crossed the threshold of industrialisation in the inter-war period not in a turbulent spurt[8] nor in a dramatic take-off[9] but encumbered by enormous difficulties, not least of which was the disproportionate development within their economies.

The most decisive indicator of the industrial level attained by any economy in the inter-war period was considered to be the share of producer goods industries in total output. In the highly industrialised economies of Europe these branches had gained increasing strength from the beginning of the twentieth century at the same time as the share of consumer goods industries diminished relatively. In this respect industrial development in the Czech Lands was the only one to proceed on a pattern similar to that of Western European economies. Although the combined shares of the metallurgical, engineering and chemical industries lagged behind in comparison with Western development, their rate of growth was faster, whilst output of the textile industry grew at a slower rate than that of total industry.[10] The output of Czechoslovakia's producer goods industries overtook between 1923 and 1937 that of her consumer goods industries and for the first time in her industrial history textile production relatively fell behind. By contrast, the share of heavy industry in Hungary's total industrial output, measured according to the value of output in the Trianon territory, remained almost stagnant between 1913 and 1938, whilst the textile and clothing industries had risen to the second largest in Hungary.[11] In South-east European countries the weight of producer goods industries was less still. In Romania, Yugoslavia and Bulgaria heavy industry was largely limited to extraction or primary processing, while mechanical and electrical engineering was still relatively underdeveloped.

It is generally held that the course of industrialisation in Central-East and South-east Europe reflects a tendency contrary to modern demands of technical development compared to the processes in Western Europe between the two wars. This is considered as proven when the inverse relationship between producer and consumer goods industries for that region is established. Yet, it is necessary to ask further questions regarding the historical stage, the nature and structural make-up of this comparative economic backwardness from the viewpoint of the countries under investigation and their own internal development. So far, little attention has been paid to changes in the branch structure within producer and consumer goods industries.

Statistics on occupational distribution (resulting from population occupational and industrial censuses) are relatively more accessible than on volume and value of industrial output. These were taken as a basis for calculations of changes in structure by employment and nothing more is claimed than to sketch a picture of likely trends on a country-to-country comparison. Table 17.3 gives absolute employment figures in section A, which are converted into percentages in section B for the 1920s and 1930s respectively, i.e. in years selected, wherever possible, coinciding with peak years of employment.[12] Changes in branch structure reveal certain common features. In all investigated countries the share of mining in total industrial employment had declined in the latter part of the 1930s as against the 1920s from a mere difference in shares of 0.1 per cent in Hungary to as much as 9.7 per cent in Romania; equally general was the fall of the employment share in the food industries, which was steepest in the comparatively most backward economies of Bulgaria (12.6 per cent) and Yugoslavia (9.6 per cent) and also in the most advanced economy of Czechoslovakia (8 per cent). A definite although not pronounced decline (except for a sharp fall in Yugoslavia) was common to the wood industry everywhere. The compensating increases in employment shares were apparent in the chemical industry throughout all six countries as well as in the metallurgical and engineering industries, where the increase was greatest in Czechoslovakia and Yugoslavia (6 per cent) in both cases). The exception was Bulgaria, where employment registered a relative although not an absolute fall in mining, metallurgy and engineering, but not in chemicals and electricity. However, the major shifts occurred by substantial increases in the absolute and relative shares of employment in the textile industry except for Czechoslovakia, where employment in textiles shrank, and Poland, where the labour force somewhat declined due to the persistent problem of unemployment. In the other countries the share of the textile industry in total employment more than doubled in Yugoslavia between 1931 and 1938, whilst in Hungary and Romania it increased by approximately a third between 1928 and 1937. On the whole, during the inter-war period there occurred definite increases in the branches of heavy industry throughout the area, intermediate industries which largely supplied inputs for consumer goods tended to decline, whilst the share of light industries showed uneven development though mainly gradual increases except for the dramatic fall in food processing and the steep rise in textiles.

The results of the comparative statistical analysis of branch structures presented here show the fast advance of the textile industry in Central-East and South-east Europe, which became the most buoyant of the consumer industries. If consumer goods industries are taken in total, they in turn expanded absolutely and relatively more than producer goods industries. These historical facts do not seem to confirm the general theory of industrialisation of backward countries in twentieth-century conditions which was expounded by Alexander Gerschenkron[13] and is widely accepted. According to it a late-industrialising economy, particularly its producer goods sector, benefits from the advanced technological level reached by the leading industrial nations, and development is heavily weighted towards iron and steel, engineering and chemicals which, as a rule, become the leading force in the twentieth-century process of industrialisation. Central-East and East European countries evidently could not fully exploit the theoretically advantageous position of latecomers because industry had not built up a modern structure and was unable to supply the best developed modern technology. The course of industrialisation in the this area is thus held to reflect a tendency contrary to modern demands of technical and economic development compared to the processes in Western Europe and is, therefore, evaluated as a definite sign of economic backwardness.[14] These conclusions are unsatisfactory and gloss over important aspects which emerge more clearly from a quantitative examination. A specific point is the inter-war development of the textile industry.

TABLE 17.3 Changes in occupational structure of industry in Central-East and South-east European countries in the inter-war period

A) *Persons employed in the main branches of industry (in 000s)*

Branch of Industry	*Czecho-slovakia*		*Poland*		*Hungary*		*Romania*		*Yugoslavia*		*Bulgaria*	
	1926	*1935*	*1928*	*1938*	*1928*	*1937*	*1928*	*1937*	*1931*	*1938*	*1921*	*1938*
Mining	116	90	143.6[a]	104.8[a]	37	44	†79[d]	†62	27	12	9.6	10.2
Metallurgy and engineering	208	215	214.7[b]	228.2[b]	77	92	41	51	46	58	4.5	6.5
Chemical industry	30	39	38.8	48.0	13	20	20	28	11	16	0.8	2.5
Wood	62	49	56.6	53.1	16	15	40	44	87	42	2.3	3.4
Stone and earth	104	82	64.9	67.9	37[c]	25	14	16	20[cg]	17[cg]	4.0[cg]	5.2[cg]
Electricity	4		6.7	9.1	9	10		2		8	0.2	1.8
Food	139	42	63.0	62.9	45	43	30	35	79	43	27.6[f]	37.4[f]
Textiles	294	205	174.8	154.0	46	75	37	70	35	75	4.5	30.6
Clothing		*58	16.1	15.9	8	11						
Leather	30	9	5.7	6.3	7	12	9	12	11	14	0.8	1.4
Paper	25	27	13.7	16.5	4	6	11[e]	15[e]	5	11[e]	1.0	1.7
Glass and ceramics	40	22				7	5	8				
Printing	21	22	11.4	12.3	10	9			10		1.3	
Building			40.7	29.4								
Miscellaneous										4		2.4
Total	1073	860	850.7	808.4	309	369	286	343	331	300	56.6	103.1

Explanatory notes

a Including coal: 112.7 in 1928 and 79.4 in 1938.
b Including iron: 46.9 in 1928 and 43.9 in 1938; and zinc and lead: 13.0 in 1928 and 5.1 in 1938
c Including glass and ceramics.
d Persons employed in 1929.
e Including printing.
f Including tobacco: 20,000 employed.
g Including cement.
* Including footwear.
† Including petroleum.

B) *Persons employed in main branches of industry (in %)*

Branch of Industry	*Czecho-slovakia*		*Poland*		*Hungary*		*Romania*		*Yugoslavia*		*Bulgaria*	
	1926	*1935*	*1928*	*1938*	*1928*	*1937*	*1928*	*1937*	*1931*	*1938*	*1921*	*1938*
Mining	10.8	10.5	16.9[a]	13.0[a]	12.0	11.9	27.7†	18.0	8.2	4.0	17.0	9.9
Metallurgy and engineering	19.4	25.0	25.2[b]	28.2[b]	24.9	24.9	14.2	14.9	13.9	19.3	8.0	6.3
Chemical industry	2.8	4.5	4.6	5.9	4.2	5.4	7.0	8.2	3.3	5.3	1.4	2.4
Wood	5.8	5.7	6.6	6.6	5.2	4.1	13.9	12.8	26.3	14.0	4.0	3.3
Stone and earth	9.7	9.5	7.6	8.4	12.0[b]	6.8	4.8	4.7	6.0[g]	5.7[g]	7.0[g]	5.0[g]
Electricity	0.4		0.8	1.1	2.9	2.7		0.6		2.7	0.3	1.7
Food	12.9	4.9	7.4	7.8	14.5	11.7	10.6	10.2	23.9	14.3	48.8[f]	36.3[f]
Textiles	27.4	23.8	20.6	19.1	14.9	20.3	13.0	20.4	10.6	25.0	8.0	29.7
Clothing		*6.7	1.9	2.0	2.6	3.0						
Leather	2.8	1.1	0.7	0.8	2.3	3.3	3.2	3.5	3.3	4.7	1.4	1.4
Paper	2.3	3.1	1.6	2.0	1.3	1.6	3.8[e]	4.4[e]	1.5[e]	3.7	1.8	1.7
Glass and ceramics	3.7	2.6				1.9	1.8	2.3				
Printing	2.0	2.6	1.3	1.5	3.2	2.4			3.0		2.3	
Building			4.8	3.6								
Miscellaneous										1.3		2.3
Total	100	100	100	100	100	100	100	1 00	100	100	100	100

SOURCES:
Czechoslovakia: *Statistická příručka Republiky československé*, IV (1932); *Statistická ročenka Protektorátu Čechy a Morava, I* (1941) (strictly confidential publication of the Central Statistical Office of the *Protectorate* with an Appendix on the First Czechoslovak Republic);
Censuses of larger industrial enterprises, usually over 6 persons employed, in 1926 and 1935:
Sčítání živnostenských závodů v Re-publice československé podle stavu dne 27.5.1930 (Praha, 1935); *Statisticky zpravodaj* (Praha, 1939)
Poland: Calculated from Z. Landau and J. Tomaszewski, *Robotnicy przemystowi w Polsce 1918-1939* (Warsaw, 1971), p. 56 – based on monthly reports concerning large- and medium-scale industry, i.e. enterprises employing over 20 workers.
Hungary: *Annuaire Statistique Hongrois* (1928 and 1938).
Romania: *Conjunctura economiei româneşti* (1936); *Anuarul Statistic al Romaniei* (1929, 1939/40).
Yugoslavia: Statistika industrije z 1938 god. in N. Vučo, EEHP
Papers 21.
Bulgaria: Inquiry into heavy and protected industry in the Kingdom of Bulgaria during 1921 (Sofia, 1925); *Statisticheski Godishnik na tsarstvo Bulgaria (1938)*.

The last part of this paper discussed some of the reasons for the inverse relationship between producer and consumer goods industries found in the industrial growth of Central-East Europe as distinct from Western experience, particularly the reasons for the special prosperity of the textile industry. The objective framework in which manufacturing industries developed powerfully influenced their individual position in the economic structure of the countries in question.

On the supply side raw material, capital and labour have to be assessed briefly. Central-East European agriculture had great potentialities for supplying raw materials to manufacturing industries but did so to a very limited extent. Essentially, apart from the agricultural industries (flour milling, brewing, distilling, sugar refining) only the textile industry consumed some domestic supplies of wool, cotton, hemp, flax and silk. Yet a substantial part had still to be imported because agriculture concentrated traditionally on wheat-growing and hampered industrial development through deficient quantitative and qualitative adaptation of its production to the needs of industry.[15] In spite of this the textile industry utilised relatively more domestic supplies than most other industries whilst heavy industries produced either semi-finished goods or processed raw materials which were exported to be manufactured in more advanced industrial countries. This contributed little to the advance of domestic industrialisation. The textile industry could also utilise available supplies of labour and its needs of capital, though urgent, were of a lower order than most of the producer goods industries. It was pointed out that the common characteristic features of Central-East European economies were a chronic lack of capital and a surplus of labour on the land which theoretically was available for factory work. Industrialisation, however, was hampered also by a shortage of skilled labour. Therefore, only certain industries could develop which were able to draw on unskilled and semi-skilled labour. Again, the textile industry could and actually did utilise the available possibilities. Hungary can serve as an example of striking growth of unskilled and semi-skilled labour in proportion to skilled labour.[16] Seen from the aspect of supply the textile industry had the least unfavourable conditions for growth.

What then was the position on the demand side. The rise in industrial production was neither significantly stimulated nor accompanied by an expansion of consumer demand. Domestic markets were characterised by a low level of consumption in general and a very limited demand for consumer durables in particular. The overwhelming part of effective demand outside state purchases consisted of the needs of the essentials of life (food and clothing). Thus the home market offered greater opportunities for textiles than for other manufactured goods precisely because of the low purchasing power of the mass of the population.

However, neither the factors on the supply side nor the demand side which favoured the growth of the textile industry could have ensured the home market for domestic textile products. They would have been unable to compete in quantity, quality and price with Western products had it not been for constantly increasing restrictions on imports to the countries of the Central-East and South-eastern European area. This was an integral part of state intervention in their economic life. The textile industry benefited from the policy of state encouragement and protection generally. At the same time as the state restricted imports of manufactured goods, it exempted machinery and raw materials from customs duties, reduced rates for rail transport of merchandise, gave tax concessions to industrial enterprises, granted them monopoly rights, subsidised them directly and placed government orders at considerably higher than world prices. This meant chiefly orders for the armed forces, also for textiles. Yet, there was little expansion of the home market in the inter-war period and this led to restrictive practices by entrepreneurs and thus to both national and international cartelisation.

Thus the growth of the textile industry, like that of other state-encouraged branches, was not primarily induced by increasing purchasing power of the population in the individual countries. But above all, the protected markets of the inter-war period brought about an expansion of consumer goods industries which was hardly disturbed by the depression and this also enabled the relatively rapid growth of the textile industry.

In conclusion, the only striking change in structure during the slow and painful growth of the Central-East and South-east European economies was the advance of the textile industry to the top in the rank order of industries in the majority of them. Can this be regarded as a sign of economic backwardness? It does not seem to be enough to ascertain economic backwardness in comparison with the most industrialised nations in the world. The analysis attempted here suggests rather that in the conditions of the inter-war period, which were largely adverse to rapid industrial development, considerable and sustained industrial growth did take place in their economies in which the traditional forces of industrialisation in the consumer goods industries, above all in textile manufacture, came into play on a pattern that was similar to nineteenth-century industrial revolutions, with the important difference that this occurred without a significant extension of the home market and without marked linkages between consumer and producer goods industries. Thus objective limits were imposed on industrialisation in the inter-war period by the historical fact that it was based primarily on import substitution.

NOTES

1. R. Olsovský *et al., Prehled hospodárského vývoje Ceskoslovenska v letech* 1918-1945 (Prague, 1963) p. 24.
2. Z.P. Pryor, 'Czechoslovak Economic Development between the Two Wars', *Papers in East European Economics.* 11 (1972).
3. Cf. I.T. Berend and G. Ránki, *Hungary: A Century of Economic Development* (Newton Abbot, 1974), pp. 94-8; also K. Fink, 'Spezielle Aspekte der Wirtschafts-und Sozialentwicklung seit der Jahrhundertwende in Ungarn', *Sudosteuropa Jahrbuch,* 9 (1969) 128.

[4]Calculated from *Economic Survey of Europe in 1948* (Geneva, 1949), p. 22.

[5]According to calculations of L. Berov, 'Economic Development of Bulgaria between the Two World Wars 1918-1944', *Papers in East European Economics* 10 (1972) 8; I. Svennilson, *Growth and Stagnation in the European Economy* (Geneva, 1954) p. 57.

[6]*Industrialization and Foreign Trade* (Geneva, 1945), p. 65.

[7]Calculated according to *Economic Development in South-Eastern Europe*, PEP (London, 1945) p. 39.

[8]Cf. A. Gerschenkron, *Economic Backwardness in Historical Perspective* (New York, 1962), p. 353.

[9]Cf. W.W. Rostow, *The Stages of Economic Growth* (Cambridge, Mass., 1960).

[10]A. Teichova, 'Structural and Institutional Change in the Czechoslovak Economy 1918-1938', *Papers in East European Economics*, 6 (1972), p. 24.

[11]Berend and Ránki, op. cit., p. 143.

[12]It has to be borne in mind that different censuses used different criteria (e.g. definition of an industrial enterprise); in the case of employment figures some adjustments can be made to attain certain comparabilities across countries. Greater difficulties arise when calculating structure by industrial output because the concept of output is not homogeneous in national statistics. The only measure available is that of value of production, mainly, however, confined to the 1930s. Divergencies in price levels and in assumptions used in official and semi-official statistics are such that no amount of sophisticated econometrics can eradicate errors, omissions and uncertainties. Additional difficulties arise because consecutive statistical yearbooks do not adhere to a systematic branch classification but deviate from time to time from their own basic assumptions. For these reasons adjustments have been needed, but wherever possible branches have been brought as closely as possible to the International Standard Classification (ISIC), of course in a simplified form.

[13]Gerschenkron, op. cit., pp. 8-10, 26, 46-7, 50, 362-3.

[14]I.T. Berend and G. Ránki, *Economic Development in Central-East Europe in the 19th and 20th Centuries* (New York, 1974) p. 318; also A. Gerschenkron, op. cit., p. 213.

[15]Cf. e.g. R. Davidovic, 'Die Industrialisierung Jugoslaviens', *Sudosteuropa Jahrbuch*, 1 (1957) 171; N. Constantinescu and V.V. Axenciuc, 'The Economic Development of Romania in the Period between 1919-1939', *Papers in East European Economics*, 21 (1972), 20.

[16]Berend and Ránki, *Hungary*, p. 157.

Part 2

Regional Economic Disparities

Part 2a Northern, Western and Central Europe

18 Regional Economic Inequality in the Netherlands since 1600

Jan de Vries

1. INTRODUCTION

This modest contribution to the subject of regional economic inequality confines itself to a description of the major trends in regional inequality and a brief consideration of the possible causes of these trends. Little systematic work has yet been done on this subject, so my remarks should be regarded as introductory and provisional.

At the outset it must be kept in mind that the study of regional disparities is sensitive to the scale of analysis. In United States economic history (at least until the Civil War) it has become customary to speak of three regions: the North-east, the North-west, and the South. Each of these regions exceeds in size most of the world's nations. In the Netherlands historical regional analysis is most conveniently pursued on a provincial basis. Since 1814 the Netherlands has consisted of eleven provinces. During the Republic there were but seven – plus the territory of Drenthe and the Generality Lands, the most important of which was the modern province of North Brabant. As is the case with most historical provinces, the Dutch province boundaries are not ideal for economic analysis. To rectify this, modern economic analysis relies on a larger number of socio-economic regions. Unfortunately, very little pre-twentieth-century data can be regrouped to conform to these modern regions. When one keeps in mind the small size of the Netherlands, the provincial units will probably provide a sufficiently nuanced picture for the crude purposes on hand. Indeed, much of my analysis will be based on a two-region division of the nation. One should recognise, however, that most of the Dutch provinces can easily be divided into distinctive socio-economic regions – regions which, in fact, played an important role in provincial history during the time of the Republic.

2. THE REPUBLIC

From the founding of the Dutch Republic to the end of the seventeenth century the economy fell almost naturally into two distinctive regions. Since the province of Holland dominated the cultural, economic, and political life of the Republic to the point of having its name stand for that of the entire nation, one might suppose that the Republic consisted of Holland and 'the rest'. From a socio-economic point of view such a dichotomy would be too crude. In fact, as I tried to argue in my book *The Dutch Rural Economy in the Golden Age* (New Haven, 1974), it is more useful to distinguish the maritime provinces (Holland, Zeeland, Friesland, Groningen, and part of Utrecht) from the landward provinces (Overijssel, Gelderland, Drenthe, North Brabant, and (in the nineteenth-century) Limburg. A sharp, distinct line divided the diluvial from the alluvial Netherlands. The following scraps of evidence should suffice to establish the gap in economic and social well-being that existed between the Netherlanders living on the two sides of that line.

Daily wages for common outdoor labour hovered around 20 stuivers (one guilder) in most locations in Holland from about 1640 into the eighteenth century. The wages paid to comparable labour in the other maritime provinces fell short of the Holland level by from two to four stuivers. In the landward provinces few quotations exceed the 10-12 stuiver range.[1] In general, common labour in the landward provinces received little more than half the prevailing wage in Holland.

The inference one is inclined to draw from the wage data, that incomes in the maritime provinces greatly exceeded those in the landward provinces, is reinforced by tax evidence. Each province maintained its own tax system, a fact which makes inter-provincial comparisons difficult. The central government budget (small relative to the budgets of the provinces) was paid by each of the provinces according to a quota system. The quotas, once they were established in 1606, remained unchanged for nearly two centuries. This constancy was obviously influenced by a political tug-of-war among the provinces, and should not be taken as evidence of inter-provincial economic stability. Still, under the assumption that even in a political tug-of-war underlying economic realities could not entirely be ignored, it is worth while to look at the distribution of the central government budget. Table 18.1 presents the 1606 quota together with the population of each province in 1795 (the year of the first national census) expressed as a percentage of the total. There exists a bit more justification for such a comparison than might at first glance be thought. The population of the Republic changed very little from the late seventeenth century to 1795,[2] and the 1606 quotas remained in force until just before the time of the census. The decimal points are surely without significance, but the broad pattern that emerges is striking. Holland, with some 42 per cent of the population, paid nearly 60 per cent of the tax; Friesland and Zeeland also paid in excess of their numbers. Groningen probably did too, since its population in the seventeenth century was almost certainly far smaller than the number shown in the 1795 census. On the other hand, Gelderland, Overijssel and Drenthe all paid about half as much as the populations of their provinces would suggest. North Brabant, which was governed directly by the central government, paid taxes outside the quota system. Here again, the sums paid fell far short of the equal per capita division of tax burden level.

Finally, the results of my recent study of passenger transportation in the Dutch Republic strengthen the argument made above, and emphasise the importance of the maritime–landward division over the more customary Holland–'the rest' division. I calculated the total passenger-carring capacity of all public conveyances in the late seventeenth century – coaches, sailing vessels, and passenger barges *(trekschuiten)*. The approximately 800,000 inhabitants of Drenthe, Overijssel, Gelderland, North Brabant and eastern Utrecht had access to a passenger-carrying capacity of about 10 million passenger-kilometres, while the 1,200,000 inhabitants of Groningen, Friesland, Holland, Zeeland, and western Utrecht enjoyed access to 105 million passenger-kilometres. On a per capita basis, the inhabitants of the maritime provinces were served by seven times the capacity of their eastern neighbours.[3] When the various transport services are plotted on a map, a striking fact emerges: the boundaries of the Republic did not materially affect the flow of passengers; the boundary of the alluvial Netherlands (i.e., the maritime provinces) altered everything.

The wage and passenger transportation data also illuminate another characteristic of regional inequalities in the Dutch Republic – the remarkable balance within the maritime zone. In the existing literature on the pre-industrial European economy the view is frequently adumbrated that the reign of the Dutch Republic was really the reign of Amsterdam, and correspondingly, that the Republic was the last of the great city-states to dominate the European economy. If this were so, one should expect to find intense spatial differentiation, with Amsterdam dominating its hinterland as London or Paris dominated theirs.

The Republic's seventeenth-century urban structure did not correspond to this image. On the contrary, a balanced, mutually interdependent system of cities emerged in which Amsterdam was the largest city, but not a primate city. The passenger transportation study mentioned above demonstrates this point.[4] The transportation network gave most Dutch cities equal access to their mutual hinterland; it did not grossly favour one city.

Besides balance among the cities, the maritime zone exhibited balance between the urban and rural sectors. The most direct expression of this balance is the absence of a substantial rural-urban wage differential. Construction workers in the villages earned approximately the same wages as their urban counterparts, while agricultural labourers' earnings were comparable to those of urban common labourers.[5] A more general demonstration of this rural-urban balance is found in the successful specialisation of agriculture in the maritime provinces. For this I refer readers to my *Dutch Rural Economy in the Golden Age.* A consequence of this rural economic development was the spread of urban cultural influences to the countryside, a phenomenon documented in the inventories produced in the probating of peasant wills.[6] The level of comfort achieved by the more prosperous of the maritime sector's peasants had no counterpart in the landward zone. There the inventories reflect grim, culturally-isolating poverty.

TABLE 18.1 Provincial quotas for Dutch Central Government tax revenue and provincial population, both expressed as percentages of the total

	Year	*Holland*	*Gelderland*	*Overijssel*	*Friesland*	*Groningen*	*Utrecht*	*Zeeland*	*Drenthe*	*N. Brabant*
Tax	1606	58.3	5.6	3.5	11.7	5.8	5.8	9.4	1.0	*
Pop.	1795	42.0	11.8	7.3	8.8	6.2	5.3	4.4	2.2	11.4

TABLE 18.2 Provincial quotas for Dutch Central Government tax revenue and provincial population, both expressed as percentages of the total

Tax	1790	62	6	3	9	5	4	3	1	5
Tax	1807	57	5	4	10	5	7	5	1	5
Tax	1808	58	6.5	4.5	10	6	5.5	4	1	5.5
Pop.	1795	42.0	11.8	7.3	8.8	6.2	5.3	4.4	2.2	11.4

SOURCES: Dillen, J.G. van, *Van rijkdom en regenten* (The Hague, 1970) p. 271; Sohama, Simon, *Patriots and Liberators* (New York, 1977) p. 518; *Volks-Telling in de Nederlandsche Republiek,* compiled by order of the Commissie tot het ont werpen van een Plan van Constitutie voor het Volk van Nederland (The Hague, 1796).

In the eighteenth century the balanced economy of the maritime zone fell victim to international forces which undermined Dutch commercial hegemony. The process of economic decline is still not fully understood, but its consequence for regional differentiation in the Dutch Republic is very clear. Both Johan de Vries, in his fundamental study of this process, *De economische achteruitgang der Republiek in de achttiende eeuw* (Leiden, 1968), and I, in my study of inter-city passenger transportation, document a long-term process of economic concentration. That is, the decline of the economy as a whole brought with it a regrouping of economic activities in the remaining strong centres. The strongest of these, Amsterdam, attracted to itself much of the activity that had formerly been spread among the cities of the Dutch urban system. As a consequence, the seventeenth-century urban balance described above gave way to an increasing primacy of Amsterdam. Both the records of the *convooien* (a tax on shipping levied by the Dutch Admiralties, analysed by Johan de Vries) and those of inter-city passenger travel demonstrate with great clarity this process of concentration.

The changing regional balance is also indicated by the increasing political pressure to alter the quota system used to allocate central government taxation among the provinces. The outlying provinces of the maritime zone in particular screamed for relief.[7] Table 18.2, which presents the revised quotas for the provinces in the last years of the Republic and during the time of the Batavian Republic, shows, when compared to Table 18.1, the collapse of Zeeland's prosperity and the relative decline of Friesland and Utrecht as well. However, the basic distinction of maritime and landward provinces still seems to be valid.

A third phase in the history of Dutch regional inequality is ushered in at some time around 1780 – the outbreak of the Fourth Anglo-Dutch War – and lasts until approximately the mid-nineteenth century. This is a period in which the magnitude of the maritime–landward gap is probably reduced, not because of prosperity in the landward area but because of the weakness of Amsterdam's economy and of commerce in general.

As the entrepôt function of Amsterdam was liquidated, only the massive concentration of capital in the hands of Amsterdam bankers and the legacy of high wages and widespread charitable disbursements perpetuated the regional pattern established in earlier times. Our best estimates of Dutch investments in foreign and domestic government loans in the last years of the Republic are in excess of 1100 million guilders, with about half that amount invested abroad. The annual income from that invested capital amounted to some 40-50 million guilders, and was highly concentrated in a small number of families residing in and around Amsterdam and The Hague. In the Napoleonic period a substantial fraction of that capital was irretrievably lost to the Dutch investors as governments defaulted on their obligations. By 1814, then, neither commerce nor finance could nurture the primacy of Amsterdam. At the same time one can, with the benefit of hindsight, see early signs of an economic reorientation that was to obliterate the maritime–landward dichotomy that had characterised the Dutch economy since the time of the Revolt. The

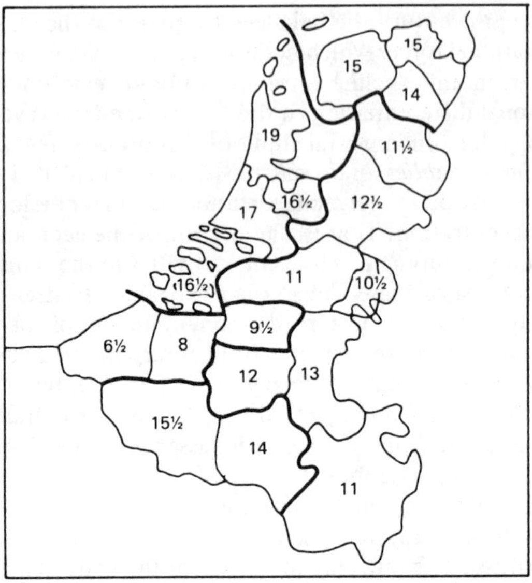

Fig. 18.1 Average adult wages in the Kingdom of the Netherlands, 1819

Province	*Daily wage in sturvers*	*Province*	*Daily wage in sturvers*
North Holland	19	Hainault	15½
South Holland	17	Naumr	14
Utrecht	16½	Liege	13
Zeeland	16½	South Brabant	12
Friesland	15	Luxembourg	11
Groningen	15	Limbourg	10½
Drenthe	14½	Antwerpen	9
Gelderland	12½	East Flanders	8
Overijssel	11½	West Flanders	6½
North Brabant	11		
Northern average	15	Southern average	9½

I.J. Brugmans, ed., *Statistieken van de Nederlandse nijverheid uit de eerste helft der 19 eeuw.* Rijks geschiedkundige publicatien. XCVIII (The Hague, 1956) 247-417. Compiled by Joel Mokyr, *Industrialization in the Low Countries, 1795-1850* (New Haven, 1976) pp. 176-7.

economic growth of the lower Rhineland increased the importance of east-west trade. Not only did the growing transit trade stimulate the growth of Rotterdam, but it affected the fortunes of towns in the eastern and southern provinces as well.[8] The earlier orientation of the maritime provinces to the sea had placed the landward provinces in an isolated position. The east-west axis following the great rivers that emerged in the course of the nineteenth century ended the economic marginality of the adjacent landward provinces (although it contributed to the new, growing economic marginality of the northern, increasingly more agricultural, provinces of Friesland and Groningen).

Little is yet known about the regional differences in the movement of Dutch wage rates in the nineteenth century. A survey of industrial wage rates made in 1819 has been analysed by Joel Mokyr. Since the Kingdom of the Netherlands then included modern-day Belgium, the Belgian provinces were included in this survey. Fig. 18.1 presents the average industrial wage for each province. The high-wage position of the maritime provinces, a situation of long standing, is still evident in these data. The landward provinces continued, just as they had in the seventeenth century, to offer wages that were from 4 to 8 stuivers per day lower than was the case in Holland. Nowhere in the Netherlands, however, does one find the truly desperate situation that characterised Flanders. I am currently working on wage data generated by mid-nineteenth century industrial surveys. My initial impression of these data is that they show a substantial lessening of the east-west wage gap. Wage rates reported for Amsterdam in 1851 show virtually no change from the seventeenth century. Quotations for many North Holland locations in 1860 show the same thing. Meanwhile, wages in the outlying provinces seem to have been creeping upward. While about 1 guilder per day, or 5 to 7 guilders per week, was the most common industrial wage in Holland, comparable quotations for rural locations in North Brabant range between 3 and 6 guilders (outlying observations excluded). In rural Limburg, 4.5 to 5.5 guilders per week brackets the bulk of all observations.[9] The catching-up process was the fruit of early industrialisation, which was concentrated outside the maritime region. Agricultural wages in the landward provinces took much longer to catch up with the maritime region.

3. INDUSTRIALISATION IN THE NINETEENTH AND TWENTIETH CENTURIES

In the nineteenth and early twentieth centuries, the period of early industrialisation in the Netherlands, powerful forces were set in motion that reduced the amount of regional inequality. By 1968 the income per taxable head in the most favoured region (the western region, comprising North and South Holland and Utrecht) was 6 per cent above the national average while the income in the least favoured region (the north, comprising Friesland, Groningen, and Drenthe) was 9 per cent below the national average.[10] What were these forces?

Both the obsolete economic structure of the urbanised western region and the favourable demographic and agricultural character of the sandy-soiled eastern provinces stimulated the development of textile production in the latter zone. This industry eventually benefited from technological changes which redounded to the benefit of the economy of the landward provinces, particularly Overijssel and North Brabant.

At the same time, the Netherlands failed to participate in the rapid urbanisation that was characteristic of most industrialising countries in the nineteenth century. Because the economy was already endowed with many large but economically obsolete cities, new economic activities tended to avoid them in favour of locations in smaller places (i.e. Eindhoven, Tilburg, Enschede). Cities in excess of 20,000 inhabitants accounted for 28.5 per cent of the Dutch population in 1830, a figure about equal to the 1795, and, presumably, 1660 percentage. By 1870, the figure was still only 28.9 per cent, despite considerable population growth. Only after that census year does urbanisation proceed. In 1909 cities with over 20,000 inhabitants comprised 40.4 per cent of the population.

Since the largest city, Amsterdam, continued to stagnate until late in the nineteenth century, and since most urban growth was taking place in small industrial cities in the landward provinces, the Netherlands escaped the agglomerative effect engendered by the rapid growth of a cosmopolitan centre. Overpopulation of the highly urbanised western provinces is today regarded as a problem warranting government intervention to speed the relocation of economic activities to the eastern provinces. But the percentage of the Dutch population in the three western provinces exceeds by very little the comparable figure for 1795, or, probably, 1660. Given the pronounced tendency found in most industrial countries for population to become less evenly distributed and to concentrate in the largest cities, this is a noteworthy fact.

Another factor contributing to the gradual, long-term reduction of regional inequality has been the successful development of specialised, commercial agriculture. The seventeenth-century 'golden age' had endowed the maritime zone with such an agricultural economy. In the nineteenth century, the agriculturally more backward eastern areas, with different soil types and rural social structures, also came to benefit from the commercial links, marketing organisations, and technological developments that had long existed in the maritime provinces.

What economic development – whether industrial or agricultural – could not accomplish for the landward provinces, interregional (and international) migration attempted to do. The economic viability of the areas that remained predominantly agricultural – most notably Zeeland and Friesland – was preserved through a large-scale out-migration.

Finally, government policies have played a role in reducing regional imbalances. But this is almost entirely a phenomenon of the very recent past, and will not be developed in this paper.

4. CONCLUSIONS

Theories of industrialisation and of modernisation often uphold as a common pattern of regional development a two-phase model in which early industrialisation brings with it growing regional imbalance and inequality while industrial maturity tends to mitigate these features. Pre-industrial regional imbalance is, presumably, not thought to be a problem. This rapid survey of Dutch regional development has found that, first of all, the pre-industrial development of an urban commercial economy in the maritime provinces did not necessarily subjugate the rural to the urban sector, but did create a striking and enormous inequality between itself and the less monetised, less urbanised economy of the landward provinces. The ability of the commercial heart of the entire European economy to integrate economically a nearby region with a low-productivity agricultural sector was, to say the least, limited. Amsterdam seems to have had closer contacts with Dithmarschen and the banks of the Vistula than it had with North Brabant and the 'Achterhoek' of Gelderland.[11]

A second conclusion is that the economic decline of the period 1670-1780 brought with it an increase in regional inequality. Contrary to the generally-held opinion that the Dutch economy was stagnant in this period but did not actually suffer a decline of per capita income, it now appears that there was a real and substantial fall in income, at least to the mid-eighteenth century. Related to this was a tendency toward disintegration of supra-regional economic ties and a corresponding increase in regional autarchy.

The final conclusion of this survey is that industrialisation, when at length it began in a Dutch economy dominated by a structurally obsolete urban sector, tended from the outset to erode the broad patterns of regional inequality. However, this was the effect of a combination of factors that may very well have been unique to the Netherlands' geography and prior economic structure. The long-delayed industrialisation of the Netherlands and the antiquated economic structure of her nineteenth-century cities have been a blessing to the country's twentieth-century inhabitants.

NOTES

[1] Vries, J. de, 'An Inquiry into the Behavior of Wages in the Dutch Republic and the Southern Netherlands, 1580-1800', *Acta Historiae Neerlandica,* no. 10, 1978, pp. 79-97.

[2] See: Faber, J.A., *et al.,* 'Population changes and economic developments in the Netherlands: a historical survey', *A.A.G. Bijdragen,* no. 12, 1965, pp. 47-113; Vries, J. de, *The Dutch Rural Economy in the Golden Age, 1500-1700* (New Haven, 1974).

[3] Vries, J. de, 'Barges and Capitalism; Passenger Transportation in the Dutch Economy, 1632-1839', *A.A.G. Bijdragen,* no. 21, 1978, ch. 3, Tables 3.4 and 3.5.

[4] Ibid., ch. 12.

[5] 'Inquiry into the behaviour of Wages', pp. 94-5.

[6] Vries, J. de, 'Peasant Demand Patterns and Economic Development: Friesland 1550-1750', in Parker, W.N., and Jones, E.L. (eds) *European Peasants and Their Markets* (Princeton, 1975) 205-65.

[7] For an interesting discussion of the struggle to revise the regional incidence of taxation see: Schama, S., *Patriots and Liberators. Revolution in the Netherlands 1780-1813* (New York, 1977).

[8] Nusteling, H.P.M., *De Rijnvaart in het tijdperk van stoom en steenkool 1831-1914* (Amsterdam, 1974).

[9] These data are drawn from the annual *Provinciale verslagen* published by the Gedeputeerde Staten of each province from 1851 to 1872.

[10] Vries, Johan de, *De Nederlandse economie tijdens de 20ste eeuw.* (Utrecht, 1973) p. 21.

[11] These observations could be developed in the context of the globalised two-sector model of Wee, H. van der and Peeters, Th., 'Een dynamisch model voor de seculaire ontwikkeling van de wereld handel en de welvaart (12^{e} - 18^{e} eeuw', *Tijdschrift voor Geschiedenis,* vol. 82, 1969, pp. 233-49. Translated in French in *Annales E.S.C.,* vol. 25, 1970, pp. 100-26. The close link forged between Amsterdam and the North Sea coastal areas is evident from the large number of migrants to Amsterdam from these areas. For this see Hart, Simon, *Geschrift en Getal* (Amsterdam, 1976).

19 Regional Differences, Differential Development and Generative Regional Growth

Herman Freudenberger and Gerhard Mensch

INTRODUCTION

What are the preconditions for the industrialisation of a region? What factors provide the changes in technology, social and economic organisation, and policy-making that transform a region from a more traditional state of existence to modern industrialisation? We wish to address ourselves to the conceptualisation of the processes by which these factors become part of the transformation phenomenon. In this context, generic developments of new technologies, institutions, etc., are being viewed as innovations. Their emergence represents an evolutionary process, e.g. like mutations in the genes, which through their selection succeed in the relevant space and time. This intellectual approach lends itself easily to an analogy between the natural economy (sociobiology) and the political economy (urban and industrial economics), as suggested 'by terminological pairs like species/industry, mutation/innovation, mutualism/exchange, and evolution/progress'.[1]

In attempting to understand the evolutionary process of regional industrialisation, we began with the case of Brno, Czechoslovakia, where in the middle of the seventeenth century a generic process of self-improvement took place that culminated a century later in what we have called a key innovation, setting the region on its course to becoming in the nineteenth century the 'Manchester' of the Habsburg Monarchy. A great textile industry and a strong machine-building industry gave the region its character.[2] Possibly not completely coincidentally to this evolution of industrial practice in Brno there took place in the nineteenth century a chain of events of major proportions for the development of modern evolution theory: it was in Brno, in 1866, that Gregory Mendel read his epochal paper: 'Versuche uber Pflanzenhybriden' to the local society for research in the natural sciences. Mendel, a member of the Augustinian order, had for years been experimenting with sweet peas in the garden of the monastery in Brno, encouraged by the head of the institution, who himself had engaged in studies and experimentation on Merino sheep breeding. Thus, it is quite clear that there existed a benevolent intellectual climate in Brno by virtue of a long-standing interest in the scientific improvement of Merino sheep, an interest that was fostered by the needs of the

Brno fine woollen cloth industry.[3] We might take notice, in passing, of another possible parallel between evolution in industrial practice and the evolution of the theory of evolution. Charles Darwin, being related by blood and by marriage to the family of the great eighteenth-century industrialist Josiah Wedgwood and whose grandfather Erasmus Darwin was a close friend of Wedgwood as well as of another well-known industrialist, Matthew Boulton, could easily have been influenced in his evolution research by his industrial environment.

MAIN HYPOTHESIS AND IMPORTANT FACTORS

The determination of historical factors that control regional economic development is conceptionally and methodologically new territory. In the conscious strategy that policy-makers may adopt to effect the economic development of the various regions in the nation, there exist at least two distinct approaches: (1) a differential approach in which central agencies evaluate a given set of criteria for different regions and then identify that region that provides the best mix of preconditions for certain innovations; (2) a generative approach, in which local agencies examine existing factors and institutional forms and their evolution with a view of drafting new institutions on a well-developed stem within their region.

Although both central and local government authorities interacted in Brno, Brno's industrial evolution fits more into the second category than the first. Firstly, it would be an exaggeration to say that national government policy-makers in the middle of the eighteenth century actually went through much screening before they chose Brno over other areas. That their development projects succeeded in their purpose in Brno may have been the result of a random occurrence. However, secondly, there is strong evidence of a generative approach taken by Brno officials, and Brno may be a good case for 'luck' *and* 'cunning'. In order to draw lessons from the Brno case, one can nevertheless determine that the success of the generative approach in the Brno region depended on a long evolution of socio-economic factors that clustered in their time of maturation in what we have called elsewhere a protostructure, leading to the key innovation in Brno with its resultant diffusion in the region and the creation of backward and forward linkages in the region and in its national and international context.

The generative approach raises a question concerning the extent to which one can generalise on the basis of a detailed examination of only one case, even though it may be laced from time to time with examples from other cases. In some ways all economic development, on whatever level, is unique. If we were solely to take this generative approach, we would be reduced to an anecdotal description of growth in a given area, be it region or country. While we are convinced that much in every historical phenomenon is unique, we also assert that definite patterns can be ascertained by careful examination of a number of cases. In our empirical work we have reached the point where we should like to compare the results of the generative approach applied to a set of regional development cases.

In economic policy-making today, regional policies play an important role. On the national economic policy level, the objective usually is the maintenance of balanced development, and a differential approach is taken to help lagging regions in reaching average standards of living, income, and service delivery: On the regional level, more often than not, particular interests in the more advanced regions cater for faster advances and higher growth rates. Thus, the differentiated approach of national policy and the generative approach of regional policy are not necessarily harmonic; in the extreme, they may in fact depart from one another and result in a widening gap; a gap which Myrdal once described as a vicious circle of poverty. By the same token, it may as easily result in a virtuous circle of prosperity: if the windfall gains from advances in the more prosperous regions pull the lagging regions faster than they can manage to advance themselves (locomotive theory of differential development).

If differential development is not *per se* viewed as an undesirable end of regional policy, which is not at all clear in modern times, then – in a world of specialisation – it is important for regional policy to capitalise on comparative advantages, say, regional differences, in order to achieve qualitative growth. This does not mean that the welfare state should or will allow regional competition to run wild in the attempt to mobilise the economic potential of the entire nation. But it means that the generative approach to regional development may deserve a more positive attention in actual practice than it currently seems to be given.

A generative approach cannot be taken by regional agencies without backing by national government agencies. This implies

1. that socio-political factors, power games, institutional linkages may play a stronger role in regional economic development than is usually assumed by economic analysis of regional growth and their preconditions; and
2. that economic factors, such as capital endowment, labour, transportation cost, etc., may turn out to be of less influence on locational choice of industries, and for a higher rate of innovative investments, in a particular region, than is usually assumed in economic policy-making.

Our *main hypothesis, therefore,* is that the generative approach to regional development cannot ignore the economic factors and comparative advantages of a region with respect to the creation or the expansion of particular industries; but the decisive condition for success of the generative approach is a favourable climate for improvement and achievement – a climate which exists, if it exists, in the hearts and brains of cultural, political, social, and economic leaders; such a climate provides external support for projects, it protects the innovator from unpredictable interventions of powerful individuals and antagonistic institutions, it motivates, remotivates, and it economises on transaction cost, which may in the final analysis be the crucial element in industrial evolution.

As a corollary to this hypothesis we may expect not the comparative advantages of some (closed) region to play the most decisive role in its industrial evolution but the region's openness for cultural stimulation, resource and technology transfer, exchange, and sharing of ideas with cultural, political, social, and economic leaders elsewhere.

Rewarding as the classical investigation of economic development seems to be, there are numerous difficulties associated with it. In focusing on regional development one tends to emphasise spatial characteristics or at the very least economic and social *factors within a spatial context.* It is then the first task to define what spatial characteristics are relevant for a region or, for that matter, a country. The main distinction that must be made from the start between a country or a nation and a region in their economic contexts is that a country is determined almost completely by the political process, whereas a region within a country can more easily be examined on the basis of objective criteria. The region is unquestionably a more open economy than the nation, with various economic and social factors being fairly free to flow in directions that upon examination seem to be natural or at least predictable. The national economy includes within it more arbitrary or unique conditions than the region. Unfortunately, no hard and fast definitions have yet evolved for the 'open boundary' of a region. Consequently, political and administrative delineations have some usefulness.[4]

It will not be our purpose at this time to attempt a convincing definition of a region. We will therefore adopt as a rule of thumb the proposition that it is a geographical entity dominated by an urban core and surrounded and supported by hinterlands that are frequently, although not inevitably, rural in nature. On a historical basis there are many problems associated even with this simplified approach since relevant data, especially on the countryside, are difficult and often impossible to obtain. In short, we feel hardly in a position to test the theoretical approaches of scholars like Thunen, Christaller, Losch or Alfred Weber. Nevertheless, their suggestions as well as those of investigators of innovation and diffusion serve as important road markers for the direction in which we wish to proceed.[5]

Relevant elements that should be examined in this process include the following. (1) Natural resource endowment. Special attention must be paid to those resources that are unique to the area and those that are ubiquitous to all areas. Greater specialisation and concentration can be expected when there are unique resources as well as when their weight is great and therefore the transportation costs are high. (2) Human resource endowment. To our judgement, this is the critical variable. Where nature produces useful commodities without the prodding of the human hand, populations tend to be highly dispersed and at low densities. If this proposition is correct, it could suggest, among other possibilities, that (3) the cost of transportation is another critical variable. The implication associated with this proposition is that people generally prefer living in small clusters. On the other hand, however, (4) agglomeration may be the result of the human propensity to associate with larger numbers of the species. The huge cities of our own day would suggest that there is hardly any limit to this propensity. If, besides agglomeration serving a social purpose, it also provided, as seems self-evident, (5) significant external economies of scale both in production and consumption and therefore improved welfare, then one of the conducive factors for change would have had to be the ease and reduction in cost of communication, especially if it is not mere facts that are communicated but wishes, visions, and innovation plans. Such information is a precious commodity which tends to flow freely only among people who know and trust one another to a certain extent.

Also of relevance for industrial change in a region are the indigenous conditions that affect the localisation and growth of industry. One might investigate the demography of the area, for example. For one thing, is there a critical size of the population? For entrepreneurs outside the area looking for the most propitious location for their manufacturing activities both a minimum and a maximum absolute population size may have useful aspects. As a rule of thumb a prospective industrialist may make part of his decision on the basis of the labour force that a particular number of population could be expected to supply. There might be a minimum population below which an industrialist might feel that it would be unlikely that a sufficient able labour supply could be generated.

Absolute size is of course only one consideration. Possibly more important is the quality of the population as disaggregated into age distribution, health and skill attributes. The importance of these factors relates to the production function of an area. The aged and the very young quite obviously do not figure in the labour force. Consequently, if the age-pyramid of a large population reveals a low percentage of employable persons in the important age groups between 16 and 40, possibly the labour force will not seem very attractive to a potential employer. Similarly, the health of the population will have an important effect. Days lost from work on account of illness reduces production. Consequently, the reports of doctors investigating in 1819 the conditions in factories in Manchester and Stockport did not merely provide information on social problems but reflected significant economic effects as well.[6] Health and nutrition today and even more in the past were closely related to each other. The provision of abundant and cheap foodstuffs becomes therefore an important consideration in the examination of regional industrialisation.[7] Food as a resource is fairly ubiquitous but its availability at low prices and in sufficient quantity has always been a major concern of urban governments. This characteristic has been very well pointed out by F.J. Fisher in an article on what might be considered modified Thunen rings around London in the sixteenth century.[8]

Another factor that cannot be ignored is the general level of education, aside of specialised training for a craft. Were the prospective workers literate? Were there schools that were accessible to them? As Herman van der Wee has pointed out for the southern Netherlands in the sixteenth century, these were certainly factors important for industrial activity. Van der Wee made the further trenchant observation that a large part of the population lived in an area where the industrial tradition was old and strong. These points were no less relevant for eighteenth-century regional industrialisation efforts than in the sixteenth century.

The size and composition of a population figures critically in the production function. It is also an essential element in the demand for goods to be produced. To be sure, here the question arises of how important local demand was for the evolving industry in the eighteenth and nineteenth centuries. In the case that we have examined in some detail, the industrialisation of Brno, the fine woollen cloth industry located there was little dependent on the demand of the local population. For that matter, we have suggested, it was also not critically dependent on the supply side either.

To try to understand the consumption pattern of the city better, one would of course have to examine in detail income and wealth distributions. On the surface this should not be an overwhelming problem. It does, however, become difficult despite the availability of fairly good data, such as income tax records where they exist,[9] because of the considerable movement of the population. This was especially true of the upper classes, who no less than the jet-set of our own day, were highly peripatetic. The rich aristocracy, especially, had many residences and generally found it desirable to make appearances at all of them during some part of the year. Nevertheless, residence itself may not be a good indicator of demand since the rich persons especially usually remained in one place only temporarily.

Income and wealth distribution should be expected to have had an effect also on the production function. The wealthier should be expected to save more and be more interested in investing their savings in profitable endeavours. Needless to say, this proposition needs careful examination in relation to aristocrats, whose profit maximisation proclivities may not have been highly developed. Since they did, nevertheless, command great resources potentially useful for industrial capital formation, their contribution should not be dismissed out of hand. To be sure, even when they did invest in industry, it may have been more a consumption matter for them than a profit orientation. A great landowner like Count Hugo von Salm-Reifferscheidt, whose major properties lay not far from Brno, was indeed deeply involved in bringing industry to the region. But one still sees the romantic cavalier even in some of these actions, as when he feigned illness while crossing the English Channel, having before embarkation strapped the plans for spinning machines under his clothing around his legs. Innovating entrepreneurs need not always be profit-maximisers; they can easily find their utilities in other directions.

At the other extreme of the income distribution were of course the paupers, who might be expected to be part of the production function as a labour force. But they proved to be of questionable value. For one thing, their skills were frequently not useful for industry. In addition, they exhibited a strong secular opposition to being included in a labour force. In Brno, for example, the textile factories existing in the late 1760s experienced labour shortages despite the fact that armies of beggars existed. Frustrated by the able-bodied beggars, the employers in this case took on the less resistant orphans and made spinners of them.[10]

Given a degree of specialisation, did industry tend to locate in a particular region? If an area harboured a skilled population, was this fact decisive or even very influential in having factories establish themselves there? The evidence on the Brno case and its prehistory is ambiguous. Originally, it had been the government's purpose to introduce the manufacture of fine woollens into the Habsburg Monarchy since large quantities were being imported from abroad. For that purpose, skilled workers had been brought in from Verviers (Belgium) to train native workers in Jihlava (Iglau) and by their example to introduce the methods of manufacturing fine woollen cloth. This attempt failed utterly because Jihlava, a city that had a long tradition in the making of cloth, was dominated by master guildsmen. Quite clearly, then, the area of specialisation was not a desirable location for new industry. Tradition prevailed against the self-evident better interest of the clothmakers, a large number of whom were unemployed and none of whom produced the type of cloth that the Belgians were trying to introduce. The Habsburg government's next step was to place the Verviers craftsmen in a rural setting where there would be no interference from guilds. There they were to train peasants who had scarcely any tradition concerning industrial production to fall back on. The result again was failure. Stubbornly insisting that this enterprise must succeed, the Empress Maria Theresa then effected its transfer to Brno. Here the results were brilliant, if the long run is the criterion.

GENERATIVE APPROACH

The industrialisation of Brno was the result of generative development. Over time, the social arrangements in this region evolved in such a way as to provide a propitious climate for the fine woollen cloth industry. This evolution had its purposeful elements but also included 'necessary' factors that may have had other goals. Moreover, it was created through a combination of exogenous and endogenous phenomena and influences.

What locational advantages did Brno have? To the best of our understanding there were few indeed that should have proved attractive to a rational decision-maker. For example, little cloth was being manufactured there before the factory came, so that in a tabulation of some 30 cloth-manufacturing centres in the Monarchy Brno was not even mentioned. In terms of other human resources it did show a fairly broad representation of skills, mainly, however, for the production of luxury goods for local consumption. One factor of production, however, stood out: entrepreneurship. There was clearly leadership here that presumably did not exist elsewhere. It is telling that the factory was offered to Jihlava and Vienna, and in both places it was unceremoniously rejected. DiTella's thesis of regional development may thus be supported by historical evidence.[11] He suggests that a group that he calls associational leaders, persons who take an active part in what might be called a 'booster' organisation, will be found where a community prepares itself for industrialisation. Membership in such a group is temporary and voluntary, having not necessarily a direct connection with the main occupation of a person. Piecing together bits and pieces of evidence, one might conclude that such a group, composed of government officials and merchants, did indeed exist in Brno. As early as the 1650s, when Brno was still reeling from the devastating blows of the Thirty Years War, a prominent citizen of the town proposed methods to the Emperor in Vienna for its improvement and development.[12] Another similar historical accident may be the establishment in Brno of a development bank in 1751. Its goal was to support and encourage the expansion of industry in Moravia in general, and it was responsible for bringing to Brno in 1764 the fine-cloth factory that we have dubbed the key innovation.

Also in the case of Brno, external influences from Vienna were of vital importance. Nevertheless, it is our conclusion that external efforts without strong internal, active support would have proved as unavailing in Brno as they did earlier in Jihlava and elsewhere. For the presence of associationist leaders in Brno we give several examples in our book. We can identify one person (Johann Anton Kehrnhofer), a government official and head of the semi-governmental development bank, as the one primarily responsible for the transfer of the factory to Brno.

There were others who could be considered associational leaders. One of these was the mayor of Brno in 1750, who is reported to have pushed through the resolution by which the municipality became a shareholder in the investment bank against considerable opposition.

Leaders who fit into this category may not follow very rational paths of action. Rational economic action would frequently dictate the largest short-term returns, which in a fairly normal, static situation also means reducing risks. Conscious efforts to industrialise an area, on the other hand, more often than not entail considerable risk and uncertainty. In the Brno case it is interesting, for example, that the wealthiest person in the city took no apparent interest at all in the development bank that was founded in 1750. His son, however, in the 1760s was in the forefront of the industrialisation drive. At the same time, the son also lost his inherited wealth in this venture; but the Brno region and for that matter the entire Habsburg Monarchy gained greatly. Several fine-cloth merchants in the city also invested in the factory and lost either all or a sizeable portion of their contribution. They of course may not fit into the 'associationist' category since they might be considered to have followed their own self-interest. Nevertheless, their problem comes up for consideration, because in terms of a rational economic approach, given the norms of the time, they acted perversely. Merchants normally restricted themselves to commercial transactions. In this case, there may well have been a mitigating circumstance. Well after the fact of their involvement, they complained that the Emperor had convinced them to participate, presumably against their better judgement. Be this as it may, in any case it proves the point that the socio-political linkages among the 'associationist leaders' provided for the push and pull which propelled the industrial revolution in the Brno region.

DIFFERENTIAL APPROACH

Based on our examination of Brno's industrialisation we may conclude that even though the generative approach seemed to have been logical for Brno, it was in fact not consciously employed. On the contrary, the differential approach was more attractive to the government planners. When they wanted to expand the woollen industry so that the Habsburg Monarchy would be less dependent on foreign suppliers and thus retain more money within its borders, they chose Jihlava, the Moravian cloth centre, for their activities. In this they were logical; this traditional cloth centre presumably had the technological basis for expansion and since many of the masters and other workers were unemployed at the time, the labour supply should have been elastic. Their calculations were reasonable but the result was not forthcoming mainly because they had ignored a number of institutional sociological variables, among them the strong disinclination of guild masters to be willing to learn from others.

Similarly, Liberec (Reichenberg) in northern Bohemia had for two centuries at least been a major centre of cloth production. Controlled by guilds and owned by a manorial lord, the city was also far from Vienna. It may for such reasons as these not have been a good candidate for an innovational breakthrough. Moreover, it had earlier in the eighteenth century displayed tendencies in opposition to proposed innovations. Interestingly enough, Brno's successful industrialisation provided the north Bohemian city with a model and an impulse for its own drive toward factory industry in the 1790s.

Olomouc (Olmütz), a city of a similar size to Brno and located not far away, was another potential candidate for an industrialisation drive. It was the seat of the Moravian archbishop and the ancient capital of the province. Moreover, it was also the site of educational institutions of some importance. In terms of demand and supply it should have been about as attractive as Brno.

In terms of economic factor endowments, there were of course some other towns and regions where decision-makers might have determined to place and promote the fine-cloth industry. On purely economic grounds, Brno seems to have been a chance choice. On closer scrutiny, however, it appears that a long period of generative development had prepared its inhabitants for its role, whereas this preparatory development was largely absent in the other likely locations.

IMPLICATIONS FOR FURTHER RESEARCH

In the near future we wish to elaborate our method by including additional criteria. In the past we have concentrated to a large extent on factors that changed, that is, on innovational processes. What about those factors that were inherited and remained unchanged? Among other things, we should evaluate more closely the relationship of law and economics. Were laws interpreted more beneficially to private economic actors, for example? Was there any push from within the Brno community to reform laws, to simplify them or to make them more malleable for industrial purposes? Possibly even more important at this time and place was the question of governmental control. There is no doubt whatsoever that the government of Maria Theresa was pushing industrialisation with all its power. Was the mere fact that some of the agencies entrusted with this task had regional headquarters in Brno significant? If so, why did not a similar configuration of government bureaux create the conditions for industrialisation in Prague or in Klagenfurt or in Graz, all of them provincial capitals? We are convinced that the crucial regional differences will be found in the socio-political network, which allows enterprising people at some places to develop the endogenous potential and to capture the external benefits from resource and technology transfer, whereas it stifles the process of innovation in other less 'open' places.

NOTES

[1] J. Hirshleifer, 'Competition, Cooperation, and Conflict in Economics and Biology', *American Economic Review,* 68 (1978) 238-43.

[2] H. Freudenberger and G. Mensch, *Von der Provinzstadt zur Industrieregion* (Brünn-Studie) (Göttingen, 1975).

[3] This hypothesis is partly based on a discussion with Dr Roger Wood, Department of Zoology, University of Manchester. See also H. Freudenberger, *The Industrialization of a Central European City* (Edington, England, 1977).

[4] Cf. A.G. Kenwood, 'Fixed Capital Formation on Merseyside, 1800-1913', *Economic History Review,* Second Series, xxxi (1978), 214n.

[5] Cf. Harry W. Richardson, *Regional Growth Theory* (New York-Toronto, 1973) 7, 55.

[6] Lords Papers 1819 (HL24).

[7] Cf. Joseph von Sonnenfels, *Von der Theuerung in den grossen Städten und dem Mittel derselben abzuhelfen* (Wien, 1770). See also Hugo Wermelinger, *Lebensmittelteuerungen, ihre Bekämpfung und ihre politischen Rückwirkungen in Bern* (Bern, 1971).

[8] F.J. Fisher, 'The Development of the London Food Market, 1540-1640', *Economic History Review,* v (1934), No. 2, 46-64.

[9] Cf. Peter Stolz, *Basler Wirtschaft in vor – und früh industrieller Zeit* (Zürich, 1977) 61ff.

[10] Freudenberger, *The Industrialization of a Central European City,* p. 102.

[11] Torcuato S. diTella, 'The Concept of Polarized Development in Regional Planning – a Sociological Interpretation', in A. Kuklinski and R. Petrella (eds), *Growth Poles and Regional Policies* (Hague-Paris, 1972) 82f.

[12] P.H. Morgenthaler came in 1653 to Brno as a judge, and he published a grandiose plan for the mercantilistic development of Habsburg provinces. Ten years later, F.S. Malivski von Maliv, a lawyer in Brno, presented the Kaiser with a similar

plan. Note that these pioneering schemes preceded the classical works of mercantilism (Thomas Munn, *England's Treasure by Foreign Trade,* 1664) and cameralism (Johann Joachim Becher, Wilhelm von Schroeder, Philip von Hörnig).

20 The Development of a Growth Pole in the Nineteenth Century illustrated by the example of Nuremberg

R. Gömmel

1. BACKGROUND

About 1800, i.e. long before the beginning of the industrial revolution in Germany, nothing – apart from the century-old crafts and trade tradition – seemed to speak in favour of a steep economic rise of Nuremberg in the nineteenth century. Still known world-wide in the sixteenth century, it lost more and more its importance. In the early nineteenth century, its population was reduced by half to 25,000 inhabitants while its debts increased to more than 12 million guilders. And finally in 1806, Nuremberg lost its legal status as free town of the German Reich and was made a part of the kingdom of Bavaria.

Nuremberg was not the only town to become impoverished. Many more towns, such as Rothenburg ob der Tauber, Ravensburg, Dinkelsbuhl, met the same fate, and nothing pointed to a change in that trend. The artisan structure of the crafts, which was not at all comparable to the industrial structure of towns such as Manchester, London, Glasgow, Paris, Lyon, etc., was still mentioned in 1827.[1] Some neighbouring towns with an equally skilled and diligent population such as Furth, Erlangen, Bayreuth and Bamberg, even experienced a certain economic upswing. Nuremberg's advantage as a traffic centre (seven important roads of the German Reich met there) vanished on account of the mercantilistic barriers built up by the neighbouring rulers, and in 1810, seven of twelve main roads were impassable for long stretches.[2] Incomes in Nuremberg were comparable to those of other towns. Workmen in the building trade, for example, had, between 1821 and 1830, a yearly income of about 180 guilders.[3] This corresponded exactly to the average income of comparable workmen in eight German towns. The incomes in Hamburg, Leipzig and Emden, however, surpassed this average by up to 25 per cent.[4]

2. THE FORMATION OF A GROWTH POLE

(a) The growth pattern

The economic development of Nuremberg is first illustrated by its population.

The growth of the towns Essen and Dortmund is, in general, regarded as typical for the industrialisation in Germany, particularly the Ruhr region. By comparing the numbers of inhabitants, one gets an impression of the importance Nuremberg gained in the course of the nineteenth century:

	Nuremberg	*Essen*	*Dortmund*
1871	80,000	51,000	44,000
1910	320,000	295,000	214,000

Nuremberg's population grew, between 1806 and 1913, at a mean yearly rate of 2.05 per cent as compared to 1.02 per cent of the total German population.

More detailed insights are gained from the growth rates of production. Between 1830 and 1843, production rose in Nuremberg at a yearly average of not quite 2 per cent.[5] The corresponding rate for Germany as a whole amounted to about 1.4 per cent.[6] This average, however, did not apply to all regions. In Prussia, for example, industrial production rose, between 1824 and 1831, at a yearly average of 3 per cent,[7] although this trend did not necessarily continue after 1831. The lower growth of Nuremberg's economy of about 2 per cent could be regarded as indicator for an economic decline between 1822 and 1842.

Nuremberg's industrial rise started shortly after 1840, although certain signs could be noticed as early as in the 1820s. Between 1843 and 1861, industrial production rose at a yearly rate of 3.5 per cent. The German Reich as a whole reached this rate only between 1850 and 1868.[8]

Another growth indicator is the development of great enterprises. Some companies expanded rapidly in 1840. The engineering company of Cramer-Klett (later called Maschinenfabrik Augsburg-Nurnberg AG, or MAN) started production with a dozen workers in 1837. The number of workers employed increased constantly, up to the crisis of 1857, to more than 2,200. This meant a yearly growth rate of almost 30 per cent. As regards the number of employees, industry caught up with the crafts by 1875/80. This means that about 13,000 of the total labour force of 44,000 were employed in industrial workshops.[9] Already before the boom of the 1890s, Nuremberg had developed into one of the most important growth poles of Germany.[10]

(b) Reasons for economic agglomeration

According to Kuznets[11] certain economic conditions are necessary for industrialisation: (i) a minimum of efficiency in some non-industrial sectors; (ii) adequate supply of labour and capital, (iii) adequate demand for industrial products; and (iv) adequate supply of entrepreneurial skills. Population growth is not expressly mentioned as a precondition. Deane, Cole, Chambers and others, on the contrary, stress the importance of a growing population for the industrialisation process.[12] The size of the population, which results in economies of scale, is also taken into account by Habakkuk. He sees, however, an interaction playing a substantial role in population growth.[13]

The excess of births over deaths being negligible in Nuremberg up to the 1860s and approaching the average of the German Reich only later on (about 1 per cent of the respective population), the growth of Nuremberg's population was largely determined by migration – much like that of many towns in developing countries today. The rate of migration to Nuremberg ranged between 1 per cent and 5 per cent, and amounted on the average to 2 per cent. This migration to Nuremberg can be traced back to various economic variables. During the first phase of industrialisation (1835-69) migration correlated with the number of newly built workshops ($r = 0.74$) and the number of unemployed ($r = -0.65$). These correlations were also effective in the period from 1875 till 1913, the coefficients being $r = 0.66$ and $r = -0.56$ respectively. More detailed investigations reveal that investments (and therewith the number of unemployed) caused the migration to Nuremberg and not vice versa.[14] This seems to confirm the thesis of Bairoch, who does not count population growth among the factors necessary for economic development.[15] It must therefore be asked what were the reasons for these investments. This question turns the attention above all to Kuznets' condition of adequate supply of entrepreneurial skills. Even leading tradesmen did not suspect such skills to be available in Nuremberg. In 1817, Nuremberg prided itself upon not wanting large factories.[16] This was wrong. Firstly, there were already dynamic entrepreneurs, W. Spath for example, who obtained the concession for a factory only in 1842.

Secondly, the skills available could only evolve when two other important conditions were met by the construction – against the will of the Bavarian Government – of the first German railroad between Nuremberg and Furth in 1835, which was by itself a major entrepreneurial achievement. Because of this (i) efficiency of the communications sector was heavily improved. The large-scale effect of industry only now became effective. Dynamic entrepreneurs made their way in various branches of industry such as the pencil-making and chemical industries. As early as 1847, J. Zeltner made his ultramarine-producing company into the leading firm in this branch in the world.[17] (ii) The construction of the railroad itself created adequate demand for industrial, in particular metal, goods. As the metal-working industry had anyway long been a leader in Nuremberg, this sector expanded strongly. While between 1823 and 1840 every fourth worker employed in the industry and the crafts worked in the metal-working sector, this applied to every third by 1861.[18] Between 70 per cent and 87 per cent of the turnover of the above-mentioned company, MAN, was attributable to rolling stock.

It must be asked why dynamic entrepreneurs were above all to be found in Nuremberg and only to a lesser extent in the neighbouring towns, which had an equally advantageous location. Among the many possible factors, two seem to be particularly responsible for that development. (i) The large supply of skilled labour and the century-old goodwill of the products were decisive for winning large markets. (ii) The economic climate in Nuremberg was favourable to entrepreneurs, as economic activities were always held in high esteem there. In addition, there were Nuremberg's trades – and craftsmen had always advocated free trade and defended strongly the teachings of Adam Smith. This is why extremely successful entrepreneurs like W. Spath and J. Zeltner migrated to Nuremberg from its surroundings to try their luck there. This seems to confirm the opinion of E. Heub, who believes entrepreneurial capabilities to be independent of the environment, their development, however, being dependent on social esteem.[19] It is, nevertheless, striking that almost all leading entrepreneurs of Nuremberg of that time were Protestants and led a life in accordance with the hypothesis of Max Weber.

(c) Effects on neighbouring regions

The industrialisation which set in rapidly after the construction of the first railroad influenced the population of the neighbouring areas to a large degree, since migration during the entire nineteenth century was almost completely restricted to nearby regions. This migration potential seems to have been exhausted at the beginning of the twentieth century, for even the strong economic upswing, lasting till the outbreak of the First World War, was accompanied by decreasing migration rates. The economic attraction of Nuremberg seems to have been so great as to have hampered the development of other towns in Northern Bavaria, although these towns were quite quickly connected to the railroad system (Furth, Bamberg and Hoff, for example). Nevertheless, these towns also experienced, in absolute figures, a considerable economic growth on account of the new means of transportation, namely the railroad. Only areas at a distance of more than four miles either side of the railroad tracks tended to stagnate, or even to decline, although their initial position about 1800 was almost equal to that of the others.[20]

3. LEVELLING-OFF TENDENCIES AND CONCLUSION

As shown, Nuremberg had a lead on the road to industrialisation of about eight years against the average of the German Reich. This was due to its traditionally high share in the metal-working industry, which received decisive impulses from the construction of railroads, which started in 1835. In the pre-industrial period, the textile industry, mainly the flax-milling and linen-weaving sectors, was generally predominant in the German Reich. On account of tightening international competition, and the replacement of linen by cotton, the textile industry had a smaller growth potential. After railroad building had lost its leading role in the mid-1850s, the industrial growth rates of Nuremberg and of the German Reich converged. During the last quarter of the nineteenth century, the trend of growth in the crafts and industry corresponded to that of MAN in Nuremberg. As the new growth industries (chemical and electrical) also achieved a rapid breakthrough in Nuremberg, the economy of the Nuremberg area followed closely the general trend of industrial development, while its lead in the number of persons employed stayed much the same in comparison with the surrounding areas.

Similar levelling-off tendencies can be observed with respect to real incomes. A comparison with average incomes of the Reich is only possible for the time after 1871, since (according to J. Kuczynski) calculations of real incomes for the time before 1871 are much too high.[21] On the whole, the index of real industrial incomes showed, between 1871 and 1913, a similar trend for Nuremberg and the German Reich.

NOTES

[1] I. Rudhart, *Über den Zustand des Königreichs Bayern nach amtlichen Quellen,* 2. Bd., *Über die Gewerbe, den Handel und die Staatsverfassung des Königreichs Bayern* (Erlangen, 1827) p. 31.

[2] F. Voigt, *Die gestaltende Kraft der Verkehrsmittel in wirtschaftlichen Wachstumsprozessen* (Bielefeld, 1959) p. 16.

[3] Stadtarchiv Nürnberg, HR 4579.

[4] D. Saalfeld, 'Einkommensverhältnisse und Lebenshaltungskosten städtischer Populationen in Deutschland in der Übergangsperiode zum Industriezeitalter', in *Wirtschaftliche und soziale Strukturen im säkularen Wandel. Festschrift für Wilhelm Abel zum 70. Geburtstag,* eds. I. Bog, G. Franz, K.-H. Kaufhold, H. Kellenbenz and W. Zorn (Hanover, 1974) p. 421. (The eight towns: Berlin, Hamburg, Leipzig, Chemnitz, Emden, Göttingen, Quedlinburg, Warmbrunn/ Schlesien.)

[5] Calculated from P. Schröder, *Die Entwicklung des Nürnberger Großgewerbes 1806-1870. Studien zur Frühindustrialisierung. Nürnberger Werkstücke zur Stadt-und Landesgeschichte,* eds. G. Hirschmann *et al.*, Bd. 8 (Nürnberg, 1971) p. 248.

[6] W.G. Hoffmann, 'The Take-Off in Germany', in *The Economics of Take-Off into Sustained Growth,* ed. W.W. Rostow (reprinted London, 1969) pp. 96, 114.

[7] Calculated from F. Lütge, *Deutsche Sozial- und Wirtschaftsgeschichte. Ein Überblick,* 2. *Auflage* (Berlin-Göttingen-Heidelberg, 1960) p. 409.

[8] Calculated from W.G. Hoffmann, *Das Wachstum der deutschen Wirtschaft seit der Mitte des 19. Jahrhunderts* (Berlin-Heidelberg-New York, 1965) Tab. 103, p. 454, 455.

[9] Calculated from R. Gömmel, *Wachstum und Konjunktur der Nürnberger Wirtschaft 1815-1914* (Stuttgart, 1978) pp. 47, 173.

[10] The term 'growth pole' has apparently been accepted first in the French literature. See F. Perroux, 'Note sur la notion de "pôle de croissance', *Economie Appliquée,* Bd. 6 (1953), p. 307.

[11] S. Kuznets, *Economic growth and structure. Selected essays* (New York, 1965) pp. 194-212.

[12] P. Deane and W.A. Cole, *British Economic Growth 1688-1959. Trends and Structure* (Cambridge, 1962); J.D. Chambers, 'Population change in a provincial town: Nottingham 1700-1800', in *Studies in the industrial revolution,* ed. L.S. Presnell (London, 1960) p. 101.

[13] H. J. Habakkuk, *Population growth and economic development since 1750* (Leicester, 1972) pp. 47, 48.

[14] R. Gömmel, op. cit., S.31.

[15] P. Bairoch, *Révolution Industrielle et Sous-Développement,* 3rd ed (Paris, 1969) p. 201.

[16]Cited from F. Voigt, op. cit., p. 16, 17.
[17]Staatsarchiv Nürnberg, D 4 IuHK Nbg Nr. 125.
[18]Calculated from R. Gömmel, op. cit., pp. 50, 173.
[19]E. Heuß, *Allgemeine Markttheorie* (Tubingen-Zürich, 1965) S. 12 f.
[20]F. Voigt, op. cit., p. 41, 50, 56.
[21]See the criticism on J. Kuczynski ('Die Geschichte der Lage der Arbeiter unter dem Kapitalismus. Darstellung der Lage der Arbeiter in Deutschland von 1789 bis 1849', Bd. 1, Berlin-Ost 1961, S. 253) in R. Gömmel, op. cit., pp. 134-8.

21 Market Integration during the Period of Industrialisation in Norway

Fritz Hodne and Ole Gjølberg

1. INTRODUCTION

The prevalence of regional disparities in the past is generally acknowledged. We know less, however, about their subsequent disappearance, and in the face of vast amounts of price and wage observations, the historian has too often resigned himself to the task of compilation rather than generalisation. Thus, it is usually assumed, less often ascertained, that disparities prevailed in the earlier stages and that with industrialisation they have either disappeared or been sharply reduced. The corollary is the idea that industrialisation can be analysed as a case of market integration. The proposition runs as follows: industrialisation implies an exchange economy in which capital, labour and commodities are bought and sold in their respective markets. With increasing information and mobility of factors the price fluctuations should, so to speak, begin to get synchronised. Once, for instance, wages in the different labour markets begin to show strong co-variation in the various regions or industries, the observer would conclude that market integration had been established. By the same token, industrialisation could be said to have been completed, having imparted its ethos and pulse to all parts of the economy. In its simplest outline, then, the proposition is that the trends towards increasing co-variation in prices and wages may be used as a measuring rod for describing and analysing the process of industrialisation. Hence two sets of problems: first, do data on wages and prices show strong sectoral and regional disparities in fluctuations in the pre-industrial era? Secondly, do the data reveal higher degrees of co-variation during the march towards the modern industrial period?

In order to throw light on these questions, the present paper reviews Norwegian data on wages and prices, most of which is unpublished so far, for the period 1830-1914. With regard to Norway the time-span covers the entire transition from the pre-industrial era to the fully industrialised economy. The paper limits itself to considering fluctuations and co-variation. Specifically, by the aid of simple correlation analysis the paper attempts to determine whether the data indicate increased economic integration in the sense that wages and prices in the various regions more strongly than before begin to fluctuate in the same direction and at the same speed. Is it possible to identify clear shifts or structural changes in the series? Increased integration should then show up in steadily higher correlation coefficients, both in the price fluctuations between regions and in the fluctuations in wages in different industries. We have contrasted modern and traditionalist sectors, i.e., urban and rural regions. The paper also includes the northern counties of Nordland and Finnmark. The selection of regions promises to capture some central disparities presumed to have existed, notably the cleavage between rural-urban and between centre-periphery regions.

The paper omits discussing the possible tendencies regarding level of wages and prices in the various regions. The study, moreover, confines itself to looking at commodity prices and wages; it does not deal with the price of capital.[1] Nor, except in passing, will the paper consider the degree of conformity between international price movements and Norwegian trends.

2. THE DATA

The wage data used stem from the historical prices archive of the late Professor Dr Ingvar Wedervang of the Norwegian School of Economics and Business Administration. Beginning about 1930 Professor Wedervang and his assistants worked in association with the International Committee on Prices with funds from the Rockefeller Foundation and other sources, and compiled prices and wages, dating back to the 1780s, from a wide range of private and public enterprises and geographic regions.[2] The archive contains a vast amount of observations: the shipping files alone comprise 1.5 million entries for seamen's wages, roughly from the 1780s to 1930. The bulk of the material however, covers the second half of the nineteenth century. Professor Wedervang did not live to see his massive work completed; it remains unpublished to this day. Some time-series, however, are now to be found in five recent theses, all completed at the Department of Economic History of the Norwegian School of Economics.[3] The wage data used in this paper are with some exceptions taken from the five theses mentioned. The price data used are published statistics from the Central Bureau of Statistics, Oslo.[4]

3. EMPIRICAL RESULTS

The Coastal Labour Market 1830-1914

As to the labour market for seamen, one would expect an initial high degree of integration. For one thing, seamen are a perennially mobile group, and the trades they trafficked in were generally competitive, so one would assume the existence of what amounted to a coastal labour market even before the modern age. Since Norwegian shipping competed in the international freight markets, wages would naturally fluctuate in line with international business cycles, much the same way in Bergen as, say, in Oslo. Yet one should not be surprised to encounter specialised markets for seamen that would contrast with the general background of high correlation in this field.

By and large, the expectations are confirmed when a series of correlations are run for nominal wages for one major group, the able-bodied seamen (ABs) in the period 1830-1914, on the basis of data from 11 towns situated along the coast of Norway from Trondheim southward (see map on page 222). Since the wage structure, i.e. the wage differentials, on board remained remarkably stable in the period mentioned, any group of seamen could have been chosen for an analysis. The ABs have been chosen, first, because they were the largest group by far; second, because the Wedervang archive contains the most complete time-series for this group.

Beginning with the sub-period 1830-60, the pre-industrial period, we have found the simple correlation coefficients between the wages in the towns studied to range from 0.6 to 0.9. Breaking the pattern are the following towns: Mandel, Risor and Kristiansund, which, when correlated with the other towns, give a coefficient around 0.4-0.5. The results point to a fairly well integrated labour market in shipping already in the pre-industrial period, despite the exceptions noted. The deviations, as may be inferred from other evidence, were due to special conditions, notably in Kristiansund, where the sailors had ample alternative income opportunities in fishing, and more easily slipped back into primary activities.

For the years 1860-1914 the results indicate a tendency towards even stronger co-variation; the coefficients now range between 0.80 and 0.97 for the bulk of the material. The observation holds also for towns located fairly far apart, which may be interpreted as affirmation that near-complete integration had been establised in this labour market. The odd town is again Kristiansund, though this time only for periods up to 1900, after which this town also joins the ranks. Correlated with Tönsberg 1887-97, Kristiansund, for example, scores 0.5, and with Trondheim 0.6 for the years 1870-99. Local deviation for sub-periods is observable also in the scores for Bergen and Risos; notably the Bergen results are puzzling for the years 1906-14. Expectedly, the towns bordering the Oslofjord show a very high degree of correlation throughout this period, their coefficients persistently ranging above 0.9.

Correlating absolute wage rates may, however, entail an optical illusion. The data may contain an underlying common trend. As a result, the correlation coefficients may turn out to be higher than warranted. In order to avoid possible distortion from such factors, we have also correlated the yearly changes in percentages. Testing the material in this way, we occasionally obtained lower coefficients. These results indicate that although the direction of the fluctuations might be identical, the yearly changes in percentages could be quite dissimilar. To illustrate, the figures for Tönsberg, Sarpsborg and Fredrikstad, which had been 0.9 when using nominal wage rates, now drop to under 0.8 for the period 1870-1914. The special characteristics of Kristiansund again show up in the results, and more strongly than before: for the entire period

1840-1914 the correlation coefficient between Kristiansund and Trondheim reaches a mere 0.3; for the period 1870-1900 it even drops to 0.2, which indicates quite convincingly that Kristiansund in this context ran against a common trend. The direction of the changes in the Kristiansund wages ran counter to the others, and the fluctuations show smaller amplitudes.

The labour market for agricultural workers

If agriculture was dominated by traditionalist notions of fair wages and patriarchal relationships between employer and employee, one would expect weak correspondence between wage fluctuations in agriculture and shipping, for instance. The latter would generally reflect market economy conditions, the former, by contrast, should reveal the predominance of traditional relationships.

In order to test the notion, we have correlated the wage rates of farm hands (the paid day labourer with board) of eastern central Norway with the

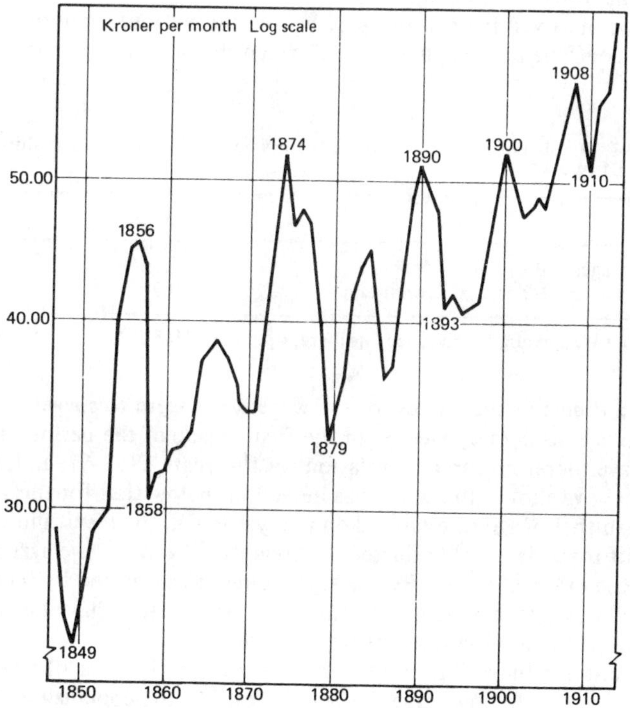

Fig. 21.1 Monthly wages for able bodied seamen (ABs) 1847-1914 recorded in Tönsberg, Norway, and their conformity with the international business cycles

SOURCE The Wedervang Archive, Norwegian School of Economics and Business Administration.

wage rates in shipping during the period 1850-80.[5] Since the timing of the so-called transformation of the old farm culture is a recurrent issue, not least among Norwegian historians, the results of such a test would appear to be of particular interest. As for the choice of farm hands rather than, say, cottars, it was assumed that unlike the cottars, who worked under severe institutional constraints, the day workers were free to exploit the job opportunities that recurred over the year's seasons in agriculture and forestry, hence that this wage rate would better reveal the market rate for paid labour, even prior to the coming of the railways from the 1850s onwards. The choice of agricultural area has been influenced by paucity of data. Since family farms dominated in the coastal regions, few data for hired farm labour can be traced there. It was only in the heartland of eastern Norway that hired help was extensively used, which is why wage-series are fairly continuous here. Shipping wages appeared a natural choice as a proxy for the modern sector linked up with the international economy. In fact, as seen from Figure 21.1, wage fluctuations in Norwegian shipping were obviously synchronised with international fluctuations in demand for sea tonnage.

As may be observed from Table 21.1 below, the computation yields correlation coefficients as high as 0.6-0.7 when the period 1853-80 is seen as a whole.

TABLE 21.1 Simple correlation coefficients for wages in agriculture and shipping in Norway 1853-1880

	1853-80	*1853-64*
Agricultural wages/AB's wages, Tõnsberg	0.64	0.11
Agricultural wages/AB's wages, Trondheim	0.70	0.03

SOURCE: The Wedervang archive, see Gjølberg, op.cit. 1974(b).

Plotted on a time axis the curves for the wage series seem to suggest that the co-variation is considerably weaker in the first decade of the period under review. We have therefore run a correlation for the years 1853-67, and, as Table 21.1 above shows, the score was indeed far below that for the whole period. When their wage rates are taken as a yardstick, the result indicates a marked shift towards a higher degree of integration between the agricultural world and the external world. By the same token, as suggested by scores of 0.11 and 0.03, wages in agriculture prior to 1870 appear to have been wholly independent of the international business cycle.

We have also for these data run the correlations on the basis of yearly changes in per cent. By and large the results confirm the conclusion drawn above. The overall figure, 0.64 and 0.70 respectively in Table 21.1, now drops to a mere 0.3 and 0.4. The inference again is that, as yet, agricultural wages, even in eastern Norway, were far less sensitive to external influences than those in shipping.

The labour market for road workers 1860-1914

To analyse the march towards integration from a different perspective, we have compared wages for road workers on public projects in different parts of the country.[6] The areas include Finnmark and Nordland, two northern counties, representing the periphery, and districts in the central county of Oppland in south-eastern Norway. The roadwork wage rates have further been compared with the seamen's wage series, taken as proxy of the international economic cycle. Usually, the road workers' wage rates were not institutional, but by decree consciously adjusted to local costs of living. As a result the variations between regional wage rates reveal the market rate for this type of labour. The observation period covers the years 1860-1914. In this period the country built 3000 km of railways, 15,000 km of public roads, added 20,000 km to its telegraph network, and saw the setting up of regular steamship traffic along the entire coast from the 1870s, all of which should have accelerated market integration.

The statistical results from the correlation analysis indicate that in the central eastern districts the labour markets for navvies were highly integrated, with scores running above 0.9 for Nord Gudbrandsdalen and Toten. This holds even for the earliest periods observed, the 1860s and 1870s. Evaluating this result, one should recall that the road workers, like the Irish navvies in England, were professionals, usually unmarried men, who easily moved from one project to another. The high mobility revealed by these scores seems to suggest at least the existence of a regional labour market in south-eastern parts of Norway.

To see how far this integration went, we also ran a correlation against the seamen's wages in Trondheim and towns along the Oslofjord. The correlation coefficients between wages on roadwork in the above areas and seamen's wages turned out to be 0.8 both in regard to Trondheim and Tönsberg. The result thus strengthens the above conclusion.

Mobility, however, did not encompass the entire country. Tests on the northern counties point consistently to a borderline across the country somewhere in Nordland (see map). South of the border wage fluctuations are generally in tune with those further south ($r = 0.6$-0.7 for the years 1879-1910). North of that border, however, the fluctuations in wage rates show a far weaker correspondence, with correlation coefficients varying between 0.25 and 0.53. The conclusion derived from a reading of the results is that correlation tends to vary inversely with distance. This reading of the material is strengthened when we look at the Finnmark scores. When correlated with roadwork wages in the south, the wages for similar work in East Finnmark in the extreme north yield a score of a mere 0.2 for 1872-1910. The existence of a border in the labour market is suggested also by a low correlation coefficient between East Finnmark and Nordland South ($r = 0.2$) and a decidedly higher figure for Nordland North ($r = 0.5$). Finally, the low degree of integration in the northern labour market shows up in a low score ($r = -0.5$ for the

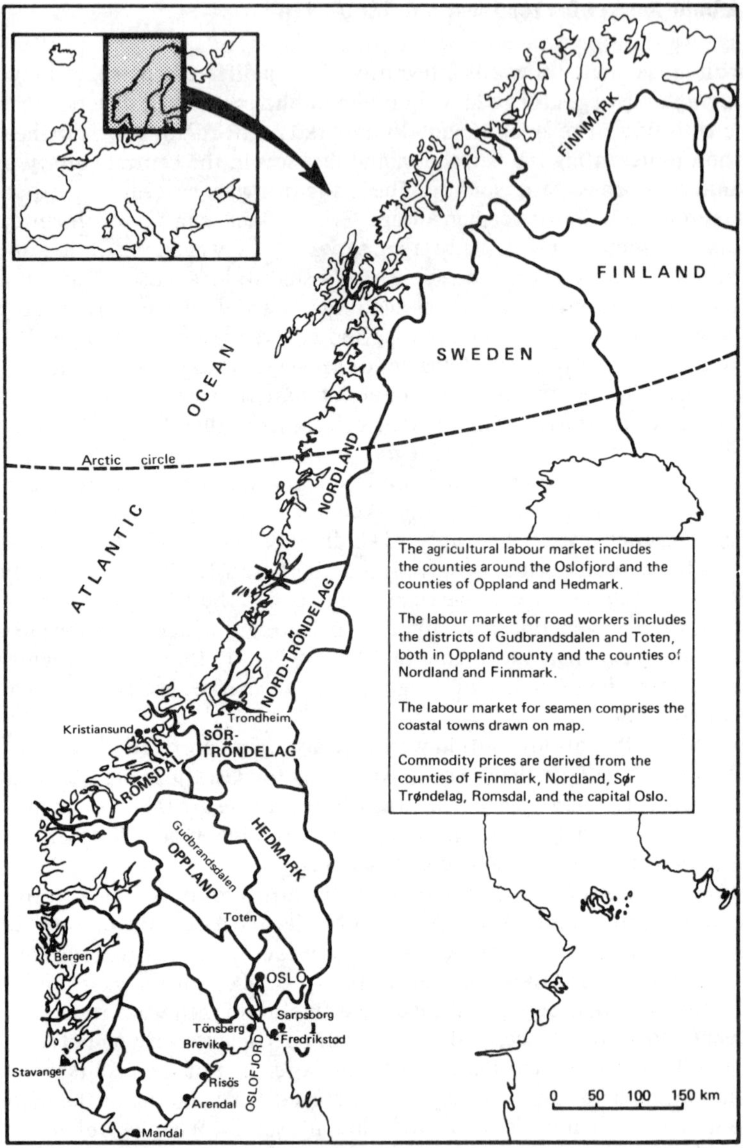

Fig. 21.2 Norway: Observation areas

years 1872-1910) when a test is run for East against West Finnmark. This result is to some extent invalidated, however, since payments to road workers in East Finnmark in the 1870s formed part of a government effort to colonise the region by Norwegian citizens in order to stem the influence of the numerous Finnish and Lapp migrants that settled in Finnmark from the 1850s. This amounted to paying institutional wages which created wage fluctuations moving independently of market rates in the surroundings.

The market for consumer goods 1830-1913

Potatoes have been chosen as an interesting article for an analysis of prices in the consumer goods market. The reason for selecting potato prices as representative is the simple one that potatoes, beside cereals and fish, formed a central part of the people's diet throughout the nineteenth century. Especially for the lower classes in town and country, herring and potatoes made up the staple of food consumption. Potatoes were grown all over the country, but some regions were sporadically, others regularly, in need of external supplies, among them the towns and the northern country of Finnmark. The surpluses were generally marketed as liquor at first, but increasingly as a food item for households when transport systems improved during the century. At any rate, potatoes were marketed at an early stage by districts having surpluses to neighbouring districts.

Against this background the fluctuations in the covariations in potato prices in Norway should allow us to identify the main features and trends in the process of market integration. A pitfall here is that local crop variations may distort the general price fluctuations; however, using observation periods of at least twenty years, it should be possible to reduce this statistical difficulty.

The choice of geographic area has been made with an eye for comprehensiveness; accordingly, we have used price data from two northern counties (Finnmark and Nordland), two midland counties (Romsdal and South Trondelag); which includes Trondheim, and Oslo, a town taken to be representative for the urban sector.

The findings suggest that the market for potatoes covered large geographic areas, apparently, even in the pre-industrial period; that is, before the 1840s. The picture that unfolds on a closer reading of the test results is that of a series of overlapping markets, each with a radius of several hundred kilometres and each stretching beyond the regional boundaries of Norway as these are conventionally understood. Within the circumference of each of the circles the co-variations are strong. Discrete jumps, however, from one circle to another consistently yield a lower score. Thus, the correlation coefficient for prices in areas as far apart as Oslo and the midland county of Romsdal, a distance of 400 km, yields an r of 0.64 for the period 1836-70. The score for Romsdal and Finnmark, similarly, a distance of 1500 km, is 0.72 for the same years. Moreover, high scores are obtained for a number of other regions located almost equally far apart.

The tendency of high correlation also shows up in the figures for the two northern counties Finnmark and Nordland. The prices of those two counties, covering vast geographic areas, poorly equipped with roads and totally lacking in railways, were nevertheless highly correlated during the entire period, reaching a score of above 0.7 in the period 1836-70. The score even climbed to 0.92 for the period 1890-1913. The result is of particular interest in view of the poor co-variation generally observed between the labour markets for road-workers in the two regions. The market circles, as noted, were not national markets, however; for, correlating the extreme northern regions with Oslo in the south, we obtained considerably lower scores, approx 0.4 for the period 1836-70.

A further observation is that the coefficients generally show no sign of a long-term increase; on the contrary, there are clear indications of diminishing coefficients even between markets previously integrated. The shift, apparently, occurred in the 1870s and lasted till around the turn of the century. To illustrate, the score for the midland county, Romsdal, and Oslo dropped to 0.40 for the period 1880-1913, down from an earlier stable level of about 0.7. Similarly, the score for Oslo and South Trondelag tumbled to 0.3 after the 1880s, from its original level of 0.7. Since on the whole correlation between the rural counties holds up, while Oslo diverges, it would seem that in this period Oslo diverged from a general trend. This is the more surprising as these were also the years when Oslo was connected by railway (1880) to the midland county of Trondelag. The fact serves as a reminder that railways do not automatically amount to market integration. The paradoxical tendency towards disintegration after 1870 could be due to a variety of factors, among them an uneven pace of change to agricultural production in the two regions. They may also be due to the greater variety of diet, so that basic shifts in the consumption of staples, potatoes for instance, might be less easy to identify from price data precisely because the railway by bringing a greater variety of food also created many subtle changes in the demand for foods, whose fluctuations may affect the staples that were measured. This would, of course, apply only to the later period.[7] It goes beyond the scope of this paper to decide the issue, but the matter does merit further attention.

4. CONCLUSIONS

No single statement sums up the findings, as the results reveal both a complex initial situation, and a few deviating and puzzling trends. As for the labour market, the findings reveal definite traces of regional dualism prior to the industrial period, in that there appears to be no conformity between wage fluctuations in shipping and farm labour up to 1870. Evidence from wages in roadbuilding, however, suggests a fairly rapid market integration in southern Norway after that date, the coastal labour market in particular achieved near complete integration from the 1870s onwards. By contrast, few traces of integration have been found in the wage data for the northern counties of Nordland and Finnmark. The findings seem to justify the continued use of terms such as centre-periphery regions. The commodity market, one segment of which has been investigated, did not evolve into a homogeneous national market; instead the findings suggest a series of market circumferences, each of them exceeding the borders of the conventional regions. Yet the data do not support the conclusion that commodity prices during industrialisation moved smoothly towards higher integration; indeed, the data show traces of disintegration, though more research is necessary for a definitive statement.

NOTES

[1] As to the capital market during this period, see J.T. Klovland, *Money and International Reserve Flows in Norway under the Gold Standard Regime 1880-1913: A Test of the Monetary Approach to the Balance of Payments,* Norwegian School of Economics (NSE), Discussion paper 02/77; and J.T. Klovland, 'Obligasjonsrenten i Norge' (*The Bond Yield in Norway*) *1852-1976, Statsøkonomisk Tidsskrift* 1976, pp. 1-35.

[2] A review of the contents of this archive is to be found in O. Gjølberg, *Professor dr. Ingvar Wedervangs pris-historiske arkiv,* NSE, 1974 (a).

[3] The theses are: O. Gjølberg, *Reallønnsutvikling og levevilkar for jord-jordbrunksarbeidere* (*The Development of Real Wages and Standard of Living for Agricultural Workers*) *ca. 1830-1880* (Bergen, 1974 (b)); L. Reinholdt, *Sjømenns lønnsforhold i Tönsberg (Seamen's Wages in Tönsberg) 1847-1914* (Bergen, 1975); H. Teigen, *Økonomisk utvikling i Nord-Gudbransdalen og på Toten. (The Economic Development in Nord-Gudbransdalen and Toten) ca. 1870-1910* (Bergen, 1976); A.S. Tjeldnes, *Vegarbeiderlønninger* (*Wages for Road Workers*) *i Helgeland og Lofoten og Vesterålen ca. 1870-1910* (Bergen, 1977); P.K. Bekkelund, *Veibygging i Finnmark (Road Construction in Finnmark) ca. 1870-1905* (Bergen, 1977).

[4] Det Statistiske Centralbyrå (CBS), *Markedspriser paa korn og poteter (Market Prices for Cereals and Potatoes) 1836-1914* (Oslo, 1915).

[5] The data are to be found in Gjølberg, op. cit., 1974 (b).

[6] The data have been derived from the Wedervang archive in the three theses by Bekkelund, Tjeldnes and Teigen.

[7] We owe this point to Professor Alan Milward, who in a written communication forwarded a possible alternative interpretation of the unexpected results for the period after 1870.

22 Regional Wages in Sweden during the Nineteenth Century

Lennart Jörberg and Tommy Bengtsson

In 1900 the share of agricultural population in the total population was slightly over 50 per cent. In one county the share was still more than 70 per cent and in three others about 40 per cent.

Non-agrarian activity was thus very small in the pre-industrial society. The iron industry in Central Sweden, trade and handicrafts in the cities were the most important sectors. During the 1830s a number of textile industries were established and the iron industry was reorganised to some extent. Timber products began to be exported from West Sweden and during the middle of the nineteenth century from Southern Norrland. Still, in 1845 the number employed in iron and manufacturing industries and handicraft was slightly over 80,000 men and 37,000 women compared to 900,000 men and 420,000 women in agriculture.[3]

The industrial expansion was, to a large extent, generated by the increase in exports, above all of timber, pulp and paper as well as of products from the iron and manufacturing industries.

The population of Sweden was 2.3 million in 1800. The increase was 23 per cent until 1830, and during the following 30-year period it rose by 34 per cent, bringing the total to 3.9 million. In eight counties the growth during the latter period was less than 30 per cent and in seven over 40 per cent. The increase was largest in Southern and Western Sweden and in Norrland, whereas the slowest growth was in the South Eastern counties. In the subsequent period, up to the turn of the century, the increase was

The Swedish economy was, as is well known, dominated by agriculture and allied sectors during the pre-industrial stage. In 1840, 20 out of a total of 24 counties had more than 80 per cent of the population engaged in agriculture. In the remaining four counties more than 70 per cent of the population were engaged in the agricultural sector.[1] In spite of this, during the eighteenth century there was some import of grains, amounting to 10-15 per cent of the production in the years of poor harvest.[2] However, the agricultural sector improved both its productivity and production volume during the eighteenth century and the import of grain was negligible in the beginning of the nineteenth century. In the 1820s, the import of grains ceased and the export of oats started. This export was substantial until the 1870s. Thereafter the grain export was replaced by the export of animal products.

33 per cent and the regional pattern of growth was similar to that of the previous period.

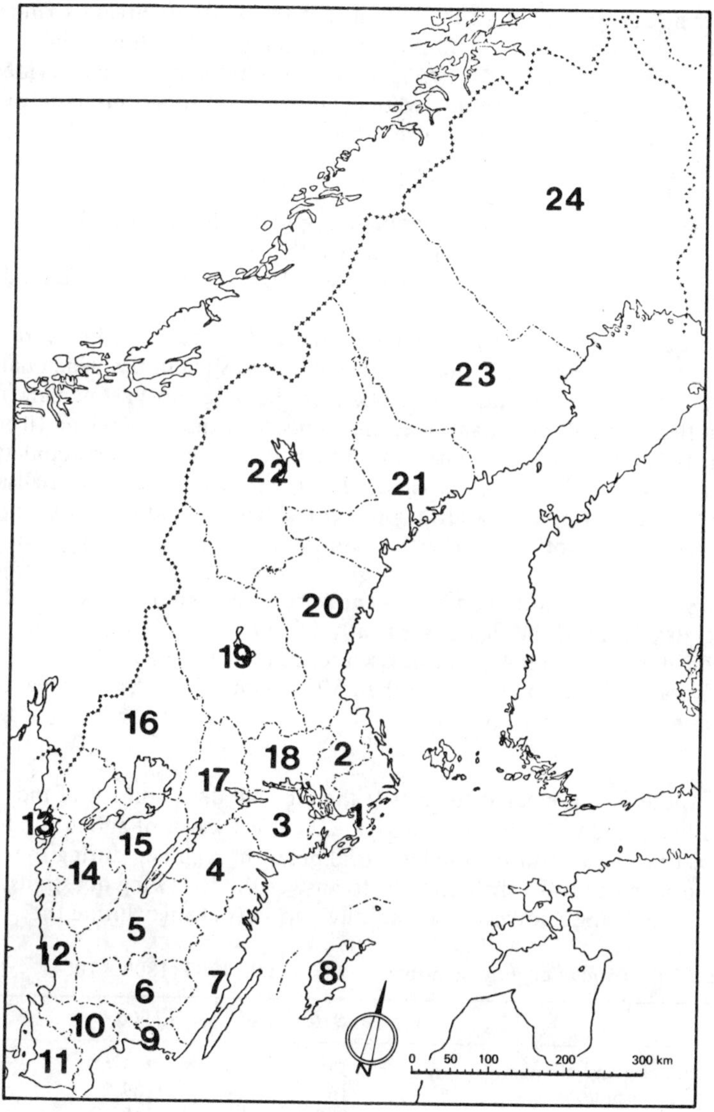

Fig. 22.1 The distribution of counties in Sweden

1. Stockholm county
2. Uppsala county
3. Sodermanland county
4. Ostergotland county
5. Jonkoping county
6. Kronoberg county
7. Kalmar county
8. Gotland county
9. Blekinge county
10. Kristianstad county
11. Malmohus county
12. Halland county
13. Goteborg and Bohus county
14. Alvsborg county
15. Skaraborg county
16. Varmland county
17. Orebro county
18. Vastmanland county
19. Kopparberg county
20. Gavleborg county
21. Vasternorrland county
22. Jamtland county
23. Vasterbotten county
24. Norrbotten county

From a regional viewpoint this meant that the Northern areas expanded both economically and in population due to, among other things, the expansion of the timber industry. Manufacturing industry was not regionally confined but was spread over the whole country, with some emphasis on the larger cities. The population also increased more in the northern areas than in the rest of Sweden, with the exception of the three counties with big cities, Stockholm, Göteborg and Malmö.

The regions with the slowest population growth also had the slowest urban growth. In the middle of the nineteenth century, the share of the urban population in the total population was 10 per cent and it had doubled by the end of the century.

In 1900, the regions with the highest degree of industrialisation were Malmöhus, Göteborg and Bohus, the Central Swedish counties which had long dominated the iron industry (Närke, Kopparberg and Västmanland), Ostergötland (textile and manufacturing industries) and Gästrikland (iron, timber, pulp). In all these counties more than 30 per cent of the population were employed in the industrial sector. The lowest degree of industrialisation was in the South Eastern Swedish counties (which also had the lowest population increase, as mentioned earlier) and in the counties of Alvsborg and Skaraborg.

In 1840 slightly more than 8 per cent were employed in industry and handicrafts. In 1870 the figure was nearly 15 per cent and by 1900 the share of industrially employed had risen to 28 per cent. In 1900 the agricultural sector employed more than 50 per cent. Thus, Sweden was still a predominantly agrarian country.

I

The purpose of this essay is to analyse the regional development of the cost of living and to study the development of real wages of agricultural workers prior to and during the industrial breakthrough i.e., during the nineteenth century. We shall attempt to answer the following questions. How did the living standard of agricultural workers change during the

TABLE 22.1 Population growth in some counties 1800-1900 (1800 = 100)

	1850	*1900*
Stockholm, city and county	126	275
Göteborg and Bohus	161	289
Malmöhus	178	288
Västerbotten and Norrbotten	176	289
Kronoberg	147	182
Skaraborg	147	178
Värmland	164	188
SWEDEN	145	219

SOURCE: Historisk statistik for Sverige Oel 1. Befolkning 1720-1967 (Stockholm, 1969) Table 5.

TABLE 22.2 Regional changes in foodstuff prices 1820-1914 (%)

	1	*2*	*3*	*4*	*5*	*6*	*7*	*8*	*10*	*11*	*12*	*13*	*14*	*15*	*16*
1820/29-50/59	52	40	51	53	50	36	70	64	55	72	47	59	62	53	59
1850/59-60/69	−1	0	−3	3	2	−1	3	−6	4	9	9	1	−1	−1	7
1860/69-70/79	7	14	16	14	13	12	8	14	9	12	6	14	6	8	2
1870/79-90/99	−5	−10	−9	−10	−10	−10	−14	−10	−9	−13	−8	−10	−5	−11	
1890/99-1905/14	+16	27	24	27	27	31	44	22	25	21	33	19	27	27	24

	17	*18*	*19*	*20a*	*20b*	*21*	*22a*	*22b*	*23*	*24*	*Whole Country*
1820/29-50/59	42	45	33	41	45	42	36	19	48	49	50
1850/59-60/69	4	2	6	5	7	9	10	9	10	9	4
1860/69-70/79	14	16	9	8	8	5	19	16	4	6	10
1870/79-90/99	−5	−7	−10	−1	−5	−1	−5	−8	−1	−1	−7
1890/99-1905/14	25	29	19	19	21	28	22	27	19	21	25

pre-industrial and industrialisation phases in the nineteenth century? Are there distinct regional differences in real wages? How did these change during the industrial breakthrough? How and why do price levels and wage levels vary regionally?

Finally, our calculations of real wages are compared with demographic data to see whether regional differences in the level of real wages are accompanied by differences in marriage rate, natural population growth, migration and net population growth. The aim was not to explain the regional demographic development as such but rather to test the validity of our calculations of real wages. If there is a correlation the results of our calculations are confirmed; if not, this may be due either to insufficient real wage calculations or to the possibility that there is no or only a low correlation between population and real wage level.

Agricultural wages are probably a good indicator of the general wage level in different parts of Sweden since a large majority of the wage earners were engaged in agriculture. The agricultural sector also supplied the expanding sectors with labour and it is therefore reasonable to assume that agricultural wages were used as norms of comparison for other groups of workers, particularly unskilled labour. Moreover, agriculture was spread over the whole country. The work was also more homogeneous than in other sectors and changed only slowly. Yet another reason for using agricultural wages for a study of regional differences in wages is simply that the data on wages in agriculture are much better and more abundant then wage series for other groups of workers.

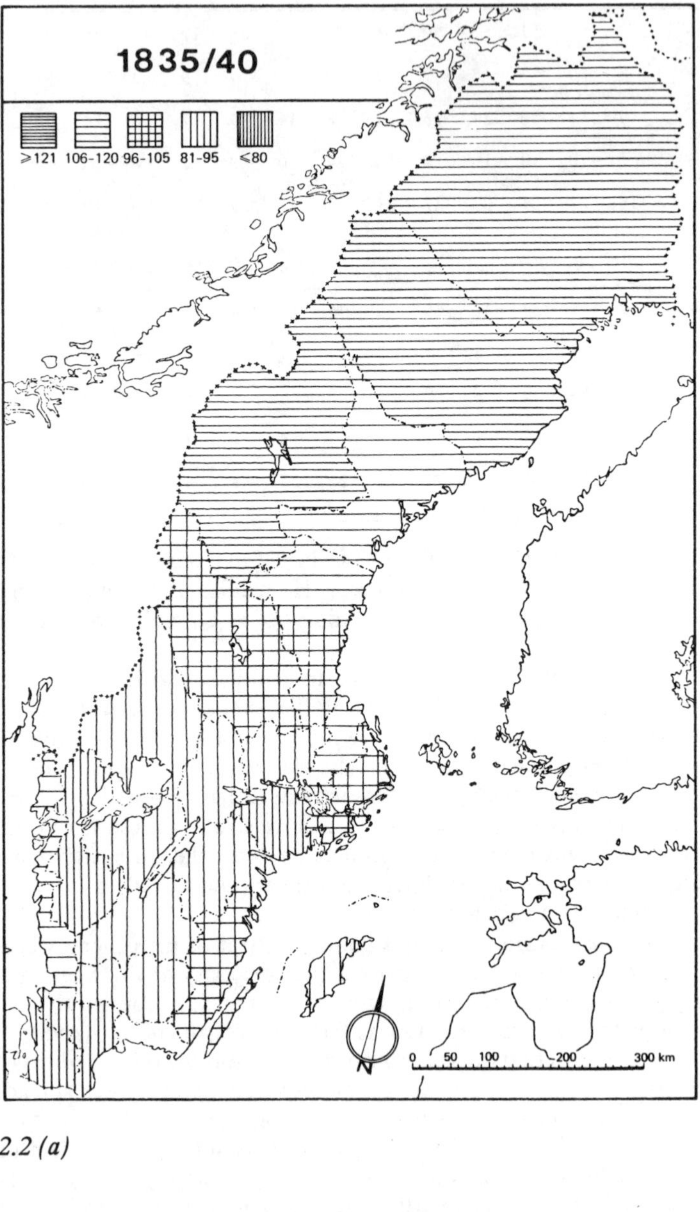

Fig. 22.2 (a)

Fig. 22.2 Regional real wage structure in 1835/40 and 1890/99

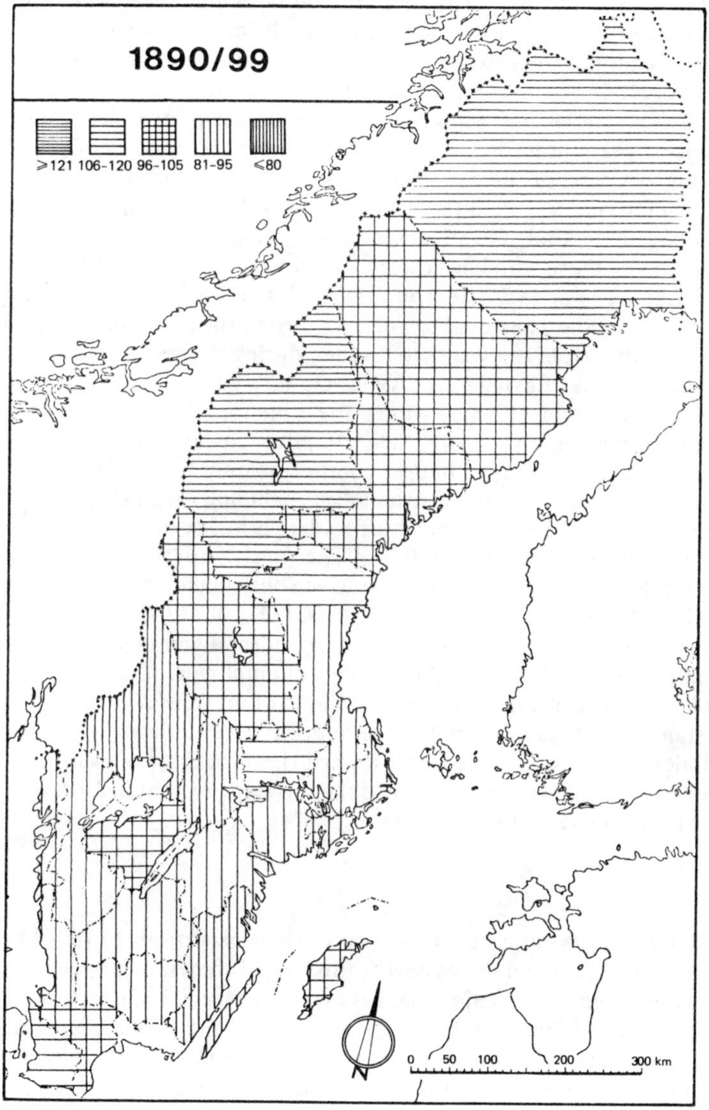

Fig. 22.2 (b)

Data on wages are available for approximately 30 regions. These regions are not homogeneous, economically or in other respects. They possess, however, certain common characteristics and should be seen as a compromise between regions with some homogeneity and dividing the country into a large number of regions. The material we have used is also determined by administrative borders, i.e., the counties and, in some cases, parts of a county.

The basic material comprises the so-called market price scales, which were fixed once a year during November and December on the basis of price data from different parts of the counties. Such data were gathered as a basis for converting into money the different charges which, according to regulations, were to be paid in kind. The price scales were subjected to thorough examination of those who had to pay as well as those who were to receive these charges. The price data correspond well with 'real' prices. The wage series are also of the same quality and have been utilised by all scholars who have dealt with prices and wages in Sweden during this period.[4] In order to construct the cost of living index we have used a given quantity of commodities in a budget which will be the same for all regions and for the whole of the nineteenth century. Since all price data are not available for all regions, we have had to use a budget comprising only foodstuffs. However, compared to a more comprehensive budget including fuel, lighting, clothing and rent, it is found that the foodstuff budget is highly correlated with a more comprehensive budget ($r = 0.9$).[5] The weights are thus constant and only the prices are varied. Thereby we have constructed an index which probably reduces the regional differences in the cost of living.[6]

The wage data consist of day-rates of agricultural workers. We have no information as regards the number of days of employment per year. Neither is there any information regarding how the working hours changed. The living standard is thus measured as the nominal wage deflated with the price index of foodstuffs. We have assumed that working hours and the number of working days are similar in the different regions, i.e. that real income is proportional to real wages.

II

Annual data on day-rates of agricultural workers exist from 1732. The development of nominal wages during this period shows, to a large extent, an increasing trend. The major changes often occurred in connection with marked periods of inflation during the first half of the 1760s, the decade around 1800, and in connection with the boom periods during the 1850s, 1870s and the 1890s. During the first half of the nineteenth century nominal wages were generally stable.

The regional indexes of foodstuffs show very good correspondence as regards the changes in the price index over time. The coefficients of variation are generally low, and the deviations from this pattern are found mainly at the beginning of the period. There is, however, a distinctly declining trend in the dispersion during the larger part of the century; from about 0.1 to about 0.04 during the 1880s, and thereafter a slightly increased dispersion.

Since each individual commodity in the budget exhibits considerably greater dispersion, the small dispersion of the foodstuffs price index means that the variations between the different types of commodities tend to cancel out.

The larger dispersion in the price indexes at the beginning of the nineteenth century is mainly due to the fact that the prices of foodstuffs in the Norrland regions did not increase to the same extent as in other regions. In other words, the price rise, particularly from the 1840s onwards, was stronger in these regions, one reason being the growth of the sawmill industry. The expansion of this industry during the 1870s is reflected in the fact that the price increases were greater in the interior regions of Norrland than in a majority of the other regions. The only regions with a similar price rise are found in southernmost Sweden, which exported agricultural products on a large scale and also went through rapid industrialisation during this period.

Changes in the foodstuff price index probably reflect the changes in economic activities in the respective regions. Strong rises would imply an expanding economy, that non-agrarian sectors increased in extent, depending upon regional migration and/or on a transfer between agriculture and other sectors within the region.

The largest increases in prices between the 1840s and the 1870s, i.e. during the initial stages of the industrial expansion in Sweden, occurred in Ostergötland, Malmöhus, Närke and in the interior of Norrland. Furthermore, above-average price increases occurred during the same period in the counties of Kristianstad, Göteborg and Bohuslän, and in Värmland.

The reasons for this vary. In some cases, a large rise in price was due to the fact that regions already well developed in non-agrarian activities continued to expand (for example Närke, Värmland and Göteborg). In other cases a price increase was probably caused by the fact that the regions previously lacked industrial activities or were undeveloped in this sector (the interior of Norrland and South Sweden). The cost of living index can thus be used to determine when the economic expansion in these regions began to accelerate, although it must be borne in mind that the relationship between economic growth and price level is complicated. For instance, the increased price level in Southern Swedish regions could be due to an increased demand for agricultural products, partly within the region and partly on the national or international market. This was also true for other regions to a lesser but varying degree. Above all, the export of oats and later that of butter could have contributed towards increasing the price level in these regions, without any non-agrarian expansion taking place. But despite this, a closer study of the changes in the regional foodstuffs price index would probably make a contribution to determining the periods when the economic expansion was initiated.

The costs of living naturally exhibit a development which largely corresponds to the changes in nominal wages. During the latter decades of the eighteenth century living costs rose more rapidly than wages and the discrepancy between the two series becomes more apparent during the war around 1800. During the subsequent inflation they followed each other, but with some relative improvement in wages. From the middle of the nineteenth century until the First World War there was a strong rise in wages while living costs showed no such increase. In some 68 price-series for different commodities, wages exhibited the largest rise during this period. In other words, there was considerable decrease in real wages from the 1770s until the beginning of the 1800s and they increased subsequently to reach the same level in the 1820s as in the middle of the eighteenth century. Thereafter there was a slight decline up until the 1840s. From the boom of the 1850s until 1914 real wages improved substantially, interrupted only by short recessions. This national average is based on a unweighted average for the thirty regions. The dispersion between the regions can be discerned in changes in the coefficients of variation.

The regional dispersion decreased continuously from the middle of the eighteenth century to about 1790. It increased later during the periods of war and inflation around 1800 and remained thereafter almost at a constant level until 1850.

Subsequently the regional wage development became more differentiated again. This was particularly marked during the period of rapid industrialisation in the 1870s when the regional wage dispersions were greater than both prior to and after this period. During the next phase of industrial development, in the 1890s, the dispersion decreased and continued to decrease until 1914. Thus it is clear that during the first phase of large-scale industrial development a regional imbalance was created. This is reflected by a large dispersion of wages (see Table 22.3).

The development of wages from the 1850s is strongly correlated with the state of industrial activities. During the earlier periods, variations in wages were influenced by periods of war with inflation as well as by agricultural harvest variations where successive years of crop failures resulted in higher prices; but often the wages did not immediately react to these changes. In the pre-industrial society the strongest improvements in real wages occurred during periods of declining prices. Changes in wages were slower than those in prices, both in the case of price increases and decreases. Co-variations with the international industrial conditions after 1850 also indicate, as we have pointed out, that the wages of agricultural workers concurred with the changes in the wages of other groups and, above all, those of unskilled industrial labour.

We have shown that the Swedish economy was already well integrated (if our point of departure is the dispersion of prices and temporal variations) during the pre-industrial phase, i.e.prior to the middle of the nineteenth century. The regional differences diminished and the variations in harvests did not, except in extreme conditions of total crop failures or very good

TABLE 22.3 Dispersion in real and nominal wages (Sweden = 100)

Region	*1835/44* N	*1835/44* R	*1890/99* N	*1890/99* R
1	113	104	84	81
2	108	112	88	84
3	80	74	87	81
4	80	84	94	93
5	95	94	88	88
6	96	89	79	80
7	99	102	77	77
8	83	80	96	96
10	72	70	101	95
11	76	78	113	106
12	99	106	81	87
13	114	106	93	84
14	72	76	82	83
15	87	87	96	96
16	90	83	83	77
17	83	85	77	71
18	95	91	110	106
19	106	96	103	99
20a	103	103	94	88
20b	106	114	110	106
21	104	108	108	100
22a	134	183	145	140
22b	134	135	156	148
23	134	133	109	102
24	131	125	167	138

harvests, have a decisive influence on regional grain prices. The variations in prices were well correlated with the international variations reflected in the prices in Danzig, Copenhagen and Amsterdam.[7]

The process of integration also affected the wages of agricultural workers. However, the differences between regions varied – though regional differences decreased – and it is possible to study the changes in the regional development of wages. The causal connection must be sought in social and economic changes as well as in the changes in population. Since wages and prices are not totally interdependent, the problem will be to explain how the variations in one variable influence and are influenced by the other variables. It is, however, often reasonable to consider prices as the independent variable and wages as the dependent. During the pre-industrial phase the share of wages in commodity prices was not large enough to exert a decisive influence on prices.

Three high-wage areas can be distinguished in pre-industrial Sweden, namely the regions around Stockholm and Göteborg and the northernmost counties. Southern Sweden was a pronounced low-wage area. Wages in the south-eastern part of Sweden were below the national average whereas the wages were above the average in the nearby northern parts of Stockholm.

In 1835/44 ten regions (out of 27) lay within ± 10 per cent of the average, 10 regions below and 7 above. The average increase in wages was 34 per cent during 1820/29 to 1850/59. Alvsborg county had the highest increase, 88 per cent, and Kopparberg the lowest with 18 per cent; expressed in absolute figures, from an average of 68 öre per day to 95 öre and in regions with extreme values, in Alvsborg from 51 öre to 96, and Kopparberg from 78 to 92 öre. This period includes the first big economic upswing, influenced by the international industrial and wartime conditions during the 1850s, namely the Crimean War. As a consequence of this boom, the wages in Alvsborg county more than doubled during 1855-80. This was an extreme reaction which resulted in a rapid fall in wages in the beginning of the 1860s, nearly 30 per cent compared with a national average of 8 per cent. The wages continued to rise in Kopparberg county during the 1860s. These patterns of reaction can partly be explained by slightly different agrarian and non-agrarian structures which were differently affected by the boom. This occurred with varying intensity in a majority of the regions. Regions with a rapid increase in wages during one period often experienced slower increase during the following period and vice versa. In this way, the differences in wage levels between different regions remained constant during a considerable period of time. It was first as a consequence of the changes resulting from the industrial breakthrough that the deviations from the earlier pattern became systematic, i.e. influenced the development in such a way that the wage structure underwent permanent changes in a particular direction.

The wage dispersion in 1890/99 was largely similar to that in 1835/44. 11 regions lay within ± 10 per cent of the national average, 11 lay below and 5 above. All of south-eastern Sweden, from Uppland and southwards, was now a low-wage area. The northernmost parts of Sweden remained a high-wage area. A new high-wage area had come into existence in the southernmost region of the country, which had been a markedly low-wage area during earlier periods.

Thus, the largest wage increase occurred in these southern regions where the day-rate rose from 55 to 170 öre between the 1840s and the 1890s, whereas the average increase in wages was between ca. 75 and 160 öre.

The coefficients of variation are largely similar for both periods of investigation, between 20 and 25; changes in the regional variations were not due to greater price dispersion but because the regions shifted within a relatively stable pattern of variation.

During 1835/44 the average wage in the regions around Stockholm was 73 öre per day while in Scania, the low-wage region, it was 55 öre. In the 1890s, the wage in Scania was 20 per cent higher than in the Stockholm regions. A very pronounced shift in the wage relations occurred between Scania and nearby Northern regions. In the 1830s and 1840s, the latter regions had similar high wages as in the Stockholm regions whereas they were more than one-third higher in Scania during the 1890s. In the Nerrland regions the average wage was 90 öre during the 1830s and 1840s, or

TABLE 22.4 Percentage change in nominal and real wages

	Region 1		2		3		4		5		6		7		10		11		12	
	N	*R*	*N*	*R*	*N*	*R*	*N*	*R*	*N*	*R*	*N*	*R*	*N*	*R*	*N*	*R*	*N*	*R*	*N*	*R*
1820/29-50/59	52	1	22	−15	37	−10	42	−9	25	−17	19	−10	57	−8	34	−13	32	−25	46	−1
1850/59-60/69	10	14	22	25	28	34	9	9	20	+19	1	1	−7	−9	18	15	21	14	14	5
1860/69-70/79	10	6	13	−1	26	10	50	31	32	17	38	22	29	18	23	10	57	38	8	3
1870/79-90/99	3	6	8	19	29	27	23	36	11	24	13	27	15	33	36	51	37	56	23	33
1890/99-1905/14	70	48	63	28	42	27	60	26	56	22	63	25	58	11	53	22	63	34	85	40

	Region 13		14		15		16		17		18		19		20a		23		24	
	N	*R*	*N*	*R*	*N*	*R*	*N*	*R*	*N*	*R*	*N*	*R*	*N*	*R*	*N*	*R*	*N*	*R*	*N*	*R*
1820/29-50/59	69	8	88	13	54	1	58	4	26	−13	31	−10	18	−12	31	−6	64	16	81	22
1850/59-60/69	−8	−9	−6	−3	14	17	29	23	16	12	24	23	14	8	13	7	13	2	−7	−15
1860/69-70/79	1	−11	12	4	35	25	10	8	27	14	35	25	41	28	47	36	37	33	36	29
1870/79-90/99	42	55	31	46	17	23	5	18	10	15	27	30	12	26	−3	−3	−6	−6	3	4
1890/99-1905/14	62	36	74	37	72	36	59	28	85	47	39	7	56	31	75	48	43	17	49	24

about one-fourth higher than in the Stokholm regions. The discrepancy had risen to over 40 per cent during the 1890s. Thus, there was a strong relative rise in South Sweden, a slightly smaller increase in Norrland, while the rate of increase in the south-eastern regions was less than both these and the national average.

During the eighteenth century and up to the 1870s, the wages in Malmöhus county were lower than in the surrounding counties and other plain regions. There was no marked difference between the plain regions of Central Sweden and the regions with a slightly more differentiated economy, i.e., regions with an iron industry, neither during the eighteenth century nor in the pre-industrial phase in the nineteenth century. During the industrial expansion from the middle of the nineteenth century wages in the Scanian counties increased strongly in comparison with the plain regions of central Sweden and the regions with an iron industry.

Thus the highest wages were paid in regions where agriculture was most developed. One probable reason for this was the changes in the conditions of employment which occurred during the latter part of the nineteenth century; this meant a large reduction in permanent employees and a rise in the number of temporary workers. This change mainly occurred on the larger estates of South Sweden.[8]

The differences in wage level came about in some relatively short periods during the nineteenth century. Between 1815 and 1845, the rise in the day-rates was very small, about an average of 5 per cent. Deviations are mainly observed in regions where some industrial activity, above all dependent upon export of timber, was slowly emerging, i.e. in the Norrland counties, in Värmland and the Göteborg regions. During the 1850s, there was a large rise in the wages in the whole country, by nearly 50 per cent. In the subsequent 20-year period, wages in the southernmost regions increased by more than double the national average, 85 per cent as compared to 38 per cent. The Norrland counties also had a higher rate of increase than the national average during this period. The decade prior to the First World War was characterised by a rapid rise in the wages in all regions: the largest regional increase was in the metropolitan areas around Stockholm, Göteborg, Malmö and Norrköping.

There is very little change in the ranking of the wage levels when deflated with the regional cost of living index. The high nominal wages in Norrland were matched by high foodstuff prices. On the other hand, Malmöhus county with extremely low wages, relatively seen, also had lower foodstuff prices than other regions far into the nineteenth century.

The foodstuff budget has been calculated for 26 regions. It is very consistent both spatially and over time. The coefficients of variation are generally about 0.05-0.07, indicating that the different components in the budget having a coefficient of 10 to 20 often had contradictory price development. This was the case as regards the prices of food grains and animal products but other commodities such as fish and poultry also exhibited similar tendencies.

Thus, the real wage development was modified by regional differences in the prices of foodstuffs; but the changes in the latter were not such that the regional pattern of nominal wages was altered when deflated with the regional cost of living index.

Normally, the nominal and real wages, relatively seen, move in the same direction. Between the 1830s and the 1890s, in relation to the Swedish average, there was a relative deterioration in 11 regions and a relative improvement in 10, both in nominal and real wages. Only in three regions did a relative improvement in nominal wages result in a relative deterioration in real wages and the opposite only in one region.

By deflating we obtain an increased dispersion during most of the decades in the period prior to the industrial breakthrough. In other words, the coefficients of variation became slightly larger. During the period 1880-90, they were to a large extent the same. In the following period, up to the First World War, the dispersion in real wages was less than the dispersion in nominal wages. At the same time they both decrease strongly, i.e., the wages converge in real as well as nominal terms.

TABLE 22.5 Percentage change in work time (day-rate) needed to buy one unit of different products, 1820-1914 (National average)

	1820/34-1860/74	*1860/74-1900/14*
Rye	−13.0	−54.8
Barley	−13.9	−46.5
Butter	+ 3.5	−31.4
Cheese	−11.0	−38.6
Beef	+ 4.4	−17.0
Pork	− 9.9	−35.7
Poultry	+14.6	−29.1
Eggs	−14.9	−26.1
Baltic herring	−31.8	−54.4
Dried fish	−14.0	−21.1
Linen	−34.4	−69.7
Coarse cloth	−21.6	−55.8

When comparing our estimates of real wages with demographic data we may ask if regional differences in real wages are reflected in differences in levels of marriage rate, population growth, migration and net population growth. If so, the results of our calculations of real wages are confirmed. The standard of living of wage earners in agriculture would in that case reflect the standard of living for large parts of the population.

There is a significant correlation on a national level between *fluctuations* of economic and demographic variables.[9] The correlation has been studied by means of spectral analysis. The regional differences will of course disappear. It is also possible that the various regions differed so much that the correlation obtained is only a statistical fiction. However, we do know that the Swedish economy was surprisingly well integrated already during the eighteenth century. The price fluctuations were similar; they had common trough and peak years and were thus strongly correlated although the levels were different. Despite these regional differences correlations between fluctuations population and economy can be studied on a national level.

In an earlier study we have shown that five-year fluctuations played an important role in the development of the price of rye in many regions during 1732-1869.[10] A comparison between rye prices and yield estimates on the national level shows that the price fluctuation can be largely explained by five-year fluctuations in the harvests. The import of rye and other grains also shows distinct five-year fluctuations during the latter part of the eighteenth century.

TABLE 22.6 Correlation between dominant fluctuations in real wages, births and deaths on national data during the three stages of demographic transition

Length of fluctuation	*Coherence square*	*Lags*	
Live births – real wages			
1749-99			
2.5 year	0.81	birth lags	6 months
5 year	0.83	birth lags	9 months
1800-69			
2.5 year	0.61	birth lags	4 months
3.7 year	0.68	birth lags	10 months
5.0 year	0.57	birth lags	5 months
1870-1914			
5 year	0.28	no lag	
10 year	0.42	no lag	
Mortality – real wages			
1749-99			
2 year	0.55	mortality lags	4 months
3.3 year	0.53	negative corr., mortality lags 10 months	
5 year	0.55	negative corr., mortality lags 1 year	
10 year	0.88	negative corr., no lag	
1800-69			
2.7 year	0.29	negative corr., no lag	
5 year	0.49	negative corr., mortality lags 15 months	
10 year	0.48	negative corr., mortality lags 9 months	
1870-1914			
2.7 year	0.59	negative corr., mortality lags 6 months	
4.5 year	0.43	negative corr., mortality lags 6 months	

About 80 per cent of the cost of living index is made up of foodstuffs and the biggest item is rye. The development of this index coincides almost entirely with the price index of foodstuffs and thus contains the five-year fluctuations.

As the day-rates for wage earners do not fluctuate as rapidly as the cost of living index, the real wages show five-year fluctuations, implying that poor harvests were not compensated by high wages.

As can be seen in Table 22.6, there are distinct correlations between fluctuations in real wage and population. The correlations are strongest during the first two periods and become less marked during industrialisation.[11]

Mortality is clearly dependent upon the economic conditions. It is lowest about a year after the peak in real wages, and consequently it is highest a year after the trough in real wages.

The number of births also exhibit a strong co-variation with the real wage. The correlation is strongest in the eighteenth century, decreases during the first half of the nineteenth century and is absent during the second half of

TABLE 22.7 Correlation between real wage and marriage, natural increase in population, migration and net increase

	1820		*1830*		*1840*		*1850*	
	*a**	*b**	*a*	*b*	*a*	*b*	*a*	*b*
real wages/marriage rate	−0.03	−0.27	0.21	−0.38	−0.10	0.28	0.10	0.08
real wages/natural increase	−0.42	0.23	−0.45	0.02	−0.27	0.40	−0.37	0.32
real wages/migration	0.01	0.09	0.14	−0.21	0.32	0.47	0.57	0.54
real wages/net increase	−0.40	0.26	−0.47	−0.10	−0.15	0.49	0.03	0.88
real wages/nominal wages	0.78	0.93	0.91	0.93	0.94	0.96	0.92	0.28

	1860		*1870*		*1880*		*1890*	
	a	*b*	*a*	*b*	*a*	*b*	*a*	*b*
real wages/marriage rate	0.40	0.18	0.43	0.70	0.29	0.66	0.32	0.41
real wages/natural increase	−0.61	−0.01	0.32	0.55	−0.34	0.59	−0.09	0.52
real wages/migration	0.55	0.55	0.34	0.60	0.27	0.61	0.26	0.39
real wages/net increase	0.21	0.64	0.19	0.77	0.14	0.68	0.18	0.52
real wages/nominal wages	0.83	0.95	0.90	0.98	0.88	0.96	0.92	0.80

**a* excluding the four northernmost counties.
b all counties.

the century. During the first two periods, real wages reach the peak about six months prior to the number of births.

The study strengthens our conclusion that Sweden was already surprisingly well integrated during the end of the eighteenth century. Despite regional differences *in levels,* the national data show a clear correlation between *fluctuations* in real wages and population.

To study real wage level and regional differences in marriage rate, natural population growth, migration and net population growth the coefficients of correlation between real wages and the demographic variables are given in Table 22.7. In the left column (*a*) the four northernmost counties have been excluded, whereas the right column (*b*) includes all counties except Blekinge, which has not been included in any calculation due to incomplete statistical data.

When the Northern counties are included in the calculation the coefficients of correlation undergo a complete change relative to the results for the whole country. In many cases a negative coefficient becomes positive. The reason for this is the very high values for both real wages and demographic variables in the Northern counties. This is so especially in the correlation between real wages and natural population growth, but other coefficients are also affected. Thus, the Northern regions of the country are markedly different from the rest of Sweden, a fact that was indicated also by our real wage calculations.

In all other parts of Sweden the natural population growth was, during the pre-industrial phase, negatively correlated to both real and nominal wages. Migration did not influence the net population growth, which instead was entirely determined by the natural population growth. Both natural and net population growth are greatest in counties with low real wages.

From the mid-nineteenth century it was, above all, migration that determined net population growth and during the latter part of our period the negative correlation between natural population growth and real wage level decreased. During the phase of industrialisation there was a migration into those counties where the real wage level was high, which is hardly surprising

The explanation might be that expansive regions attracted people because of higher real wages or that the real wages were higher because productivity, prices and the degree of employment were higher in these regions.

The present analysis does not establish any *causal* relationship but attempts to show that our real wages calculations fit into a general picture of the regional demographic development during the phase of industrialisation. The findings neither falsify the results of our calculations of cost of living nor our assumption that the day-rates for agricultural workers are a good indicator of the general wage level.

NOTES

[1]Wohlin, N., *Den jordbruksidkande befolkningen i Sverige 1751-1900* (The Agricultural Population in Sweden) (Stockholm, 1909).

[2]Amark, K., *Spannmalshandel ooh Spannmalapolitik i Sverige 1719-1830* (Grain Trade and Grain Policy in Sweden) (Stockholm, 1915).

[3]*Historisk statistik for Sverige. Del 1. Befolkning 1720-1967* (Historical Statistics of Sweden. Part 1. Population) (Stockholm, 1969) Table 22.

[4]Jörberg, L., *A History of Prices in Sweden 1732-1914* (Lund, 1972) Vol. 1, chs 2 and 3.

[5]Ibid., Vol. II, p. 349.

[6]We do not claim that our calculations of regional costs of living reflect the actual regional pattern of consumption. The budget that has been used for all regions is a subsistence budget, and consequently the possibilities of substitution are limited. To obtain a different regional pattern of the development of costs of living a

pronounced shift between animal and vegetable products would be required. Regional patterns of consumption are worth an analysis *per se.,* since they reflect regional differences in standard of living. If separate regional budgets had been used instead of one budget for all regions, changes and differences in standard of living would have been confused with development of cost of living.

In those cases where no data on price were available, the national average has been used. If, instead, price data from bordering counties are used, then the dispersion is slightly larger (0.069 instead of 0.058). For the period 1860-65 the different price estimates are highly correlated (0.92). Since the technique used gives less dispersion, the observed differences in the costs of living between different parts of the country cannot be ascribed to the method of calculation.

Another alternative is to reduce the budget when price data are lacking. It can then be assumed that the price development of those commodities lacking price data follows the price development of other commodities. This is a less acceptable assumption since it is primarily prices for animal products which are lacking. The price of animal products fluctuates in a direction opposite to that of foodgrains. A reduction of the budget would lead to an overestimation of the costs of foodstuffs when grain prices increase and to an underestimation when the prices decline. Since the number of price data varies from county to county, such a procedure would lead to an overestimation of the difference in the costs of living between the regions.

[7] Jörberg, op. cit., Vol. II and Jörberg, L. and Bengtsson, T., 'Market Integration in Sweden during the 18th and 19th centuries. A spectral Analysis of Grain Prices', *Economy and History,* Vol. XVIII:2, 1975, pp. 93-106.

[8] Bagge, G. (ed.), *Wages in Sweden 1860-1930* (Stockholm, 1935).

[9] Bengtsson T. and Ohlsson, R., 'Population and Economic Fluctuations in Sweden 1749-1914' (forthcoming).

[10] Jörberg, L. and Bengtsson, T., op. cit.

[11] Coherence square is interpreted as the multiple correlation coefficient and lies, by definition, between 0 and 1. Although coherence square for the first period is fairly high, especially in the correlation between real wages and mortality, the amplitudes of the fluctuations are much smaller than for earlier periods, consequently real wages are of less importance during the last period. A more detailed discussion is found in a forthcoming article (see note 9).

23 Regional Differences in the Position of Peasants in the European Part of Russia in the Nineteenth Century

J. Kahk and I. Kovalchenko

The accelerated development of productive forces and the animation of trade relations, which appeared in Europe after revolutions and bourgeois reforms at the end of the eighteenth century and in the first half of the nineteenth century, brought about a remarkable increase in the influence of the international market on the local markets of separate countries. The most backward countries began to participate in the international market. Medieval partitions between geographical regions and social estates and layers began to break down. Though the general picture of socio-economic development is quite clear to us, the same cannot be said about concrete problems and even general tendencies. A peculiar contradiction takes place as a result of the development of capitalism. The development of the international market causes a definite levelling of prices, but at the same time it favours regional specialisation, i.e. in some regions it creates better conditions for the production of certain goods than in other regions. Creating a number of new jobs, the development of industry equalises the chances of the workers on the labour market to a certain extent. But on the other hand, social differentiation increases as well. In this relation a question arises – whether the differences in the position of the people in different regions have increased in any country during the nineteenth century or not.

Before studying the concrete data about the position of rural workers in Russia, we present some general propositions. We must not forget that, in essence, the small peasant holding appeared in different ways in France and Russia. In France small peasant and bourgeois land-holding had already appeared as a result of fierce competition over the sale of the former estates of the church and emigre-noblemen at the end of the eighteenth century. In Russia the peasant allotment landownership appeared as a result of a thoroughly prepared reform, in the course of which precise norms of peasant landownership were established.

Therefore we may suspect that at least for some period of time the realisation of the reform may have caused a certain levelling of peasant landownership.

In Russia the development of capitalism was also accompanied by the development of commodity agriculture and the agricultural market. The process of 'specialisation of the *commercial* (and capitalist) agriculture appears in all the capitalist countries, it appears in the international division of labour and in Russia during the reform.'[1]

In relation with these cases of unification and standardisation of certain sides of economic life, which undoubtedly took place in connection with the development of capitalism in Russia, we have interesting facts that have been obtained after studying the process of the formation of the All-Russian agrarian market.

The intensive construction of railways in the 1860s-70s resulted in providing those regions with corn where the need was the greatest. The formation of that market especially speeded up in the middle of the nineteenth century.

In the middle of the eighteenth century we can distinguish four, and at the beginning of the nineteenth century seven, local regions in the European part of Russia where it is possible to ascertain general tendencies in the movement of rye prices, the general correlation of prices in the whole European part of Russia being quite high already (the coefficient of correlation:0.75).

But towards the end of the nineteenth century all these regional corn markets formed one big All-Russian market, everywhere prices began to move in the same way and the general coefficient of correlation rose to 0.9.[2]

We can see a strong tendency towards unification and standardisation – everywhere in the European part of Russia the levels of prices of agricultural products are converging and differences between various regions are becoming less in this sense.

How much land people had in their possession may be regarded as one of the main indices of the position of the rural population.

For the end of the eighteenth century and the 1850s we have data about the amount of dessiatinas of land per man among the corvee peasants in 31 districts of 11 provinces. At the end of the eighteenth century an average of 2.86 dessiatinas belonged to one person and the variational coefficient of this index was 25 per cent; in the middle of the nineteenth century the average index was 2.96, but the amplitude of its variation did not appear to be so considerable – the index of variation was 14 per cent.[3]

In the years 1842-50 in fifty provinces of the European part of Russia an average of 1.01 dessiatinas belonged to each person of the *whole peasant population* and the variational coefficient of this index was 31 per cent.[4] When we took the land under corn cultivation in 50 provinces of the European part of Russia in 1901 and divided it between all the peasants counted during the census of 1897, the average index obtained was 0.96 dessiatinas and its variation appeared to be rather high – the coefficient of variation was 58 per cent.[5]

We must admit that the results obtained are not strictly comparable – the data were collected in different places and we do not know whether the methods applied were similar or not. Therefore we shall be careful with our conclusions and at the present stage of investigation we can fully affirm only the following. It is possible that within large regions *geographical differences* in the size of the peasant holdings may have lessened as a result of the reform in 1861 with its precise norms of peasant allotments that were rather similar in principle. But soon after the reform had been put into practice, spontaneous competitive forces became more powerful than they had been during the times of serfdom and again even geographical differences began to grow rapidly.

In 1877 the well-known geographer and statistician P.P. Semenov-Tyan-Shansky compared the position of the peasants in the volost of Murayevezhesk in the Dankov District (the province of Riazan) with their position before the reform of 1861. He wrote that 'on the one hand a great proportion of prosperous and rich households appeared . . . but the proportion of well-to-do households to poor ones hardly ever grew. At the same time, the proportion of poor households became bigger and indigent households appeared such as hardly existed before 1861.'[6]

But to Marxist historians the problem of increase in the *differences between different social groups,* between the disintegrating peasant poverty and the arising rural bourgeoisie is of greater interest and importance than the problem of increase in *geographical differences.* That is just the problem that V.I. Lenin discussed very successfully with Narodism-biased publicists who thought that the reform of 1861 and the existence of the community 'saved Russia from the vices of capitalism' including the increasing differences between different groups of peasants.

'Everywhere we can see that the actual division of the whole land at the peasants' disposal has nothing in common with the equalising character of allotments', V.I. Lenin writes on the basis of the analysis of the statistical data of Zemstvo about peasant landownership at the end of the nineteenth century.

> 35-50 per cent of the whole land belongs to 20 per cent of the households and only 20-30 per cent of the land belongs to 50 per cent of the households. . . . All the general data about the economy of our village testify a continuous and rapid increase in differentiation: on the one hand peasants neglect their land and rent it out, the number of horseless people is growing, 'peasants' run to towns, etc.; on the other hand progressive tendencies of the peasant housekeeping appear as well: 'peasants' buy new land and improve their housekeeping.[7]

Some data support the supposition that together with the increase in the differences between different layers of peasants, the indices characterising the geographical position of peasants increased as well (or at least they *did not decrease*).

On the basis of the data about budgetary investigation S.S. Klepnikov calculated the daily amount of calories per head in 13 different provinces of the European part of Russia in the years 1899-1911. An average of 4477 calories were found per head and the coefficient of variation of this index was found to be 35 per cent.[8] Consequently, at the end of the nineteenth century and at the beginning of the twentieth century differences in the economic position of peasants, found by such a thorough research method as budgetary investigation, turned out to be rather considerable when the position of peasants living in different parts of the European part of Russia was compared.

NOTES

(The following references have been translated from the original Russian sources.)

1 V.I. Lenin, *The Development of Capitalism in Russia* (Moscow 1952) p. 13.

2 I.D. Kovalchenko and L.V. Milov, 'The agrarian market in Russia in the beginning of the XXth century'. *An Essay in qualitative analysis* (Moscow 1974) pp. 94, 133, 159, 187, 190.

3 I.D. Kovalchenko, *Peasants' serfdom in Russia in the first half of the XIXth century* (Moscow, 1967) pp. 160-1.

4 I.D. Kovalchenko, 'About the economic conditions and the state of peasants in the private estates of European Russia in the 40s and the 50s of the XIXth century. Scientific publications of post-graduate schools'. *Historical Sciences,* 1259 (2).

5 Series of economic statistics on agriculture in Russia and in a few foreign countries. Year 1, St Petersbourg, 1907. First general census of the population of the Russian Empire, 1897.

6 *History of the USSR,* Book V (Moscow, 1968) p. 130.

7 V.I. Lenin, *The Development of Capitalism in Russia,* pp. 145, 150.

8 S.S. Klepnikov, *The Alimentation of Russian peasantry,* Part 1. *Utilization standards of the main food products* (Moscow, 1920) p. 12.

24 Regional Disparities in Wages: the Cotton Industry in Nineteenth-century Germany – Some Methodological Considerations

Hubert Kiesewetter

> The wages of labour are the encouragement of industry, which, like every other human quality, improves in proportion to the encouragement it receives.
>
> Adam Smith, 1776

I dedicate this essay to Karl R. Popper on his seventy-fifth birthday, 28 July, 1977. It is impossible to express here how much I owe to his scientific work and his personal inspiration. I am indebted to Knut Borchardt, Wolfram Fischer, Patrice L.-R. Higgonet and Carl-Ludwig Holtfrerich for comments and valuable criticism of an earlier draft.

The industrial revolution which followed political unification in France, Britain, the United States and Sweden necessarily preceded it in Germany. Although the idea of unification had been, for other than economic reasons, very strong all over Germany since the war against Napoleon, the political constellations in Europe in the first half of the nineteenth century prevented its realisation. In a description of the Hambach Festival of June 1832, Gustav Freytag wrote in 1870:

> There lies a certain irony in the fact that, while enthusiastic popular speakers accused their sovereigns with some justice of being deadly enemies of Germany's unity and liberty, these same sovereigns created, by joining the *Zollverein,* a long-lasting basis for German unity . . . and that rough, selfish businessmen who had no interest in political matters, by raising levels of production and floating railway stocks, extirpated with greater effect the frontiers than the official spokesmen of unification.[1]

For the student of German history, then, the study of economics and of economic indicators has a pronounced political dimension.

The early history of the industrial revolution in Germany must be set in the context of the times, a context which was politically, and therefore statistically, complex. For historians of this first phase of industrialisation in Germany the available published data are scanty, unreliable, and difficult to compare. The methods of data collection differed from state to state, and their reliability was often dependent on the abilities and the funds of the directors of the statistical bureaus. Confronted with the task of inquiring into economic disparities in regional development in nineteenth-century Germany I was naturally tempted, like many other economic historians, to restrict myself to the latter part of the century, where the material is quite abundant and lends itself better to regional comparison. None the less, I am convinced that we cannot understand the social, economic, and political problems of industrialised Germany unless we have better explanations and greater knowledge of various regions in the first half of the century.

The bulk of recent work on economic development by region has focussed on the data for incomes.[2] With this in mind, my purpose in this essay is to consider some of the methodological difficulties that arise in these comparisons of wage data for nineteenth-century Germany. Many statisticians and historians of the nineteenth century, it may be added, were already aware of these problems, and tried to collect and interpret as much data as they could find.[3] We now know, however, that their findings are insufficient for the purpose of detailed comparisons of the development, economic change, and reciprocal entanglements and influences of the various regions of Germany, because the modes of collection had been different. Rising or falling per capita income, for example, is without doubt a good indicator of economic change of a particular sort, but it does not give us much information about larger problems such as living standards, social status, or possible class structures. In addition, there are the problems of different income-tax systems in Germany, changes in income tax, and the nearly incomparable modes of assessment before 1900. Bo Ohngren has shown for Sweden, for example, where the available data are much more solid, that the incomes used by the taxation authorities to calculate the income tax are in general too low.[4] Even if there is little doubt that the economic growth of regions in nineteenth-century Germany was very uneven, with higher incomes in the west, we do not know very much about the factors and consequences of these regional differences.

The complexity of the problem in relation to regional disparities of development in terms of differences in wages is exemplified by the situation of cotton workers, especially spinners and weavers. Their case can serve as our model, because a variety of factors complicate the use of their wages as an indicator of change. (1) Throughout the nineteenth century, we find in the cotton industry domestic workers as well as factory workers. Thus we can test the long-disputed thesis that the poverty and misery of the workers was a result of the factory system and the alleged decline in *real* wages. (2) In Germany, as in the other European nations, it was necessary to import raw material from overseas.[5] Disruptions in the trade of cotton, price changes, booms and slumps consequently had immediate effects on industry and

TABLE 24.1 Yearly wages of spinners, 1800-1913 (in Marks per capita)

Year	*Baden*	*Bavaria*	*Rhineland*	*Saxony*	*Württemberg*
1800	67				
1805		104			
1811	79		44		
1812		52			
1820			182		
1822			230	252	
1824			238		330
1825	275		255		
1828	275				
1830				408	333
1835				252	
1836			185		
1839				369	
1840			201	360	375
1841			204		
1842			217		
1843			279		
1844			304		
1848	317				
1850				584	374
1853		233			
1855		295	753	695	416
1856			756		
1857		240	774		
1858			743		438
1860			763		550
1861			810		
1863			720		
1864			713		
1865			708	504	457
1866		379	749		
1868			819	232	407
1869		380	840		
1872					691
1874	354				
1875		492			
1878			557		
1879			562		
1880	519		583		
1881			588		587
1882			540		
1883					470
1885	606	494			
1887	550				526
1888	557				529
1890	577			840	549
1891	587	522			548
1892	581		625		553
1893			751		
1896	553				
1900	682				
1903		960	1,087	890	
1904	633				
1905	684				
1906	720	1,020	1,050	706	
1911			1,080		
1912			820		
1913		709	745		

SOURCE: Calculated from Kirchhain, G., *Das Wachstum der deutschen Baumwollindustrie im 19. Jahrhundert.* (Diss, Münster, 1973). Appendix, pp. 256-63.

TABLE 24.2 Yearly wages of weavers, 1805-1913 (in Marks per capita)

Year	*Baden*	*Bavaria*	*Rhineland*	*Saxony*	*Württemberg*
1805		340			
1811			73	260	
1812		272			
1813				713	
1820				357	
1825				564	
1830					350
1833				322	
1838				725	
1840				302	358
1841		212	563		
1842			387	501	
1843			384		
1844			385		
1847		254		644	
1848	299	187			
1850				394	357
1851		142			
1852				265	
1855			219		429
1856			200	290	
1858			231		388
1859		466	314	403	
1860		482	346	338	525
1861		722	380	403	
1862			345		
1863			330	244	
1865		430	370	432	498
1866			404		
1867			398		
1868			406	324	
1869			407	456	
1871		600	360		
1872			482		682
1874	372		532	576	
1875			544		
1876			530		
1877			547	432	
1878			704		
1880	630	670	701		580
1881			725	433	
1882			705		
1884			719	289	
1885			722	318	
1886		580	890		
1887			945		
1888			939	720	
1890		643	951		
1891		664	945		
1892			977		
1893			917		
1895			1,000		
1896	568		1,035		
1897			995		
1898			989	1,175	
1900	1,060		1,058		
1902			1,043	960	
1903		770	1,065	576	
1904	669		1,090		
1905	770		1,110		
1906	720		1,164	672	
1907			1,198	671	
1911			1,150		
1913		795			

SOURCE: Calculated from Kirchhain, G., op. cit., pp. 265-74.

wages. (3) Almost any industrial or political measure affecting the production of cotton in the United States, the main producer, and Britain, the main consumer of cotton, influenced the German industry and forced it to react. (4) Though closely connected, the degree of mechanisation differs widely between spinning-mills and weaving-mills. Regional disparities in wages can possibly be dependent on the level of mechanisation or the resistance to it. (5) Differences in wages, especially if calculated on an annual basis, are most often the result of the fact that the percentage of women and children is much higher in spinning-mills than in weaving-mills. (6) The relatively low price of cottons compared to woollen, linen or silk goods enabled a greater part of the workers to buy new cottons with their rising wages. (7) The influence of fashion is perhaps greater in textiles than in other industries. This was felt very strongly in 1883/84, when woollen goods became fashionable and reduced to a considerable extent the consumption of cottons.[6] (8) The rapid development of the cotton industry in the early phase of industrialisation tends to support the thesis that this manufacturing branch was one of the leading sectors in the process of economic and technical growth. One should therefore be able to see the impact of the cotton industry in the changes of wages in different regions.

Of course, I cannot present here definitive correlations of these factors. Indeed, despite the vast literature on the subject there are many questions yet to be answered about regional development in Germany. The literature on wages, for example, by G. Bry, A.V. Desai or R. and J. Kuczynski, most often presents annual average wages, which if separated by region or town[7] do show huge differences. But can we assume these wage differences are truly due to regional disparities? More careful investigation casts doubt on the validity of these assumptions.

For example, in the years around 1875, the annual wages in weaving-mills were 600 Marks in 1871 in Bavaria, 682 Marks in 1872 in Wurttemberg, 372 Marks in 1874 in Baden, 544 Marks in 1875 in the Rhineland, 580 Marks in 1874 in Silesia, and 432 Marks in 1877 in the Kingdom of Saxony.[8] In order to assess the significance of these differences between regions, we should at least know the pattern of wages within regions. Victor Bohmert, the director of the statistical bureau in Dresden, in his valuable description of the annual wages of 444 looms in a weaving-mill in Merane, one of the centres of the cotton industry in the Kingdom of Saxony,[9] shows that the lowest wage from 1 June 1876 till 31 May 1877 was 323 Marks, the highest wage 874 Marks, i.e. a difference of 170 per cent. The weaver with the lowest wage was absent from his loom for *only* three weeks during this period, while the man with the highest wage was always present. Even greater differences appear if we look at the weekly wages. The range between the lowest and the highest weekly wage of the first weaver goes from 2.25 to 11.50 Marks, i.e. 411 per cent, while the range of the second weaver reaches from 4.60 to 33.75 Marks, i.e. 634 per cent. And the lowest weekly wage of the second weaver is more than twice as much as that of the first weaver, while the highest weekly wage is nearly three times as much. There are many reasons for these differences which I cannot consider here in detail. But we can see that the wage fluctuations in this one weaving-mill are greater than the fluctuations in the various regions in Germany.

It is not difficult to find other patterns of difference that are even more striking. In a spinning-mill in Chemnitz a child earned in 1847 15 *Neugroschen* a week, a spinner 76, an engine fitter 95 and a willow master 210 *Neugroschen* a week.[10] In Silesia in the textile industry in 1874 the wages for children between 12 and 14 years of age were 1.8 Marks a week, for girls between 14 and 16 years 3 Marks, for women 3-6 Marks, for day-workers 8 Marks, for weavers 9 Marks, for spinners 9-12 Marks, for master weavers 13-16 Marks a week.[11] A solid explanation of the wage structure in weaving- and spinning-mills has to separate first of all the wages of men, women and children, then of masters, skilled and unskilled workers and journeymen. Annual average wages in spinning-mills include the low wages of children and women, while the wages in weaving-mills tend to be higher due to the fact that the majority of wage earners are skilled workers. In addition, we should wherever possible separate wage categories, which are numerous throughout the nineteenth century. This leads to astonishing results.[12] With the help of frequency distributions we are in a position to eliminate the influences of the extreme wages.

Even if we can separate nominal wages according to skill, age, working time, etc., our insight into the situation of workers in different regions over a long period remains partial and inadequate. The maintenance of a family depends on many other factors: the number of children, the health of the family, the amount of property and other things which are not directly related to wages. Because wages all over Germany were extremely low, at least in the first half of the nineteenth century, the price of food played an enormous part in the attempt to escape the vicious circle of poverty. Therefore many economic historians of the nineteenth century take rye or corn as a deflator in order to ascertain real wages. Although I do not want to discuss here the problem of indices, for a reliable comparison of economic disparities in regional development we do have to consider some of the difficulties.

Already near the minimum subsistence level and often below, workers were indeed very sensitive to changes in the price of food. When the price of rye or corn rose, they lived, for example, on potatoes, eggs, milk and herring.[13] In the nineteenth century rye was usually the main staple, and the biggest expense of a common working-class family. Changes in diet, however, were so great during the different periods of the nineteenth century that the deflation of nominal wages with rye is, I think, a rather unreliable index for real wages. If the nominal wages are quite stable, a diagram which deflates these wages with the prices of rye will essentially show the fluctuations of rye prices. If the wages fluctuate parallel to price development, then they reinforce the fluctuations. Wages anticyclical to prices level the diagram.[14] Even if we could find a cost-of-living index for the nineteenth century, it would not be uniformly applicable to the different regions, some of which were self-sufficient, while others were heavily dependent on food imports. Thus the comparison between indices of wages and cost-of-living indices of nineteenth-century Germany by Kuczynski and others[15] gives us an unreliable picture.

Figure 24.1 compares a non-index development of the annual average prices of rye at the Munich market with annual wages of textile workers in a factory in Ettlingen (Baden), and the average prices of raw cotton between 1801 and 1913. There is no direct correlation between the three curves. The great fluctuation in rye prices during the whole nineteenth century is very similar to the price indices of rye, corn, barley, oats, potatoes and peas which we know from Jacobs and Richter.[18] The development of wages has a rather steady upward trend since 1849, with downward movements during economic recessions. All that I have said before about the reliability of those wages applies here too. But if we can rely on Schmoller,[19] who found that the share of bread amounted to the greater part of the budget of a common working-class family up to 1914, it then seems obvious that the increase in average wages from 345 Marks in 1839 to 885 Marks in 1913 allowed our textile workers to raise their living standard. One acceptable indicator is the consumption of meat, which increased from 21.6 kg in 1840 to 23.3 kg in 1861, 29.5 kg in 1873, 32.5 kg in 1892 and 46.8 kg in 1904/5 per capita in Germany.[20]

There are many other problems affecting regional disparities in wages in the economic development of Germany during the nineteenth century which I have not yet mentioned. To improve our knowledge we have to separate the patterns of compensation, such as wages for piecework, hourly wages, premiums, profit-sharing, or summer and winter wages.[21] We must also consider the differences in working hours, the variations in the customs of nutrition, etc. Wieck[22] for example tells us that textile workers in the Kingdom of Saxony refused to work more than five days a week in 1812 because their wages were sufficient. Engel[23] says in 1866 that many branches of industry calculate on a basis of 10 working months a year. Domestic weavers were unemployed two or three months a year even in the early twentieth century.[24] For wage comparisons, I think, we should return to a weekly basis, not only because of these factors but also because the majority of workers in the nineteenth century calculated their spendings within this time-span.

Although the statistical material is not easy to attain, we ought not to be too pessimistic. The annual reports of the chambers of commerce and business, which exist for every industrial town, provide possibly the best source of wage data, in spite of the fact that they were put forth by entrepreneurs. Dispersed material is also available in reports of exhibitions or of factory inspectors, in anniversary publications, journals, etc. While I do not wish to underrate the usefulness of computer projects that rely on complicated mathematical and economic models, I wish to emphasise that we still need to locate basic data for this type of quantitative work. Along the lines of my motto, borrowed from Adam Smith, I think it important to encourage

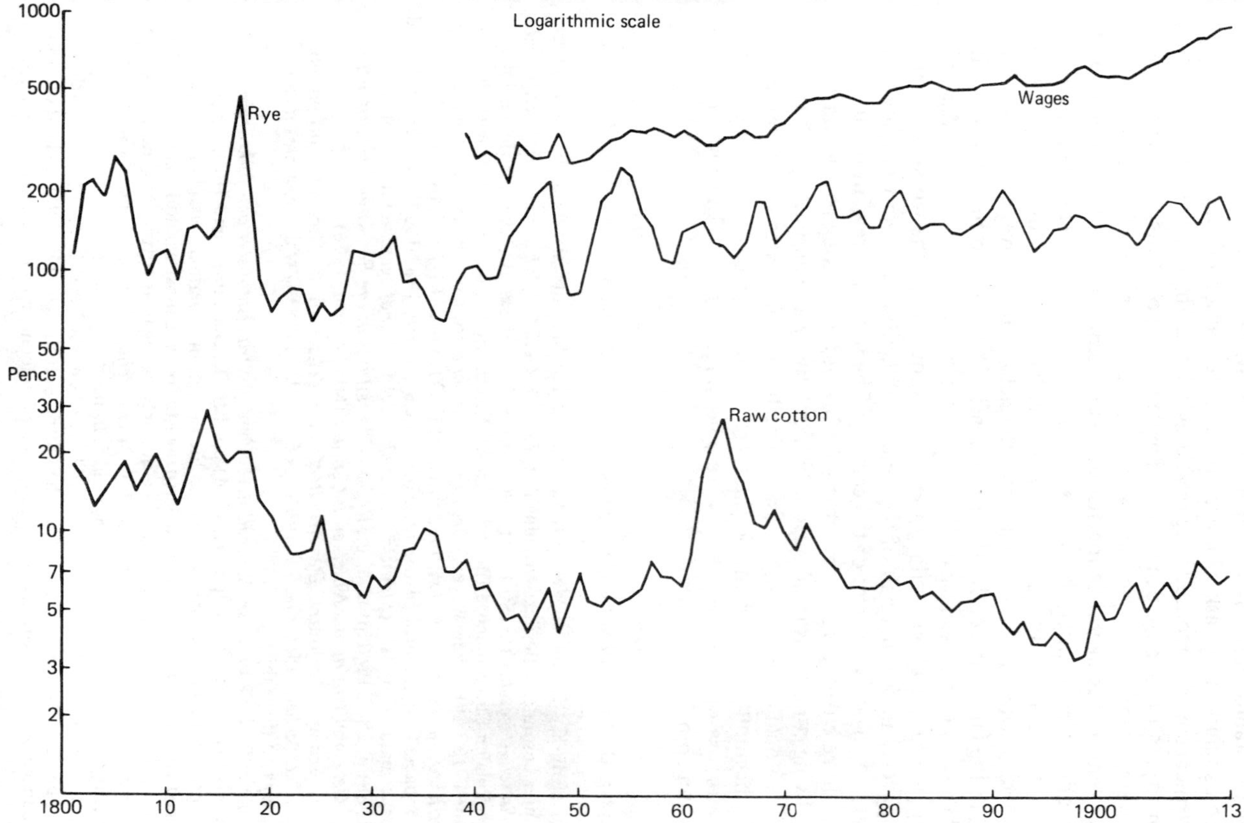

Fig. 24.1 Annual average prices of rye, 1801-1913, average prices of raw cotton, 1801-1913,[16] *and annual wages of textile workers, 1839-1913*[17]

young scholars to produce an imaginative economic history based on stimulating interpretations and refined explanatory hypotheses. Otherwise we are going to establish a form of quantitative positivism.

To conclude, if we ask whether or not there was a tendency towards convergence or divergence in regional wages during the nineteenth century in Germany,[25] the answer cannot be a simple yes or no. In the cotton industry the average tendency of nominal as well as real wages to rise was clearly dependent on the degree of mechanisation in spinning- and weaving-mills, and on productivity, capital, the acquisition of skilled labour and market conditions. Thus, for example, manual weavers in Bavaria, living in the countryside, had to work 15 hours a day with the help of their wives and children even in the late nineteenth century, to reach the minimum subsistence level, while a weaver in Augsburg or Hof could afford a relatively high standard of living, working 10 hours a day or less.[26] Without doubt the workers' misery and poverty in the first half of the nineteenth century all over Germany had largely changed by the end of the century. The industrial revolution, in spite of the huge changes it imposed upon the life of the working people, improved their living conditions in all regions both relatively and absolutely. Thus, while regional disparities in wages were perhaps even greater at the end than at the beginning of the century, the social and economic situation of cotton workers rose to a level where they were no longer forced to live a life unworthy of a human being.

NOTES

[1] Freytag, G., *Karl Mathy. Geschichte seines Lebens* (Leipzig, 1870) pp. 56-7. All translations are mine.

[2] Borchardt, K., 'Regionale Wachstumsdifferenzierung in Deutschland im 19. Jahrhundert unter besonderer Berücksichtigung des West-Ost-Gefälles', *Wirtschaft, Geschichte und Wirtschaftsgeschichte* (Stuttgart, 1966) pp. 325-39; Hesse, H., 'Die Entwicklung der regionalen Einkommensdifferenzen im Wachstumsprozess der deutschen Wirtschaft vor 1913', in Fischer, W. (ed.) *Beiträge zu Wirtschaftswachstum und Wirtschaftsstruktur im 16. und 19. Jahrhundert* (Berlin, 1971) pp. 261-79; Orsagh, T.J., 'The Probable Geographical Distribution of German Income, 1882-1963', in Giersch, H. and Sauermann, H. (eds.), *Quantitative Aspekte der Wirtschaftsgeschichte* (Tübingen, 1968) p. 280-311; Tipton, F.B., *Regional Variations in the Economic Development of Germany During the Nineteenth Century* (Middletown, 1976).

[3] See for example the journal *Der Arbeiterfreund. Zeitschrift des Centralvereins für das Wohl der arbeitenden Klassen,* vol. 1 (1863); vol. 52 (1914) which contains many essays on this subject.

[4] Ohngren, B., *Folk i rörelse. Samhällsutveckling, flyttningsmönster och folkrörelser i Eskilstuna 1870-1900* (Uppsala, 1974) pp. 126 ff., Diagrams 9 and 10.

[5] Few people, I feel, can have believed, as Fichte did, that Germany would no longer need cotton if peasants could be persuaded to sow the most wool-like grass, to produce in time a fibre that would be not only as cheap as cotton, but the source of a new and healthy food. See Fichte, J. G., *Der geschlossne Handelsstaat* [1800] (Leipzig, 1943) Book III, chap. 6, p. 115, footnote.

[6] Another example is the cholera year of 1831, when wool was thought to be a remedy for cholera. The factory owners in the cotton industry complained heavily about the reduced selling of cottons. See 'Das Berliner Cholerajahr 1831', *Vossische Zeitung,* No. 208, 1 Sep. 1931.

[7]Kuczynski, J., *Löhne und Ernährungskosten in Deutschland 1820 bis 1937* (Libau, 1937) III: Wages in the textile industry, pp. 19-23; Kirchhain, G., *Das Wachstum der deutschen Baumwollindustrie im 19. Jahrhundert* (dissertation, Münster, 1973) Appendix, pp. 255-84.

[8]Kirchhain, G., op. cit. pp. 265-75.

[9]Böhmert, V., 'Weberlöhne einer Fabrik in Merane', *Zeitschrift des K. Sächsischen Statistischen Bureau's,* Vol. XXIII, 1877, pp. 47-64.

[10]Strauss, R., *Die Lage und die Bewegung der Chemnitzer Arbeiter in der ersten Hälfte des 19. Jahrhunderts* (Berlin, 1960) p. 49. For a thoughtful discussion of this problem with different examples see Fischer, W., 'Innerbetrieblicher und sozialer Status der frühen Fabrikarbeiterschaft', in Fischer, W. and Bajor, G. (eds.), *Die soziale Frage* (Stuttgart, 1967) pp. 215-52.

[11]Frief, A., *Die wirtschaftliche Lage der Fabrikarbeiter in Schlesien* (Breslau, 1876), pp. 39-44.

[12]See Fischer, W., op. cit.

[13]A touching description thereof is given by Schneer, A., *Uber die Zustände der arbeitenden Klassen in Breslau* (Berlin, 1845).

[14]Saalfeld, D., 'Lebensstandard in Deutschland 1750-1860' in Bog, I., *et al.* (eds.), *Wirtschaftliche und soziale Strukturen im säkularen Wandel,* Vol. II, (Hannover, 1974) pp. 417-43. Saalfeld overlooks the effect of the rye prices. See Diagram 2 and text on p. 422. Jörberg, L., 'The Development of Real Wages for Agricultural Workers in Sweden During the 18th and 19th Centuries', *Economy and History.* Vol. XV, 1972, pp. 41-57, who deflates nominal wages with the prices of rye over a period of more than 180 years. I leave out here the question of the influence of monetary and real effects upon price movements. See Kessel, R.A. and Alchian, A. A., 'The Meaning and Validity of the Inflation Induced Lag of Wages behind Prices', *American Economic Review,* Vol. L, 1960, pp. 43-66.

[15]Kuczynski, J., op. cit., pp. 38-43, for wages in the textile industry. Blumberg, H., *Die deutsche Textilindustrie in der industriellen Revolution* (Berlin, 1965) pp. 317, 324, compared the wages in spinning-mills in Württemberg with the cost-of-living indices. For contradictory findings see Neumann, A., *Die Bewegung der Löhne der ländlichen "freien" Arbeiter im Zusammenhang mit der gesamtwirtschaftlichen Entwicklung im Königreich Preussen gegenwärtigen Umfangs vom Ausgang des 18. Jahrhunderts bis 1850* (Berlin, 1911) p. 258; Saalfeld, D., 'Handwerkereinkommen in Deutschland vom ausgehenden 18. bis zur Mitte des 19. Jahrhunderts. Ein Beitrag zur Bewertung von Handwerkerlöhnen in der Ubergangsperiode zum industriellen Zeitalter', in Abel, W. (ed.), *Handwerksgeschichte in neuer Sicht* (Göttingen, 1978) p. 68, Diagram 1; Tenfelde, K., *Sozialgeschichte der Bergarbeiterschaft an der Ruhr im 19. Jahrhundert* (Bonn-Bad Godesberg, 1977) p. 108, note 9.

[16]Data for rye from Jacobs, A. and Richter, H., *Die Grosshandelspreise in Deutschland von 1792 bis 1934* (Berlin, 1935) pp. 52/53. From 1801 to 1880 socalled "Schrannenpreise", from 1881 to 1913 Bavarian middle, loco. See also Grohnert, C., *Die Bildung der Roggenpreise bei freier und gebundener Wirtschaft* (Jena, 1926) p. 178, Table 3. The annual average prices are in Reichsmark per 1000 kg. Data for raw cotton from Mitchell, B. R., *Abstract of British Historical Statistics* (Cambridge, 1962) p. 491. Average prices of Upland or Middling American in pence per lb.

[17]See Schmieder, L., *Chronik der Gesellschaft für Spinnerei und Weberei Ettlingen. Ein Beitrag zur Wirtschaftsgeschichte des Albtales und zur Geschichte der badischen Textilindustrie 1836-1936* (Karlsruhe, 1936) p. 134 (diagram), and Kirchhain, G., op. cit., p. 279, Table 96.

[18]Jacobs, A., and Richter, H., op. cit., p. 52 ff. The price indices of other goods are considerably different.

[19]Schmoller, G., 'Die Tatsachen der Lohnbewegung in Geschichte und Gegenwart', *Schmollers Jahrbuch für Gesetzgebung, Verwaltung und Volkswirtschaft im Deutschen Reiche,* Vol. 38, 1914, p. 544 ff. For a discussion of rye as a relatively

stable market good see Seelhorst, C. von, *Der Roggen als Wertmass für Landwirtschaftliche Berechnungen* (Jena, 1888). Rye as the 'chief nutriment of the manual working classes' in the 1840s, as described by Reden, F.W. von, 'Vergleichende Zusammenstellung der Preise der nothwendigsten Lebensbedürfnisse, sowie der Verhältnisse der handarbeitenden Volksklassen in Hamburg, Bremen, Lübeck und Frankfurt a.M.', *Zeitschrift des Vereins für deutsche Statistik*, Vol. 1, 1847, p. 1041; and Saalfeld, D., 'Methodische Darlegungen zur Einkommensentwicklung und Sozialstruktur 1760-1860 am Beispiel einiger deutschen Städte', in Winkel, H. (ed.), *Vom Kleingewerbe zur Grossindustrie* (Berlin, 1975) pp. 227-9.

[20] Abel, W., *Agrarkrisen und Agrarkonjunktur* (Hamburg/Berlin, 1966) p. 247. Also Saalfeld, D., 'Steigerung und Wandlung des Fleischverbrauchs in Deutschland 1800-1913', *Zeitschrift für Agrargeschichte und Agrarsoziologie*, Vol. 25, 1977, pp. 244-53.

[21] See Roberts, E., 'Working-Class Standards of Living in Barrow and Lancaster, 1890-1914', *Economic History Review*, vol. XXX, 1977, p. 309.

[22] Wieck, F. G., *Industrielle Zustände Sachsens* (Chemnitz, 1840) p. 181.

[23] Engel, E., *Der Preis der Arbeit* (Berlin, 1866) p. 43.

[24] Wilbrandt, R., *Die Weber in der Gegenwart. Sozialpolitische Wanderungen durch die Hausweberei und die Webfabrik* (Jena, 1906) p. 104.

[25] See for income levels Easterlin, R. A., 'Interregional Differences in Per Capita Income, Population, and Total Income, 1840-1950', *Trends in the American Economy in the Nineteenth Century* (Princeton, 1960) pp. 73-140.

[26] Grabmann, J., *Die Entwickelung der Augsburger Industrie im 19. Jahrhundert* (Augsburg, 1894) pp. 163-87; Schmid, K., *Die Entwicklung der Hofer Baumwoll-Industrie* (Leipzig/Erlangen, 1923) pp. 74-89.

25 Regional Disparities in Brabantine Urbanisation before and after the Industrial Revolution (1374–1970): Some Aspects of Measurement and Explanation

Paul M. M. Klep

This text is a revised version of a paper, entitled 'Urbanization in a Pre-Industrial Economy. The Case of Brabant, 1374-1930', published in: Belgisch Tijdschrift voor Nieuwste Geschiedenis, *7(1976). I wish to thank Prof. Herman Van der Wee for his very interesting suggestions.*

This contribution examines the level of urbanisation as a specific indicator of structural differences between some regions in Belgium. The purpose is to describe and to analyse very long-term changes in the regional dispersion of urbanisation. A distinction has to be made between the study of disparities of aggregates and structures. My discussion will not be directed to regional gaps in wages, prices or (per capita) product. The disparities will concern the increasing or declining unevenness of structural socio-economic development during the periods before and after the Industrial Revolution.

Brabant has a long tradition of highly developed commercial and industrial activity. From the twelfth century onwards, an important non-agricultural home market and export industry, especially in textiles, developed in this region. Agricultural techniques were among the best in Europe. The commercial and industrial activity of this region reached a climax in the first half of the sixteenth century, when the international market of Antwerp stretched from the north to the south and from the west to the east of Europe.[1]

The Wars of Religion between 1568 and 1648 divided the Netherlands into a southern and northern part. International conventions, dominated by Dutch and English commercial interests, isolated the Brabantine economy from the international markets, at least partially. We have to wait for the nineteenth century for a second period of such fast commercial and industrial development. The modern transformation of the Brabantine economy started very slowly about 1800. Although the population had been growing faster and faster since 1755, the real breakthrough to modern economic growth is only after 1850.[2]

The level of urbanisation will be defined as the ratio of the urban population to total population. As urban population I include people residing in communities with a centre of at least 5000 inhabitants. This rather high level is necessary because we find in Brabant very extensive rural communities with populations of 3000 or 4000 inhabitants. One could debate whether a community of 5000 is indeed an urban unit, but the timing of changes is quite insensitive to our urban definition. In Table 25.1 I have collected the levels of urbanisation in six Brabantine regions (and combinations of them).

TABLE 25.1 Urban ratios and population in Brabant, 1374-1970 (total population in millions)

Region	*1374*	*1437*	*1480*	*1526*	*1565*	*1615*	*1665*	*1709*	*1755*	*1806*	*1846*	*1890*	*1930*	*1970*
Antwerp	22	43	60	63	76	71	67	64	51	48	49	75	85	90
Mechelen	43	62	68	65	64	55	51	51	40	35	35	49	57	66
Turnhout	0	0	0	0	15	0	0	12	13	14	14	17	37	52
Brussels	26	35	40	37	41	52	51	51	37	34	45	72	78	86
Leuven	34	34	39	38	36	25	32	40	27	30	28	35	36	41
Nijvel	10	15	17	0	0	0	0	15	0	7	6	11	16	40
Total	24	33	39	39	46	41	41	45	32	30	34	57	68	75
A + B	25	38	47	50	51	61	58	56	43	39	47	73	80	88
M + L	34	43	48	48	48	37	40	46	33	32	31	41	45	52
T + N	6	7	8	0	7	0	0	13	7	10	9	14	27	47
AMT	20	34	45	45	61	51	48	48	38	35	37	58	71	77
BLN	28	32	36	36	30	33	35	43	28	27	33	56	64	73
Total population	0.33	0.38	0.37	0.38	0.45	0.36	0.48	0.48	0.50	0.72	1.10	1.81	2.84	3.68

Source: P.M.M.Klep, *Bevolking* . . ., p. 8.

TABLE 25.2 Incremental urbanisation ratios ($\Delta\frac{U}{P}$) in Brabant, 1374-1970 (percentages)

Region	*1374-1437*	*1437-1480*	*1480-1526*	*1526-1555*	*1555-1615*	*1615-1665*	*1665-1709*	*1709-1755*	*1755-1806*	*1806-1846*	*1846-1890*	*1890-1930*	*1930-1970*
	length of period (years)												
	63	*43*	*46*	*39*	*50*	*50*	*44*	*46*	*51*	*40*	*44*	*40*	*40*
Antwerp	21	17	3	13	−5	−4	−3	−12	−4	1	26	10	5
Mechelen	19	6	−3	−1	−9	−4	0	−11	−5	0	14	8	9
Turnhout	0	0	0	15	−15	0	12	1	2	0	3	20	15
Brussels	9	5	−3	4	11	−1	0	−14	−3	11	27	6	8
Leuven	0	5	−1	−2	−11	7	8	−13	3	−2	7	1	5
Nijvel	5	2	−17	0	0	0	15	−15	7	−1	5	5	14
Total	9	6	0	7	−5	0	4	−13	−2	4	23	11	7
A + B	13	9	3	11	0	−3	−2	−13	−4	8	26	7	8
M + L	9	5	0	0	11	3	6	−13	−1	−1	10	4	7
T + N	1	1	−8	7	−7	0	13	−6	3	−1	5	13	20
AMT	14	11	0	16	−10	−3	0	−10	−3	2	21	13	6
BLN	4	4	0	−6	3	2	8	−15	−1	6	23	8	9

Like Jeffrey Williamson in his study on American North-east Urbanisation[3] I have taken as an index of the rate at which urbanisation occurs a rather primitive measure, that is, the incremental urbanisation ratio $\Delta \frac{U}{P}$ (see Table 25.2). This ratio directly captures the share of the population transferred during a certain period.

By examining the timing of Brabantine urbanisation, we see that Brabant witnessed two broad periods of increasing levels of urbanisation: the first in the fourteenth, fifteenth and first half of the sixteenth century, and the second in the nineteenth and twentieth century. This is consistent with the Commercial and Industrial Revolutions in those centuries.

The de-urbanisation of the second half of the sixteenth century coincides with the loss of important export markets and a disrupted domestic market, caused by the eighty-year Wars of Religion. The seventeenth century brings stability. The crisis in the Brabantine skilled-labour industries of the first half of the eighteenth century generates a further de-urbanisation, and during the strong agricultural expansion in the second half of this century the process of de-urbanisation continues.

I believe that we cannot speak of Brabantine 'urban booms' either in late medieval times or in the nineteenth century. Nineteenth-century urbanisation in Brabant was much slower than, for example, in the industrialising centres of the United States. Incremental urbanisation ratios of 35 per cent, measured over only three decades, can be observed in Rhode Island, Eastern Pennsylvania, New Jersey, New York, Maryland, and other American industrial and commercial regions. In the nineteenth century the Brussels area had a long and intensive urbanisation period, of five decades from 1830 to 1880, starting from 35 per cent with decennial incremental ratios of about 6½ per cent. On the other hand the Antwerp area had its urban acceleration between 1846 and 1890, over four-and-a-half decades, starting from 45 per cent, with decennial incremental ratios of 6 per cent.

We have to conclude that the nineteenth-century urban acceleration developed after a 50-year period of slow urbanisation. It also departed from high established urban ratios: 34 per cent in the total Brabantine region and almost 50 per cent in the Antwerp-Brussels area, where the acceleration was nevertheless the highest.

The highest incremental urban ratios are negative and pre-industrial. Some data suggest that in the three or four decades after 1565 Brabant underwent strong de-urbanisation. The region of Antwerp, especially, lost quite a lot of urban population. In 1565 there were 100,000 citizens, but about 1600 the maximum was 50,000. I am not absolutely sure about the evolution of the rural population but it is not unlikely that the negative incremental urban ratio for the Antwerp area is about 35-40 per cent in the last three decades of the sixteenth century.

The timing of the Brabantine urbanisation supports our conventional historical knowledge. However, by comparing the evolution of the incremental urban ratios, it could be interesting to make a further study of the chronology of the urbanisation in the Brussels and Antwerp areas. There are reasons to believe that in the fourteenth/fifteenth century, as well as in the nineteenth century, urban acceleration started earlier in the Brussels area than in the Antwerp area. This suggests a possible interdependency, which could indicate the importance of internal Brabantine growth-forces in the expansion of Antwerp's urban population. This possible interdependency seems to weaken the importance attributed to specific commercial factors, developed by the Antwerp merchants in non-Brabant-oriented international trade. Perhaps the earlier increase in the level of urbanisation and industrialisation in the Brussels area was a necessary but insufficient condition to Antwerp's expansion?

How far can the changes in the levels of urbanisation be explained by migration, and to what extent are they due to variations in the rate of natural increase? If I could estimate the surpluses of births over deaths in urban and rural areas, I should in principle get an answer to this question. However there are a great number of practical obstacles to such a procedure: for example, we have no data about births and deaths before 1600.

If I take as hypotheses (1) that rates of urban natural increase were negative in the fourteenth to sixteenth centuries and were positive in the nineteenth century, and (2) that rates of natural rural increase were more positive in the nineteenth century than in late medieval times, I can try to deduce some kind of answer to this question.[4]

I will compare two periods of increasing levels of urbanisation: the first from 1437 to 1565 (with percentages increasing from 33 per cent to 46 per cent and a second period from 1806 to 1855, with almost the same percentages: 30 per cent and 44 per cent (see Table 25.3, line 5).

TABLE 25.3 Data concerning two urbanisation periods in Brabant

1.	Period	1437-1565	1806-1866
2.	Length (years)	128	60
3.	Urban population (000)	123-209	218-563
4.	Total population (000)	378-452	717-1292
5.	Urban ratios (%)	33-46	30-44
6.	Annual rate of increase of the urban population (%)	0.42	1.60
7.	Annual rate of increase of the total population (%)	0.14	1.0
8.	6 relative to 7 (ratio)	3.0	1.6
9.	Annual rate of increase of the rural population (%)	−0.038	0.63
10.	Annual rate of natural increase of the urban population (assumed, %)	−0.4	0.2
11.	Annual rate of increase of the urban population by immigration (6-10, %)	0.82	1.4
12.	Annual rate of natural increase of the rural population (%) (from 3,4,10)	0.31	1.24
13.	Annual rate of decrease of the rural population by emigration (12-9%)	0.35	0.61

If we assume that the urban population in the late medieval period has an annual rate of natural increase of, say, –0.4 per cent and in the nineteenth century one of 0.2 per cent (working hypotheses), then we have to conclude that in the first period a high proportion of the flow from the rural districts to the towns was devoted to neutralisation of the natural decrease of the urban population. The late medieval increase of urban population seems to be totally caused by immigration, while the nineteenth-century increase is partially generated by the natural growth of the urban population – which is positive now – and partially by immigration.

In the case of Brabant a certain absolute growth of the towns would seem to require more immigration in the fifteenth and sixteenth centuries than in the nineteenth century. In addition the medieval rural natural increase is creamed off, while in the nineteenth century migration costs only about 50 per cent of the natural rural increase (see Table 25.3, lines 12-13).

Of course this had an effect on the evolution of the urban ratios. The levels of urbanisation could increase relatively fast in the medieval circumstances. An annual rate of increase in the Brabantine urban population of only 0.4 per cent is enough to reach high levels of urbanisation in 128 years. The same performance over 60 years should require an annual urban growth of only 0.85 per cent. In the nineteenth century increased rates of natural population growth have a doubly negative effect on the rise of urban levels. First, urban natural growth is now positive. Immigration comes into competition with natural urban growth. Second, natural rural increase is much higher now than four centuries ago. The result is that the Brabantine urban population has to grow 1.6 per cent a year in order to raise the level of urbanisation from 30 per cent to 44 per cent within 60 years (see Table 25.3, line 6).

We have to conclude that in Brabant the early nineteenth-century increase of urban ratios required a much higher rate of growth of non-agricultural employment than the classic late medieval expansion of the Brabantine cities (see Table 25.3, line 6). The fact that their natural increase was negative and had to be surpassed by immigration from a rural sector with a low positive natural increase led to astonishingly high urban ratios, induced by a relatively small growth of non-agricultural employment.

But as suggested in Table 25.3, line 7, there is an important difference between the annual rate of increase of total population in the two periods: 0.14 per cent and 1.0 per cent respectively. This implies that in the fifteenth century urban population had to grow more than three times as fast as total population in order to bring about a given increase in urban ratios. The nineteenth-century urban population had to grow only 1.6 times as fast as total population (see Table 25.3, line 8). In terms of employment, late medieval non-agricultural employment had to grow more intensely than nineteenth-century non-agricultural employment.

The levels of urbanisation were not the same in the different regions. Those of Antwerp and Brussels always had a high degree of commercial and industrial activity. Urbanisation in this area is high, and displays important fluctuations. (See Table 25.1, the percentages of group A + B.)

The regions of Mechelen and Leuven (group M + L) also have a high level of urbanisation, but the fluctuations in the long run are relatively small. This region has no particular history of an expansion of commerce and industry, except during the period before 1400. As a compensation for its declining wool industry Leuven got its University in 1425.[5] Mechelen had been the residence of a very rich and important archbishopric since 1559. Till 1800 the county of Mechelen was a politically independent entity.

The regions of Turnhout and Nijvel (group T + N) are strongly agricultural. Before 1800 the cities of Turnhout and Nijvel never exceeded 10,000 inhabitants. The Turnhout area has relatively infertile soil. The villages mostly encompass more than 2000 hectares (5000 acres) and are composed of a range of hamlets. The Nijvel area, in the south, is very fertile, has small communities and impressive farms, which contrast very favourably with the poor peasant farms in the Turnhout area.[6]

Regional variation in levels of urbanisation has some interesting aspects. Overall urbanisation is to be observed in two distinct periods: from 1374 to 1480 and from 1846 to 1970. There are no periods of overall de-urbanisation, but the first half of the eighteenth century shows negative values in five regions.

In the first period the incremental urbanisation ratios of the *arrondissement* of Mechelen seem to follow those of the Antwerp area, but at a more modest pace. After a period of historically very high rates of urbanisation in the fourteenth century, the level of urbanisation decreases from 1500 onwards till about 1820, and recovers relatively slowly thereafter. The level of urbanisation in this region in 1930 is lower than that in the fifteenth and sixteenth centuries!

The Turnhout and Nijvel areas reveal stability or erratic fluctuations in incremental urban ratios. At the end of the nineteenth century some new small urban centres appear.

Just as in the case of the Antwerp area, the region of Brussels has enjoyed two urbanisation periods, one in the fifteenth/sixteenth century, and one in the nineteenth/twentieth century. The de-urbanisation in the seventeenth/eighteenth century is not so considerable as in the Antwerp area.

The region of Leuven has low incremental urban ratios over the whole period, except for the strong de-urbanisation in the eighteenth century. No drastic nineteenth-century urbanisation occurs. This area indeed witnesses its high incremental ratios in the twelfth to the fourteenth centuries.

The historiography of the socio-economic history of Brabant suggests that relatively rapid structural change, as in the second half of the nineteenth century, but also during some period in the fourteenth, fifteenth and sixteenth centuries, had a disequilibrating effect on the total economy. Regional divergence would be typical for the growth periods of the Brabantine economy. In particular, the explosive growth of medieval and late nineteenth-century Antwerp would be a unique case in Brabant.

TABLE 25.4 Percentage mean deviation of urban ratios in Brabant during two urbanisation periods

Year	*p.m.d.*	*Δp.m.d.*	*year*	*p.m.d.*	*Δp.m.d.*
1374	41		1806	37	
1437	40	–1	1829	40	3
1480	42	2	1846	40	0
1526	47	5	–	–	–
1565	47	0	1866	44	4
1615	52	5	1880	45	1
1665	45	–7	–	–	–
1709	37	–8	1900	41	–4
1755	39	2	–	–	–
1806	37	–2	1920	37	–4
			–	–	–
			1970	28	–9

$$\text{p.m.d.} = \frac{\Sigma\, u_a - 1.00}{n} \times 100$$

n = the number of regions

u_a = the urban relative = $\dfrac{U_a}{P_a} : \dfrac{U_{\text{Brabant}}}{P_{\text{Brabant}}}$

divergence = increasing values
convergence = decreasing values

In Table 25.4 I have indicated some spatial dimensions of Brabantine urbanisation.[7] The mean absolute deviation measures the average absolute difference between, on the one hand, the individual urban ratio of each region relative to the Brabantine urban ratio, and, on the other, to unity (see my note on Table 25.4).

Table 25.4 shows very clearly that the disparity in the regional levels of urbanisation in 1970 was much lower than the value of any previous year. Second, the deviations of 1526-1615 are bigger than those of the second half of the nineteenth century. Although this second wave of urbanisation was much stronger than the first one, the dispersion was not only very moderate (till 1880), but actually decreasing (since 1880).

The 1374-1615 period appears to be one with divergence. This seems to underline traditional historical knowledge, although it is surprising that Antwerp's sixteenth-century boom had no disequilibrating effects (at least in terms of urbanisation) on Brabant. I will return to this point.

In the second period of urbanisation, beginning slowly in 1800, and in fact getting under way about 1830, we first see divergence, and then, when the acceleration of urbanisation loses momentum after 1880, we see a slow convergence of regional urban ratios. Urban ratios are at best only very crude measures of economic structure, but this would support the generalisation that the six regions of Brabant find their economic structures becoming slowly similar after 1880, that is, after the period with the highest incremental ratios. Convergence after 1880 seems to be a result of two sub-waves of urbanisation. The first is some extensive process of maturing, penetrating each corner of Brabant, even the self-sufficient villages of the Turnhout area. The second (after the Second World War) is a more intensive process of maturation and redistribution of economic activity, affecting the whole of Brabant. Perhaps a flight from the old over-urbanised areas will follow.

Another secular movement of convergence seems to develop from 1615 to 1806, i.e. the period of stagnating and decreasing levels of urbanisation. The very rapid de-urbanisation of the Antwerp area especially, and the Mechelen area too, is responsible for this. This convergence can at least partially be identified as a consequence of a loss of export markets. As long as the penetrating forces of the industrial revolution are not at work, we could say that convergence in this territory must be the expression of a reruralisation of the economy.

How to explain the long trend variation (divergence-convergence before the Industrial Revolution, and again divergence-convergence after the Industrial Revolution) of the Brabantine regional disparition of urbanisation? We will try to point out some elements.

First we examine some effects of population variables on a system with an existing urban disparity (as in 1374 and 1806). We have to realise that the evolution of the percentage mean deviation (p.m.d.) (see Table 25.4) is independent of changes in the relative weight of the regional populations. Differential population growth of regions as a whole is not important here.

Table 25.3 indicates that there is a difference between the natural increase of the urban population and the rural (total) population in both the first and the second urbanisation periods. These differences do not necessarily affect the regional dispersion of urban levels. Assume there is no migration. The urban relatives and p.m.d. (see Table 25.4) will remain the same as long as the proportion of the urban growth rate to the total growth rate (expressed in multipliers) is the same for all regions. In these circumstances the urban ratios of the six regions and Brabant will not change (if the proportion is equal to unity) or will decrease at the same rate (if the proportion is lower than unity, as in Table 25.3).

This hypothetical situation approximates reality in the first half of the eighteenth century, when migration to the towns was reduced very strongly. The urban population decreased from 219,000 to 160,000. Rural migration to the towns was distorted too during the first half of the Eighty Years War (1565-1615), but the city of Brussels continued to function as a growth pole and considerably increased the disparity. In most periods migration must have been a very important factor in changing the p.m.d. We find intra-regional migrations as well as inter-regional flows. The Turnhout area has been an almost constant loser, for example.

If we want to know something more about peak urbanisation in Brabant, or if we wish to pay more attention to the concept of growth, we have to weight the urban relatives by their shares in total population (see Table 25.5).[8]

The renewed measurement shows a positive increase in the dispersion of urban ratios between 1526 and 1565. Secondly the (weighted) p.m.d. already declines from 1856 onwards, as a result of the diminishing impact of the least urbanised districts. The share of the *arrondissements* Turnhout, Leuven and Nijvel in total Brabantine population is 38 per cent in 1846 and 37 per cent in 1856, but drops to 33 per cent in 1866 and 28 per cent in 1890. The (unweighted) p.m.d. ignores this evolution. We can interpret the opposite

TABLE 25.5 Unweighted and weighted p.m.d. of urban ratios in Brabant 1374-1970 (1806 = 100)

Year	*p.m.d. (unw.)*		*p.m.d. (w.)*		*Year*	*p.m.d. (unw.)*		*p.m.d. (w.)*	
1374	111		117		1806	100	− 5	100	− 4
1437	108	− 3	91	−28	1846	108	+ 8	120	+20
1480	114	+16	98	+ 7	1856	116	+12	131	+11
1526	127	+13	126	+28	1866	119	+ 3	127	− 4
1565	127	0	139	+13	1880	122	+ 3	116	−11
1615	141	+14	151	+12	1890	119	− 3	114	− 2
1665	122	−19	128	−23	1930	100	−19	84	−30
1709	100	−22	97	−31	1970	76	−24	70	−14
1755	105	+ 5	104	+ 7					
1806	100	− 5	100	− 4					

Weighted p.m.d. = $\frac{\sum u_a - 1 \; P_a}{n} \cdot 100$

P_a = share in total popul.

movement of the p.m.d.s as a change in demographic sources of urbanisation. Early urbanisation must have been mainly an intra-regional process, whereas urbanisation in later stages was fed by immigration from the rural districts. Thirdly, the amplitude of the w.p.m.d. is much greater than that of the u.p.m.d. Peak-urbanisation of Antwerp and Brussels has been measured more explicitly.

How can we explain changes of the p.m.d. by economic variables which dominate the processes of migration and urbanisation before and after the Industrial Revolution? It is not impossible that the high standards of Brabantine agriculture produced high rents from the beginning of the period now studied. In my view they explain a great part of the high *level* of urban ratios in the pre-industrial period. Some reasons exist for accepting the hypothesis that non-agricultural demand of property-owners was unevenly distributed in Brabant, but I doubt whether the long-term influence of changes in rents[9] on urban dispersion would be important.

The demand of urban activity can be seen as a total of foreign demand and domestic demand. If demand for export activity is growing the existing uneven distribution of export activity will be still more uneven. Changes in exports are very important in the pre-industrial urbanisation period. As an indicator we can use the evolution of urban real wages.

If an urban population gets higher real wages (as an effect of lower agricultural prices and/or increased export activity) the law-of-Engel-effect raises the propensity to consume urban products. The demand for urban workers will increase. If cities differ in size, we can expect more demand for workers in great cities than in small cities. Will this effect raise the p.m.d.? We can answer this question only if we know something about the demographic characteristics of the economy. Table 25.4 shows that urban growth requires immigration from rural districts. In the case of a higher demand for urban workers rural people will go to the cities and change *U*/*P* drastically. In the case of Brabant this change will be the smallest in the rural areas with the lowest urban ratios and causes therefore divergence of urban ratios. In the long run this real income effect may be an interesting factor explaining some changes in the dispersion of urban ratios.

The levels of the percentage mean deviation of Brabantine urban ratios seem to be related to the levels of real wages earned by a journeyman-bricklayer in the city of Antwerp (as composed by Dr E. Scholliers for the 1427-1800 period).[10] (See Figure 25.1.)

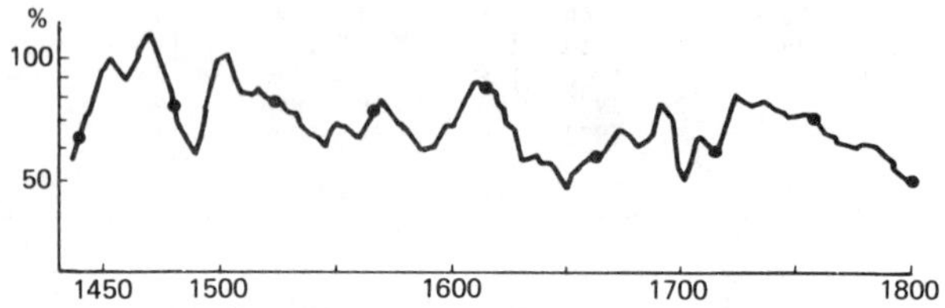

Fig. 25.1 The evolution of real wages earned by a journeyman-bricklayer, Antwerp, 1427-1800 (1460-1479 = 100)

We find a highly significant, and rather strong correlation of $r = 0.66$ (u.p.m.d. and real wages) and 0.49 (w.p.m.d. and real wages). This may indicate the importance of domestic demand created by wage earners. Of course, the influences of disease and war disturb the correlation. Since the w.p.m.d. is very sensitive for export-induced reallocation of population, it is quite normal that in this case the correlation should be 0.17 points lower.

After 1806 the positive correlation of p.m.d. and real wages virtually does not exist any more. Real wages first decrease by 50 per cent (1750-1850), grow slowly from about 1860 onwards, and increase much faster from 1880 till today. On the other hand the p.m.d. rises during the period 1806-80 and declines afterwards.

Other factors have to be introduced. Modern population growth (since 1755) creates strong pushing forces on an overpopulated (agricultural) rural sector to the existing towns; and, secondly, modern economic growth (since 1850-70) releases most workers from the necessity to produce essential foods, not only in the old urbanised regions, but also in the traditional rural areas.

These remarks conclude my investigation, which is still mainly descriptive and explorative. The Brabantine long-term urbanisation process shows highly interesting pre-industrial features, which can contribute to our knowledge about the phenomenon of economic inequality of regions or nations.

More specifically my long-term series of urban ratios suggests the existence of a strong regional inequality in the sixteenth/seventeenth and nineteenth centuries. Economic and demographic conditions of the two periods are totally different. The seventeenth century can be seen as a failed transition to mature economic growth, while the twentieth century was successful, and produced regional convergence of urban ratios as well as higher levels of real income.

There are many problems which are left to be solved in this study. Of course, there is the question of getting more regional macro-economic data on pre-industrial economies in order to offer explanations of dispersion and changes in dispersion. On the other hand we need more fundamental knowledge about the social and economic mechanisms in pre-industrial times by which differentials persist, increase, stabilise and diminish.

NOTES

[1] H. van der Wee, *The Growth of the Antwerp Market and the European Economy* [fourteenth/sixteenth centuries] (The Hague, 1963) 3 vols.

[2] P.M.M. Klep, *Bevolking en arbeid in transformatie: Brabant 1700-1900* (forthcoming).

[3] J. Williamson, 'Urbanization in the American Northeast, 1820-1870', in R. Fogel and S. Engerman (eds.), *The Reinterpretation of American Economic History* (New York, 1971).

[4] R. Mols, *Introduction à la démographie historique des villes d'Europe du XIVe au XVIIIe siecle* (Leuven, 1955-56) 3 vols. passim.

[5] R. van Uytven, *Stadsfinancien en stadsekonomie te Leuven van de XIIe tot het einde der XVIe eeuw* (Brussels, 1961).

[6] P.M.M. Klep, *Groeidynamiek en stagnatie in een agrarisch grensgebied. De economische ontwikkeling in de Noordantwerpse Kempen en de Barcnie van Breda, 1750-1850* (Tilburg, 1973).

[7] In order to avoid erratic fluctuations caused by 0-values (see Table 25.1), I have taken a value 10 for each 0 (with corrections for total *U/P*).

[8] J. G. Williamson, 'Regional Inequality and the Process of National Development: A Description of the Patterns', in *Economic Development and Cultural Change*, 13,4 (II) (1965).

[9] W. Abel, *Agrarkrisen und Agrarkonjunktur* (Hamburg, 1966).

[10] E. Scholliers, 'De Materiele vershijningsvorm van armoede voor de industriele revolutie', in *Tijdschrift voor Geschiedenis*, 88 (1975).

Part 2b France

26 Regional Inequalities and Economic Development: French Agriculture in the Nineteenth and Twentieth Centuries

Marc Auffret, Michel Hau and Maurice Lévy-Leboyer

Are regional inequalities in income per head a permanent feature of modern economies that have existed at every stage of their development; from the pre-industrial period to the present? Or, instead, are they to be conceived as a by-product of the industrialisation process itself – a sort of temporary penalty due to the slow diffusion of technological change or to the imperfect working of the market? On the assumption that significant changes first appear in a single region, it has been convincingly asserted that a few centres in the main industrial countries were able to improve their position from the start by attracting labour (and the most active), by concentrating capital for investment and the power to innovate, while the rest of the country suffered from restricted markets, loss of skilled hands, and, increasingly from the sheer inability to adapt to change. In such a situation, so long as the lack of inter-regional linkages prevailed, any dispersion of wages between regions was likely to rise in a cumulative way until the reduction of transport costs, the spread of education and wage increases lowered internal barriers and brought about a major transfer of surplus labour from agriculture to industry, and the levelling of marginal productivities.[1] The outcome should be a two-stage sequence of widening and narrowing spatial inequality which is often presented as a standard pattern to be found in all industrialising countries.

These views have been well documented in a number of countries. But, at least in the case of France, even though empirical studies have confirmed the fact that regional incomes present a broad pattern of convergence after the 1860s, and that labour migration did play a role that contributed to that result, attempts at testing the model have proved disappointing. Historians and economists, working independently, have demonstrated that wage disparities were not a prime force in moving labour, and so in building and in closing up the gap; the wage elasticity of the labour supply is almost non-existent over the long term.[2] Furthermore, the process of industrialisation in France did not conform initially to that of other developing countries. The creation of a modern sector was achieved, for a long period of time, without

TABLE 26.1 Regional income disparities and rural migrations

	Income per head index 1864	Agriculture income index, 1864	Agriculture share % 1864	Wage levels indust. index 1882	Wage levels agricult. index 1882	Rural depopul. total (000) 1872	Rural depopul. share % 1911	Migrants' share among residents Paris 1911	Migrants' share among residents Province 1911
Northern plains	106.7	133.3	52.1%	102.6	127.9	1,154	18.1%	22.7%	3.6%
Region of Paris	175.1	145.3	12.1	135.4	182.3	25	3.6	5.6	1.0
Region of Lyons	86.3	95.1	57.0	99.8	81.9	725	20.2	2.7	1.5
Massif Central	79.2	73.2	58.9	84.3	94.4	577	21.4	7.1	1.7
Mediterranean	93.3	105.4	51.4	93.0	113.5	196	11.9	1.2	1.0
S.-W. Atlantic	93.7	94.3	61.5	86.7	95.9	678	18.4	2.8	1.9
Western Regions	83.8	79.9	61.0	83.3	75.8	1,240	20.0	6.7	1.7
Average or total	100.0	100.0	49.2%	100.0	100.0	4,541	18.3%	48.8%	12.4%

SOURCE: Income per head, total and agricultural (base: French average), and agriculture's share in incomes for the year 1864: N. Delefortrie and J. Morice, *Les revenus départementaux en 1864 et en 1954* (Paris, 1959); Industrial and agricultural wages (base: French average): L.M. Goreux, 'Les migrations agricoles en France depuis un siècle et leurs relations avec certains facteurs économiques', *Etudes et conjoncture*, no. 4 (1958), pp. 327ff. Rural depopulations (total number and share of the 1872 stock): P. Merlin, *L'exode rural* (Paris, 1971); Migrants (as a percentage of total residents, classified by regions of origin): *Recensement de la population* (Paris, 1911). For the definition of the regions, cf. note 5.

the major redistribution of the labour force which is held responsible for regional inequalities. In the earlier part of the nineteenth century, instead of pulling workers into urban employment, factories were often transferred out of the cities, where the new technologies had been first tried out, in order to reduce wage costs; the ruralisation of industry was used as a substitute for labour migrations and so it contributed to spread work over the country as a whole.[3] Of course, at a later date, when techniques became more capital-intensive, a structural readjustment took place: with the decline of the rural industries and the displacement of service activities, once the railroad had been completed, labour became redundant in the country and was forced to move. Then a sharper divergence between regions became possible. But, at the time, it seems doubtful whether a cumulative widening of income levels could occur. The period of transition until the period of revival of industry was too short to allow for the creation of a labour reserve: local monographs have often made the point that industrial workers were not left behind, but contributed sometimes in a greater number than farm hands to the rural depopulation; about 1.15 million people, one-fourth of the total who moved out over the years 1872-1911, migrated from the more industrialised *departements* of Northern France. And the outflow was almost at the same level throughout the country; migrants amounted to some 18 or 20 per cent of the original stock of rural population in the majority of provincial regions (Table 26.1, column 7). Besides, existing data tend to suggest that no serious gap between regions developed until the end of the great depression: the coefficients of variation for industrial wages, at the level of the *departements*, were of 16.7 per cent in 1852 and 16.0 per cent in 1882, against a coefficient of 36.8 per cent at the latter date for agricultural wages; further, when profits and other sources of revenue are included in the estimates, the levels of non-agricultural incomes per head were not significantly higher than the agricultural ones perhaps until after the 1890s, when the urban and rural sectors moved apart.[4] So it seems fair to conclude that, over the past century as a whole, industrialisation was probably not the major source of inequalities between regions.

Sharp contrasts, on the other hand, have always been characteristic of the agricultural sector for reasons that may be explained in terms of climate, land fertility or past historical experience: in 1852, productivities in some areas north of Paris were three or four times those to be found in more outward regions. And such a situation was bound to last or even worsen over the years, since the working of the market obviously differed in the various regions according to their distance from Paris. The capital had of course only 7 per cent of the French population at the turn of the century, but one-fourth of the urban population; the levels of income per head in the city were some two-thirds above the French average, and so it had an influence upon the market that was disproportionate to that of the other cities. The growth of urban construction, to take one instance at the time when the railroads were being built, had an immediate impact in the North: over the country as a whole, 600,000 labourers, almost one-tenth of the agricultural workforce,

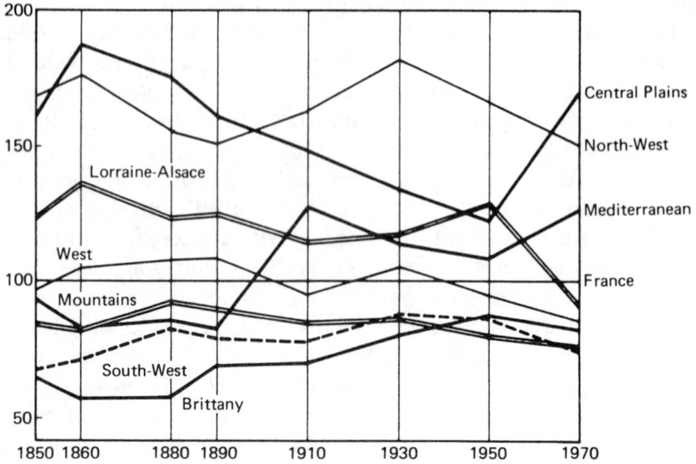

Fig 26.1 Agricultural output per head in each region as a percentage of France's average, 1850-1970
SOURCE: Table 26.2

were said to have left the farms in the early 1850s; but the greater part came from the plains that supplied Paris with food crops, and this for reasons that are related to the creation of a market economy: there were conflicts, at an earlier date here than in the rest of the country, over the determination and use of money wages, the division of common lands, as well as crop shortages. However, when the same opportunities and the consequent rise in wages came, with a lag, in other regions, the outcome was different: as price competition had increased with the lifting of the cornlaws in 1861, and with the unification of internal markets by railroads, the squeeze on profits made it a necessity for many landowners to break up their estates and sell out. Market pressures had therefore had opposite results: in one case, marginal productivity probably improved with labour migration, assuming no change in production levels; in the other, division of land property was achieved at the expense of efficiency and market adaptation; the number of proprietors reached an all-time peak in the early 1880s.[6] And this process was repetitive. At the turn of the century, to take the reverse case, as a wave of farm concentration reduced sharply the number of productive units (more specifically those of 1 to 10 hectares), the fall in the small farms was greater in the North than at the periphery: their share was reduced from 75 per cent of the total stock (with slight variations among the regions) in 1882, to respectively 56.7 per cent and 64.2 per cent in the two areas by 1929. Clearly regional inequalities in agriculture were a legacy of the past that economic growth, because of the unequal diffusion of technical change, had failed to alleviate.

This seems to be the real issue. France does not offer the case of a country where industrial centres had attracted from the start skills and capital, leading thereby to a true imbalance between regions. Its originality comes from two

TABLE 26.2 Agricultural output per head in the major regions: levels and dispersion, 1852-1970

Regions	*1852*	*1862*	*1882*	*1892*	*1912*	*1929*	*1948*	*1970*
Central plains	161	186	175	161	146	135	122	171
North-western	169	177	157	151	163	181	166	151
Lorraine-Alsace	122	136	123	124	114	117	129	90
Mediterranean	91	82	86	84	128	114	109	126
Western	96	105	107	108	95	105	95	86
Rhone-Mountains	84	83	92	89	84	85	80	78
S.-W. Atlantic	68	72	82	78	77	86	85	77
Brittany	65	57	58	68	73	79	86	82
France	100	100	100	100	100	100	100	100
Coeff. of variation:								
France (total)	41%	51%	43%	39%	41%	39%	34%	43%
Sample Regions	38%	48%	42%	38%	32%	39%	22%	41%

SOURCE: *Enquêtes agricoles;* L.M. Goreux, op. cit.; Service central des Enquêtes et Etudes statistiques, *Etude* no 160 (1971).

For each date, the value of agricultural output of the main regions has been divided by the number of men active in agriculture and expressed as a percentage of the French average. The coefficients of variation were estimated from data collected at the level of the départements. For the definition of the regions, cf. note 5.

opposite elements. First, major inequalities had been inherited from the past in the agricultural sector (which still contributed more than 40 per cent of the national product in the 1880s); and they were not significantly reduced over the years. As it appears by comparing the values of agricultural output per head in the main regions (Table 26.2), the Northern and Central sections, within a moderate distance from Paris, held a leading position for a century and a half, with product per head at 35-50 per cent above the national average; while the Western and some of the Southern regions, as well as the mountainous areas, tended to cluster at 15-20 per cent below the same level. The cleavage between the two groups should be considered as a permanent feature of the economy that certainly had a lasting influence upon the local structure of the economy. Second, going against this trend, a broad pattern of convergence is also registered in Table 26.2: it may be inferred from the movement of the individual series, more particularly in the case of the Central Plains and of Brittany between 1862 and 1948; and from the reduction, during the same period, of the coefficient of variation (from 51 to 34 per cent). Obviously, there were forces at work which contributed to narrow the gap between regions. But opposite tendencies were also evident. Inequality increased on two occasions, in the mid-nineteenth century and again after the 1950s, so that in the end all progress had been cancelled; the dispersion of regional income levels was of about the same size in the initial and terminal periods. Furthermore, there were clear cases of departure from the trend; the Mediterranean region in the pre-war years, the North West in the 1920s, and even the Central plains after a long period of decline moved sharply against the general pattern. In other words, for reasons that are still to be clarified, new inequalities were superimposed upon the older ones.

These are, in short, the two problems to which this paper is addressed: why the survival of wide disparities between the centre and the periphery (to use an inadequate expression)? And why the creation of new ones? So, rather than an analysis of economic regions conceived as adapting in a passive way to the lead of a modern sector, it is a brief survey limited to the agricultural sector and its modernisation that is attempted here, in order to determine not so much the sources of productivity changes and their contribution to the growth of the sector, but the obstacles that have prevented their use in a more effective way to equalise income among the various regions.

1. LONG-TERM TRENDS IN AGRICULTURAL PRODUCTION

The first step, in this survey, was to collect production data so as to scale down individual regions according to their performance over time. However, not to deal with too great a number of cases, a sample of eleven regions was selected, using types of farming and income levels as criteria. The sample, as it stands, may be held as fairly representative, although its coverage increases during the period of study – from 32.4 to 37.9 per cent of the French gross production value and, in about the same proportion, of the labour force. This slight discrepancy is not due to an over-representation of the high income regions (here, those of Picardie, Champagne and Beauce); their share in the sample and that of the low-income regions (Brittany, Maine, Basse-Normandie) are of 24.9 and 34.4 per cent respectively for the 1823-1970 period, against an average of 27.3 and 47.5 per cent for the same categories in the French total figures. The bias comes rather from the fact that, among the poorer regions, some were losing ground (and are not included in the sample), while those in the Western sections, in spite of heavy population outflow, managed to adapt to the demand and improved their position. All the regions that have been selected – at a high, a low and an intermediate level – reacted positively to market changes.

In fact, it is this bias in the structure of the sample that explains its sensitivity to the long-term trends of the French economy. Changes in the income dispersion of the eleven regions are identical in amplitude and timing with those observed for the country as a whole; the coefficients of variation for the two sets of data, in Table 26.2, move alike: the gap widened for both, with coefficients reaching a peak around 50 per cent at the end of the 1850s; in a second stage, it tended to close down (in spite of a mild upturn in the 1920s); and rose again in the post-1950s period up to 41-43 per cent. In a similar fashion, the trend exhibited by the eleven series of agricultural production follow closely those of the French commodity output index: there is a break in the growth rates – for each of the sample regions – at the end of the 1860s, when the economy was slowing down (the rates became

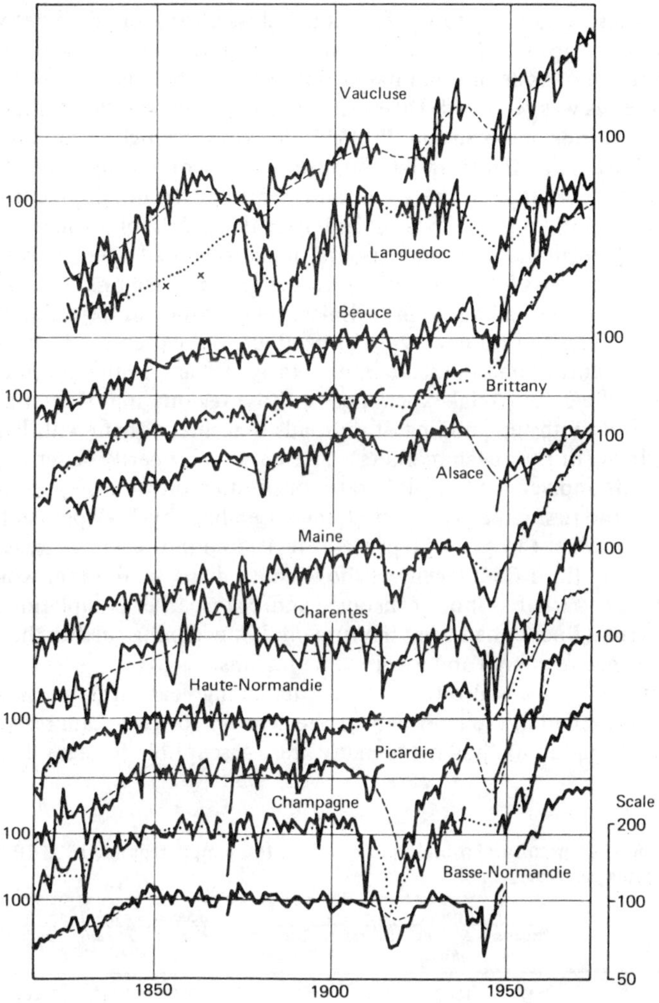

Fig. 26.2 Agricultural production by regions, 1815-1970 volume index (basis: 1908-1912 = 100)

negative for the sample as a whole, falling from +1.30 to –0.20 per cent p.a.); then, a long period of stagnation that can be explained by the great depression and by the lack of linkages during the inter-war and war years between agriculture and industry; and, last, a strong revival with a sharp increase in the growth rates – they averaged 3.5 per cent p.a. in the 1952-70 period, five times the rate of 0.7 per cent at which the regions had stagnated for more than a century, from 1823 to 1952 (Figure 26.2).

What these data bring to the fore is the close correspondence between dispersion and growth. Long-term trends in output explain to a great extent why a pattern of widening and narrowing variation between the eleven regional series was recorded. Divergence accompanied the two (initial and terminal) periods of expansion. Probably because the high-income regions, having a greater flexibility and a better knowledge of consumer needs, were able to take advantage, in the 1840s and 1850s, of the development of urbanisation and internal demand; and after the 1950s, of a wider access to home and foreign markets, once international trade had opened up again. These opportunities benefited of course the group of regions close to Paris, as they had always had a lead in technical innovation and were able in both periods to diversify into new types of product. But expansion in the mid-nineteenth century had the same impact in Alsace and in the South-east because of the commercial experience of those regions and of their urban environment; with the building of railroads that linked them with Paris and later with North European markets, older crops were partly superseded by wines, fruits and vegetables, while rates of production were stepped up: output, in the first expansion period, increased here by 1.42 per cent p.a., which is equivalent to the 1.50 per cent registered in the wheat areas, but much beyond the 1.05 per cent of the Western districts. In other words, access to the market – shorter distance and/or an earlier completion of the railroad trunk lines – had been instrumental in widening further the disparities between high and low-income regions.

But the reverse was also true of the intervening years of depression. Convergence prevailed in the later part of the century for two main reasons. (1) Forced production had made many areas susceptible to plant disease

TABLE 26.3 Agricultural production trends in the sample regions, 1823-1970 (growth rates per year)

	First period: 1823-1936				*Second period: 1936-70*			*Total*
	Expans.	*Turning point*	*Depres.*	*Total*	*Stagnat.*	*Expans.*	*Total*	*General*
Beauce	1.42%	1862	0.46%	0.79%	1.95%	3.11%	2.56%	1.20%
Haute-Normandie	1.00	1868	0.20	0.52	0.52	4.45	2.60	1.00
Picardie	1.13	1874	0.01	0.51	1.18	4.43	2.90	1.05
Champagne	1.28	1864	−0.01	0.46	0.43	4.71	2.70	1.00
Basse-Normandie	0.88%	1874	−0.24%	0.27%	2.17%	3.65%	2.95%	0.90%
Charentes	2.13	1874	−0.78	0.53	−0.06	4.36	2.28	0.95
Maine	1.44	1874	0.15	0.73	0.34	4.60	2.60	1.15
Brittany	1.12	1868	0.55	0.78	2.27	3.16	2.74	1.25
Vaucluse	2.47%	1857	0.77%	1.32%	1.22%	1.74%	1.50%	1.36%
Bas-Languedoc	1.52	1874	0.37	0.89	−0.74	2.00	0.71	0.85
Alsace	0.94	1875	0.53	0.72	−2.21	1.55	−0.22	0.50
Total (sample)	1.28%	1869	0.17%	0.69%	0.83%	3.52%	2.25%	1.05%

The weights used in aggregating the series are the contributions of each region at every bench-mark year to the agricultural gross production value. The turning point, between the stagnation and the expansion periods of second period 1936-1970, is the year 1952. For the definition of the regions, cf. note 5.

(such as the vineyards in the 1870s). And (2) the over-extension of land under cultivation had pushed costs upward to such levels that large areas became vulnerable; entire districts did not resist the cheapening of foreign wheat (in the 1880s) and the opening abroad of alternative sources of supply for silk, dyes, wool, etc. Instead of a cumulative widening of incomes in their favour, the leading regions bore the brunt of the downturn: negative rates (–0.63 per cent p.a.) were registered at the time of the great depression in the regions that supplied Paris. But production, on the other hand, was maintained or improved at the periphery, either because the rise of urban real incomes maintained the demand for new products such as those of the South-eastern regions, or else because some regions were not fully integrated into the market and so were spared the effects of the depression. This was the case of Brittany and Maine, the former more than the latter, since the region, at that time, was reducing its grain shipments to other parts of France and England (Brittany had supplied half the French wheat exports in the 1840s), and was moving to a more isolated position, though with stable rates of growth – at some 0.40 per cent p.a. over the 1874-1911 period.

An alternative explanation for the economic deceleration and the income convergence that developed in the later part of the nineteenth century might be found in the movements of the labour supply. There was a break in the development of production in most of the regions adjoining Paris. It antedated the 1880s depression – by some twenty years (Figure 26.2) – and cannot therefore be explained simply by later changes in the market, especially by the substitution of foreign imports for home production; besides, the stagnation in agriculture for those regions was to last up to the inter-war years in spite of the early recovery of French industry. So, rather than to external circumstances, the downturn should be related to supply factors, namely to the slowdown in the population growth in the rural districts and to labour migrations. The outflow, already mentioned at the beginning of the railroad period, certainly hampered the regions close to Paris and other cities such as Rouen and Lille, by breaking the complementarity between industry and farming, and by reducing the workforce. It fell by one-fifth – in the four central regions of the sample – between 1861 and 1911, and by an equivalent percentage in the post-war years, while the steady growth of population in Brittany and immigration in the South-east contributed, on the opposite side, to maintain the development of production there up to the war. The land-labour ratios in the Central plains were twice those to be found at the periphery; there were 9.6 hectares per man in 1861, 11.7 in 1931, against 5.5 and 6.4 per man in the rest of the sample. High labour costs therefore should have undermined their ability to compete: the relative decline of cattle-farming in Basse-Normandie has been explained primarily by a gap in wages and cattle-prices in the 1860s-70s; the loss of industrial and other labour-intensive crops came in the same areas for similar reasons; and the slow organisation of a seasonal labour force, as a substitute for sedentary hands, prevented or at least limited the extension of new crop-rotations from the northern to the southern districts of the Central plains.

In other words, leaving aside the two periods of prosperity and concomitant dispersion of regional incomes, and also the development of the periphery when labour supply and market integration made it possible, the main fact that is brought out by the production series is the unusual length of the stagnation period (1860s-1930s) for the Central plains and the importance this had in closing the gap between the regions. This pattern is open to two interpretations. Either the depression of the economy had a greater impact on the regions close to Paris, because of their dependence on the market – they had to pay the penalty of a more mature structure. Or else, labour shortage, and perhaps low profit and low investments, prevented them from playing, after the first agricultural revolution, their traditional role of innovators and technical leaders. In one case, stagnation in agriculture may be held as induced from the economy at large; in the other, it was due to autonomous factors and should have contributed in an independent way to the series of difficulties the country went through.

2. *TYPOLOGY OF THE AGRICULTURAL REGIONS*

In order to differentiate further between these two interpretations and also to determine the factors that shaped the French agricultural regions (beyond the opposition centre-periphery), a factor analysis was undertaken at four peak or recovery time-periods (Figure 26.3). The aim of the procedure was to classify the sample regions in a most objective way – according to eleven independent variables. They were selected so as to compare in each regions: (1) supply factors (measured by land-labour ratio, cattle stock per man, farm size, wage cost, labour outflow); (2) the intensity of market demand (using an index of income per head, the percentage of urban population, that of the population occupied out of agriculture, railroad density); and (3) the adaptation of each region to the market: two indices were calculated here, one to measure the degree of branch-specialisation, and the other the price of the agricultural output, both with reference to a national average.[7] Without going into the details of the estimates, it might be useful to mention that the results were quite high: the percentage of inertia explained by the two first axes (the only ones which are taken into account) reached 23.5 per cent for the first three periods (1861-1911-1931), and 56.8 per cent in 1970; the difference between the two estimates (which is similar when the first four axes are included, the total reaching then 40.9 and 80.3 per cent comes from the fact that two variables were left out in the 1970 analysis (the railroad density and the price coefficient), because of their reduced importance at that date.

The plane – as determined by the two first axes and reproduced on Figure 26.3 – tends to validate the comments that have seemed relevant so far. The first axis presents the scattering of the regions on the plane (from left to right, i.e. from low to high values) according to price-indicators – income per

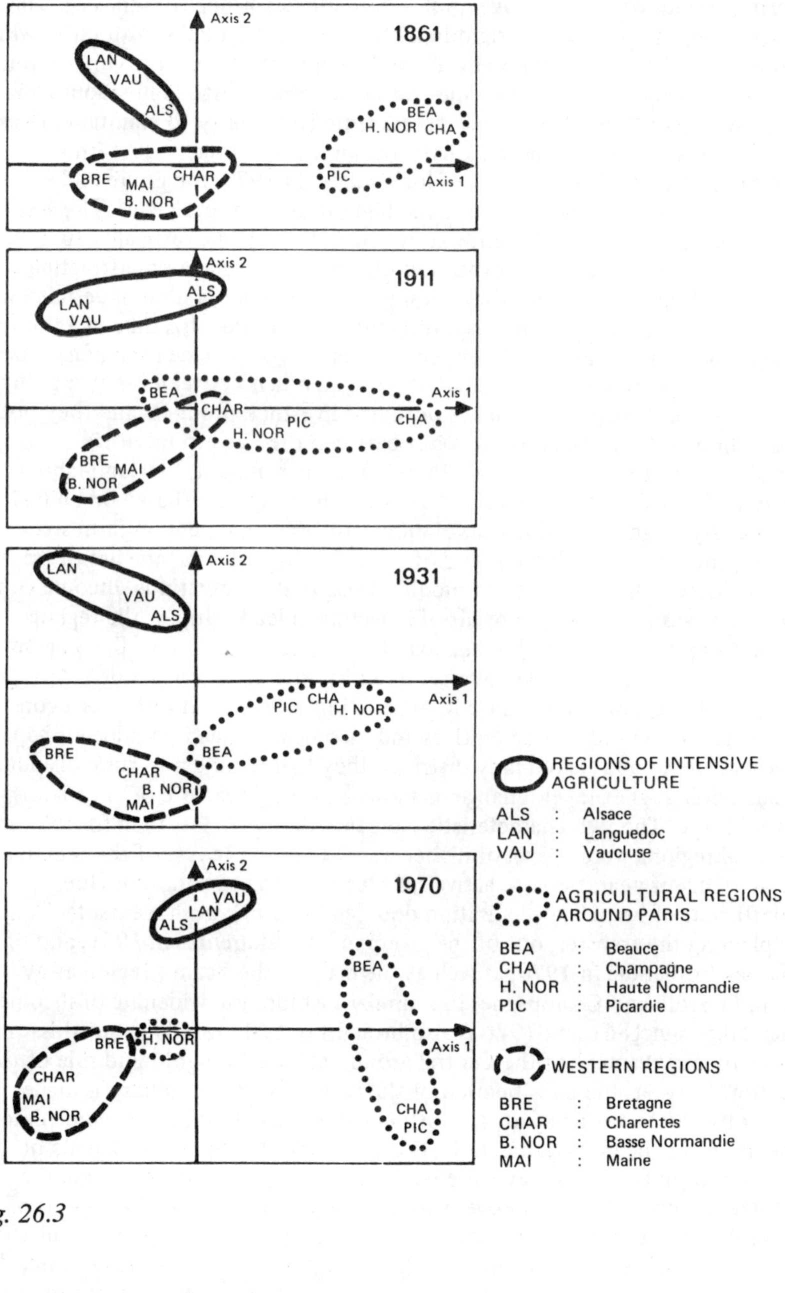
1861
Axis 2
Axis 1
LAN
VAU
ALS
BEA
H. NOR
CHA
PIC
BRE
MAI
CHAR
B. NOR
1911
ALS
LAN
VAU
BEA
CHAR
PIC
H. NOR
CHA
BRE
MAI
B. NOR
1931
LAN
VAU
ALS
PIC
CHA
H. NOR
BEA
BRE
CHAR
B. NOR
MAI
1970
VAU
LAN
ALS
BEA
BRE
H. NOR
CHAR
MAI
B. NOR
CHA
PIC
REGIONS OF INTENSIVE AGRICULTURE
ALS : Alsace
LAN : Languedoc
VAU : Vaucluse
AGRICULTURAL REGIONS AROUND PARIS
BEA : Beauce
CHA : Champagne
H. NOR : Haute Normandie
PIC : Picardie
WESTERN REGIONS
BRE : Bretagne
CHAR : Charentes
B. NOR : Basse Normandie
MAI : Maine

Fig. 26.3

head, product prices and wage level – and also according to farm size. The scatter concentrates on the right-hand side of the diagram – with ranks which varied over the years – the Central and North-western regions. This grouping is explained by three elements they had in common: high land-labour ratios and high income per head; market leadership (the ability to maintain prices at a higher level than other regions); and some lead in techniques (in so far as the farmers could bear the cost of high wages; in 1970, the group had still the highest labour cost, but no longer the highest incomes per head). The second axis uses more quantitative criteria: it orders the regions vertically, first in terms of urban density and migration movements (urban areas attracting immigrants are at the top, while rural districts with a population deficit cluster at the bottom of the diagram); and, second, but this time in an order inverse to the axis, railroad density, cattle per man and, once again, farm size.[8] The scatter here helps to differentiate, not so much between the two groups of Central and Western regions – both had livestock products and they both lost labour through migrations – but between the Eastern intensive agriculture (with a strong urban, in-migrant environment, low land-labour ratio and low farm size) and the Western farming system (based on animal husbandry, high railroad density, labour out-flow and medium farm size).

So, the increase in the number of variables, in particular the use of price and income indicators, has not modified our first observations. Income convergence was primarily the result of a decline in leadership of the regions close to Paris: they moved, along axis 1, towards the centre of the diagram between 1861 and 1911 (to a lesser extent in the inter-war period). And this not simply because of a change in production growth, but rather as a consequence of the fall of staple prices and incomes per head: conditions had become unfavourable in many districts: they had to adjust to rural disindustrialisation, higher taxes, change in status and the departure of large landowners, etc. The two characteristic elements that were left then for the Central regions were a level of higher wages than in the rest of the sample and, in recent years, a more active search for new crop-rotations (the coefficient of branch-specialisation doubled in 1970), both elements explaining the transfer, out of the group, of the Charentes in 1931, and of the Haute-Normandie in 1970, as well as the drift of the Beauce region away from Picardie and Champagne. In a similar fashion, the widening of income inequalities in 1861 and 1970 is also brought out, along axis 1, but this time, by a movement of the Central group back to the right-hand side of the scatter. Further, the classification of the regions at the periphery is made easier by the factor analysis, as it offers two criteria that have become determinant after the great depression. They are, first, the high coefficients of specialisation (in 1970 they were twice as high in the South-east as in the Central group), and an improvement in incomes per head of the regions of intensive agriculture – although prices moved against the Languedoc in 1911 and 1931; and, second, the increasing specialisation in cattle-farming and the consequent drift to the lower end of the diagram of the Western group, without substantial changes here – except for Brittany – of the relative wage and income position of the member regions. Actually, these elements contribute to the paradox of the growth pattern: there were positive results, gains in income and production, a greater specialisation among farming regions; but, in spite of this, no definite progress in the narrowing of income disparities between them.

3. CAUSAL FACTORS

This brings this study to the last point. It has been possible so far to determine three separate groups of regions and to isolate individual cases of good performance (such as those of Brittany and Vaucluse). But no explanation has been offered for the broad movement of convergence that prevailed during most of the period, and for the deviations from trend which were observed after the 1950s in the Central plains and the South-eastern regions (Figure 26.1). Of course if labour had moved within the country according to the differences in wage levels, the problem would be solved; convergence would have come, as recalled earlier, from the labour outflow in the lagging regions and the consequent increase in productivity, and from the continuity of capital investment in the leading ones. But, perhaps because of the unusual length of the agricultural depression, most of these conditions were not met in the French case. Labour migrated equally from the low and the high-wage regions – in our sample, from the West and the Centre. Productivity improved in each group between 1861 and 1936; but the gains were twice as high in the regions where the rural depopulation was moderate (the Eastern group, Brittany, Maine and Beauce) as in those where the fall was steep.[9] And, in a similar fashion, rural investments – measured in a crude way by the change in the value of real estate per head between 1911 and 1931 – were not maintained in the leading regions: the index (with the French average used as a base) declined in the Central regions (from 163 to 154); while its progression was slight, but positive, in the West (it moved from 104 to 107), and more substantial in the East (with 54 and 76 at the two dates).[10] In short, all our findings have been mostly negative. And the two questions are still unanswered.

In fact, the basic model is somewhat misleading because it oversimplifies the situation and gives too much weight to factor movements. It assumes that agriculture acted as a kind of reservoir for low-productivity labour, with no future except for those who moved out of the sector. But in a country of low densities, where the population had been declining since the 1860s, things were not so. A breakdown of the sources of productivity change gives evidence that, during most of the period of study, migrations were responsible for a major part of the fall in production (Table 26.4). In the Central crop-farming regions, where labour was already scarce, they induced at the same time, because of their complementarity, a loss of hands and a fall in the land

TABLE 26.4 Sources of productivity change in agriculture by regions (percentage changes per year)

	1861-1911			*1911-31*			*1931-70*		
	East	*Centre*	*West*	*East*	*Centre*	*West*	*East*	*Centre*	*West*
Labour	+0.35%	−0.32%	+0.14%	−0.80%	−1.27%	−0.94%	−2.19%	−1.87%	−1.85%
Land	+0.38	−0.13	+0.16	−0.53	−0.30	−0.06	−0.13	+0.31	+0.20
Cattle	+0.52	+0.29	+0.46	−1.10	+0.31	+0.72	−0.03	+2.07	+1.03
Traction	−0.24	−0.32	−0.82	+1.13	+1.01	+0.79	+7.64	+9.67	+9.20
Subtotal	+0.41%	−0.16%	+0.18%	−0.52%	−0.44%	−0.43%	−0.89%	+0.11%	−0.25%
Other factors	+0.56%	+0.08%	+0.10%	+0.46%	+1.01%	+0.91%	+1.61%	+2.77%	+2.85%
Agricult. output	+0.97%	−0.08%	+0.28%	−0.06%	+0.57%	+0.48	+0.72%	+2.88%	+2.60%

The table is at best tentative because rates of growth are calculated from benchmark years, and not continuously from the intervening years; and also because no satisfactory documents have been found that could be used to estimate weight coefficients. The average coefficients for labour (45%, 60% and 67%) are therefore regression coefficients, based on the labour and production data; those for land and the two other factors have been taken from L.M. Goreux, op. cit., Appendix VI. The year 1892 has been substituted for 1911 on line 4.

area under cultivation over the 1861-1931 period; and this could not be overcome, even though some productivity gains were registered in the 1920s – new methods and machinery being used for the first time at a substantial rate. In the other regions of the sample, labour and land inputs moved alike: they increased in steps in the pre-war years and were reduced in the 1920s, but this time with better results in the West, the region having the benefit of a larger market, with a greater consumption of dairy products by the public, and of the slow reconstruction of the regions that had been devastated during the war. It is therefore only in the years after the Second World War that major changes made agriculture more autonomous. Then, in spite of a sharp reduction in the workforce (the number of hands was halved in the sample between 1931 and 1968), increases in productivity reached very high levels indeed, not simply because of the consolidation of estates and the widespread use of machinery and other labour-saving devices (traction, measured in h.p. per hand, reached 26.4 in the Central regions by 1967, against 0.44 in 1929), but also because improvements in seeds and breeds, and the use of new fertilisers and feeds, which had been progressive in other countries, came in one single period, making the sector more independent of land and changing thereby the production structure. In other words, the convergence of regional incomes was unavoidable so long as agriculture had been labour-and land-intensive, the leading regions, at the Centre, having the highest land-labour ratios and the highest rate of labour outflow (Table 26.4, line 1). And the situation was reversed when production became more technical and probably – but it has not been possible to make specific estimates – more capital-intensive.

Prices should also have contributed to a narrowing of the gap for at least three reasons. (1) Regions at the periphery – together with the Centre – had had the benefit of the first industrialisation: they gained access, but with more lasting results, to cheaper manufactured goods; the terms of trade between agriculture and industry improved in favour of the former, the index moving from 42.6 to 100 between 1820 and 1880, when stability was reached. (2) The same process applied to the inter-regional trade: the building of the railroads, together with rebates on long-distance hauls, the difference in labour costs – which was of 40 per cent in 1861, and still of 25 and 19 per cent in 1911 and 1931, between the West and the Centre – gave farmers on the periphery the possibility of competing with those in the Central regions for the market in Paris; the margin for wheat was still of 10 per cent in the 1860s.[11] (3) Change in consumer demand and international competition made for a drastic fall in the price structure: wheat, wine and industrial crops, which had been the basis of the first agricultural revolution – in the Centre and South-eastern regions – lost ground; their index, measured as a percentage of national supplies, fell by one-fifth in the 1861-1911 period, while fruit, vegetables and livestock products rose by some 30 per cent and improved further in the 1920s. The results of this price competition as far as regional incomes are concerned are not as clear-cut as for production; since part of the extra profit may have gone to middlemen and large-scale producers or simply to pressure groups having special interests and the power to manipulate the market or to influence government policy. Still it seems fair to assume that the animal and crop-farming regions close to the capital, which had led the market up to the 1860s, faced stern competition – internal and external – during the depression, and that their revival came not so much from a price recovery (the regional price index for Beauce, Champagne, Picardie and Haute-Normandie was at 81.0 per cent of the French average in 1970, against 109.4 per cent in 1931), but from a change after the 1970s in the choice of processes and products more in line with market demand and relative factor costs

To sum up the argument, French agriculture offers the case of a country where the leading regions were not able to keep a cumulative advantage over the lagging ones, and where income convergence between them was paid at a price, that of an unusual long-term stagnation. Of course, France is only one case that may be disregarded. There are several other countries where inequalities resulted from a lack of labour mobility at the periphery: agricultural regions have often been plagued with overpopulation problems; depressed areas in industrial Europe have also had surplus labour struck by unemployment – the linen districts in the 1840s, the coal, steel and cotton regions in the inter-war period, etc. It is only fair, in such instances, to look for responsibilities since the development of major centres had no 'spread effects' on the rest of the economy. But there might be a danger of overstating the negative aspects of economic concentration. And this may be inferred from the French case: there, (1) regional inequality was a fact that had been inherited from the pre-modern period; it was not simply the end-result of the industrialisation process; (2) the lead of the farmers in the central regions, who had built a market, was beneficial to those at the periphery since they could develop their production through price competition and product diversification; and (3) their temporary decline brought about a slowing down of technical change – at least in the agricultural sector – and a deceleration of the economy that were not made up for until recent years. Inequality may have been of some usefulness in the past.

NOTES

[1] L.M. Goreux, 'Les migrations agricoles en France depuis un siècle et leurs relations avec certains facteurs économiques', *Etudes et conjoncture*, no. 4 (1958), p. 327; M. Quelenec, *Analyse structurelle du développement économique des régions francaises, 1864-1970* (Université de Paris-I, PhD. thesis, 1972).

[2] L. Chevalier, *La formation de la population parisienne au XIXe siècle* (Paris, 1950) p. 94; M. Hau, *La croissance économique de la Champagne de 1810 à 1969* (Strasbourg, 1976) p. 17. L.M. Goreux has found a low wage elasticity of the labour migration of 0.01 over the period 1862-1946, i.e. a difference of wages of 50 per cent between industry and agriculture would induce a reduction of 0.5 per cent p.a. in the farm labour-force. An independent estimate of migrations (y), in relation with wage disparities (w) and distance to Paris (D), based on a sample of 11 regions, has given also a low coefficient: $y = -7.89 + 0.048\,w + 0.006\,d$, with $R^2 = (0.499)^2$.

[3]People working in the rural industries have been estimated at 1.16 million in 1848, while the total population occupied in the industrial sector was of about 4.0 to 4.5 million; F. Charpenel and A. Magot, *L'industrie rurale en France d'après l'enquête de 1848* (Université de Paris-X Nanterre, MA thesis, 1971).

[4]The data used are those of L.M. Goreux, op. cit., and of N. Delefortrie and J. Morice, *Les revenus départementaux en 1864 et en 1954* (Paris, 1956). According to these authors, agricultural incomes per head were superior in 1864, and still equal in 1882, to non-agricultural incomes.

[5]Official regions have been put together under the names of: North-West (Nord, Picardie, Haute-Normandie); Central Plains (Champagne and six départements south of Paris, from Loir-et-Cher to Côte d'Or); Lorraine-Alsace – these three regions are labelled Northern Plains in Table 26.1; Région Parisienne (is listed as independent in Table 26.2, but included in the Central Plains of Table 26.2); Region of Lyons (Franche-Comté, Rhône-Alpes, Saône-et-Loire); Massif Central (Auvergne, Limousin and four départements further north) – these last two are listed as Mountains in Table 26.2; Mediterranean (Languedoc, Provence-Côte d'Azur); S.W. Atlantic (Midi-Pyrénées, Aquitaine, Poitou-Charente); West (Basse-Normandie, Pays de la Loire, Brittany).

[6]L. de Lavergne, *Economie rurale de la France* (Paris, 1877); A. de Foville, *Le morcellement. Etude de la propriété foncière* (1885); J. Pautard, *Les disparités régionales de croissance de l'agriculture francaise* (1965).

[7]The method used is that of J. Benzecri, *L'analyse des données* (Paris, 1973). The price coefficient, among the variables, is a weighted average of regional prices expressed as a percentage of a similar index, based on regional weights and national prices (unity implies similarity of regional and national prices; more than unity superiority of the first over the second; inferiority the reverse case). The coefficient of branch-specialisation is built according to the same principles; it has a minimum of unity (when the structure is similar in the region and in the country); it increases the smaller the number of products in the region.

[8]Relationships between variables are not linear. So, the variables used to structure the factorial plane are not ordered along straight lines. For instance, farm sizes are at a minimum at the upper end of the plane, on the left-hand side; medium farms tend to concentrate on the same side, but at the lower part of the plane; and from there sizes increase from left to right along axis 1. Another case is that of incomes per head: they are at a minimum on the left-hand side; at a medium range on the right (still at the same level); and at a maximum on the upper end of the diagram near axis 2.

[9]Leaving aside Haute-Normandie, where population statistics seem to be mistaken (the number of male farm hands fell in the official publications from 125,617 to 66,425 between 1861 and 1911), and the Charentes because of the disruption of the wine production (and the stability of the work-force at about 140,000 male hands), production per hand increased by 54.9 per cent between 1861 and 1936 in regions where the share of the rural population was of 33.6 per cent (Champagne, Picardie and Basse-Normandie), while the increase of labour productivity was of 96.3 per cent for the rest of the sample, where the average decline was only of 20 per cent (–7.6 per cent in Alsace, +0.6 per cent in Languedoc, etc.).

[10]P. Cornut, *La répartition de la fortune privée en France* (Paris, 1943) pp. 327-8.

[11]M. Lévy-Leboyer, 'L'héritage de Simiand: prix, profit et termes de l'échange au XIXe siècle', *Revue historique,* 493 (1970), pp. 77ff.; J. Toutain, *Les transports en France, 1830-1965* (Paris, 1967) pp. 160-7; E. Labrousse (ed.), *Le prix du froment en France au temps de la monnaie stable, 1726-1913* (Paris, 1970).

[12]Government price regulations were also instrumental in bringing back parity between regions, as in the Bas-Languedoc where prices had reached ruinous levels in the pre-war period.

27 The Spread of Agricultural Growth over the Departments of France from the Mid-nineteenth to the Mid-twentieth Century

Nicole Soubeyroux

Since the nineteenth century the European countries have undergone fast, far-reaching changes in their economy. It was the progress made in agriculture which made the start-up of the industrial revolution possible as early as the end of the eighteenth century.

In this paper we propose to examine how the French agricultural growth which accompanied the industrial revolution spread into the regions; we shall then try to trace how a multi-dimensional analysis of the data can be used to measure the regional effects of this growth since the middle of the nineteenth century.

In France, just as in Europe, industrialisation developed in a chiefly rural environment whose population had become too great for the tasks to be performed; exchanges of goods were limited. Industry used the excess population and agriculture took off at the same time so that its surplus production could be directed towards urban consumers.

The decrease in the agricultural and rural populations has been constant (the rural population represented 71 per cent of the total population in 1861 and 37 per cent in 1961). Currently in France the rural exodus is not yet over. From the strictly economic standpoint, this evolution has been favourable to our society. From the social and human standpoints the very difficult conditions for many people under which the rural exodus, industrialisation and urbanisation took place ought not to be overlooked.

At the outset of the movement, two ways were open to French agriculture. All the European countries had a choice: either the abandoning of part of their agricultural activity compensated by imports, as in England (the shifting of crops has become international on account of the development of extensive cereal-growing areas in North America); or else regional specialisation within the frontiers with, if possible, an exportable surplus, as in France or Germany, thereby implying considerable growth in agricultural production.

Agriculture became bound up in the other sectors. The agricultural, rural population was closely involved in the economic movements. By remaining it had to adapt; by going, through appeal or repression depending on the period and the place, it changed character and way of life, without wholly losing its ties with its origins.

An increase in agricultural productivity and yield resulted from the population departures and a new way of performing production tasks. Farmers were compelled to resort to means supplied by industrial technology to improve and develop crops and to enter into a distribution system to sell their produce to the urban consumers. The level of salaries and income, which went up by itself, became competitive with what industry was offering. The pressure was sometimes very great at the regional level.

By improving their production the farmers had to subject themselves to financing and credit systems. Most of them had little money available at the time when investment had become necessary to go over to the modern agricultural stage. They had to buy fertiliser, selected cattle, more efficient tools and, later, machinery.

French agriculture participated in the general growth, but its place in the economy, which was according to the Physiocrats in the eighteenth century the prime and sole creator of wealth, fell off. It progressed materially, becoming all the while less independent. The growth was a cumulative process which transformed the agricultural population and production. It stemmed from the geographical and sectoral transfers of population. The agricultural workers who stayed on became more qualified and more capable of assimilating what was new: their productivity rose. Agricultural production changed in style; the farmer cultivated less and less for his own keep and became a supplier to markets. Famine was wiped out in the nineteenth century in Europe. To meet the demand, produce improved and new crops appeared. Cattle were reared more for meat and dairy produce rather than for work and to produce fertiliser. An increasing amount of produce was processed by industry before being consumed.

Industrialisation gave rise to the setting up of an ever-improved exchange system. Industrial production, especially that of the chemical and light metal industries, contributed to the rise in agricultural productivity and yield. What was new and profitable to agriculture generally originated from the industrial sector. The dependence of agriculture was technological. Regions flourished according to how well they were able to break the hold of a certain passivity. The dependence was also financial on account of the growing investment requirements. Land ownership had long linked some farmers to the bourgeoisie of the towns (it has been estimated that on average in the nineteenth century 45 per cent of the land belonged to non-farmers).

The income of farmers rose less quickly over a long period than that of the other categories. There was a major obstacle to continuous growth in agricultural production and this was the low elasticity in the demand for food-produce relative to consumer income (Engel's law).

During the period being considered, agriculture was for ever having to adapt since it was very sensitive, regionally speaking. A slow, structural transformation emerged through choices, delays and cyclical periods of crisis and prosperity. The farmer had to choose individually about staying or going, about adapting his cultivation methods to meet new needs or keeping to his traditional way of life and about running into debt or going on living in a more or less closed economy.

In France some economic, social and political resistance checked general agricultural modernisation and slowed down the population decrease necessary. French agricultural growth was curbed around 1880, particularly through difficulty in organising the internal and external cereal market, through disease in the vineyards, etc. All these deep-rooted transformations were variously felt in the different regions.

1. REGIONAL DISPARITIES IN AGRICULTURAL DEVELOPMENT

Regions and departments reorganised their structures in terms of the natural conditions and adaptation capabilities of the agricultural population which was less numerous but better equipped. It became possible to separate the producer from the consumer, something which removed a constraint and allowed regional specialisation.

(a) The natural factors

The regional variety of natural factors is very great in France: soils, climate, relief, etc. Geography accounts for the primary breakdown of local activities: between rich and poor regions as regards agriculture, and also as regards industry because sites have often been set up on account of natural facilities (mines, waterways, ports).

The distance between the industrial development centres and the agricultural areas occurs sometimes the opposite way. A rich agricultural region like the North was simultaneously the leading industrialisation area in France in the nineteenth century. On the other hand, an out-of-the way region like Brittany remained backward for long with substantial agricultural potential. Cyclical accidents determined localised situations: the phylloxera outbreak in the last quarter of the last century caused the organisation of the vineyards to be overhauled and their extent to be reduced; the discovery of chemical colourants upset the economy of the Vaucluse department, formerly devoted to madder-growing.

(b) The population

At the national level only the intersectoral flows are known. At the regional level it is possible to observe the qualitative selection caused by the departure of workers: the poorest and least useful left first (in the category of agricultural salaried staff and mother's helps). The optimum, however, did not always result from it: the breakdown by age and sex of the agricultural working population and natural population movements were locally modified. Generally beneficial, these movements sometimes caused distortion through the ageing of the population in the poorest regions and shortage of labour in those which had been abandoned by the salaried staff.

The geographical flows of agricultural and rural emigration were an important determinant in the transformation of the regions. Regional modifications were born of the population exchanges and property exchanges which resulted in transformed town/countryside relations. In the northern half of France rich agricultural areas grew up in an industrial, urban environment. In the southern half, physically more varied, the adaptation was more difficult, except when a specialised activity was able to settle in (orchards or vineyards).

Since distance was no longer an obstacle, the crops were redistributed according to the natural agricultural calling of each region. Under the old regime it was vital to grow cereals, the basic food, everywhere. Their production was limited to more appropriate areas, chiefly the northern half of France and the South-west (15,620 thousand hectares in 1862, 9260 in 1962, i.e approximately a 40 per cent reduction). Changeovers took place: expansion of meadows to meet an increased demand for meat, development of new crops like the potato and beet. The conversion of Normandy into an intensive rearing area is a model in this respect. The Massif Central, on account of its contours, its harsher climate and difficult communications had more trouble in adapting to the same activity.

All these changes did not take place without difficulties and the greatest resistance was apparent at the regional level. The increase in yields and productivity which characterised this period was not uniform since the rationalisation of the crops was slow. In the least rich regions (like the Centre) and in those which remained overpopulated (like the West), less progress was made. The separation between agricultural activities proper and those which were related and industrial in type, like the textile or small-scale metal industries, which constituted extra resources for the farmers, marked certain regions like Normandy or the East. Part of the agricultural labour force went off to the factories to carry out these activities. Those who stayed mainly devoted themselves to agricultural production which was beneficial for their productivity.

Some regions have always been richer than others. The development of land is often a heritage from the past: even today, in the Centre and South-west, there are farms where sharecropping is practised and this system holds progress back.

In the aggregate, urban attraction was a factor in the numerical equilibrium of the agricultural population. Local scarcity situations became apparent – lack of salaried labour and excessive departures of young people likely to have ensured the continuation of the farms, a trend which was heightened by schooling and successional law inherited from the Revolution and Empire.

The presence of towns is generally a factor of equilibrium for a region.

The North continues as the leading producer of cereals and beet; its substantial urban network, developed from long-standing industrialisation, represented both an outlet for the possible excess agricultural labour and an opening for its products. The West, on the contrary, suffered for long from its remoteness from the attractive industrial urban centres and this region remained overpopulated. In the Mediterranean Midi quite a dense urban network, the origins of which dated back to Roman times, made up for the shortage of industrialisation sufficiently to welcome the rural exodus and let very specialised agriculture remain (chiefly in the vineyards). On the other hand, Paris, by dominating all the other French towns, often exercised too strong a centralising attraction on its environment; the rich agriculture of the Paris Basin suffered from this proximity, Haute Normandie more especially.

A split occurred between the regions which adapted themselves to modern agriculture and the others. In the poor regions of France agricultural activity was not totally forsaken and it is still today practised in an often archaic and traditional fashion with small-size, unprofitable farms.

The mountainous regions cover an extensive part of the country: their contours were an obstacle to the modernising of cultivation methods, particularly to the introduction of mechanisation and the development of communications. The total area of agricultural land has, however, little varied over a century since the abandoning of fallow land and the clearing and draining operations performed extensively in the nineteenth century increased the amount of usable agricultural ground. A certain expansion of the woods and forests made up for the escheated land.

The French agricultural regions can be classified into three types:

(i) The adapted agricultural regions. Some are predominantly agricultural. Brittany reached this stage slowly. In other regions, like the North, there is room for prosperous agriculture alongside the other activity sectors. Also in this group can be found regions where there is specialised agriculture (wine, market-garden and fruit produce in certain Midi departments). Production problems are not always easy to resolve in this type of region: modernisation, finance and internal and external marketing match the size of the farms and production. These problems are currently occurring in the functioning of the Common Market.

(ii) The regions in which agriculture declined without the set-off of the establishment of other sectors to use up the surplus population, which had to leave in droves. Unsuitable agricultural activities still go on there, however (in certain departments of the Centre and in mountainous areas in general).

(iii) The regions where the development of industry and urbanisation has prevented modernised agriculture from being maintained, except for limited products (in the East, the vineyards of Champagne or Alsace).

There are many restraints in agriculture and evolution is slow, unlike industry. It is frequently necessary to wait for the renewal of generations as it is the youngest workers who adapt best to innovation. The old structures were not always forsaken. The total shifting of an industrial or commercial activity is possible, but this is not so when it comes to crops. It is rather a question of doing away with marginal cultivation areas, the least profitable ones, replaced by more suitable crops or plantations of forests (in the East and in mountainous regions), when the agricultural population is insufficient.

Since the economic start-up at the beginning of the nineteenth century, the progression of agriculture had, first of all, established an equilibrium between production and consumption at the national level (by wiping out famine), then it had to meet new needs and improve the quality of the food.

Agriculture in France has resisted international competition quite well, but often at the expense of its own modernisation, by resorting at times to protectionism, so as to maintain a certain variety of produce corresponding to the variety of the regions. The farmers profited from the political consequences of the Revolution but they were never able to become dominant because their number did not stop going down. At the same time their economic dependence grew, but they were able to secure an ever-increasing share of the ownership of the land they cultivated.

This situation was accompanied by a relative worsening of the level of their income which was lower and which progressed less quickly than that of the other categories. The mainly agricultural regions were at a disadvantage because of it. These regions were generally situated in the western half of the country.

The many factors we have just put forward affect or have affected simultaneously the evolution of agriculture. We are going to examine how we can use the facts and figures corresponding to these factors, which are available at the departmental level, to measure the effects.

2. THE APPLICATION OF A MULTI-DIMENSIONAL ANALYSIS OF THE DATA TO A SPACE-TIME PROBLEM

The long-term evolution of agriculture at the regional level results from the combination of many variables which have just been set out descriptively. Having departmental data over a long term available, we must search for the solution of a space-time problem which is of interest not only to those who study long-term movements, since they may be able to derive a forecasting instrument from it, but also to economic historians who seek instruments suitable for their own work and to those who study inter-regional or international economic relations.

Now, despite the efforts of econometricians, no satisfactory solution has really been found to date to this problem. There is always a lack of information from the space or time standpoints or else inadequate processing of the data.

As regards the evolution of French agriculture, we introduce in a geographical dimension, for a given duration, an economic dimension materialised by a certain amount of data. The three dimensions are the following, including the example studied here:

the geographical space of the French departments;
the time-space made up by the period of a century from 1861 to 1962 with two 50-year sub-periods (on the basis of the data supplied by the censuses and enquiries of the Statistique Generale de la France and the INSEE);
the data-field represented by variables relating to the population and agricultural production, expressed in quantities.

The methods possible do not enable all the information to be used at one and the same time. One of the dimensions has to be sacrificed: reduce the geographical field, limit the periods or lower the number of variables.

Multi-dimensional analysis of the data seems more suitable than other methods to introduce a large number of time variables in an organised system, these variables being left to the user's choice with no consistency constraints. Later on we present the application of a factor analysis of the correspondences to the dimensions of our problem: the departmental evolution of French agriculture from 1861 to 1962. There are two sorts of data: economic and departmental variables. If they can be distributed over a contingency table, then the factor analysis of the correspondences is applicable. If not, then main component analysis must be resorted to. The time is integrated through simultaneous use of identical variables at different dates. When there are very many variables available it is possible to compare operations carried out at several periods (providing that the intervals are not too short).

The interpretation of a factor analysis of the correspondences

The results of a factor analysis of the correspondences leave the user faced with a certain number of choices as regards their interpretation.

The variables presented in contingency tables represent a cluster of points with many dimensions. The factor analysis of the correspondences makes it possible to reduce this cluster to a small number of dimensions materialised by planes formed by two axes on which the points are projected. We choose the number of axes necessary to obtain the maximum amount of information the loss of which is indicated by the percentage of unexplained variance of each axis.

Two sorts of point are represented on these planes. In our example (see Figure 27.1) there are department-points and variable-points, a point in each category representing the linear combination of the corresponding data of the other category. The variable-points resume all the departmental information about them; the department-points synthesise the variables and depend on the prior choice of the latter. One has to examine the position of the points relative to one another and their position relative to the axes:

two points are all the closer on the plane formed by two axes in that there is a very great correlation between them;
the correlation between one variable and a factor-axis is measured by the coordinate of this variable with the axis.

The interpretation of the factor axes leads to a definition of the most discriminating variables, i.e. those which have the greatest correlation (positive or negative) relative to the axes. We thus obtain the leading characteristics of the phenomena we are looking at.

The interpretation of the position of the points consists in distinguishing clusters of points of the same type: groups of departments indicating regionalisation or dispersion; sets of variables giving information on the possibility of a reciprocal action on the part of the corresponding factors. Seeking proximities between points of different categories (departments and variables) is most enlightening as it can lead to distinguishing regionalisation and is essential to the understanding of the space dimension. Space has been privileged in our example, i.e. we have distributed the frequencies over the departments on the one hand, and the variables relating to the three years selected, namely 1861, 1911 and 1962, on the other. The interval of fifty years is likely in a survey on agriculture when changes come about slowly.

The possibility of employing this method is reduced when the interval is great: long-period annual data, for example. It is useful, however, when mixed data are available since the choice is free and without constraint.

A certain doubt remains in the interpretation. The proximities noted between the points do not allow any causality to be concluded between them. Sometimes it is necessary to look beyond the obvious links which show up at times: for instance, beyond the breakdown of the departments according to their agricultural characteristics, the comparison at differing dates can throw light on the passing of the economy of the departments from a past state to a recent situation. This analysis cannot thus constitute an end in itself. It is merely a stage in an explanatory process. It is very useful to draw up a regional typology or sort out a large number of variables when the latter possibly contribute to the explanation of a complex phenomenon.

THE COMMENTS

The calculations related to 45 variables representing the total, urban and male agricultural working populations, the areas of the main crops, the working population productivity and the wheat yields for the years 1861, 1911 and 1962 together with their variations during these periods. On Figure 27.1 we have presented the cluster of department-points and that of variable-points separately so that it remains legible. As there is not enough space, only the chief conclusions are going to be presented.

The variables which have the greatest correlations relative to the axes are tillable land (positive correlations), traditional crops having provided human food since the beginning, and urban population density (negative correlations). The discriminating factors are thus the old structure of agriculture as opposed to urbanisation. The link-ups of points highlight various situations: little urbanisation in great ploughland areas (Eure, Aisne, Seine et Marne); the

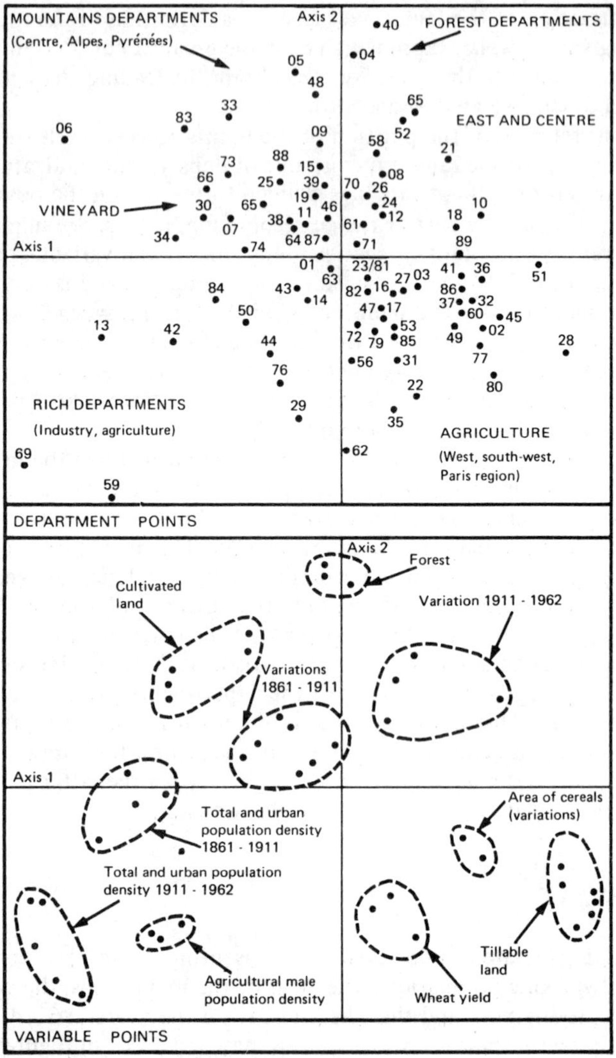

Fig. 27.1

simultaneous presence of towns and agricultural cultivation zones (Pas-de-Calais). Geographically, these variables relate to the Northern part of France, the most developed economically speaking.

The second factor brings in the areas of forest, a variable negatively linked to the density of the urban population and the agricultural working population; forests cover the regions which are at once underpopulated and have

Key to Figure 27.1

DEPARTMENTS

01	AIN	31	HTE GARONNE	61	ORNE
02	AISNE	32	GERS	62	PAS DEICAL
03	ALLIER	33	GIRONDE	63	PUY DE D.
04	ALPES H.P.	34	HERAULT	64	PYR. ATL.
05	HTES ALPES	35	ILLE ET VIL.	65	HTES PYR.
06	ALPES MAR.	36	INDRE	66	PYR. OR.
07	ARDECHE	37	I. ET LOIRE	69	RHONE
08	ARDENNES	38	ISERE	70	HTE SAONE
09	ARIEGE	39	JURA	71	S. ET LOIRE
10	AUBE	40	LANDES	72	SARTHE
11	AUDE	41	LOIR-ET-CHER	73	SAVOIE
12	AVEYRON	42	LOIRE	74	HTE SAVOIE
13	B. DU RHONE	43	HTE LOIRE	76	SEINE MAR.
14	CALVADOS	44	LOIRE ATL.	77	S. ET MARNE
15	CANTAL	45	LOIRET	79	DEUX SEV.
16	CHARENTE	46	LOT	80	SOMME
17	CHAR. MAR.	47	L. ET GAR.	81	TARN
18	CHER	48	LOZERE	82	T. ET GAR.
19	CORREZE	49	MAINE ET L.	83	VAR
21	COTE D'OR	50	MANCHE	84	VAUCLUSE
22	COTE DU NORD	51	MARNE	85	VENDEE
23	CREUSE	52	HTE MARNE	86	VIENNE
24	DORDOGNE	53	MAYENNE	87	HTE VIENNE
25	DOUBS	54	M. ET MOS.	88	VOSGES
26	DROME	55	MEUSE	89	YONNE
27	EURE	56	MORBIHAN		
28	E. ET LOIRE	58	NIEVRE		
29	FINISTERE	59	NORD		
30	GARD	60	OISE		

been forsaken by farmers during the period. This is the negative aspect of the adaptation of agriculture.

The third factor combines the agricultural workers and the new agriculture born of urban consumer demand (market garden produce and pastures). This produce often calls for a relatively abundant labour force. On the corresponding plane the position of the departments in Britanny is tied up with their insufficient productivity as long as they remained overpopulated, despite extensive agricultural production.

Since the first three axes have a total inertia of 50.4 per cent (30.2 per cent for the first two and 10.2 per cent for the third), the departmental breakdown of the variables is accounted for in the first place by the maintaining of the great food crops and their regrouping, then by the use to which the land no longer cultivated is put (forestry in the best cases), and lastly by the development of new produce, with the phenomena of the falling off in the agricultural population and of urbanisation being underlying.

The search for proximities between the variable-points reveals the adaptation-modes at the departmental level of the population and agriculture: great accelerated urbanisation during the second period (1911-62), distribution of the agricultural population favourable to the rich departments, dwindling of the extent of tillable land which is concentrated in the most suitable areas.

Improved yield and productivity is noted in the privileged departments. New crops came along in the other departments. When they lose their population the area of forest rises (in the East, South-east and South-west).

When we bring in the time, both sub-periods present different characteristics. Urbanisation speeded up during the second half of the period, but the transformation of agricultural production was seemingly older and more regular. There is anteriority in the evolution of agriculture relative to the other economic phenomena: industrialisation and urbanisation can go ahead only after the agricultural infrastructure has been set up.

The departmental breakdown between rich and poor, industrial and agricultural comes over clearly. It was the structure of the whole country which changed at this time. Traditionally the North, always better off, was opposed to the South. This distinction continues into the historical, political and ethnic standpoints. Since the nineteenth century, the economic division has tipped in the opposite direction. The North-east zone, through industrialisation, has acquired a real advance over the South-west, even in the agricultural sector.

These two divisions are superimposed on each other in such a way that it is now possible to split France up into four economic zones, centred about Paris:

the North-east quarter, which is the richest and most industrialised, representing as a whole a substantial part of the agricultural production and national wealth;

the North-west quarter, whose wealth is mainly agricultural and in which a better equilibrium is being sought between the economic activities;

the South-west quarter, agricultural and more backward, where adaptation is difficult,

the South-east quarter, which is very varied: there are rich agricultural regions in the Rhone valley, poor ones in the mountains, small-size yet sometimes very important industrial areas like the region of Lyons and dense, long-standing urbanisation.

From this commentary it can be seen that the factor analysis of the correspondences has made it possible to arrange the space and time variables and bring out the leading characteristics. Above all, it appears that the choice of the variables is especially important in attaining the research goal. In the example which has just been given, the narrow field of the variables selected does not allow a sufficiently explanatory analysis to be made. We have undertaken a study to this end, but the results of it were not available when this paper was drawn up.

BIBLIOGRAPHY

Annales de l'I.N.S.E.E., no. 4, 1970.

M. Agulhon, G. Désert and R. Specklin, *Histoire de la France rurale,* vol. 3, 'Apogée et crise de la civilisation paysanne 1789-1914' (Paris, 1975-6).

Ph. Aries, *Histoire des populations françaises et de leurs attitudes devant la vie depuis le XVIIIe siècle* (Paris, 1971).
R. Badouin, *Economie rurale* (Paris, 1971).
P. Bairoch, *Le tiers-monde dans l' impasse* (Paris, 1971).
—— *Révolution industrielle et sous-développement* (Paris, 1963).
—— *Agriculture and the Industrial Revolution* (London, 1969).
J.P. Benzecri, *L'analyse des données* (Paris, 1976).
P. Boyer and A. Richard, 'Eléments d'analyse de la transition démographique', *Population,* nos 4-5, July-October 1975.
J.-L. Guigou, *Théorie économique et transformations de 1 'espace agricole,* (Paris, 1972).
J.-P. Jobard, *Les disparités régionales de croissance* (Paris, 1971).
P. Houee, *Les étapes du développement rural* (Paris, 1972).
A. Sauvy, *Théorie générale de la population* (Paris, 1963-6).
N. Soubeyroux, 'L'emploi agricole, typologie départementale et perspectives d'évolution', *Recherche sociale,* no. 59, July-September 1976.
J.-C. Toutain, *La population de la France 1700-1959,* Cahiers de l' ISEA, no.3.

28 The Uneven Growth of Regional Incomes in France from 1840 to 1970

Jean-Claude Toutain

1. The uneven development of the various regions in France is in evidence for every one of us. However, what we know about it today poses more problems than it solves. Like all the inequalities which go hand in hand with general economic growth, whether they be reduced or increased by this growth, it has been the subject of much less work, relative to other economic phenomena, both theoretically and empirically. Modern societies, the nation states, have all had and still have, whatever their regime, a tendency to force the unequal distribution of the fruits of growth out of the national conscience. As for the 'National Developers', faced today with the practical problem of re-balancing regions, they have to cope with problems for the solution of which they do not have an operational theoretical grasp (how the regional inequality comes about and works) or even a definite analysis of the inequality phenomenon (what is regional inequality? What are its significant criteria?). They don't even have an exhaustive measure of the most basic inequalities at their disposal.

Historical analysis makes no exception to this inadequacy with the outcome that, from the political viewpoint itself, the results of inter-regional exchanges which have occurred over the past two centuries are considered without proof, depending on what is required, as a sharing out by the rich regions of their intertemporal surpluses with the poor regions or as a colonisation of the poor regions by the rich ones without which the latter would not have experienced growth.

The fact that the phenomenon of regional inequalities has been statistically, analytically and theoretically ignored is especially evident in France where the studies looking into this problem carried out over the last 150 years could be counted on one hand.

2. Does a theoretical tool for guiding statistical analysis exist?
It is not the basic statistical data which is unavailable. On the contrary, it is abundant. All the data which exist for the whole of France since early in the nineteenth century also exist for each department. The problem lies in the difficulty of grasping these numerous bits of data (90 per parameter), whereas it is already long-winded and drawn-out to work on national data, and, having grasped and transformed them into meaningful statistical figures, then finding a theoretical tool capable of accounting for the variations between each of these departmental 'items'.

Regional growth can be considered as spreading out over a neutral and homogeneous space and the regions as companies or as nations allowing us to study their production functions. This is the simplest way and to a certain extent this sort of theoretical reasoning should be integrated into a regional analysis and the data making it possible to be done should thus be collated; but in so doing one ignores the specific nature of the regional problem, namely the unchanging localisation of the region with the resulting relative immobility of the factors and the secular inertia of the structures. Moreover, this theoretical approach does not allow the articulation of the various types of growth to be studied.

We can also attempt to apply the methods of analysis derived from the theories of international exchanges to the regional phenomena, and try to understand the mechanisms behind the regional-specific nature and the favourable or unfavourable effects of these exchanges. However, it would then be necessary to take another look at the fundamental assumption of immobility of the production factors peculiar to these theories.

Finally the regional problem can be broached using the models derived from the von Thunen analysis, which attempt to explain how the process of regional polarisation developed. Here too, in assuming that we succeed in isolating the various activities from the laws of polarisation, we would not, for all that, account for the regional-specific nature, a sort of indeterminate residual element or a melting-pot where the prime data (geography, distance, climate), the sociological and cultural facts, or basically the makings of regional phenomena, blend together.

In the face of the recognised bounds to these theories, would it perhaps be necessary to resort to topological analysis so as better to grasp the forms of dependence and liberty of the region sub-sections in the nation system?

3. Our aim here is quite modest with respect to these lines of research. It comes down to presenting the initial results of an endeavour to *re-create* a given region's gross internal product as a first quantitative element in any analysis of the regional phenomenon.

France is a country which stands out for this from the Anglo-Saxon ones from the economic history viewpoint: although the concern over measuring economic phenomena goes back to late in the seventeenth century with Vauban, first estimator of the national income, although his statistics departments were amongst the earliest (the Service de la Balance du Commerce was set up in 1715) and although it experienced a flourish of impressive statistical work between 1750 and 1850, France has today only a limited number of historical statistical works, despite the fact that economic history strives, either for valid scientific reasons or for a mere influence from pure science, to build up a good temporal statistical series. Consequently we have, as I have already said, over and above the well-known and incomplete stock of official publications, only less than half a dozen studies, and moreover all of them concerning agriculture.

I thus had to undertake the re-creation of all the elements enabling the regional phenomenon to be measured. Even the working population is only known for each region from the years 1862-66 and again the estimation concerning farmers' wives tends to be arbitrary: on the basis of the latest reckonings, the proportion of wives in the working agricultural population can be estimated as lying in the 30-45 per cent bracket, the national figure. On the regional scale, one is reduced either to taking the national ratio or to correcting this bracket for the difference, in the censuses, between the working agricultural female population regional rate and the national one, assuming in this way the error or indetermination relative to this homothetic rate having these differences. This first bias is of importance.

For agricultural production, I have reverted to the major enquiries of 1840 to 1929, but, with the exception of the 1929 enquiry, extremely complex corrections that I can't go into here had to be applied for fruit and vegetables, meat and dairy produce.

For industrial production, the major enquiries of 1840 and 1860 and the semi-enquiries of 1911 and 1931 were essentially used, together with the population censuses, which provided the basis for evaluation of the 'produce per working person' per sector and per region. For each period we are presenting here – 1862-66, 1892-96, 1929-31 and 1968-70 – the complete re-creation of the square table product per region-product per sector was drawn up from the basic 'value added per working person'.

The fact shouldn't be hidden that some considerable biases are introduced by the calculation methods used. These biases are unavoidable: until historians are allowed, using as yet unexploited regional sources, to correct and complete the known statistical data, we will only be able simply to modify the bias by modifying the recreation technique: we will not reduce it.

I have been quite brief in expounding the re-creation methods which in some aspects resemble to a certain extent archaeological ones. Any value in this re-creation lies in the choice of the basic units which will serve as a basis for the conclusion and in connection with the operations.

The biases which I believe can be chosen as 'the least biases' must therefore be mentioned here. The first bias concerns the agricultural female population, already referred to above. In connection with agricultural production, I postulated that the inter-regional exchanges of intermediate products could be neglected; they still are today, for the most part, by the departments of the Ministry of Agriculture. I have subtracted nothing relating to animal consumption for dry vegetables and potatoes and, for the cereals, I took into account as animal consumption all the production of oats, corn and barley. This assumption unfavourably treats those regions which could consume this produce or sell it to towns (horses) or factories (breweries). But it seemed to me less far-reaching than a series of arbitrary deductions regarding the department based on livestock.

For industry, the chief bias stems from the triturations which had to be applied to the 'apparent-productivity-of-the-working population' unit of each region and each sector so that it represents the productivity of all working people, whereas industrial enquiries don't take account, as a rule, of the activity of small-scale industry and the modern enquiries (1970) only take a census of those firms having a staff of more than five. So as to make up complete regional accounts, not only did these data for obtaining all the firms or working people present in each region have to be triturated, but also the whole productive set-up had to be re-created: in 1865, for example, the enquiry covered only about one third of the industrial production. The data we are arriving at are thus only temporary: in the near future, the industrial production will have to be carefully reconstituted, *arrondissement* by *arrondissement,* by comparing the results of industrial enquiries, population censuses and fiscal documents case by case.

To finish, the few results we have arrived at suffer from the absence of the tertiary industries which play an essential part in the development of the differential productivity and standard of living in a region. Even if Easterlin was satisfied, for evaluating American industry's production in 1840, in using very approximative national 'intermediary product'/'value produced' ratios, he did on the other hand include a section of the tertiary industries (mainly commerce). We are reckoning on adding these industries in future.

Last bias, but not least – that which stems from the nomenclature: as will be seen later on, certain specific aspects of the regional differences, and perhaps the regional-specific nature itself, are only the consequence of approximations in measuring and the difference factors being insufficiently taken into consideration.

It should be noted that the 90 departments have been grouped into 21 regions, an imperfect but convenient arrangement. Fishing, it should also be noted, has not been included under physical product. This omission brings down the income chiefly in Brittany and the North, but only to the extent of between 1 and 3 per cent of the physical product from these regions. For the other coastal regions, fishing represents an even lower percentage of the product.

4. *The population.* Data concerning the population are the easiest to collate. Two regions saw their population drop before 1850: Basse-Normandie and Midi-Pyrénées. The other regions in the West and South-west were to wait until 1890 for the rural exodus to become evident there. In the East, only Auvergne and Franche-Comté followed this movement. Finally it was the turn of the 1914 war to see the population of all the regions in the Paris Basin, except in Haute-Normandie, drop. Contrary to this is the long-period growth of the populations in the Paris region and Haute-Normandie, the North and East and the Mediterranean regions: Rhône-Alpes, Languedoc and Provence.

A curious fact comes to light in that all regions experiencing long-period population growth saw their population decrease between 1931 and 1946 and those regions in long-period population decrease saw theirs rise during the same period. The Great Depression and the 1939-45 war were, for a time, to check the secular 'modernisation' movement of the economic structures (indirect proof that population movements are strictly dependent on the 'modernisation' process – which is still to be defined), a movement which imposed itself slowly from the first half of the nineteenth century onwards and hit those regions resisting it one after the other.

In 1946, a time of low demographic ebb, a certain number of regions almost reverted to the levels of 1801: Champagne, Picardie, Bourgogne, Franche-Comté, Midi-Pyrénées, Limousin and Auvergne. After 1946, all regions saw their population rise, except Basse-Normandie, which, in 1970, had less inhabitants than in 1801! It should be noted that all regions experiencing high demographic growth over the last 25 years were precisely those which were showing a long-period demographic growth from 1801 onwards: we have there an initial index of the deep secular establishment of the distribution of contemporary wealth.

It can be ascertained, finally, on relative values that up until approximately 1840-50 regional populations were stable, with a slight tendency towards falling, whereas the Paris region, Rhône-Alpes and the North were already draining the population surplus. After 1850, all regions, except for the aforementioned ones joined by Provence, saw their relative drop become more marked. This relative fall was not to experience any lasting interruption. Alsace and Lorraine are the only regions to maintain stable relative positions.

5. The *Physical Product* at today's values is not the best indicator of regional differences because it compares regional products with no reference to their population or their extent, or quite simply with no reference to a quantity making them comparable. Having said this, this aggregate measures the gross wealth produced by each region and its development over time is after all significant. In this way, the difference between regions, as can be seen, carried on widening from 1861 onwards:

Physical Product Variation Coefficients

	1865	*1896*	*1931*	*1970*
With Paris	0.46	0.59	0.78	1.04
Without Paris	0.33	0.38	0.44	0.57

The gap didn't stop widening between the rich and poor regions, the rich ones (Paris region, Rhône-Alpes, the North) or those becoming richer (Provence, Lorraine) being precisely those whose population continued to grow or at least remained stable (Lorraine). But what is most striking, is the relative secular fall in *all* the provinces other than the above-mentioned five.

6. Let us now look at the relative *Incomes* (product) *per inhabitant* (i.e. expressed as a percentage of the national income (product) per inhabitant). Figure 28.1 and Table 28.1 show that from 1865 to 1930 these incomes per inhabitant converged but that between 1930 and 1970 – from a date we have not yet fixed but which is most likely after the Second World War – the dispersion increased, to reach a variation coefficient in 1970 equal to that of 1865. This contrasts with what had been observed by Easterlin and Williamson for the United States.

TABLE 28.1 Physical product per inhabitant as a percentage of the national physical product per inhabitant

1785		*1865*		*1970*	
R.P.	280	R.P.	160	R.P.	129
H.-Nie	160	–	–	–	–
Champ., Pic., Bas.-Nie.	115	Nord. Champ., Pic., H.-Nie	126	Rh. Champ., H.-Nie	118
Cent., Loi. Rh.	100	Bourg., Loire Als., Lor., Cent.	100	Nd., Pic., Cent., Lorr., F.-C.	102
Nd., Bourg., Lang., Pro.	90	F.-C., B.-Nis., Aq., Midi-P., Lang., Pro.	89	Als., Bourg., Aq.	90
Aq., Midi-P., Poit., Auv.	75	Lim., Poit., Auv., Rh.	81	B.-N., Loire, Poit., Auv., Pro.	83
Lorr., Als., Lim., F.-Comte	60	–	–	Lim., Lang., Midi-P.	74
Bret.	54	Bret.	68	Bret.	64

NOTE:
Key to abbreviations and numbering of the 21 regions. This key relates also to Figures 28.1 and 28.2, and to Tables 28.2 and 28.3.

1. Nord : Nd.
2. Lorraine : Lor.
3. Alsace : Als.
4. Franche-Comte : F.-C.
5. Champagne : Champ.
6. Picardie : Pic.
7. Haute-Normandie : H.-Nie.
8. Centre : Cent.
9. Basse Normandie : B.-Nie.
10. Bourgogne : Bourg.
11. Loire : Loi.
12. Bretagne: Bret.
13. Poitou : Poit.
14. Aquitaine : Aq.
15. Midi-Pyrénées : Midi-P.
16. Limousin : Lim.
17. Auvergne : Auv.
18. Rhône-Alpes : Rh.
19. Languedoc : Lang.
20. Provence : Pro.

R.P. : Paris region.

Variation Coefficients (without Paris)

1784	*1865*	*1896*	*1931*	*1970*
0.29	0.18	0.15	0.12	0.18

The minimum record, held by Brittany, in 1865 was 68; it stands today at 64 (see Table 28.1).
From the general aspect viewpoint of the development of the physical product per inhabitant, the regions can be classed into four groups:

> The North, Champagne, Picardie and Haute-Normandie were, along with the Paris region (160-129), the strongest provinces in 1865 as in 1970 (although the North and Picardie did drop behind: 111 in 1970).
> They were joined in 1970 by Lorraine, Franche-Comte and the Rhone-Alpes region (89 in 1865; 111 in 1970).
> Bourgogne, the Centre and Alsace remained at the national average throughout the whole period, with a slight tendency to drop (103 in 1865, 97 in 1970).

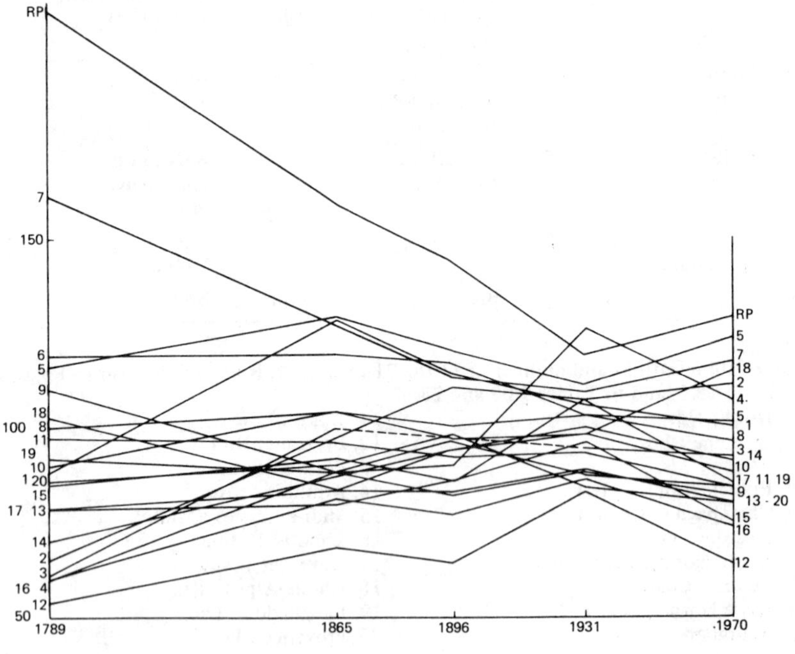

Fig. 28.1 Physical product per inhabitant

All the remaining regions can be classed in the *poor* sector with a distinction between:

(i) the regions which remained poor and are hardly better off today (relative to the national average) than in 1865 – Basse-Normandie, Loire, Aquitaine, Auvergne.
(ii) the average or poor regions which tended to join Bretagne at the lowest level: Midi-Pyrenees, Limousin, Languedoc.

We can try to make the comparison with those years preceding the Revolution by using the taxes per person, although the taxation system differs from that existing during the nineteenth century and we disregard the relationships between the tax per person and the product per person for the eighteenth and nineteenth centuries. This comparison makes it possible however to put several assumptions forward:

The Paris region was way ahead of the others.
Haute-Normandie was already the wealthiest region after the Paris region: following, but not yet equal to this region were Champagne, Picardie and above all the North, which was to join it by 1865.
Basse-Normandie was at the time one of the richest regions.
Bretagne was already at the bottom of the list as regards economic growth and Limousin was not much better off.
Centre, Bourgogne, Midi-Pyrenees and Poitou already had similar relative wealth, which they were to maintain until 1970.
Rhone-Alpes was to see its relative wealth fall between the Revolution and the Second Empire, but it re-established its privileged position in the twentieth century.
Loire and Languedoc were to decline slightly as a result of their agricultural preponderance.
Lorraine, Alsace and Franche-Comte on the other hand were to enter a period of growth, like the North, after the Revolution.
Putting the Paris region and Haute-Normandie aside, the dispersion of incomes per person was no greater in 1865 than in 1789.

What is thus most striking here, is the high significance of the structures and the deep-rootedness up until the eighteenth century of the then existing inequalities.

The 1970 data enable us to introduce two modifications to the foregoing observations:

(*a*) If we add the tertiary industry's incomes to the regional ones of 1970, the regional dispersion of the average income (product) per person is attenuated (0.12 instead of 0.18) – the 1970 figures should be compared with those of 1865 and 1931, but the data are not available for the time being.

(*b*) The further we were going, in 1970, towards poverty (relatively speaking), the greater was the portion of the salaries paid by the tertiary sector. This means that France today is apparently reducing its regional inequalities via the tertiary industries. To be more precise, we are seeing a very close inverse correlation between the portion of tertiary industries' salaries and the physical product per inhabitant up to a certain threshold – represented here by Franche-Comte (income per inhabitant at index 107) – above which the ratio between the level of physical product per inhabitant and the tertiary portion in the regional product is inverted, and becomes positive (see Table 28.2).

TABLE 28.2

	1970 without tertiary sector *	*1970 with tertiary sector* *	*Portion of tertiary industry salaries in the total salaries*
R.P.	1.39	1.51	53
Lor., Champ. Rh., H.-Nie	1.26	1.04	45
Pic., F.-C., Nd.	1.10	0.98	37
Bourg., Cent. Als. Aq.	1.00	1.02	48
B.-Nie, Auv. Poit., Prov., Loi.	0.89	0.97	51
Midi-P., Lim., Lang.	0.79	0.95	56
Bret.	0.68	0.93	59
France	1.00	1.00	50
Variation coefficients	0.18	0.12	

*All these calculations are made with respect to France, excluding the Paris region.

7. *Productivity:* the variations in the total regional product or regional product per person stem from variations in the working population and from variations in productivity. But what does this term productivity signify? Product per person, that can stem from a simple adjustment of the number of working people to the needs of production; concealed recession in unemployment – as must have been the case for agriculture in quite a number of regions; the mechanical product of the rural exodus with no change in the yield from the ground or in the technical conditions of the production only measures the apparent rise in productivity and not the rise in real productivity (something which could only be measured by the rise in yield from the ground per work unit). For industry, the phenomenon is comparable for those sectors in recession, i.e. where the decline in production combined with a stagnation in real productivity leads to lay-offs which only increase the apparent productivity of the remaining workers. Finally, an increase in apparent productivity could be the result of a rise in market prices. In an accurate analysis of the

rise in productivity and above all in a comparative analysis, the distinction should be clearly made between the rise in apparent productivity (mechanical rise in the output quantity per active person) and monetary productivity (rise in the value of output per active person) and the rise in real productivity (rise in output quantity per input unit per active person).

The dispersion in physical product per active person indicates an unquestionable fall since 1840.

Variation coefficients in physical product per active person

1840	*1865*	*1896*	*1931*	*1970*
0.44	0.37	0.30	0.22	0.24

The convergence of regional productivities is perfectly clear: but as far as 1931 the process seems to have reached its maximum point. This convergence

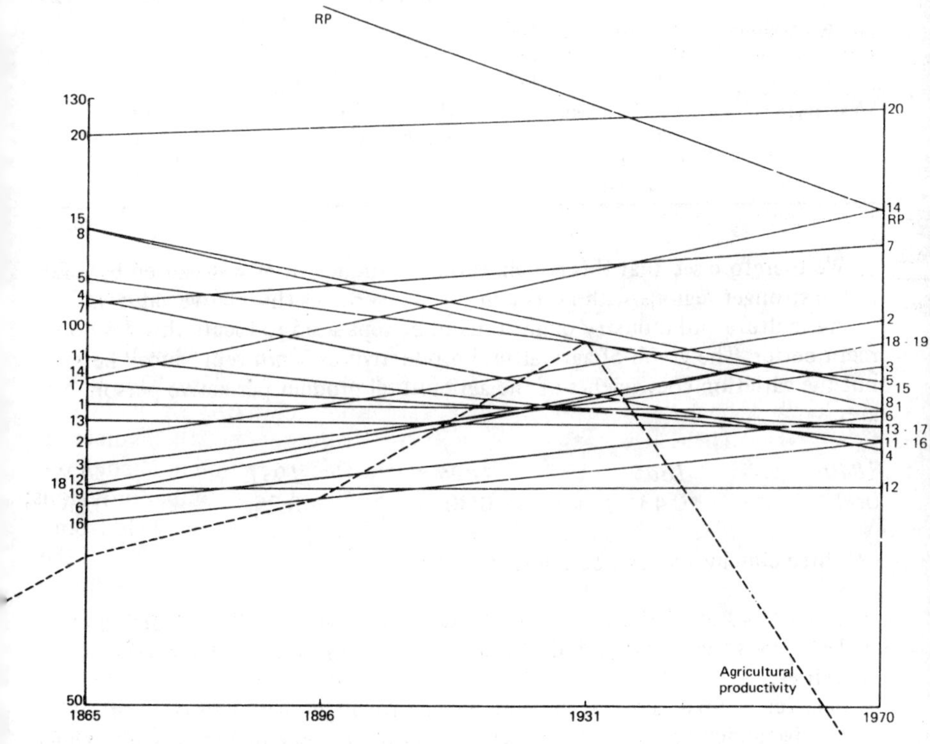

Fig 28.2 Industrial product per working person

of regional productivities is somewhat interesting, since it means that the production factors have been fairly mobile within the system so as to improve the localisation of the activities. However, on close examination of Figure 28.2 we see that this convergence came about as a result of a considerable drop in the high relative productivity of the wealthy regions (in 1865, Champagne, Picardie, Nord, Haute-Normandie: average index = 140; Paris region: index = 230 with respect to the national average = 100), whereas the 16 other regions whose relative productivity lay between 60 and 110 saw this productivity narrow down to lie between 60 and 100 (Table 28.3).

TABLE 28.3

	Relative regional productivity					
	1865		*1931*		*1970*	
Strong regions	R.P. H.-N., Pic. Champ., Nd.	230 140	R. P. H.-N. Pic. Champ. Nd. Lorr. Pro.	105 to 120	R. P. H.-N. Pic. Champ. Nd. Lorr. Pro.	105 to 120
Average regions	Als., Lorr. Cent. Bourg.	100 to 110	–		–	
Weak regions	The 12 other regions: from 60 to 100 excluded.		The 15 other regions: from 70 to 100.		The 15 other regions: from 60 to 100.	

We therefore see that this equalisation of productivities was caused by a fall in the stronger regions with no rise in the weaker ones (in relative values).

Agriculture and industry ought thus to be separated to locate this development better. The graph of agricultural productivities is not reproduced here but the variation coefficients of the agricultural product per active person are:

1840	*1865*	*1896*	*1931*	*1970*
0.41	0.43	0.30	0.25	0.38

Three conclusions can be drawn from this:

From 1840 to 1865, there is most likely no variation in the dispersion;
1865-96 is the major period of equalisation of the agricultural productivities;
between 1896 and 1931, the apparent narrowing-down movement of relative agricultural productivities slowed up or, more precisely, it continued for most regions, but the two most industrial provinces (excluding Paris),

Lorraine and Nord, saw their agricultural productivity increase significantly thereby preventing the overall dispersion from closing up.

In 1865, agricultural productivities were spread out between 65 and 210; in 1896 between 70 and 165; in 1931 between 75 and 145 except for Lorraine, which reached index 180, and Nord, index 160.

In 1970, Limousin was at index 50 and the Paris region above 210. The secular movement was reversed, the first signs of which were indicated in 1931 by Lorraine and Nord. Inequality is today at its peak, even if we compare 1970 with 1840. As regards this agricultural productivity, it ought to be added that its narrowing down between 1840 and 1930 didn't upset the original bits of data: all those regions below the national average (100) in 1840 (i.e. the six regions in the West and South-west, Basse-Normandie, Auvergne and Rhone-Alpes) were still below it in 1931 and 1970; all those above it in 1865 were still above it in 1970 with the exception of the three provinces in the North-east: Franche-Comte, Lorraine and Alsace. Yet there is however a certain equilibrium between the 12 regions which were, from the agricultural productivity standpoint, above the national average and those nine below it.

This is not the case for *industrial productivity,* whose development is shown by Figure 28.2. The variation coefficients are decidedly lower than the agricultural productivity ones and are also more stable.

Variation coefficients of the industrial product per active person (excluding Paris)

1865	*1896*	*1931*	*1970*
0.16	0.13	0.12	0.13

Figure 28.2 does however show us:

An unquestionable secular narrowing down of regional industrial productivities.

The three most productive regions in 1865 (Paris region, Haute-Normandie and Provence) were still the most productive in 1970 and have only been joined by Aquitaine (the three latter provinces profit from the high productivity of the petrochemical industry). All the other provinces lay between 80 and 100 in 1970 as against 74 to 113 in 1865.

Finally, agricultural productivity, which had caught up with industrial productivity in 1931 following a secular rise which carried it from 50 to 100 between 1840 and 1930, dropped back in 1970 to the level 35 (still relative to industrial productivity). The secular equalisation of the agricultural productivities between themselves and with the industrial productivity seems then to have been entirely cancelled out by the policies followed since the Second World War. The reason behind these relative movements of productivity should be looked for in the type of specialisation and the behaviour of prices which have prevailed at one time or the other. This is why an analysis of the regional growth and secular development of productivities ought, in the first place, to be accompanied by an analysis of relative prices and structural transformations of the regions. Due to the lack of space we can only touch on this topic, one which will be studied elsewhere.

What do we notice to begin with as regards the regional and sectorial differentations of productivity? It is not easy to take into account at one and the same time differences in the apparent productivity per region and those per sector, together with the transformation of this matrix from one point in time to another.

If we analyse our first results, we observe that in 1860 the difference between average regional productivities, taking all industries together, was 0.20; the difference between sectorial productivities, taking all regions together, was 0.56 (variation coefficients). In 1970, the phenomenon was the same: the inter-sectorial difference, 0.55, was clearly more significant than the inter-regional one which was 0.14. The differences, calculated on identical aggregates from one date to the other, had thus only slightly changed. In other words, from the lowest to the highest sectorial productivity, there was a difference of 1 to 2 in 1865 and of 1 to 1.5 in 1970; from the lowest to the highest regional productivity, there was a difference of 1 to 5 or 6 in 1865 as in 1970.

We must not rely solely on these average differences because the graph of apparent industrial productivities per region indicates a clear narrowing down of the relative productivities above the average for the majority of regions and an increasing drift of Haute-Normandie, Aquitaine and Provence above the average, as a result chiefly of their petrochemical industry. The apparent narrowing or apparent stability of the average regional productivities can thus cover various inter-regional structures. It can also cover very dissimilar inter-regional systems. The variation coefficients of the sectors are proof of this – see Table 28.4.

TABLE 28.4

	Textiles	*Metals*	*Wood, paper*	*Ceramics building*	*Chemicals*	*Food*
1865	0.30	0.37	0.28	0.24	0.42	0.33
1970	0.22	0.13	0.10	0.18	0.37	0.17

	Agriculture	*Industry*	*Agriculture † Industry*
1865	0.43	0.20	0.37
1970	0.38	0.14	0.24

Two sectors thus saw their regional productivities become much narrower: the wood-paper sector and the metals one, and on the other hand it is in the chemicals sector that the differences in productivity changed the least.

Agriculture is also a sector where the productivity reveals inter-regional variation coefficients as high as those of the chemical sector. Now, although the dispersion on the part of the agricultural sector in the physical product of regions remained stable between 1840 and 1929, it then rose over the period 1929 to 1970.

Variation coefficients for agriculture

1840	*1892*	*1929*	*1970*
0.32	0.30	0.32	0.47

Conjugation of the structure variations in the industrial system and of a growing agricultural specialisation of certain regions explains away a sizeable part of the changes in average regional productivities and the widening differences between regional products per inhabitant. These variations in the regional specialisation do not however account for everything. As regards industry, structural differences in 1865 only accounted for one-third and in 1970 only two-thirds of the regional differences in productivity. We have started the analysis of salaries and prices which most likely account for the remainder of the difference, but it is too early to draw any conclusions from this work.

Be that as it may, the growth in income (product) which thus results – and which was eight and a half for the whole of France between 1865 and 1970 – was, compared with this national average taken as a basis (index 100), at index 200 for the Paris region, which implies that Paris grew twice as fast as the rest of France. Rhone-Alpes, Provence and Lorraine were, in 1970, at index 135 with respect to the national average growth; Nord at index 110, Franche-Comte at 100; Haute-Normandie and Aquitaine at 88; Champagne, Picardie, Centre, Loire, Bretagne, Poitou, Auvergne and Languedoc at 71; Basse-Normandie, Bourgogne, Midi-Pyrenees and Limousin at 55 which means that these last four regions grew twice as slowly as France as a whole and four times slower than Paris.

Let us draw two brief conclusions from this overall picture:

the inertia of the relative regional positions, or the plurisecular deep-rooted nature of the contemporary differences between regions;

after one century of decrease in regional differences, the contemporary explosion of the inequalities, which appears to call into question the currently existing theory and contravene asserted policies.

Part 2c Southern Europe

29 Regional Inequalities in Italy

A. Graziani

At the end of the Second World War economic conditions in Southern Italy were extremely precarious. The southern regions were still dominated by agriculture, the agricultural sector being itself extremely unequal and, in general, very poor. All along the coasts one could detect tiny strips of intensively cultivated land, where density of population reached extremely high peaks. But even along the coasts one could find extensive marshes, where pastures, alternated with wheat growing, were the only kind of land use that malaria made possible. In the inner areas, where deforestation had produced an extensive erosion of natural resources, and where property was mainly in the form of big estates, dry crops were the rule. In those areas, small parcels of land were cultivated by peasant families who, not being the owners of the land, were tied to absentee landowners by contracts which were widely different from area to area. Here and there, a few scattered islands of modern industry were also present (such as steel and mechanical industries around Naples, or chemical industries at Crotone). But even such industry as existed was mainly oriented to war production, and it was now necessary to reconvert it to other lines of production in order to make it meet the requirements of the market. The remaining industries of Southern Italy were in the nature of a mix of traditional activities, mainly concentrated in the sectors of food, wood, and clothing. As for technologies and size, these activities could be considered midway between industry and handicraft. In the past, the deep imbalance between population and resources had been taken care of by means of intense and continuous migrations. Even in the inter-war period, when any open debate concerning the problems of the underdeveloped South had been banished, a reduced, slow, but uninterrupted movement of population from south to north of Italy had never ceased to exist. During the war years, even this outlet had disappeared. The problem of the South was thus taking more and more the appearance and the substance of a social problem, since it was increasingly hard to keep within the same national border groups of population enjoying such widely different income levels. The problem was made all the more serious by the fact that the population in Southern Italy was no longer prepared to accept such miserable living conditions. Cases of riots and of occupation of estates on the part of peasants had already passed the stage of local dissatisfaction, and were acquiring, as to extent and strength, the substance of a true class fight.

It was thus clear that inequalities between North and South Italy made it

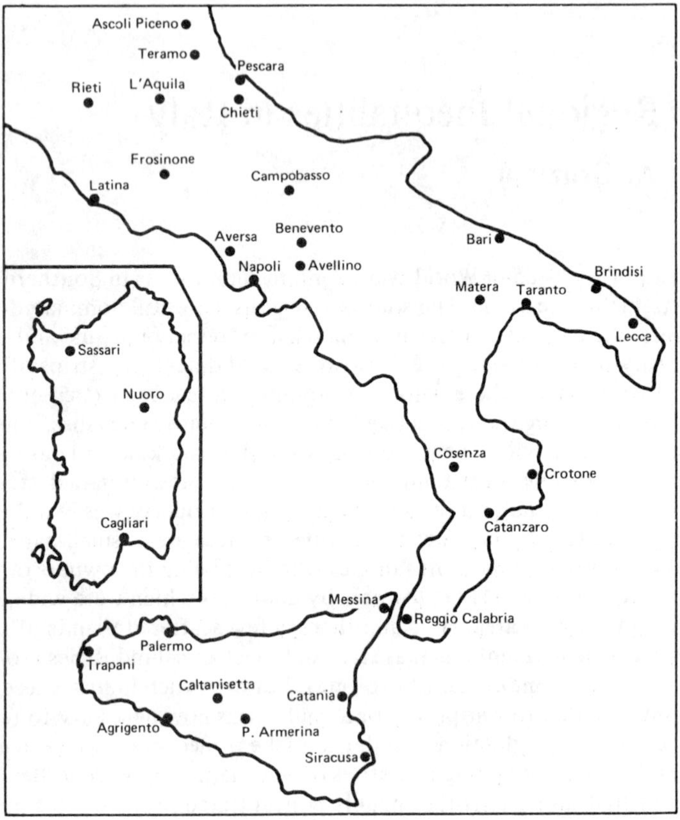

Fig 29.1

unavoidable to take measures to produce a more balanced situation. On the other hand, it was by no means clear what kind of measures it would have been possible to introduce. A regional development policy designed for Southern Italy was to be consistent with the overall national development policy, of which it was going to be a part. National development policy, on the other hand, was following a well-defined design, being mainly centred on the goal of European economic integration. This policy line imposed on Italian industry the burden of a quick modernisation, in order to acquire a greater competitiveness in international markets. According to the prevailing opinion, the only way of reaching that target was to concentrate efforts on industry located in Northern Italy, avoiding any temptation to extend the process of industrialisation to any new regions, where industry could not count on a well-established tradition. The economic problem of Southern Italy was therefore one of raising per capita incomes without any industrial development and in the absence of migration outlets. As a consequence, the only possible way was to develop an extended policy of public works and agricultural improvements, without any serious intervention in the industrial sector. Such a policy was going to meet no objection in the industrial circles of Northern Italy. It was clear to anybody that public expenditure in Southern Italy was going to increase national income and therefore exports from the North towards the South, thus producing an increase in the regional income of the North as well. A policy of public works could also rely on a theoretical basis, such as the theory of social overhead capital as developed by R. Nurkse, or the doctrine of prerequisites to industrialisation as developed by W. Rostow. On such theoretical grounds, the Italian Government could well declare that the final aim of intervention was industrialisation, public works performing the necessary function of a preliminary endowment. On the other hand, the same policy design met consistent objections in circles reflecting interests dominant at the time in the South. The development policy included Land Reform, a measure which was bound to meet the opposition of big landowners, resolved not to lose their own properties.

In order to meet these opposing views, the initial programme had to be revised in various directions. On the one hand, as we shall see, Land Reform was so designed that the less productive lands were the only ones expropriated, while good land practically escaped expropriation, under the motivation that, in those cases, landowners had proved to be able to achieve efficient management. On the other hand, opposition was reduced by the fact that landowners were paid their indemnities in bonds, which, although not saleable at that moment, allowed them finally to acquire new properties in the form of urban land, a kind of investment which in the long run proved to be much more profitable than the original agricultural properties. Finally, while it is true that landowners felt that their position had been assailed on grounds of principle, it is also true that the dominant classes, under the farsighted guidance of De Gasperi, were ready to give up the traditional system of alliances based on the support of Southern aristocracy, and to replace it by new alliances established with other social groups. Along these lines, a base was created for the development of a new bureaucracy in charge of administering public expenditure in Southern Italy, a bureaucracy which is now one of the main centres of power in the South.

On such terms, it was possible to gather political support for a development policy in Southern Italy, the main measures of which were approved by Parliament between 1949 and 1950. The development programme was based on three main points, being respectively Land Reform, the creation of the *Cassa per il Mezzogiorno* (a new development fund for Southern Italy), and new provision for credit on easy terms for local industry.

In principle, Land Reform was to be regulated by one single law, covering the whole national territory. In fact, it was only possible to introduce fragments of regulation. Calabria got its own law, the remaining regions of continental Southern Italy got another partial law *(Legge stralcio),* Sicily was ruled by a still different law, approved by the Sicilian Regional Parliament. According to the so-called *Legge stralcio,* big properties were to be expropriated according to a specific rule determining the amount of land to be expropriated as a direct function of property size and as an inverse function of average product per acre. As a consequence, the most inefficient and neglected properties were the hardest hit. But, as already said, it also happened that expropriated lands were the less fertile ones and those where improvements and investments were most needed. In total, some 450 thousand hectares were expropriated in Southern Italy and some 350 thousand more in the rest of the country. Expropriation was carried out by newly-created Land Reform Agencies *(Enti per la Riforma agraria).* Agencies carried out the distribution of land, which was subdivided into small parcels, the so-called *poderi* (farms), if considered adequate to the needs of an average peasant family, or *quote* (portions), if smaller. The average extent of a farm was very limited: three or five hectares as a rule, with the exception of only a few cattle-raising farms in Sardinia, where acres of up to 15 to 20 hectares were reached. A network of family peasant farms was thus created, which was in accordance with the principles inspiring the whole operation. The adoption of peasant families as the unit of management made it possible to keep on the available land a larger population. In peasant farms, labour is rewarded according to average productivity, so that even those workers can be employed who, having a zero or negative marginal productivity, would be condemned to unemployment if hired as wage labour. According to the Land Reform law, peasants, by paying a number of annuities, could acquire the ownership of the farms that had been allotted to them. As a consequence, the operation was meant to transform a class of landless wage workers into a class of small landowners, ensuring a higher social stability to the whole sector. The results of Land Reform were widely different from area to area. In the plains, where, by means of costly investments, irrigation was introduced, and cultivation was shifted to new and more profitable crops, Land Reform produced excellent results in the form of a large increase in peasant incomes. In the inner areas, where even after Land Reform dry crops prevailed, income levels did not increase much and the whole operation ended in failure.

The *Cassa per il Mezzogiorno* was created in 1950 with a ten-year programme, subsequently extended again and again over time. Its function was to carry out block or large-scale public works, closely connected with what Land Reform had started in agriculture, with the specific aim of improving living conditions. It seemed then certain that, in the absence of deep structural changes in production, the regional distribution of population was bound to remain fairly stable all over the country. Intervention by the *Cassa* was therefore equally spread all over the Southern regions. Chosen targets were, for instance, to bring drinking water and electric power to every community, ensure an equal endowment of roads, schools, hospitals, and the like. It must also be remembered that in the *Cassa's* programme intervention for agricultural improvements had a considerable place.

The third point in the development programme for the South, credit for industry on easy terms, was also the weakest. On the one hand, its introduction was belated. Even if foreseen from the very beginning, it was only in 1953 that the three industrial credit agencies for Southern Italy were created *(Isveimer, Irfis, Cis)*. On the other hand, no direct investment in industry was performed at the beginning, and the only action taken was to offer financial subsidies, in the hope that private investors would decide to take advantage of their existence. It is not surprising therefore that such action produced very limited results. Only after 1958, and owing to totally different factors, did any considerable amount of industrial investment take place in Southern Italy.

Basic industry. It soon appeared that the policy design for the development of Southern Italy had been overtaken by external events. The idea of concentrating efforts on social fixed capital as well as on agriculture was consistent with the image of a stagnating national economy, without perspectives of industrial development and with no migration outlets. During the ten-year period between 1950 and 1960 both assumptions proved to be wrong. Starting with 1955, Italian industry went through a process of rapid growth and deep structural change. In the past, the traditional sectors of textiles, food and mechanical industries had supplied most of the employment. Now, steel, chemicals and automobiles became the leading sectors of industry – all of them had existed in the past, but had always been very limited in size. Such deep change took place through a quick increase in exports, so that industrial development and an improvement in the balance of payments took place hand in hand. At the same time, similar developments were taking place in the most industrialised European countries and, since the same countries were experiencing a labour shortage, new migration outlets were opening to Italian labour. Migration outlets were now no longer present only in faraway countries, as before the First World War, but in the much closer countries of Northern Europe. Since Italian industrial development of those years was concentrated in the North, Southern labour got access to two possible migration outlets, the one inside, the second outside the country. Thus a second great migration flow from Southern Italy began. The first big flow had taken place at the turn of the century, and had reached its peak in 1913. When in 1971 a population census was taken, it was found that, during the preceding twenty years, no less than four million people had left the South for Northern Italy or for some foreign European country. The destinies of Italian migrants were very different over the years. At first, Italian migrants could only find employment in the most dangerous activities (such as mining), or in the less well-paid jobs (such as construction). It was only later that Italian workers were admitted to the manufacturing sectors.

Such enormous population movements were bound to reverse the kind of economic and social equilibrium that had been gradually reached in Southern Italy. The low income levels that could be earned on Land Reform farms were no longer attractive if compared to the much higher and safer incomes that could be obtained by means of migration. A limited number of areas all along the coasts, where irrigation had made possible a shift to more profitable crops, did not suffer greatly from migration and, especially in urban areas, experienced in fact an increase in population. But in all inner mountainous areas a process of increasing abandonment started.

Given the prevailing conditions, it was clearly useless to insist on the initial lines of action. Such lines had brought into being investments the majority of which seemed now to be deprived of any function. After 1958, two main changes took place in the philosophy of intervention, as well as in the ruling legislation. On the one hand, Government expenditure in Southern Italy, which had previously been spread uniformly all over the area, was gradually concentrated on a reduced number of development areas *(poli di sviluppo).* On the other hand, intervention was shifted away from infrastructures and agriculture in favour of industry, a sector which received, between 1960 and 1970, nearly half of the funds administered by the *Cassa.* Once more, this policy line had its own theoretical basis, which was no longer the old theory of prerequisites of industrial development, but the modern theory of development areas, a theory expounded by F. Perroux and A.O. Hirschman, on the original older nucleus of the external economies theory of Alfred Marshall. At first, the policy of development areas was conceived as creation of a severely limited number of industrial poles. Later on, under the pressure of local interests, the Government was made to approve the creation of a very large number of development areas as well as of smaller development nucleuses. In each of them, associations of local administrative institutions, assisted (and when necessary replaced) by the *Cassa,* were supposed to locate areas for new industrial plants, and to endow them with basic overhead capital. Firms locating their plants inside the chosen areas were enabled to enjoy a number of privileges in the attribution of financial subsidies provided by law.

In fact, the development areas where considerable development did take place were the same ones where, owing to independent investment decisions, the location of one or more big industrial plants took place. In the Taranto area a big steel plant was created; close to Brindisi, the private firm Montedison located a chemical plant; at Siracusa, an oil refinery and a petrochemical plant were built; in Sardinia, years later, Sir created a new chemical plant; close to Naples, where a small industrial structure was already present, Alfa-Sud, a firm belonging to the Government-owned holding Iri, created an automobile factory.

The policy of infrastructures was gradually coordinated along the new lines of intervention. In the past, considerable funds had been appropriated for the creation of a network of local roads (an undeniable requirement of all Southern regions). Now a priority was being recognised for long-distance roads, connecting production centres in the North to the growing markets of Southern Italy.

The five-year period between 1958 and 1963 was a most remarkable one, both for the development of the South and for the Italian economy as a whole. For the Italian economy, it was the peak of the so-called economic miracle. Industrial production reached the highest levels ever touched in the post-war period, and investment attained the record figure of 25 per cent of national income. It was only towards the end of the period that monetary equilibrium was broken by a first wave of inflation, while the balance of payments, which had nearly reached an equilibrium, turned again to a net deficit position. In the South, the years following 1958 were characterised by the first considerable increase in industrial investment. Two different kinds of industrial investment could be distinguished. In the first place, big autonomous investment took place, owing to decisions taken by the major national concerns. Such investments led to the creation of giant plants, mostly in the basic sectors (steel, chemicals, petrochemicals), with very limited employment effects and, given their nature of vertically integrated processes, equally limited effects on surrounding production structures. On the other hand, smaller local investments took place, mostly due to entrepreneurs already active in Southern Italy. Only a small part of such minor investments were located in sectors connected to the activities of big plants, and could be interpreted as induced by them. The majority of smaller initiatives, due to local entrepreneurial forces, were located in construction or in related sectors. Government expenditure and subsequently big industrial investments had given rise to an increasing concentration of population in the major towns, and as a consequence to a considerable increase in residential construction, generously assisted by bank finance. Construction was the main outlet of local entrepreneurial forces, who seemed unable to discover the opportunities for investment in manufacturing, a sector where risk was considerably higher and management problems much more daunting.

Since both new industrial plants and the richer agricultural areas were located along the coasts, Southern Italy was gradually acquiring an unbalanced structure that subsequent events could only accentuate. While coastal areas, and in particular those areas where big industrial plants had been located, seemed to become more and more affluent, and were experiencing an increase in population, internal areas were experiencing increasing depopulation, which meant the loss of the more efficient members of the labour force. Southern Italy was thus reproducing, inside its own borders, the same unbalanced situation that had been for such a long time the main feature of the whole country.

Years of crisis. The year 1963 was a critical year in the history of the Italian economy. In 1963, a period of quick economic growth, coupled with price stability and a balance of payments equilibrium, came suddenly to an end. After 1963 a new phase began, during which the Italian economy went through a number of inflation and depression crises, thus becoming more and more similar to other advanced economies. It is important to recall a number of events which took place in the national economy in those years and by which the economy of Southern Italy was greatly influenced. First of all, conflicts between capital and labour became much more violent. Secondly, new and deep conflicts, of a nature previously unknown, divided the main industrial sectors. In this general picture, three main phases can be distinguished. *(a)* The first phase took place between 1964 and 1969. All through those years, deflation was used as the main instrument in order to fight the trade union movement. The 1964-65 depression, the short boom of 1966, the new monetary restrictions of 1969 were the result of an attempt to control the economy avoiding peaks of full employment. Such attempts turned out to be fruitless when, in 1969, in spite of high unemployment, the trade unions, in the process of negotiating new national collective bargains, led a fight of unexpected violence, which is still known as the 'hot autumn' of 1969. *(b)* With 1970 a new phase began which lasted until 1973, during which the attempt was to get a reduction in labour costs by means of what was called restructuring of production (increase in production rhythms inside the factories, intensified mechanisation in big plants, decentralisation of production processes by means of a greater utilisation of small satellite firms as well as of cottage work). *(c)* In 1973, such procedures were integrated by new instruments, the main element being the external devaluation of the lira coupled to an increasing domestic inflation. The two operations were followed by an increased development of exports and by a fall in real wages.

In Southern Italy such events were followed by considerable repercussions. After 1964-65, Southern Italy was no longer the traditional poor country of the past, and was gradually becoming an attractive market as far as consumption goods were concerned. In 1964, the first recession took place, as a consequence of monetary restrictions placed during the summer of 1963. The same recession arrived only somewhat later in the South, where at first the flow of government expenditure had kept its usual pace. Industrial firms located in Northern Italy found it therefore more and more convenient to enter massively into Southern markets, by means of a systematic effort of commercial penetration which destroyed for good the situation of *de facto* protection that Southern markets had enjoyed so far. It was then that local industry in the South started showing symptoms of deep crisis. In the more traditional sectors (the food, clothing, and wood industries) employment started to decline. The situation was made more and more serious by the fact that, at the same time, migration outlets in foreign countries appeared to be almost exhausted. Migrations towards the regions of Northern Italy came to a halt as a result of the industrial crisis. Migration flows towards other countries declined as a consequence of totally different factors. The enforcement of the Common Market Treaty had assured to Italian migrant workers equality of treatment as compared to national workers belonging to host countries. A consequence was that for European industries Italian migrant workers were no longer the cheap labour force of the past, and were rapidly becoming more expensive as compared to workers coming from third countries (Yugoslavia, Turkey, Spain, Greece, Algeria). In 1963, Italian migrations to European countries started declining. In the preceding years, the number of Italian workers who had found employment abroad had been constantly higher than the number of jobs created in Italian manufacturing industries. After 1963, the reverse situation prevailed, and by 1969, when the Italian Government finally made officially known how serious the situation was, migration flows had fallen to negligible levels.

The economic situation of the Southern regions was thus becoming more and more desperate, since the sources of new employment appeared to be in the process of being exhausted one after the other. Agriculture was no longer offering employment, and especially in the mountainous areas the flight from the fields became a flood. Industrial employment was declining because of the crisis in local industry, unable to resist competition from industry located in other regions. Possibilities of finding employment in the North or in other countries, as we have already said, were rapidly vanishing.

Given the situation, the only possible way out was of deliberately creating new employment by means of an adequate increase in industrial investment. In fact, between 1968 and 1973 a new flow of investment took place in Southern industry. Industrial investment in the South touched record levels, and in one year it covered nearly 50 per cent of national industrial investment. Such enormous increase in industrial investment has been the object of various interpretations. A first version connects the increase in investment with innovations introduced in he legislation concerning financial incentives. The increase in financial subsidies and the possibility of extending benefits to big plants within the framework of the so-called 'negotiated programming' (a procedure by which the Government was entitled to negotiate financial subsidies if the firm made a commitment to undertake well-defined industrial investments) would have been at the root of a renewal interest in the Italian South, and would have pushed big national firms to locate there a considerable portion of total investment. A different interpretation brings attention to the fact that the increase in industrial investment took place after the wave of strikes of 1969. Such an increase could therefore be interpreted as the consequence of an attempt on the part of Italian industry to select new locations in regions where unions were weaker. In fact, this interpretation does find support in some historical events. It is true, for instance, that, as a consequence of the 'hot autumn' of 1969, Fiat decided to locate in Southern Italy some ten small plants, each of them specialising in the production of a specific component of the car. The particular case of Fiat, which anyhow achieved its programme only partially and belatedly, cannot explain the whole of the phenomenon. If we analyse the structure of industrial investment in Southern Italy in those years, the dominant presence of Government-owned industry appears clearly. During this phase, Government-owned industries led the process of industrialisation in the South. Once more, therefore, the causes of revival of industrial investment in Southern Italy can be found outside the Southern regions, and precisely in the conflicts which developed among the leading industrial and financial groups. Government-owned firms, in the past only a secondary element in the industrial structure of the country, could by now private industry. Public industries, thanks to political support, could enjoy a privileged access to financial subsidies, and could therefore consider the South as a preferential location. It so happened that, owing to a number of factors, both of an economic and political nature, Government-owned industries gradually shifted their industrial base to the regions of Southern Italy. As a consequence of investments realised between 1968 and 1973, the expansion of public industry produced two different results. At the national level, Government-owned industries became one of the main financial and industrial groups in the country, and certainly the biggest industrial group in Southern Italy. Within Southern Italy, the massive investments and the newly-created employment inside the big plants gave birth to a small but not negligible group of permanently employed workers, something which resulted in becoming an important, even if inadequate, remedy for the problem of structural unemployment. At the same time, the creation of a small but strong group of unionised workers allowed trade unions to overcome the weak position which had been a constant condition of the past.

Inequalities today. The problem of economic development in Southern Italy does not exhaust the list of regional inequalities in Italy. On the contrary, the regional articulation of the Italian economy has undergone a process of change over the last thirty years, so that while in the past it was still correct to mention the existence of two Italies (the group of the industrialised Northern regions being opposed to the agricultural and poor regions of the South), today the structure is much more complex and any description, no matter how approximate, of the Italian economy has to allow for at least three different and widely opposed realities. The three structures can be identified, from a geographical point of view, as follows. The first is located in the so-called industrial triangle (Piedmont, Lombardy, Liguria); the second, in the Central and North-eastern regions (Veneto, Emilia-Romagna, Tuscany); the third in the South.

The first group of regions was the cradle of Italian industry. Here the first industrial revolution of the country took place, and the first Italian capitalism, mainly based on family fortunes, developed. Here one can find a limited number of big firms still owned by private capital. The industrial structure of these regions is based on the model of one big enterprise, surrounded by smaller satellite firms, which are tied to the main firm by extremely complex relationships. One can detect market relationships (the main firm buying products from the smaller ones), financial relationships (the bigger firm, by determining payment conditions, is able to supply or to extract finance from the smaller ones), technological relationships (the big firm supplies designs and new models to the smaller ones). Such a structure finds its most typical example in the area around Turin, where the Fiat factory is the pivotal firm. This same structure draws today new force from the practice of production decentralisation, a practice giving new and wider functions to smaller firms. In the past, this group of regions used to dominate the Italian economic scene. Today, their relative position is definitely less influential, as a consequence of the fact that, while in the past their industrial structure was the only relevant one in the country, today there are at least two other industrial areas deserving equal consideration.

The second group of areas, located in the Central and North-eastern regions, shows a completely different industrial structure. All these regions were dominated, until some thirty years ago, by agriculture: a very rich agriculture in Emilia-Romagna, an extremely poor one in Veneto. Nowadays, the same group of regions has an extensive industrial sector, based on a network of small and medium-sized firms, mostly in the sectors of light industry (construction materials, clothing, wood, leather goods, footwear, electrical appliances). Such small firms, mostly active in the field of consumption goods, do not gravitate around any major firm, and are directly present on the market, both in Italy and abroad. In the same region, a situation of full employment prevails, industrial relations are much more peaceful than elsewhere, the political structure is homogeneous in trend, being dominated by one main political party (the Christian-Democrat party in Veneto, the Communist party in Emilia-Romagna and Tuscany), a situation making for considerable cohesion and widespread consensus.

The third group of regions covers Southern Italy. Southern Italy has derived its industrial model from the industrial triangle, and a number of giant firms are located there. There is however a difference, in that in the North big firms give birth to a number of smaller concerns, while in the South the image of 'cathedrals in the desert' often seems more adequate. As already said, the Southern industrial structure is dominated by Government-owned industry, which means that relationships between industry and political parties are strong. Here lives the typical inefficient parasitic industry, which in Southern Italy shows an even more marked mixture of inefficiency and political connections.

In the past, Italian political life was dominated by heterogeneous political alliances, which were a consequence of economic disparities among regions. The alliance between Northern industry and big landownership in the South, a well-established one at the turn of the century, is well known. Once more to-day, economic inequalities produce agreements between heterogeneous forces, the only difference being that the terms of the agreement have changed. In the North, alongside the old industrial capital, a new structure of small firms has been growing up. In these regions, and mainly in Emilia-Romagna and Tuscany, the dominant party is the Communist party. In a considerable measure, it is due to the dominant role that the party plays in those regions that the Communist party has become a necessary element in political equilibrium at the national level. In the South, in the place of the old landowners, whose influence has disappeared, we have the new presence of Government-owned industry and a new class of public servants, who are the controllers of public funds and constitute the so-called state bourgeoisie.

The economic structure of Southern Italy is strongly unequal. With regard to a limited number of areas, one could speak of a 'productive South'. In those areas, the most modern agricultural firms and the largest industrial plants are located. A second typical situation is represented by a less eye-catching sector that might be described as 'productive but absent', being made up of people who live on gifts coming from migrant workers. Finally, a third situation must be considered, the 'subsidised South', subsidies being supplied by public expenditure, both in the nature of employment-creating expenditure and in the form of old age pensions or of illness subsidies, which are extended by means of highly generous practices.

Economic inequalities produce deep social disruption. In the rich sectors of agriculture and industry, small groups of unionised workers have appeared. But nothing like a corresponding industrial bourgeoisie exists. In fact, big industry in Southern Italy, no matter whether public or private, is the creature of national financial groups, which means that the South gets only industrial plants but no managerial centres. Managers and technicians who work in the big plants of Southern Italy take care only of problems concerning production in the strict sense of the word. The cultural and political life of the regions where industry is located is left in the hands of other social groups. In spite of the fact that Southern Italy is by now a partially industrialised region, bureaucratic circles still control both the labour and the capital markets. Local political parties and bureaucracy still control enrolment in big factories as well as financial flows, a situation in which both the labour and the capital market can only work in a typical 'clientelistic' way. The absence of a true class of capitalistic entrepreneurs, the fragmentation of the working class between a minority of factory workers and a vast number of dispersed workers employed in smaller concerns or self-employed, or not employed at all, bring more and more power to social groups which are not interested in, when they are not hostile to, a process of industrialisation. Such social disruption is the main factor which prevents the Italian South from making further progress on the way of industrialisation and growth.

BIBLIOGRAPHY

V. Castronovo, 'La storia economica', in *Storia d'Italia,* vol. iv (Turin, 1975).

M. Rossi-Doria, *Dieci anni di politica agraria nel Mezzogiorno* (Bari, 1956).

E. Sereni, *Il Mezzogiorno all'opposizione* (Turin, 1948).

G. Barbero, *Riforma agraria italiana* (Rome, 1960).

Svimez, *Il Mezzogiorno nelle ricerche della Svimez* (Rome, 1968).

M. Rossi-Doria, G. Galasso and others, *Nord e Sud nell 'economia e nella societa italiana* (Turin, 1968).

P. Saraceno, *Il meridionalismo dopo la ricostruzione* (Rome, 1974).

C. Daneo, *La politica economica della ricostruzione* (Turin, 1975).

P. Allum, *Potere e societa a Napoli nel dopoguerra* (Turin, 1975).

G. Bonazzi, A. Bagnasco and S. Casillo, *Industria e potere politico in una provincia meridionale* (Turin, 1972).

A. Bagnasco and M. Messori, *Tendenze dell'economia periferica* (Turin, 1975).

A. Bagnasco, *Le tre Italie* (Bologna, 1978).

30 Regional Development in Portugal (1929-1977): an Assessment

Jean Mayer

INTRODUCTION

The present paper will have three sections. First, the evolution of regional[1] disparities in Portugal in the last decades will be presented, under such headings as demographic and economic structures, living conditions and employment creation. Secondly, from an analysis of the plan documents, together with an overview of the decision-making structures, critical observations will be offered with regard to the strengthening throughout the successive planning periods from 1953 onwards of the industrial basis of the two urban metropolises and the well-off coastal regions. Finally, it will be pointed out that a reversal of this trend will only be made possible by the adoption of a radically different strategy, such as the one suggested in the great options of the medium-term plan, 1977-80; being both distributive, attacking poverty and based on the real resources and basic needs and regions, its originality consists in the fact that it combines production and well-being.

I

EVOLUTION OF REGIONAL DISPARITIES

From the demographic point of view, regional disparities disclose a growing tendency, in the last few decades, towards urban concentration and an enormous drain on the active element in agriculture. This has been a constant trend in the country, as a result of the Napoleonic wars, sweeping epidemics, an unyieldingly rigid structure (subjection laws) and the usual inability of the agricultural sector to produce the required foodstuffs. This unequal evolution is shown in Table 30.1, showing population growth characteristics.[2]

It is of course necessary to establish, as Table 30.1 does not refer to out-migration, that the proportion of migrants to the natural increase of the population has constantly been high since the last century: with the exception of the 1941-50 decade, characterised by a war situation and the closing of borders, each decade from 1891 till now has seen a loss of between 25 and 78 per cent of the additional population, and more than 100 per cent in the North inland districts, as shown in Table 30.2.

Out-migration, which represented about 2.8 million exits between 1880 and

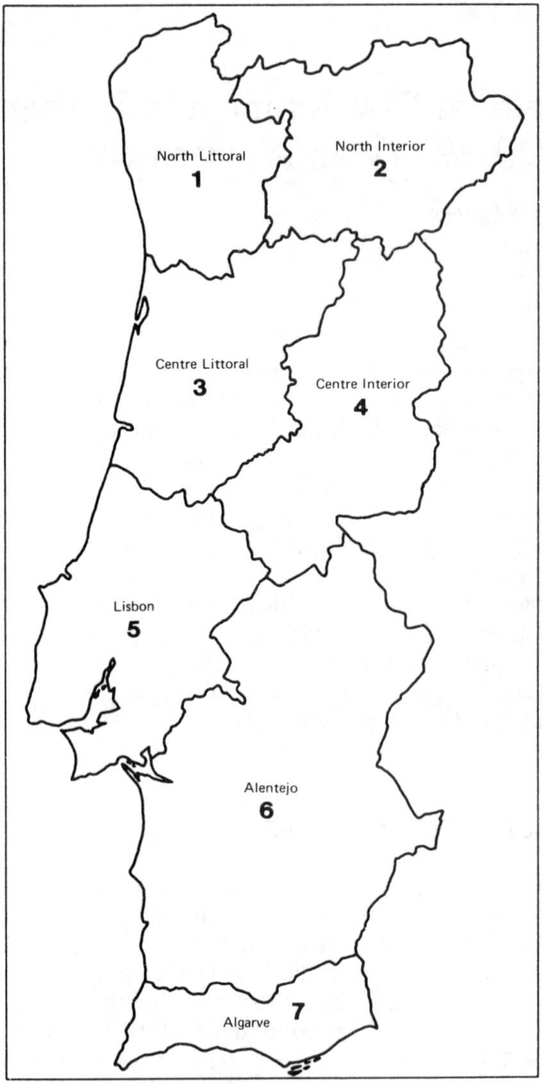

Fig 30.1 Portugal: proposed planned regions

1975 (1.7 million of them between 1950 and 1975), accounted for more than 50 per cent of the increase in the population, which grew from 4.2 million in 1880 to 9 million in 1975: out-migration may well have been a useful safety valve, but the process has undoubtedly contributed to depriving Portugal of her potentially most active strata. This is confirmed by the consider-

TABLE 30.1 Regional population growth

Region	*1864*		*1960*		
	Population	*%*	*Population*	*%*	*+%*
North inland	1,355,700	35.4	1,849,200	22.4	36
Western strip	1,217,800	31.8	2,617,000	31.7	115
Lisbon	291,100	7.6	1,378,700	16.7	374
Porto	218,300	5.7	825,600	10.0	278
South	746,800	19.5	1,585,000	19.2	112
	3,829,700	100.0	8,255,500	100.0	116

able fall in the agricultural population, which lost 35 per cent of its workforce between 1950 and 1970 in the country as a whole, and an even higher proportion in the districts of the interior.

This tendency has resulted in an excessive concentration of the population in the coastal regions 1, 3 and 5, which in total contain 80 per cent of the 9 million inhabitants of the mainland, while the districts of Braga-Oporto-Aveiro-Lisbon-Setubal contain nearly 60 per cent. This growth has engendered two series of effects on employment: on the one hand, in this same littoral fringe, an influx of migrants coming from regions in the interior – to which has recently been added the biggest part (77 per cent) of the flood of returning expatriates (which, in spite of positive factors such as feminine participation and growing urbanisation, has increased in these areas essentially urban social problems relating to housing, transport, health, etc., in addition to unemployment); and on the other hand, in the regions of origin, an undeniable tendency towards the creation of a species of human desert, allied to demographic ageing and weak urbanisation.

Between 1960 and 1975, the four regions of the interior, already sparsely populated, have lost 480,000 inhabitants – mainly active adults – while the three coastal regions have had an increase of 1.1 million units; 490,000 of them in the Lisbon region alone. Between 1970 and 1975, the non-coastal regions lost 58,200 jobs, a fall of 9 per cent. Everything points to the fact that the absence of prospects for employment and revenue in the interior of the country, together (secondarily) with the poor living conditions existing there, are at the root of this process leading to a particularly unbalanced distribution of the population.

It is also noticeable that *production* structures are also excessively concentrated, a process which is furthermore cumulative; thus, the three coastal regions (1, 3 and 5) account for 86 per cent of the GDP (with region 5 alone contributing 48 per cent) and 89 per cent of the industrial production.

With regard to investments, in spite of the absence of data on the spatial distribution of these before 1974, one can nevertheless see a striking convergence in the practice of the private sector and the public sector. The tendency towards geographical concentration in the former sector is illustrated by

TABLE 30.2 Proportion which emigrated in relation to total demographic growth, by district (%)

	1891-1900	*1900-1911*	*1911-1920*	*1920-1930*	*1930-1940*	*1940-1950*	*1950-1960*	*1960-1965*	*1890-1960*
Viana do Castelo	50- 80	50- 80	80-120	20- 50	10- 20	10- 20	20- 50	80-120	41- 50
Braga	20- 50	50- 80	80-120	20- 50	0- 10	0- 10	10- 20	20- 50	21- 30
Vila Real	121	101	269	50- 80	10- 20	0- 10	20- 50	20- 50	51- 60
Braganca	20- 50	50- 80	297	50- 80	20- 50	10- 20	50- 80	50- 80	61- 70
Porto	50- 80	20- 50	50- 80	20- 50	10- 20	0- 10	10- 20	10- 20	31- 40
Aveiro	50- 80	50- 80	80-120	73	20- 50	10- 20	20- 50	20- 50	51- 60
Viseu	80-120	101	120-200	50- 80	29	10- 20	50- 80	20- 50	61- 70
Guarda	20- 50	50- 80	120-200	50- 80	10- 20	10- 20	67	80-120	51- 60
Leiria	20- 50	20- 50	50- 80	20- 50	0- 10	0- 10	20- 50	80-120	21- 30
Coimbra	80-120	50- 80	120-200	50- 80	20- 50	10- 20	20- 50	20- 50	51- 60
Castelo Branco	0- 10	0- 10	20- 50	10- 20	0- 10	0- 10	10- 20	80-120	6- 10
Santarem	0- 10	0- 10	10- 20	10- 20	0- 10	0- 10	10- 20	50- 80	6- 10
Lisbon	20- 50	0- 10	20- 50	10- 20	0- 10	0- 10	0- 10	20- 50	11- 20
Portalegre	0- 10	0- 10	0- 10	0- 10	0- 10	0- 10	0- 10	10- 20	0- 5
Setubal	20- 50	0- 10	20- 50	10- 20	0- 10	0- 10	0- 10	10- 20	0- 5
Evora	0- 10	0- 10	0- 10	0- 10	0- 10	0- 10	0- 10	0- 10	0- 5
Beja	0- 10	0- 10	0- 10	0- 10	0- 10	0- 10	0- 10	20- 50	0- 5
Faro	0- 10	0- 10	20- 50	20- 50	10- 20	10- 20	20- 50	130	11- 20
Portuguese mainland	49	42	78	39	10	8	25	39	32

Without counting illegal emigrants or emigration to the colonies.
SOURCE: From figures given by Joao Evangelista, 'Um Seculo de Populacao Portuguesa (1864-1960)' (1971; The Population of Portugal over a Century).

Table 30.3 on the evolution of industrial production between 1953 and 1970, that in the latter is indirectly demonstrated by the persistence with which the State, after the Revolution, neglected the regions of the interior, which received only 20 per cent of the investments under the programmes for 1977 of the Public Administration (PIAP), and 32 per cent under the programme of the sector of State enterprises (PISEE). It is clearly a question of deeply-rooted administrative practices.

TABLE 30.3 Evolution of industrial production

		1953	*1959*	*1964*	*1970*
Region	1	27.9	27.8	26.4	28.4
	2	2.1	1.5	1.1	0.6
	3	13.3	13.9	14.6	11.9
	4	4.9	3.8	3.0	2.8
	5	46.3	48.0	50.7	53.1
	6	3.8	3.2	2.6	2.2
	7	1.7	1.6	1.6	1.0
	Continent	100.0	100.0	100.0	100.0

Similarly, it is disturbing to note that, sectorially, the PISEE programme for 1977 does not provide for any investment in agriculture, for regions 2, 3 and 7; in industry, either no project is envisaged (regions 4 and 7) or it is a question of projects with no real regional benefits (electrical energy and a railway for transporting iron ore in region 2, the Sines complex in region 6); in construction 98 per cent of the programme is devoted to the metropolitan zones of Lisbon and Oporto; in tourism, 82 per cent of the investments is devoted to the Algarve, thus increasing the extent of its monopoly still further.

Finally, with regard to industrial production, it is striking to note that concentration here has been exclusively on the increase over the last twenty years, as shown by the evolution of production in the manufacturing industries and in construction between 1953 and 1970 – the distribution by districts has been regrouped in accordance with the present-day division by regions.[3]

It will be noted that in the three coastal regions, industrial production has increased from 87.5 per cent in 1953 to 93 per cent in 1970. In 1964, Lisbon and Oporto alone concentrated 55 per cent of the industrial enterprises having more than 100 wage-earners.

Of the 610 industrial enterprises created between 1970 and 1974, 532 (87 per cent) were placed in the already industrialised districts along the coast. This phenomenon is even more striking if one compares the creation of enterprises having more than twenty wage-earners: during the same period, no single unit of that size was placed in the districts of the interior, while the coast, which already had a 91.4 per cent concentration, attracted 52 new enterprises. In addition, in the already developed regions, the phenomenon of concentration has sometimes had a double effect, the peripheral districts experiencing in the food industries a reduction in the number of their establishments, in favour of Oporto and Coimbra, which during the same period increased the number of their enterprises having more than 20 wage-earners.

The agricultural sector also reveals considerable structural disparities, which show an insufficient use of arable land. The great inequality in land distribution is reflected in two ways: on one hand, 2 million hectares relate to fragmented smallholdings of less than 20 hectares each, which maintain 95 per cent of the total rural population; whilst, at the other extreme, 3 million hectares, corresponding to estates of more than 20 hectares each, are controlled by 5 per cent of the same group. Rather than a West-East cleavage, the agricultural census figures give a fairly clear image of a North-South division, with hundreds of thousands of small properties to the north of the River Tagus and large estates which have grown up in the south of the country, many of them used solely as hunting land and for extensive exploitation.

These structural desequilibria are also reflected in the very large regional variations in *productivity*. For the time being, the contribution to GDP per person employed is twice as high (76 contos) in region 5 as in regions 2, 4, 6 and 7 respectively, regions 1 and 3 reaching, as expected, levels in between. At the level of sectors, the comparisons are even more striking; if one ignores the aberrant case of electricity (which differs in accordance with whether thermal or hydro-electric power-stations are in question), and also the case of mines (where the added value differs considerably according to the product), it will be seen that the manufacturing industries in region 5 present figures (123 contos) twice as high as those in regions 1, 3 and 4, and three times as high as those in regions 6 and 7; even agriculture is more productive there, having a figure which exceeds the Alentejo, and is nearly double the two supposedly agricultural regions, the North Interior and the Algarve. On the whole, it appears that variations in productivity by region and sector have not been significantly reduced in the last 25 years; in any case, except for the chemical industries, the productivity of each branch of the Portuguese industrial sector has been kept at a lower level (sometimes by half), than that registered in Greece and Spain. The regional analysis of *living conditions* makes it possible to demonstrate even more clearly the disparities in satisfaction of basic needs.

It is true that the housing sector shows generalised shortcomings for the whole country: overcrowding in exiguous or inappropriate dwellings or, in nearly every second home, the absence of at least one of the four elements of comfort considered as the minimum – drinking water, electricity and sanitary facilities (bath and WC). Quantitatively, the serious backwardness in the construction of housing for private use is equally apparent in all the regions, especially in Lisbon where this is twice as serious in relation to the resident population. Similarly, backwardness in *education* is equally common in nearly every part of the country: too low a rate of compulsory education and insufficient secondary education (except in Lisbon), lack of classrooms, without mentioning here the concentration of secondary, technical and higher education in Lisbon and Oporto, which allows the assumption that the displacement of students outside their region is often only the prelude to their non-return as adults.

On the other hand, when the question of *health* is considered, the regional differences become more pronounced, the ratios doctors and nurses/population or hospital beds/population ranging from one to two or even four as between the metropolitan areas of Lisbon, Coimbra and Oporto and the rest of the country – a situation which evidently explains the differences noted between the rates of non-assisted births and between those referring to infant mortality.

Interesting data which confirm the regional disparities already noted have just been provided by an unpublished study on the importance of the banking, health and educational services. They show that, for the values obtained, Lisbon, Oporto and Coimbra have nearly twice as many services of this type as the 25 urban centres coming after them.

Finally, under the heading of *accessibility*, it has been found that the density of the road network is from two to three times higher in the coastal regions than in the interior, and that 80 per cent of the railway infrastructure is concentrated on the Braga-Setubal axis. With regard to the time and distance involved in benefiting from the essential goods and services, the problems of congestion in the urban centres seem to be less crucial than the difficulties of intra-regional mobility.

A ranking of living conditions in relation to the degree of satisfaction with regard to housing, health, education and mass communications shows that there exists very great homogeneity within each region between the various indicators (three regions out of six have the same four indices, and in the three others the difference does not exceed unity); and on the other hand, rather than finding once again dissymmetry between East and West, one observes generally speaking an improvement in living conditions as one proceeds from North to South (the North littoral is almost as badly provided for as the North Interior, the median position of the Centre Interior is similar to that of the Alentejo, and the Algarve shares the top rank with Lisbon). A similar observation can also be made with regard to non-material needs where the differences between cultural and participation levels do not follow the usual regional pattern. A first conclusion is therefore self-evident: the concentration of growth and employment in the littoral fringe has not had a direct effect on the levels of life, which are practically the same as in the geographically-corresponding interior zones. This demonstrates the weak spatial diffusion of the fruits of the recorded growth.

II

INADEQUACY OF THE SYSTEMS OF REGIONAL PLANNING IN USE

This is the place to ask ourselves how this imperfect division of the national space came about. In order to do this, it is necessary to recall how the attempts at regionalisation in Portugal developed, and to point out the gaps in their fundamental orientations, in order to bring out how such efforts to achieve socio-economic re-balance were vitiated from the start, as is revealed by the aggravation in disequilibria of all kinds that existed at the very moment when attempts were being made to attack them by global planning.

After the serious economic crisis in 1929-31 that helped to shape the theoretical justification for government intervention in economic activities, the gradual extension of programming methods to various sectors of national life began with the 'Port Plan' of 1929 calling for an important investment in works on ports over a three-year period, and the law of Economic Reconstruction of 1935, which organised the main programmes and projects in the public sector over the next 15 years. However, the projects were exclusively concerned with infrastructure, and the planning was limited to working out a set of sectorial programmes, subjected to financial coordination; moreover, no regional objectives nor spatial project allocations were pursued.

It is only in the fifties that a growing process of global planning took place, starting with the First Development Plan for the period 1953 to 1958, which though a partial plan made provision for strategic priority investments; nevertheless the regional implications of these were ignored, as well as the contribution of the existing natural resources to development. In its turn, the Second Development Plan 1959-1964 does not concern itself with regional disparities but, to the extent that it aims at attracting the private sector into new industrial projects, within the context of an emerging EEC as a competitor, it pays some attention to decentralising industrial employment. As a matter of fact, however, 50 per cent of the investment, both public and private, was still confined to the Lisbon and Setubal areas.

While the first idea of regional development in order to retain in place the rural populations goes back to the Second Plan of 1958, the idea of administrative decentralisation began in 1962, the year in which the Corporative Chamber, called upon to pronounce on a government project for a decree-law proposing the creation of an Office for regional economic planning, suggested the establishment in each of the regions of organs for consultation and coordination, supported by technical planning departments. This idea, which was not implemented, was taken up again during the preparatory work for the Intermediate Development Plan.

This latter plan, however, does no more than pay lip-service to regional development, since it gives overall priority to growth and admits that such a strategy could not have much effect on the correction of existing desequilibria.

The practical administrative necessities of the various technical departments, confronted in Lisbon with the difficulties of regional development, meanwhile led the Ministry of Economy to create district technical commissions, and the Ministry of Public Works to undertake work of great importance for regional development, and other ministries to get their feet more on the ground. The government felt the need to coordinate these various initiatives and in 1966 created, within the technical secretariat of the Presidency of the Council, a division of regional planning. At the same time, provision was made for the establishment in the capitals of the four regions (Oporto, Coimbra, Lisbon and Evora) of a consultative regional commission, representative of the public sectors and private interests, whose task was to support the preparation of regional plans and programmes. However, in reality, no important devolution of executive responsibilities took place for the benefit of the regions concerned and the mechanisms for consultation provided were of little use except to authorise the steps taken by the technical departments of the capital, in most cases to the detriment of the regions, so much so that it can be said that regional development came to nothing for want of a propitious framework.

The disclosure of the regional desequilibria, and of the planning of actions intended to correct these, was in fact basically due to the preparation of the Third Development Plan 1968-1973, which for the first time included specific treatment of regional planning. Whilst the gradual elimination of defined disparities is retained as one of the three fundamental planning priorities, development still depends on a sustained increase in growth rate. This industrialisation strategy, therefore, is concentrated in the few points of the national territory which possess important comparative advantages from the point of view of infrastructures. This theme, linked to that of spatial physical planning was taken up again and amplified by the Fourth Development Plan 1974-1979, prepared before the Revolution of 25 April 1974.

Generally speaking, on examining the contribution made by fifteen years of reflection on the regional problems of Portugal, one cannot fail to be struck by the contrast between the accuracy of the analyses of the existing shortcomings and the contradictory nature of the means proposed for remedying them.

Thus, by 1967 the following had been correctly pointed out:

the excessive depopulation of the district of the interior and the Southern littoral, to the detriment of the production and agricultural employment in these regions;

the cumulative nature of the industrialisation and urbanisation process in the metropolitan zones of Lisbon and Oporto, likely to increase the existing regional desequilibria;

the uneven distribution of social facilities, relegating the districts of the interior and the South to unfavourable levels of infrastructure with regard to housing, energy, health, education, transport, etc.

At that time, the division of the national territory into four planning regions (North, Centre, Lisbon, South) was based on several correct considerations: (*a*) the potentialities of the urban centres; (*b*) the need to have a minimum demographic size; (*c*) the urgent need to compensate for the excessive attraction of Lisbon and Oporto; (*d*) the inter-regional economic complementarity. For each of the four regions thus already defined in 1967, the plan put forward some concepts which have not since been repudiated: the use of natural resources, the diversification of the pattern of economic activities, the creation of industrial poles, the reinforcement of the urban hierarchy, the decentralisation of enterprises and administrations, the radical improvement of the social infrastructure.

This same Third Plan 1968-1973 seems, on the other hand, to have been inspired by an ultra-liberalism which was little conscious of the opposition to the carrying out of such intentions, when it drew up the catalogue of regional policy measures. For example, it presents as spontaneous the mechanisms for the diffusion of the fruits of growth 'trickling down' from the traditional centres of polarisation, and for the preferential location by the private sector of productive activities in new urban foci which might compete with the above-mentioned centres. Similarly, the reinforcement of the social infrastructures is envisaged without questioning the very principle of the emigration of the rural population, which is presented as a general trend.

These same contradictions are accentuated in the Fourth Plan 1973-1979. Recognising the enlargement of the regional desequilibria, this plan attributes responsibility for it to the evolution of techniques and to the mobility of people, both due to industrial growth and the development of transport and communications, without enquiring into the rigidity of modes of production, the immobilisation of capital, the resistance of the private sector and of the State sector itself. Beginning by attributing the depopulation of rural zones to the lack of employment, the same document relies on these migrations to stimulate the modernisation of the economy and society, especially in order to 'help agriculture to develop and to decrease the demographic pressure'. Similarly, the pursuit of greater regional specialisation, and the intensification of sentiments of interdependence born within each region according to their potentialities, should according to the authors of the plan proceed via the participation at different levels of the social organisation; something which it is known has not begun to happen. Furthermore, the emergence in the area of signs of a complex of basic industries is considered to be 'a first great option with regard to spatial physical planning' through the definite impact which this is supposed to have on the amount of population and the organisation of the activities in this region; whereas it should have been clear even at that time that industries so highly integrated, creating little or no direct or indirect employment, hardly bring to or borrow anything at all from their immediate environment.

Still more worthy of criticism would appear to be the central theses of the regional planners of 1973, for whom the development of the different regions should be 'compatible with the requirements of the growth-rhythm of the national economy', something which explicitly leads to the idea that the measures to be taken should not 'hamper the expansion of the urbano-industrial areas of Lisbon and Oporto or compromise their later development', while the actions to be taken in favour of the other regions finally appear only as attenuations of the growth applications from which the metropoles are suffering. While purporting to increase the satisfaction of the basic social needs – this expression occurs for the first time – the same frankness is expressed by the leitmotif that the creation of employment serves to modernise agriculture and to develop industry and services, which should encourage internal migrations. With regard to areas not able potentially to contribute to the global growth, it is equally baldly stated that their inhabitants will be granted 'as a temporary and provisional solution' the necessary social facilities to reach a decent level of life.

One is therefore faced with an apparent regionalisation, which has been characterised as

> an industrialisation strategy based on highly capital-intensive, export-oriented branches, using a low-paid, submissive manpower; . . . the development model which is followed aims at strengthening the existing dual society, out of which a modern sector emerges, isolated from the economic spaces of the countries and from an overall underdevelopment context. Regional disparities are therefore not generated by underdevelopment but are the very reflection of this dual society.[4]

This dualism is dramatically shown in the domination, which has been maintained during decades of an authoritarian regime, of an urban class owning the power in industry, agriculture, bank, trade, information and decision-making, without any possible opposition from parties or unions. This group, which owned half of the income and the land and concentrated in only 70 industrial enterprises the manpower of more than 1000 wage-earners, undoubtedly contributed to a rapid industrial expansion – industrial growth rate increased by 11.6 per cent per annum in the period 1960-70, and by 10 per cent between 1970 and 1974. However, this expansion was not accompanied by a substantial income redistribution, nor by commensurate job-creation.

III

NEW PROSPECTS OF A REAL REGIONAL DEVELOPMENT

The medium-term plan for the period 1977-80 was based on a different approach – the satisfaction of basic needs – which opens up new avenues for the regional development of Portugal, inasmuch as it is based on the development of existing potentialities, whether it is a question of the human, natural or financial resources of the different regions or of a greater utilisation of the production capacities already installed.

The development of human resources stems from the necessity to have available, to prepare and to renew the human capital in order to take advantage of regional potentialities. In the regions of the interior of Portugal, where there has taken place in the last fifteen years a creaming-off of the most dynamic layer of the active population, the execution even of a plan based on the essential needs of the whole population – including the part located along the coast – must include a reduction of unemployment in the above-mentioned zones of the interior, but also retention, and even attraction, of active personnel necessary for the realisation of the national objectives of production, in agriculture as well as in industry. One can see an element of proof in the undoubtedly positive contribution of the returning expatriates ('retornados') to the economy of the North and North-east, where the concrete conditions for their integration have been achieved – apparently much more successfully than in the metropolitan zones of Lisbon and Oporto, where the mechanisms of social marginalisation have been at work.

Furthermore, it is necessary to consider the demographic structure of the regions in each of their aspects, and in particular to measure the dynamism stemming from a high and growing rate of feminine participation, as well as the rate of urbanisation, the degree of skill of the workers, and their propensity to associate together (in cooperatives, trade unions and other forms of community life) in order to disclose correctly the specifically human levels of regional development.

The development of the *natural resources* of the regions can obviously be seen to be even more important when one puts forward as a principle the satisfaction of basic needs. A rapid inventory of the regional potentialities discloses important trump cards for the development of hitherto neglected regions.

The existence of agricultural and mining resources in the neglected regions (2, 4, 6 and 7) has three important consequences: (*a*) these resources being insufficiently utilised, a complementary effort by the public sector should be sufficient to intensify a process which has usually already been started; (*b*) since these resources are relatively well distributed between each of the regions, none of them has in fact a smaller chance of development than any other, which reinforces the conviction that the existing desequilibria stem from the failure of the State to introduce a truly distributive regional policy; (*c*) finally, since these resources are neither strongly concentrated, nor widely dispersed within the interior of each region, their intensive exploitation within a series of locations linked together would permit the reinforcement, or the introduction, of an urban network which, in addition, would provide more continuity between the towns and the countryside. (As a matter of fact, the urban hierarchy appears in Portugal very unbalanced, with the absence of towns of the second rank – except Oporto – able to function as regional capitals, and the absence of district capitals having a sufficient dimension.)

Finally the idea of developing the *financial resources* of the regions is based on the need to better redistribute the fiscal receipts concentrated in the hands of the central power, as well as on the existence of a regional savings system, the remittances of migrants being three times higher in Lisbon, the North and North-east than elsewhere.[5] In other words, potentially, financial resources could be mobilised, provided that a centralising financial and fiscal policy did not divert them.

The double verification of a concentration of growth in the coastal regions and of under-utilisation of the potentialities of the interior zones leads therefore to a very definite recommendation to launch new economic activities in the less-developed regions. To begin with, these could profit from the existence of the regions' own resources, in exploiting which they are at an advantage compared with the rest of the country.

We have calculated the various regional economic bases from the data provided by the 1960 and 1970 censuses. The most striking points to be learned from these would appear to be the following:

(*a*) The regions of Lisbon and Oporto (1 and 5) provide an economic base which is both important and diversified, linked to both productive and non-productive activities, by contrast with the regions of the interior and the South (2, 4, 6 and 7) where the base, although it does indeed exist, seems small and should be amplified.

(*b*) The specialisations of the coastal regions (1, 3 and 5) mostly relate to the use of mobile resources, while those of the other regions mostly relate to the exploitation of immobile resources.

(*c*) The multipliers of employment are higher in the regions of the interior (average 1.44) than in the coastal regions (average 1.28).

(*d*) Specialisations, and also multipliers, evolve only slowly throughout the decade and for each of the eighteen districts – a successful regionalisation can therefore only be voluntary.

(*e*) However, over a long period, it is the specialisations based on the immobile resources – whether these relate to developed or retarded regions – which show the clearest amount of development, while those based on mobile resources are either stagnant or in decline.

(*f*) The 'population-serving ratios' confirm, if it is necessary to do so, the structural disequilibrium between the coastal and the interior with regard to supporting activities – the difference varying from one to two (0.17 employment of the residential type per inhabitant in the North interior, against 0.32 in Lisbon).

In view of the fact that, in the actual state of the structure of inter-regional exchanges, the necessary inputs to the regions of the interior must, as to a third, still come from Lisbon,[6] it must realistically be admitted that regional specialisation is insufficient, if it is not accompanied by inter- and intra-regional diversification and integration. On the one hand, rather than limiting themselves to making primary non-manufactured products, regional activities should tend towards the creation of a flow of intermediate and final goods, stimulated by the internal and external demand of the region, and necessarily leading to an output of industrialisation, taking over from agriculture, for exports and mining. In this respect, the sectors most able to create employment and to satisfy the basic needs – agriculture and construction – are also the ones which are best placed (in the proper sense of that term) for calling upon a local light-industrial infrastructure, with industries connected with food, wood, furniture, non-metallic ore, etc. On the other hand, the economic integration necessary for the structuring of the country has the best chance of coming to fruition when the industrialisation is oriented towards national needs: in this sense, an initial advantage for the State may consist in the fact that the road transport and railway network for merchandise should not, in spite of its insufficiency, be altered in its actual configuration, as would be the case if it were a question of corridors leading directly to the ports from which are despatched the raw materials intended for abroad. Moreover, integration into EEC, following a sharp decline in seaborne trade with Africa, would bring as an advantage a development of the Portuguese railway system towards the Spanish part of the peninsula.

It seemed to us that it would be interesting to provide a concrete example, taken from the application of criteria for the localisation of global and sectorial objectives for the creation of employment, derived from the strategy of basic needs.[7] An attempt has thus been made to distribute spatially between regions, by sector, branch or product, the total of 350,000 new work posts envisaged at a given moment in our planning exercise, without any later modification in the size of this objective altering the lessons to be learnt from it.

Whatever the limitations of this method, and the concrete difficulties in applying it, it remains true that the attempt at the regionalisation of employment presented here offers an indication – in our view one of a fundamental character – with regard to the necessity for, and the possibility of, reducing the asymmetries in the growth of employment: it is essential, for example, to observe that the regions of the interior have attributed to them, under the least of our hypotheses, 135,000 new jobs for the period 1977-80, viz. 42 per cent of the total, while between 1970 and 1975 they have in fact lost nearly 60,000: it is thus the reversal of a trend which should be taking place.

CONCLUSIONS

In the terms of this analysis, the model for regional planning seems to stand out clearly. On the one hand, fifteen years of apparent regionalisation, characterised by the absence of transfers of investments and of responsibilities to the peripheral zones and the impoverishment of the countryside, solely for the benefit of industrial growth in an urban environment without any true sharing or distribution, have led to a picture of a country in deep disequilibrium, tending towards making a desert of the interior. On the other hand, by means of applying a strategy of basic needs, the possibility emerges of developing the natural and human resources of parts of the national whole which have so far been neglected, and in the light of the pressure of the international crises, of leading Portugal towards a better restructuring of its internal development.

In order to apply this strategy there is but one way, which democratisation of economic and social life since 25 April 1974 has caused to be inscribed in the Constitution: to enable the regions to participate in their own destiny by giving them the necessary means for decision and participation. Without doubt this is one of the very last chances to put a brake on the dramatically increasing marginalisation of the most neglected regions and social groups.

NOTES

1 The new Portuguese Constitution recognises planning regions, to be defined by law (art. 95). A draft law in this sense is still under discussion in the Assembly of the Republic on the basis of work undertaken by the Ministry of Plan and of Economic Coordination, which has put forward the seven regions appearing in the map at the beginning of the chapter. While approval of this proposal is awaited, preparatory work on the main options of the 1977-1980 Plan, has been based on the district units – a division maintained up to the institution of the regions (Constitution, art. 263) – regrouped for the purpose of an example, according to the scheme of the proposed seven regions. It should be noted that a different delimitation, into five regions, has been proposed by the Ministry of Internal Affairs, in order to meet another constitutional requirement, namely the creation of administrative regions, the territory of which should correspond to the territory for the application of the regional plans (art. 256, 1º and 2º). In our research, the division of the country into seven regions will therefore be used.

2 David Baytelman, *The Agricultural Sector in Portugal,* excerpt from *Planning for Employment and Basic Needs in Portugal* (forthcoming, ILO, Geneva).

3 *IV Plano de Fomento,* p. 60, as regards 1953, 1959 and 1964, *Relatorio de Politica Regional,* Plano *1977-1980*, Lisbon 1977, p. 11 as regards 1970.

4 *Documento de Trabalho preliminar com vista a um esquema de ordenamento do territorio* (Centro de Estudos de Planeamento Lisbon, July 1977) p. 13.

5 Vasco A. Corregedor da Fonseca, *A Poupanca ao nivel regional* (Banco de Fomento nacional, Lisbon, 1975) pp. 42-4.

6 A. Simoes Lopes, *Desenvolvimento regional em Portugal,* Conferencia sobre economia portuguesa, October 1976, p. 601, Gulbenkian ed. (Lisbon).

7 Thus to the base activities have been applied location criteria combining location quotients, potentialities not used or under-used, and industrial capacity already installed. On the other hand the multipliers of employment of the previous period have not been applied to the derived residential activities: for transport, we have distributed the employment according to the relative weight of the sector, retaining as a hypothesis an improvement in inter- and intra-regional accessibility; for construction, distribution has been made in proportion to the housing deficits, with adjustment in regions 1 and 5 to take into account the existing capacity of the enterprises and their possibility of going outside the limits of the regional market; finally, the estimation of the services sector has taken into account reasonable 'tertialisation' objectives, both as concerns support for base activities and with a view to catching up with the delays in creating social facilities (health, education, administration).

Part 2d The Third World

31 Regional Inequalities in Brazil during the Second Half of the Nineteenth Century

Mircea Buescu

1. There seems to be no doubt that there are economic inequalities which are caused by the development process itself. Francois Perroux has said that 'growth is disequilibrium'.[1] At the national level, disparity in development is evidenced by the presence of poles of growth that stand apart from backward regions and give rise to actual dualism within the economy,[2] as Jacques Lambert has shown in the case of Brazil.[3] The cumulative mechanism of development – Gunnar Myrdal's 'circular causality'[4] – merely sharpens such disparities. These disparities are not only inevitable: certain economists, such as Alberto Hirschman, regard them as a necessary feature of sound economic development strategy.[5]

Do these inequalities arise only in the decisive stage of economic development, during and after take-off? Or can they be detected in preceding periods? The purpose of this paper is to identify regional income disparities in Brazil in the second half of the nineteenth century, thus well before the take-off, and to try to explain their causes.

2. The first step is to find evidence for the existence of income inequalities. This is mainly a question of methodology in view of the scarcity of statistical information for the period. So far economists have been content to use pure conjecture. Thus, Celso Furtado compares an arbitrary rate of growth of regional income with the population rate in order to estimate the rate of growth of per capita income. For instance, he says: '*We assume* [my italics] that the absolute growth of income in the Northeast was equal to half the population growth', and so on.[6]

What are the data that could be used? For the second half of the nineteenth century, the 1872, 1890 and 1900 population censuses provide data which could be used, but population growth alone does not tell us anything about the level of economic development.[7] The censuses include also the distribution of occupations by region, but comparison leads only to contradictory conclusions, as I have found out for myself. All that can be said is that population structure does not seem to have changed much between 1872 and 1900, a sign that growth was still slow. Equally useless for the purpose of this study are the data showing the regional distribution of illiterates and of urban growth. It has already been pointed out that the latter is not always a sign of economic development.[8] Certain social indicators seem to be more significant, but are far too vague: the number of doctors, or of dwellings with several floors, or of teachers. Coastal shipping and ocean shipping statistics are more significant as indicators. The latter show strong concentration in the large traditional ports of Salvador (Bahia), Recife (Pernambuco) and, most of all, Rio de Janeiro. Railway concentration follows a slightly different pattern: in 1889, the provinces of Rio de Janeiro, Sao Paulo and Minas Gerais – these were the coffee-growing areas – had 3169 kilometres of railroad or 65 per cent of the total, while the remainder of the country had 1699 kilometres or 35 per cent. A sampling of tax revenues in different typical regions shows the same concentration covering the provinces of Rio de Janeiro, Bahia and Pernambuco, but any conclusions from this are of doubtful value. One may already notice between 1850 and 1900 the growth of Sao Paulo as a major coffee centre, to later become the major centre of industry, yet in 1900 Sao Paulo still lags far behind Rio de Janeiro, and even Bahia, in terms of tax revenue. This suggests that the taxation system was linked rather to centres of consumption than to centres of production.

I have therefore thought it necessary to attempt a more precise, but inevitably less reliable quantification. The method has been described in a previous paper.[9] It is based only on the more reliable of the available data: population, exports and imports, and national income estimated using exports and an export factor extrapolated for the period, as shown elsewhere.[10]

For any year, one can say that:

$$R = E + A,$$

where R is the national income, E the portion of income contributed by exports, and A the portion contributed by the non-exporting or autonomous sector, and that:

$$R = x.E,$$

where x is the extrapolated export factor. It should be pointed out that, for the purposes of this paper, any error in the value of x is of no significance whatever, since we are concerned with the distribution of R and not with its absolute value. For a given region, its income r shall be given by:

$$r = e.E + k.A,$$

where e is the percentage share of the region in total exports and k is the factor for the share of the income generated by the autonomous sector. This factor is basically proportional to the regional population (h), but the proportion is weighted with the factor for the region's share in total imports (factor i), since propensity to import implies higher income. Thus:

$$k = h.i,$$

where k is the region's percentage share in $(h.i)$ of the country. Combining all these formulas, we obtain:

$$r = e.E + (h.i.)\,A.$$

To apply this method, I have chosen the 1872 and 1900 census years, the data for which are used to determine the h factor, as the limiting dates. R was obtained by assuming an export factor of 0.2, which seems to be fairly consistent. For E and e, statistical data which are directly available for the budget year of 1872/1873 were used. Lastly, the i factor was determined using import statistics. After obtaining the income for each region in this way, the same method was applied using this income to estimate total and per capita revenue for each Province (or State during the Republic). The results are shown in Table 31.1.

3. Analysis of the figures is very instructive. From the statistical angle, marked economic inequalities can be observed from 1872 onwards. Concentration occurs in the East region, whose per capita income is nearly three times that of the North-east region and nearly four times that of the South and the North regions. Comparison of the Provinces discloses the marked superiority of Rio de Janeiro which includes the capital of the Empire of Brazil and also the export and import trade of the Province of Minas Gerais, which has no other outlet to the sea. However, the income of Pernambuco is significantly high, while both Rio Grande do Sul and Bahia rank ahead of Sao Paulo. The ratio of Rio de Janeiro to Piaui is 85:1, a spread that will persist for very many years.

In terms of growth, one notes that the country experienced a very moderate rate of growth from 1872 and 1900: total income increased at an annual rate of 2.8 per cent, while per capita income, weighed down by a substantial expansion in the population, rose only 0.7 per cent. Furthermore, this growth was uneven. If we split the country into two blocs, one comprising the provinces from Espirito Santo and Minas Gerais to the south (Zone I) and the other the remainder of the country (Zone II), we find that the ratio between per capita incomes increased from 3.1:1 in 1872 to 3.5:1 in 1900. Furthermore, this ratio between Rio de Janeiro and a backward State as, for instance, Sergipe, was 176:1.

But this is not all. Both regions and States in some cases grew at rates lower than population growth. Although per capita income for the East region increased only 4.1 per cent during the period, for the North-east it declined 23.3 per cent. On the other hand, the South advanced 219.4 per cent, and the North 275.8 per cent. Among the States, Rio de Janeiro still ranked first, although its per capita income increased only 3.5 per cent, followed closely by Sao Paulo whose per capita income rose 423.3 per cent. The differences have increased, for some States which formerly ranked high have dropped back: Bahia by 2.5 per cent, Pernambuco by 18.2 per cent, and Rio Grande do Sul by 31.9 per cent.

TABLE 31.1 Regional total income and per capita income in Brazil, 1872 and 1900

	Total (£ millions)		*Per capita (£)*	
	1872	*1900*	*1872*	*1900*
North Amazons and Para	1.1	8.6	3.3	12.4
North-east	13.3	14.3	4.3	3.3
Maranhao	0.8	0.6	2.4	1.3
Piaui	0.0	0.1	0.2	0.3
Ceara	1.6	0.7	2.2	0.8
Rio Grande do Norte	0.1	0.1	0.4	0.2
Paraiba	0.2	0.3	0.5	0.5
Pernambuco	10.2	11.6	12.1	9.9
Alagoas	0.4	0.9	1.0	1.4
East	58.2	102.4	12.3	12.8
Sergipe	0.2	0.0	0.9	0.1
Bahia	5.5	8.2	4.0	3.9
Espirito Santo	0.0	0.5	0.0	2.2
Rio de Janeiro	52.5	93.7	17.0	17.6
South	4.8	40.3	3.1	9.9
Sao Paulo	2.5	35.7	3.0	15.7
Parana	0.2	0.7	1.9	1.9
Santa Catarina	0.1	0.2	0.3	0.7
Rio Grande do Sul	2.0	3.7	4.7	3.2
Centre West (Mato Grosso and Goias)	0.1	0.4	0.5	1.1
Brazil	77.5	166.0	7.8	9.5

4. Two questions suggest themselves: (*a*) why did these inequalities exist in 1872; and (*b*) why can new inequalities be observed in 1900?

To find the answer to the first question one must go back into the past, since regional disequilibrium has a long history. Regional inequalities make their appearance during the colonial period as a consequence of a mercantilistic policy under which production efforts were concentrated on those products that had the readiest export market – the Brazilian economy's well-known 'cycles' which established themselves within limited regions. In fact, Frederic Mauro characterised these cycles as 'a spontaneous policy of unbalanced development'.[11] Since exports were the main source of income, they were the cause of concentration. At the beginning of the seventeenth century, 90 per cent of the sugar exports came from the North-east region. Since sugar accounted for nearly 90 per cent of total exports and since exports produced about 80 per cent of the monetary income, this region (18 per cent of the total inhabited land area) concentrated about 65 per cent of the country's monetary income.[12] By the middle of the eighteenth century, the gold cycle had shifted the economic centre of gravity southward, but concentration remained strong in the economically engaged region from Pernambuco to Minas Gerais.

It is likely that, towards the end of the eighteenth century and the beginning of the nineteenth, this concentration had become weaker as a result of the decline of the gold cycle and the diversification of economic activity despite the rise of a stronger concentration in Rio de Janeiro caused by the growth of secondary and especially tertiary activities around the nation's new capital. From a territorial standpoint, concentration is restricted to the coast from Pernambuco to Rio de Janeiro. If we again take exports as the major indicator of income, we shall find that they are highly concentrated: in 1800, the ports of Rio de Janeiro, Bahia and Pernambuco accounted for 77.8 per cent of the country's total exports in value. There is little information concerning regional population, economic occupation of the land or urban growth, but imports provide a fairly reliable indicator of expenditure at a time when demand was mainly directed overseas. The three ports mentioned above accounted for 86.1 per cent of the total value of imports at the beginning of the nineteenth century. They imported 94.4 per cent of the salted salmon, 86.6 per cent of the salt, 80.1 per cent of the wine, and 57.9 per cent of the olive oil. However, one must keep in mind the possibility that these ports may have served far larger areas.

On the other hand, there was no true circular movement capable of further increasing regional inequalities. This was due, in the first place, to the low level of per capita income and its slow growth. After 300 years under the colonialist-mercantilist model, Brazil's domestic per capita income had dropped to its lowest level, about £3.00, one seventh of Great Britain's per capita income in 1800. In addition, because of the economy's overseas orientation – its 'external polarisation'[13] – there were no reflexes inland. The 'circular causality' could not be triggered without available factors of production, entrepreneurial spirit, technological level, infrastructure and suitable political conditions.

A new stage of growth begins in 1808. During the period from the arrival of the Portuguese Court in Brazil till the middle of the nineteenth century, which I have called the 'watershed period', despite the moderate growth, certain major events occurred: independence, the abolition of the slave trade (about 1850), the inception of protectionism (the 1844 Alves Branco tariff), and particularly the expansion of coffee exports. During the 1830s, the downward secular trend of exports was reversed thanks to coffee: by 1840, this product already accounted for 43 per cent of the value of exports. Exports per capita which had declined to £0.6 in 1830, rose to £0.9 in 1840 and had reached £1.8 by 1900.[14]

5. Returning to the situation in 1872, it is difficult not to relate it to the export position, since exports represented the dynamic sector of the economy. In 1872 we have a continuation of past situations with the addition of a decisive element, coffee, which implied a shift of the economic centre of gravity towards the coffee-growing area. Concentration, however, was not

as yet very high. The region that I have labelled Zone II provided only 35.3 per cent of total export revenues. Rio de Janeiro, the major coffee exporter, alone accounted for 47.6 per cent of these revenues, but other provinces such as Pernambuco, Bahia and Rio Grande do Sul still maintained a favourable position. Although very moderate, the multiplier effect of exports, and urban concentration determined by political reasons or merely surviving from the past, are reflected by a high import coefficient. Pernambuco and Bahia account for 26.7 per cent of total imports, while Sao Paulo accounts for only 2.4 per cent. Rio de Janeiro's share is 54.1 per cent. The export multiplier, not only for coffee, also had an effect on the incipient industrial sector. According to Stanley Stein,[15] in 1866 there were six textile factories in Zone II as compared with three in Zone I. In 1875, 46.7 per cent of the country's textile factories were located in Zone II, but this percentage was down to 31.3 per cent in 1885. Roberto Simonsen[16] provides similar information.

6. The second question is more important: why didn't the initial disparities initiate a genuine process of 'circular causality' which would have perpetuated and strengthened concentration while preventing its southward shift? Nathaniel Leff[17] states the question differently: he assumes the existence of a balanced regional position at the beginning of the nineteenth century which was subsequently disturbed by the different ways in which the coffee market, on the one hand, and the sugar and cotton markets, on the other, developed. Based on the concept of 'optimum currency', he believes that the application of the same rate of exchange for coffee was detrimental to the North-east region because this prevented the region from being adequately compensated for its sugar and cotton exports. However, I think that it is more important to find out the reasons for the lack of competitiveness of these products, as David Denslow Jr has attempted to do,[18] both from the demand side and the supply side, in other words, by basically looking for the causes of the North-east's backwardness. One can agree with Leff that a different exchange-rate policy might have corrected the disequilibrium: a lower exchange rate for the North-east would have amounted to a transfer of funds to the benefit of this region. This would have been a remedy. but it does not provide us with an explanation. What we should ask ourselves, both in the case of the North-east and in the case of other regions such as Rio de Janeiro, is why did they begin to lose their momentum before provoking a genuine cumulative development process? Moreover, if it is true that coffee did enjoy comparative advantages on the international market, this would have affected Rio de Janeiro as much as it did Sao Paulo.

I believe that one must consider a set of conditions that determine the acceleration of economic development within a region. In fact, development cannot be regarded as a simplified phenomenon subject to a single cause. It is true that, given the economic structure of Brazil in the nineteenth century, the export sector continued to be the main driving force. We have seen that the concentration of income in the region of Rio de Janeiro was due to exports and to coffee, and that the enduring privileged positions enjoyed by certain regions such as Pernambuco and Bahia may be explained in the same way.

The supremacy of exports could apparently be used in support of Leff's conclusion, although the latter implies that, if the exchange rate problem had been corrected, development would have followed a parallel course in both regions. This is an unfounded assumption which does not seem to be supported by the facts. In fact, there were differences in development even in the coffee-growing areas: the figures show that the growth of Rio de Janeiro between 1872 and 1900 was much lower than that of Sao Paulo which adapted itself better to export market conditions and to the domestic market conditions for factors of production. This question has already been thoroughly discussed.[19] Even more significant is the case of rubber, which enjoyed circumstances more favourable than those for coffee between 1870 and 1910, although on a smaller scale. We have already seen the steep increase in per capita income of the North region, which is the natural rubber area. In 1899, the region's per capita exports amounted to £12.4 as against £4.5 for Sao Paulo. The total value of rubber in 1910 was as high as 97.8 per cent of the value of coffee exports. Some idea of the terms of trade may be obtained from the fact that, between 1870 and 1900, the selling price for rubber (in current money) increased 497.0 per cent, while the increase in coffee prices did not exceed 139.6 per cent. Nevertheless, this was a passing triumph with which we shall not concern ourselves further. It merely suggests that a set of circumstances must exist to set off the mechanism of 'circular causality'.

7. A different kind of process was about to begin in Sao Paulo. Of course, one must not exaggerate the advances achieved prior to 1900. Even in the case of these preferred regions that blossomed out as a result of their participation in the world economy, the results were meagre. In the first place, the benefits obtained were directed overseas, particularly towards England – the 'external polarisation' mentioned earlier. Similar cases are common to other Latin-American countries.[20] Furthermore, the general income level was very low, so that the possibility of setting off the circular process was limited. Nevertheless, certain regions benefited more than others and as concentration shifted towards the former, it became more intense. The basic question is what were the opportunities for steadier economic growth in Brazil in the second half of the nineteenth century.

These opportunities become stronger and stronger towards the end of the century, but in 1900 Brazil's per capita income is still very low: my historical reconstruction method[21] yields a figure of US$70 which today corresponds to countries that still have a long way to go before their take-off. The exporting model itself prevented other sectors of the economy from beginning to develop. Agriculture is the first to suffer: coffee attracts all the factors of production, and farming for local consumption is abandoned. Similar situations have been identified for Latin America in general, and for Chile and Mexico.[22] What actually occurs is a process of 'replacement by imports' whereby agricultural products which were formerly produced within the country have to be imported. Coffee revenues are mostly spent overseas. Economic policy is directed towards protecting coffee. Customs duties, despite the advance of protectionist ideas, are still very mild.

It is important to understand that the required conditions for major industrial development were still absent. Capability for growth was very limited: I have estimated that in 1890 the net capital formation rate was about 4.5 per cent of the domestic product. The slavery system prevented the growth of a skilled labour force for industry. Technological training was minimal, and there was a lack of enterprise. The market was restricted because of low and ill-distributed total income as a result of the overseas orientation and the importance of non-monetary and self-sufficient economies even in the large coffee plantations.

The trend of income concentration was increasingly in favour of Zone I and, within that Zone, of Sao Paulo. It did not produce any outward spreading movements that might have benefited Zone II, either through trade, which mainly involved foreign markets (the cotton industry obtained its raw material within Sao Paulo itself), or by attracting labour which, due to the isolation of centres of production, the lack of transportation, and to other reasons that are hard to identify, consisted mainly of foreign immigrants (at first there were some transfers of slaves and even free workers from Zone II to Zone I, without causing any significant change; internal migration within the North-east region re-established any disequilibrium that may have existed), or through any redistributive policy using the exchange rate, as Leff would have wished, or taxation. Even the great drought of 1877-79 in the North-east was unable to hold the attention of the South for long.

Even in the more developed region, the cumulative process was proceeding slowly. However, its speeding up was foreshadowed by certain changes brought about by coffee: the rise of entrepreneurial spirit, the development of a transportation infrastructure and, coming somewhat late, as in the rest of Latin America, the growth of a banking and business system. But, above all, the human factor must be emphasised: the massive inflow of better-educated and more skilled European immigrants.

There is general agreement among historians that the abolition of slavery and the resulting immigration from Europe proved to be one of the decisive factors in Brazil's industrialisation process. This is applicable to the development of Sao Paulo. Immigration increased towards the end of the nineteenth century: 221,918 foreign immigrants or 41.8 per cent of the country's total between 1881 and 1890, and 719,497 foreign immigrants or 65.1 per cent of the total between 1891 and 1900. The importance of this immigration may be judged from the fact that, from 1881 to 1890, the population of the province of Sao Paulo rose by 312,940 inhabitants, while immigration totalled 221,918 persons or 70.9 per cent of the population increase. Immigrant labour originally sought the rural areas and the coffee plantations. However, under the influence of its patterns of consumption, it ended up by devoting itself to subsistence farming, and to such an extent that, after 1900, local produce began to replace agricultural imports. Unfortunately, we have no information concerning the effect on agricultural productivity. A similar growth model to that proposed by Paul Bairoch[23] could apply in this case.

The fact remains that the factors already cited: the growth of income thanks to the coffee trade, the opening up of new cultural horizons, greater decisiveness on the part of government, all contributed towards a speedier, although still moderate, growth of the industrial sector. The positive factors that worked on behalf of Sao Paulo caused greater industrial expansion in this State, and consequently greater concentration as compared even with the nation's capital. By 1915, Sao Paulo's textile industry had already moved ahead of that of Rio de Janeiro. However, this period of history, the disparities in the twentieth century during the take-off, is beyond the time-frame of this paper.

The general conclusion is that the growth of the Brazilian economy has always produced regional inequalities. The low income level and the presence of less advantageous local conditions – distance, educational level, economic structures – have delayed or even suspended the process. At a certain point in time, progress itself and new conditions permitted the start of a genuine mechanism of 'circular causality'. This happened in Sao Paulo in the twentieth century, but its beginnings may be traced back to the last quarter of the nineteenth century, as I have attempted to demonstrate.

NOTES

[1]Perroux, Francois, *L'économie du XX-ème siècle* (Paris, 1964).
[2]Leon, Pierre, *Economies et sociétés de l'Amérique Latine* (Paris, 1969).
[3]Lambert, Jacques, *Os dois Brasis* (Sao Paulo, 1969).
[4]Myrdal, Gunnar, *Economic Theory and Underdeveloped Countries* (London, 1957).
[5]Hirschman, Alberto O., *The Strategy of Economic Development* (New Haven, 1958).
[6]Furtado, Celso, *Formacao economica do Brasil* (Rio de Janeiro, 1959).
[7]Bairoch, Paul, *Le Tiers Monde dans l'impasse* (Paris, 1971).
[8]Bairoch, Paul, *Révolution industrielle et sous-développement* (Paris, 1963).
[9]Buescu, Mircea, 'A mensuracao das disparidades regionais no Brasil na segunda metade do século XIX', in the periodical *Verbum,* Rio de Janeiro, 1978.
[10]Buescu, Mircea, 'Pour une quantification globale de l'économie brésilienne depuis l'époque coloniale', in *L'histoire quantitative du Brésil de 1800 à 1930* (Paris, 1973). See also Buescu, M., *Evolucao economica do Brasil* (Rio de Janeiro, 1974).
[11]Mauro, Frederic, *Cycle de l'or et cycle du café au Brésil* (Paris, 1969).
[12]Buescu, Mircea, *Exercicios de história econômica do Brasil* (Rio de Janeiro, 1968).
[13]Boudeville, Jean, 'Pôles de développement et pôles de croissance brésiliens au XX-ème siècle', in *L'histoire quantitative . . .*
[14]Buescu, Mircea, *Evolucao . . .*
[15]Stein, Stanley, *The Brazilian Cotton Manufacture* (Havana, 1957).
[16]Simonsen, Roberto C., *Evolucao industrial do Brasil* (Sao Paulo, 1973).
[17]Leff, Nathaniel H., 'Desenvolvimento economico e desigualdade regional: origens do caso brasileiro', in *Revista Brasileira de Economia* (Rio de Janeiro, 1972).
[18]Denslow Jr., David, 'As origens da desigualdade regional no Brasil', in *Formacao Economica do Brasil,* ed. Versiani-Barros (Rio de Janeiro, 1977).
[19]Stein, Stanley, *Vassouras – A Brazilian Coffee County* (Cambridge, 1957).

[20]Pepelasis, A., Mears, L., and Adelman, I., *Economic Development* (Berkeley, 1961).
[21]Buescu, Mircea, 'Pour une quantification . . .'
[22]Leon, Pierre, op. cit.; Pepelasis, A., *et al.* op. cit.
[23]Bairoch, Paul, *Révolution industrielle* . . .

Part 3

Relation Between Regional and National Disparities

32 Regional and International Economic Disparities since the Industrial Revolution: the Indian Evidence

Dharma Kumar and J. Krishnamurty

Two general hypotheses dominate the literature on historical trends in regional disparities in income. The first holds that regional disparities increase within a country in the early stages of development, since the process of growth starts in a few areas; in time, growth will spread and regional incomes converge. The second holds that the process of increasing disparity is cumulative, and that differentials widen over time (e.g. Myrdal, 1957, especially chs 3-5). This again can be applied both to differences within and between nations, but will apply more strongly to international differences, since the equalising factors, such as the movement of factors of production or government policies, will be weaker in the international case; on one view, indeed, disparity has been increased by imperialist exploitation, leading not only to slower growth of the colony but to actual immiserisation. Thus both hypotheses predict an increase in regional and international disparities in the initial stages of development; they diverge only about the later stages. To test either of them, one must define the phases of development. There is, of course, no single unambiguous definition but various measures of the degree of development within a country have been used: level of per capita income, structure of the labour force, composition of national income, and so forth.

In this paper we examine the Indian data on national and regional income, and other indicators of levels of living, and ask whether they support either of the hypotheses on trends in international and inter-regional inequality. Our aim is modest: we have no grand theory to propose and do not evaluate the various 'explanations' of growing disparities in India, since we are sceptical about the facts themselves. There are enormous inadequacies of data, but it is still possible to show that certain hypotheses can be fairly firmly ruled out, such as that the development of the international economy over the last 100 years has led to the impoverishment of India, and that others have at present little support from the facts, such as that there has been a growth in regional disparities within India during the same period. We take up first the evidence on the disparity between India and the West, and then the evidence on regional incomes within India.

INTERNATIONAL DIFFERENCES, 1860-1970

As one of India's national income statisticians has remarked with respect to India's per capita income, 'our knowledge about the period 1850 to 1900 is nearly non-existent' (Mukherjee, 1969, p. 37), and this is equally true of earlier periods. Fortunately for this paper, Mukherjee has gone on none the less to estimate national and per capita income for this period 1860-1900, largely on the basis of scattered point estimates made by earlier writers.

For the 40-year period 1860-1900 Mukherjee found that national income grew by 0.9 per cent per annum, population by 0.5 per cent and hence per capita income by 0.4 per cent. There were fluctuations within the period: 1865-85 saw a rapid increase in per capita income of 1.2 per cent (the population grew at 0.5 per cent); while between 1885 and 1900 per capita income declined, a conclusion which some other writers dispute (Lidman and Domress, 1970, pp. 333-4).

There are much better data after 1900, though it is only after 1951 that a systematic official series has been compiled. Of the various non-official national income series,[1] far and away the best available series is by Sivasubramoniam, who has made direct estimates for each year from 1900-1 to 1946-47 (Sivasubramoniam, 1965). His estimates show that between the two five-year periods ending 1904-5 and 1929-30, per capita income increased by around 20 per cent or 0.8 per cent per annum; during the depression per capita income declined but started to rise again after 1940-41. Between 1900-1/1904-5 and 1942-3/1946-7 real per capita income rose by only 19 per cent.

How does this rate of growth (19 per cent) compare with that of other countries for about the same period? India's per capita income growth was roughly similar to that of Asia; it was much lower than that of Latin America (70 per cent, but this may be an overestimate), or the LDCs as a whole (36 per cent, but also overestimated, if the Latin American rates turn out to be too high), or the DCs (113 per cent) (Bairoch, 1975, p. 191). Thus the gap between India and most of the world outside Asia has been growing in the twentieth century.

Going back to 1860-1900, it is almost certainly the case that the gap between India and the West and Japan increased, if one considers that the latter grew at rates well above those estimated for India during this period (Kuznets, 1966, pp. 64-5). India's per capita income may well have grown more slowly than many other tropical countries, including some Asian countries like Thailand. At least, this appears to be true for the period 1800-1913 (Lewis, 1970, p. 28).

It is well known that official exchange rates underestimate the relative real value of the income of LDCs, so that international comparisons can exaggerate international disparities of income. This bias may also affect comparisons over time. Heston has made some adjustments for purchasing power, and estimated that the ratio of Indian to UK per capita income, corrected for purchasing power disparities, declined from 30 per cent in 1870 to 12 per cent in 1970, and compared to the US from 24 per cent in 1870 to 7 per cent in 1970. At the official exchange rate the decline is a little faster: from around 10.0 per cent of the US and UK levels in 1870 to 3.7 per cent of the UK and 2.5 per cent of the US level in 1970 (Heston, forthcoming).[2] It might be argued that immiserisation in India took the form of a deterioration in the quality of life measured by demographic and social indices. It is difficult to find support for this hypothesis. If we consider the period from 1881/1901 to 1951, there was a decline in the death rate over the period from 41 per cent in the 1880s to 27 per cent around 1951, though this improvement really dates from 1921. Similarly infant mortality rates in India declined from 295 per thousand live births in 1901 to 199 in 1951; we have no reason to believe that they were *lower* in the late nineteenth century. The literacy rate too shows a marked improvement in the twentieth century, from 5.4 per cent in 1901 to 16.7 per cent of the population in 1951. One might argue that income distribution became more skewed in India over the period, but data do not exist to test this hypothesis. One can, however, assess the per capita availability of food to the population. Certainly Blyn's estimates (Blyn, 1966) indicate that per capita availability of food declined after the 1920s, but Blyn's figures are based on the official data on agricultural yields which Heston (1973) suspects underestimate the growth of agricultural output. Alternatively we could consider direct estimates of nutritional availability based on field surveys, but these are sporadic and unrepresentative. For what they are worth, the evidence of the surveys conducted in the 1930s and early 1940s suggest that 30 per cent of the population got less than 2300 calories per consumption unit.[3] The evidence for 1972-73 based on the results of the National Sample Survey suggest that 46 per cent of the Indian population got less than the poverty norm (2400 calories in rural and 2100 calories in urban India per consumption unit). This does support the view that there has been immiserisation, but the empirical basis is not sound enough to enable us to reject the hypothesis of improvement in living standards suggested by the national income and other demographic data.

It is important to note that the Indian data for the period after 1860 do not support the hypothesis that the growth of international trade and the world economy led to immiserising growth in the LDCs. The gap between India and the advanced countries widened, and also probably between India and the many other LDCs. But this was because Indian per capita income grew at a relatively slow *positive* rate, not because it declined.

REGIONAL DISPARITIES IN INDIA, PAST AND PRESENT

The data problems are even more serious when one turns to regional disparities within India. With one unsatisfactory exception, discussed later, there are no complete regional breakdowns for the pre-Independence period: and even since 1951, although the collection and processing of national income statistics has greatly improved, the regional figures are unsatisfactory. The Indian Union is at present divided into 23 States of greatly varying size.[4] Practically the only regional breakdowns available are for Statewise distribution of income. For testing many hypotheses about the causes of regional disparities, the State is often not the natural unit to study as it may contain a number of agro-climatic zones, or regions displaying widely varying cultural patterns and socio-economic characteristics. But data are often the by-product of administrative procedure and usually cannot be recast to fit into 'economic regions', howsoever defined.

But it is still worth considering the distribution of income between States in the post-war period, since the figures show that regional income disparities are not very large in India by international standards. Further, the regional income distribution can fruitfully be compared with other indicators of the level of living. Let us consider 1961, a census year and one for which a fairly good non-official estimate of Statewise income distribution is available.[5]

TABLE 32.1 Ranking of states according to per capita income, 1960-61 (current prices)

	1960-61	
State	*Per capita income (Rs.)*	*Rank*
Andhra Pradesh	289.1	11
Assam	328.4	6
Bihar	222.0	14
Gujarat	402.8	4
Kerala	326.2	7
Madhya Pradesh	293.4	9
Madras (Tamil Nadu)	343.8	5
Maharashtra	479.4	1
Mysore (Karnataka)	313.2	8
Orissa	267.9	13
Punjab	441.3	3
Rajasthan	272.0	12
Uttar Pradesh	291.7	10
West Bengal	461.9	2
All India	336.3	

SOURCE: NCAER, 1967.[5]

The State with the highest per capita income in 1961 was Maharashtra which contains Bombay City, the second richest was West Bengal, whose capital is Calcutta. These are also large States with populations in 1961 of 40 million and 35 million respectively. The poorest States, Orissa and Bihar, both in the east, are also large. There would be broad agreement on this ranking.

TABLE 32.2 The percentage distribution of NDP by broad sector in the Indian States, 1960-61

State	*Agriculture (including allied activities)*	*Manufacturing (including mining)*	*Services*	*Total*
1. Maharashtra	36.5	22.4	41.1	100.0
2. West Bengal	36.6	23.7	39.7	100.0
3. Punjab	57.0	14.1	28.9	100.0
4. Gujarat	46.0	20.9	33.1	100.0
5. Madras (Tamil Nadu)	46.4	16.9	36.7	100.0
6. Kerala	56.0	15.8	28.2	100.0
7. Mysore (Karnataka)	57.3	15.2	27.5	100.0
8. Madhya Pradesh	60.6	12.5	26.9	100.0
9. Uttar Pradesh	67.4	9.2	23.4	100.0
10. Andhra Pradesh	56.9	9.5	33.6	100.0
11. Rajasthan	63.8	7.5	28.7	100.0
12. Orissa	67.0	8.0	25.0	100.0
13. Bihar	57.0	17.2	25.8	100.0
India	52.3	15.7	32.0	100.0

SOURCE: NCAER (1967)[5], Table 10, p. 62.

TABLE 32.3 Shares of broad sectors in the male working force of the Indian States, 1961

States (ranked by per capita income 1960-61)	*Share of agriculture (including allied activities) in the male working force % 1961*	*Share of manufacturing in the male working force % 1961*	*Share of services in the male working force % 1961*
1. Maharashtra	64.5	14.4	19.5
2. West Bengal	59.5	15.1	21.9
3. Punjab	66.6	11.3	18.3
4. Gujarat	67.3	12.7	17.8
5. Madras (Tamil Nadu)	64.5	13.7	18.5
6. Kerala	55.0	14.6	26.5
7. Mysore (Karnataka)	73.4	9.7	13.7
8. Madhya Pradesh	78.8	8.0	10.5
9. Uttar Pradesh	77.4	8.2	12.5
10. Andhra Pradesh	72.2	10.7	14.6
11. Rajasthan	78.4	6.0	12.8
12. Orissa	84.2	5.7	8.9
13. Bihar	79.5	6.7	10.9

SOURCE: Krishnamurty, 1971, Table 6.1, pp. 182-3.

TABLE 32.4 Some indicators of levels of development in the Indian States around 1960-61

States	*Per capita income (Rs.) 1960-61*	*percentage of male work force in agriculture and allied activities 1961*	*percentage of male work force in manufacturing 1961*	*percentage of male work force in services 1961*	*Birth rate percentages 1950s*	*Death rate percentages 1950s*	*Percentage of population literate 1961*	*Expectation of life at birth (male 1950s)*	*Infant mortality per thousand live births, 1950s*
(1)	(2)	(3)	(4)	(5)	(6)	(7)	(8)	(9)	(10)
Maharashtra	479.4	63.5	14.7	21.8	42.8	19.3	29.8	45	109
West Bengal	461.9	59.5	15.1	25.4	42.9	20.9	29.3	45	120
Punjab	441.3	66.6	11.3	22.1	44.7	18.9	24.2	49	110
Gujarat	402.8	67.3	12.7	20.0	45.7	23.5	30.5	41	N.A.
Madras	343.8	64.5	13.7	21.8	34.9	22.5	31.4	40	109
Assam	328.4	85.5	3.5	9.2	49.3	26.9	27.4	37	184
Kerala	326.2	55.0	14.6	30.4	38.9	16.1	46.8	49	120
Mysore	313.2	73.4	9.7	16.9	41.6	22.2	25.4	49	120
Madhya Pradesh	293.4	76.8	8.0	13.2	43.2	23.2	17.1	40	175
Uttar Pradesh	291.7	77.4	8.2	14.4	41.5	24.9	17.6	39	186
Andhra Pradesh	289.1	72.2	10.7	17.1	39.7	25.2	21.2	38	111
Rajasthan	272.0	78.4	6.0	15.6	42.7	19.4	15.2	48	177
Orissa	267.9	84.2	5.7	10.1	40.4	22.9	21.7	41	159
Bihar	222.0	79.5	6.7	13.8	43.4	26.1	18.4	38	145
India	336.3	71.7	10.1	15.5	41.7	22.8	24.0	41	140

SOURCES: Col. 2: NCAER 1967[5]
Cols. 3, 4, 5: Krishnamurty, 1971, Table 6.1
Cols. 6-10: Bhattacharjee and Shastri, 1976, Tables 9, 11, 12, 16, 22, 37, 38.

As one would expect, the richer States derived relatively higher shares of their income from manufacturing and relatively lower shares from agriculture. Punjab is an exception, with a relatively high share (57 per cent) of its income coming from agriculture. Similarly most of the poorer States depended heavily on agriculture; Bihar, the poorest State, was an exception, with a large mining and manufacturing sector.

Again, if we compare the structure of the male working force in 1961 with the per capita income of different States (excluding Assam), we find a fairly marked positive association between per capita income and the respective shares of manufacturing and services in the workforce; conversely, there is a marked negative association between per capita income and the share of agriculture in the work force of 13 States which were considered.

As we know, per capita figures in themselves are an inadequate guide to the quality of life. The expectation of life, the rate of literacy, standards of health and nutrition, depend on the distribution of income, the standard of public services and other social factors. (For instance, literacy is higher in States where missionaries were active.) Thus, most demographic variables like birth and death rates, or the expectation of life at birth or the dependency rate, do not appear to be closely correlated with per capita State income. How ever, infant mortality rates are negatively associated to some degree with per capita State income with the exception of Andhra Pradesh. Literacy rates were above 24 per cent in States with per capita income above Rs.300 per annum, and below 22 per cent in States with per capita income below this level.

While high infant mortality or low literacy are associated with low average per capita State income, they (and perhaps other demographic variables) ought to be related to the extent of absolute poverty within a State. In rich States like Punjab and Gujarat, the percentage of the 'poor' to total population was relatively small, as one would expect. But in Maharashtra, the richest State, the percentage of the 'poor' was above the national average and the estimates for West Bengal for the period 1956-57 to 1973-74 suggest rather a large percentage below the poverty line – the results for 1960-61 for West Bengal appear exceptional. Of course this could be because we consider the percentage below the poverty line in rural areas only and Maharashtra and West Bengal have the large cities of Bombay and Calcutta respectively within their boundaries.

One should note that the extent of regional disparity is not in fact large by international standards. Maharashtra's per capita income was only about twice Bihar's. The relative variation of State per capita incomes was 24 per cent compared to 36 per cent in the US in 1929 and 23 per cent in the US in 1955 (Perloff *et al.*, 1960, p. 504; NCAER, 1967[5], p. 48). Again if, following Williamson, we use the share of agriculture in the workforce as an indicator of relative backwardness, India in 1951 turns out to have a rather *low* degree of regional inequality; the coefficient of variation in shares of agricultural workforce was 9 per cent. This is lower than that of Brazil,

TABLE 32.5 Percentage of the population below the poverty line in the Indian States 1960-61 and 1973-74 (rural areas)

States	*1960-61*	*1973-74*
1. Andhra Pradesh	50.1	39.8
2. Assam	25.6	39.3
3. Bihar	41.5	58.4
4. Gujarat	31.6	35.6
5. Karala	57.8	49.3
6. Madhya Pradesh	43.8	52.3
7. Madras (Tamil Nadu)	53.9	48.3
8. Maharashtra	48.4	49.8
9. Mysore (Karnataka)	39.1	46.9
10. Orissa	62.4	58.0
11. Punjab (including Haryana)	18.8	23.0
12. Rajasthan	32.3	29.8
13. Uttar Pradesh	37.9	47.3
14. West Bengal	40.4	66.0
India	42.0	47.6

SOURCE: The World Bank (1978): Paper by Montek S. Ahluwalia, Table 3(a), p. 17. The basic data are from the 16th and 28th Rounds of the National Sample Survey. The poverty line was set at Rs.15 per head per month at 1960-61 prices for all India, but account was taken of differences in prices in different States in that year. For each State in each year, the poverty line in current prices was estimated using the consumer price indices for agricultural labourers.

13 per cent; the same as the US (9 per cent); and significantly lower than that of Italy, Finland, Austria, Spain, Japan and Sweden (Williamson, 1965, Table 7a).

Our main interest is in changes in regional disparities in the nineteenth and twentieth centuries, but unfortunately there are no reliable estimates of regional incomes before 1951. For the nineteenth century, there are only a few imprecise estimates for a few regions. Even for the first half of the twentieth century only one set of estimates, by B. Natarajan, seems usable and even this is doubtful. His ranking of Provinces in 1938-39 and 1949-50 is startlingly different from the 1961 estimates we have used, even when account is taken of changes in territorial coverage, etc. Natarajan found that West Bengal was the second poorest Province and that this was the case not only in 1938-39 but in 1949-50 as well (Natarajan, 1949, p. 15). No other estimate for the period around 1950 agrees with this result (except the West Bengal State Statistical Bureau's estimate for 1958-59), and one cannot but suspect that Natarajan's figures for Bengal are underestimates. Natarajan does not directly estimate income in each State sector by sector; instead he allocates national sectorial totals among the States on the basis of a variety of indicators. The NCAER 1960-61 figures, on the other hand, are based on direct estimation, and are reinforced by evidence that in Bengal the share of the workforce engaged in manufacturing and services was rising fairly rapidly, while that in agriculture was declining between 1901 and 1951 (Krishnamurty, 1977, pp. 21-3). If West Bengal was poor, East Bengal must have been poorer and hence undivided Bengal must have been poorer than West Bengal. Yet even for undivided Bengal, the share of agriculture fell and the shares of manufacturing and services in the workforce rose between 1911 and 1951. This does not suggest economic decline during the twentieth century.

For the period 1911-51 we can obtain a summary measure of regional inequality by taking the coefficient of variation in the shares in different States of agriculture in the workforce. Using this measure we find that regional inequality rose marginally from 6 per cent to 9 per cent over this period. So there is evidence that regional disparities did not rise rapidly between 1911 and 1951 at least.

Even this type of calculation cannot be made for the nineteenth century and only some general speculations are possible. There are practically no historical studies of regional development, but there have been several studies of individual sectors, such as agriculture (Blyn, 1966) or processes, such as 'deindustrialisation' (Thorner, 1962; Krishnamurty, 1976; Bagchi, 1976), many of which suggest very unequal regional growth. How can these be reconciled with the findings that the regional distribution of income was not in fact particularly unequal in 1961?

The qualitative assessments of historians suggest that there were vast disparities in regional income in 1800 or even earlier (Morris *et al.*, 1969). It is, therefore, difficult to argue that regional inequality *per se* has increased over time in India; though of course it is perfectly possible that the fortunes of individual regions may have altered substantially. In 1800 Bengal was regarded as one of the richest parts of India; it was free from famine, had flourishing handicrafts, an active merchant community and large prosperous towns. Between 1893 and 1947 agricultural output per head may have declined somewhat.[6] Gujarat and Madras were areas which, in the early nineteenth century, had been at least partly commercialised and which in 1961 were in the top six States. Kerala, which was a highly developed area in the nineteenth century, was at the margin of inclusion among the developed States of 1961. But the area around Agra, which used to be highly developed, is now submerged in the large backward State of Uttar Pradesh.[7] Again, neither Maharashtra nor Punjab were regarded as developed areas early in the nineteenth century, and these two States were among the top three States in 1961. It is likely that there have been some striking changes in fortunes in the State/Provincial league tables since 1800.

One possibility is that the growth of formerly backward regions was offset by the decline of once prosperous regions, with little change in overall regional disparity. Another possibility is that regional disparities were actually reduced, for example, by the levelling down of the richest regions, or by the spread of impulses of growth, as transport improved and markets widened. Political changes are of great importance too, but their significance is not yet clear – how do the differences in the governments of British India and the native States before Independence compare with the differences between the successor States? It at least seems probable that political unification within the Indian Union has reduced regional disparities, particularly since the reduction of such disparities is now an explicit policy goal.

We cannot take the discussion much further without much more work on the first half of the nineteeenth century, and, in particular, on the regions. However, it may be worthwhile to summarise some recent work on South India, shaky though its empirical basis is, to illustrate the dangers of generalising from one factor, such as a fall in the exports of manufactures. In the first half of the nineteenth century Madras Presidency, which was once a major exporter of textiles, became mainly an exporter of primary commodities. The total volume of exports expanded greatly, but at least from 1821-22 bullion was exported abroad in large quantities to finance net invisible payments. These are pointers to a 'drain' and to 'deindustrialisation', but it is not at all clear that they did in fact lead to impoverishment. It is not even clear that total employment in weaving fell, since the fall in exports may have been matched by the expansion of domestic demand. On the other hand, skilled weavers lost employment and it seems probable that there was actually a decline in literacy, perhaps a consequence of the increasing dependence on agriculture. However, population expanded – often taken as a sign of prosperity; agricultural output also grew, and at least some groups of the population prospered, such as the larger farmers producing cash crops, and if there are no signs of a widespread rise in living standards, there are equally none of a widespread fall (Kumar, forthcoming). This casts doubt on many generalisations made about the first half of the nineteenth century, such as that it was a period of actual immiserisation.

To conclude, India's per capita income almost certainly grew between 1860 and 1947, and those of the Indian Union and Pakistan certainly grew between 1947 and 1970. The gap between India and the West widened, since the rate of growth of income was comparatively low. In comparison with many other countries, such as the US, Brazil or Italy, regional disparity was relatively low in Independent India. There is evidence of significant regional disparities in, say, 1800, but not of marked growth in overall regional disparities. There have been various social, political and economic forces at work affecting regional growth, but the net result of these forces is unknown.

NOTES

[1] Mukherjee (1969) provides an excellent description of the various types of data and estimates from 1860.

[2] Heston has pointed out that Sivasubramoniam (and others) may have underestimated the rate of growth of agricultural output (Heston, 1973), he has therefore reworked the estimates of national income (Heston, forthcoming). Heston's figures agree broadly with Sivasubramoniam's estimates as to trend. On Sivasubramoniam's estimates the gap between India and the West would have widened even further, but there would still be no immiserisation.

[3]See Aykroyd, 1941. According to Aykroyd, 'in about 30 per cent of the groups, average daily calorie intake per consumption unit was below 2300, that is below any reasonable standard of requirements. . . .' These observations cannot legitimately be generalised into a statement of the extent of undernutrition in India, because the sample of the population – about 1,500 families – investigated was small, and cannot in any strict statistical sense be taken as typical of the country as a whole.

[4]Most of the estimates used in this paper relate to 14 larger States using the boundaries in force in 1961.

[5]NCAER, 1967. These were based on direct estimates of agricultural output and factory manufacture. For most other sectors, 1961 Workforce estimates and appropriate output-worker ratios were used.

[6]A recent careful study (Islam, 1973) suggests that there may not have been the sharp decline in food output reported by George Blyn (Blyn, 1966).

[7]The share of agriculture (including allied activities) in the work force of Agra Division remained rather high, around 69 per cent during the period 1911-61 (unpublished estimates of Krishnamurty). This is not low in an absolute sense, but is the second lowest among the 9 Divisions of Uttar Pradesh for which we have comparable data.

REFERENCES

Aykroyd, W.R. (1941), 'Problems of Nutrition in India', *Indian Journal of Social Work,* December 1941.

Bagchi, A.K. (1976), 'Deindustrialization in India', *Journal of Development Studies,* Vol. 12, No. 2 (January 1976) pp. 132-50.

Bairoch, P. (1975), *The Economic Development of the Third World since 1900* (London).

Bhattacharjee, P. J. and Shastri, G. N. (1976), *Population in India* (Delhi).

Blyn, G. (1966), *Agricultural Trends in India. 1891-1947, Output, Availability, Productivity* (Philadelphia).

Desai, Ashok V. (1978), 'Revenue Administration and Agricultural Statistics in Bombay Presidency', *Indian Economic and Social History Review,* Vol. XV, No. 2 (April-June 1978) pp. 173-85.

Heston, A. (1973), 'Official Yields Per Acre in India, 1886-1947: Some Questions of Interpretation', *Indian Economic and Social History Review,* Vol. X, No. 4 (December 1973) pp. 303-32.

Heston, A. (1978), 'A Further Critique of Historical Yields Per Acre in India', *Indian Economic and Social History Review,* Vol, XV, No. 2 (April-June 1978) pp. 187-210.

Heston, A. (forthcoming), Chapter on National Income of India, 1857-1947 in *Cambridge Economic History of India,* Vol. II.

India, Planning Commission Delhi (1978), *Draft Five Year Plan 1978-83* (Delhi).

Islam, M. M. (1973) 'The Quality of Official Crop Statistics of Bengal (1920-1947)', *Bulletin of Quantitative and Computer Methods in South Asian Studies,* No. 1 (July 1973) pp. 23-4.

Krishnamurty, J. (1971), 'The Industrial Distribution of the Working Force in India, 1901-1961: A Study of Selected Aspects', PhD thesis, University of Delhi, (mimeo).

Krishnamurty, J. (1976), 'Deindustrialization Revisited', *Economic and Political Weekly,* Vol. XI, No. 26 (26 June, 1976) pp. 964-7.

Krishnamurty, J. (forthcoming), Chapter on Occupation in *Cambridge Economic History of India,* Vol. II.

Kumar, Dharma (1974), 'Changes in Income Distribution and Poverty in India: A Review of the Literature', *World Development,* Vol. 2, No. 1 (January 1974) pp. 31-41.

Kumar, Dharma (forthcoming), Chapter on the South Indian Economy, 1757 to 1857, in *Cambridge Economic History of India,* Vol. II.

Kuznets, Simon (1966), *Modern Economic Growth: Rate, Structure, Spread* (New Haven).

Lewis, W. Arthur (ed.) 1970), *Tropical Development, 1880-1913* (London).

Morris, M. D., *et al.* (1969), *The Indian Economy in the Nineteenth Century: A Symposium* (Delhi).
Myrdal, G. (1957), *Economic Theory and Underdeveloped Regions* (London).
Mukherjee, M. (1969), *National Income of India, Trends and Structure* (Calcutta).
Natarajan, B. (1949), *An Essay on National Income and Expenditure in India* (Madras).
National Council of Applied Economic Research (1967), *Estimates of State Income* (New Delhi).
Perloff, H. S., *et al.* (1960), *Regions, Resources and Economic Growth* (Baltimore).
Sivasubramoniam, S. (1965), 'National Income of India, 1900-01 to 1946-47', PhD thesis, University of Delhi (mimeo).
Thorner, D. and A. (1962), *Land and Labour in India* (Bombay).
Williamson, J. G. (1965), 'Regional Inequality and the Process of National Development', *Economic Development and Cultural Change,* Vol. 13, pp. 3-45.
World Bank (1978), *India, Occasional Papers,* World Bank Staff Working Paper No. 279, (Washington): paper by Montek S. Ahluwalia.

33 Inequality and Regional Development: the View from America

Jeffrey G. Williamson

1. WHAT IS WRONG WITH CONVENTIONAL WISDOM?

The conventional wisdom on regional per capita income performance in American history suffers from five weaknesses.

First, conventional regional 'histories' were built with little or no attention to the national determinants of growth and structural change. Without a theory of national growth, there can be no useful theory of regional divergence or convergence, however elegant the models or careful the archival research.

Second, the empirical literature was based primarily on experience since 1880 generally and since 1919 in particular. This is unfortunate since it fails to appreciate the sources of disequilibrium which produced the initial disparities in American regional incomes in the first half of the nineteenth century, disequilibrium forces that reappear in the first third of the present century. A very special theory emerges which is primarily relevant to an economy approaching 'steady state'. If we wish to derive lessons which are useful to contemporary Third World economies or even to the contemporary American setting of resource-scarcity shocks, then the long-term history between 1880 and 1970 is likely to be far less relevant than the history between 1800 and 1860, or the shorter-term experience between 1900 and 1929.

Third, America is usually treated as a whole, and after the Civil War there were *two* regional plays being acted out, not just one as the literature implies. In the North, states and regions were playing out a development process initiated by disequilibrating conditions set in motion by modern economic growth itself. In the South, the spectacular destruction of wealth created a whole new set of disequilibrium conditions, not unlike those in Europe and Japan created by inter-war and Second World War events. There is no reason why these two regional dynamics should exhibit the same characteristics since the disequilibrating shocks were quite different. Thus, sections 2 and 3 will offer a theory of *Northern* regional development within the context of modern economic growth. This does not imply that the 'North-South problem' has been unimportant, since it has dominated the American scene for a century. But the North-South problem is special, experience upon which no general theory of regional inequality should be based. In addition, there are important price, cost-of-living and 'sunshine' effects which make the North-South problem unique.

Fourth, the literature has almost totally ignored the influence of prices and cost of living. Not only is their inclusion central to welfare and distributional judgements, but they are an important endogenous ingredient of regional performance during national development.

Finally, I believe that labour markets were very efficient in America even during periods of extraordinary stress. Alleged inter-regional and intra-regional labour market 'failure' has been grossly overdrawn. This is especially true of intra-regional labour markets, and the interpretation is central to understanding growth as well as to making correct welfare inferences. This flaw in the literature lies in part with inadequate attention to labour heterogeneity and living costs. Furthermore, the key to factor immobility conditions in American history seems to have been intra-regional capital market imperfections and lags in adjustment. Non-farm inter-regional capital market imperfections, on the other hand, rarely played a significant role.

2. NATIONAL GROWTH AND DISTRIBUTION: THE GRAND DESIGN

What follows is a comprehensive narrative stating my position regarding the forces driving American nineteenth-century experience with growth, accumulation and distribution. The historical narrative offers an inter-dependent view of the process of development from an initial pre-industrial agrarian society exhibiting egalitarian attributes across and within regions, to a mature industrialised economy with high and pervasive inequality within regions, but not between. I begin by isolating the shocks which appear to have set the economy in motion along a path of modern economic growth. The endogenous response will then be traced through ten subsequent decades. The formal attributes of the general equilibrium model can be found elsewhere (Williamson and Lindert, 1979), so I shall rely here on a verbal statement of the model.

Disequilibrating Shocks and the Early Nineteenth Century

The primary initial disturbances to the early national economy were two, and they are distinctive by their magnitude as well as by their persistence over the half-century following 1820: rising rates of labour force growth, especially among the unskilled, and sharply unbalanced rates of total factor productivity growth across sectors.

The American economy had been characterised by high rates of population growth throughout the seventeenth and eighteenth centuries. Thus, the gentle upward drift in rates after the first decade of the nineteenth century may appear modest by comparison, but labour force growth, on the other hand, rises from a per annum rate of roughly 2 per cent in 1800-10 to approximately 3.8 per cent in 1840-50. An important part of this labour force acceleration can, of course, be explained by immigration. Furthermore, the most recent econometric research (Williamson, 1974, ch. 11) documents that the vast majority of the observed nineteenth-century immigration to America was of the 'push' variety. The finding of low 'wage elasticity' on this side of the Atlantic strongly supports the view that immigration, and thus labour force growth, was exogenous to the early nineteenth-century economy. There are abundant qualitative accounts which confirm the econometrics, such as those which emphasise European blight, famine, and demographic 'transition', as well as the sharp decline in direct and indirect steerage costs.

The second, and more important, exogenous shock lay with technological change and its bias. The conjectures offered by modern economic historians appear to document an unambiguous acceleration in total factor productivity growth (TFPG) in manufacturing in particular and in 'modern' machine-cum-skill intensive sectors in general. During the period 1800-35, these conjectures imply a modest rate of TFPG somewhere in the neighbourhood of 0.75 per cent per annum. The rate accelerates thereafter, reaching something like 3 per cent per annum during the last two decades of the ante-bellum period. 'Traditional' unskilled-cum-resource-intensive sectors lagged behind. The evidence suggests that agricultural TFPG underwent retardation over the period, from about 0.5 per cent per annum prior to 1835, to no improvement at all after the 1830s.

In short, the ante-bellum period can be characterised by high and sharply rising *unbalancedness* in sectorial rates of TFPG.

Laws of Motion: The Ante-bellum Response

What was the nature of the endogenous, economy-wide response to these two disequilibrium shocks?

First and foremost, unbalanced TFPG produced a striking decline in the relative price of modern goods (Williamson and Lindert, 1979, chs 5, 9 and 10). Nowhere in nineteenth- and twentieth-century experience is the decline more rapid. This supply-induced relative price decline had an inevitable impact: it produced a dramatic shift in output mix out of traditional goods production. Nowhere in American experience is the rate of industrialisation more dramatic or agriculture's relative demise more impressive. Some of this mix-response can be attributed to domestic demand and price-elastic shifts into modern goods, and some of it to import substitution and the displacement of foreign manufactured imports. While this shift in the composition of output was further reinforced by Engel effects associated with per capita income improvement, its unusual rate compared with the late nineteenth century must be assigned instead to the unbalanced character of technical progress.

The unbalanced output growth raised the relative demand for factors used intensively in the favoured modern sectors, namely machines and skills. The net impact was unskilled 'labour-saving' in the aggregate. Inequality indicators rose markedly in response, and along a broad front (Lindert and Williamson, 1976). Pay ratios drifted upwards, urban skill premia rose, profit shares increased, and the share of national income accruing to the impecunious unskilled dropped sharply. What had been an economy characterised by 'dear labour' in the 1820s had become an economy of abundant labour and scarce skills by the Civil War. What had been an agrarian society of relative egalitarianism in the eighteenth century had become an economy dominated by high urban wealth concentration. While the exogenous forces of accelerating unskilled labour supply and unbalanced TFP growth were producing these endogenous nominal distribution trends, they were also tending to produce distributional influences on the expenditure side. Increasing land scarcity and unbalanced TFPG both tended to drive the relative price of traditional consumption goods upwards. Since the low-wage unskilled worker was a heavy consumer of traditional and resource-intensive wage goods – fuel, light, food and rents – he found his relative income position deteriorating even further in real terms (Williamson, 1976b, 1977b). While the urban worker found his relative standard of living being eroded on the expenditure side, the producer of some of those traditional goods – farmers located most extensively in backward regions – received a benefit in the form of rising output prices, a rise reinforced by improvements in long-haul transport costs to American and European urban markets. Thus, the 'price' forces were far more deleterious on distribution *within* regions than between.

The impressive structural change in the ante-bellum economy could never have taken place without high and rising rates of capital formation. The net reproducible capital stock rose from a 4.5 per cent per annum growth rate prior to the mid-late 1830s to 5.5 per cent afterwards. Both of these figures exceed by a factor of five or ten the rates typical of the two centuries before 1805. Part of the explanation for the surge in accumulation rates after 1805 (Williamson, 1978) lies with the impact of population growth on demographically sensitive investment like housing. Part of it appears to be explained by induced inequality forces. The major portion, however, seems to lie with the unbalanced character of technological change itself. The shift in output mix towards more machine-cum-skill-intensive activities tended to raise rates of return to saving, and accumulation rates rose as a consequence. Furthermore, TFPG in capital goods sectors in general, and in the producer durables sector in particular, accelerated at an extraordinary rate (Williamson, 1978). The resulting cheapening of machines fostered capital deepening, mechanisation and labour-saving at the firm level throughout the economy, even on the farm. It also supplied an additional impetus to the rise in accumulation rates and investment shares.

What was the impact of accelerating rates of conventional capital accumulation on the inequality drift already set in motion by economy-wide labour-saving? It served to suppress the rise in profit rates and profit shares, but the ameliorating influence ceased there and for three reasons. First, capital formation fostered the expansion of the modern sectors (the Rybczynski effect) where raw labour was used least intensively. Unbalanced output growth was exacerbated and labour-saving in the aggregate reinforced. Second, since skills and machines appear to be complementary in production, the relatively dramatic growth in conventional capital tended to raise the relative demands for skills, pay ratios rose, and thus the drift towards *earnings* inequality was augmented. Third, since producer durables are capital-cum-skill-intensive (Williamson and Lindert, 1979, ch 8), the relative expansion of capital goods production tended to augment the demands for machines and skills still further.

The American economy was thus set in motion across the ante-bellum period. Unbalanced TFP and labour force growth acceleration set in motion the classic correlates of modern economic growth. The relative price of traditional, resource intensive consumption goods tended to rise, fostering a deterioration in the relative income position of the low-wage urban unskilled on the expenditure side. Nominal inequality trends were even more apparent. Distribution shifted across a broad front which included lagging unskilled wages, declining unskilled labour shares, rising pay ratios, and earnings inequality. Conventional wealth concentration followed apace.

'Equilibrating' Shocks and the Late Nineteenth Century

The motion of the American economy was altered in the mid-nineteenth century. First, overall labour force growth retreated from the peak rates achieved in the 1840s. The rate of growth in total man-hours employed underwent an even more spectacular decline. Second, technological unbalancedness appears to have fled from the American scene. According to Kendrick (1961), industry and agriculture exhibited approximate TFPG balance over the late nineteenth century. This characterisation also seems to apply to the capital-consumption goods dichotomy since the relative price decline of both producer durables and investment goods slows down and almost ceases over the period (Williamson, 1978). These 'price dual' calculations supply the inference that measured rates of TFPG unbalancedness must have sharply diminished between these two sectors as well.

These new exogenous conditions had an inevitable impact on the motion of the late nineteenth-century economy. The rate of change in the commodity price structure slowed down markedly (Williamson and Lindert, 1979, chs 5, 9 and 10). This induced a diminution in the rate of industrialisation, so that the aggregate rate of labour-saving diminished and the drift towards inequality was retarded. In addition, the rise in the saving rate slowed down as the favourable forces generating its increase dissipated.

The structural transformation of the American economy certainly didn't halt after the 1850s. Nor did the downward drift in the relative price of modern goods cease. Nor did the rate of accumulation fall back to the levels of the early nineteenth century. Nor did the economy-wide bias in the rate of labour-saving disappear. Rather, as the *intensity* of these forces dissipated so too did their influence on relative factor demands which had served to raise pay ratios, the non-labour share, earnings inequality, and wealth concentration for some four or five decades of modern development. What resulted, therefore, was a high plateau of inequality quiescence which persisted up to the turn of the century (Lindert and Williamson, 1976).

Lessons for the Twentieth Century? 1900 and Beyond

Around the turn of the century America witnessed another change in the motion of the key exogenous forces which had been driving inequality trends for the previous century. Disequilibrating forces reappear. From the late 1890s to shortly before the First World War the downward trend in labour force growth halted. In fact there was a modest rise in growth rates up to 1910 or 1913, and it appears to have been steeper for the unskilled, given the shifting bias of immigration towards the less advanced regions of Europe. Most importantly, however, there is persuasive evidence that technological unbalancedness reappears between 1900 and 1929, centred with special drama on the 1920s (Kendrick, 1961; Williamson, 1976a). Since similar exogenous forces re-emerge around the turn of the century, it seems plausible to expect the 'nineteenth-century model' to account for the rise in American inequality up to 1929 as well (Lindert and Williamson, 1976).

Finally, we note that following 1929 'technological balancedness' returns to the American scene (Kendrick, 1961: Williamson, 1976a), especially in the form of impressive TFPG in the farm sector. Furthermore, the rate of labour force growth also declines following the 1929 'turning-point', in part due to the cessation of immigration. Finally, the rise of government expenditure shares in GNP seems to have had a greater unskilled labour-intensive demand than the private expenditures which they replaced.

3. *REGIONAL DIVERGENCE AND CONVERGENCE: THEORY*

Regional Divergence and Early Industrialisation

We shall find it useful to follow the development and regional growth literature by decomposing aggregate economic activity along dualistic lines. Regional output per worker can be separated into its agricultural ('traditional' sector) and non-agricultural ('modern' sector) parts:

$$y_j = \alpha_j^m y_j^m + \alpha_j^a y_j^a ,$$

where $\alpha^m_j = (1 - \alpha^a_j$ = share of jth regions's non-ag labour force in the jth region's total labour force,

y^m_j = non-ag income per non-ag worker,

y^a_j = ag income per ag worker.

Suppose regional inequality is measured by the weighted coefficient of variation, V, or its square, V^2. Then the regional variance in y_j can be decomposed into the following 'sources of regional growth' expressions:

$$V^2 = \left\{ \sum_j w_j (\alpha^m_j)^2 \left[\frac{y^m_j - y^m}{y}\right] \right\}^2 + \qquad (A)$$

$$+ \left\{ \sum_j w_j (\alpha^a_j)^2 \left[\frac{y^a_j - y^a}{y}\right] \right\}^2 + \qquad (B)$$

$$+ \left\{ 2 \sum_j w_j (\alpha^a_j \, \alpha^m_j) \left[\frac{y^m_j - y^m}{y}\right] \left[\frac{y^a_j - y^a}{y}\right] \right\} + \qquad (C)$$

$$+ \left\{\left[\frac{y^m - y^a}{y}\right]\right\}^2 \cdot \left\{ \sum_j w_j (\alpha^m_j - \alpha^m)^2 \right\} + \qquad (D = F \cdot G)$$

$$+ 2\left\{\left[\frac{y^m - y^a}{y}\right]\right\} \cdot \left\{ \sum_j w_j (\alpha^m_j - \alpha^m) \left(\alpha^m_j \left[\frac{y^m_j - y^m}{y}\right] + \alpha^a_j \left[\frac{y^a_j - y^a}{y}\right] \right) \right\}, \qquad (E = 2 \cdot H \cdot J)$$

where w_j is region j's share in the national labour force and the expressions in brackets are relative income 'gaps'. Each of these five terms,

$$V^2 = A + B + C + (F \cdot G) + (2H \cdot J),$$

has a specific interpretation as a statistical 'source of regional inequality'. Furthermore, changes in regional inequality between two points in time can be written as

$$dV^2 = [dA + dB + dC] + [G \cdot dF + 2J \cdot dH] + [F \cdot dG] + [2H \cdot dJ].$$

These four components of dV^2 can be given the following labels: (1) the contribution of changing variance in sectorial incomes per worker; (2) the contribution of changes in economy-wide sectorial productivity 'gaps'; (3) the contribution of changing variance in industrial structures; and (4) a changing covariance term.

The first term in our V^2 equation, A, denotes the contribution of non-ag income per worker variance. If sectorial TFPG were truly region-specific in early growth stages, then we would expect that some portion of the rise in aggregate regional inequality would be explained by increased variance in y_j^m. The question is an empirical one, but it certainly seems reasonable to expect increasing *Northern* variance in y_j^m during periods of dramatic rates of TFPG in the non-farm sector. This would include the ante-bellum period as well as the period between 1900 and 1929, especially the 1920s. It may also include the South over the Civil War decade. After all, the war may have created conditions during which the inter-regional transfer of new 'modern' technologies were interrupted, creating increasing gaps between best and average practice in Southern non-ag sectors.

The second term in our V^2 equation, B, denotes the contribution of ag income per worker variance. Agricultural labour productivities are likely to exhibit far more extensive regional variance and for two reasons: first, the quality of immobile resources matter far more in this case; second, the mobility of agricultural capital and farm labour is likely to be far lower between regions than is true of urban-specific factors of production. Yet capital scarcity is a regional phenomenon, so low agricultural productivities are likely to be associated with regional poverty in general. Thus, the variance in y_j^a should be positively correlated with variance in y_j^m, and furthermore the variance in y_j^a should exceed that of y_j^m at any point in time.

It is the *changing* variance in y_j^a which is our focus, however. Inter-regional factor immobility *within* agriculture may well cause increased disparities in farm capital availabilities, the richer regions enjoying the higher capital intensities for long periods in the presence of continued disequilibrating growth. Outside the North, the Civil War most assuredly had the same disequilibrating impact. Since the war was especially destructive of agricultural capital stocks, and given the reduction in voluntary labour supplies associated with emancipation, we expect even greater variance in v_j^a shortly after the Civil War when the South is included.

The fourth term in the 'source of regional growth' expression has attracted the most attention in the literature. D measures the contribution of the variance in 'industrialisation' to aggregate productivity variance across states. The term has two components, both of which may have a profound impact on regional inequality trends: the average productivity gap between two sectors, and the variance in industrialisation levels themselves. These two effects are called 'differential shift' and 'proportionality shift' by regional economists, but they became a staple in the literature when Kuznets introduced them in 1955 to account for inequality patterns. If national demand or technological forces tend to raise $(y^m - y^a)$, those regions already committed to industry will find their incomes favoured. The previous section stressed the impact of unbalanced TFPG in generating those 'gaps', but subsequent Engel effects and rising capital formation shares would tend to produce demand-side reinforcement. Similarly, tariff policy favours expansion of the gap, although recent analysis suggests that the Metzler effect may have served to benefit Southern cotton producers through favourable terms of trade changes.

There are other offsetting forces to consider. Unbalanced TFPG favouring non-agriculture would produce an offsetting improvement in agriculture's terms of trade and thus would benefit regions specialising in farm production. Transatlantic and internal transport cost reductions also served to raise the relative price of farm products in the backward regions. While these induced and endogenous price effects may have played an offsetting role, systematic demand and technological forces associated with early modern economic growth must on net serve to drive the sectorial gap upwards.

During periods of balanced sectorial TFPG, the gap may stabilise or even decline as increasing land scarcity raises labour productivity on the farm and as rising capital intensity follows in the wake of out-migrating farm labour. Since technological unbalancedness is characteristic of both the ante-bellum and the 1900-29 periods, rising gaps should be typical of those historical episodes and regional inequality forces should be most apparent then too. Obviously, there may have been other exogenous forces driving the gap, and one will be emphasised in section 4: the exogenous behaviour of cotton prices.

Given the sectorial income gaps in D, any increase in the variance of industrialisation levels across regions would tend to raise aggregate regional inequality as well. Since early industrialisation is region-specific, and both scale economies and specialisation serve to reinforce that specificity, more rapid rates of industrialisation are most likely to prevail in the initially advanced states where, after all, the modern sector TFPG is centred.

Extending the Argument to Convergence

How long these disequilibrium forces persist depends on two factors: (1) the size of the initial shock and its persistence over time; and (2) the speed of inter-regional adjustment through factor markets. We have already argued that the post-1850s and post-1929 periods are indeed ones of technological and demand 'quiescence'. In each of these periods of 'quiesence', therefore, the issue centres on the speed of factor market adjustment. Certainly the rate of growth of unskilled labour in the more advanced states should tend to exceed the national average either through inter-regional migration to high-wage states, or by foreign immigrants selecting the more favoured states for location. Either historical force would tend to have the same influence: the capital-labour ratio in backward states would rise while it would tend to fall towards the national average in the richer states.

There is an additional force for equalisation to consider: the diffusion of new technologies. New technologies initially centred in non-farm sectors located in industrial states may spread to other non-farm sectors, sectors which are less region-specific. More importantly, the new technologies should spread *within* sectors to other regions in much the same fashion that the gap between best and average practice has been eroded among post-Second World War developed economies. The rate of diffusion, however, would be influenced by the poorer regions' abilities to shift capacity into the dynamic sectors, and underlying the process is accumulation in the dynamic sectors located in the 'backward' states.

What conditions would ensure that capital stock growth would be higher in backward states (label them s) relative to richer states (label them n) during periods of 'quiescence'? Contrary to the popular view, it is not necessary that investment per worker (I/L) be higher in the backward region to yield higher capital stock growth and thus convergence. Regional capital stock growth differentials can be written as

$$(G_s^k - G_n^k) = (I/L)_s \cdot k_s^{-1} - (I/L)_n \cdot k_n^{-1} .$$

Based on Soltow's (1975) estimates of wealth per active male, for example, k_n exceeded k_s by a factor of about 2 in 1870 (where the comparison is for aggregate North and South). It follows that investment per worker in the South need only have exceeded 50 per cent of the Northern figure to have enjoyed a higher capital stock growth and thus convergence.

'Differential shift' should also favour convergence. Nevertheless, we shall argue in section 5 that inter-regional convergence in industrial output mixes is to be explained by human and non-human capital formation forces rather than by the extent of initial 'labour market failure' in backward regions and subsequent success in removing such alleged market misallocations. If I am correct, then convergence of industrialisation levels across states simply serves as a proxy for capital-labour ratio equalisation.

The final force producing regional convergence lies with the economy-wide behaviour of the sectorial 'productivity gap'. After disequilibrating forces have driven the gap upwards, what influences would serve to reverse that trend, thus contributing to regional income convergence? First, the disappearance of unbalanced TFPG would tend to halt those forces which drove the gap upwards in the first place. Second, the out-migration of labour from the farm sector would tend to raise land and capital endowments among those farm workers left behind. The combined effect, of course, is to induce a downward drift in the sectorial productivity gap over time. Clearly, the poorer regions specialising in agricultural activities derive the greater benefit and thus regional convergence is fostered on this score as well.

4. REGIONAL DIVERGENCE AND CONVERGENCE: FACT

Trends in Regional Inequality

Table 33.1 confirms conventional wisdom. Since 1880, the American economy has undergone regional convergence in per worker incomes. Although we do not report the calculation here, it has also been shown (Williamson, 1977c) that labour participation rates play a minor and unsystematic role in regional per capita income trends. Theory would have suggested otherwise. That is, what might be called the 'conventional labour supply model' would predict that high-wage regions tend to have higher labour participation rates (LPRs). Thus, the variance in per capita incomes should exceed the variance in per worker incomes, and those forces producing convergence in incomes per worker should produce even larger convergence in per capita incomes. The latter prediction is confirmed everywhere in America between 1929 and 1970 and in the North between 1840 and 1880. It is rejected in all other episodes. Even for the North from 1840 to 1880, only 5 per cent of the convergence in per capita incomes can be explained by the convergence in LPRs. Explanations for differing regional income per capita growth must therefore centre on the behaviour of differing regional labour productivity growth.

More to the point of this paper, note the episodic deviations from the post-1880 convergence trend and the contrasting behaviour over the 1804-80 period. First, pronounced regional convergence prevailed within the North between 1840 and 1880, a result consistent with the technology-induced unbalanced growth of early industrialisation. Second, and in contrast, regional divergence was true of the North and South combined over the same period – the well-known Civil War impact, but the decomposition is not supplied in Table 33.1. Third, convergence took place everywhere in America between 1880 and 1900 – a result consistent with the relatively balanced character of sectorial TFPG over the late nineteenth century. The convergence was far more pronounced in the North, however, suggesting that there were additional forces at work in the South which inhibited convergence. Fourth, this long-term convergence was interrupted between 1900 and 1929. Indeed, these were decades of regional divergence in per capita incomes, especially so during the twenties. Once again, the result is consistent with the evidence of technological unbalancedness across sectors during the first third of the twentieth century. Yet, the divergence was far more pronounced in the North, suggesting that there were additional forces at work specified to the South which tended to offset the impact of unbalanced growth. Fifth, the period 1929-70 records convergence everywhere, a result consistent with balanced growth typical of the mid-twentieth century.

Why Regional Productivity Growth Rates Differ: Looking for Sources

Since the changing variance in regional per worker incomes is the result of

TABLE 33.1 The sources of changing regional inequality in America, 1840-1970: decomposing changing regional income per worker variance

Decomposition	*Period* 1950-70	1929-50	1900-29	1880-1900	1840*-80*	1880-1970
			1. Northern states only			
Total ΔV^2, of which due to	+0.000012	−0.024217	+0.012210	−0.010347	−0.040891	−0.022342
1. A var sectorial incomes per worker combined	+0.000959	−0.010503	+0.002553	+0.001662	−0.016384	−0.005329
1.1 var NFI per wkr	+0.001275	−0.010518	+0.012023	+0.001757	−0.002611	+0.004537
1.2 var FI per wkr	−0.000391	+0.000122	−0.005499	−0.001903	−0.008286	−0.007671
1.3 cov	+0.000075	−0.000107	−0.003971	+0.001808	−0.005487	−0.002195
2. var indust. structure	−0.000891	−0.000603	−0.011880	+0.000372	+0.006147	−0.010257
3. sectorial prdvty gap	+0.000863	−0.009225	+0.003726	−0.000446	−0.021909	−0.004043
4. residl cov forces	−0.000919	−0.003886	+0.017811	−0.011935	−0.008745	−0.002713
			2. Northern and Southern states combined			
Total ΔV^2, of which due to:	−0.019449	−0.072053	0.038747	−0.000900		−0.131149
1. var sectorial incomes per worker combined	−0.010065	−0.020496	−0.009936	+0.005461		−0.035036
1.1 var NFI per wkr	−0.003876	−0.019199	+0.030192	+0.003614		+0.010731
1.2 var FI per wkr	−0.001398	−0.000165	−0.028926	−0.005991		−0.036480
1.3 cov	−0.004791	−0.001132	−0.011202	+0.007838		−0.009287
2. var indust structure	−0.000934	−0.003711	−0.021746	+0.007093		−0.018699
3. sectorial prdvty gap	−0.002788	−0.031558	−0.13892	−0.001870		−0.055852
4. residl gov forces	−0.005662	−0.016288	+0.006827	−0.011584		−0.21562
			3. America combined			
Total ΔV^2, of which one to:	−0.017594	−0.066157	−0.049537	−0.009559		−0.142847
1. var sectorial incomes per worker combined	−0.009853	−0.019068	−0.17806	+0.004776		−0.41951
1.1 var NFI per wkr	−0.002937	−0.018043	+0.024654	+0.003360		+0.007034
1.2 var FI per wkr	−0.001538	−0.000130	−0.028930	−0.006749		−0.037347
1.3 cov	−0.005378	−0.000895	−0.013530	+0.008165		−0.011638
2. var indust structure	−0.000834	−0.002787	−0.020371	+0.004237		−0.025762
3. sectorial prdvty gap	−0.001558	−0.030642	−0.015179	−0.002957		−0.046794
4. residl cov forces	−0.005349	−0.013660	+0.003819	−0.015615		−0.028340

SOURCES AND NOTES: See text section 3 for dV^2 decomposition formula. Lines 2 and 3 use Paasche weights, except for 1880-1970 which uses 1929 weights. Weighted coefficient of variation used throughout. 1840* and 1880* refer to comparable regional groups with state observations in both years (e.g., excluding Minnesota, the Dakotas, Kansas, Texas and Oklahoma). The data sources and fuller details can be found in Williamson (1977c).

differing regional growth rates, the decomposition reported in Table 33.1 offers an empirical accounting of the sources of these disparate regional growth rates. How much of America's long-term regional experience is explained by differing regional productivity growth within sectors? How much by the convergence and divergence in regional industrial structures? How much by the behaviour of economy-wide experience with productivity gaps between sectors? The answers are central to any effort in modelling long-term regional inequality experience.

An earlier work of mine (Williamson, 1965) showed that the weighted coefficient of variation across states in 1840 was about the same as for France in 1864 or 1951, a country where 'pôle de croissance' had its intellectual beginnings. The figure is almost comparable to that of inter-war Italy, a nation with perhaps the most studied North-South problem. In short, America was already beset by regional inequalities in 1840, and they were marked by the international standards of the late nineteenth or early mid twentieth centuries.

An important source of the high regional inequalities in 1840 was the sectorial productivity gap. Indeed, a central prediction of section 3 was that sectorial productivity gaps should rise in response to technological unbalancedness in early development. These gaps were indeed on the rise early in the nineteenth century and reach a peak in the 1850s (Williamson, 1977c). Agricultural labour productivity growth lagged behind and, as a consequence, non-farm income per gainful worker in 1879 prices was from 2.5 to 2.8 times that of farm labour in the 1850s. The size of the gap was very large compared with that of 1839 and, presumably, even larger compared with the 1820s. The American gap was larger, for example, than Italy in either the 1870s or the 1950s, than France in the 1870s, than Japan in early Meiji, and was approximately the same as Soviet Russia on the eve of the First Plan. Clearly, sectorial productivity gaps were already very much part of the American scene by the 1850s, and they reflected the disequilibrating influences associated with the previous decades of unbalanced TFPG.

Northern regional growth experience over the four decades following 1840 can be summarised in the following terms (Table 33.1): there was no convergence in industrial structure, converging non-farm labour productivities played a minor role, converging farm labour productivities played a far larger role, and the decline in the farm-non-farm labour productivity gap played the major role. These trends appear to be consistent with technological quiescence following the late ante-bellum period.

Is the 1840-80 Northern pattern repeated for the North and South combined following 1880? The nation-wide decline in the sectorial gap accounts for 43 per cent of the convergence in state per worker incomes between 1880 and 1970, while the convergence of sectorial incomes per worker accounts for only 27 per cent. Furthermore, it is the convergence of farm income per worker which explains *all* of the sectorial income convergence. 'Differential shift' made a positive but small contribution. Once again, the main source of long-term convergence lies with farm-non-farm productivity gaps and interstate differentials in farm labour-productivities.

Demand Shocks. Technology Shocks and Unbalanced Growth

Can we account for departures from long-term regional inequality trends within the past century? Consider first the Northern regional inequality trends in Table 33.1. The period 1880-1900 records a continuation of the previous four decades of convergence, but at a slower rate as the states approach parity. The next three decades record a reversal in those trends. Between 1929 and 1950, the convergence resumes, but at an astounding rate. Indeed, the total convergence between 1929 and 1950 exceeds the convergence for 1880-1970 as a whole. Between 1950 and 1970, Northern regional inequality indices remain relatively stable.

Why the reversal in trend 1900-29 and the spectacular resumption 1929-50? The source of the reversal lies with two influences: (1) a rise in the sectorial productivity gap, and (2) an increase in the regional variance in non-farm income (NFI) per worker. Both of these forces can in combination account for all of Northern regional divergence over the first third of the twentieth century. Converging farm productivities and converging industrial structures tend to produce income per worker convergence, but the other two divergence influences dominate. It seems to me evident that both of these influences are precisely those associated with technological unbalancedness favouring the non-farm sector. It served to raise relative non-farm productivities, increasing the gap, and it also served to increase the variance in NFI per worker since the rapid rates of TFPG were centred in those sectors location-specific to high-income states, that is, in skill and machine-intensive sectors. These forces reverse in sign following 1929, a result fully consistent with the evidence of technological and demand balancedness which characterises the two decades up to 1950. Changes in the variance in state industrial structures play *no* role in accounting for the reversal after 1900 or for the resumption of convergence after 1929. The same holds for changes in the variance of farm income per worker. Indeed, both of these variables were operating in the opposite direction.

When one turns from Northern regional inequality experience over the past century to economy-wide experience, some interesting contrasts emerge. First, however, let us review the similarities. The overall convergence in state per worker incomes between 1880 and 1970 was even more pronounced in America as a whole than in the North. The 'sources' of that long-term convergence appear to be similar. The nation-wide decline in the productivity gap accounts for 33 per cent; the convergence of sectorial incomes per worker accounts for 29 per cent, all of which is explained by the convergence of farm incomes, and none by non-farm productivity behaviour; convergence in state industrial structures accounts for a much smaller share, 18 per cent. As with the North, explanations of differences in long-term regional rates of productivity growth must lie primarily with the behaviour of the economy-wide productivity gap and with interstate differentials in farm productivity growth. Similarities with the Northern regional experience appear within shorter-term episodes as well. The dramatic convergence between 1929 and 1950 reappears economy-wide, and the sources of that convergence are roughly the same. That is, 46 per cent of the per worker incomes convergence between 1929 and 1950 is attributable to the sharp decline in productivity gaps, a notable departure from the much lower contribution from this source in the 1900-29 period. The convergence of state industrial structures following 1929 accounts for only 4 per cent of the total convergence in per worker incomes, an even smaller contribution than in the preceding 1900-29 period. Finally, it appears that almost all of the contribution of converging sectorial incomes per worker after 1929 is attributable to the declining variance in NFI per worker. In contrast, the 1900-29 period records a divergence in state NFI per worker, a result fully consistent with trends in the North.

What, then, are the differences? There are two, and they both centre on the 1900-29 episode. First, the convergence in state farm productivities was much more dramatic economy-wide than in the North. This served to offset the divergence in state NFI per worker, thus producing a net contribution towards convergence in sectorial income variance combined. Since this result appears for the North and South combined, we conclude that the 1900-29 period contained unusually favourable farm productivity forces specific to the South. Second, while farm-non-farm productivity gaps rose in the North after 1900, they declined economy-wide. True, the decline was far less extensive than in the 1929-50 episode, but the contrast with Northern experience during the first third of the twentieth century is still striking.

What is it about Southern agricultural productivity performance which serves to make American regional inequality experience between 1900 and 1929 different from that taking place within the North? I believe the answer lies in large part with cotton prices. Between 1900 and 1920, the relative price of cotton underwent an extraordinary rise, far in excess of farm products generally. To some extent, the same is true of the 1929-50 period. In contrast, cotton prices collapsed during the twenties, but the total rise from 1900 to 1929 still exceeds that of farm products generally. These relative price movements may well explain the contrasting regional inequality behaviour within the North, on the one hand, and the North and South combined on the other: farm incomes per worker converge at a far less dramatic rate within the North, 1900-29; sectorial productivity gaps rise in the North but fall economy-wide over the same period; thus, regional divergence occurs in the North but not economy-wide. Furthermore, these relative price trends suggest that contrasting regional inequality behaviour should have been centred on the 1900-20 decades, while comparable behaviour should have characterised the 1920s. The evidence confirms this prediction (Williamson, 1977c). It seems plausible, therefore, that the exogenous trends in cotton prices may account for America's departure from the 'Northern model of regional divergence' operating during the first third of the twentieth century.

Cost-of-Living Impact and Converging Price Structure

Since comparisons of labour productivity and income per capita differentials across American regions are used to make both welfare and labour market efficiency judgements, cost-of-living adjustments should be introduced wherever possible. While published cost-of-living data for the twentieth century have always been available, such adjustments have never, to my knowledge, been attempted. In addition, recent research has now supplied the necessary data to make such adjustments even for the nineteenth century.

We can only report the results of those adjustments briefly here (Williamson, 1977c). Cost-of-living differentials have always been pronounced in America and they have always been lower in backward states. Thus, the variance in real state incomes per worker are smaller than the variance in nominal incomes in *every* year since 1840, with one exception. (For the North and South combined, real disparities are higher than nominal in 1840, primarily due to the high costs of living which prevailed in the South Atlantic at that time.) There is no indication from the last century of American experience that the living cost differentials have declined in importance. On the contrary, from 1880 to 1970 regional income convergence was *steeper* in real than in nominal terms. Thus, nominal incomes understate the 'true' convergence in America over the past century. The result is not simply a North-South 'sunshine' phenomenon, since the same finding appears within the North itself.

5. FACTOR MARKET FAILURE AND THE WELFARE IMPLICATIONS OF REGIONAL HISTORIES

What are the welfare implications of these regional inequality trends? If real wages for identical worker 'types' were equated across states and if rates of return to capital were also so equated, one would be hard pressed to argue that regional inequality indicators serve well as measures of market failure, or that regions really matter in analyses of historical trends in income distribution. We conclude with two brief comments that relate to this issue.

First, we now have the evidence which shows little consistency between regional and national inequality trends. For example, high and persistent national inequality between 1880 and 1929 was consistent with the regional income convergence. Regional convergence after 1950 was not accompanied by national egalitarian trends either. The implication seems to be that trends in 'between'-state income variance have never been an important ingredient

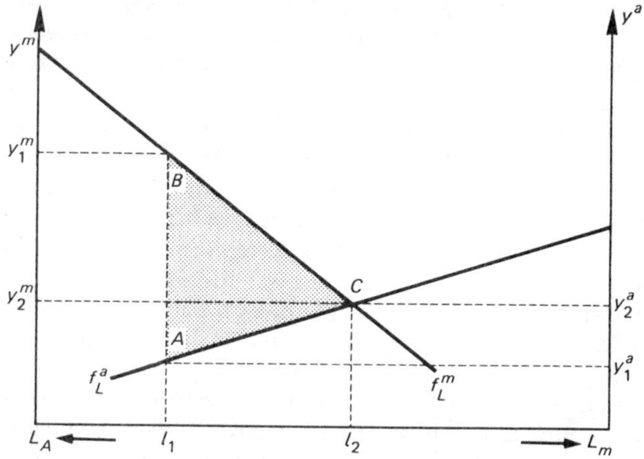

Fig. 33.1

of total inequality trends in America, and that trends in 'within'-state variance have dominated.

Second, factor market failure appears to have been grossly overdrawn in the literature. Sectorial income gaps and wage differentials are hardly the same thing, although the literature seems to suggest otherwise. An example is offered by New England in 1890. (See Williamson, 1977c, section 3.) Nominal wages of urban common labour were only 9 per cent higher than farm labour during that year in New England. For the same region the ratio of service income per worker in the non-ag compared to the ag sector was 3.68 in 1880 and 3.45 in 1900. In the late nineteenth century, approximate nominal wage equalisation *intra*-regionally in New England was consistent with enormous differentials in average labour productivities (or service incomes per worker). The latter is an irrelevant index of the former. Apparently the same is true for the early and mid-nineteenth century. With the exception of Vermont in the 1840s and 1850s, no region exhibited significant non-farm-farm wage gaps for labour of comparable skill. The average ratio of these wages for both the North and the US as a whole was 0.99, evidence which unambiguously rejects the thesis of *intra*-regional labour market failure even during a period of extensive regional inequality.

The implications are important since the intra-regional 'labour market failure' view is central to Borts and Stein's (1964) regional model. It is also central to Denison's (1967) decomposition of the sources of international differences in rates of post-war growth. The argument is familiar. The two sectors diagrammed in Figure 33.1 illustrate the actual distribution of employment l_1, and the equilibrium distribution l_2, for a given region. We observe large sectorial labour productivity gaps between agriculture and non-agriculture early in American development. Borts and Stein and Denison infer that there are too many labourers in agriculture. Subsequent success in transferring workers to non-agricultural employment produces regional income gains as the *intra*-regional 'labour market failure' is removed. The more rapid the rate of industrialisation in the backward region, given the size of the alleged market failure, the larger will be the growth of the backward region. The key to this analysis is the doubtful assumption that sectorial income gaps can be equated with gaps in marginal productivities of homogeneous labour. There is little in the history of American labour markets to support such a view. *Intra*-sectoral differences in wage rates for homogeneous labour were never large, *intra*-sectorial labour markets were typically efficient, and the alleged gains in regional GNP from the reduction in the size of the triangle *ABC* are illusory.

There is an alternative view of market failure which would instead stress intra-regional capital immobility. The alternative view can be seen in Figure 33.1 if rates of return were to replace the service income indicators and if we now imagine the horizontal axis describing the intra-sectorial distribution of capital. If it can be established that rates of return in non-agriculture in general, and manufacturing in particular, were higher with the advent of modern economic growth and that they persisted, then we would have an alternative explanation for convergence even in the absence of labour market failure. Recent research for the 1850s would appear to substantiate this position. (For a summary of the evidence, see Williamson, 1977c.)

REFERENCES

Borts, G., and J. Stein, *Economic Growth in a Free Market* (New York: Columbia University Press, 1964).

Denison, E. F., *Why Growth Rates Differ: Postwar Experience in Nine Western Countries* (Washington, D.C.: The Brookings Institution, 1967).

Kendrick, J. W., *Productivity Trends in the United States* (Princeton: Princeton University Press, 1961).

Lindert, P. H., and J. G. Williamson. 'Three Centuries of American Inequality', in P. Uselding (ed.), *Research in Economic History,* Vol. I (Greenwich, Conn.: Johnson Associates, 1976) 69-123.

Soltow, L., *Men and Wealth in the United States, 1850-1870* (New Haven: Yale University Press, 1975).

Williamson, J. G., and P.H. Lindert, *A Macroeconomic History of American Inequality* (Academic Press, 1979).

Williamson, J. G., *Late Nineteenth Century American Development: A General Equilibrium History* (Cambridge: Cambridge University Press, 1974).

Williamson, J. G., 'American Prices and Urban Inequality since 1820', *Journal of Economic History,* 36 (June 1976b) 303-33.

Williamson, J. G., 'Strategiv Wage Goods, Prices and Inequality', *American Economic Review,* 67 (March 1977b) 29-41.

Williamson, J. G., 'Inequality, Accumulation and Technological Imbalance: A Growth-Equity Conflict in American History?', *Economic Development and Cultural Change* vol. 27, no. 2 (January 1979), pp. 231-53.

Williamson, J. G., 'The Sources of American Inequality, 1896-1948', *Review of Economics and Statistics,* LVIII, No. 4 (November 1976a) 387-97.

Williamson, J. G., 'Regional Inequality and the Process of National Development', *Economic Development and Cultural Change*;XIII, No. 4, Part II (July 1965), Supplement.

Williamson, J. G., 'Unbalanced Growth, Inequality and Regional Development: Some Lessons from American History', paper presented to the Symposium 'A National Policy Toward Regional Change: Alernatives to Confrontation', 24-27 September 1977c (Austin, Texas).

Part 4

Methodology for Measurement of Economic Disparities

34 Comparison of Development Levels: Inequalities in the Physical Structures of National Economies

Eva Ehrlich

Highly complex economic categories, as e.g. the economic development level of a country at a given date, can be less and less determined true to reality with the aid of a single indicator as e.g. GNP or GDP or national income, though, undoubtedly, this is most palpable. Still, practically every international comparison makes efforts to express economic development finally compressed into a single indicator, and that into a comprehensive synthetic indicator which, for lack of a better one, is considered as suited for an imperfect and simplified quantification of the development level and which is widely used by economic historians, economists and politicians as well.

Though I believe that the expression of economic development level with a single simplified indicator is an 'impermissible simplification', yet I apply it. In addition, however, I make an attempt to approach the economic development level on the basis of several physical indicators, in a many-sided way, and to present and analyse its internal pattern and components in a diversified manner. By relying on these I will try to draw a few conclusions, to be regarded for the time being as hypotheses, about the present-day interpretation of international regularities (international average norms).

1. ECONOMIC DEVELOPMENT LEVELS AND PROPORTIONS

Aided by a team I have recently concluded a major experimental project, whose aim was to compare from several aspects the economic development level of countries in the 1960s and 1970s. In the course of work we have succeeded in collecting and using a wide basis of physical data. Of course I have to refrain from reviewing the data basis and the detailed analysis. At this place I shall dwell only on those statements of the experimental analysis, to be regarded only as hypotheses, which are related mainly to international economic inequalities.

'Technically', the short-cut method[1] was applied which had been worked out by Ferenc Janossy [1][2] and whose development can be traced through several works, as e.g. [2], [3], [4], [5], [6] and [7]. In the course of time the system of indicators strongly expanded, also under the effect of the widening possibilities provided by international statistics. (In Janossy's work there were 16 indicators, while in the work mentioned as [8], 43 physical indicators were used.)

The expansion and differentiation of the system of indicators is not merely a quantitative change and does not only facilitate more exact computations. It is a meritorial, qualitative development that the present set of indicators comprises, beside the physical indicators having the nature of a flow, almost an equal number of indicators which relate to stock. Accordingly, the so-called corrected GDP per capita values obtained with the 'old method' but on the basis of the new set of indicators, differ also in contents from the GDP per capita values used as a starting basis and, by their nature, having the character of a flow.

Namely, the corrected GDP per capita indicator obtained with our method is a complex synthetic indicator which tries to express not only the current utilisation of a country at a given date (i.e. the value of GDP), but also its wealth accumulated in the course of time (i.e. the reproducible national wealth of a country), that is, its stock, in a combined manner – even if imperfectly. Let us call this complex synthetic indicator hereafter 'economic development level' per capita.

It has to be emphasised that the results of the (for the time being

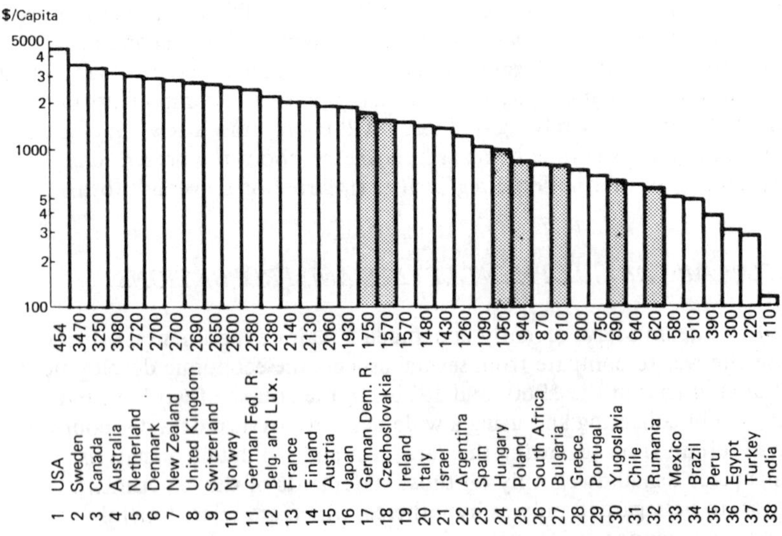

FIG. 34.1 EDL values of 31 capitalist countries and Hungary in 1970

experimental) computations may necessarily deviate from the results of other international comparisons, as this one measures the EDL values of the countries on a different scale and, as can be seen, it interprets the notion of economic development level in a different way: for details see [10].

It is necessary to call attention to the fact that on the lowest levels of economic development (as e.g. India) the value of EDL obtained by our method may imply mistakes because of the used set of indicators and the statistical unreliabilities. Perhaps another set of physical indicators may characterise the EDL of the developing countries better.

2. PHYSICAL STRUCTURES, GROWTH PATHS

Our method relies on the assumption that the size of the physical indicators allows us to determine the level of economic development. In our earlier analyses (e.g. in 9) it already turned out that the values of the physical indicators representing areas of production and consumption are influenced not only by the economic development level: certain deviations – within a domain – may be observed between the physical indicators even with the same level of economic development. Obviously, such deviations may be caused by geographical relations, various endowments, customs, traditions and orders of value, the cultural levels developed and determined by historical and economic antecedents, by the various aspects of international relations, etc.

Our assumption is that if we work by relying on a sufficient number of physical indicators representing the main aspects of socio-economic processes for a sufficient number of countries, there is a way of learning and characterising the structure of the countries from a physical aspect, in other words, the so-called physical structure of the countries. On this basis, it becomes possible:

to identify the specific features of differences between countries;

to place the shifts over time of the physical structures of the individual countries in the process of development;

to grasp the general features of development and differences in development level as appearing in the physical structures.

We have 43 physical indicators. These indicators seem to be suited for characterising various aspects of the socio-economic development level. There are indicators which represent personal consumption and others which show the investment process. There are indicators expressive of productive consumption and its structure. Within all these there are indicators of flows (output) and of stocks (wealth).

In our judgement the set of indicators in itself is insufficient for pointing out the differences, for characterising the physical structure of the individual countries, for interpreting and evaluating the particular features. It allows, however, depending on the extent of general orientation in the subject-matter, to point out some general and important interrelations of the physical structures. The analysis will be performed in the course of our work by two kinds of approach. First the relative dispersion of the physical indicators (see the formula in Table 34.1) by countries will be shown and analysed, and then the levels computed from the set of flow and stock indicators will be analysed.

(a) Relative dispersion is an essential characteristic of the physical structure

It is a methodological-computational principle of the analysis that to a definite level of economic development at a given date (to the value of EDL) there belongs on international average a definite magnitude of a physical indicator (e.g. steel consumption – kg per capita). As a reciprocal of this approach it may be also said that a definite value of the physical indicator corresponds to a partial fictitious EDL value determined according to the regression line expressing the international average. From the partial fictitious EDL values of a country (43 in our case), the usual indicator of relative dispersion may be easily computed. Economically interpreted: the higher the value of the indicator of relative dispersion, the stronger the

TABLE 34.1 Relative dispersion* in capitalist countries and Hungary in 1970

Country number	*Country*	*Relative dispersion*	*Country number*	*Country*	*Relative dispersion*
1	Austria	0.330	17	Turkey	0.499
2	Belgium-Luxemburg	0.347	18	India	0.530
3	Denmark	0.430	19	Israel	0.428
4	United Kingdom	0.300	20	Japan	0.507
5	Finland	0.462	21	South Africa	0.330
6	France	0.364	22	Egypt	0.412
7	Greece	0.567	23	Canada	0.308
8	Netherlands	0.334	24	USA	0.355
9	Ireland	0.567	25	Argentina	0.620
10	Italy	0.423	26	Brazilia	0.920
11	Norway	0.291	27	Chile	0.270
12	German Fed. Rep.	0.322	28	Mexico	0.920
13	Portugal	0.502	29	Peru	0.561
14	Spain	0.392	30	Australia	0.353
15	Sweden	0.361	31	New Zealand	0.482
16	Switzerland	0.268	32	Hungary	0.418

*Relative dispersion $= \frac{s}{\bar{x}}$

where $$s = \sqrt{\frac{n^1/x1 - \bar{x}/^2 + n^2/x2 - \bar{x}/^2 + \ldots + n_r/x_r - \bar{x}/^2}{n^1 + n^2 + \ldots n_r}}$$

$$\bar{x} = \frac{n_i x_i + n2x2 + \ldots + n_r x_r}{n^1 + n^2 + \ldots + n_r}$$

deviation of the physical structure of the given country or group of countries from the international average of economic development level as a 'norm'.

It is remarkable that the countries where relative development is high, belong, almost without exception, to the medium zone. The question arises: is there a relationship between the EDL values of the countries and the magnitude of dispersions; and if so, of what kind?

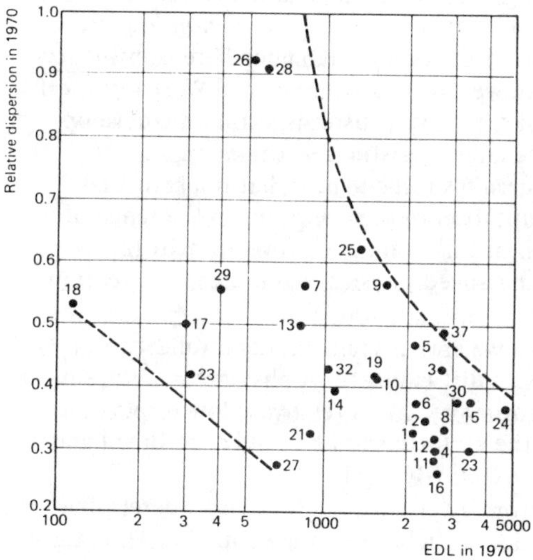

1 Austria
2 Belg.+ Lux.
3 Denmark
4 UK
5 Finland
6 France
7 Greece
8 Netherlands
9 Ireland
10 Italy
11 Norway
12 GFR
13 Portugal
14 Spain
15 Sweden
16 Switzerland
17 Turkey
18 India
19 Israel
20 Japan
21 South Africa
22 Egypt
23 Canada
24 USA
25 Argentina
26 Brazilia
27 Chile
28 Mexico
29 Peru
30 Australia
31 New Zealand
32 Hungary

FIG. 34.2 Relationship between dispersion and the value of EDL in capitalist countries and Hungary in 1970

The points of individual countries indicating dispersion in the graphs relate to logically interpretable interrelations.

With a low EDL the physical structure of the countries is characterised by a certain traditional equilibrium and a corresponding similarity. In this domain, therefore, the indicators of dispersion are on a low level. Here belong the points of countries on a lower development level than $400 per capita. (The small number of countries makes the statement rather uncertain.)

In the domain of 500 and 1500-dollar EDL we find the countries on the road to industrialisation. In this domain an extremely strong differentiation of the physical structure seems to occur. Different areas of development obtain emphasis in the countries, economic processes may accelerate in different domains, economic policy may prefer and disprefer various areas in a differentiated manner on different principles. The rather high value and scattered situation of the indicators appearing in this domain is probably also related to the fact that the countries situated in this domain differ very greatly from each other from the social point of view, in geographical location and, as a consequence, also in respect of traditions and customs:

we find here Hungary and capitalist countries, and a group of developing South American countries also belongs here. At the same time, it is also probable that in this period of the economic development process some economic and social disequilibrium is unavoidable and maybe even necessary: it is a disequilibrium which is both a cause and a consequence of considerable social and economic tensions.

On a high EDL level again, the countries are characterised by low dispersion indicators and, accordingly, by similarities in the physical structure of the countries, and by a balanced state in the *economic sense*. It must be noted that the situation of the points belonging here is influenced also by the fact that in this domain we find mostly advanced West European countries, for which a similarity of traditions, customs, economic development and intensive interactions are characteristic. But this is only a motivating factor. The assumption seems to be logical that the high EDL already attained allows a close adaptation of consumption to the range of needs appearing on the given level. In this domain of development this is presumably the real cause for the balanced physical structures, for a certain degree of 'uniformity'.

It seems that those described above are of a fairly general validity and also characterise the situation of socialist Hungary. A physical structure most conforming to the international norm and thus a relatively low dispersion, is found in Hungary too. Among the countries to be found here Brazil and Mexico's dispersion indicators are extremely high.

Analysis of the physical indicators by countries allows us to determine the particular features of the physical structures of the countries. Thus e.g. the physical indicators of Greece indicate an accelerated expansion of investments and growth, a relatively high nutritive content of food consumption and, at the same time, a low agricultural productivity. In Mexico an up-to-date network of transportation, on the one hand, and a low level of public infrastructure, as well as low indicators of personal consumption, point to considerable discrepancies.

The countries presented only for the sake of illustration and having characteristically unbalanced physical structures (high relative dispersion) are on the upswing in the industrial development process. These are countries situated in the medium domain of development and which have been characterised in the last 10-15 years by a high rate of absolute[3] economic growth, generally exceeding 5-6 per cent annually. By examining the growth rate between 1961-1970[4] and the relative dispersion in 1970, together with its interrelations, we get also in general terms the proposition that to higher rates of growth there belong higher values of dispersion, and conversely. From the interrelations there emerge different 'paths of dispersion and growth': on the highest path are situated Brazil and Mexico with a high dispersion relative to their growth rates and the lowest path – as will follow from what has been said – is that of the West European capitalist countries.

Two statements meet here: we have seen that the indicators of dispersion are highest in the zone of medium-developed countries and we have found a positive correlation between the growth rate and the size of dispersion. Examining then the relationship between EDL in 1970 and growth rates between 1961 and 1970, we find that in economically more developed countries, with the progress of growth, the rates of growth become smaller – more exactly, in the countries in the 'second line' there is a possibility of an acceleration of the growth rate. The relationship between EDL and the growth rate throws a different light on our statements made up to now. With an EDL between $500 and $1000 per head growth rates fluctuate in many countries between 5 and 8 per cent, in the development zone above it between 3.5 and 5.0 per cent and later they clearly fall below this rate. Thus significant deviations in the physical structures of countries (high dispersion) are characteristic of moderately developed countries, related to the fact that growth generally accelerates with such development level, which, by the nature of things, involves strong structural rearrangements, imbalances, tensions, 'structural uneasiness'.

If the size of relative dispersions and their relations with development level are examined also for 1960 and compared to the relationship presented in Figure 34.2, the following tendencies emerge:

the indicator of dispersion of the countries was generally higher in 1970 than in 1960;

the magnitude of dispersions increased fast in countries on a lower level of development:

the growth of dispersion is remarkable also in the most developed countries.

The reasons, the main explanation of these tendencies, may be found in the following:

(1) Apart from the reconstruction period after the Second World War, the decade in question was the period of fastest growth in the countries examined. In addition, this period was characterised by the fast spread of very important technical-technological changes which, by the nature of things, considerably changed the range of choice as regards the possibilities and needs of productive and final consumption. All that necessarily entailed a relatively quick modification in the physical structure and a growing uneasiness. This, in turn, increased the differences in physical structures between countries and led to a rise in the level of the relative dispersions.

The general tendency may be observed in Hungary too.

(2) It had already turned out when the relative dispersions for 1970 were presented that in the beginning or in the early stages of industrialisation the dispersions of the countries are situated on a relatively high level. In our opinion the related effects strengthened between 1960 and 1970 because technical-technological progress and the intensification of international relations demanded the specification of physical structures in these countries. This is indicated by the fact that the relative dispersions conspicuously increased in some countries, e.g. in Greece, Portugal, Egypt etc.

(3) The increasing relative dispersion in the most developed countries in respect of the given set of indicators is caused from the economic point of view – beyond those mentioned under (1) – by the fact that saturation has been approached, which is expressed methodologically in the 'flattening of regression curves'. At a given stage of growth in these countries, in respect of the relatively easily observable traditional physical indicators, it is no longer the growth of volume but qualitative improvements and differentiation that are the order of the day. Therefore small differences in volume find expression as large differences in development level and thus the indicators become insensitive to development and growth. (This problem emerges otherwise with international comparisons, also in general terms.)

(b) Main components of development level: differences in the levels of flows and stocks

In the preceding subsection we presented the economic development levels and proportions determined on the basis of the total set of indicators. We may also compute development level indicators from a partial set of the total of indicators and deepen the analysis with the aid of such indicators of level and their comparison.

The rather big number of physical indicators in the set allows us to separate and use two partial sets of indicators, to characterise on the one hand current productive and personal consumption (henceforth flow level) and on the other hand to characterise the order of magnitude of material wealth (henceforth stock level).[5]

As can be seen from Table 34.2, in some countries the flow level and in others the stock level is higher and, accordingly, the order of countries by flow and stock levels differs. The direction and extent of the deviation between the flow and stock levels is made palpable by the quotient of the two: the flow/stock quotient (column 5). It should be self-evident that a quotient with a value higher than unity means that in the given country relatively advanced flow indicators are coupled with a lower level of stock indicators, and conversely if the quotient is smaller than unity. The greater the deviation from unity, the sharper the difference in level determined by the flow and stock indicators, the greater – in this respect – the deviation from the international average or norm of the country.

Is there a relationship between the growth rate and the flow/stock quotient?

Examining 32 countries, from among the set of indicators around the value of 1.0, first of all Hungary and the fast-developing South European countries occupy a separate place. It can be also shown with the aid of a model that the acceleration of the growth rate entails for some time a particular discrepancy in relations between the current output and the elements of material wealth having the character of stock. Acceleration of the growth rate first necessarily materialises in the growing volume of

TABLE 34.2 Values for stock and flow levels by countries in 1970.

Country	*Flow level*		*Stock level*		*Quotient of flow/stock*	*Order according to EDL*
	rank	*per head*	*rank*	*per head*	*2/4*	
	1	2	3	4	5	6
USA	1	4370	1	4750	0.92	1
Sweden	2	3560	3	3360	1.06	2
Australia	3	3050	5	3060	1.00	4
Canada	4	2970	2	3410	0.87	3
Netherlands	5	2830	11	2610	1.08	5
GFR	6	2620	12	2360	1.11	11
Switzerland	7	2620	8	2710	0.97	9
United Kingdom	8	2570	9	2690	0.96	8
Finland	9	2520	16	1750	1.44	14
Norway	10	2470	10	2630	0.94	10
Belgium and Lux.	11	2450	13	2300	1.07	12
Denmark	12	2450	4	3080	0.80	6
New Zealand	13	2430	7	2850	0.85	7
France	14	2230	6	2920	0.76	13
Austria	15	2010	14	2100	0.96	15
Japan	16	1790	15	2100	0.85	16
Italy	17	1500	18	1530	0.98	18
Ireland	18	1480	17	1650	0.90	17
Israel	19	1290	19	1520	0.85	19
Hungary	20	1200	22	860	1.40	22
Spain	21	1160	21	940	1.23	21
Argentina	22	940	20	1270	0.74	20
South Africa	23	940	23	760	1.24	23
Greece	24	900	25	680	1.32	24
Portugal	25	790	24	700	1.13	25
Chile	26	620	26	650	0.95	26
Mexico	27	560	27	615	0.91	27
Brazil	28	520	28	510	1.02	28
Peru	29	400	29	390	1.05	29
Turkey	30	350	31	240	1.38	31
Egypt	31	270	30	350	0.77	30
India	32	121	32	94	1.29	32

output, whose increased volume allows only later that the increased production capacity should be embodied in stocks (wealth). In our opinion it is basically this law which becomes manifest in the separation of the countries mentioned.

Acceleration of economic growth in the South European countries, Spain, Greece and to a lesser extent in Portugal, was promoted, beside spontaneous processes, also by efforts of economic policy and economic policy instruments put at the service of these efforts. Obviously, in these countries economic policy efforts were orientated towards increasing output. But the operational mechanisms of the capitalist economy leave rather narrow scope for the movement of economic policy.

It is a welcome change that the quotient of Hungary in 1970 is somewhat lower than that of Finland and not much higher than in the South European capitalist countries with a higher rate of growth. In socialist countries, including Hungary, economic policy has a much higher degree of freedom and a qualitatively different one. From the point of view of the deliberate and planned development of the economy this is a huge advantage. But the higher degree of freedom also conceals dangers. Objective laws of movement also assert themselves in the socialist economy – the 'physical structure' of the economy cannot be shaped at will. If economic policy in our countries pursues, using the higher degree of freedom, a strongly output-oriented trend of 'catching-up' and represses on this account certain fields too much in the course of development, then as occurred in Hungary in the 1950s, significant disproportions may come about which, on the one hand, may entail disproportions in the physical structure and consumption and also related tensions; and, on the other hand, a sharpening of the tensions may endanger the success of the output-oriented development itself.

It is justified to have a closer look at the situation of the flow/stock indicators by countries, as well as the internal structure of the relatively low stock indicators. The quotient indicators of the fast-developing capitalist countries are relatively near to each other. As regards the internal structure of the stock indicators, no significant agreements (similarities) between countries can be discerned.

As regards the internal structure of the stock indicators of Hungary those indicating a relatively high development level are to be found among the less capital-intensive, so-called 'relatively easy to develop stock indicators' such as radio and TV sets, hospital beds and so on. At the same time we find among the worst-situated indicators the 'slowly developing stock indicators' e.g. rooms (23), water (24) and WC (25) indicators. But the indicators for the stock of passenger cars (30) and trucks (31) also show a low value. The low level of the former group of indicators is a sign of the underdevelopment of the capital-intensive infrastructure belonging to living standards, while the indicators for cars and trucks are related today above all to the lack of quality roads and the underdevelopment of a service-station network. These features of the structure of stock indicators are also related to the historical inheritance of Hungary. But, as a matter of fact, because of the economic policy aimed at increasing volumes, asserted in the course of socialist development, the requirements of equilibrium were frequently pushed into the background.

3. 'DISSOLUTION' OF THE INTERNATIONAL STANDARD (NORM)

From the facts presented and the few comments on them it has emerged that, first of all *in the domain of the now industrialising countries* and mainly after 1960, a strong differentiation of physical structures within and between countries, and through this, a gradual 'dissolution' of the 'international standard' has occurred.

It is worthwhile to emphasise at least the following aspects of this process:

(1) The number of national economies now joining the international road to economic growth and the international division of labour on a wider scale is on the increase. It follows that the process of industrialisation becomes a dominating force in countries situated geographically far apart, having different traditions and situated outside the European sphere of culture.

(2) Intensification of the international division of labour and the fact that it is more and more assuming the nature of integration allows, particularly for countries with relatively small or medium-sized population, to develop their production structures rather one-sidedly, and thus being about significant 'disproportions' within the country, which has a direct determinative effect first of all on the pattern of productive consumption.

(3) The technical-technological and cooperation constellation in the world economy and the present-day capitalism increase and expand the centralisation of gross domestic product, particularly in the now industrialising countries, and increase the scope of influence as well as the degree of efficiency of economic policy.

These are perhaps the most important reasons why physical structures are strongly differentiated in this domain and lead to the emergence of multi-level and highly diversified economies. Therefore, the determination of the international average becomes rather uncertain in a certain interval and the possibility of error in using it as a standard becomes greater.

In the domain of high development, though from a different aspect, the 'dissolution' of the international standard also asserts itself. The problem of the domain of 'flattened regression curves' has been already mentioned when discussing the changes in the indicator of relative dispersion: in the interval belonging to a high economic development level small differences in volume of the physical indicator are already reflected as big differences in development level (e.g. in the case of the radio indicator, where on the high-development level the regression curve – that is the relationship between physical indicator and EDL value – is flattening.) The rise in development level brings more and more physical indicators registered in international statistics to the critical stage where a statistically traceable change in the consumption of the given physical volume hardly indicates a rise in economic development level.

It should be emphasised that the problems of measurement and of methodology related to the differentiation of the industrialising countries and to the flattening of the regression curve emerge not only with the given method, but with every method attempting a many-sided international comparison. At the same time, we have no doubt that the levels of economic development – as far as they have indeed an important effect on the lives of people – are internationally measurable in a comparative manner, even if with larger margins of error; they are measurable through several kinds of careful approach, in a less simplified manner, not condensed into a single indicator, but many-sidedly – in other words, more realistically.

It should be obvious that, in view of the new problem which has emerged, our method and our set of indicators have to be modified and expanded. This correction must adapt itself to the analytical problems which become increasingly important internationally: to learning and characterising the various types of economic and consumption patterns changing over time, to drawing the conclusions therefrom for economic history and economic policy and for the determination of long-term development tasks in the individual countries.

NOTES

[1] A short review of the method and the physical indicators used in the computations contained in Appendix 1.

[2] The references below are indicated in the text by superior numbers.

[3] The development level and progress in it are generally measured with the aid of per capita indicators, since it should be obvious that, e.g. from the viewpoint of productivity or living standards, such indicators are important. However, as regards structural changes and their velocity, their balanced or unbalanced state, it is not so much the per unit as the absolute indicators which are significant. The faster the growth in absolute terms, the stronger the assertion of quick and unbalanced structural changes may be. Thus here, from this aspect, the countries which show big growth in absolute terms (but slow growth in per capita indicator because of large demographic development) are considered as countries with high growth rates.

[4] Economic growth rates were taken on the basis of the official data of the capitalist countries and Hungary on GDP per head at unchanged prices.

[5] The flow level was determined on the basis of 24 physical indicators and the stock level on that of 19. From the partial fictitious GDP per head values of the 24 flow indicators and the 19 stock indicators the geometrical mean has been computed and the values of the flow and stock levels have been arrived at accordingly.

REFERENCES

[1] Ferenc Janossy, 'A gazdasagi fejlettseg merhetosege es uj meresi modszere' [The measurability and a new measuring method of economic development level (Kosgazdasagi es Jogi Konyvkiado, Budapest, 1963).

[2] Eva Ehrlich, 'An examination of the interrelation between consumption indicators expressed in physical units and per capita national income', *Czechoslovak Economic Papers* (Academic Publishing House of the Czechoslovak Academy of Sciences, Prague, 1966-7).

[3] Eva Ehrlich, 'Mezhdunarodniye sopostavleniya natsionalnovo dohoda na dushu naseleniya v sotsialisticheskih i kapitalisticheskih stranah', *Metologicheskiye problemi mezhdunarodnih soizmerenyj stoizmosmih pokazanyelei* (NAUKA, Moscow, 1968).

[4] Eva Ehrlich, 'International analysis for the Hungarian long-term planning', Volumes 'A', 'B', 'C' (Institute of Economic Planning of the Hungarian Planning Office, 1968) Number 2.

[5] Eva Ehrlich, 'Dynamic international comparison of national incomes expressed in terms of physical indicators', *Oesteurope Wirtschaft*, Koln, 1969/1.

[6]Eva Ehrlich, 'The level of GDP per head in 29 market economies and 8 socialist countries in 1960', Interoffice Memorandum (European Commission for Europe, Geneva, 1968). See also 'Survey 1969' [United Nations: prepared by the Secretariat of the Economic Commission for Europe, Geneva].

[7]Eva Ehrlich, 'Economic development and personal consumption levels: an international comparison', *Acta Oeconomica,* 1971, Vol.. 6.

[8]Eva Ehrlich and workmates Gy. Partos; M-ne Csorba; P. Szarvas, 'Economic development levels, rates and structures', Volume I-II, manuscript, (Budapest, 1977).

[9]See in details Attila Osernok, E. Ehrlich and Gyorgy Szilagyi, 'Infrastruktura. Korok es orszagok' [Infrastructure. Ages and countries] (Kossuth Konyvkiado, Budapest, 1975); 'A hundred years of infrastructural development: an international comparison', *Acta Oeconomica,* Vol. 9, 1972/1; and E. Ehrlich, 'On the Condition, Terms and Trends of Development of Hungarian infrastructure' (Gazdasag, 1977/2); Dr Eva Ehrlich, *An international comparison of infrastructural development; International Economics-Comparisons and Interdependences, Internationale Wirtschaft-Vergleiche und Interdependenzen.* ed. F. Levcik. (Springer Verlag, Wien-New York, 1978) pp. 15-36.

[10]Dr I. Csahok-Dr. Gy. Szilagyi, 'A nemzetkozi osszehasonlitasok meresenek skalai' [Measurement scales of international comparison], *Statisztikai Szemle,* Vol. 56. No. 8-9, 1978, pp. 842-55.

APPENDIX 1 THE SHORT-CUT METHOD OF MEASURING ECONOMIC DEVELOPMENT LEVEL

The main steps leading to the determination of the economic development level are as follows.

1st step: selection of the countries to be included in the investigation and a first, approximate, estimation of their development level. As a preliminary standard of development level the per capita GDP converted to dollars at the official rate of exchange may be taken.

2nd step: selection or formation of the physical indicators and working out their volumes from the statistical data of the countries to be examined.

3rd step: a separate graph is drawn for each of the physical indicators: on the horizontal axis the per capita GDP, on the vertical one the scale of the given physical indicator is represented.

Then the data of the selected physical indicators of the selected countries are plotted on these graphs, by indicating the consumption of the volume of the indicator in question at the place corresponding to the per capita GDP of the country in question. Thus every country is represented by a point whose abscissa is the per capita GDP of the given country and its ordinate is the value of the given indicator belonging to the given per capita GDP of the country.

The set of points in the diagrams is situated in a narrower or wider zone depending on the closeness of correlation between the given indicator and the level of economic development.

4th step: determination of the middle line of the set of points in the diagrams of each physical indicator. The method does not apply mathematical specification, but establishes the functions empirically, in a graphical manner. The medium line (regression line) denoted graphically and controlled with the aid of the least-squares method thus derived illustrates the relationship between the physical indicator and the level of economic development: in other words, the regression line expresses what international average or 'normal' quantity of the physical indicator belongs to a given development level.

5th step: determination of the economic development level of the countries examined. This happens in such a manner that in the diagrams of each physical indicator a horizontal line is drawn from the point indicating the country's consumption of the indicator in question and at the point of intersection with the regression line the size of the partial fictitious EDL indicator belonging to it is read.

The geometrical mean of the partial EDL values (43 in our case) thus obtained will yield the corrected GDP per head for the given country, that is, the EDL.

This procedure of computation is followed and completed by iterative steps. In its course the corrected EDL values obtained as a result of the preceding step are built into the function, replacing the initially used GDP converted at the official rate of exchange. In this manner the whole computation is repeated and the whole procedure continued until the corrected EDL values of the countries no longer show deviations from the results of the preceding iteration.

6th step: with the aid of the function thus determined the EDL indicators of such countries may also be approached whose data were not taken into account when constructing the function. With this method it becomes possible to compare the economic development level of Hungary with the capitalist countries in identical terms.

		Definition of the indicator	*Flow (F) or Stock (S)*
I		*Characterising industrial development*	
	1.	Steel consumption, kg/head	F
	2.	Total consumption of energy, in coal equivalent, kg/head	F
	3.	Productive consumption of electric energy, kWh/head	F
	4.	Petroleum consumption, kg/head	F
	5.	Cement consumption, kg/head	F
	6.	Aluminium consumption, kg/head	F
	7.	Zinc consumption, kg/head	F
	8.	Lead consumption, kg/head	F
	9.	Copper consumption, kg/head	F

	Definition of the indicator	*Flow (F) or Stock (S)*
	10. Plastics consumption, kg/head	F
	11. Wrapping paper consumption, kg/head	F
II	*Reflecting the development level of agriculture*	
	12. Tractors, units per 1000 persons, employed in agriculture	S
	13. Total fertiliser consumption, in effective substance, kg/person, employed in agriculture	F
	14. Inhabitants maintained by an agricultural worker, heads	S
	15. Ratio of those employed in agriculture to the total employment, per cent	S
III	*Characterising food consumption*	
	16. Cereals consumption, kg/head	F
	17. Animal protein consumption, grams/head/day	F
	18. Consumption of milk and dairy products, calories/head	F
	19. Sugar consumption, kg/head	F
	20. Consumption of coffee, cocoa and tea, kg/head	F
IV	*Characterising the level of clothing*	
	21. Consumption of traditional textiles, kg/head	F
	22. Consumption of synthetic textiles, kg/head	F
V	*Characterising housing and its equipment*	
	23. Number of persons per living room	S
	24. Ratio of dwellings with running water to the total, per cent	S
	25. Ratio of dwellings with WC to the total, per cent	S
	26. Electricity consumed by households, kWh/head	S
VI	*Reflecting the development of transportation*	
	27. Ratio of electric and diesel engines to the total, per cent	S
	28. Total freight-ton-kilometres per head	F
	29. Length of motorways and main roads, km/1000 inhabitants	S
	30. Stock of registered passenger cars, units/1000 inhabitants	S
	31. Stock of registered trucks, buses, and semi-trailer combinations, excluding trailers and farm tractors, units/1000 inhabitants	S
VII	*Characterising the standards of health service*	
	32. Deaths under one year of age per thousand live births	S

	Definition of the indicator	Flow (F) or Stock (S)
	33. Total health personnel per 1000 inhabitants (doctors, dentists, nurses with or without diploma, midwives)	S
	34. Number of hospital beds per 1000 inhabitants	S
VIII	*Reflecting the level of services*	
	35. Ratio of those employed in the tertiary sector to the total, per cent	S
	36. Number of inhabitants per one commercial employee	S
IX	*Characterising cultural standards*	
	37. Consumption of household paperware and special thin paper, kg/head	F
	38. Consumption of printing paper (other than newsprint), kg/head	F
	39. Newsprint consumption, kg/head	F
	40. Internal correspondence (annual amount of letters sent or received), units/head	F
	41. Stock of telephone sets (extensions), units/1000 inhabitants	S
	42. Stock of radio receiver sets (including wired transmission), units/1000 inhabitants	S
	43. Stock of TV sets, units/1000 inhabitants	S

35 National Product Series in Historical Analysis: a Case Study of Sweden, 1861–1975

Olle Krantz and Carl-Axel Nilsson

1. THEORETICAL AND METHODOLOGICAL BACKGROUND

In our method for analysis of economic historical patterns, national product[1] estimates play an essential role. Our methodological approach has been applied to one country, Sweden, but it could be used in international and inter-regional studies of economic disparities as well.

In general terms our empirical analysis is founded on a theoretical conception of how a capitalist market economy functions. Thus, it is assumed that prices are determined under conditions of competition and that they are allocative instruments, i.e. they form a basis for the decision-makers in the economic sphere in their choice of products, quantities, etc.

These decisions are normally taken on the basis of historical experience. As such, they have a conservative bias. A continuous adaptation of the economy to changing mechanisms of expansion is prevented, leading to structural crises. These crises can be interpreted as demarcating periods of structurally different growth patterns.

The variations in prices and quantities, which are fundamental ingredients in the decision process, are also the point of departure for our methodological approach to the analysis of historical change. We are specially interested in the long-term patterns of change. One important aspect thus will be to determine and characterise homogeneous periods.

In this economic historical perspective, neo-classical or Keynesian theory cannot constitute a methodological basis. Those theories are of a short-term character or rather they have an 'imaginary' time perspective.

Our basis for analysis corresponds to a certain degree with the ideas put forward by Johan Akerman – an economist out of the main stream of Swedish economic science. In his opinion,

> Contrary to the unitary, transcendental equilibrium theory, the theory for a real society is *dualistic*: on the one hand one obtains models of calculus, i.e. rationalisations of the plans of the relevant groups in a given time-located society; on the other hand a reconstructing causal analysis of the economic process during a certain period of time.

The former, the models of calculus, are instruments of action, which 'must both in reality and in the scientific rationalization be separated from the process in time so as to take the form of a logical cause-effect-relation'. The causal analysis on the other hand is the attempt by the researcher to understand the total process, which continuously changes the setting around these instruments of action and thereby the instruments themselves. This causal analysis 'is based directly on the time-series; its reconstruction rests upon calculated and discussed causal relations within given periods of time'. Hereby different time-scales are obtained: 'on the one hand the imaginary time or reference scale of the model of calculus . . . and on the other hand the actual calendar time-scale of the causal analysis.'[2]

Certain concepts play a central role in Akerman's view of the causal analysis. One such concept is structure, to which he pays a lot of attention.[3] Structural differences lead to different periods in the economic process and these differences are connected to the driving forces – another of the basic concepts of the causal analysis.

The structural conditions could be measured by means of structural indicators. These are material for 'statistical analysis through which a systematization of constant tendencies and perhaps periodicities might emerge'.[4]

Thus the term structure might mean 'a, within given time-limits, *the structural boundaries,* fairly constant economic mechanism, whereby the constance may be established through a study of the mutual relations of the different variables during upward and downward phases of the economic cycles.'[5]

It is Akerman's theoretical conception rather than his empirical studies that are of specific interest for our analysis. One cannot, as he mostly does, simply rely on existing series and treat them as if they were historical facts. Instead, data have to be reorganised in order to make them directly suited for the analytical reconstruction of a certain process defined with regard to space and time. This means that the theoretical conception must contain criteria for the empirical constructions.

2. *THE ANALYTICAL METHOD*

We have applied the principles described above in our work on national product estimates.[6] Thus, a concrete historical analysis based on national accounts must not mean an uncritical acceptance of the data as they are presented in the official publications. On the contrary, it is an important task for the historian to revise the data in many respects in order to attain the intended purpose of the analysis. Our theoretical framework offers a more flexible approach to the possibilities of analysing NP data than is usually the case.

We agree to a large extent with the generally accepted ideas of what series of national product should contain and we have also more or less adopted the prevailing methods of grouping NP data into different sub-aggregates. In our grouping we have utilised two totalities: Domestic Supply (DS) – i.e. the sum of domestic consumption and domestic investments – and Domestic Product

(DP) – i.e. the sum of production of the country, both for exports and home market.

Our primary aim to construct series suitable for analysing long-term historical patterns of change implies that we need not necessarily cover the entire economic system with all flows of goods and services. In our opinion it is possible to use only certain aggregates out of the total number of goods and services.

Conventionally a country's economy is summarised in Gross Domestic Product by expenditure which can be considered as a balance of resources with a Credit side including consumption, investments and exports and a Debit side including imports and Gross National Product. Prognoses based on such a balance are almost always concentrated to the components of the Credit side. These are the components that are to be influenced by various measures of economic policy. The effects are then to be shown in the development of the GNP. One consequence is that when measured at constant prices the two sides of the balance must be equal.

In our opinion an alternative approach would be more fruitful. The economy has, in a figurative sense, a revenue side and a cost side.

The former, DS, consists of goods and services for immediate consumption together with investment for future consumption. The latter, DP, comprises production for use at home and for exports. Thus, over a period of time, the changes in DS can differ from the changes in DP, when measured at constant prices.

We have constructed historical long-term series for DS and DP at constant prices. Thereby, we have obtained a specific series showing the changes of production over time, i.e. among other things production for export. Furthermore, we have obtained a series showing the results of this production, i.e. also imports of manufactured goods for consumption and investment.

The problem of deflation is of special importance in our analysis. As historians we are forced to pay special attention to the problem of achieving comparability over time, considering the large shifts of price and commodity structures that usually occur. In the short run and above all at current prices it might be sufficient to base the analysis on the assumption of a consistent totality, summarised in a balance of resources.

For our analysis with its relatively long-time perspective it is important to work with different NP totals. At a given moment of time and at current prices the totals are largely identical in nominal terms, but they are different with regard to the composition of goods and services. The degree of difference between the compositions of the two totals also varies over time.

Thus, the deflation of current values is not a step in an analysis of the interconnections and interactions of the various parts of the economy at a given moment of time. It is merely a method of measuring volumes, with the intention of picturing the pattern of change in aggregates and sub-aggregates comparable over time.

We intend that Paasche price indices should be used to obtain Laspeyre volume indices. However, we have not had the opportunity of employing this principally superior deflation technique. With our limited resources the amount of necessary work would have been unreasonably large. Therefore, we have had to choose a second-best alternative, using Laspeyre price indices to obtain Paasche volumes. The entire period of investigation was divided into a number of sub-periods, deflation periods. These periods must be separated in such a manner that they can be expected to represent different price structures. Deflation periods of a length roughly similar to Kuznets cycles, i.e. periods of 15 to 25 years, were chosen under the assumption that the important elements determining such cycles are differences in the economic structure. Somewhat arbitrarily, peak years were used as period boundaries.

Within each deflation period Laspeyre deflators were constructed for as many goods (services) or in some cases groups of goods (services) as possible. The aggregation was done by means of weights taken from the years of recession in the beginning of each deflation period. The series for the different periods – altogether amounting to six during the total period of 115 years – were then chained together to form continuous series.

Separate deflators must be constructed for each aggregate. Since the various aggregates are constituted by, to a large extent, different elements of the total balance of resources we also obtain differences in the composition of goods. Separate deflators, as far as possible constructed by using price indices for each commodity, should normally give different volume indices for the different aggregates.

This is the basis for our analytical method. Firstly, we are able to relate two different aggregates – DP and DS or relevant sub-aggregates within these – to each other. They both summarise the same economy but nevertheless they can show differences in the development of volumes over time and these differences can be analysed. Secondly, each one of the aggregates consist of parts, unitarily constructed, with the same base years within each deflation period. Consequently the base years can be changed and used for construction of deflators for previous or later periods. New volume series are obtained, which in turn are comparable to the original series. Also in this case the differences can be analysed.

This method makes possible an analysis of a different kind from the conventional analyses of national accounts. One can decide rather exactly where boundaries are to be found in periodisations and one can analyse structural shifts within the economy. The method does not, however, make it possible to analyse thoroughly the changes and the underlying conditions behind the shifts.

However, the analysis can be extended even further. It is quite clear that the differences between DP and DS appear as an effect of the fact that DP includes exported goods whereas DS includes imported goods. Of course, the differences are not a consequence of changes in the balance of trade. Instead, differences in the deflators totally determine the shape of the patterns. One can isolate those effects originating from differences in the deflators by constructing specific deflator series only for those products within the DP that may be exported, and the products within the DS that may be imported. The ratio between these new deflator series – MPDP/MPDS, i.e. Material Products in DP in relation to Material Products in DS – is mainly a measure of the impact of foreign trade on the total economy. It is a better measure of the real exchange conditions than conventional terms-of-trade measures, since it measures the changes in the volume of imported goods for domestic consumption and domestic investment which a given volume of exports has made possible.

Thus, this terms-of-trade-measure is derived from national product series containing only those sectors or items in which the export and import goods directly appear. The entire export will be included in the MPDP, but only those parts of the import are included in the MPDS that comprise goods for immediate consumption and investment. Other parts of the imports, i.e. different kinds of inputs, including fuel for domestic production, are not included.

A reasonable estimate is that about 40 per cent of inputs imported to Sweden were used for export production (1969). Of course, the prices of these 40 per cent of the imported inputs have already influenced the deflators in the MPDP and should not influence the corresponding estimates of the MPDS.

The rest of the imported inputs were used for production of goods and services for the domestic market. The major part of this production has to compete with the corresponding foreign products that are included in the import of manufacturers for consumption and investment. Thus, the prices of those inputs favour or disfavour both domestic and foreign producers on the same domestic market to roughly the same degree. Consequently they do not influence an analysis of the conditions of foreign trade based on deflator series, which measure the net exchange.

3. LONG-TERM PATTERNS OF CHANGE IN THE SWEDISH ECONOMY, 1861-1975

These theoretical and methodological considerations have formed the basis for an empirical study of the Swedish economy during a 115-year period following 1860. In the present paper we have concentrated the summary of the results on those parts of the investigation where the specific methods mentioned above were used. First we summarise the analysis of shifting the weight bases and then the analysis of the DP/DS and MPDP/MPDS ratios.

Our analytical method with shifting the weight bases is a development of the method used by Alexander Gerschenkron in his analysis of a phase in the economic history of Bulgaria. He posed the problem whether Bulgaria in the period 1909-39 may have undergone 'the great upsurge of its industrial development'. If such a concept should be applied to a specific period, the transformation process must, according to Gerschenkeron, have certain special characteristics. There must exist a considerable production of goods, that initially were produced in small quantities at relatively high prices. During the period, however, the goods will be produced in greatly increasing quantities at relatively falling prices.[7]

It should also be possible to identify goods which initially play a dominant role in production but whose quantities increase at a much lower rate and whose prices tend to rise relative to others. Such effects are often referred to as 'Gerschenkron-effects'.

An investigation using changing weight-bases makes it possible to determine the very existence of these Gerschenkron-effects. Relative price decreases combined with increasing quantities lead to falling deflator values when shifting the weight-bases. In the opposite case the result will be increasing deflator values.

For each one of the deflation periods we have constructed two deflator series. First, we have the original deflator values, i.e. those which are aggregated with weights from the beginning of each deflation period. Second, we have constructed new deflator values by using weights within each period taken from the beginning of the following deflation period. We have calculated such pairs of deflators for both DP and DS and for sub-aggregates within each aggregate.

In most cases, the result of the two measurements was that different values were obtained for each pair of deflator series. These differences form the basis for our analysis of structural changes in the Swedish economy during the period as a whole.

Two periods, 1890-1907 and 1930-51, are characterised by pronounced Gerschenkron-effects. Both periods are dominated by sectors and branches with rapid growth of production and relative price decreases. These changes took place in the manufacturing sector and in the branches of transport and communication closely attached to manufacturing and for the later period also in commerce. During these periods the investment ratio also rose rapidly to new and durable levels.

The earlier period shows the most pronounced Gerschenkron-effects. At the same time the share of manufacturing in the total production increases very rapidly. These and other facts point to the conclusion that the definite industrial breakthrough in the Swedish economy occurred during this period.

Apart from this, a major result of the investigation was that the deflator values generally tend to increase when the weight-bases are shifted forward, i.e. the deflator series for one period with the weight-base taken from the following period have higher values than the series with the weight-base from the beginning of the actual period. This means that the production with the fastest rate of growth also has a relative increase in price. Thus, the periods 1890-1907 and 1930-51 are exceptions to the general pattern.

There is probably no simple explanation of this pattern. One might point to the effect of rising income levels. The consumption of goods and services with high price-elasticity increases in relation to necessities. Services are no less important, the production of which further on might imply fewer possibilities of lowering costs.

Another reason might be a relatively increasing importance of costs for research and development in connection with a growing national product. Thereby the tendency towards decreasing relative prices could have a less marked effect. A further possible explanation might be changes in competition as an effect of growing units of production.

The changes in the DP/DS ratio over time show the extent to which the domestic production must change in order to allow for a certain change in the domestic use of goods and services. An increasing DP/DS ratio means that production must increase in order to keep up a given level of consumption and investment; a decreasing ratio means the opposite.

From an economic historical point of view it is natural to try to find clearly depictable regularities in the changing DP/DS ratio. For our period, 1861-1975, this was definitely the case. Four separate periods with different characteristics were found. The first one comprises the period roughly until the turn of the century, 1900, the second one includes the three first decades of the twentieth century and the third period covers the subsequent years until the early 1950s. The fourth period continues until the early 1970s.

During the latter part of the nineteenth century there is a long-cycle pattern with the following cycles, counted from trough to peak to trough:

1861 – 1868 – 1874
1874 – 1879 – 1885
1885 – 1893 – 1899 (or 1900)

It must be emphasised that trough and peak refer to the variations in the DP/DS ratio and not to the general business cycles. As a matter of fact, the DP/DS ratio increases during periods of recessions and decreases during periods of expansion. This is true during the twentieth century as well.

It seems as if the lengths of the nineteenth-century cycles were gradually extended, but this conclusion is uncertain, not least since the series does not go back prior to 1861, and we do not know anything of the pattern during that period. It is difficult to specify exactly the year when the pattern of the twentieth century became dominant, but 1901 – a year of depression – seems suitable.

From this year until 1933 there is a steadily upward trend in the DP/DS ratio. This was a consequence of the conditions of competition within the international economy, which with the given production possibilities in Sweden made it necessary for production to increase more than consumption and investment.

However, the conditions became different during the period from 1933 to the early 1950s; 1953 was chosen as a boundary year. During this period the DP/DS ratio decreases – gradually a relatively smaller production increase is needed for an increase in DS. The tendency in the DP/DS ratio from 1953 to 1973 is once again increasing. Thereby the pattern is similar to that of the period 1901-53.

The pattern for the development of the DP/DS ratio is largely connected with the changes of the international competition and the position of the Swedish economy towards this competition. Therefore the analysis can be extended by separation of the sectors in DP with export production. A specific deflator, MPDP, has been calculated for agriculture, manufacturing industry and transport. In the same way a specific deflator, MPDS, has been constructed for those items in DS which include imports. These items are consumption of goods and investment in machinery.

A number of characteristics of the performance of the MPDP/MPDS ratio during the last one hundred years can be recorded. Firstly, a periodisation similar to the one for DP/DS can be depicted. The cyclical pattern for the latter part of the nineteenth century could be found also in the new series, although somewhat less pronounced than in DP/DS. A downward trend characterises the first three decades of the twentieth century. However, there was a marked interruption during the years of war in the 1910s. The 1930s and the 1940s were characterised by an upward trend but also in this case there was an interruption during the period of war. The MPDP/MPDS ratio shows quite clearly a decrease during the 1950s and the 1960s. During the former decade it was slow but it accelerated later on.

Secondly, there was a 20 per cent long-term decrease of the MPDP/MPDS ratio during the hundred years from the 1860s to the 1960s. Since, as mentioned above, this ratio expresses the impact of foreign trade on the domestic economy, i.e. the terms of trade, it is natural to make a comparison with the traditional measure, Net Barter Terms of Trade. The long-term decrease of the MPDP/MPDS ratio shows a striking contrast to the Net Barter Terms of Trade, which increased by 140 per cent during the entire period. From the 1870s the increase was slightly over 80 per cent. Thus there was a very large increase in the Net Barter Terms of Trade between the 1860s and the 1870s.

The difference between MPDP/MPDS and the Net Barter Terms of Trade is a consequence of the fact that the latter includes directly all imported goods, i.e. also raw materials and semi-manufactured goods. Relative to finished goods these commodities had a generally falling price trend during the whole period, which tends to lower the total performance of the import prices. But such products are used partly for production for domestic use and partly for export. Thus foreign and Swedish producers roughly have the same advantages from the falling prices of inputs, and this is no competitive advantage for Swedish production. The possible existence of such advantages must in other words lie in the different stages of processing, the development of which can be shown by means of changes in the MPDP/MPDS ratio. A decrease in this ratio might be taken as an indicator of Swedish production, having developed in a less favourable way relative to competing production. But the falling prices of inputs and the increase in productivity has of course been important, which means that for the economy as a whole the development need not have been 'bad'. It might well have been characterised by increasing real wages and consumption.

Thirdly, the decrease of the MPDP/MPDS ratio is to a large extent concentrated in three short periods, during the 1880s, around 1930 and during the 1960s. In those periods productivity has increased rapidly, but simultaneously the performance during these periods has pointed to the increasingly acute need for transformation. Thus, the rapid decreases have anticipated structural crises, and at least in the first two crises, where we have a historical perspective, new structural patterns emerged which made rapid economic expansions possible.

4. *CONCLUDING REMARKS*

Our analysis has shown that National Product series, if properly constructed, can be used to systematise 'constant tendencies and perhaps periodicities' in the process of economic development. They can form structural indicators which can be material not only for establishing structural shifts between periods with different characteristics but also for throwing light on the nature of the changes.

Thus, the field of inquiry is not the same in our study as in studies in which often ready-made NP series are considered as indicators of the process of economic growth during a more or less arbitrarily chosen period. Instead, a study of the growth process should be an integral part of an analysis of the periodisation pattern.

Due to lack of space, growth indicators have not been treated in the present summary. However, our extended studies clearly show that when using our analytical framework in a comprehensive analysis of the process of economic development new and important results can be arrived at.

NOTES

1 Our calculations refer to Gross National Product (National Product, abbreviated NP), i.e. where investment is treated as a gross figure, thus including capital depreciation.

2 Akerman, J., 'Ekonomisk kalkyl och kausalanalys' (Economic Calculus and Causal Analysis), *Ekonomisk Tidskrift,* 1942: 1, p. 5.

3 See e.g. Akerman, J., *Ekonomisk teori I* (Economic Theory, part I) (Lund, 1939, pp. 261 ff.).

4 Ibid., p. 272.

5 Akerman, J., 'Strukturgranser i svensk ekonomi' (Structural Boundaries in the Swedish Economy), *Ekonomisk Tidskrift,* 1949: 1, p. 1.

6 Krantz, O. and Nilsson, C-A., *Swedish National Product 1861-1970. New Aspects on Methods and Measurement* (Kristianstad, 1975). See also *Structural Changes in the Swedish Economy 1950-1975* (forthcoming).

7 Gerschenkron, A., 'Some Aspects of Industrialization in Bulgaria 1878-1939', in *Economic Backwardness in Historical Perspective* (Cambridge, Mass., 1962). See especially Part I.

Index

Compiled by B. Etemad

Abel, W., 257, 258, 269
Adamson, A. H., 57
Adelman, I., 358
Agriculture
    productivity, 3
    role in industrialisation, 79, 290
    value added per worker, 3
    see also under individual countries
Agulhon, M., 300
Ahluwalia, M. S., 368, 372
Akerman, J., 411-12, 419
Alchian, A. A., 257
Allum, P., 330
Alpert, P., 45
Amark, K., 242
Andic, S., 24
Arango, M., 109
Aries, P., 301
Arrubla, M., 108
Ashworth, W., 139, 148
Auffert, M., 273-288
Austria
    economic leadership, 145-6, 173
    employment distribution, 167, 173
    industrial production, 169-70
    migrations, 143-4
    national product per capita, 146, 167, 172
    population, 167
    rate of growth, 167, 168-9, 170, 172
Austria-Hungary, 137-47, 165-74, 175
    capitalism, 166-7
    debate on economic unity, 139-41
    economic backwardness, 165-6
    economic integration, 138-9, 145
    income per capita, 144, 146
    interest rates, 142-3, 146
    literacy rates, 144
    national product, 165
    national product per capita, 165-6, 172
    political institutions, 137-8, 147
    population, 145
    prices, 141-2, 146
    railways, 171
    socio-political forces, 171
    technology, 171-2
    trade, 141
    see also under Brno
Axencinc, V. V., 186
Aykroyd, W. R., 371

Backwardness, *see* economic backwardness
Badouin, R., 301
Bagchi, A. K., 85, 369, 371
Bagge, G. (ed), 243
Bagnasco, A., 330
Bairoch, P., 3-17, 79-80, 84, 85, 117, 118, 146, 150, 214, 301, 357, 358, 362, 371
Baran, P., 84
Barbero, G., 330
Barton, G. T., 88
Bauer, P. T., 45
Baytelman, D., 345
Becker, W., 131-136
Bekkelhund, P.K., 225
Benedict, R., 85
Benedikt, H., 148
Bengtsson, T., 226-243
Benzecri, J. P., 301
Berend, I. V., 170, 174, 185, 186
Berov, L., 177, 185
Bhagwati, 110
Bharier, J., 77
Bhattacharjee, P. J., 371
Billinger, R., 137
Bjork, G., 57
Blumberg, H., 136
Blyn, G., 363, 369, 371
Böhmert, V., 257
Bonazzi, G., 330
Bonnet, M., 110, 118
Borchardt, K., 117, 119, 248, 256
Borda, O. F., 108
Borts, G., 389, 390
Boserup, E., 78, 84
Boudeville, J., 357
Boulding, R. E., 84

Bourgeoisie, 131-35
Boyer, P., 301
Brabant, 259-69
 economic structure, 265
 employment, 263, 267
 income, 267-8
 migrations, 263, 266, 267
 trade, 262, 266, 267
 wages, 268
Braudel, F., 153, 154, 162
Brazil, 349-57, 396-403 passim
 exchange rate problem, 354-5, 356
 export sector, 352, 353-4, 355
 income per capita, 351, 352, 353, 355
 industrialisation, 356-7
 population, 349
 taxation system, 350
 terms of trade, 355
Brno
 comparison with other cities, 207-8
 factors of development, 200, 206-7
 industrialisation, 204-8 passim
 textile factories, 205-6
Brodell, A. P., 88
Brown, A. J., 148
Buescu, M., 349-58
Burrows, E. M., 148
Bushnell, D., 108

Capitalism, 117, 131-6, 173, 405, 411
Caracciolo, A., 162
Casillo, S., 330
Castronovo, V., 330
Central-East Europe, 175-85
 agriculture, 175-6, 177, 179, 184
 economic backwardness, 176, 180, 181, 185
 economic leadership within, 177
 foreign loans, 176, 178
 income per capita, 177
 industrial output, 179-80, 184
 occupational distribution, 178, 180-1, 182-3
 rate of growth, 179
 textile industry, 181-2, 184-5
 unemployment, 181
Chambers, J. D., 214
Chambers, R. L. (ed.), 77
Charpenel, F., 289
Chevalier, L., 288
China, 117
 national product, 10, 14
 national product per capita, 14
 population, 14
Ciocca, P., 164
Clark, C., 81, 85
Cole, W. A., 56, 214
Colmenares, G., 108
Colombia, 98-108, 116
 as a colonial economy, 99-101
 export expansion, 102-4
 exports per capita, 99, 102
 limit to export expansion, 104-8
  foreign investment, 104
  forms of production, 104-5
  speculation, 105-6
Colonies, 9, 16
 British North American, 46-56
  income per capita, 50-1, 52-3, 54-5
  population, 46-7, 54
  slavery, 46-56 passim
  specialisation, 48
  sugar, 49, 53-4
  trade, 48-9, 54
 French, 29-33
 Spanish, 99
 see also under dualism
Colonna, M., 163
Comparative levels of development, 3-14, 20-3, 35, 244, 361, 362-3, 367-8, 370, 385
 indicators measuring, 70-72, 120-22, 168, 366-7, 395-410, 413
 Middle East, 69, 70-72
 Western Europe, 166-7, 168
 see also under economic gap and national product
Constantinescu, N., 186
Cook, M. A., (ed.), 77
Cooper, M. R., 88
Coquery-Vidrovitch, C., 29-33
Corbino, E., 162
Cornut, P., 289
Crouzet, F., 117, 119, 162
Csahok, I., 407
Csorba, M., 407
Curtin, P. D., 56
Czechoslovakia, *see* Austria-Hungary, Brno and Central-East Europe

Daneo, C., 330
Davidovic, R., 186
De Rosa, L., 163
Deane, P., 48, 56, 214
Deerr, N., 49, 54, 57
Delefortrie, N., 289
Denison, E. F., 389, 390
Denslow, D., 354, 357

Desia, A. V., 371
Désert, G., 300
Di Tella, T. S., 208
Diejomaoh, V. P., 45
Domress, 362
Drake, M., 84
Dualism, 38, 80, 147, 349, 378-80
  see also under colonies and economic gap

East Asia countries
  agriculture, 123-4
  industrialisation, 123-6
  stages of economic development, 122-3
Easterlin, R. A., 97, 258
Economic backwardness, 135
  Austria-Hungary, 165-6, 168
  Central-East Europe, 176, 180, 181, 185
  United States South, 86-7
  within Netherlands regions, 196
Economic development, *see under* comparative levels of development, economic backwardness, economic leadership, economic gap, factors of economic development, industrialisation, national product, rate of growth
Economic gap, 35, 126, 201, 362, 363
  and population growth, 78-82
  and technology transfer, 82-84
  between developed world and third world, 7-9, 120
  between Egypt, Iran and Turkey, 70
  between India and advanced countries, 362-3
  between low-income, middle-income and industrialised countries, 20-3
  inside developed world, 9-13
  inside third world, 13-14
  inside world, 3-5
  see also under comparative levels of development
Economic leadership
  national
    Central-East Europe, 177
    China, 10
    France, 167, 168
    Germany, 136, 167, 168
    Middle East, 77
    United Kingdom, 9, 10, 12, 132-3, 136, 167, 168
    United States, 10, 136
  regional
    Austria-Hungary, 145-6, 166, 173
    India, 369
    Netherlands, 190-1
  see also under economic backwardness
Eddie, S., 137, 149
Egypt, 65-77 passim, 123
  capital goods, 67, 69
  defence expenditures, 71
  development attempts, 67-8
  economic decline, 66
  factors of development, 73-7
  foreign debt, 68-9
  income per capita, 69
  industrialisation, 71
  national product per capita, 72
  population, 65, 70-2 passim, 74
  rate of growth, 71
  trade, 66, 67, 68
  transport, 66, 68, 60-72 passim
  see also under Muhammad Ali
Ehrlich, E., 395-410
Eisner, G., 54, 57
Ekundare, R. O., 34-45
Eldem, V., 77
Engel, E., 258
Engel's law, 267, 375, 381
Engels, F., 136
Engerman, S. L., 46-57, 86, 97

Faber, J. A., 197
Factors of economic development
  cost of transportation, 202
  demography, 78-81, 203, 212
  distinct approaches, 200-1
  education, 203
  external forces, 76-7
  human resources, 15, 16, 74-5, 202
  in Middle East, 73-77
  income distribution, 204
  location, 73-4
  nation-region distinction, 202
  natural resources, 9, 15-16, 74, 202
  political system, 36-7, 75-6
  specialistation, 205
Factors of economic underdevelopment
  in United States South, 86-96
  population growth, 80-1
Fellner, F., 170
Feudal system, 166-7, 131-2
Fichte, J. G., 256
Fieldhouse, D. K., 58-64
Fink, K., 148, 149, 185
Fischer, W., 119, 150, 248, 257
Fisher, F. J., 208

Fogel, R. W., 56-57
Fohlen, C., 163
Fonseca, V. A. C. da, 345
Foreign trade, 9, 413-15; *see also under* individual countries
Fossati, A., 162
Foville, A. de, 289
France
agriculture, 273-88
incomes, 274, 275, 277, 278, 285, 291
migrations, 274, 275, 285, 293, 294
population, 290, 292
prices, 287-8
production, 278-82, 291
productivity, 285-7, 291, 293
rate of growth, 290-300
colonies, 29-33
economic leadership, 167, 168
income per capita, 307-10
industrialisation, 79, 273-4, 288
physical product, 306-7
population, 79, 305-6
productivity, 310-15
rate of growth, 20, 136
regional incomes, 302-15
terms of trade with Latin America, 110-17
Frank, A. G., 110, 111, 117, 118
Fremdling, R., 137
Freuendenberger, H., 149, 199-208
Freytag, G., 248, 256
Friede, J., 108
Frief, A., 257
Furtado, C., 85, 117, 349, 357

Galasso, G., 330
Galli della Loggia, E., 164
Gap, *see* economic gap
Germany
cities, 210
cost of living, 253, 254
cotton industry, 248-56
economic leadership, 136, 167, 168
employment distribution, 167
industrialisation, 79, 248-9
population, 167, 211
rate of growth, 20, 136, 167, 170, 211
see also under Nuremberg
Gerschenkron, A., 154, 155, 181, 186, 419
Gini coefficient, 12, 19-23 passim
Gjølberg, O., 216-25
Gomez, F., 108
Gömmel, R., 210-14, 215
Gonzalez, M., 108
Good, D. F., 137-50
Goodrich, C., 45
Gordon, H. J. and N. M. (eds), 148
Goreux, L. M., 277, 288, 289
Grabmann, J., 258
Gray, L., 57
Graziani, A., 319-30
Green, W.A., 57
Grifone, P., 163
Grohnert, C., 257
Gross, N., 139, 148, 149, 169, 174
Gross domestic product, *see under* national product
Gross domestic product per capita, *see under* national product per capita
Gross national product, *see under* national product
Gross national product per capita, *see under* national product per capita
Gualerni, G., 164
Guarneri, F., 164
Guignon, J. -L., 301

Habakkuk, H. J., 78, 84, 163, 214
Haberler, G., 118
Habib, I., 85
Habsburg monarchy, *see* Austria-Hungary
Hall, D., 57
Hanak, P., 148, 170, 172
Harrison, J. R., 109
Hart, S., 198
Hau, M., 273-288
Haynes, W., 163
Hazlewood, A. (ed.), 45
Hebga, J., 118
Hecksher and Ohlin, 138
Henderson, W. O., 79, 84
Hertz, F., 139, 140
Hesse, H., 150
Heston, A., 18-24, 363, 370, 371
Heu, E., 215
Hewett, E., 137
Hicks, J., 81, 85
Higgaret, P., 248
Hirschman, A. O., 324, 349, 354
Hirshleifer, J., 208
Hobsbawn, E., 162
Hocevar, T., 149
Hodne, F., 216-25
Hoffmann, W. G., 162, 214

Holtfrerich, C. -L., 248
Honee, P., 301
Huertas, T., 137, 149
Humphreys, R. A. (ed.), 119
Hungary, 175-85 passim, 396-404 passim, 408
  industrial growth, 170, 172
  national product, 170, 172
  rate of growth, 172, 173
Hurd, J., 149

Imlah, A. H., 117, 118, 119
Income per capita, 3, 35
  Austria-Hungary, 144, 146
  Brazil, 351, 352, 353, 355
  British North American colonies, 50-1, 52-3, 54-5
  Central-East Europe, 177
  Egypt, 69
  France, 307-10
  India, 362-3, 364, 370
  Iran, 69
  Italy, 146
  Turkey, 69
  United States, 50-2, 383, 386-7, 388, 389
  United States South, 50-3, 86
  see also under national product per capita
India, 82, 123, 146, 361-70
  economic gap, 362-63
  deindustrialisation, 81
  immiserisation, 363, 370
  income per capita, 362-3, 364, 370
  indicators of development, 366-7
  national product, 365
  'poverty line', 368-9
  working force, 365
  see also under Unilever
Industrialisation, 9, 16, 151-62, 400-5 passim
  Africa, 38-9
  Austria-Hungary, 165, 166-70 passim
  Brazil, 356-7
  Brno, 204-8 passim
  Central-East Europe, 175-85
  East Asia countries, 120-6
  economic conditions necessary for, 211, 216
  Egypt, Iran, Turkey, 70-3
  Europe, 131-6
  France, 79, 273-4, 288
  French colonies, 29-33
  Germany, 79, 248-9
  Italy, 151-62
  Netherlands, 195-6, 197
  Norway, 216-25
  role of agriculture in, 79, 290
  role of population growth in, 211-12, 78-9
  technology transfer and, 82-4
  United Kingdom, 78-80, 132-3
  United States, 134, 135
Iran
  capital goods, 69
  development attempts, 67
  economic decline, 66
  factors of development, 73-7
  foreign debt, 69
  income per capita, 69
  industrialisation, 72-3
  national product, 72
  national product per capita, 72
  oil revenues, 73, 74
  population, 65, 70-2 passim
  rate of growth, 72
  trade, 66, 67, 68
  transport, 66, 68, 70-2 passim
Islam, 66
Islam, M. M., 371
Issawi, C., 65-77
Italy, 151-62, 319-30
  banks, 154, 158, 160-1
  economic crisis, 325-6
  employment, 327, 328
  fascism, 157, 159
  income per capita, 146
  industrial structure, 158-60, 162, 328-9
  industialisation, 151-62 passim
  investment, 322-3, 324-5, 327
  land reform, 321
  migrations, 323-4, 325, 326
  national development policy, 320-1
  population, 151
  real wages, 161
  socio-political forces, 155-8, 329-30
  trade, 151, 155

Jacobs, A., 257
Janossy, F., 396, 406
Japan, 135, 146, 172
Jaquier, N., 84
Jaramillo, G. G. (ed.), 108
Jaszi, O., 139, 148
Jobard, J. -P., 301
Jones, A. H., 50, 51, 56
Jones, W. O., 93, 97
Jöberg, L., 226-243, 257

Kahk, J., 244-247
Kaisel, A., 174
Kaiser, G., 117, 119
Kalmanovitz, S., 109
Katus, L., 149, 170, 174
Kausel, A., 146
Kellenbenz, H., 117, 119
Kendrick, J. W., 390
Kenessey, Z., 24
Kenwood, A. G., 208
Kessel, R. A., 257
Kiesewetter, H., 248-56
Kirchhain, G., 250-1, 257
Klein, H. S., 56
Klep, P. M. M., 259-65
Klepnikov, S. S., 247
Klima, A., 149
Klovland, J. T., 225
Kovalchenko, I. D., 244-47
Krantz, O., 411-19
Kravis, I. B., 18-24
Krishnamurty, J., 361-71
Krizek, J., 148
Kuczynski, J., 257
Kula, W., 163
Kumar, D., 361-71
Kuznets, S., 84, 97, 214, 371, 380

Labriola, A., 153, 154, 155, 163
Labrousse, E., 289
Lambert, J., 349, 357
Landes, D., 84, 85
Laurence, K. O., 57
Lavergne, L. de, 289
Lefebvre d'Ovidio, O., 164
Leff, N., 354, 356, 357
Lenin, V. I., 153, 246, 247
Leon, P., 357, 358
Lévy-Leboyer, M., 117, 118, 273-89
Lewis, K., 149
Lewis, W. A., 45, 371
Lidman, 362
Lindert, P. H., 374, 375, 377, 390
Lopes, A. S., 345
Lorenz curves, 19-22 passim
Lütge, F., 214
Luzzatto, G., 163

Macesich, G., 149
Machado, A., 109
Machine tool industry, 133, 134, 136
Machlup, F., 148
Maddison, A., 146, 150
Magot, A., 289
Maitra, P., 78-85
Mandle, J., 86-97
Maraviglia, M., 164
Marshall, A., 152, 324
Martin, R. M., 47
Marx, K., 82-3, 85, 111, 118, 131, 136, 153
März, E., 148
Mauro, F., 352, 357
Mayer, J., 331-345
McCusker, J. J., 47
McFarlane, A., 108
McGreevey, P., 109
Mears, L., 358
Meier, C.S., 161, 164
Mendels, F., 137, 162
Mensch, G., 199-208
Merli, S., 156
Middle East
  European intervention, 66-7, 76-7
  terms of trade, 69
  see also under Egypt, Iran and Turkey
Milov, L. V., 247
Milward, A., 255
Mitchell, B., 48, 49, 162, 257
Mols, R., 169
Moore, W. E., 177
Moreland, W. H., 85
Mori, G., 151-164
Morice, J., 289
Morley, J., 163
Morris, M. D., 369, 372
Mottek, H., 136
Muhammad Ali, 66, 67, 68, 75, 76, 163
Mukherjee, M., 362, 370, 372
Mulhall, M., 166, 168, 174
Müller-Armack, A., 117, 119
Mynt, H., 45
Myrdal, G., 138, 139, 148, 349, 357, 361, 372

Natarajan, B., 368, 372
Nath, D., 57
National income, *see under* national product
National product, 6, 8, 9-10, 13, 18, 395-6, 405, 408, 412-15
  Austria-Hungary, 146, 165, 170, 172
  China, 10, 14
  developed countries, 7
  India, 365
  Iran, 72
  Nigeria, 44
  Sweden, 412-19 passim

third world, 7, 9
world, 7
National product per capita, 4-6, 19, 20, 21, 396, 407-8
Austria-Hungary, 146, 165-6, 167, 172
China, 14
developed countries, 4, 7, 10-13
Egypt, Iran, Turkey, 70, 72
Russia, 13
third world, 4, 6-7, 13-14
United Kingdom, 10, 12
United States, 10
world, 7
see also under income per capita
Needham, J., 117, 119
Netherlands, 131-4 passim, 189-97
economic decline, 193, 197
industrialisation, 195, 196, 197
investments, 193
population, 190, 192, 196, 204
tax system, 190, 192, 193
transport, 191
urban-rural balance, 191, 193, 196, 197
urbanisation, 196
wages, 190, 191, 194-5
Neumann, A., 257
Nieto Arteta, L. E., 109
Nigeria
agriculture, 41-2
development planning, 39-42
industry, 42
sector contribution to national product, 43-4
Nilsson, C. -A., 411-419
Norway, 216-225
economic disintegration, 224
prices, 223
wages, 216-25 passim
Nuremberg, 210-14
communications, 212
economic attraction of, 213
entrepreneurs, 212-3
growth industries, 213-4
investments, 212
population, 210, 211-12
rate of growth, 211
real incomes, 214
Nurske, R., 321
Nustching, H. P. M., 197

Ocampo, J. -A., 98-108
Ohlsson, R., 243
Ohngren, B., 249, 256
Olsovsky, R., 185
OPEC countries, 125
Organski, A. F. K., 163
Ortiz, S. E. (ed.), 108
Osernok, A., 407

Paglin, M., 24
Pantard, J., 289
Parker, W. N., 97
Partos, G., 407
Peacock, A. T., 24
Pecters, T., 198
Pelacz, C. M., 111, 117, 118
Pepelasis, A., 358
Perloff, H. S., 367, 372
Perroux, F., 110, 153, 154, 162, 214, 324, 349, 357
Pitkin, T., 51
Platt, D. M. C., 119
Polanyi, K., 154, 163
Polk, W. R. (ed.), 77
Pollard, S., 153, 162
Popper, K. R., 248
Population, 8, 20-1, 211-12
deindustrialisation and, 81
industrialisation and, 78-80
third world, 80
western Europe, 78-80
see also under individual countries
Portugal, 331-45
agriculture, 336
economic planning, 338-41
industrial production, 333, 335-6, 341
migrations, 332-3, 334
population, 331-3
productivity, 336
social conditions, 336-7
unemployment, 341-4 passim
Prebisch, R., 110, 117, 118
Preti, O., 164
Prussia, 134-5, 146-7
Pryor, Z., 137, 185
Pyatt, G., 25

Quelenec, M., 288

Radwan, S., 77
Ranki, G., 148, 165-74, 185, 186
Ransom, R., 86, 88, 89, 90, 97
Rate of growth, 7, 35, 400-2
Austria, 167, 168-9, 170, 172
Central-East Europe, 179
Egypt, Iran, Turkey, 71
France, 20, 136

Germany, 20, 136, 167, 170, 211
Hungary, 172, 173
industrialised countries, 20-3
Japan, 20
low-income countries, 20-3
Sweden, 416
see also under comparative levels of development and economic gap
Reden, F. W., 258
Redlich, F., 45
Reinholdt, L., 225
Restrepo, J. M., 108
Ricardo, 153
Richard, A., 301
Richardson, H., 148, 208
Richter, H., 257
Rioux, J. P., 162
Roberts, E., 258
Robinson, E. A. G. (ed.), 162
Rockoff, H., 137
Rodriguez, J. E., 109
Romeo, R., 155
Rosenberg, H., 148, 164
Rosenberg, N., 95, 96, 97
Rossi-Doria, M., 330
Rostow, W., 186, 321
Rudhart, I., 214
Rudolph, R., 149, 169, 170, 174
Russia, 168
agricultural prices, 245
development of capitalism, 244-5
GNP per capita, 13
peasant holdings, 245-6
Rybczynski, B., 377

Saalfeld, D., 214, 257, 258
Safford, F. R., 108, 109
Sapelli, G., 164
Saraceno, P., 330
Sarti, R., 161, 164
Sauvy, A., 301
Schmid, K., 258
Schmoller, G., 257
Schmookler, J., 89, 92
Schneer, A., 257
Schneider, J., 110-19
Schnieder, L., 257
Scholliers, E., 269
Schröder, P., 214
Seelhorst, C. von, 258
Sereni, E., 330
Shastri, G. N., 371
Shepherd, J. F., 51, 56
Sheridan, R., 50, 56
Sievers, A. M., 109
Silvasubramoniam, S., 362, 370, 372
Simoniya, N. A., 120-7
Simonsen, R., 354, 357
Singer, C., 82, 85, 110
Sinha, N. K., 85
Slicher Van Baih, B. H., 185
Smiley, G., 137, 150
Smith, A., 56, 248
Soltow, L., St, 382, 390
Sonnenfels, J. von, 208
Soubeyroux, N., 290-301
Specklin, R., 300
Stein, J., 389, 390
Stein, S., 357
Stolper, W. F., 36, 45
Stolz, P., 208
Struass, R., 257
Street, J. H., 92, 97
Stull, W., 137
Summers, R., 18-24
Supple, B. E., 45
Sutch, R., 86, 88, 89, 90, 97
Svennilson, I., 162, 186
Sweden, 146, 415-419
agriculture, 226, 228, 229, 232, 235
economic integration, 234-5, 241
industry, 226, 228, 234
national product, 412-19 passim
population, 227, 228, 229, 239, 241, 242
prices, 229, 232, 233, 239-40
structural changes, 415-19
terms of trade, 418
trade, 226, 233
Szabad, G., 142, 149
Szarvas, P., 407
Szilagyi, G., 407

Tarle, E. V., 163
Tchistosvonov, A., 136
Teichova, A., 175-86
Teigen, H., 225
Temin, P., 87, 97
Tenfelde, K., 257
Terms of trade, 18-19
between France and Latin America, 110-17
countries with favourable terms, 114-15
countries with deterioration in terms, 116
see also under individual countries
Thompson, E. T., 93, 97
Thorner, D. and A., 85, 372
Tjeldnes, A. S., 225

Tolly, R., 84
Toniolo, G., 164
Toutain, J. -Cl., 289, 301, 302-15
Tranter, N., 84, 85
Tremel, F., 148
Turkey, 65-77 passim
  capital goods, 65
  development attempts, 68
  economic decline, 66
  factors of development, 73-7
  foreign debt, 69
  industrialisation, 70-2
  migrations, 72
  national product per capita, 72
  population, 65, 70-2 passim
  rate of growth 72
  trade, 66, 67, 68
  transport, 66, 68, 70-2 passim

Unilever, 58-64
  colonial status, 60
  effects of decolonisation on, 60-2
  manufacture in India, 58-60
  profitability, 63-4
  productive capacity, 62-3
United Kingdom
  economic leadership, 9, 10, 12, 132-3, 136, 167, 168
  industrialisation, 78-80, 132-3
  national product per capita, 10, 12
United States, 9, 23, 45-56 passim, 51-3, 134-5, 146, 189, 261, 367, 373-90
  capital formation, 376-7, 378, 382
  cost-of-living differentials, 388
  diffusion of technologies, 382
  economic leadership, 9, 10, 136
  income per capita, 50-2
  industrialisation, 134, 135, 374-82 passim
  labour force, 374-5, 377, 389-90
  national product per capita, 10
  population, 47, 51
  prices, 375-6, 377, 381
  productivity, 375, 379, 380, 382, 385, 386-7
  trade, 48
United States South, 46-56 passim, 86-96
  factors of underdevelopment
    characteristics of plantation economy, 93-6
    cotton, 87, 88-95 passim
    slavery, 86, 93-5
    technological change, 88-96
  income per capita, 50-3, 86
  population, 47, 51
  trade, 48
Uribe, J. J., 108
Urrutia, M., 108
Uytven, R. van, 269

Vargas, P. F. de, 108
Vasquez, L. O., 108
Villamarin, J. A., 108
Voigt, F., 214, 215
Vries, J. de, 189-197

Walton, G. M., 51, 57
Wedervang, I., 217
Wee, H. van der, 198, 203-4, 259, 269
West Indies, *see* Colonies, British North American
Whiteside, A., 148
Wieck, F. G., 258
Wilbrandt, R., 258
Williamson, F. G., 139, 148, 269, 368, 372, 373-91
Winkel, H., 117, 119, 258
Wohlin, N., 242
Wolfe, M., 137
Wright, G., 87, 88, 89, 90, 97

Yamamura, K., 149